Curriculum and Assessment for Students
with Moderate and Severe Disabilities

Curriculum and Assessment for Students with Moderate and Severe Disabilities

Diane M. Browder

THE GUILFORD PRESS
New York   London

KH

© 2001 The Guilford Press
A Division of Guilford Publications, Inc.
72 Spring Street, New York, NY 10012
www.guilford.com

Printed in the United States of America

This book is printed on acid-free paper.

Last digit is print number: 9   8   7   6   5   4   3   2

Library of Congress Cataloging-in-Publication Data

Browder, Diane M.
    Curriculum and assessment for students with moderate and severe
disabilities / Diane M. Browder.
        p. cm.
    Includes bibliographical references and index.
    ISBN 1-57230-615-7 (hardcover)
    1. Handicapped children—Education—United States—Curricula.
2. Handicapped—United States—Functional assessment.   I. Title.
LC4031 .B695   2001
371.9´044—dc21

                                                    00-051382

To my husband, Wallace Boswell,
and to my sons, Ben and Andrew

About the Author

Diane M. Browder, PhD, is currently the Snyder Distinguished Professor of Special Education, an endowed chair, at the University of North Carolina at Charlotte. At UNC Charlotte, Dr. Browder is leading the development of a new doctoral program in special education. Through her research and work with local schools, she is also exploring ways to use the outcomes of alternate assessment to improve student progress. Prior to accepting the position at UNC Charlotte, Dr. Browder was on the faculty of Lehigh University in Bethlehem, Pennsylvania, for 17 years. While at Lehigh, Dr. Browder helped establish the Life Skills Program for students with autism and severe behavior disorders at Centennial School. She also founded a community-based job training and leisure program for adults with severe disabilities who had resided at Pennhurst. In the mid-1990s, she established Lehigh University Supported Employment and Assessment Services which provided evaluations and job support for individuals with a wide variety of disabilities. Dr. Browder continues to be actively involved in educational planning for individuals with disabilities through her consultation to schools in North Carolina and across the United States. She is well known in the special education research community and has over 90 publications in print. She has served on numerous editorial boards and was guest editor for the *Journal of Special Education*'s special issue on Research in Severe Disabilities. Much of Dr. Browder's research has been conducted in applied settings in collaboration with teachers and other practitioners. As part of her commitment to bridging the gap between research and practice, she was the founding editor of *Innovations*, a new publication of the American Association on Mental Retardation established for practitioners.

Preface

ONE OF THE MOST IMPORTANT DECISIONS we make in planning educational programs for students with moderate and severe disabilities is *what to teach*. In the current era of educational accountability, a question that also must be answered is this: *What have students learned?* This book primarily offers guidance in designing a curriculum—that is, determining what to teach and what students have learned. The book offers a curriculum-building model of assessment; information is also offered on instruction (i.e., *how* to teach), because curriculum and assessment are intertwined with instruction. While offering information on assessment and instruction, this book nevertheless emphasizes curriculum, because the most powerful or intricate instructional technology will be worthless if it is not applied to skills that are relevant for the student, the student's family, and current and future environments.

The term I use for the planning process described here is "ecological assessment," which is a blend of person-centered planning and behavioral assessment. Although many professionals have used the term "functional assessment" to talk about life skills planning, I now prefer the term "ecological assessment" because it reflects how planning should consider not only the student, but also his or her environments (e.g., cultural context, learning opportunities, family life). The term "functional assessment" also has been strongly linked to determining the functions of problem behavior (discussed in Chapter Eleven).

In writing this book, my goal has been to honor the teachers, families, and students who have taught me so much. It is one of the joys of my career that for the two decades I worked in Lehigh University's field-based programs, I was able to be involved in both university work and direct service. While at Lehigh, I helped teachers plan and solve problems for individuals with a wide range of moderate and severe disabilities (autism, mental disabilities, traumatic brain injury, severe behavior disorders, physical disabilities). These teachers, who worked in the university-affiliated programs and were my graduate students, impressed me with their ability to take ideas and create excellent services in planning for students who had complex learning challenges. They also questioned me when what I recommended seemed unattainable. The wonderful times were when we made ideas real. The hard times were when I realized that ideas that intrigue researchers and philosophers do not always meet the needs of students and their

teachers. From walking this bridge between research and practice in the last two decades, I have tried in this book to offer teachers the best of what I have learned from
both. This learning process continues, and as I packed up the final draft of this book to
send it to the publisher, it was difficult to feel "finished" when every day still brought
new insights and new ideas. So my hope is that I not only have offered some concrete,
usable ideas, but also have offered strategies that will help teachers continue the process of innovation.

The "teachers" I hope to reach with usable ideas are not just the professionals employed in K–12 classrooms, but also parents, paraprofessionals, job coaches, adult service providers, and therapists. My goal is for this book to contain useful information for
anyone who is involved in planning education for students with moderate and severe
disabilities. I also hope that some of the research applications and practical recommendations jog researchers to ask new questions. The conversation between research and
practice in special education needs to become more active and effective to meet the
needs of students with complex learning challenges.

To honor families and students, I have tried to emphasize family-centered planning and self-determination in this book. Families and students can teach us what we
need to know about planning for students if we will listen and learn. Sometimes, as
professionals, we rush in with tickets before we know the destination. Families and students can tell us, "Here is where we want to go." We then can work together to determine how to get there. Sometimes families and students need new ideas about where
they might go. Sometimes state accountability systems dictate some of the destinations.
But even in these circumstances, we need to invest time in understanding families' and
students' priorities.

I decided to use some brief stories as well as facts and suggestions in these chapters. As these stories evolved, I realized that some were coming from my experiences
with real people. With the help of The Guilford Press, I found guidelines for disguising
case material to protect confidentiality while not presenting fiction. When the cases are
fictional (i.e., the people I describe are not real), I let the reader know this in footnotes.
One of the things I contemplated as I wrote this book was the common practice in
"how-to" books and articles of making up fictitious stories to illustrate points. Sometimes the reader is unable to determine whether these illustrations describe what has
actually *been* achieved or simply offer creative ideas of what *might* be tried. I thought
my readers might like to know when I was writing fiction or nonfiction. Both provide
useful ways of illustrating a concept, but it is not fair to consumers to present a fictitious case study as if it were true. The risks in using true cases are (1) violating the privacy of persons with disabilities and their families, (2) taking credit for someone else's
achievements, and (3) changing a case so much for purposes of illustration that it is no
longer "true." To avoid these pitfalls, I have followed Clifft's (1986) guidelines for disguising case material and have only used cases in which either I or the coauthor of a
particular chapter was part of the planning team.

There is one brief story in this book about my niece Beth that is not disguised (with
the consent of her parents), because it is also part of my story. At the end of Chapter
Five, I share a little about what it is like for me to cross the bridge from being a professional to being a family member. I am grateful to my brother Mike and his wife, Susan,
and to Beth, for encouraging me to share what I am learning from watching Beth's life
unfold.

In addition to the teachers, families, and individuals with disabilities who have helped me learn so much of what is shared in this book, I am grateful to the contributors who made writing much of it possible. All of the people who have written chapters with me in this book are also folks with whom I have walked the bridge between research and practice. I invited their coauthorship not only because they know research and write well, but, more importantly, because of the impact their work is having on the lives of people with moderate and severe disabilities. Levan, Sharon, Karena, Kim, Barbara, and Ed, thank you for all you did to make this book possible.

There are others I would like to thank who contributed in other ways to this book. I am grateful to my colleagues at the University of North Carolina at Charlotte, who gave me the flexibility to finish this book after I accepted a position there. I am also thankful to Caroline DiPippi (Lehigh) and Anna Lichtenwalner and Meagan Karronen (UNC Charlotte) for their proofreading assistance, and to the reviewers for their feedback. On a personal note, I thank my husband, Wally Boswell, and my sons, Ben and Andrew, who have been great sources of encouragement in the various stages of this project. To God be the glory.

REFERENCE

Clifft, M. A. (1986). Writing about psychiatric patients: Guidelines for disguising case material. *Bulletin of the Menninger Clinic, 50,* 511–524.

Contents

ONE

Introduction

IN THE EARLY 1980s, *while teaching a course on assessment of individuals with severe disabilities, I had the honor of getting to know a boy named Tommy[1] and his teacher, Doris. A 12-year-old with spastic quadriplegia, blindness, and medical complications, Tommy probably had more assessment information available than any student I had ever met. Despite these extensive descriptions of Tommy, none provided useful guidance in determining what or how to teach him. The available developmental assessments offered a pessimistic view, suggesting that Tommy scored at the 1-month level. Most of the remaining information described Tommy's medical and physical complications.*

When Doris and I decided to design behavioral assessments of age-appropriate functional skills for Tommy, we were challenged by his physical limitations. In fact, we were able to identify only two observable responses that Tommy made: He clicked his tongue and could slide one fist a few inches. The breakthrough in planning came for Tommy when Doris discovered a way to use one of these responses for choice making. She taught Tommy to click his tongue for "yes" by using trial-and-error learning with preferred and nonpreferred foods. She asked, "Do you want yogurt? Click for yes," and clicked her own tongue to model the response. She then waited for Tommy's click before giving him a spoonful of yogurt. Next she asked, "Do you want applesauce?" and when he grimaced at getting it, she would say, "Don't click." Although it took many trials across several days, Tommy learned to click when he heard "yogurt" and to be silent when he heard "applesauce." To our amazement, he quickly generalized clicking "yes" to other food choices and to other types of questions: "Do you want to go outside?" "Do you want a sweatshirt?" His grandmother was delighted with this new beginning and offered more ideas for Tommy's choice making.

From this small but powerful response, a curriculum was designed for Tommy (Browder & Martin, 1986). Many others have made similar discoveries about students' abilities and the power of choice. The terms "person-centered planning" and "self-determination" have been used to describe processes that honor and encourage this ability. This chapter introduces the concepts and values to be used in a curriculum-building process—not only for students like Tommy, but for students with a wide variety of labels (e.g., autism, moderate mental retardation, developmental disabilities, severe disabilities) who have been underserved in traditional approaches to curriculum and assessment.

---

[1]Tommy's is a true story; it is adapted from Browder and Martin (1986). Copyright 1986 by The Council for Exceptional Children. Adapted with permission.

WHY FOCUS ON CURRICULUM?

A "curriculum" is a defined course of study. It provides a blueprint for learning that teachers can follow in designing instruction. Just as a contractor follows a blueprint to build a house that meets the customer's expectations for quality, following a curriculum helps an educator meet community, parental, and student expectations for quality in education.

There are several reasons for focusing on curriculum in educational planning for students with moderate and severe disabilities. First, there is rarely an established curriculum that will meet the needs of all students from low-incidence populations. Even when educators are planning inclusion in the general education curriculum, or utilizing a specially developed functional curriculum, it is rarely clear how to determine what to teach students with complex learning needs. Because of these complex learning needs, educators need tools for designing personalized curricula (Knowlton, 1998). Planning for students with moderate and severe disabilities must include determining priorities for instruction. This book focuses on the design of a personalized curriculum for students with moderate and severe disabilities.

A second reason to focus on curriculum is to ensure that instruction will achieve desired life outcomes. Unless curricular priorities are defined, educational planning may not target skills that enhance the quality of a student's life. In reviewing the literature on quality of life, Hughes, Hwang, Kim, Eisenman, and Killian (1995) identified several potential outcomes that have been described as indicators of a good quality of life:

- Social relationships
- Personal satisfaction
- Employment
- Self-determination
- Recreation and leisure
- Personal competence
- A home
- Normalization
- Support services
- Personal development
- Social acceptance and status
- Material well-being
- Civic responsibility
- Other personal indicators

One of the most important of these indicators is self-determination. An individual with self determination can define for him- or herself what constitutes a good life and then pursue it. For students with moderate and severe disabilities, self-determination may be enhanced as they discover preferences and make choices. To focus on curriculum is to target skills that relate to the student's desired outcomes, or to focus on what to teach that will enhance quality of life.

Clearly, teaching is only one tool in enhancing quality of life. In the 1970s and 1980s, professionals sometimes overemphasized skill acquisition as a means of obtaining new opportunities. For example, it was thought that once individuals gained a certain set of community skills, they could "earn" the right to a home in the community. This thinking was challenged by people like Smull and Bellamy (1991), who called for professionals to shift their focus from the limitations of individuals to the constraints of environments. With this shift in focus, professionals began to explore ways to help individuals with disabilities to gain access to life opportunities, *regardless of current skill deficits*. Groups began to meet to develop and implement action plans for gaining this access. Several terms emerged for this process, such as "lifestyle planning" (O'Brien, 1987) and "personal-futures planning" (Mount & Zwernik, 1988). In schools, the McGill Action Planning System (MAPS; Vandercook, York, & Forest, 1989) was sometimes used. The general term "person-centered planning" was adopted by many to describe these various action-planning strategies. Many students have gained new opportunities through such planning, such as inclusion in general education and transition to jobs in the community. Unfortunately, most students with more severe disabilities do not obtain opportunities in inclusive settings. Clearly, action planning is still needed. This action planning, referred to in this text as "person-centered planning," is a strong component of the curriculum-building process described in this book.

Besides the need to personalize curricula and target quality-of-life indicators, a focus on curricula for students with moderate and severe disabilities is also needed for educational accountability. Students attend school to gain an education, and current educational reforms focus on accountability for this education. For example, statewide standardized testing in states such as North Carolina has been implemented to answer parental and community concerns about students' educational achievement. With the reauthorization of the Individuals with Disabilities Education Act (IDEA) in 1997, special education services must include alternate assessment for students exempted from this testing (Council for Exceptional Children [CEC], 1998). Planning this alternate assessment can be confusing for students who are not pursuing the standard course of study. Usually in states with standardized testing, there is a close match between the academic curriculum and this testing. In contrast, there is no set curriculum that all students with moderate or severe disabilities can or should achieve. Does this mean there need not be accountability in educational services for these students? When there is no curriculum, and no specific alternate assessment procedures exist, it can be difficult for parents to know whether their children are making educational gains. Similarly, potential employers may not understand students' abilities and may inadvertently rely on stereotypes about disabilities. For the sake of accountability, educational planning for students with severe disabilities needs to define curriculum priorities and provide information on student outcomes.

This curriculum focus is not incompatible with person-centered planning, but rather complements action plans with specific educational objectives. The students' future opportunities are *not* made contingent on mastering these objectives; rather, teaching and advocacy provide a twofold approach to enhancing students' opportunities.

This book describes specific methods for conducting alternate assessment of students with disabilities that will meet state standards (where these exist), developing an individualized education plan (IEP), and assessing progress on target objectives to improve student learning. The approach described in this book is consistent with trends in curriculum-based assessment described for students with mild disabilities (Tucker, 1985; Taylor, 1997). The difference is that for students with severe disabilities, professionals first must define an individualized curriculum before planning specific assessment. This specific assessment will often use behavioral assessment strategies, but may also include qualitative appraisals such as portfolio assessment.

WHO DETERMINES THE CURRICULUM FOCUS?

Curriculum decisions can become heated debates, because they reflect the cultural values people want to pass on to their children. Professionals sometimes do not realize that their personal and cultural values influence how they make curriculum decisions. For example, whether to utilize community-based instruction in inclusive schools or to focus more on academic and social skills is a curriculum decision. How is such a decision made? One alternative is to develop professional consensus about "best practice." Although such consensus can be a helpful starting point, only a team of people who know an individual student can achieve the development of a personalized curriculum.

Who participates in the team that will make these individual curriculum decisions for students with moderate and severe disabilities? Since the implementation of the original legislation granting education rights to students with disabilities (the Education for All Handicapped Children Act, PL 94-142), parental participation has been required. Unfortunately, parents have often been underrepresented in this planning process. When cultural diversity is considered, this underrepresentation becomes even more notable (Lynch & Stein, 1982; Sontag & Schacht, 1994). Families need to be part of the team that decides what students with disabilities will learn. For students with moderate and severe disabilities who are not pursuing the standard course of study in a school district, parental participation becomes even more crucial, because there are more curricular decisions to be made. Some of these decisions require understanding a family's culture and values. For example, many skills of daily living (e.g., what to eat, how to socialize) are culturally determined (Lim & Browder, 1994). To make curriculum decisions that are culturally relevant and related to how the family defines quality of life, educational planning for a student with moderate or severe disabilities must go beyond simply inviting family participation to being family-centered.

This educational planning also needs to be student-centered. In recent years, advocates of self-determination have helped professionals realize the importance of having the student involved in educational planning. Much has been written about the importance of self-determination for students with disabilities (e.g., Wehmeyer, 1992). In describing the principle of normalization, Nirje (1972) noted:

> One major facet of the normalization principle is to create conditions through which a handicapped person experiences the normal respect to which any human being is entitled. Thus the choices, wishes, desires, and aspirations of a handicapped person have to be taken into consideration as much as possible in actions affecting him. (p. 176)

Sometimes it is difficult to translate self-determination guidelines into realistic expectations for students who do not have a symbolic system of communication. How can students define their future goals and gain more control of their education when they are unable to express these complex concepts? An important beginning point is to realize that every student has preferences, whether or not they are expressed through a formal system of communication. To involve students in curriculum development requires understanding and honoring these preferences. Specific guidelines for preference assessment are described in Chapter Six of this book.

While the planning team for curriculum development should always include the family, the student with disabilities, and the professional who will coordinate the personalized curriculum process, the other members of the team may vary across students. Usually the team will include professionals who teach the student or provide related services. The participation of one or more general education teachers can be especially useful as the team considers academic objectives and goals for inclusion. The team should also include people the family and student identify. These participants may be other professionals, or family friends who are committed to the student's future goals.

To summarize the "who" in the process of curriculum development, the team should include the student, the student's family, the professional coordinating the process, and other individuals selected by these key participants who can make a contribution in planning the student's future. Once the team members are identified, the process of planning can begin. This process of designing a personalized curriculum can be viewed as a form of assessment. "Assessment" is a process of gathering information about a student to make educational decisions. Sometimes assessment is direct, including observations and testing of the student. Assessment may also be indirect, utilizing strategies such as family interviews and review of prior records. Students with severe disabilities like Tommy (described at the beginning of this chapter) have often experienced prolific assessments with few educational benefits. To make any assessment purposeful, it is important to begin by defining its purpose.

THE PURPOSE OF ASSESSMENT:
CAPACITY BUILDING VERSUS DEFICIT FINDING

Assessment of students with disabilities is conducted for several purposes, including eligibility for special services, development of an IEP, planning positive behavioral supports, and monitoring progress. All of these purposes have curricular implications.

In determining eligibility for special services, assessment teams focus on the criteria for classification. For example, if intellectual level is a qualifier, a standardized intelligence test may be administered. For consideration of autism, a test such as the Psychoeducational Profile—Revised may be administered (Schopler, Reichler, Bashford, Lansing, & Marcus, 1990). Although numerous standardized tests have been used to assess individuals with moderate and severe disabilities, many of these have been inappropriate (e.g., tests designed for infants) or resulted in students' being labeled "untestable" (Sigafoos, Cole, & McQuarter, 1987).

As an alternative, school psychologists may use standardized adaptive behavior scales such as the Vineland Adaptive Behavior Scales (Sparrow, Balla, & Cicchetti, 1984) for the normative data needed to make eligibility decisions. Adaptive behavior scales use indirect assessment methods, such as interviews or checklists completed with parents or teachers, and thus are applicable for students who do not respond well to structured testing. Adaptive behavior scales also focus on life skills, which may have relevance to a student's curricular focus. In contrast, even adaptive behavior scales may overlook the capability of students with the most severe disabilities by failing to include items that are specific enough to reflect subtle progress. For example, although a student may receive no credit for "preparing meals or snacks" (a broad skill typical of adaptive behavior scales), he or she may be able to use an adaptive switch to operate a blender or to pour a drink. Thus, while adaptive behavior scales may be more appropriate than some other types of standardized assessments for making eligibility decisions that focus on what students *can* do (i.e., life skills), they will not be adequate to reflect all students' capabilities or specific enough to serve as a curriculum.

Table 1.1 provides a list of adaptive behavior scales that may be useful in initial assessments. This table also provides information on the quality of each instrument and the number of items it covers in each life skill area. When an evaluator is selecting an instrument, primary consideration should be given to the age and disabilities of the student to be evaluated.

In the process of providing evidence for service eligibility, it can be difficult to avoid describing the student's limitations in detail. For families, this information may be no more than an ongoing "deficit-finding" activity. Students with moderate and severe disabilities have usually received medical or psychological evaluations early in life to determine the reasons for their delay. Once these students reach school age, evaluation of eligibility may seem unproductive to families who know well the student's need for specialized services. This process, and all assessments, can become more productive if the team members focus on "capacity building" rather than "deficit finding."

"Capacity building" is a term used by O'Brien and Mount (1991) to refer to planning that focuses on a person's strengths and preferences. In the initial assessment of eligibility for services, a professional can focus on capacity building by noting things a student does well, the student's personal attributes, and his or her achievements. This capacity-building approach can also set the stage for continued educational planning. Unfortunately, a deficit-finding approach is often applied and carried over into the next phases of educational planning. Educational opportunities, IEP objectives, and plans for progress monitoring may all lack vision and accountability when driven by a litany of the student's shortcomings. The absence of a curriculum development process can contribute to this perseverance in deficit finding. Because professionals have not identified a personalized curriculum for the student, the student makes few gains, which are then blamed on diagnosed deficits. What is needed instead is a commitment to gathering information for the purpose of enhancing the student's capacity.

There are several steps that can be taken to focus on capacity rather than deficits when conducting evaluations. First, an evaluator can refrain from repeating negative information about a student from past files that is not current or relevant to educational planning. Second, the evaluator can avoid the use of standardized assessments that are not appropriate to a student because of his or her physical or sensory impairments or cultural differences. Third, evaluators can be careful not to use terms for individuals with disabilities that are outmoded or stigmatizing. Fourth, evaluators can use observations of a student and interviews with family members and teachers to describe the student's strengths and recent achievements. Box 1.1 illustrates the type of information that will be generated when an evaluation shifts from deficit finding to capacity building.

TABLE 1.1. Comparison of Adaptive Behavior Scales

	AAMD Adaptive Behavior Scales	Adaptive Behavior Inventory	Comprehensive Test of Adaptive Behavior	Functional Skills Screening Inventory	Pyramid Scales	Scales of Independent Behavior	Vineland Adaptive Behavior Scales
Reference	Lambert et al. (1981)	Brown & Leigh (1986)	Adams (1984)	Becker et al. (1986)	Cone (1984)	Bruininks et al. (1984)	Sparrow et al. (1984)
Age	3–adult	5–18	0–21	6–adult	0–adult	0–adult	0–18
Informant and format to administer	Teacher or caregiver questionnaire or interview	Teacher questionnaire	Teacher or caregiver questionnaire or interview	Observation and caregiver interview	Observation and caregiver interview	Caregiver interview	Caregiver interview or questionnaire
Areas assessed and no. of skills	Self-care—17 Communication—9 Motor—6 Social—7 Vocational & academic—17 Maladaptive behavior—17	Self care—30 Communication—32 Social—30 Vocational—28 Academic—30	Self-care: Male—11 Female—14 Communication & academic—68 Home—135 Motor—51 Social—45 Vocational—87	Self-care—> 100 Communication—20 Social—35 Community & vocational—85 Academic—20	Self-care—> 100 Communication—> 50 Social—35 Vocational & academic—> 100	Self-care—195 Communication—33 Motor—34 Social—16 Vocational & academic—48	Self-care—92 Communication—67 Motor—34 Social—16 Vocational & academic—48 Maladaptive behavior—36
Standard score	No—percentile ranks	Yes	No	No	No	Yes	Yes
Comparison group[a]	Nondisabled or with MR	Nondisabled or with MR	Nondisabled or with MR	Not applicable	Not applicable	Nondisabled	Nondisabled or with MR, ED, VI, HI
Standardization	Large sample, not nationally representative	Excellent	Small sample	Small sample	Small sample	Good	Excellent
Reliability and validity	Questionable	Good	Questionable	Good	Poor	Good	Excellent
Comments	Provides profile of strengths and weaknesses. Maladaptive behavior scales unreliable.	Most useful in screening for educational eligibility.	Useful to describe current skills. Lacks standardization.	Useful to describe current skills. Lacks standardization.	Useful to describe current skills and applicable to subjects with physical disabilities. Lacks standardization.	Can evaluate adaptive behavior scores in relation to score on Woodcock–Johnson Cognitive Ability Scales.	Complex to administer. Yields standard scores useful in eligibility decisions. Scores fluctuate across ages—not good for longitudinal comparisons.
Reviews	Elliott (1985); Perry & Factor (1989)	Evans & Bradley-Johnson (1988); Ehly (1989)	Evans & Bradley-Johnson (1988)	Browder (1989)	Svinicki (1989)	Ipsen (1986)	Oakland & Houchins (1985); Perry & Factor (1989)

Note. Adapted from Browder (1991). Copyright 1991 by Diane M. Browder. Adapted by permission.
[a] Abbreviations for comparison groups: MR, mental retardation; ED, emotional disability; VI, visual impairment; HI, hearing impairment.

BOX 1.1. **Capacity Building versus Deficit Finding**

Our educational planning efforts can focus on either capacity building or deficit finding. Consider how these two descriptions of the same person will influence professionals' perceptions and expectations for the student.

Deficit-Finding Perspective

Chandra Washington[1] has an IQ of 21 and a mental age of 1 year, 18 months. Her scores on the Vineland Adaptive Behavior Scales were below basal levels. She has Down's syndrome and severe mental retardation. Chandra cannot use the toilet or eat independently and will require lifelong assistance for personal care. She is nonverbal except for some random vocalizations. Chandra sometimes engages in aggressive behavior including spitting, hair pulling, and slapping.

Capacity-Building Perspective

Note that this second description also contains information needed to determine eligibility for services, but gives more weight to the student's positive attributes and achievements.

Chandra Washington is a 16-year-old girl with brown eyes and black hair who has been medically classified with Down's syndrome. Her scores below basal levels on the Vineland Adaptive Behavior Scales and the Wechsler Intelligence Scale for Children—Revised support her ongoing eligibility for intensive special education services. Chandra is highly social and greets others using eye contact, smiles, a wave, and an occasional hug. She makes her needs known by moving to an area or obtaining materials (e.g., her bathing suit to go swimming). She can sign "eat" to request food. Chandra has strong preferences and is self-assertive. Because she does not yet have a consistent "no" response, she will sometimes protest physically (e.g., slap or pull hair) until a change is made. Although she needs some assistance in personal care, she works with her caregiver. For example, she can eat with a spoon and point to food choices. She lifts her arms and legs in dressing, and helps to pull up her clothes. Chandra has obtained a part-time job in a school office and has mastered use of the photocopying machine. Chandra and her family are active in the community, and she is an enthusiastic fan at her brother's soccer games. Chandra and her family have begun planning for the future. Although options are still being explored, her interest in her copying job, her love of swimming, and her delight in being with people all provide important clues about Chandra's desires for her future.

---

[1]Chandra Washington is a real person. The guidelines for disguising case material recommended by the American and World Psychiatric Associations have been followed to protect the student's confidentiality (Clifft, 1986).

PITFALLS OF ASSESSMENT
WITHOUT CURRICULUM DEVELOPMENT

One of the reasons why assessments of students with severe disabilities have been deficit-oriented is the absence of a curricular focus. Within special education, there has been a trend away from using standardized assessments to using curriculum-based assessments (Shapiro & Lentz, 1986). In curriculum-based assessment, educational objectives with direct links to the academic curriculum are identified. By contrast, in the absence of an established curriculum for students with severe disabilities, assessment has often been a futile process, producing little of value for developing the IEP.

The futility of traditional assessment for students with severe disabilities was empirically validated by Bricker and Campbell (1980). In their project, multidisciplinary teams invested several weeks in conducting comprehensive assessments of students with severe disabilities. Although the teams made 397 recommendations, only 29% were judged to be adequate to formulate long- or short-term goals, and only 11% were eventually implemented. One reason recommendations were not implemented is that as the professionals got to know the students better, they discovered the recommendations were not applicable.

In the search for alternatives to standardized assessments or developmental checklists, many professionals have found Brown et al.'s (1979a, 1979b) ecological inventory model useful. In this approach, students' current and future environments are defined, and skills needed for these environments are identified. This process helps to generate personalized curricula. Building on this work, professionals have published curricula focusing on life skills (Ford et al., 1989; Wilcox & Bellamy, 1987) and a life skills assessment approach (Browder, 1991; Browder & Snell, 1988; Gaylord-Ross & Browder, 1991). With the push toward inclusion, professionals have tried to determine ways to select skills from general education curricula (Ryndak & Alper, 1996). Although this is not its actual intent, the life skills curriculum development approach sometimes contributes to a school program that separates students with moderate and severe disabilities from their peers with typical abilities. Because the curriculum is designed for relevance to life in the community, it sometimes bears little resemblance to what other students experience in their school day.

Ryndak and Alper (1996) have recommended a twofold planning approach in which the curriculum is developed from both ecological inventories of life routines and adaptations of the general education curriculum. Their twofold approach is shown in Figure 1.1. As this figure illustrates, the planning team focuses on both determining functional life skills a student needs and ways to enhance participation in general education.

A second curriculum development model that can incorporate both general education and life skills planning is Choosing Outcomes and Accommodations for Children (COACH; Giangreco, Cloninger, & Iverson, 1998). In the COACH model, the first step is for the professional to collaborate with the parents or other family members to define curricular priorities. These priorities may include (1) being safe and healthy; (2) having a home, now and in the future; (3) having meaningful relationships; (4) having choice and control to a degree consistent with one's age and culture; and (5) participating in meaningful activities in various places. Figure 1.2 illustrates how these priorities are reviewed with the family. With these prioritized outcomes, the professional and family

FIGURE I.I. Ryndak and Alper's (1996) process for identifying both general education and functional curricular goals. From Ryndak and Alper (1996). Copyright 1996 by Allyn & Bacon. Reprinted with permission.

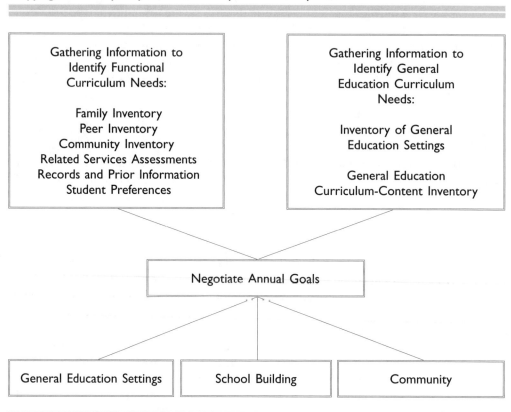

members then review skills lists (a life skills curriculum) to select those that are most important for the next year's priorities. Finally, the team determines how to incorporate these skill targets in inclusive settings.

In the MAPS (Vandercook et al., 1989), mentioned earlier in this chapter, skills are generated by comparing the student's current day to the day of a student of the same chronological age who is nondisabled. The discrepancies between the two can help the planning team generate ways to make the student's day more inclusive. This discrepancy analysis can also be useful to build a personalized curriculum. An illustration of the MAPS approach is shown in Table 1.2.

The strength of all of these newer assessment models is that they generate curricula for students with disabilities that are relevant both to their life skills needs and to their public school experience. This book builds on these models by offering an assessment approach that incorporates planning steps gleaned from several published models and my own practical experience in providing assessments for students with disabilities. This model is described in detail in Chapter Two. Before I describe the model, however, it will be helpful to consider the history of assessment that led to this new curricular focus.

FIGURE 1.2. An illustration of helping families determine their curricular priorities within the COACH model. From Giangreco, Cloninger, and Iverson (1998). Copyright 1998 by Michael F. Giangreco. Reprinted with permission.

Having Meaningful Relationships

Question: "Are you (family member) interested in answering questions on this topic?"

Circle (YES) or   NO

5. With whom does [student's name] have relationships and friendships? With whom does [student's name] like to spend time?   *family, relatives; has 3 close girlfriends at school; has many school acquaintances.*

6. How, if at all, would you like [student's name] relationships to change or expand in the near future? *Some of her friends may move away after high school so she needs to develop a wider local network of relationships. Chelsea says she wants a "boyfriend."*

Having Choice and Control
that Match One's Age and Culture

Question: "Are you (family member) interested in answering questions on this topic?"

Circle (YES) or   NO

7. What kinds of choices and control does [student's name] have now that match his or her age and family/community situation? *Chelsea has the opportunity to make many of her own choices, but she tends to be passive and waits for others to make decisions for her.*

8. How, if at all, would you like to see [student's name] choices and control change or expand in the near future? *More confidence and assertiveness to make her own choices and advocate for herself.*

TABLE 1.2. An Illustration of a Discrepancy Analysis: Catherine's Day, Compared to a Typical Third-Grade Day to Note Possibilities for Change

Catherine's priority needs identified by family, friends, and educators		
Family	Friends	Educators
For others to know she is not helpless Music and time to listen to it Affection To be with people To change environments and surroundings often Healthy foods	More friends Support to get more places and learn things there A lot of opportunity to walk and use her hands As an adult, to live in a small home with friends in a community where she is accepted Teachers to accept her To learn to hang onto the book when a friend is reading with her	More friends Support to get more places and learn things there A lot of opportunity to walk and use her hands Opportunity to let people know what she wants and a way to communicate that with more people To increase the opportunity and skill to make more choices Affection People to know how to: deal with her seizures, help her stand up, and accept and deal with her drooling

Tuesday morning schedule for Catherine: Moving toward the ideal school day			
Time	Catherine's day (current)	3rd-grade day (current)	Possibilities for change (proposed)
9:00–9:30	Take off coat Use restroom Adaptive P.E.	Pledge of Allegiance Seat work directions Spelling	Breakfast (could eat with nondisabled peers if school arrival coincided)
9:30–10:00	Breakfast Work on lip closure, holding the spoon, choosing objects she wants	Reading Group I Others do seat work, write stories, read silently	Switch center (in 3rd-grade reading) Transition to center, reaching, touching picture, activating tape player
10:00–10:45	Switch center Transition to center, reaching, touching picture, activating tape player using microswitch (leisure activity)	Physical education (10:00–10:20) Mousercize, Exercise Express, use restroom Reading Group II (10:25–10:45)	Physical education (with 3rd grade) Skills related to maintaining ambulation and mobility (weight shifting, balance reactions, strength exercise) Cooperation with peer partner Rest time
10:45–11:10	Reading Group III (with 3rd grade) Makes transition to floor, responds to greeting from peer, reaches for peer's hand, holds onto book, looks at book, closes book, makes transition to standing	Reading Group III	Maintain current activity with 3rd grade
11:10–11:30	Library (with 3rd grade) Return book, choose book, look at it, check it out, return to class	Library	Maintain current activity with 3rd grade

Note. Adapted from Vandercook, York, and Forest (1989). Copyright 1989 by the Association for Persons with Severe Handicaps. Adapted with permission.

HISTORY OF ASSESSMENT OF STUDENTS
WITH MODERATE AND SEVERE DISABILITIES

In describing the history of individualization in special education, White (1981) noted that the profession's starting point was to use stereotypes about disability labels to select accommodations. For example, if a student was blind, mobility training and Braille were taught. For students with physical disabilities, various therapies were prescribed. Students with behavioral challenges were given behavior modification programs. For students with mental retardation, the general education curriculum was "watered down" and taught at a slower pace. These approaches were oriented to the students' disability labels, not the individual needs of the children.

With the advent of PL 94-142, many professionals faced planning school services for students with severe disabilities for the first time. There was no existing match between students with severe disabilities and a specific type of service, because these students had often been excluded from public schools. In this same era (the early 1970s), the field of special education was moving toward the use of a diagnostic–prescriptive approach to special education. In this approach, instructors or diagnosticians gave students a battery of tests. For individuals with academic skills, these often included tests in math, reading, and language skills. In early childhood, developmental checklists were the core of these assessments. Several problems emerged with this model. Assessment was often comprehensive, but episodic (e.g., once a year). With no clear progress monitoring, students might stagnate for months before a new diagnosis was made. Also, the match between the assessment and the students' curriculum was not always clear.

Recognizing this diagnostic–prescriptive error, but continuing to try to match students by label to a certain type of service, professionals tried using both developmental and standardized assessments for students with severe disabilities. As described earlier, the information obtained yielded little usefulness for educational planning (Bricker & Campbell, 1980). Sometimes the outcome was an educational program that was not age-appropriate. For example, activities and materials similar to those found in preschool programs were used for teaching students with moderate and severe disabilities at all age levels.

Parallel to the trend in using a diagnostic prescriptive approach, other professionals such as Lindsley (1964) were describing how to use applied behavior analysis for educational planning. Lindsley's work became the basis for the precision teaching model (White & Haring, 1980). This model and other forms of behavioral assessment strongly influenced the fields of school psychology and special education (Shapiro & Kratochwill, 1988) The appeal of this model was that testing was "criterion-referenced" (i.e., based on mastery criteria) rather than "norm-referenced" (i.e., based on comparison to a peer group). Students' performance could be monitored across time to note demonstrations of mastery.

In the late 1970s, professionals sometimes used a combination of precision teaching and developmental assessments. Professionals selected specific skills from a developmental checklist and then tracked them via behavioral assessment. Brown et al. (1979a) challenged this "bottom-up" curriculum model, in which students with severe disabilities had to begin at the bottom of typical developmental sequences and progress upward. Students rarely progressed beyond preschool skills even in late adolescence and adulthood. Instead, Brown et al. (1979a) proposed using a "top-down" curriculum approach, in which the students' environments were reviewed to generate curricular options. This "functional" approach to curriculum development became widely adapted in services for students with severe disabilities and continues to be described in most texts for this population (e.g., Cipani & Spooner, 1995; Snell, 1993; Westling & Fox, 1995).

In the 1980s, professionals continued to apply behavioral assessment strategies because of the progress monitoring offered, but now focused on skills that were "functional"—that is, useful in daily living. A form of behavioral assessment called "task analysis" was especially compatible with assessing functional skills (e.g., Cuvo, Leaf, & Borakove, 1978; Tucker & Berry, 1980).

By the late 1980s, behavioral assessment of life skills, sometimes called "functional assessment," was further developed. Among the important developments of this era were published curriculum guides that featured life skills, such as the Syracuse Community-Referenced Curriculum Guide (Ford et al., 1989) and the Activities Catalog (Wilcox & Bellamy, 1987). Some teachers found conducting multiple environmental inventories tedious. Others found making the transfer from using a developmental model (i.e., preschool curricula) to functional skills difficult. Many welcomed the advent of life skills ("functional") curriculum guides, whether commercially published or developed by their school districts. I (Browder, 1987, 1991) described an assessment strategy that incorporated both behavioral assessment and this life skills curriculum focus. During this same era, curriculum-based assessment became popular within special education in general (Tucker, 1985). Professionals moved away from using standardized tests to using their target curriculum materials for assessing students. Some professionals offered ways to use a life skills curriculum in a similar manner (e.g., Ford et al., 1989).

Concurrent with these developments in curriculum-based assessment in the late 1980s was the movement toward the use of person-centered planning. Just as students in a developmental model might not ever "graduate" from a preschool focus, students in the life skills model sometimes never "earned" control of their own lives because they did not have enough "entry skills." For example, individuals who lost their community placements and returned to institutions were noted to lack certain daily living and social skills (Schalock & Harper, 1978), and those who made a successful transition to the community were noted to have these skills (Crnic & Pym, 1979). Families were also frustrated that students never "earned" their way into general education, and indeed might spend their entire day outside of school (e.g., in the community). Planning strategies emerged that focused on creating access to new opportunities, such as work, a community home, or general education inclusion, through the work of a team committed to the individual (Mount & Zwernik, 1988). This person-centered planning focus was used in planning both for school (Vandercook et al., 1989) and for transition to the community (Miner & Bates, 1997). During the 1990s, this person-centered planning approach complemented the priority of self-determination by making the student's preferences and goals the focus of planning. Some professionals combined this person-centered planning focus with behavioral assessment; others moved away from traditional assessment strategies altogether. During this era, new resources emerged to facilitate planning for participation in inclusive settings (e.g., Downing, 1996).

As special educators interacted more with general educators, new ideas for utilizing "portfolio assessment" emerged (Taylor, 1997). Portfolio assessment involves maintaining a collection of representative student work to demonstrate achievement. Portfolios include samples of students' work collected across time rather than during a single observation. They can also include samples of tasks performed during the course of the student's natural routine. Determining what to teach usually includes some student participation.

During the late 1990s, pressures for school reform gave impetus to the use of statewide standardized tests to demonstrate accountability for student learning. In some states, such as North Carolina, students had to meet minimal criteria in such testing to obtain a high school diploma. With the effort for inclusion in special education, these broader assessment trends were also translated into planning for the individual needs of students with disabilities. The 1997 amendments of IDEA required alternate assessments for all students not included in statewide testing (CEC, 1998).

In this era of school reform, with the mandate for accountability for students with special needs, educators are searching for meaningful ways to assess students with severe disabilities. Although earlier assessment practices have had their shortcomings, each has also contributed strategies for creating individual services for students with disabilities. These advantages and disadvantages are shown in Table 1.3. The challenge for the future is both to glean the best from this past, and to develop new options, so that students' educational needs can be fully met. This book provides a broad perspective on curriculum building and assessment for students with moderate and severe disabilities—a perspective that synthesizes the best of the past, while also offering new directions for this process. To begin this process, it is important to define some values or "quality indicators" for this curriculum development process.

VALUES FOR CURRICULUM BUILDING

In personalized curriculum building, the specific skills selected will reflect the values of the participants. This is why it is crucial to have the student and family at the center of this planning. Given that the *content* of the curriculum will reflect these values, the *process* of educational planning can be built on specific values. These values are reflected throughout this book and are now described.

1. *Self-determination.* Educational planning should honor students' own preferences in setting goals for the future. As students enter the transition years, they need opportunities and encouragement to define their future as adults and to take steps toward achieving it.

2. *Family- and culture-centered planning.* Educational planning should focus on each family's priorities and be sensitive to cultural values. In planning life skills, it is especially important to know family preferences.

3. *Educational accountability.* All students can learn and deserve the opportunity to receive high-quality instruction. Curricular priorities need to be specific enough that assessment can be designed to track student progress. The purpose for such progress monitoring is twofold: to provide accountability to students and their families, and to adjust instruction to improve learning.

4. *Personalized curriculum.* Although some students with moderate and severe disabilities may pursue the standard course of study (i.e., the general education academic

TABLE 1.3. Methods Used to Assess Students with Moderate and Severe Disabilities

Method	Information obtained	Example of information	Shortcomings	Contributions to current practice
1. Match label to service (e.g., students with physical disabilities receive physical and occupational therapy)	Students' diagnostic labels.	Based on Mark's scores on the Psychoeducational Profile—Revised and the Childhood Autism Rating Scale, he can be classified as autistic.	Stereotypes student based on labels; not all students with same disability have same educational needs.	Helpful to administrative planning in determining staff and services to have available.
2. Diagnostic–prescriptive teaching	Students' deficits that should be targeted for instruction.	On a test of language function, Mark did not use greetings or other interactive language except for requesting.	Deficit-oriented; may not be a link between testing and the curriculum; if based on preschool curriculum, not age-appropriate for school-age students.	Writing an IEP requires some identification of target skills that a student needs; this can be achieved by using curriculum checklists based on life skills and general education.
3. Precision teaching	Specific skills to teach, defined as observable behaviors; data collected on ongoing progress.	In an object-matching task, Mark matched 6 of 10 objects.	Sometimes focuses on trivial or splinter skills because these are easier to define; skills tracked may not be functional or age-appropriate.	Provides a strong model for ongoing progress monitoring that can be made meaningful by using curriculum development to select skills.
4. Ecological inventories and "top-down" curriculum	Lists of skills student can use in current and future environments.	Environment: Grocery store Activities: Selecting produce Using a list Pushing a cart Paying cashier Environment: Home Activities: Snack preparation Toy play Dressing	Can be tedious to conduct ecological inventories for all environments and all students; may overlook planning for school inclusion.	Ecological inventories continue to be important tools for curriculum development. Process can be made less tedious by using published curricula as a starting point. Ecological inventories can be applied to general education settings.

Assessment	Description	Example	Limitations	Advantages
5. Task analysis and other behavioral assessments	Student's specific performance in real-life activities.	Purchasing a soda: 1. Take out coins – 2. Insert coins – 3. Push button + 4. Pick up can + 5. Take change – Total correct 2/5	Can be deficit-oriented (student must master task before getting the opportunity to work, live in community, etc.)	Behavioral assessments provide important tools for determining students' current level of functioning in various curricular areas; they also provide excellent tools for progress monitoring.
6. Curriculum-based assessment	Student's current skills in the target curriculum for his or her age group.	Passage from reading series: John saw the tree. He wanted to climb. He saw apples on the tree. He wanted an apple. Words read per minute: 2.4 Errores: 6	Typically utilized in academics; impossible to use when there is no curriculum.	Published life skills curriculum and adaptations from general education can be used to conduct assessment (e.g., skills checklist) and then to develop a personalized curriculum.
7. Person-centered planning	Student's strengths, preferences, and future life goals.	Our dream for Mark's future: • Mark will have friends. • Mark will go with his family on community outings. • Mark will have a job in the community when he graduates.	May not provide enough information to create personalized curriculum or define what student is to learn for IEP.	An important strategy for making planning student- and family-centered; can be supplemented with additional curriculum development strategies.
8. Portfolio assessment	Samples of student's work in various curricular areas.	Handwriting sample for September 8th: [handwriting] Handwriting sample for December 1st: [handwriting]	May be difficult to apply to life skills; more applicable to academics; progress monitoring can be highly subjective.	Provides an important tool for qualitative assessments; useful in tracking progress in general education settings.
9. Alternate assessment	Accountability that student is learning when student has been exempted from statewide testing. May use any of the above described assessment methods.	Mark had 33 skills in the life skills curriculum in September and 72 skills as of June. This reflects excellent progress.	May exclude student from obtaining high school diploma. May be difficult to plan for students with severe disabilities.	Can provide an important link to general education by maintaining expectations that all students can show progress.

curriculum), many will need alternatives. These alternatives can draw both from adaptations of an academic curriculum and from the life skills the students need for their current and future environments.

5. *Inclusion.* Educational planning should encourage opportunities in inclusive classrooms, schools, jobs, and the community. Curriculum planning should focus on skills that enhance participation in inclusive settings.

6. *Functional and age-appropriate skills.* A personalized curriculum needs to reflect skills that are functional—that is, usable in daily living. Skills also need to be appropriate to students' chronological age.

7. *Choice.* A component of self determination, choice making increases students' active participation in their learning day. The curriculum should include a focus on skills that teach and encourage choice making.

8. *Research as a resource for practice.* Data-based intervention research provides an important resource for curriculum building by offering examples of both what and how to teach students with moderate and severe disabilities.

SUMMARY

This first chapter has described the importance of curriculum development for students with moderate and severe disabilities. Just as a contractor needs a blueprint to build a house, defining skills for instruction helps the educator focus on teaching skills that will be related to enhancing a student's quality of life. For students with moderate and severe disabilities, personalized curricula will be needed to meet their complex learning needs. A published curriculum that focuses on functional life skills can be a helpful starting point, but needs to be individualized to (1) honor a student's own preferences, (2) reflect family and cultural values, (3) incorporate planning for general education, and (4) meet the student's unique learning needs.

The process of planning a personalized curriculum is a form of assessment. Students with moderate and severe disabilities have often experienced many evaluations that focus on finding their deficits and provide little guidance for educational planning. In contrast, assessment needs to be focused on building capacity—from evaluation for eligibility for services, through development of the IEP, to ongoing progress monitoring.

A historical view of assessing students with moderate and severe disabilities reveals an increasing focus on individualization. In its early phases, individualization went no further than trying to match students to services based on their disability labels or their scores on standardized tests. Because there was no easy match for students with severe disabilities, professionals sometimes followed preschool models, adapting developmental checklists and early childhood curricula to teach this population. As special education shifted from diagnostic–prescriptive teaching to precision teaching, applied behavior analysis provided tools for tracking progress. By the late 1970s, professionals realized that developmental curricula would not achieve optimal outcomes for older students with moderate and severe disabilities, and a new focus on functional life skills emerged. Behavioral assessment of life skills, such as task analyses, were widely used.

As inclusion and self-determination emerged as priorities in the 1990s, professionals explored using new alternatives, such as person-centered planning meetings and planning for inclusion. Some combined this new focus with behavioral assessment of life skills, whereas others moved away from direct assessment of specific skills. By the end of the 1990s, school reform, with its emphasis on educational accountability, renewed interest in methods that would assist with documenting student progress. The reauthorization of IDEA in 1997 provided impetus to defining alternate assessment for students who would not participate in statewide testing.

This book provides a comprehensive approach to planning for students with moderate and severe disabilities. Multiple strategies are synthesized to offer alternatives to meet the heterogeneous needs of this population. Although the primary focus is on the values of self-determination and family-centered planning, recommendations are also provided for educational accountability. Such accountability has been counterproductive when used to determine whether students "qualify" for opportunities such as inclusive schools and community jobs and homes. In contrast, when focused on the student's and family's priorities, such accountability can be important in demonstrating that values such as self-determination are actually being implemented in the educational program.

This book takes a curriculum-planning focus. In the next chapters, the steps for curriculum building are introduced first, and then specific curricular areas are described in more detail. The purpose of this book is to provide strategies for determining what to teach students with moderate and severe disabilities and for tracking progress in this curriculum. These recommendations are applicable to students with a wide variety of disabilities, such as autism, mental retardation, severe behavior disorders, and multiple disabilities. Throughout the book, references are made to the research literature. These data-based interventions offer not only examples of what to teach, but evidence that students with moderate and severe disabilities can learn a wide range of skills that can enhance quality of life. Each chapter also includes examples and brief stories about students with moderate and severe disabilities. Many of these stories are true and come from my own experiences (see the Preface). A wise person once said that our students will guide us to know how to teach them if we listen to them and observe them closely.

More about Tommy

In the beginning, some of the professionals who provided care for Tommy (see the vignette that begins this chapter) were dubious about whether he was making intentional choices or just clicking his tongue randomly. Perhaps in jest, given Tommy's blindness, a staff person asked him whether he wanted to wear a green shirt. Tommy clicked "yes." Surprised, the staff person asked again, and again he clicked "yes." So she asked about another color: "Do you want to wear a red shirt?" Silence. "Do you want to wear blue?" Silence. "Do you want to wear green?" Click! Tommy's choice was the source of considerable discussion that day among the staff. Had he really chosen a color? How could this happen, given his blindness? Could he really understand the concept of color? When one staff person heard the discussion, she said, "I know why Tommy chose green. He has the most beautiful green eyes, and whenever he wears green, a lot of people compliment him, saying, 'Look at how that green shirt makes your green eyes so bright!'" What we had never realized until that day was that Tommy understood our words! (Tommy's curriculum chart can be found in Browder & Martin, 1986.)

REFERENCES

Adams, G. L. (1984). *Comprehensive Test of Adaptive Behavior.* Columbus, OH: Charles E. Merrill.

Becker, H., Schur, S., Paoletti-Schelp, M., & Hammer, E. (1986). *Functional Skills Screening Inventory.* Austin, TX: Functional Resources Enterprises.

Bricker, W. A., & Campbell, P. H. (1980). Interdisciplinary assessment and programming for multi-handicapped students. In W. Sailor, B. Wilcox, & L. Brown (Eds.), *Methods of instruction for severely handicapped students* (pp. 3–46). Baltimore: Paul H. Brookes.

Browder, D. M. (1987). *Assessment of individuals with severe disabilities: An applied behavioral approach to life skills assessment.* Baltimore: Paul H. Brookes.

Browder, D. M. (1989). Functional skills screening inventory. In J. C. Conoley & J. J. Kramer (Eds.), *Tenth mental measurement yearbook* (pp. 315–317). Lincoln: University of Nebraska Press.

Browder, D. M. (1991). *Assessment of individuals with severe disabilities: An applied behavioral approach to life skills assessment* (2nd ed.). Baltimore: Paul H. Brookes.

Browder, D. M., & Martin, D. K. (1986). A new curriculum for Tommy. *Teaching Exceptional Children, 18,* 261–265.

Browder, D. M., & Snell, M. E. (1988). Assessment of individuals with severe handicaps. In E. S. Shapiro & T. R. Kratochwill (Eds.), *Behavioral assessment in schools* (pp. 121–160). New York: Guilford Press.

Brown, L., Branston, M. B., Hamre-Nietupski, S., Pumpian, I., Certo, N., & Gruenewald, L. (1979a). A strategy for developing chronological age-appropriate and functional curricular content for severely handicapped adolescents and young adults. *Journal of Special Education, 13,* 81–90.

Brown, L., Branston-McLean, M. B., Baumgart, D., Vincent, I., Falvey, M., & Schroeder, J. (1979b). Using the characteristics of current and subsequent least restrictive environments as factors in the development of curricular content for severely handicapped students. *AAESPH Review, 4,* 407–424.

Brown, L., & Leigh, J. E. (1986). *Adaptive Behavior Inventory.* Austin, TX: Pro-Ed.

Bruininks, R. H., Woodcock, R. W., Weatherman, R. F., & Hill, B. K. (1984). *Woodcock–Johnson Psycho-Educational Battery: Part 4. Scales of Independent Behavior.* Allen, TX: DLM Resources.

Cipani, E. C., & Spooner, R. (1994). *Curricular and instructional approaches for persons with severe disabilities.* Boston: Allyn & Bacon.

Clifft, M. A. (1986). Writing about psychiatric patients: Guidelines for disguising case material. *Bulletin of the Menninger Clinic, 50,* 511–524.

Cone, J. D. (1984). *The Pyramid Scales: Criterion-referenced measures of adaptive behavior in severely handicapped persons.* Austin, TX: Pro-Ed.

Council for Exceptional Children (CEC). (1998). *IDEA 1997: Let's make it work.* Reston, VA: Author.

Crnic, K. A., & Pym, H. A. (1979). Training mentally retarded adults in independent living skills. *Mental Retardation, 17,* 13–16.

Cuvo, A. J., Leaf, R. B., & Borakove, L. S. (1978). Teaching janitorial skills to the mentally retarded: Acquisition, generalization and maintenance. *Journal of Applied Behavior Analysis, 11,* 435–355.

Downing, J. (Ed.). (1996). *Including students with severe and multiple disabilities in typical classrooms.* Baltimore: Paul H. Brookes.

Ehly, S. (1989). Review of the Adaptive Behavior Inventory. In J. C. Connolly & J. J. Kramer (Eds.), *Tenth mental measurements yearbook* (pp. 20–21). Lincoln: University of Nebraska Press.

Elliott, S. N. (1985). AAMD Adaptive Behavior Scale. In O. K. Buros (Ed.), *Ninth mental measurements yearbook* (p. 3). Highland Park, NJ: Gryphon Press.

Evans, L. D., & Bradley-Johnson, S. (1988). A review of recently developed measures of adaptive behavior. *Psychology in the Schools, 25,* 276–287.

Ford, A., Schnorr, R., Meyer, L., Davern, L., Black, J., & Dempsey, P. (1989). *The Syracuse Community-Referenced Curriculum Guide for students with moderate and severe disabilities.* Baltimore: Paul H. Brookes.

Gaylord-Ross, R., & Browder, D. (1991). Functional assessment: Dynamic and domain properties. In L. H. Meyer, C. A. Peck, & L. Brown (Eds.), *Critical issues in the lives of people with severe disabilities* (pp. 45–66). Baltimore: Paul H. Brookes.

Giangreco, M. F., Cloninger, C. J., & Iverson, V. S. (1998). *Choosing Outcomes and Accommodations for Children* (2nd ed.). Baltimore: Paul H. Brookes.

Haring, N. G. (Ed.). (1988). *Generalization for students with severe handicaps: Strategies and solutions.* Seattle: University of Washington Press.

Harris, S. L., Belchic, J., Blum, L., & Celiberti, D. (1994). Behavioral assessment of autistic disorder. In J. Matson (Ed.), *Autism in children and adults: Etiology, assessment, and interventions* (pp. 127–146). Pacific Grove, CA: Brooks/Cole.

Hughes, C., Hwang, B., Kim, J., Eisenman, L., & Killian, D. (1995). Quality of life in applied research: A review and analysis of empirical measures. *American Journal of Mental Retardation, 99,* 623–641.

Ipsen, S. M. (1986). Test review: Scales of Independent Behavior: Woodcock–Johnson Psycho-Educational Battery: Part Four. *Education and Training of the Mentally Retarded, 21,* 153–154.

Knowlton, E. (1998). Considerations in the design of personalized curricular supports for students with developmental disabilities. *Education and Training in Mental Retardation and Developmental Disabilities, 33,* 95–107.

Lambert, N., Windmiller, M., Taringer, D., & Cole, L. (1981). *American Association on Mental Deficiency Adaptive Behavior Scales.* Monterey, CA: CTB/McGraw-Hill.

Lim, L., & Browder, D. M. (1994). Multicultural life skills assessment of individuals with severe disabilities. *Journal of the Association for Persons with Severe Handicaps, 19,* 130–138.

Lindsley, O. R. (1964). Direct measurement and prosthesis of retarded behavior. *Journal of Education, 147,* 60–82.

Lynch, E. W., & Stein, R. C. (1982). Perspectives on participation in special education. *Exceptional Education Quarterly, 3,* 56–63.

Miner, C. A., & Bates, P. E. (1997). The effect of person centered planning activities on the IEP/transition planning process. *Education and Training in Mental Retardation and Developmental Disabilities, 32,* 105–112.

Mount, B., & Zwernik, K. (1988). *It's never too early, it's never too late: A book about personal-futures planning for persons with developmental disabilities, their families, and friends, case managers, service providers, and advocates.* St. Paul, MN: St. Paul Metropolitan Council.

Nirje, B. (1972). The right to self determination. In W. Wolfenberger (Ed.), *Normalization: The principle of normalization* (pp. 176–193). Toronto: National Institute on Mental Retardation.

Oakland, T., & Houchins, S. (1985). A review of the Vineland Adaptive Behavior Scales: Survey. *Journal of Counseling and Development, 63,* 585–586.

O'Brien, J. (1987). A guide to life-style planning: Using the Activities Catalog to integrate services and natural support systems. In B. Wilcox & G. T. Bellamy (Eds.), *A comprehensive guide to the Activities Catalog* (pp. 175–190). Baltimore: Paul H. Brookes.

O'Brien, J., & Mount, B. (1991). Telling new stories: The search for capacity among people with severe handicaps. In L. H. Meyer, C. A. Peck, & L. Brown (Eds.), *Critical issues in the lives of people with severe disabilities* (pp. 89–92). Baltimore: Paul H. Brookes.

Perry, A., & Factor, D. C. (1989). Psychometric validity and clinical usefulness of the Vineland Adaptive Behavior Scales and the AAMD Adaptive Behavior Scales for an autistic sample. *Journal of Autism and Developmental Disabilities, 19,* 41–55.

Ryndak, D., & Alper, S. (Eds.). (1996). *Curriculum content for students with moderate and severe disabilities in inclusive settings.* Boston: Allyn & Bacon.

Schalock, R. L., & Harper, R. S. (1978). Placement from community-based mental retardation programs: How well do clients do? *American Journal of Mental Deficiency, 86,* 170–177.

Schopler, E., Reichler, R. J., Bashford, A., Lansing, M. D., & Marcus, L. M. (1990). *Psychoeducational Profile—Revised (PEP-R).* Austin, TX: Pro-Ed.

Shapiro, E. S., & Kratochwill, T. R. (1988). *Behavioral assessment in schools* (pp. 1–13). New York: Guilford Press.

Shapiro, E. S., & Lentz, F. E. (1986). Behavioral assessment of academic behavior. *Advances in School Psychology, 5,* 87–140.

Sigafoos, J., Cole, D. A., & McQuarter, R. (1987). Current practices in the assessment of students with severe handicaps. *Journal of the Association for Persons with Severe Handicaps, 12,* 264–273.

Smull, M. W., & Bellamy, G. T. (1991). Community services for adults with disabilities: Policy, changes, and the emerging support paradigm. In L. H. Meyer, C. A. Peck, & L. Brown (Eds.), *Critical issues in the lives of people with severe disabilities* (pp. 527–536). Baltimore: Paul H. Brookes.

Snell, M. E. (1993). *Instruction of students with severe disabilities* (4th ed.). Columbus, OH: Charles E. Merrill.

Sontag, J. C., & Schacht, R. (1994). An ethnic comparison of parent participation and information needs in early intervention. *Exceptional Children, 60,* 422–433.

Sparrow, S. S., Balla, D. A., & Cicchetti, D. V. (1984). *Vineland Adaptive Behavior Scales.* Circle Pines, MN: American Guidance Services.

Svinicki, J. G. (1989). Review of the Pyramid Scales. In J. C. Conoley & J. J. Kramer (Eds.), *Tenth mental measurements yearbook* (pp. 671–673). Lincoln, NE: University of Nebraska Press.

Taylor, R. L. (1997). *Assessment of exceptional students* (4th ed.). Boston: Allyn & Bacon.

Tucker, D. J., & Berry, G. W. (1980). Teaching severely multihandicapped students to put on their own hearing aids. *Journal of Applied Behavior Analysis, 13,* 65–75.

Tucker, J. A. (1985). Curriculum-based assessment: An introduction. *Exceptional Children, 52,* 199–204.

Vandercook, T., York, J., & Forest, M. (1989). The McGill Action Planning System (MAPS): A strategy for building the vision. *Journal of the Association for Persons with Severe Handicaps, 14,* 205–215.

Wehmeyer, M. (1992). Self-determination and the education of students with mental retardation. *Education and Training in Mental Retardation, 27,* 302–314.

Westling, D. L., & Fox, L. (1995). *Teaching students with severe disabilities.* Columbus, OH: Charles E. Merrill.

White, O. R. (1981). *Making daily classroom decisions.* Paper presented at the annual meeting of the American Educational Research Association. Los Angeles.

White, O. R., & Haring, N. G. (1980). *Exceptional teaching.* Columbus, OH: Charles E. Merrill.

Wilcox, B., & Bellamy, G. T. (Ed.). (1987). *The Activities Catalog: An alternative curriculum for youth and adults with severe disabilities.* Baltimore: Paul H. Brookes.

TWO

Ecological Assessment and Person-Centered Planning

ALTHOUGH TIMOTHY[1] WAS ONLY 8 YEARS OLD, *he already had a long list of labels to describe him. He had been described as psychotic, as severely mentally retarded, as having a mental age of 2 years, as having an IQ of 27, as having severe behavior disorders, and as having a pervasive developmental disability. His school file contained over 50 sheets of paper from various professionals, using these and other terms. If you had searched his file for information on his educational needs, you would have found few if any descriptions of what Timothy could do, wanted to do, or needed to learn. Although his past IEPs listed objectives, it was difficult to find a relationship between these objectives and all the other written material describing Timothy. Timothy's parents objected to his current IEP, which they found redundant with the previous 3 years' plans and lacking in vision for Timothy. If you had recently accepted a position with this school district and had been asked to lead the team that would develop a new IEP for Timothy, how would you have approached this task?*

This chapter provides an overview of the ecological assessment and person-centered planning process described in further detail in the rest of this book. These steps can provide a method for planning for, and with, a student like Timothy and other students from low-incidence populations who have complex educational needs.

Chapter One has provided a historical overview of the various approaches for assessing students with severe disabilities. This chapter describes a specific process for planning a curriculum for such a student, using both ecological assessment and person-centered planning strategies. To some extent, "assessment" versus "planning" approaches have been distinctive alternatives in developing individualized education plans (IEPs) for students with severe disabilities. Campbell, Campbell, and Brady (1998) describe the "assessment" approach as one that uses a diagnostic–prescriptive process. The steps in this process include delineating a sequence of skills, assessing the student's performance within this sequence, and selecting instructional objectives based on assessment results. In contrast, in a "planning" process, a team of people familiar with the student establishes curriculum goals in partnership with the student and family. In the ecological assessment process described in this chapter, both assessment *and* plan-

---

[1]Timothy's case is a fictitious composite of details from the cases of several real children.

ning strategies are used to develop a personalized curriculum and IEP. There are several advantages to this blended approach. Assessment of the student may provide information to the planning team that was not previously known; when this assessment includes giving the student opportunities to try new tasks and activities, new preferences and abilities can be discovered. Using planning processes as well enables the student's and family's preferences to be used as the priorities for selecting skills; new options may be considered through brainstorming as a group.

WHAT IS ECOLOGICAL ASSESSMENT?

An "ecological assessment" is a person-centered planning method to identify instructional priorities based on a student's current and future environments and the student's and family's preferences. This method of assessment differs from standardized assessment in that standardized tests are rarely used in the process. Similarly, it differs from developmental assessment in that the terms of typical child development inventories (e.g., "mental age") are not applied.

Alternative Terms for Ecological Assessment

Two alternative terms that are sometimes used for ecological assessment are "functional assessment" (Linehan & Brady, 1995) and "life skills assessment" (Browder, 1991). The term "functional assessment" has at least two other meanings in the special education literature. First, the term has been used to describe the procedure in which the function of a behavior is identified through observations of antecedents and consequences that maintain it. This procedure is used in planning positive behavioral support (Horner, 1994). The term has also been used to refer to the process of identifying the level of mental health functioning of individuals with severe mental illness (Weiner, 1993) or the physical functioning of individuals with cerebral palsy (Wright & Boschen, 1993). The term "life skills assessment" has fewer alternative meanings but also may not be fully descriptive of the process, since ecological assessment may include curriculum planning based on general education environments and academic content.

The term "ecological assessment" comes from the focus on a student's environments in conducting planning. Brown et al. (1979) used the term "ecological inventory" to describe how to generate curriculum priorities by surveying a student's current and future environments. These inventories have been primarily applied to the domains of daily living, such as the community, home, and work, but can also be applied to general education contexts (Ryndak & Alper, 1996). The term "ecological assessment" is used to refer to assessments based on these inventories (Downing & Perino, 1992; Parker, Szymanski, & Hanley-Maxwell, 1989). The term has gained added meaning as professionals blend assessment and planning processes, because "ecology" refers to a student's social relationships as well as places. Mental health professionals have used the term "ecological mapping" to refer to the process of understanding family relationships, resources, and their impact on children (Hartman & Laird, 1983). An ecological assessment uses a family- and culture-centered approach that requires understanding these social relationships. As Overton (1996) notes, an ecological assessment involves analyzing "a student's total learning environment" (p. 276). Consideration is given not only to the student's current level of performance, but also to the way in which the student's environment affects this performance. The classroom's physical and social environment, materials the teacher uses, the way time is used in the classroom; and the interactions among the student, peers, and the teacher can all influence how a student performs. In an ecological assessment, the focus is not only on students, but also on the opportunities and supports available in their environments.

Research on Ecological Assessment

Ecological assessment arose out of dissatisfaction with trying to adapt standardized assessments for students with severe disabilities. As described in Chapter One, Bricker and Campbell (1980) evaluated the use of a wide battery of standardized assessments with individuals with severe disabilities, and found that the information obtained had a minimal impact on educational planning. Professionals have also noted the inappropriateness of adapting standardized assessments to this population, because (1) students with severe disabilities are rarely included in the standardization sample (Sigafoos, Cole, & McQuarter, 1987); (2) administration procedures often cannot be followed (Blankenship, 1985); and (3) the tests are insensitive to small changes in functional behavior (Cole, Swisher, Thompson, & Fewell, 1985).

Some researchers have contrasted the impact of ecological and traditional assessment models. Downing and Perino (1992) developed three assessment reports for the same 8-year-old boy with severe disabilities. Teacher ratings of the educational usefulness of the three reports revealed significantly higher ratings for the options that included the ecological assessment information. Similarly, Linehan, Brady, and Hwang (1991) compared ecological and developmental assessments. Educators who read the ecological reports gave significantly higher ratings of expected educational outcomes than those reading developmental assessments. Linehan and Brady (1995) prepared similar contrasting reports for a 19-year-old student with severe disabilities and asked two groups of educators to write IEP objectives and suggest placements. Educators who read the developmental/standardized report were more likely to recommend more related services and restrictive settings.

These studies provide evidence that using an ecological assessment approach will yield more educationally useful information and may create higher professional expectations for a student's outcomes. This approach can be further strengthened by including a person-centered planning perspective.

WHAT IS PERSON-CENTERED PLANNING?

The philosophy of being "person-centered" is one that values directing service delivery to the goals, preferences, and needs of the individual being served. Rather than matching the person to services that already exist, services are developed based on the person's priorities and unique situation. Professionals who are "person-centered" in planning an IEP will focus on the student's agenda. The terms "person-driven" and "person-controlled" have been used to emphasize that the person being served sets the agenda (Marrone, Hoff, & Helm, 1997). Being person-centered can enhance self-determination as students are encouraged to make decisions, set their own goals, and run their own meetings.

Formats and Principles of Person-Centered Planning

"Person-centered planning" is a process for implementing this person-centered philosophy (Mount, 1994). There are a variety of formats for this process including lifestyle planning (O'Brien, 1987), personal-futures planning (Mount & Zwernik, 1988), the McGill Action Planning System (MAPS; Vandercook, York, & Forest, 1989), outcome-based planning (Steere, Wood, Pansocofar, & Butterworth, 1990), essential lifestyle planning (Smull & Harrison, 1992), group action planning (Turnbull & Turnbull, 1992), PATH (Planning Alternatives for Tomorrows with Hope; Falvey, Forest, Pearpoint, & Rosenberg, 1994), and whole-life planning (Butterworth, Hagner, Heikkinen, DeMello, & McDonough, 1993). Although each format has its own specific process for planning, all share some broadly defined principles (O'Brien & Lovett, 1993):

1. The primary direction for planning comes from the individual.
2. Family members and friends are involved in planning. Personal relationships are viewed as a primary source of support to the student.
3. Planning focuses on the individual's capacities and assets versus deficits.
4. An emphasis is given to the settings, services, supports, and routines available in the community or school at large versus those designed for people with disabilities.
5. Planning tolerates uncertainty, setbacks, false starts, and disagreement.

Person-centered planning formats were developed to include individuals with disabilities more centrally in the process of developing goals, and to involve family members as partners with professionals (Stineman, Morningstar, Bishop, & Turnbull, 1993). To be meaningful, the process must also involve taking action as well as planning. The outcome of a person-centered planning process includes a list of actions participants will take to help the individual with disabilities achieve his or her goals. For a school-age student, the process may produce both objectives for the student's IEP and action goals for the team. The creative brainstorming that is a part of the process can be especially beneficial for students with severe disabilities, who may have experienced limited options in their educational programs. Often one person will serve as the "facilitator" to coordinate the planning process.

Research on Person-Centered Planning

Research on person-centered planning provides evidence that using this approach can encourage participation by the family and individual with disabilities (Hagner, Helm, & Butterworth, 1996; Miner & Bates, 1997). The process can also increase the number of preferred, integrated activities in the person's schedule (Mallette et al., 1992).

Hagner et al. (1996) used in-depth participant observation to study the process of person-centered planning for six high school students with varying levels of mental retardation (mild to severe). The five-step creative problem-solving process, based on that of Butterworth et al. (1993), included (1) organizing the participants, setting a time and place for planning, and developing the facilitation strategy; (2) developing a personal profile; (3) constructing a vision of the future; (4) planning specific action steps; and (5) supporting ongoing implementation and networking. The researchers found that family members and friends were active participants in these meetings. They also were more likely to attend home-based meetings, whereas more professionals attended the school-based meetings.

Mallette et al. (1992) evaluated the use of person-centered planning with four unique individuals. These included (1) a woman with dual sensory impairments and severe intellectual disabilities; (2) a man who had spent much of his life in an institution; (3) a girl with autism; and (4) a girl with Sanfilippo's syndrome, a progressive degenerative neurological disorder. Mallette et al.'s (1992) research demonstrated that person-centered planning strategies can be applied to individuals with a wide variety of disabilities and personal priorities.

Miner and Bates (1997) evaluated the use of a person-centered planning meeting as a means to increase student and family participation in the IEP/transition planning meeting. In this person-centered planning process, the facilitator scheduled a meeting prior to the school's IEP/transition meeting with the student and family, to brainstorm some goals for the future that could be discussed at the school's meeting. This process increased both family participation and satisfaction with the transition planning process.

Although person-centered planning encourages student and family participation, implementing the process on a systemwide basis may be complex for many school districts. Even experts in person-centered planning warn that widespread implementation may be untenable (Hagner et al., 1996; O'Brien & Lovett, 1993). Although an open-ended series of meetings may be beyond most school district's resources, a family-focused meeting before the formal IEP meeting, such as the one utilized by Miner and Bates (1997), may be both feasible and productive in encouraging student and family participation. This modified approach to person-centered planning can be combined with ecological assessment strategies to strengthen the curriculum-planning process. Figure 2.1 shows what the agenda for a person-centered planning meeting may be.

BLENDING ECOLOGICAL ASSESSMENT AND PERSON-CENTERED PLANNING PROCESSES

Examples of Blended Approaches

An alternative to using only ecological assessment or only person-centered planning is to blend these approaches to make the curriculum-planning process as individualized and meaningful as possible. *Choosing Outcomes and Accommodations for Children* (COACH; Giangreco, Cloninger, & Iverson, 1998) is a model for blending these two approaches that has been empirically validated. In the COACH approach, the educator first interviews the family members to determine their priorities for educational planning. In a collaborative meeting with the family and professionals, a curriculum list of life skills is reviewed to select potential priorities. The group also plans how to incorporate priorities across educational settings (e.g., general education classes). The utility of the COACH model has been demonstrated with students with severe disabilities (Giangreco, Cloninger, Dennis, & Edelman, 1993) and with students who are deaf–blind (Giangreco, Edelman, Dennis, & Cloninger, 1995). The COACH approach is a highly useful guide for developing an IEP for students with severe disabilities. Figure 2.2 provides an illustration of the summary information obtained in a COACH model

FIGURE 2.1. Agenda for a person-centered planning meeting, based on the one used in the research of Miner and Bates (1997). Dave is a fictitious student.

Agenda for a Person-Centered Planning Meeting

Develop a Personal Profile

1. Draw the student's "support circles" (four concentric circles).

   Middle: Student's name
   Circle 1: Closest and most important people (e.g., Mom, Sally)
   Circle 2: Close, but not quite as close (e.g., neighbor—Mrs. Fields)
   Circle 3: People from church, sports teams, clubs, or other associations (e.g., Sam)
   Circle 4: People paid to be in student's life (e.g., teacher, bus driver)

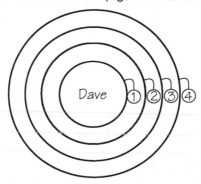

2. Draw a "community presence map": Include the community settings that the student uses daily, weekly, or occasionally.

   Grocery store   Restaurant

   Church   Uncle Bill's House

3. List the student's preferences.

   Likes   **Dislikes**
   Ice cream   Vegetables
   Kind people   Being teased
   Cars   Cold weather
   Being outside

(cont.)

FIGURE 2.1. (cont.)

4. List the student's capacities.

What Do People Like about Dave?
Great smile!   Works hard   Great listener

Describe a Desirable Future

1. Future living situations?
2. Community participation?
3. Employment?
4. Recreation/leisure?

Dave's Future
Work around cars
Outdoor fun—ski, hikes
Deliver newspapers like Uncle Bill
Join the football booster club

Action Plan

Goal	Action	Person responsible	Next step
1. Get a job	Job tryouts	Transition specialist	Schedule tryout.
2. Be outside more	Go hiking	Dave and Sam	Dave will set date.
3. Be in booster club	Sign up	Dave with Uncle Bill	Get the form.

Note Any Systems Change Needed

Currently job tryouts are only offered to students with mild disabilities—will need to advocate for Dave to have this chance.

The booster club currently has no members with mental retardation. Dave will be a "trailblazer."

Summarize the Meeting

Review goals, activities required to move toward a desirable future, and person responsible for each activity. Consider future meetings to continue planning process: Whom to invite? when to meet? where to meet?

planning process. Although the COACH is useful for a wide range of students with severe disabilities, expanded curricular options may be needed to use this approach for students with autism or moderate mental retardation. More resources may also be needed if teachers want to do some situational assessments in which students try new activities to discover more about their skills and preferences.

A similar model that combines person-centered planning and ecological assessment is the Team Environmental Assessment Mapping System (TEAMS) approach (Campbell et al., 1998). TEAMS was designed as a practical tool to gain information both about a student's environments and about his or her social relationships. TEAMS is a planning process implemented with a group of people including the student, family, teachers, and others familiar with the student. The first step, from an ecological assessment approach, involves determining the student's current and future environments (e.g., home, school classes, bus, family home, park, etc.) In the second step, from

FIGURE 2.2. An illustration of the summary information obtained in a COACH planning session. From Giangreco, Cloninger, and Iverson (1998). Copyright 1998 by Michael F. Giangreco. Reprinted with permission.

Ranking Valued Life Outcomes
to Emphasize this Year

Directions: Ask the person being interviewed, "Please rank the Valued Life Outcomes (where 1 is the most important) to help the team understand which ones you feel are most important for [student's name] this year." Terms that are presented in bold are abbreviations for use in Steps 1.5, 10.1, and 10.2.

Rank

_4_   Being **Safe** and **Healthy**

_5_   Having a **Home**, Now and in the Future

_1_   Having Meaningful **Relationships**

_2_   Having **Choice** and Control that Match One's Age and Culture

_3_   Participating in Meaningful **Activities** in Various Places

*** Relationship to Next Steps ***

This information about the student's Valued Life Outcomes will set the context for the selection of individualized learning outcomes and general supports.

a person-centered planning perspective, the student's relationships are identified for each of these environments. In the third step, a TEAMS meeting is held. This meeting can be a preparation for the IEP meeting or can be the IEP meeting itself, depending on how flexible IEP meeting times can be. In this meeting, the group plans for the student's future (person-centered planning), using questions that stimulate brainstorming. In the fourth step, the TEAMS map is drawn; this is a map that shows the student's current and future environments and relationships. In the fifth step, the team makes decisions based on this information, using four questions as guides:

1. What does it all mean? (Review of the map.)
2. What are the student's current and potential resources in these different environments?
3. What are the student's needs in these different environments?
4. Which of these needs could be affected by instruction and support?

From the fourth question, IEP objectives can be generated. The third question generates action plan goals for ongoing person-centered planning (e.g., development of supports needed to participate in general education). Figure 2.3 provides an example of a TEAMS map. The TEAMS approach will be especially strong in identifying relationships that can serve as natural supports to the student in various environments. In contrast, developing a personalized curriculum from this process may require more resources for students whose curricular needs are complex.

Using a Blended Approach to Develop the IEP

The Individuals with Disabilities Education Act (IDEA; PL 101-476) requires that all students identified with disabilities have an IEP. The IEP is a written commitment that the student will receive needed special education and related services. To be consistent with federally mandated procedures, the written statements in the IEP are developed by the IEP team, using information from assessments conducted in all areas of the student's disability. This chapter provides an example of how such assessments can be conducted for students with moderate and severe disabilities. Sometimes each professional participating in the IEP process provides a separate assessment report, and these are then synthesized to develop the IEP. The following list (paraphrased from Council on Exceptional Children [CEC], 1998, p. 75) gives the components that must be included in the IEP, according to IDEA and its amendments of 1997 (PL 105-17).

- *A statement of present levels of educational performance*, including how the student's disability affects involvement and progress in the general education curriculum.
- *A statement of annual goals, including benchmarks or short-term objectives* related to (1) meeting the student's needs that result from the student's disability, to enable the student to be involved in and progress in the general education curriculum; and (2) meeting each of the student's other educational needs that result from the disability.
- *Special education and related services to be provided*, and any program modifications or support for school personnel necessary to attain goals or participate in the general education curriculum or extracurricular activities.

FIGURE 2.3. An example of a TEAMS map. From Campbell, Campbell, and Brady (1998). Copyright 1998 by The Council for Exceptional Children. Reprinted with permission.

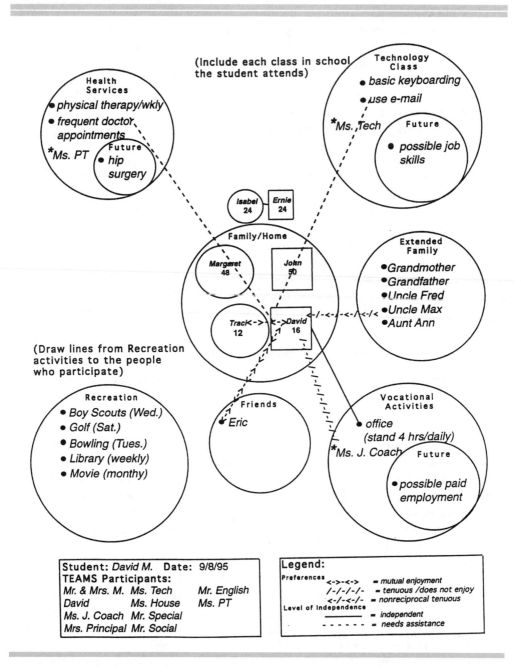

- An explanation of the extent, if any, to which the student *will not participate with students without disabilities in general education.*
- *A statement of any modifications in the administration of statewide or districtwide assessments of student achievement.* If the student will not participate in this assessment, a statement of why and how the student will be assessed must be provided.
- *Projected dates for the initiation of services, and the duration of services,* as well as projected frequency and location.
- *Statement of how the student's progress toward annual goals will be measured,* and how the student's parents will be informed of progress (at least as often as parents of students without disabilities).
- Beginning at age 14, *a statement of needed transition services*—including a statement of the interagency responsibilities (beginning at age 16), and a statement that the student has been informed (at least 1 year in advance) that rights will be transferred to the student at the age of majority.
- *Additional considerations,* depending on the student's unique needs:

  - Student's behavioral needs and whether positive behavior interventions are needed.
  - Language needs of a student with limited English proficiency.
  - Provision of instruction in Braille, if appropriate for a student who is blind or visually impaired.
  - Communication needs and modes of the student, especially if he or she is deaf or hard of hearing.
  - Student's need for assistive technology devices and services.

Constructing the IEP is an annual planning process. After the initial IEP is written, the school district must assume responsibility for reviewing and revising it annually. The people who attend the IEP meeting include the student; the parent(s); at least one special education teacher; at least one general education teacher (if the child is, or may be, participating in general education); any individuals who have conducted an evaluation of the student (e.g., physical therapist, school psychologist); a representative of the school district administration; and, in the case of an older student receiving a transition plan, representatives of adult service agencies (e.g., the local office of vocational rehabilitation).

In describing the student's current performance level, the IEP team will need to rely on some type of assessment information. Information obtained through the ecological assessment process can be especially helpful in providing educationally relevant information. Most often, this information is provided for each curricular area: (1) major life domains—home and personal care, community skills, leisure and recreation, employment skills; (2) basic skills—communication and social skills, functional academics; and (3) participation in the general education curriculum. The student's annual goals and objectives are based on this current level of functioning. These goals should reflect parental priorities and the student's preferences. A complete behavioral objective will be written to include the following "ABCs":

A—*Antecedent:* Conditions for performing the skill.

  Example: When working with a peer tutor in fourth-grade math and when us-
    ing her school schedule . . .

B—*Behavior:* The observable, measurable response the student is to make.

  Example: . . . Karen will identify clock times to the nearest quarter hour . . .

C—*Criterion:* The level of mastery expected.

  Example: . . . for 5 of 6 times across 2 days.

Complete objective: When working with a peer tutor in fourth-grade math and
    when using her school schedule, Karen will identify clock times to the nearest
    quarter hour for 5 of 6 times across 2 days.

In addition, the IEP must describe the annual evaluation procedures for these objectives. These may include task-analytic assessment, repeated opportunities, or other
procedures described in Chapter Four of this book. The IEP will also specify the student's placement and the extent of the student's participation in general education.
The projected data for the initiation and duration of special services are also described.

From these legal requirements for the IEP process, the following criteria will need
to apply to any assessment and planning process designed to generate an IEP:

1. Planning will include the student.
2. Planning will include the family.
3. Assessment will be specific enough to describe the student's current level of
   functioning and to generate objectives that can be measured.
4. Planning will be related to the student's environments, including participation
   that is targeted for general education (and, for a student of transition age, planning for future adult environments).
5. Planning will include a team process involving the student, the family, other
   professionals who are involved with the student, and others the family and student choose to include (e.g., extended family, friends, outside professionals).

The IDEA specifies what *must* be included in the IEP. Individualized planning for
students will often go beyond these basic requirements. Two important ways these
basics may be extended are by using person-centered planning and by developing a
personalized curriculum. As described earlier, using person-centered planning strategies can enhance the family's participation. Using these strategies in the IEP meeting,
however, can be difficult for two reasons. First, the requirement that all relevant professionals be present can overwhelm the family. Both the number of professionals
present and their use of technical jargon in presenting their evaluations can make the
meeting professionally driven. Also, the time constraints of administrators, who legally must attend the IEP, often make the open-ended discussion needed for person-
centered planning difficult. For example, Miner and Bates (1997) found that schools
often only allotted 30 minutes for IEP meetings, which does not allow sufficient time
for group planning. Similarly, participants may be intimidated in considering systems

change in this context. What is needed is a person-centered planning process to *prepare* for the IEP meeting. Often a special education teacher or other professional (e.g., guidance counselor, school psychologist, therapist) will serve as the facilitator of this process in preparation for an upcoming IEP meeting. To be person-centered, the planning process will encourage students and their families to take the lead in setting priorities for the IEP or transition plan. The facilitator can help the family identify a "circle of friends," including extended family members, neighbors, and other friends who are strongly committed to the student's future and are willing to help with this planning. The planning agenda will then be developed to affirm the student and create a positive tone.

Students with moderate and severe disabilities also need a personalized curriculum (Knowlton, 1998). Because students with moderate and severe disabilities are probably not following the school district's standard course of study, alternative curriculum planning is needed. A school district may develop a "functional curriculum guide" that outlines skills related to major life domains and basic skills. Such a guide will be highly useful in planning for a particular student, but will need to be further individualized according to the student's abilities, individual circumstances, support needs, and priorities. *An IEP is not the same as a curriculum.* The IEP outlines the priorities for the student's specially designed instruction. These priorities provide important direction to the educational program; they also provide specific objectives that can be measured to demonstrate the student's progress. However, IEP objectives are not comprehensive enough to cover the entire scope and sequence of what a student is to learn. The content taught by most special educators goes far beyond what is written in the IEP. Sometimes special educators try to incorporate an entire curriculum into the IEP, resulting in an overly long, detailed IEP. In other situations, the IEP is brief, and the curriculum the student will be learning is vague or undefined.

Like person-centered planning, developing a personalized curriculum is a longitudinal planning process. The IDEA mandates annual planning through the IEP. This does not preclude taking a more longitudinal planning focus. Using person-centered planning will help set priorities that are based on the student's future goals. Developing a personalized curriculum will offer the scope and sequence of what to teach to move toward these goals.

One important reason to develop a personalized curriculum is educational accountability. The 1997 amendments of IDEA require that the state or local education agency develop guidelines for the participation of children in alternate assessments if they cannot participate in statewide or districtwide assessment programs. If a student is to participate in an alternate assessment, the IEP must specify the rationale and process for this. States must also establish performance indicators that are consistent to the maximum extent possible with goals and standards for children established by the state. The development of a personalized curriculum can complement the process of alternate assessment by (1) clarifying the need for such assessment through identifying the student's curricular needs as different from the standard course of study; and (2) defining the student's curriculum so that he or she is prepared to meet the state's performance indicators. More information on alternate assessment is provided in Chapter Three. Table 2.1 summarizes the criteria to use for individualized planning.

TABLE 2.1. Criteria for Individualized Planning for Students with Moderate
and Severe Disabilities

I. Criteria from the IDEA for the IEP
- Include the student.
- Include the family.
- Plan with a team consisting of the student; the family; professionals (special education teacher, general education teacher, outside agency representatives if the student is of transition age) who are, or may be, involved with the student; and others the family and student choose to include.
- Use assessment that will indicate the student's current level of functioning and can lead to specific goals and objectives.
- Identify assessment that can providing ongoing evaluation.
- Plan the student's level of participation in general education.
- If the student is of transition age, plan toward functioning in adult environments.

II. Criteria from a person-centered planning perspective
- Encourage student self-determination (e.g., honor the student's preferences).
- Encourage ways for planning to be family-centered.
- Include people in planning who have a long-term commitment to the student.
- Brainstorm short- and long-term future plans.
- Focus on quality-of-life issues.
- Plan and implement action goals for creating the student's desirable future.

III. Criteria for planning a personalized curriculum
- Plan for the student's current and future environments in and out of school.
- Identify priorities for the curricular focus with the student and family.
- Plan curriculum across life domains, basic skills, and general education (a published or district curriculum may be used as a guide).
- Prioritize within curriculum planning for the student's IEP.

PLANNING WHAT TO TEACH STUDENTS WITH MODERATE AND SEVERE DISABILITIES: STEPS IN CONDUCTING AN ECOLOGICAL ASSESSMENT

One of the most important educational decisions to be made is determining what to teach students with moderate and severe disabilities (Browder, 1997). Educators are often confused about this process because of the lack of a "standard course of study" or other definitive curriculum, as well as the lack of published diagnostic tests that can be used for this purpose. Guidelines are now offered for conducting an ecological assessment, from a person-centered planning perspective, that will help determine the goals and objectives for an IEP and generate a personalized curriculum.[2] For each step, references to data-based research, legal requirements of IDEA, and descriptive resources are included, both here and in subsequent chapters that describe these steps in further detail. As shown in Table 2.2, these steps can be used in developing the IEP only (see the third column) or in conducting an evaluation of the student that will include a formal written report as preparation for the IEP process (see the fourth column).

[2]I field-tested the guidelines for ecological assessment offered in this book during my term as Director of Lehigh University Supported Employment and Assessment Services.

Step 1: Summarize What Is Known about the Student

The beginning point in planning with any student is to get to know the student. Although all of the steps to follow are ways of getting to know the student, it is helpful to begin by summarizing the information that is already available. To meet IDEA requirements in developing an IEP, the team will need to consider the strengths of the student, to review the most recent evaluation conducted on the student, and to define the student's present level of educational performance, including how the student's disability affects participation in the general education curriculum (CEC, 1998). Whether team members are writing a full assessment report, or focusing solely on the development of the IEP, the beginning point is to summarize the most recent information on the student.

If the team begins with summarizing the student's *strengths* and *positive attributes*, this can set the tone for the entire information-gathering process to be one of "capacity building" for the student versus "deficit finding," as described in the Chapter One. Research on the impact of written assessment reports has shown that the way a student is described can influence what teachers expect of the student in writing IEP objectives (Linehan & Brady, 1995). The extended example to follow introduces the case of Roberto Gomez (a fictional, but realistic, individual), whose information is provided in describing each step of the ecological assessment process.

In Roberto's case, the assessment purpose was twofold: to develop a written assessment report that would be used as part of his reevaluation, and to develop the IEP. Roberto's special education teacher, Ms. Becker, had the primary responsibility of writing the educational assessment report. She was also coordinating the members of the multidisciplinary team who were contributing to Roberto's reevaluation. Her contributions to this team would be to identify Roberto's curricular and support needs, and to determine whether he needed to participate in alternate assessment or the state's standardized testing. As Roberto's teacher, Ms. Becker was also responsible for writing the IEP. She decided to use two overlapping teams for the planning process: a "circle of friends" and a formal IEP team. The "circle of friends" would include Roberto's extended family and friends and the professionals they chose to invite to conduct person-centered planning. A subset of this circle, including Roberto, his parents, and any others the parents chose to include from the circle of friends, would join with the group of professionals who would serve as the IEP team. These professionals included the principal, the director for exceptional children, a speech therapist, an occupational therapist, an English as a Second Language (ESL) instructor, two general education teachers, the school guidance counselor, and school psychologist. Because of the number of people involved, the difficulty in meeting both family members' and professionals' schedule needs, and the need to encourage family involvement, these overlapping teams seemed to be the best approach. Because Ms. Becker had taught Roberto for a year, she volunteered to summarize some information on his strengths as a capacity statement. This is what she wrote and shared with the members of both teams.

CAPACITY STATEMENT

Roberto is an attractive 12-year-old boy with expressive brown eyes and black hair. Roberto focuses well on functional academics and seatwork when given a structured

TABLE 2.2. Steps in Conducting an Ecological Assessment to Develop an IEP

Step	Information obtained	Development of the IEP	Summary for assessment report (if applicable)
STEP 1. Summarize what is known about the student's strengths, educational performance, and disability.	• Capacity statement. • Notes from educational records. • Summary of progress on IEP.	• Use information obtained in describing "current level of performance." • IDEA requires that the IEP team consider the strengths of the child. • Team must also consider the most recent evaluation of the student and determine how the disability affects participation in general education curriculum.	Part I. Description of student and purpose of assessment.
STEP 2. Facilitate family involvement, using person-centered planning strategies, prior to the actual IEP meeting.	• Family's perspective on student's preferences. • Student's life story (if family considers it relevant to current planning). • Family and cultural values to honor in planning. • "Dreams"/goals for the long-term future. • Priorities for IEP.	• IDEA requires that the IEP team consider the concerns of parents for enhancing the education of their child. • Identify priorities to consider in writing annual goals, benchmarks, and objectives.	Part II. Person-centered planning: • Student's history and priorities. • Family's priorities.
STEP 3. Encourage student self-determination.	• Student preference chart. • Data from systematic preference assessment and situational assessments. • Information on student's skills in, and support for, self-determination. • Plans for student's involvement in the IEP.	• Encourage student participation in the IEP.	Part III. Student self-determination: • Student's preferences. • Student's skills in self-determination and ways to encourage these. • Recommendation for how to involve student in the IEP meeting.

| STEP 4. Define the student's personalized curriculum (skill needs). | • Indirect assessment using curriculum inventory.
• Priorities established with family and student (use these to focus subsequent information gathering).
• Ecological inventories of general education classes and community sites.
• Discrepancy analyses.
• Situational assessments, in which student tries new activity, material, setting (as needed).
• Functional assessment if needed for problem behavior.
• Curriculum chart. | • Pinpoint specific skills to be targeted in writing short-term objectives.
• Use specific skills to set benchmarks (e.g., for alternate assessment).
• Review special considerations such as need for behavioral support, English as a Second Language (ESL) services, Braille, augmentative communication system, or assistive technology.
• Involve general education teacher through curriculum and inclusion planning. | Part IV. Current skills and curriculum priorities:
• Description of student's skills and skill needs in each priority curricular area.
• Appendix: The curriculum chart. |
| STEP 5. Develop the IEP and/or assessment report. | • Annual goals, short-term objectives, and benchmarks.
• Method of progress monitoring for each goal.
• Schedule matrix showing recommended time in general education and IEP objectives for each goal.
• Support needs. | • Create the draft IEP to be considered by the team for formal approval. | Part V. Recommendations for the IEP:
• Priorities for consideration in developing the IEP.
• Recommendations for general education inclusion.
• Recommendations for related services and other support needs. |

environment. Roberto enjoys birds and can imitate several bird songs. Although he is nonverbal, he is able to comprehend words and short phrases in both English and Spanish.

Next, team members reviewed Roberto's prior records for educationally relevant information. Ms. Becker reviewed the prior year's progress on IEP objectives to write the statements on "current level of educational performance" for the IEP. Because she had used some data collection, she had specific information for most prior objectives. When available, data-based summaries can help teachers be more accurate in determining student progress and making the types of instructional decisions needed (Holvoet, O'Neil, Chazdon, Carr, & Warner, 1983; Utley, Zigmond, & Strain, 1987). The following are Ms. Becker's summary notes. An illustration of how she used these notes and other information she knew about Roberto to write the current level of performance on the IEP is given later in this chapter.

SUMMARY OF ROBERTO'S PROGRESS ON PAST IEPs

GOAL	PROGRESS
1. Put on own jacket.	Mean is 84%; mastered all steps of task analysis except zipping.
2. Recognize name on lunchbox.	Mastered and generalized to name on other materials.
3. Greet peers when he enters class.	No progress; mean of 20% with variability in data (flat trend).
4. Make choices across school day.	Minimal progress (no data)—need better method to track progress.
5. Identify numbers on math sheet.	Excellent progress and near mastery (95%); a highly preferred task.
6. Work quietly during math class.	Quiet for most days (95%); disruptions when confused by changes in routine.
7. Self-initiate toileting every 2 hours.	Mastered early in year by using watch alarm.
8. Eat with utensils.	Mastered task analysis for spoon use; will not use a fork or knife.
9. Comprehend 50 new English words.	Showed comprehension of 70 new words!

In developing a formal assessment report as part of Roberto's reevaluation, Ms. Becker reviewed his most recent psychological, medical, and therapy evaluations. Sometimes reviewing past records entails wading through pages of disparaging and deficit finding reports. To keep a positive focus, educators can "talk back" to such statements and challenge their validity as they read. The educator's notes on such a file may look something like the following.

SIFTING THROUGH ROBERTO'S PAST RECORDS: KEEPING A POSITIVE VIEW

Record says:	My comments:
IQ is 23	Not reflective of Roberto's ability or classification.
	Stigmatizing—irrelevant and may be discriminatory, given cultural heritage.
	Don't make reference to this score.
Classification of autism	Important—current classification.
Grand mal seizures	Important—check medication currently used.
	Side effects of medication? Sun-sensitive?
	Talk with mother; consult with school nurse.
	Symptoms of seizures? Watch for how seizures affect responding. Make team aware of this challenge.

From this preliminary information, Ms. Becker began to draft her assessment report as shown in Figure 2.4.

Step 2: Plan with the Student and Family

The second step is a person-centered planning process and involves meeting with the family *prior* to the actual IEP meeting. As described in the research of Miner and Bates (1997), this preliminary planning can increase the family's participation in the IEP pro-

FIGURE 2.4. Example of Part I of a written assessment report.

Written Assessment Report:
Part I. Statement about Student and Purpose of Assessment

Student: Roberto Gomez   **Evaluator:** Meg Becker
School: Sun Valley Middle School   **Date:** May 1, 20—

Roberto Gomez is a student with autism who receives educational services through the Mid-Central School District at Sun Valley Middle School. Roberto is an attractive 12-year-old boy with expressive brown eyes and short black hair. When given the support of a consistent routine and predictable environment, Roberto shows a keen interest in his schoolwork. Roberto has recently begun to attend general education classes in his middle school. The purposes of the current assessment are to develop a personalized curriculum for Roberto that will coordinate his life skills priorities with involvement in the general education curriculum, and to recommend priorities for his IEP.

(This report continues.)

cess. Not only is recruiting family participation legally mandated by IDEA, but students themselves note the importance of having their families involved (Morningstar, Turnbull, & Turnbull, 1996). Nevertheless, research on families has often shown estrangement from the IEP process, especially if the family is not from the predominant culture (Harry, Allen, & McLaughlin, 1995). To develop family collaboration and avoid such estrangement, the facilitator should work closely with the primary family contact (e.g., the mother) to establish a convenient time and place for a preliminary planning session. More family members and friends may participate if the meeting is held at home rather than school (Hagner et al., 1996). Sometimes it may be helpful if the facilitator makes a phone call or home visit to establish rapport with the family and to explain the person-centered planning process. Some families prefer to meet in a school context and to keep the meeting more formalized (in the style of a business meeting). What is most important is that the student's and family's preferences are honored in setting up this meeting for their convenience. In general, the majority of people at this meeting will be those who have a long term commitment to the student with disabilities (family and friends).

In setting up Roberto's person-centered planning meeting, Ms. Becker called his mother Mrs. Gomez to talk about the concept of a "circle of friends" and what a person-centered meeting would involve. Mrs. Gomez was delighted with the idea because their friends and family would be able to share their ideas to help Roberto. They discussed some options for the meeting and then Ms. Becker followed up with this written invitation:

AN INVITATION TO PLAN FOR ROBERTO'S FUTURE WITH A "CIRCLE OF FRIENDS"

I have enjoyed having Roberto in my class this year. I would like to have the opportunity to get to know you better and to talk with you about your dreams and goals for Roberto's future. This is an invitation to do some planning before the IEP meeting that will be held next month. By meeting together now, we will have more time to talk about Roberto's future. This is Roberto's meeting . . . and your meeting. You and Roberto can invite anyone you like . . . anyone who might help us plan for Roberto's future because they are involved in Roberto's life. I would be glad to come to your home to meet with you, Roberto, and the "circle of friends and family" that you invite. Or, if you prefer, I would be glad to set up this meeting here at school. I will be calling you soon to discuss this planning meeting.

Any of the person-centered planning formats described earlier in this chapter can be used to develop the meeting's agenda. Whatever format is used, it is important to (1) affirm the student and keep a positive perspective, (2) brainstorm about the student's future together, and (3) set some specific priorities and action plans for the coming IEP.

In Roberto's case, the family chose the home visit option. Mrs. Gomez was glad for Ms. Becker to invite the other professionals involved in Roberto's life. She promised to invite her family and friends. Because the meeting was held in the evening in the family's home (a time and place convenient for the family), only three professionals were able to attend: Ms. Becker, Ms. Jacobson, and the ESL teacher (who was also available to translate if needed). In contrast, the meeting was highly successful in involving a strong "circle" of family and friends for Roberto. Here are the minutes of this meeting.

MINUTES FROM ROBERTO'S PERSON-CENTERED PLANNING MEETING

PRESENT AT THE MEETING

Roberto, Mrs. Gomez, Mr. Gomez, Grandmother Gomez, Grandmother Ricardo, Aunt Rosa, "Angel" (Mr. Diaz—a friend who worked in the family's grocery store), Father Hernandez (family's priest), Ms. Jacobson (school psychologist), Ms. Becker (special education teacher and meeting facilitator), Mr. Santos (ESL teacher).

DATE AND LOCATION OF MEETING

March 26th at the Gomez home.

WHAT DO WE LIKE ABOUT ROBERTO?

He is gentle.
He can sing beautiful bird songs.
He is handsome.
He is family.

WHAT DOES ROBERTO LIKE?

Birds!!!!!
Being outside.
Being at church.
Spring.
Being warm.
Being with Aunt Rosa.
Sweet food.
Being in sixth-grade math class.

WHAT DOES ROBERTO DISLIKE?

Sudden, loud noises.
Being physically forced to do something.
Too many people talking to him at once.
A lot of walking.

HOW ELSE IS ROBERTO UNIQUE?

Has a large family whose members live together in the same neighborhood.
Sometimes spends the day with his father in the family's grocery store.
Puerto Rican and Roman Catholic heritage.
Has traveled to Puerto Rico to see extended family.

WHAT IS ROBERTO'S LIFE STORY?

Born in Puerto Rico.
Typical child development, began to talk, then regression at age 2.
Attended an early intervention program in Puerto Rico.
Relocated to Pennsylvania when Roberto was 5; mother got administrative position in
    large company with good medical benefits; Roberto was sick a lot and had seizures.

Extended family came to help father start a store.

Roberto was very unhappy in elementary special education class.

When Roberto was 9, parents took him to specialist in Puerto Rico, who classified him as autistic; also got help for his seizures from specialist in New York.

Family asked for Roberto to be reevaluated; district classified him as autistic.

Roberto was happier in new special education class for children with autism.

District began to try inclusion when Roberto was 10.

Roberto started middle school when he turned 11.

WHAT DOES OUR FAMILY VALUE MOST?

Stay close as family.

Catholic faith.

WHAT ARE OUR HOPES AND DREAMS FOR ROBERTO?

That he will always have family and not be lonely.

That he can work in the family store.

That he be healthy—no more seizures!

That he be able to tell us more about what he wants.

That he learn to communicate.

That he learn to read and write.

WHAT ARE OUR TOP PRIORITIES FOR ROBERTO'S SCHOOL PROGRAM AT THIS TIME?

Communication skills!

Learn "real skills" (e.g., reading, math)—no more "baby work."

Be able to go see neighbors on his own (e.g., street crossing).

Find more classes like math (more inclusion).

ACTION GOALS

1. Observe and select classes for general education inclusion.
2. Assess Roberto's safety skills in the community and plan instruction.
3. Develop communication system for Roberto.
4. Include academic skills on IEP.

When the person-centered planning meeting is complete, the notes taken from the meeting can be used in developing the IEP. Ms. Becker used the information from this meeting to note priority areas to follow in developing the IEP: (1) communication, (2) functional academics, (3) inclusion, and (4) community safety. For the formal written report, Ms. Becker summarized the family preplanning as shown in Figure 2.5.

Step 3: Encourage Student Self-Determination

The person-centered planning meeting held with the family is an important beginning point to encourage self-determination. The student's presence and participation in this meeting enhance the team's understanding of the student's priorities. As a follow-up to this meeting, the facilitator should spend some additional time preplanning the IEP

FIGURE 2.5. Written Assessment Report: Part II. Person-Centered Planning

On March 26, a meeting was held with Roberto's family and friends at the Gomez home to plan for his future priorities. The family shared Roberto's life history. Roberto was born in Puerto Rico and had typical child development, including some speech, until age 2. Roberto lost these skills for unknown reasons during his second year of life and attended an early intervention program in Puerto Rico at ages 3 and 4. The family relocated to Pennsylvania when Roberto was 5, so that the family would have access to more options and benefits for his medical care. In early elementary school, Roberto did not respond well to his educational program in a classroom. An outside evaluation from Dr. Juan Diaz (see report in files) resulted in Roberto's being reclassified as having autism. Roberto also received medical treatment for his grand mal seizures, which are now partially controlled with medication. The family reports that Roberto has made good progress since having teachers who know more about autism. Since he was 10, Roberto has been responding well to opportunities to participate in general education with his typical peers. Roberto is now a middle school student who spends one period a day in general education and the rest in a self-contained special education class. His family's priorities are for Roberto to have more inclusion at the middle school and to learn more academics.

The family members noted that their long-term goals ("dreams") for Roberto are that he be able to communicate with them better and tell them more about what he wants; that he remain in his family's neighborhood and perhaps work with his father; that his seizures be decreased or eliminated; and that he be able to read and write. Their priorities for his next IEP are (1) communication skills, (2) functional academics ("real skills") and life skills, (3) inclusion in general education, and (4) street crossing and community safety.

(This report continues.)

with the student to strengthen the student's influence on the outcome of the IEP. Also, the student's preferences may not be fully identifiable in a meeting format. The student may need time to try new options through systematic preference assessment. Taking this extra time to understand the student's perspective is an important investment in developing a high-quality IEP. Research on choice has shown that students' performance can be enhanced by offering and honoring choices (Kern et al., 1998). Research has also revealed that if students' preferences are included in a written individualized plan, they are more likely to be considered when educators are planning daily activities (Newton, Horner, & Lund, 1991). However, nonverbal students like Roberto cannot state their preferences for their IEPs directly; instead, systematic preference assessment methods are needed (Lohrmann-O'Rourke & Browder, 1998).

During this third step, the facilitator uses systematic preference assessment by making notes on the student's typical choices, talking with others who know the student, and giving the student the opportunity to try new options. The teacher may also use a checklist to consider the student's skills and opportunities for self-determination. Some thought should be given to how to involve the student in the IEP meeting. Does the student need the opportunity to learn more about the meeting process? Will the student need support to participate or be present? After considering how to encourage Roberto's self-determination through preference assessment, evaluation of his self-determination skills, and planning for his involvement in the IEP meeting, Ms. Becker made the following notes.

HOW CAN I ENCOURAGE ROBERTO'S SELF-DETERMINATION?

PREFERENCE ASSESSMENT

- Food preferences: Likes all types of sweet food; mild preference for spicy food.
- Leisure preferences: On 8 of 10 occasions over 3 days, chose being outside and view-ing bird books. When bird books not available, chose other options in this order: (1) cassette tape of music, (2) video game, (3) blacklight art.
- New activities: Showed strong interest in a walk in a nature preserve, a visit to a natural history museum, dusting shelves in his father's store, and walking in his neighborhood; disliked bagging groceries, food at the deli, pep rally.
- I can incorporate Roberto's preferences into the daily schedule.

SKILLS IN SELF-DETERMINATION

- Follows a schedule; needs verbal prompt to begin activity.
- Clear about dislikes by pulling away.
- Uses self-monitoring of behavior with checklist during some lessons.
- Needs opportunities to make choices; needs communication skills to ask for prefer-ences that are not visible in environment.

INVOLVING ROBERTO IN HIS IEP MEETING

- Roberto stayed present at the table during the first 30 minutes of his person-cen-tered planning meeting, and then sat on the other side of the room with Aunt Rosa.
- Roberto can be present at his IEP meeting, but may need a support person in case he tires of the process.
- Because Roberto is nonverbal and a nonreader, I will need to use picture symbols for each objective whenever possible during the IEP meeting, and to show these to Roberto as they are discussed. I will consider his reaction and notes from his prefer-ence assessments as each objective is discussed.
- I need to be careful not to lose sight of Roberto's preferences during the meeting.

Ms. Becker then summarized these notes in her formal report, as shown in Fig-ure 2.6.

Step 4: Define the Student's Personalized Curriculum

As described earlier, students with moderate and severe disabilities need personalized curricula, since they typically are not following the school district's academic standard course of study. Consideration also needs to be given to the form of alternate assess-ment that will be used if a student will not participate in district and state testing (more information is provided on alternate assessment in Chapter Three). This personalized curriculum is not meant to prevent a student from participating in general education, but rather to define how to make this participation meaningful for a student whose reading and math skills may be below the first-grade level. IDEA emphasizes this in-volvement in general education by requiring (1) a statement of how the student's dis-ability affects involvement and progress in the general education curriculum; (2) mea-surable goals, objectives, and benchmarks related to involvement and progress in the

FIGURE 2.6. Example of Part III of a written assessment report.

Written Assessment Report:
Part III. Student Self-Determination

Systematic preference assessment was conducted with Roberto over a 1-week period by offering him choices during his daily routine and creating opportunities for him to sample new activities. Roberto showed specific preferences (see below) by reaching for items, by looking at items for a prolonged time, or by not refusing (e.g., not trying to leave the area). In considering ways to encourage Roberto's self-determination, staff members should offer Roberto more opportunities for choice making and should encourage him to request objects and activities not seen by using picture cards. Roberto can participate in his IEP with a support person by being present and by having the opportunity to see pictures of the objectives being discussed.

Student Preference Chart for Roberto

Foods	Leisure items	Activities and settings
Sweets	Bird books	Outside, hiking, birds
Some spicy foods	Cassette tapes	Nature museums
	Video games	Dusting at father's store
	Blacklight art	Math class

(This report continues.)

general education curriculum; and (3) involvement of the general education teacher, to the extent appropriate, in the development of the IEP (CEC, 1998).

Developing this personalized curriculum will be easier if the district has both a functional curriculum guide and well-defined indicators for student achievement of state standards and outcomes. If these do not exist, several commercial functional curricula are available, including the Syracuse Community-Referenced Curriculum Guide (Ford et al., 1989), Life Centered Career Education (Loyd & Brolin, 1997), the COACH model (Giangreco et al., 1998), and the Activities Catalog (Wilcox & Bellamy, 1987). Sometimes adaptive behavior scales can be used for this purpose (see Table 1.1 in Chapter One). The present book also provides many skill charts that can be used as guides for developing functional curricula and for embedding life skills or functional academics in general education activities.

To develop a personalized curriculum, an evaluator needs to begin with broad assessments and then move to specific assessments. In planning for life skills, it is impossible to conduct direct assessment of all, or even many, of the activities of daily living. Unlike assessing skills in the general education curriculum, in which tests can be designed that sample mastery in a group testing format, "tests" of life skills may require having many days and settings for each student to be evaluated. The entire school year could be devoted to testing life skills, with no time left for teaching! The alternative is to use indirect assessment with a life skills inventory (e.g., a life skills curriculum checklist) to summarize the student's skills and potential needs in each life skills area. Unfortunately, indirect assessment, though necessary, is not sufficient because life skills are influenced by culture and context (Lim & Browder, 1994). These skills are also so numerous that an indirect assessment cannot possibly be specific or comprehensive enough to contain all possible objectives. To determine the student's specific instructional needs, the evaluator can follow this sequence of general to specific assessment: (1) curriculum inventory, (2) ecological inventories, (3) discrepancy analysis, (4) situational assessment, and (5) functional assessment of problem behavior (if needed).

First, the evaluator completes a curriculum inventory and then reviews priorities established during person-centered planning with the family and student. Next, the evaluator considers the specific contextual skills needed by conducting ecological inventories—that is, observing the student's current and future environments that are relevant to this planning. For example, if general education music and social studies classes are priorities, what is the classroom routine in these settings? What skills will the student need? What support is needed? Similarly, if a new job-training setting is planned, what skills will be needed in the new job site? What natural supports are available? In the third step, the skills needed can then be specified further by using a discrepancy analysis, in which the evaluator asks, "What would a nondisabled peer of the same age do in this setting? What can/does this student do now? What new skills are needed for him or her to participate more like a same-age peer?" This discrepancy analysis may result in planning curriculum adaptations. For example, the student might participate in social studies daily, but with a focus on functional academic skills such as reading sight words and writing his or her name. Or the student might have the goal of learning basic information, such as learning the name of the current U.S. president and local representatives to Congress when the class studies a unit on the branches of government.

From these ecological inventories and discrepancy analyses, most IEP objectives can be generated. But sometimes even more specificity is needed. In this case, the evaluator can use a situational assessment, in which the student is given the opportunity to try a new activity, material, or setting. For example, the evaluator may help the student try a day in the second-grade class or an outing to purchase a snack at the convenience store. The evaluator takes data on the student's performance and preferences during this sampling. When problem behavior is a concern, a functional assessment may be implemented to clarify the function of the behavior and plan positive behavioral support. For example, the evaluator considers the antecedents that occur before the behavior, its consequences, and the possibility that the behavior may reflect the need for training in communication or social skills. This book contains numerous examples of using ecological inventories, discrepancy analyses, and situational assessments for functional academics, home and community skills, and planning for inclusion and transition. The following describes how all this was done in the case of Roberto.

For Roberto, Ms. Becker selected Life Centered Career Education (the version for moderate disabilities; Loyd & Brolin, 1997) as a curriculum guide and completed the checklists. An example of this evaluation for one curricular area is shown in Figure 2.7. Ms. Becker used this curriculum inventory to revise her descriptions of Roberto's current level of performance to be broader than just her prior year's data on IEP objectives. She also used this information, plus the information she had obtained from the first

FIGURE 2.7. Roberto's Life Centered Career Education evaluation in the area of daily living skills. The form is from Loyd and Brolin (1997). Copyright 1997 by the Council for Exceptional Children. Reprinted with permission.

LIFE CENTERED CAREER EDUCATION

Competency Rating Scale-Modified

Record Form

DAILY LIVING SKILLS

Student Name _Roberto Gomez_ Date of Birth _Oct. 4, 19—_ Sex _Male_

School _Sun Valley Middle_ City _Any Town_ State _Any State_

Directions: Please rate the student according to his/her mastery of *each* item using the rating key below. Indicate the ratings in the column below the date for the rating period. Use the NR rating for items which cannot be rated. For subcompetencies rated 0 or 1 at the time of the final rating, place a check (✔) in the appropriate space in the *yes/no* column to indicate his/her ability to perform the subcompetency with assistance from the community. Please refer to the CRS manual for explanation of the rating key, description of the behavioral criteria for each subcompetency, and explanation of the *yes/no* column.

Rating Key: 0 = Not Competent 1 = Partially Competent 2 = Competent NR = Not Related

To what extent has the student mastered the following subcompetencies?

Subcompetencies	Rater(s)	Becker								Yes	No
	Grade Level	7									
	Date(s)	4/15									
DAILY LIVING SKILLS DOMAIN										Yes	No
1. Managing Money											
1. Count Money		1	—	—	—	—	—	—	—	—
2. Make Purchases		1	—	—	—	—	—	—	—	—
3. Use Vending Machines		1	—	—	—	—	—	—	—	—
4. Budget Money		0	—	—	—	—	—	—	—	—
5. Perform Banking Skills		0	—	—	—	—	—	—	—	—
2. Selecting and Maintaining Living Environments											
6. Select Appropriate Community Living Environments		0	—	—	—	—	—	—	—	—
7. Maintain Living Environment		0	—	—	—	—	—	—	—	—
8. Use Basic Appliances and Tools		0	—	—	—	—	—	—	—	—
9. Set Up Personal Living Space		0	—	—	—	—	—	—	—	—
3. Caring for Personal Health											
10. Perform Appropriate Grooming and Hygiene		1	—	—	—	—	—	—	—	—
11. Dress Appropriately		1	—	—	—	—	—	—	—	—
12. Maintain Physical Fitness		1	—	—	—	—	—	—	—	—
13. Recognize and Seek Help for Illness		1	—	—	—	—	—	—	—	—
14. Practice Basic First Aid		1	—	—	—	—	—	—	—	—
15. Practice Personal Safety		1	—	—	—	—	—	—	—	—

three steps of the assessment process, to draft a curriculum chart for Roberto. She cross-referenced the skills with the state's standards in preparation for his alternate assessment.

As Ms. Becker looked at the curriculum chart, she realized that there was still work to do to generate specific, measurable IEP objectives for Roberto. She also realized that the chart was not yet fully "personalized." To personalize his curriculum, she went back to her notes on his person-centered planning and highlighted these priorities—communication, functional academics, inclusion, and community safety. She would now try to get more information on these skill areas. Her first step was to conduct ecological inventories of Roberto's current and future environments. Given the priorities of functional academics and inclusion, she focused on an inventory of potential seventh-grade classes for Roberto's next year's schedule. She included a communications class, given this priority need. Here are some of her notes:

ECOLOGICAL INVENTORY OF MIDDLE SCHOOL ENVIRONMENTS

Environment: Middle school classes.

Subenvironment: Wood shop.
  Activities: Student project—birdhouse or wooden clipboard.
  Supports available: Students work in pairs; teacher uses some picture and color cues.
  Target skills: Measure using metric rulers, sand materials, follow written assignment (use picture/sight words for Roberto?), use band saw, varnish (sight word directions?).

Subenvironment: Consumer math class.
  Activities: Work problems in text, lecture, computer simulations, group projects.
  Supports available: Computer for each student, teacher gives 1:1 feedback.
  Target skills: Number recognition, use of calculator, use of computer.

Subenvironment: Communication class.
  Activities: Lecture, written composition, speeches, reading.
  Supports available: "Warm" classroom environment and encouraging teacher; students taught to affirm each other's communication styles.
  Target skills: Name writing, sight words, listening skills, communication wallet use.

From the inventories of potential future classes for Roberto, Ms. Becker got some new ideas for his personalized curriculum chart. For his functional math, she included teaching Roberto to match numbers and letters on a card to a keyboard, and to learn general use of a computer. She also included calculator use. For functional reading, she noted the need to teach reading of the picture/sight word instructions that would be used in wood shop. She also included high-frequency sight words from the communications textbook that Roberto could use to follow the titles and picture captions. She would also use teacher-made stories with controlled vocabulary to help Roberto learn passage reading.

Next, Ms. Becker used a discrepancy analysis to consider how Roberto's day could be enhanced by making it more age-appropriate, enriching it with choice opportunities, and encouraging his self-direction. Here are her notes.

DISCREPANCY ANALYSIS FOR ROBERTO

Roberto's typical day	Typical day of Kenneth (11-year-old peer who is nondisabled)	Ideas to encourage more age-appropriate activities	Ideas to encourage more choice and communication	Ideas to encourage more self-direction
Mother helps him dress and eat.	Dresses himself; fixes own cereal.	Have him dress himself (needs to learn to zip and button). Have him fix cereal.	Have him choose what to wear. Teach him to request what to eat.	Teach him to follow picture schedule for morning routine.
Goes to SpEd class to wait for school to start.	Waits in cafeteria with peers for school to start.	Teach him to walk to cafeteria on his own (locate it from bus).	Have him choose peers with whom to sit. Have him choose whether to talk or look at books.	Teach him to manage own behavior, using reminder checklist (e.g., stay seated).
Goes to morning circle.	Goes to homeroom and locker.	Have him go to a homeroom. Help him learn to open a locker.	Have him choose seat if not assigned.	Teach him to keep track of his own bookbag and schedule.
Goes to SpEd class or to a general class (inclusion with aide).	Goes to classes.	Have aide work with whole class vs. shadow Roberto.	Encourage him to greet peers.	Teach him to read schedule and select materials needed.
Lunch in SpEd class; cartoon lunchbox.	Has lunch with own friends who all buy lunch.	Have him eat lunch in cafeteria. Help him learn to buy own lunch or pack paper bag lunch.	Encourage him to greet peers. Have him choose menu items to buy. Have him point to items needed in food line.	Help him pace self to finish lunch by end of time. Teach him to use relaxation to cope with noise.

From this information, Ms. Becker was able to personalize Roberto's curriculum chart and to begin drafting IEP objectives. She decided she needed more information about Roberto's community safety and communication with peers. To assess these priorities, she used situational assessments of two activities: using the city bus to go to the mall, and assisting the manager of the boys' soccer team. Here are her notes on the bus ride to the mall.

SITUATIONAL ASSESSMENT

Student: Roberto Gomez

Setting: Bus and Eastland Mall

Routine task analysis	Level of assistance needed	Preferences
1. Wait at bus stop.	Verbal direction, modeling.	Liked being outside.
2. Pay fare.	Partial physical guidance.	Anxious? Twirled hair.
3. Find seat.	Independent.	Sat near window.
4. Disembark at mall.	Verbal direction, modeling.	Eager to get off bus.
5. Cross street to mall.	Partial physical guidance.	Not attentive to traffic.
6. Go to food court.	Verbal direction, modeling.	Interest in mall lights.
7. Select food counter.	Verbal direction, modeling.	Disliked noise; yelled.
8. Place order.	Physical guidance to give order card.	High interest in food— leaned over counter.
9. Pay for order.	Physical guidance to give money.	Focused on the food.
10. Find seat.	Independent! Chose seat!	Motivated to sit and eat.
11. Eat food.	Independent.	Liked soda and chicken, did not eat fries.
12. Discard trash.	Resisted; would not do.	Strong dislike; pulled away, yelled.
13. Shop for model car.	Resisted; ran to mall exit.	Ready to go after eating; shop first?

Conclusions: Roberto can use the city bus and eat at the mall with minimal verbal directions and the model of an escort. He showed no awareness of traffic and needs systematic instruction in street crossing. He also needs instruction to learn to place and pay for an order. His strong preferences for being outside and for fast food make this a good alternative for community-based instruction. Some more planning is needed for behavioral challenges. For example, Roberto needs an age-appropriate way to communicate refusal of an activity versus running and yelling. He also seems to prefer to leave the mall after eating, so it may be better to do any shopping before eating.

Because Roberto's problem behavior created disruptions in his general education class and occasionally put him in danger in the community, Ms. Becker worked with the school psychologist, Ms. Jacobson, to conduct a functional assessment in preparation to develop a positive behavior support plan. Ms. Jacobson reviewed Ms. Becker's notes she had kept after each outburst that described the antecedent, specific behavior, and consequences (ABC analysis). Then, using checklists on the communicative function of behavior (Demchak, 1996), she noted that the function of Roberto's outbursts seemed to be to escape unpleasant situations. She also noted that he had no other way to communicate refusal. She conferred with the speech therapist and ESL teacher to discuss how communication might affect Roberto's behavior. She concluded that offering choices and teaching him a "no" response would be two ways to offer Roberto positive behavioral support. The ESL teacher also noted that although Roberto received all his instruction in English, he might need some directions in Spanish when he became confused. Ms. Becker asked the ESL teacher to prepare a list of Spanish commands to share with the IEP team and to be incorporated into a behavior support plan.

Ms. Becker used the ecological inventory, discrepancy analysis, and situational assessments in developing the next portion of the formal written report. She attached a final draft of the curriculum chart, which was now personalized based on Roberto's priorities and specific environments. Figure 2.8 provides the fourth section of Ms. Becker's report, and Figure 2.9 gives the curriculum chart.

Step 5: Develop the IEP and Assessment Report

By Step 5, the information gathering is complete, and recommendations can be developed for the IEP. Given the time constraints of most IEP meetings, the teacher or other professional acting as a facilitator may draft the IEP in advance and discuss it with the family and student informally prior to the meeting. In this discussion, it will be important to give examples of how the parents' and student's priorities have been included in the final plan. The facilitator may also share the curriculum chart to show how the IEP targets priorities for specially designed instruction, but he or she should make it clear that the student will also be taught many more skills.

If a formal written assessment report is being developed, the concluding section will usually restate the priorities and recommend educational supports that are needed. This lays the foundation for the IEP. Another way to encourage family and student participation is to share this written report prior to the IEP meeting, to see whether their priorities have been accurately reflected.

Ms. Becker used Roberto's curriculum chart and the other information she had collected to make a recommendation for Roberto's level of participation in the general education curriculum (partial participation) and to write a justification for use of alternate assessment. Roberto's state used external evaluation of portfolios for alternate assessment at the same time periods when other students in the state received testing (5th, 8th, and 11th grades). Teachers could submit one portion of the portfolio a year in advance for a "preview," to obtain feedback on what would need to be achieved for the portfolio to be scored "adequate" or above. Ms. Becker recommended that a benchmark for Roberto be that this sample receive a score of "adequate" or better. Ms. Becker also included recommendations for Roberto's specially designed instruction and related services. These are shown in Figure 2.10, which depicts the final section of the formal report.

When a formal assessment report is not required, the teacher may still want to summarize the ecological assessment steps to share the process used in developing the IEP. This summary may be simplified by using a short form like the one shown in Figure 2.11.

Development of Roberto's IEP

The IEP the team developed for Roberto is shown in Figure 2.12. When the IEP is compared to the written assessment report (Figures 2.4, 2.5, 2.6, 2.8, and 2.10), it is clear that these objectives came directly from the team's assessment and planning efforts. When the IEP is compared to the personalized curriculum chart (Figure 2.9), it is also notable

FIGURE 2.8. Example of Part IV of a written assessment report.

Written Assessment Report: Part IV. Personalized Curriculum

To develop a personalized curriculum for Roberto, a curriculum-based assessment was conducted, using Life Centered Career Education (the version for students with moderate disabilities). Ecological inventories were conducted of three general education classes including interviews of the teachers in these classes. A discrepancy analysis was used to identify ways to make Roberto's day more inclusive, age-appropriate, and self-directed by comparing his current day to that of a peer who is nondisabled. Situational assessments were implemented in which Roberto tried some new activities, including taking the bus to the mall to eat in the food court and assisting with the school's soccer team. A functional assessment of Roberto's yelling and running was also conducted in collaboration with the school psychologist, Ms. Jacobson. This assessment suggested that the function of the problem behavior is escape and that Roberto's positive behavioral support plan should include a communicative alternative for "no." From these assessments, Roberto's skills and instructional needs can be summarized as follows.

Functional Academics

Roberto currently has few academic skills. He can recognize his own name and some numbers. He cannot yet tell time or count money. In contrast, Roberto shows a strong interest in academics. For example, he likes to carry books in his bookbag, to circle numbers on worksheets, and to attend a general education math class. His family also has a strong preference for him to learn to read and write. Sight word instruction would be a good starting place for moving toward this goal.

Community Skills

Roberto has a strong preference for being outdoors and likes waiting at a bus stop, walking to the store, going to the park, or any other activity that involves some time outside. He likes purchasing sweets and fast foods, but needs assistance in placing an order and paying. He shows no awareness of traffic and needs instruction in street crossing. He also needs instruction in riding the bus. During a situational assessment in which Roberto took the bus to the mall, he showed a preference for the entire activity until he finished eating, when he wanted to leave. Because Roberto lacked the necessary communication skills to protest shopping and ask to leave, he relied on running and yelling to make his preference known.

General Education Inclusion

Roberto has shown a strong interest in his current math class. He likes to carry the textbook in his bookbag and to work on number identification worksheets from his folder during class. His parents also want more activities like this one. Ecological inventories were conducted of several potential seventh-grade classes, including wood shop (a potential hobby), consumer math, and communication. Because one class project in wood shop is making a birdhouse, this seems like a possible match for Roberto. He will need the adaptation of picture/sight word directions and systematic instruction to learn to follow these. He will also need training in measurement and use of the shop tools. In consumer math, Roberto may be able to participate with further instruction on use of the computer and a calculator, building on his number recognition skills to input numbers. In communication, Roberto will need to learn some key sight words and to use simple passages the teacher generates as alternatives to the text's stories.

(cont.)

FIGURE 2.8. *(cont.)*

Home and Personal Care Skills

Roberto's family enjoys taking care of him and assists him in eating and dressing. In contrast, as a middle school student, at school he is expected to eat without assistance and to dress himself in gym. With direct instruction in zipping and buttoning, and encouragement to eat without assistance, Roberto can probably master these skills in the coming year.

Communication and Social Skills

Roberto's family members use both English and Spanish in their home. Although Roberto is nonverbal, he comprehends a wide variety of words in both English and Spanish. Roberto uses a picture communication wallet to make simple requests, but needs to expand his wallet use to include a broader range of requests and to fulfill other communicative functions (e.g., interaction with peers). He will have some specific communication needs related to his general education classes that also should be incorporated. Roberto's use of his picture communication wallet and expansion of his receptive language should be jointly planned with his ESL instructor, speech therapist, and classroom teachers, so that a consistent approach is used. Based on the family's preference and recommendation of the ESL instructor, Roberto receives all of his instruction in English. However, when Roberto seems confused, a teacher may need to repeat a direction in Spanish.

Roberto currently has few social interactive responses except proximity. In his family, he initiates and responds to social interactions by sitting or standing close to others. At school, he has occasionally moved close to a peer. Roberto needs direct instruction to learn to interact with peers. A beginning point will be to teach him to respond to peers' questions by using a photo communication book. He can also be taught to share materials and take turns during cooperative learning activities.

To enhance Roberto's self-determination, he needs to be given more opportunities to make choices during his day and to learn some problem-solving skills. The shop class should provide an excellent setting to begin training in problem solving. Roberto also needs to learn an age-appropriate "no" response to replace screaming and running. This may include both a picture symbol for "no" and shaking his head "no."

Vocational Skills

Roberto has not yet reached the age at which the team needs to begin formal transition planning, but the team has begun career exploration. A shop class is recommended to provide another opportunity for inclusion and to expand his functional academics skills. His interest in his family's store can be encouraged by teaching him to dust and stock shelves and to keep money secure.

Recreation Skills

Roberto likes to spend time alone, but does not have a personal hobby. He will hold and spin objects, but has few "play" responses. Given his age, it would be helpful for Roberto to learn some age-appropriate leisure skills that he can enjoy alone or with peers. Teaching him to use games and do crafts that have intense visual stimulation may be the most appealing to Roberto (e.g., blacklight art, Lite Brite, video games).

(The personalized curriculum chart is included as an appendix to this part of the report. The report continues.)

FIGURE 2.9. Example of a personalized curriculum chart (as an appendix to Part IV of a written assessment report).

Personalized Curriculum Chart for Roberto Gomez

Functional Reading

Sight words related to directions in wood shop
Community sight words (Edmark Functional Reading)
High-frequency (Dolch) sight words to use for simple stories
School schedule words (e.g., "consumer math")
Computer letters and sight words (e.g., "enter")

Functional Math

Number entry for 0–9 for calculator and computer
Addition with a calculator
Counting dollars and paying, using "next-dollar" strategy
Metric measurement to nearest centimeter

Community Skills

Riding the city bus—paying fare and boarding/disembarking
Crossing the street and watching for traffic
Paying for food or other purchases using one dollar bills
Using picture wallet to communicate choice or ask to leave
Carrying emergency information card and showing it to security guard
Using computer and calculator with peer in consumer math
Keeping pace with stories in communication, using teacher-generated story summaries

Home and Personal Care Skills

Eating without verbal prompting
Dressing self at home and after gym
Zippering and buttoning when dressing in gym
Fixing simple snacks and breakfast foods

Recreation Skills

Developing a hobby like woodworking or blacklight art
Learning to play a video game on the computer with a peer
Assisting the manager of the school soccer team

Vocational Skills

Learning to keep money safe
Helping straighten and dust shelves after wood shop
Exploring career alternatives through visits to area businesses

Communication and Social Skills

Using a picture communication wallet
Using pictures to request food and leisure items
Using wallet to show identification to authority figures

(cont.)

FIGURE 2.9. *(cont.)*

Using wallet to answer questions when working or playing with peer
Sharing leisure materials or other objects to initiate social contact
Taking turns during cooperative learning activities
Eliminating running and yelling through positive behavioral procedures, such as offering choices and teaching to shake head "no"
Learning problem solving during wood shop

General Education Curriculum *(developed in interviews with general education teachers to define partial participation in their curriculum)*

CONSUMER MATH

Learning the "big idea" of each unit (e.g., value of money, banks hold money, some items cost more)

COMMUNICATION

Learning to sequence (pictures) as parallel to writing stories
Choosing pictures for teacher developed stories
Participating when others give speeches by applauding
Giving a speech by using pictures

WOOD SHOP

Measuring to the nearest inch
Hand sanding
Use of a hammer
Cleanup and dusting

that the IEP only contains a subset of the numerous skills identified in the assessment process for Roberto. As discussed earlier in this chapter, an IEP is not meant to restate a student's entire curriculum, but rather to provide specific objectives for 1 year's specially designed instruction. Roberto's school day would definitely include instruction on these IEP objectives, but the teachers would also address *more* than the IEP in their daily schedule. Roberto's personalized curriculum would give them a guide for planning this additional work. This personalized curriculum would serve as a bridge to the general education curriculum, including basic skills that could be incorporated into Roberto's general education classes. The curriculum was also linked to the outcomes in the state's alternate assessment for students with disabilities.

SUMMARY

This chapter describes the specific steps in conducting an ecological assessment that includes a person-centered planning process. Research on ecological assessment indicates that this approach provides more educationally relevant information and encourages higher teacher expectations than standardized or developmental assessments. Research on person-centered planning demonstrates that this process encourages both

FIGURE 2.10. Example of Part V of a written assessment report.

Written Assessment Report: Part V. Recommendations for the IEP

Recommendation for Alternate Assessment and General Education Participation

Roberto Gomez is a student with autism and moderate cognitive disabilities whose academic skills are below the first-grade level. His personalized curriculum needs are life skills, social skills, and functional academics. His participation in general education can be encouraged by having him focus on these areas in the context of some selected seventh-grade classes. He will also need opportunities in his day to learn life skills in other contexts (e.g., the community and special education class), and to receive ESL instruction, speech therapy, and occupational therapy related to his autism and communication needs. Given the priorities of Roberto's educational needs, his level of autism, and the partial participation recommended for his general education classes, it is recommended that he receive the state's alternate assessment instead of the standardized testing that is conducted in eighth grade. The preparation of the portfolio for this alternate assessment should begin next year. A recommended IEP benchmark is that this seventh-grade portfolio draft sample receive a rating of "proficient" or above in the assessment.

Specially Designed Instruction

Based on his family's preferences, Roberto's preferences, and the needs of his middle school year, Roberto's highest priorities at this time are to expand his expressive communication skills by using pictures; to eliminate yelling and screaming through the use of a "no" response and improved choice-making skills; to expand his functional academic skills; to become completely independent in personal care skills (eating and dressing); to gain skills in community safety; and to gain some skills in social interaction in his general education classes.

The educational supports Roberto will need to achieve these goals include opportunities to participate in general education classes, with the assistance of a paraprofessional; community-based instruction; and additional direct instruction in the special education class. He also needs a positive behavior support plan related to his yelling and running. Roberto's family is a strong resource in his life, and ongoing communication with the family will help him practice new skills in his home setting.

Related Services

Roberto continues to need speech therapy and ESL instruction. Team collaboration is needed to develop his communication system in ways that will honor his linguistic diversity and expand his picture communication system. Because Roberto has a history of grand mal seizures and takes medication, he will need the services of the school nurse to administer medication, monitor seizures, and train his teachers in first aid for seizures. Roberto also continues to need services from the occupational therapist who has been focusing on his sensory integration and relaxation needs.

FIGURE 2.11. A simplified form summarizing the assessment and planning for the IEP (to be used as an alternative to a formal assessment report).

Annual Assessment and Planning for IEP Development

Student's Name: Roberto Gomez   **Teacher's Name:** Ms. Becker

Date: May 1, 20—   **School:** Sun Valley Middle School

1. *Student Background:* Roberto Gomez is a 12-year-old student with autism who is sixth-grade age. He has begun to attend general education classes in his middle school and shows an interest in math class.

2. *Person-Centered Planning with Student and Family:* A person-centered planning meeting was held with Roberto's extended family and friends in March. Their priorities included communication, functional academic skills, life skills, inclusion in general education, and street crossing and community safety.

3. *Encouraging Student Self-Determination:* Roberto needs more opportunities for choice making in his daily routine. Preference assessment revealed interests in sweets, some spicy foods, anything related to birds, nature museums, cassette tapes of music, video games, blacklight art, dusting in his father's store, and being in math class.

4. *Development of the Personalized Curriculum:* Assessment conducted included use of the version of Life Centered Career Education for students with moderate disabilities (a life skills curriculum), a discrepancy analysis comparing Roberto's day to that of a nondisabled peer of the same age, ecological inventories of general education classes, and situational assessments of two activities (taking the bus to the mall and assisting with the soccer team). Observed skills are summarized on the IEP as "Present Levels of Performance." A personalized curriculum chart was also developed for Roberto.

5. *Recommendations for the IEP:* Current priorities are to expand Roberto's functional academic skills; to eliminate yelling and running through positive behavior support, including teaching a "no" response and choice making; to increase independence in personal care; to teach community safety skills; and to encourage social interaction with peers in general education classes. Roberto continues to need speech therapy and ESL instruction to expand his communication system, and occupational therapy to help him with relaxation and sensory integration. Because of his seizures, Roberto will need the services of the school nurse for medication administration, record keeping, and staff training in first aid for seizures.

FIGURE 2.12. An example of an IEP.

Mid-Central School District
Individualized Education Plan (IEP)

Date: May 1, 20—   Student's Name: Roberto Gomez   Date of Birth: 10/4/—   Grade: 6

Parents' Name: Juan and Maria Gomez   Home Phone: 322-3333   Work Phone: 233-3333

Date for Initiation of Services: May 1, 20—   Annual Review Date: May 1, 20—

Eligibility Classification: Roberto Gomez has been classified with autism and a moderate cognitive disability.

Recommended Special Education and Related Services: It is recommended that Roberto Gomez receive full-time special education services designed to address the challenges of autism. Recommended related services include speech therapy, English as a Second Language (ESL) instruction, and support from a paraprofessional when Roberto is in general education classes. Roberto's primary language of instruction is English. His primary mode of communication is a picture communication system. Roberto needs a positive behavior support plan for yelling and running. The school nurse will also administer Roberto's medications, train his teachers in first aid for seizures, and maintain a seizure log.

Participation in General Education: Roberto Gomez will participate in general education classes for half of his school day, including homeroom, lunch, and three course periods. His instruction in general education will be jointly planned by the general and special education teachers and will be supported through the assistance of a paraprofessional. The other half of Roberto's day will include specially designed instruction to meet his needs for community safety awareness and other life skills needs, speech therapy, occupational therapy, and ESL instruction.

Participation in State/District Testing: Roberto Gomez will not participate in the state and district standardized assessment. Instead, he will participate in alternate assessment through the development of a portfolio that documents his progress in his personalized curriculum, and that will be evaluated in adherence with state guidelines for alternate assessment.

Measurement of Student's Progress: Roberto Gomez's parents will receive quarterly reports consistent with the school's report card schedule that will summarize progress on IEP goals and objectives. Progress will be monitored via teacher-made assessments (e.g., task-analytic assessment) and ongoing data collection. Reports will be prepared jointly by Roberto's general and special education teachers and specialists.

This IEP is a statement of the services to be provided to my child. I agree with the goals and objectives, my child's placement, and the provision of related services as indicated. I realize that this is not a contract, and does not guarantee achievement of stated goals and objectives. I have been given a copy of my rights.

_____

Parent's Signature   **Date**

_____

Parent's Signature   **Date**

(cont.)

FIGURE 2.12. *(cont.)*

Individuals present at the meeting and serving on the IEP team:

Signature   Position   Date

_____   _____   _____

_____   _____   _____

_____   _____   _____

_____   _____   _____

_____   _____   _____

_____   _____   _____

Present Levels of Performance

Specific Abilities and Interests: Roberto has a strong interest in birds and can imitate a wide range of bird songs. He enjoys any activity that is outdoors, especially when the weather is warm. Roberto attends a general education math class. He has shown an interest in this setting by working diligently on his functional math folder and seeking his own set of any materials the other students obtain (e.g., the textbook, handouts, folders).

Overall Health: Roberto is an attractive boy who is slightly small for his age. His overall health is good, but he receives ongoing treatment from a neurologist for partially controlled grand mal seizures. During this past IEP planning year, Roberto has had two grand mal seizures at school.

Progress on Prior IEP: Roberto mastered four objectives, including recognizing his name, self-initiating toileting, and eating with a spoon. He mastered putting on his coat except for zipping it (84% of task analysis) and was close to mastery on identifying numbers on a math worksheet (95% correct). He also worked quietly on most days in math (95% of days), but sometimes disrupted the class with yelling (e.g., when he disliked the activity). He made no progress on greeting peers (mean of 20%) or making choices across the school day (teacher observation).

Academic and Related Skills: Roberto currently has few academic skills. During the prior IEP year, Roberto mastered and generalized reading his own name and was near mastery on identifying numbers. Roberto's parents have a strong preference for him to learn academics.

Life Skills: In a curriculum-based assessment using the Life Centered Career Education curriculum for students with moderate disabilities, Roberto was found to have mastered 22 of these skills. In the last IEP year, Roberto mastered putting on his own jacket but could not zip it. He has many personal care skills, but does not dress himself at home or gym class and relies on verbal prompts to eat. He does not currently make snacks or perform chores. In the community, Roberto enjoys traveling outdoors and can partially participate in making a purchase. He has no awareness of traffic or other community safety issues. Roberto likes to spend time alone, but does not have hobbies or other leisure skills.

Transition Needs: Roberto has not yet received specific vocational training. Through participation in general education, he is learning prevocational skills such as being on time, completing assignments independently, and respecting the property of others. The only form of self-determination observed for Roberto is his requesting with his pictures or with gestures or protesting.

(cont.)

FIGURE 2.12. *(cont.)*

Behavioral Needs: Roberto will sometimes react to confusing or unwanted situations by yelling and then running. This behavior disrupts his classroom settings and sometimes puts him in danger. A recent functional assessment revealed that Roberto's yelling and running function to allow him to escape a task or setting. Roberto does not have a "no" response. Positive behavioral support is needed that will include choice making and use of a "no" response.

Communication and Social Skills: Roberto can comprehend a wide range of words and phrases in both English and Spanish. Although he can use his voice (e.g., to imitate birds), he does not speak but instead utilizes a picture communication system. Currently, he only uses about six pictures to request food and other items. Based on the family's preference and the recommendation of his ESL specialist, Roberto receives all school instruction in English. In his ESL instruction, Roberto has learned the English term for 15 words he knew in Spanish in the last year. Roberto does not interact with peers except occasionally to stand close to someone, which seems to be a form of social initiation.

Goals, Objectives, and Benchmarks

FUNCTIONAL READING AND MATH

Annual Goal: By the end of the school year, Roberto will be able to recognize 50 new sight words and compute simple addition problems using a calculator.

Short-Term Objectives:

1. When shown sets of 3 community and school words, Roberto will point to the correct word for 2 of 2 days for 25 new sight words taught in sets of 5. (Special ed. teacher)
2. When given an activity involving sight words, Roberto will look at the word and demonstrate what it means for 2 of 2 days for the 25 new sight words. (Special ed. teacher and general ed. teachers)
3. When given 10 one-digit math problems, Roberto will perform addition with 80% accuracy, using a calculator or computer software program. (Special ed. teacher and math teacher)

COMMUNITY SKILLS

Annual Goal: By the end of the year, Roberto will be able to make community purchases safely.

Short-Term Objectives:

1. When crossing the street, Roberto will look for cars and wait for his escort to signal "all clear" before stepping off the curb for 10 of 10 times across 2 months. (Special ed. teacher)
2. In a variety of stores and restaurants, Roberto will purchase a snack performing all steps of the task analysis correctly for 3 of 3 times. (Special ed. teacher)

HOME AND PERSONAL LIVING

Annual Goal: By May, Roberto will master at least three new daily living skills.

Short-Term Objectives:

1. After gym, Roberto will redress himself (including zipping and buttoning), performing all steps of the task analysis correctly for 3 of 3 days. (Special ed. teacher)
2. During lunch, Roberto will complete his lunch (without verbal reminders to eat) by the end of the lunch period for 4 of 5 days. (Special ed. teacher)

(cont.)

FIGURE 2.12. *(cont.)*

3. Given the materials needed, Roberto will prepare a simple snack, performing all steps of the task analysis correctly for 2 of 2 days. (Special ed. teacher)

VOCATIONAL SKILLS

Annual Goal: By the end of the year, Roberto will be able to work independently for at least 30 minutes and to gain assistance when needed.

Short-Term Objectives:

1. When missing an item or needing assistance, Roberto will use problem-solving steps and his communication wallet on 3 of 5 occasions. (Special ed. teacher and industrial arts teacher)
2. When given a workbench task, Roberto will complete the task and work without prompting for 10 minutes by November, 20 minutes by February, and 30 minutes by May. (Special ed. teacher and industrial arts teacher)

COMMUNICATION AND SOCIAL SKILLS

Annual Goal: By the end of the year, Roberto will increase his social skills by using his communication wallet for at least 15 new symbols, by taking turns, and by shaking his head "no" instead of yelling.

Short-Term Objectives:

1. Using his communication wallet, Roberto will master at least 15 new symbols; at least one of these will be used with peers on 3 of 5 opportunities. Benchmarks: 5 new symbols by November; 10 new symbols by February; 15 new symbols by May. (Special ed. teacher, ESL teacher, and speech therapist)
2. In his general education classes, Roberto will respond socially by taking turns and sharing materials on 4 of 5 opportunities across 2 weeks. (Special ed. teacher and general ed. teachers)
3. When confused or to refuse, Roberto will shake his head "no" or point to a symbol of "no" without yelling or running for 15 of 15 days. (Special ed. teacher, speech therapist, and ESL teacher)

student and family participation. Blending these two approaches is possible if time is spent with the family and student prior to the formal IEP meeting to establish future goals and priorities.

In this "blended" ecological assessment approach, the planning team begins by summarizing what is known about the student. The teacher or other professional acting as a facilitator may use progress on the prior year's IEP in beginning to develop statements of current level of performance for the IEP. If a formal reevaluation is being conducted, the facilitator may also review records for recent evaluations by psychologists, physicians, and other professionals. The second step is to hold a person-centered planning meeting with the student, the student's family, and the "circle of friends" they choose to include. This session provides more extended planning time than the typical IEP meeting and may encourage more family participation. Once priorities are established through this person-centered planning, the facilitator will probably want to spend more time with the student to clarify his or her preferences further and decide on ways to encourage self-determination in this process. Once priorities have been established with the family and student, the facilitator and other team members can focus their assessment efforts. These can be implemented in a broad-to-specific sequence to save time. By beginning with a life skills curriculum inventory, the team gains an overview of the student's skills and instructional needs across areas. This can then be supplemented with ecological inventories of the general education class and community environments and with discrepancy analyses. Sometimes situational assessment will be needed to pinpoint preferences and skill needs by giving the student the opportunity to try new activities. If problem behavior is a concern, functional assessment may also be used to plan positive behavioral support.

The outcome of this ecological assessment process is an IEP that is based both on the student's and family's priorities and on the student's specific instructional needs. This information can also be used to generate a written assessment report for a reevaluation. If a formal evaluation is not required, the assessment notes may be summarized on a brief form or shared informally in the IEP meeting.

Timothy's Planning Process

At the beginning of this chapter, Timothy was described as a child with many labels, but little information about what he wanted or needed to learn. His parents objected to his current IEP as being redundant with prior years' planning and lacking in vision for Timothy. You were invited to consider how you would have planned for Timothy. Before reading on to discover what John Maddox did, take a few minutes to outline the steps you would have taken to plan for Timothy. Compare your plan with what Mr. Maddox tried.

John Maddox the professional who led an initiative to develop a new plan for Timothy, started by getting to know him better. He spent time observing Timothy and read through his educational file. After reading his file and studying his prior IEPs, he discovered that Timothy had indeed been working on the same objectives for several years, and that little information existed on his educational needs. Mr. Maddox then spent time with Timothy and his parents to discuss their concerns in more detail. He was able to establish rapport with them and to hear their story about Timothy's educational history. He began to generate a chart of the parents' preferences as he listened to what they valued most. With the family's help, he formed a planning team. Because Timothy's parents preferred having a formal team of professionals, Mr. Maddox recommended including the speech therapist, the special education teacher, a third-grade general education teacher, a behavior specialist, and a paraprofessional who provided support for Timothy. He asked the team to make a commitment to two meetings. At the first, they would develop a vision for Timothy's education, using person-centered planning strategies. At the second, they would develop the IEP, using information they gathered about Timothy and his environments related to these priorities.

At the first meeting, Mr. Maddox introduced Timothy and his parents. He then opened the meeting by having each person present describe one or more of Timothy's abilities or appealing characteristics. Although Timothy only used a few manual signs to communicate, he sometimes would sign or laugh when he heard someone mention a familiar term or preferred activity. Mr. Maddox encouraged Timothy's participation by speaking directly with him. He then asked Timothy's parents to share their story of Timothy's education. Next, the team used the MAPS approach to envision an ideal day for Timothy. From this, they were able to develop broad goals for his future. Using these as priorities, Mr. Maddox asked the team to return to the IEP meeting with more information about Timothy's preferences, abilities, and educational needs related to these priorities. At the end of the meeting, Mr. Maddox talked privately with Timothy's parents to check their impression of the meeting. They were both excited and cautious about how the team would proceed.

Mr. Maddox took the role of identifying Timothy's needs for learning life skills and functional academics. He began by conducting preference assessments of Timothy's responses to various teaching materials and activities. He built a personalized curriculum for Timothy by noting skills he needed in his current and future environments. He used a published life skills curriculum to help describe more fully what Timothy could do and what he might learn next. He then met with the third-grade teacher to review scope and sequence charts from that curriculum to target some ideas for Timothy. To validate some of these ideas, he conducted situational assessments of Timothy in some new activities and settings, and took data on his preferences and his performances. Mr. Maddox summarized his ideas in both a formal assessment report and a personalized curriculum chart, which he shared with the parents in advance of the IEP meeting. The report included recommendations for Timothy's life skills and academic goals.

When the team met again, Mr. Maddox began by asking participants to describe any ways they had been surprised by their discoveries of Timothy's abilities and interests. He then asked Timothy whether he enjoyed the assessment activities. Although Timothy did not respond, his mother described why she thought Timothy liked trying the new activities. Each participant then described his or her list of Timothy's preferences and abilities. Mr. Maddox used a laptop computer with a projection screen to type these into his IEP as the team reached consensus. (Timothy's parents both used computers in their own professions and found this format appealing.) He then typed in target goals and objectives as they were shared. Finally, the team developed a tentative schedule showing Timothy's time in general education, special education, speech therapy, and other target activities (e.g., a school computer club). Timothy's parents took a copy of the draft IEP to study further. Mr. Maddox also wanted a few days to work through the details of Timothy's new schedule in general education. The parents were then ready to sign their approval the next week, after a few negotiated revisions related to Timothy's time and activities in general education.

REFERENCES

Blankenship, C. S. (1985). Using curriculum-based assessment to make instructional decisions. *Exceptional Children, 52*, 233–238.

Bricker, W. A., & Campbell, P. H. (1980). Interdisciplinary assessment and programming for multi-handicapped students. In W. Sailor, B. Wilcox, & L. Brown (Eds.), *Methods of instruction for severely handicapped students* (pp. 3–46). Baltimore: Paul H. Brookes.

Browder, D. M. (1991). *Assessment of individuals with severe disabilities: An applied behavioral approach to life skills assessment* (2nd ed., pp. 1–68). Baltimore: Paul H. Brookes.

Browder, D. M. (1997). Educating students with severe disabilities: Enhancing the conversation between research and practice. *Journal of Special Education, 31*, 137–144.

Brown, L., Branston, M. B., Hamre-Nietupski, S., Pumpian, I., Certo, N., & Gruenwald, L. (1979). A strategy for developing chronological age-appropriate and functional curriculum content for severely handicapped adolescents and young adults. *Journal of Special Education, 13*, 81–90.

Butterworth, J., Hagner, D., Heikkinen, B., DeMello, S., & McDonough, K. (1993). *Whole life planning: A guide for organizers and facilitators.* Boston: Children's Hospital, Institute for Community Inclusion.

Campbell, P. C., Campbell, C. R., & Brady, M. P. (1998). Team Environmental Assessment Mapping System: A method for selecting curriculum goals for students with disabilities. *Education and Training in Mental Retardation and Developmental Disabilities, 33,* 264–272.

Cole, K. N., Swisher, V., Thompson, M. D., & Fewell, R. R. (1985). Enhancing sensitivity of assessment instruments for children: Graded multi-dimension scoring. *Journal of the Association for Persons with Severe Handicaps, 10,* 209–213.

Council for Exceptional Children (CEC). (1998). *IDEA 1997: Let's make it work.* Reston, VA: Author.

Demchak, M. (1996). *Assessing problem behaviors (Innovations No. 4).* Washington, DC: American Association on Mental Retardation.

Downing, J. E., & Perino, D. M. (1992). Functional versus standardized assessment procedures: Implications for educational programming. *Mental Retardation, 30,* 289–295.

Falvey, M., Forest, M., Pearpoint, J., & Rosenberg, R. (1994). Building connections. In J. Thousand, R. Villa, & E. Nevin (Eds.), *Creativity and collaborative learning: A practical guide to empowering students and teachers* (pp. 347–368). Baltimore: Paul H. Brookes.

Ford, A., Schnorr, R., Meyer, L., Davern, L., Black, J., & Dempsey, P. (1989). *The Syracuse Community-Referenced Curriculum Guide for students with moderate and severe disabilities.* Baltimore: Paul H. Brookes.

Giangreco, M. F., Cloninger, C. J., Dennis, R. E., & Edelman, S. W. (1993). National expert validation of COACH: Congruence with exemplary practice and suggestions for improvement. *Journal of the Association for Persons with Severe Handicaps, 18,* 109–120.

Giangreco, M. F., Cloninger, C. J., & Iverson, V. S. (1998). *Choosing Outcomes and Accommodations for Children* (2nd ed., pp. 29–95). Baltimore: Paul H. Brookes.

Giangreco, M. F., Edelman, S. W., Dennis, R. E., & Cloninger, C. J. (1995). Use and impact of COACH with students who are deaf–blind. *Journal of the Association for Persons with Severe Handicaps, 20,* 121–135.

Hagner, D., Helm, D. T., & Butterworth, J. (1996). "This is your meeting": A qualitative study of person-centered planning. *Mental Retardation, 34,* 159–171.

Harry, B., Allen, N., & McLaughlin, M. (1995). Communication versus compliance: African-American parents' involvement in special education. *Exceptional Children, 61,* 364–377.

Hartman, A., & Laird, J. (1983). The family in space: Ecological assessment. In A. Hartman & J. Laird (Eds.), *Family centered social work practice* (pp. 157–186). Beverly Hills, CA: Sage.

Horner, R. H. (1994). Functional assessment: Contributions and future directions. *Journal of Applied Behavior Analysis, 27,* 401–404.

Holvoet, J., O'Neil, C., Chazdon, L., Carr, D., & Warner, J. (1983). Hey, do we really have to take data? *Journal of the Association for the Severely Handicapped, 5,* 56–70.

Kern, L., Vorndran, C. M., Hill, A., Ringdahl, J. E., Dunlap, G., & Adelman, G. (1998). Choice as an intervention to improve behavior. *Journal of Behavioral Education, 8,* 151–169.

Knowlton, E. (1998). Considerations in the design of personalized curricular supports for students with developmental disabilities. *Education and Training in Mental Retardation and Developmental Disabilities, 33,* 95–107.

Linehan, S. C., & Brady, M. P. (1995). Functional versus developmental assessment: Influences on instructional planning decisions. *Journal of Special Education, 29,* 295–309.

Lim, L., & Browder, D. (1994). Multicultural life skills assessment of individuals with severe disabilities. *Journal of the Association for Persons with Severe Handicaps, 19,* 130–138.

Linehan, S. C., Brady, M. P., & Hwang, C. (1991). Ecological versus developmental assessment: Influences on instructional expectations. *Journal of the Association for Persons with Severe Handicaps, 16,* 146–153.

Lohrmann-O'Rourke, S., & Browder, D. M. (1998). Empirically based methods of preference assessments for individuals with severe disabilities. *American Journal on Mental Retardation, 103,* 146–161.

Loyd, R. J., & Brolin, D. E. (1997). *Life Centered Career Education: Modified curriculum for individuals with moderate disabilities.* Reston, VA: Council for Exceptional Children.

Mallette, P., Mirenda, P., Kandborg, T., Jones, P., Bunz, T., & Rogow, S. (1992). Application of a lifestyle development process for persons with severe intellectual disabilities: A case study report. *Journal of the Association for Persons with Severe Handicaps, 17,* 179–191.

Marrone, J., Hoff, D., & Helm, D. T. (1997). Person-centered planning for the millenium: We're old enough to remember when PCP was just a drug. *Journal of Vocational Rehabilitation, 8,* 285–297.

Miner, C. A., & Bates, P. E. (1997). The effect of person centered planning activities on the IEP/transition planning process. *Education and Training in Mental Retardation and Developmental Disabilities, 32,* 105–112.

Morningstar, M. E., Turnbull, A. P., & Turnbull, H. R. (1996). What do students with disabilities tell us about the importance of family involvement in the transition from school to adult life? *Exceptional Children, 62,* 249–260.

Mount, B. (1994). Benefits and limitations of personal futures planning. In V. J. Bradley, J. W. Ashbaugh, & B. C. Blaney (Eds.), *Creating individual supports for people with developmental disabilities* (pp. 97–108). Baltimore: Paul H. Brookes.

Mount, B., & Zwernik, K. (1988). *It's never too early, it's never too late: A booklet about personal-futures planning for persons with developmental disabilities, their families and friends, case managers, service providers, and advocates.* St. Paul, MN: St. Paul Metropolitan Council.

Newton, J. S., Horner, R. H., & Lund, L. (1991). Honoring activity preferences in individualized plan development: A descriptive analysis. *Journal of the Association for Persons with Severe Handicaps, 16,* 207–212.

O'Brien, J. (1987). A guide to life-style planning. In B. Wilcox & G. T. Bellamy (Eds.), *A comprehensive guide to the Activities Catalog: An alternative curriculum for youth and adults with severe disabilities* (pp. 175–189). Baltimore: Paul H. Brookes.

O'Brien, J., & Lovett, H. (1993). *Finding a way toward everyday lives: The contribution of person-centered planning.* Harrisburg: Pennsylvania Office of Mental Retardation.

Overton, T. (1996). *Assessment in special education: An applied approach* (2nd ed). Columbus, OH: Charles E. Merrill.

Parker, R. M., Szymanski, E. M., & Hanley-Maxwell, C. (1989). Ecological assessment in supported employment. *Journal of Applied Rehabilitation Counseling, 20,* 26–33.

Ryndak, D. L., & Alper, S. (Eds.). (1996). *Curriculum content for students with moderate and severe disabilities in inclusive settings.* Boston: Allyn & Bacon.

Sigafoos, J., Cole, D., & McQuarter, R. J. (1987). Current practices in the assessment of students with severe handicaps. *Journal of the Association for Persons with Severe Handicaps, 12,* 264–273.

Smull, M., & Harrison, S. B. (1992). *Supporting people with severe reputations in the community.* Alexandria, VA: NASMRPD.

Steere, D. E., Wood, R., Pansocofar, E. L., & Butterworth, J. (1990). Outcome-based school-to-work transition planning for students with severe disabilities. *Career Development for Exceptional Individuals, 13,* 57–69.

Stineman, R., Morningstar, M., Bishop, B., & Turnbull, H. R. (1993). Role of families in transition planning for young adults with disabilities: Toward a method of person-centered planning. *Journal of Vocational Rehabilitation, 3,* 52–61.

Turnbull, A., & Turnbull, R. (1992, Fall–Winter). Group action planning. *Families and Disability Newsletter* (Beach Center on Families and Disability, Lawrence, KS).

Utley, B. L., Zigmond, N., & Strain, P. S. (1987). How various forms of data affect teacher analysis of student performance. *Exceptional Children, 53,* 411–422.

Vandercook, T., York, J., & Forest, M. (1989). The McGill Action Planning System (MAPS): A strategy for building the vision. *Journal of the Association for Persons with Severe Handicaps, 14,* 205–215.

Weiner, H. R. (1993). Multi-function needs assessment: The development of a functional assessment instrument. *Psychosocial Rehabilitation Journal, 16,* 51–61.

Wilcox, B., & Bellamy, G. T. (1987). *The Activities Catalog: An alternative curriculum for youth and adults with severe disabilities.* Baltimore: Paul H. Brookes.

Wright, F. V., & Boschen, K. A. (1993). The Pediatric Evaluation of Disability Inventory (PEDI): Validation of a new functional assessment instrument. *Canadian Journal of Rehabilitation, 7,* 41–42.

THREE

Alternate Assessment
and Quality Enhancement

IT'S MAY IN NORTH CAROLINA. *The days are warm and the irises are in full bloom, but no one would accuse the teachers of having "spring fever." Next week the students will participate in the state's end-of-grade testing program, and classroom preparations are intense. The teachers give students daily practice drills as the testing dates grow near. By the time the summer's sun is blazing in July, some teachers will learn that they work in a "North Carolina Exemplary School," which has received this designation based on these test scores. This award will be more than a banner for the front of their school; it will also include cash bonuses for each teacher, as well as school rewards. In this "high-stakes" accountability system, schools that do not meet the standards set for their students will be publicly identified and will face contingencies for improvement. Most students with moderate and severe disabilities will not take these standardized tests, but instead will participate in an "alternate assessment." Portfolios of their work will be developed according to state standards and submitted to external evaluators. How will their evaluations be used? Will their scores make a difference in how their schools are rated? Will they make a difference in decisions made about the students' educational programs?*

The use of alternate assessments in state accountability systems is a topic of ongoing national debate. This chapter provides guidelines for developing alternate assessment based on several states' models, and for using these results for ongoing quality enhancement.

By the end of the 1990s, most state departments of education had, or were developing, frameworks of educational standards, state assessments, and accountability systems (Roeber, Bond, & Braskamp, 1997). The development of these accountability systems has been part of an overall movement in school reform with influences at the national, state, and local levels. For example, the passage of Goals 2000: The Educate America Act (U.S. Congress, House of Representatives, 1994) influenced the school reform movement by setting these goals for the year 2000:

1. All children in America will start school ready to learn.
2. The high school graduation rate will increase to at least 90 percent.
3. All students will leave grades 4, 8, and 12 having demonstrated competency over challenging subject matter including English, mathematics, science, foreign languages, civics and government, economics, arts, history, and geography.

4. The U.S. teaching force will have access to programs for the continued improvement of their professional skills.

5. U.S. students will be the first in the world in science and mathematics achievement.

6. Every adult American will be literate and will possess the knowledge and skills to compete in a global economy.

7. Every school will be free of drugs, violence, and the unauthorized presence of firearms and alcohol and will offer a disciplined environment conducive to learning.

8. Every school will promote partnerships that will increase parental involvement and participation.[1]

Although many schools did not achieve these national goals by 2000, the strong interest in education reform and accountability continued. This interest was also reflected in reports on skills needed for the workplace. The U.S. Department of Labor's SCANS Report (Secretary's Commission on Achieving Necessary Skills) identified the "know-how" high school graduates need to enter the job market (Wagner, 1995). For example, graduates need to be able to use computers to process information; to have basic skills in reading writing, arithmetic, speaking, and listening; and to have personal qualities such as individual responsibility, self-esteem, sociability, self-management, and integrity. As the push for school reform increased, some professionals voiced concern that students with disabilities were being bypassed in decision making. The professionals at the National Center on Educational Outcomes (NCEO) called attention to the fact that large numbers of students with disabilities were excluded from state assessment and accountability systems (Erickson, Thurlow, & Thor, 1995). Their concern was that if students were out of sight in assessment and accountability systems, they would be out of mind when policy decisions were made. The NCEO responded to this dilemma in several ways. First, it identified desired goals and outcomes for students with disabilities (Ysseldyke, Thurlow, & Gilman, 1993). These goals targeted academic and functional literacy, personal and social adjustment, contribution and citizenship, responsibility and independence, and physical health. The NCEO also developed guidelines for including larger numbers of students with disabilities in national and state assessments (Ysseldyke, Olsen, & Thurlow, 1997). After the passage of the 1997 amendments to the Individuals with Disabilities Education Act (IDEA), the NCEO provided recommendations for alternate assessment for students who are not working toward a regular high school diploma (Ysseldyke & Olsen, 1999). This chapter focuses on alternate assessment for students with moderate and severe disabilities.

ALTERNATE ASSESSMENT FOR STUDENTS WITH MODERATE AND SEVERE DISABILITIES

In this era of school reform and educational accountability, it is important that students with moderate and severe disabilities not be excluded. Their inclusion in educational accountability systems was legally mandated in the 1997 amendments to IDEA. Specifically, according to the amendments, the state or local agency

(i) develops guidelines for the participation of children with disabilities in alternate assessment for those children who cannot participate in State and district-wide assessment programs; and

(ii) develops and beginning not later than July 1, 2000, conducts those alternate assessments. (IDEA Amendments of 1997, Sec. 612(a)(17)(A); quoted in Council for Exceptional Children, 1998)

The state educational agency also must make available to the public the number of children who participate in alternate assessments and their performance on the alternate assessments, if doing so is statistically sound and does not result in the disclosure of performance results identifiable to individual children.

Planning alternate assessment for students with moderate and severe disabilities is complex, for two primary reasons. First, all students with moderate and severe disabilities within a district typically do not have a common curriculum. They often are not pursuing a regular high school diploma and may only "audit" the standard course of study in inclusive settings. Many of their indvidualized education plan (IEP) objectives may focus on functional life skills. In contrast, most state and local standardized testing and other assessments evaluate what the NCEO has identified as "academic and functional literacy" outcomes (Vanderwood, Ysseldyke, & Thurlow, 1993). In developing alternate assessment, states have had to develop functional equivalents of the academic skills they measure, or to expand their assessments to focus on other outcomes (e.g., life skills).

A second problem in planning alternate assessment is that districts frequently lack a defined curriculum for students with moderate and severe disabilities that is comparable to a district's standard course of study in academics. As described in Chapter Two, professionals have sometimes relied on the IEP as the sole curriculum. The use of a published life skills curriculum can be an important resource for both IEP development and determining domains to be included in an alternate assessment. Table 3.1 provides several examples of published life skills curricula and the domains that they include. Some districts develop their own life skill curriculum guides with similar domains, but with more relevance to their specific geographic region. Although the use of a life skill curriculum guide may help in planning the domains for alternate assessment, it does not fully resolve the dilemma for two reasons. First, curricula for students with moderate and severe disabilities must be *personalized* (Knowlton, 1998). Nearly all published life skills curriculum guides recommend some process for prioritization. For example, the Choosing Outcomes and Accommodations for Children (COACH) model (Giangreco, Cloninger, & Iverson, 1998) uses a parent interview process to set priorities and pick specific areas from the curriculum. The Syracuse Community-Referenced Curriculum Guide (Ford et al., 1989) recommends considering parent, student, and professional input to set priorities during the IEP meeting. To decide that all students must achieve certain outcomes in the leisure/recreation domain, for example, ignores the person-centered planning process that may identify other priorities for an individual student (e.g., functional academics, personal care).

The second reason a published life skills curriculum may not resolve the issue of what domains to use for alternate assessment is that students with moderate and severe disabilities may be actively engaged in the general education curriculum through their inclusive educational settings. When validating performance indicators for Kentucky's alternate assessment with 44 national experts in severe disabilities, Kleinert and Kearns (1999) received mixed feedback on the use of "functional outcomes." Although overall the respondents gave "functionality" the second highest rating as a performance indicator (after the top-rated "integrated environments"), their written comments indicated some ambivalence about basing an alternate assessment on functional life skills. The respondents noted the need to use academic settings to achieve functional outcomes, and the need not to underestimate the ability of students with moderate and severe disabilities to participate in the general education curriculum. In response to this feedback, Kentucky changed the focus of its reporting system (i.e., portfolio) from functional domains (personal management, recreation/leisure, and vocational) to academic ones (e.g., language arts, math, science, social studies, and arts/humanities) (Kleinert & Kearns, 1999). To take a general education approach to curriculum planning for students with moderate and severe disabilities, professionals reviewed each of the academic expectations set for all students and defined functional alternatives as shown in Table 3.2.

Another challenge in planning alternate assessment is that life skills and functional equivalents of academic skills (e.g., "Requests assistance," "Problem-solves in new or novel situations") do not lend themselves well to standardized testing. Unlike typical academic skills that can be sampled via paper-and-pencil tests, most life skills and functional academics require using diverse settings and real materials. Ysseldyke and Olsen (1999) identify four ways to gather information on students: (1) observation, (2) recollection (via interview or rating scale), (3) record review, and (4) testing. As states develop and refine their alternate assessments, a variety of these strategies have been tried.

DECISIONS IN PLANNING AND USING ALTERNATE ASSESSMENT

In a statewide survey in Kentucky, Kleinert, Kennedy, and Kearns (1999) found that teachers generally had favorable attitudes about the inclusion of their students in school and state accountability measures, and that they saw benefits for students in the process. In contrast, respondents also expressed many negative comments reflecting the stress of being involved in a "high-stakes" accountability environment. Kleinert, Kearns, and Kennedy (in press) emphasize the importance of teachers' being involved in decisions about a state's or district's alternate assessment process. This section describes some of the decisions to be made in the ongoing development and refinement of these procedures, and the implications for students with moderate and severe disabilities. This discussion is based on Kleinert, Haigh, Kearns, and Kennedy's (in press) description of developing alternate assessments in Kentucky and Maryland, as well as on information gleaned from other states.

Decision 1: How Will the Alternate Assessment Information be Used?

In some states like Kentucky, Maryland, and North Carolina, comprehensive statewide educational reform has included holding schools accountable for clearly delineated student outcomes. Some states focus assessment primarily on *school* accountability (e.g., funding contingencies based on student scores); others target *student* accountabil-

TABLE 3.1. Published Life Skills Curricula

		Curriculum		
	COACH	Syracuse Guide	Activities Catalog	Life Centered Career Education
Reference	Giangreco, Cloninger, & Iverson (1998)	Ford et al. (1989)	Wilcox & Bellamy (1987)	Loyd & Brolin (1997)
Home and personal care skills	Personal management (12) Home (8)	Eating and food preparation (7) Grooming and dressing (5) Hygiene and toileting (3) Safety and health (13) Budget/schedule (7) (Numbers of skills from high school charts)	Food (4) Space and belongings (25) Personal business (9) Self-care (7)	Eating (6) Home care (5) Health (6) Sexuality (2) Clothing care (2)
Recreation/leisure skills	Leisure/recreation (4)	School, activities (10) Alone (6) With family/friends (7) Fitness (5) (Numbers of skills based on high school goals)	Exercise (21) Games/hobbies (20) Events (3) Media (8) Other (7)	Leisure (4)
Vocational skills	Vocational (11)	(Gives examples of school and community jobs)	Job categories (9)	Locate placement (2) Make placement choice (5) Apply for job (3) Appropriate work skills (6) Physical–manual skills (4) Training (no specifics)
Motor skills		Position (5) Mobility (6) Manipulation (7) Oral motor (4) Visual (3)		

Communication and social skills	Communication (12)	Social functions (11) Communication functions (11)		Self-identity (4) Responsible behavior (7) Social relationships (2) Independent behavior (3) Informed decisions (4) Communicate with others (3)
Community skills	Community (8)	Travel (4) Safety (2) Shopping (3) Eating out (4) Using services (3)	Eating out or buying food (7)	
Academics: Reading and writing	Academics (15) School (9)	Word identification (2) Materials (11) Comprehension (3) Interest (4) Writing (8) (From Cluster II)		
Functional math		Money: Cluster I (2) Cluster II (2) Cluster III (over 50) Time: Cluster I (3) Cluster II (4) Cluster III (over 40)		
Individualizing the curriculum	Parents identify valued life outcomes and help select specific curriculum items with team	Set priorities at the IEP meeting based on parent, student, and professional input	Choose among activities, similar to placing an order from a catalog; consider quality-of-life issues	Expect all skills to be mastered by graduation, or seek additional training or request support

Note. Numbers in parentheses indicate the number of skills listed in the curriculum for each category.

TABLE 3.2. Examples Given in Kentucky's Alternate Assessment Validation Survey for Interpreting "Academic Expectations for All Students" to Include Students with Moderate and Severe Disabilities

Kentucky academic expectation	Interpretation (example) for student with moderate/severe disabilities
Accessing information. Students use research tools to locate sources of information and ideas relevant to a problem.	Requests assistance.
Reading. Students construct meaning through print for a variety of purposes through reading.	Reads environmental, pictorial print.
Writing. Students communicate ideas and information for a variety of purposes through writing.	Constructs printed or pictorial messages; uses personal signature.
Democratic principles. Students recognize issues of justice, equality, responsibility, choice, and freedom, and apply these democratic principles.	Makes choices; accepts consequences.
Nature of scientific activity. Students use appropriate and relevant scientific skills to solve problems in real-life situations.	Problem-solves in new or novel situations.

Note. From Kleinert and Kearns (1999). Copyright 1999 by the Association for Persons with Severe Handicaps. Reprinted with permission.

ity (e.g., graduation or promotion contingent on test scores); and still others incorporate both. Although the 1997 IDEA amendments (hereafter referred to simply as IDEA 1997) require that all students be included in state and district educational assessments, and that outcomes be reported for alternate assessment, they do not specify that the scores on alternate assessments be part of the school's measure of *accountability*. An important decision to be made is whether the scores for students with moderate and severe disabilities will be used as part of a school's accountability measures. For example, in Kentucky, where *all* students are included in a school's accountability measures, the outcomes for students with severe disabilities can have an important influence on whether a school meets state standards (Kleinert, Haigh, et al., in press). If students with severe disabilities are excluded from the rating of a school, the potential exists that they will also be excluded from the resources to strengthen a school that underachieves, or from the rewards for a school that meets the state's goals.

Decision 2: Who Will Receive an Alternate Assessment?

IDEA 1997 requires alternate assessments for students who cannot participate in state or district testing, even with accommodations. Many students with disabilities will be able to participate in the typical assessment procedures, especially with well-designed accommodations. When a student cannot participate in the typical assessment, the IEP must designate whether the student will need an alternate assessment. States have defined the eligibility criteria for this alternate assessment based on graduation outcomes (e.g., students' not pursuing a regular diploma), curricular priorities (e.g., life skills or instruction in multiple, community-referenced settings), and the need for alternative outcome indicators (Kleinert, Haigh, et al., in press; Olsen & Thompson, 1999). The implication of these types of eligibility criteria is that while most, or even all, students with moderate and severe disabilities in a district may be designated as qualifying for alternate assessment, this designation will be based on a specific, educational rationale and not on the label "moderate" or "severe."

Decision 3: What Will Be Assessed?

Whether or not alternate assessment achieves the goal of educational accountability will depend largely on *what* is assessed. Careful planning is needed to determine the focus of alternate assessment. First, the planning group needs to review the standards or performance indicators that have been set for students in general in the state or district, to determine whether these same outcomes or modifications of these outcomes are applicable for students with moderate and severe disabilities. For example, Kentucky identified a relevant subset of the state's "learner outcomes" and then defined a "critical function" that could include students with significant disabilities, as shown in Table 3.2. In contrast, Maryland stakeholders (e.g., teachers, parents, and students with disabilities) identified what they wanted the students to be able to do when they left school. From there, the stakeholders used a backward mapping process to identify outcome indicators aligned with both general education and the life skills curriculum (Kleinert, Haigh, et al., in press). From this process, they identified the content domains (personal management, community, career/vocational, and recreation/leisure) and the skill domains (communication, decision making, behavior, and academics) to be assessed.

Once the group selects the curricular domains to be assessed, they need to consider whether a student's IEP will be used, and if so, how there will be performance expectations for all students that transcend the IEPs. For example, in North Carolina, the IEP serves as the foundation for a student's portfolio (Lee, 1999). The advantage of linking alternate assessment to the IEP is that it honors individualization of curriculum. In the last two decades, professionals have recommended personalizing curricula for students with moderate and severe disabilities (Brown et al., 1979; Ford et al., 1989; Giangreco et al., 1998; Knowlton, 1998). An alternate assessment that focuses on the IEP can be highly individualized across students. The disadvantage of such individualization is that it becomes difficult to conduct external evaluations and to compile meaningful information about groups of students for purposes of comparison. Even if IEPs are the focus of the alternate assessment, some external standards will need to be set to determine accountability. For example, North Carolina specified that student work must include communication, personal and home management, career/vocational, and community domains, and must give attention to self-determination, literacy, numeracy, and technology in environments that promote generalization of skills, self-determination, inclusive learning opportunities, and contextual learning (Lee, 1999).

Besides the decisions about which general curricular areas are to be assessed, and whether these will come from the IEP, decisions are needed about the quality indicators to be used to rank performance. First, will the quality indicators focus on a student's performance only, or also consider a student's environment? For students with moderate and severe disabilities, quality indicators should focus on both. Although professionals once focused on having students with severe disabilities "earn" outcomes such as jobs, school inclusion, and community access through skill acquisition, this perspective was challenged by the advocacy work in the late 1980s and 1990s that created inclusive opportunities and offered appropriate supports. Smull and Bellamy (1991) articulated this paradigm shift by challenging professionals to focus on environmental constraints rather than students' limitations.

To determine what these environmental opportunities should be, planning groups can use stakeholder consensus that has been published (e.g., Kleinert & Kearns, 1999; Meyer, Eichinger, & Park-Lee, 1987; Williams, Fox, Thousand, & Fox, 1990) or that is generated through local surveys or discussions. For example, in the national validation study of Kentucky's performance indicators, Kleinert and Kearns (1999) found that the following indicators were rated most highly (above 4.0 on a 5-point scale):

1. Integrated environments
2. Functionality
3. Age-appropriateness
4. Choice making
5. Multiple settings
6. Communication
7. Academic expectations
8. Natural support
9. Targeted skills
10. Friendship
11. Parent involvement
12. Assistive technology

Just as states vary in the standards set in their overall assessment systems, the performance indicators for students taking alternate assessment also vary. In Michigan, performance expectations are developed for four levels of participation: Level 4, full independence; Level 3, functional independence; Level 2, supported independence; and Level 1, partial participation. Performance expectations for supported independence (Level 2) are for students to (1) complete personal care, health, and fitness activities; (2) complete domestic activities in personal living environments; (3) manage personal work assignments; (4) complete activities requiring transactions in the community; (5) participate effectively in group situations; (6) respond effectively to unexpected events and potentially harmful situations; (7) manage unstructured time; and (8) proceed appropriately toward the fulfillment of personal desires. In partial participation (Level 1), the expectations are for students to (1) engage in typical patterns of leisure and productive activities in the home and community; (2) engage in typical patterns of interactions; (3) participate in effective communication cycles; (4) participate in personal care, health, and safety routines; and (5) reach desired locations safely within familiar environments (Parshall, 1999).

Decision 4: How Will the Alternate Assessment Be Conducted?

Because the purpose of alternate assessment is educational accountability, student outcomes are usually evaluated by external professionals (i.e., professionals not in the students' schools) using defined performance indicators. The assessment format many states have adopted for the process is portfolio assessment, because of the advantages this method offers. In states using portfolio assessment as part of the evaluation for all students, the alternate assessment can yield similar outcome information (e.g., rubric scoring). Also, portfolio assessments are "doable" for all students. In contrast, testing or conducting direct observations of students with moderate and severe disabilities may not be feasible if the domains to be sampled are nonacademic or if the students lack traditional test-taking skills. Portfolio assessments also yield "permanent products" that lend themselves well to external review. Although teacher and parent interviews or surveys are an option, they can be difficult for external evaluators to implement on a statewide basis and may be viewed as "biased" in high-stakes accountability systems. In contrast, information from direct observations and interviews can be important components of a portfolio that will also include other information.

Portfolio assessment involves the collection and evaluation of student work samples. These samples may include drafts or steps toward final products, as well as the final products themselves, and are selected by the students and teachers. Students usually participate in evaluating their own work in the portfolio by reflecting on their own work. Rubrics, checklists, and other tools can be used to guide student and teacher evaluation of the portfolio (Bigge & Stump, 1999). In Kentucky, the alternate portfolio to be submitted for evaluation must include the following components (Kleinert, Kearns, & Kennedy, in press):

1. A description of the student's primary mode of communication.
2. The student's daily/weekly schedule. This must also include a description of how the student uses the individualized schedule and performance data on how well the student is learning to follow this schedule.
3. A student letter to the portfolio reviewer in which the student rates his or her best or favorite entries. This letter can be developed with a typical peer as long as the level of assistance is specified.
4. Portfolio entries including individual and group projects and clear documentation of learned skills (e.g., systematic instructional data). The entries should involved nondisabled peers and relate to the content area of the general education curriculum to the maximum extent possible.
5. A work resume for students in the 12th grade indicating job experiences and an employer evaluation.
6. A letter from the student's parents or guardian about their satisfaction with the portfolio entries and the extent to which the student can apply skills learned in school.

Maryland uses a portfolio assessment, but also requires a videotape of the student performing a task that is prescribed each year by the state department of education. For example, in 1999, the "IMAP task" for 17-year-old or junior students was "developing a schedule." To complete this portion of the portfolio, teachers videotaped their students making a schedule for their day and initiating the first task. At the end, each student was interviewed on video about the task.

In addition to determining the specifics of the alternate assessment process, a decision is needed about when the alternate assessment will be administered. Typically, the alternate assessment will follow the state's requirements for all students. For example, if the state's requirement is that students are assessed in the 4th, 8th, and 12th grades, the alternate assessment may be administered when students are the age of other 4th- and 8th-graders and when they are in their last year of school (e.g., age 21).

Decision 5: How Will the Alternate Assessment be Scored?

Professionals have expressed ongoing concerns about the validity and reliability of portfolio assessment (Kleinert, Haigh, et al., in press). For example, interrater reliability has been a concern in Kentucky's alternate assessment (Kleinert, Kearns, & Kennedy, 1997). Several strategies can be used to strengthen the validity and reliability of these assessments. First, performance indicators should be clearly defined and validated with stakeholders. Kleinert, Haigh, et al. (in press) validated Kentucky's performance indicators with a national panel of experts. North Carolina and other states involved stakeholders in defining the performance indicators. Second, clear guidelines should be developed for scoring. Table 3.3 shows the revised scoring rubric used for the Kentucky alternate portfolio. A third way to increase reliability and validity in portfolio assessment is to recruit evaluators (e.g., teachers) who know the types of programs being assessed, and to train them to reach high levels of agreement in using a checklist, rubric, or other scoring method. Whatever method is used to develop and score the alternate assessment, consideration needs to be given to how the results will be used.

QUALITY ENHANCEMENT

Alternate assessment is a form of program evaluation. "Program evaluation" can be defined as the "systematic collection of information about the activities, characteristics, and outcomes of programs for use by specific people to reduce uncertainties, improve effectiveness, and make decisions with regard to what those programs are doing and affecting" (Patton, 1986, p. 14). There has been worldwide demand for program evaluation of many human services (Patton, 1986). Often this demand stems from a concern about the cost–benefit analysis of services provided at taxpayer expense. Similarly, recent school reform efforts have been focused on obtaining information about the quality of educational programs.

In any program evaluation, there will be: (1) objectives, (2) means, and (3) measures for the purposes of accountability and feedback. As described in this chapter, the objectives of school accountability systems vary. The focus may be student accountability, school accountability, or both. The means for measuring accountability also vary widely across states. In some instances, teachers themselves participate in the evaluation; in others, external review alone is used. As described earlier, the measures likewise vary widely, although many states rely on portfolio assessments as the basic format.

Because of the complexities of designing and implementing program evaluation strategies, professionals sometimes lose sight of its purpose, which should be *to have an immediate effect on decision making*. Unfortunately, much more has been written in the professional literature on how to develop alternate assessment than on what to do with the information obtained. If alternate assessment information is not used to make decisions, there will be no benefit for students with disabilities. Patton (1986) notes that one

TABLE 3.3. The Revised Scoring Rubric Used in Kentucky's Alternate Assessment

	Novice	Apprentice	Proficient	Distinguished
Performance	Student participates passively in portfolio products. No clear evidence of targeted skills. Little or no linkage to academic expectations.	Student performs specifically targeted IEP goals/objectives that are meaningful in current and future environments. Planning, monitoring, and evaluating are limited or inconsistent. Some evidence of academic expectations.	Student work indicates progress on specifically targeted IEP goals/objectives that are meaningful in current and future environments. Student consistently plans, monitors, and evaluates own performance. Academic expectations clearly evidenced in most entries.	Student work indicates progress on specifically targeted IEP goals/objectives that are meaningful in current and future environments. Planning, monitoring, and evaluating progress [are] clearly evident. Evaluation is used to extend performance. Extensive evidence of academic expectations in all entries.
Settings	Student participates in a limited number of settings.	Student performs targeted IEP goals/objectives in a variety of integrated settings.	Student performs targeted IEP goals/objectives in a wide variety of integrated settings within and across most entries.	Student performance occurs in an extensive variety of integrated settings, within and across all entries.
Support	No clear evidence of peer supports or needed adaptations, modifications, &/[or] assistive technology.	Support is limited to peer tutoring. Limited use of adaptations, modifications, &/or assistive technology.	Support is natural with students learning together. Appropriate use of adaptations, modifications, &/or assistive technology.	Support is natural. Use of adaptations, modifications, &/or assistive technology evidences progress toward independence.
Social relationships	The student has appropriate but limited social interactions.	The student has frequent, appropriate social interactions with a diverse range of peers.	The student has diverse, sustained, appropriate social interactions that are reciprocal within the context of established social contacts.	The student has sustained social relationships and is clearly a member of a social network of peers who choose to spend time together.
Contexts	Student makes limited choices in portfolio products. Products are not age-appropriate.	Student makes choices that have minimal impact on student learning in a variety of portfolio products. All products are age-appropriate.	Student consistently makes choices that have significant impact on student learning. All products are age-appropriate.	The student makes choices that have significant impact on student learning within and across all entries. All products are age-appropriate.

Note. From University of Kentucky, Human Development Institute (1999). Reprinted with permission of the University of Kentucky Human Development Institute.

of the major problems in the application of program evaluation is the "utilization crisis." That is, will decision makers use the information they receive, and if so, how? He describes the outcome of many program evaluations as follows:

> . . . the advisory board explains its frustration with the disappointing results of the evaluation ("data just aren't solid enough"). The county board representatives explain why their decisions are contrary to evaluation recommendations ("we didn't really get the information we needed when we wanted it and it wasn't what we wanted when we got it"). The room is filled with disappointment, frustration, defensiveness, cynicism, and more than a little anger. There are charges, countercharges, budget threats, moments of planning, and longer moments of explaining away the problems . . . (Patton, 1986, p. 11)

As states and local districts begin to review the results of alternate assessments, it becomes evident that some students, and some schools, are not meeting the standards that have been set. The temptation exists to spend "longer moments of explaining away the problems" than making decisions to effect change. Another temptation decision makers face is to respond by "satisficing"—or that is, finding a course of action that is "good enough" without creating real change (Patton, 1986). In contrast, alternate assessment information can be used for the benefit of students with disabilities if it becomes a foundation for quality enhancement for these educational programs. What educators often need is a process for developing this quality enhancement.

Using "Total Quality Management" Principles to Respond to Alternate Assessment Outcomes

Since the 1980s, American businesses and schools have considered principles of "total quality management" (TQM) to enhance their work (Marchese, 1991). TQM is both a philosophy and a set of tools for creating a "culture of quality." It requires a shift in thinking from individualism and "if it works, don't fix it" to teamwork and constant improvement. The principles of TQM can be helpful in responding to the outcomes of an alternate assessment. The following are some of the principles of TQM, with examples of how each can be applied to responding to data received from alternate assessments of students with moderate and severe disabilities.

Making Quality the Goal

The starting point in quality enhancement is to set the goal of having a high-quality program. When disappointing results are obtained in an external evaluation, energy can be wasted in belittling the evaluation itself or in making excuses for why the standards could not be achieved. Although there may be real problems with both the evaluation and the resources available, a team that is committed to excellence will respond to these challenges with problem solving, rather than viewing them as reasons not to respond. The fact that many states and districts with accountability systems did not include students with moderate and severe disabilities until the IDEA 1997 mandates suggests that these students were overlooked in initial discussions of school reform. If TQM principles are to be applied, *all* students will be included in goals for quality enhancement of schools.

Customer-Driven Services

A common TQM expression is to "delight the customer." The goal of excellence is to surpass customer needs and expectations and to turn to customers themselves to define quality. Encouraging family-centered services and self-determination are two ways to make special education services customer-driven (Chapters Five and Six discuss family-centered services and self-determination, respectively). The district or school can form a quality enhancement team that includes families and students with disabilities to develop program improvement plans.

Continuous Improvement

In TQM, quality enhancement is not episodic, but continuous. Planning teams are always seeking ways to do their work better. There is no finish line in the journey toward quality. Once formed, a quality enhancement team will become an ongoing part of planning for the educational programs of a school or district. Also, these teams will not be static committees, but dynamic groups that solve specific problems and are empowered to make things happen.

Making Processes Work Better

As a problem-solving team, those most directly involved with the process need to be included in creating solutions. Teachers, therapists, paraprofessionals, and others who work with students with moderate and severe disabilities can often recognize what led to a disappointing alternate assessment outcome. For example, was there a mismatch between the curriculum and the performance indicators of the assessment? Were there no opportunities to demonstrate some performance indicators (e.g., social inclusion)? Did the teachers need technical assistance to know how to achieve some of the standards (e.g., self-determination for students with significant disabilities)? Some of these specific problems are now considered.

Specific Quality Enhancement Strategies to Improve Alternate Assessment Outcomes

Curriculum Development and Training

As stakeholders define standards to be measured in alternate assessments, curriculum development work needs to keep pace. For example, if the domains to be measured in an alternate assessment include life skills such as personal maintenance, leisure/recreation, vocational, and community skills, do teachers have access to a written curriculum containing skills in these areas that are relevant for their students? Many states and districts have included academic outcomes in their performance indicators to encourage access to the general education curriculum for students with moderate and severe disabilities. Do teachers have curriculum guides identifying skills for each academic area that are applicable to students with few or no reading or math skills? Once curricula are updated, teachers must be trained in their use. Training is needed to help teachers know how to assess students' skills in a curriculum and how to set priorities for personalizing the curriculum and writing the IEP, as described in Chapter Two. Box 3.1

describes one school district's creative approach to the challenges of curriculum development.

"Teaching to the Test"

A second way to enhance quality is to use the performance indicators for an alternate assessment when planning students' instruction. As mentioned earlier, some states sample specific skills in their assessments. For example, in 1999, the videotape sample in the Maryland assessment described above required each student to create and follow a schedule. To the extent that specific skill areas are known, teachers will want to be sure to include these in IEP planning and daily instruction. For example, if one of the domain areas is communication, the teacher will want to be sure each student has a communication system. In most states, performance indicators are defined for the alter-

---

BOX 3.1. Pursuing Quality: One District's Approach to Curriculum Development

During the summer of 1999, the Charlotte–Mecklenberg School System in North Carolina initiated a quality enhancement effort with teachers of students with severe disabilities. This large, rapidly growing district provides services for hundreds of students with significant learning problems. Although the district had a "functional" curriculum, many teachers of students with the most severe disabilities found it difficult to translate these skill lists into achievable objectives. Interests in encouraging inclusion and responding to new requirements for alternate assessment also fueled the interest in curriculum development for this population. To develop a new curriculum guide, the teachers worked together in the summer, first defining strategies to generate curricular ideas. These included (1) reviewing other published curricula; (2) considering principles of partial participation, inclusion, age-appropriateness, and self-determination (e.g., choice making, students' preferences); (3) conducting ecological inventories of community environments; (4) reviewing general education curricula; (5) conducting discrepancy analyses by comparing their students' day to a typical day of a same-age peer who was nondisabled; (6) interviewing parents, students, and employers; and (7) creative brainstorming. After deciding how to generate the curriculum ideas, the teachers divided into work groups defined by curricular area (e.g., vocational skills, home and personal living, functional academics, communication). Each work group used the seven strategies described above to develop a skill list for its section of the curriculum. Once these lists were complete, they were presented to the entire group for feedback and revision. They were then presented to a panel of external "experts" (e.g., students with disabilities, parents, district program specialists, university faculty members) who reviewed the final product. This group also gave awards for the groups' efforts in a fun, supportive manner. For example, an award was given for the skill considered "most creative." Others were given for skills that "encourage self-determination" and "create links to the general education curriculum."

nate assessment (see Table 3.3). By using these when planning the IEP, teachers may enhance students' achievement.

Creating Opportunities

Some performance indicators will require creating new opportunities for students. If self-determination is a performance indicator, teachers may need to create opportunities for students to express preferences, make choices, initiate tasks, and self-evaluate (see Chapter Six). If interaction with students who are nondisabled is a performance indicator, schoolwide planning may be needed to create more inclusive opportunities for students with moderate and severe disabilities. If secondary students are expected to have a resume of job experiences, district-level planning may be needed to create more access to job placements and training for students with moderate and severe disabilities.

Will It Cost More?

Because of their responsibility to taxpayers for cost containment, administrators are sometimes wary of quality enhancement activities that may create demand for new resources. Quality enhancement planning may need to include financial planning, but does not necessarily increase costs. Sometimes students with moderate and severe disabilities are not receiving their fair share of resources within a school or district, and some reallocation is needed. For example, when new computers are allocated, do students with moderate and severe disabilities get access to them? Sometimes the cost will be time. For example, developing the school's schedule may require extra time to plan for inclusion of all students. In some instances, financial planning may mean realigning the budget with changing priorities.

SUMMARY

> There can be no acting or doing of any kind, till it be recognized that there
> is a thing to be done; the thing once recognized, doing in a thousand
> shapes becomes possible.
>
> THOMAS CARLYLE (as quoted by Patton, 1986, p. 180)

As part of the school reform movement, many states have adopted an accountability system for measuring student outcomes. Sometimes these are "high-stakes" systems with contingencies for schools, students, or both. As of July 1, 2000, schools have been required by IDEA 1997 either to include students with disabilities in these accountability measures or to develop alternate assessments. Many students with moderate and severe disabilities participate in alternate assessments.

In developing alternate assessments, states and local districts must determine their purpose, implementation schedule, content, format, and scoring. If the evaluation is focused on school accountability, it is important for students with moderate and severe disabilities to be included. For this to occur, the alternate assessment will need to be scheduled in the same time frame as the state or district evaluation of students who receive the typical assessment (e.g., standardized testing). Many states and districts have adopted the use of portfolio assessments that are rated by external evaluators using checklists or rubrics. The content for these portfolios varies and reflects the field's struggle with balancing a focus on functional life skills with access to the general education curriculum for students with moderate and severe disabilities.

The meaningfulness of this alternate assessment will depend both on how it is designed and how it is used. As a form of program evaluation, alternate assessment runs the risk of developing a "utilization crisis" in which results are not used for decision making. To make this process beneficial to students, quality enhancement strategies can be used to plan continual improvements. TQM provides one resource to guide this quality enhancement process.

REFERENCES

Bigge, J. L., & Stump, C. S. (1999). *Curriculum, assessment, and instruction.* Belmont, CA: Wadsworth.

Brown, L., Branston, M. B., Hamre-Nietupski, S., Pumpian, I., Certo, N., & Gruenwald, L. (1979). A strategy for developing chronological age-appropriate and functional curriculum content for severely handicapped adolescents and young adults. *Journal of Special Education, 13,* 81–90.

Council for Exceptional Children. (1998). *IDEA 1997: Let's make it work.* Reston, VA: Author.

Erickson, R. N., Thurlow, M. L., & Thor, K. (1995). *State special education outcomes, 1994.* Minneapolis: University of Minnesota, National Center on Educational Outcomes. (ERIC Document Reproduction Service No. ED 404 799)

Ford, A., Schnorr, R., Meyer, L., Davern, L., Black, J., & Dempsey, P. (1989). *The Syracuse Community-Referenced Curriculum Guide for students with moderate and severe disabilities.* Baltimore: Paul H. Brookes.

Giangreco, M. F., Cloninger, C. J., & Iverson, V. S. (1998). *Choosing Outcomes and Accommodations for Children* (2nd ed.). Baltimore: Paul H. Brookes.

Kleinert, H. L., Haigh, J., Kearns, J., & Kennedy, S. (in press). Alternate assessments for students with disabilities and IDEA 97: Lessons learned and roads to be taken. *Exceptional Children.*

Kleinert, H. L., & Kearns, J. F. (1999). A validation study of the performance indicators and learner outcomes of Kentucky's alternate assessment for students with significant disabilities. *Journal of the Association for Persons with Severe Handicaps, 24,* 100–110.

Kleinert, H. L., Kearns, J. F., & Kennedy, S. (1997). Accountability for all students: Kentucky's alternate portfolio system for students with moderate and severe cognitive disabilities. *Journal of the Association for Persons with Severe Handicaps, 22,* 88–101.

Kleinert, H. L., Kearns, J. F., & Kennedy, S. (in press). Including all students in education assessment and accountability. In W. Sailor (Ed.), *Inclusive education and school/community partnerships.* New York: Teachers College Press.

Kleinert, H. L., Kennedy, S., Kearns, J. F. (1999). The impact of alternate assessments: A statewide teacher survey. *Journal of Special Education, 33,* 93–102.

Knowlton, E. (1998). Considerations in the design of personalized curricular supports for students with developmental disabilities. *Education and Training in Mental Retardation and Developmental Disabilities, 33,* 95–107.

Lee, F. M. (1999). *Models of alternate assessment in four states: North Carolina alternate assessment portfolio.* Paper presented at the annual meeting of the Council for Exceptional Children, Charlotte, NC.

Loyd, R. J., & Brolin, D. E. (1997). *Life Centered Career Education: Modified curriculum for individuals with moderate disabilities.* Reston, VA: Council for Exceptional Children.

Marchese, T. (1991, November). TQM reaches the academy. *AAHE [American Academy of Higher Education] Bulletin,* pp. 3–13.

Meyer, L., Eichinger, J., & Park-Lee, S. (1987). A validation of program quality indicators in educational services for students with severe disabilities. *Journal of the Association for Persons with Severe Handicaps, 12,* 251–263.

Olsen, K., & Thompson, S. (1999). *Issues and strategies in alternate assessment: Strand session #2: How are states linking alternate assessments to standards?* Paper presented at the annual meeting of the Council for Exceptional Children, Charlotte, NC.

Parshall, L. (1999). *A guide to measure and improve the performance of students with disabilities.* Paper presented at the annual meeting of the Council for Exceptional Children, Charlotte, NC.

Patton, M. Q. (1986). *Utilization-focused evaluation.* Beverly Hills, CA: Sage.

Roeber, E., Bond, L., & Braskamp, D. (1997). *Annual survey of state student assessment programs.* Washington, DC: Council of Chief State School Officers.

Smull, M. W., & Bellamy, G. T. (1991). Community services for adults with disabilities: Policy, changes, and the emerging support paradigm. In L. H. Meyer, C. A. Peck, & L. Brown (Eds.), *Critical issues in the lives of people with severe disabilities* (pp. 527–536). Baltimore: Paul H. Brookes.

University of Kentucky, Human Development Institute. (1999). Revised scoring rubric. In *Kentucky alternate portfolio online teacher's guide* [Online]. Available: http://www.ihdi.uky.edu/project/KAP/ [2000, August 15].

Vanderwood, M., Ysseldyke, J., & Thurlow, M. (1993). *Concensus building: A process for selecting educational outcomes and indicators* (Outcomes and Indicators No. 2). Minneapolis: University of Minnesota, National Center on Educational Outcomes.

Wagner, T. (1995). What's school really for, anyway? And who should decide? *Phi Delta Kappan, 76,* 393–399.

Williams, W., Fox, T. J., Thousand, J., & Fox, W. (1990). Level of acceptance and implementation of best practices in the education of students with severe handicaps in Vermont. *Education and Training in Mental Retardation, 25,* 120–131.

Wilcox, B., & Bellamy, G. T. (Eds.). (1987). *The Activities Catalog: An alternative curriculum for youth and adults with severe disabilities.* Baltimore: Paul H. Brookes.

Ysseldyke, J., & Olsen, K. (1999). Putting alternate assessment into practice: What to measure and possible sources of data. *Exceptional Children, 65,* 175–185.

Ysseldyke, J., Olsen, K., & Thurlow, M. (1997). *Issues and consideration in alternate assessments* (Synthesis Report No. 27). Minneapolis: University of Minnesota, National Center on Educational Outcomes. (ERIC Document Reproduction Service No. ED 415 656)

Ysseldyke, J., Thurlow, M. L., & Gilman, C. J. (1993). *Educational outcomes and indicators for students completing school.* Minneapolis: University of Minnesota, National Center on Educational Outcomes.

FOUR

Evaluating Progress
to Plan Instructional Supports

ALLEN AND TINA[1] WERE 10-YEAR-OLD TWINS. *Tina had a moderate cognitive disability, and Allen was nondisabled. When they first started school, Allen would bring home his report card and wait with anticipation for his parents' reaction. Allen usually did well in school, and his parents were enthusiastic with their praise. Because Allen's mother was a former elementary school substitute teacher, she was familiar with the type of curriculum and instruction the teacher used with Allen. When Allen struggled with learning to add, she knew what to ask his teacher and how to help him at home. In contrast, Tina's teacher did not use any type of report card. Although her parents attended her individualized education plan (IEP) meeting and read the teachers' daily logs, they were not clear about Tina's program and whether or not she was making progress. Tina wanted a report card like Allen's and carried a copy of his report card in her bookbag. When the twins started fourth grade, Tina's special education teacher developed a way to summarize her progress on an adapted report card. Tina and her parents were pleased with these new ongoing progress reports.*

This chapter briefly reviews what specialized instructional supports may include, and provides a model for the assessment and evaluation of ongoing progress.

Students with moderate and severe disabilities can participate in a wide variety of inclusive school and community environments with adequate supports. Among the most important forms of this assistance in a school program are instructional supports. "Instructional supports" are environmental arrangements, teaching strategies, and student-directed activities that are specially designed for an individual student's learning. Although direct teacher instruction is a key element for student learning, natural supports, cooperative learning, peer tutoring, classroom arrangements, and self-management all play important roles as well.

This chapter describes strategies to evaluate students' progress on their IEPs. To be consistent with the Individuals with Disabilities Education Act (IDEA) 1997 requirements, teachers will need to (1) monitor progress on a regular basis; (2) describe the extent to which this progress is sufficient to achieve objectives by the end of the year; (3) inform parents of students' progress at least as often as reporting occurs for

---

[1]Allen and Tina's example is fictitious.

students who are nondisabled (e.g., report cards); and (4) describe the method to be used for progress monitoring on the IEP. For students with moderate and severe disabilities, the purpose of progress monitoring is not to assign "grades," although grades may be used as part of their participation in general education classes. Instead, the purpose of monitoring progress on the IEP is to modify instruction as needed to enhance student performance. By planning appropriate instructional supports at the onset of the IEP, monitoring is more likely to reveal progress that is on track toward mastery. When progress is not adequate, this information can be used to enhance these instructional supports. To emphasize that the purpose of progress monitoring is to plan instructional supports, this chapter begins with a description of these supports, and then provides information on the assessments and decisions needed to modify them when necessary.

PLANNING INSTRUCTIONAL SUPPORTS

The special education teacher's use of systematic instruction has been an important foundation for learning by students with moderate and severe disabilities. Systematic instruction involves teaching specific, measurable responses via prompting and feedback procedures. As students with moderate and severe disabilities experience more inclusive settings and acquire skills in self-determination, instructional supports become more multifaceted. Systematic instruction continues to be essential in inclusive contexts, but may be delivered by more than one person. For example, therapists, paraprofessionals, job coaches, general education teachers, and peers all may play a role in the delivery of this instruction. To enhance self-determination, teachers can also encourage students to take more responsibility for their own learning through choice making, self-instruction, and self-evaluation. Teachers can also enhance learning by creating environments that help focus learners' attention, encourage social interaction, and maximize natural cues and consequences. The components of instructional supports include (1) natural supports, (2) environmental supports, (3) student-directed learning, (4) systematic instruction, and (5) other special strategies, as shown in Figure 4.1. In this hierarchy, more applications would be expected for the supports toward the top (e.g., enhanced natural supports and environmental arrangements), and fewer applications would be expected for the supports toward the bottom (e.g., systematic instruction and other individualized interventions). By following this sequence in planning, teachers will reserve the intensive time required to plan and implement systematic instruction and other highly specialized interventions for priority areas.

Enhanced Natural Supports

When creating opportunities for students to be included in general education, community, job, and other learning contexts, it is important to capitalize on the instructional supports typically available in these contexts. These typically available resources are called "natural supports" (Nisbet, 1992). To "enhance" these natural supports simply means to identify them; to be sure the learner has access to them; and, if necessary, to accentuate them so the learner can attend or respond to them more easily. Some of the

FIGURE 4.1. Components of instructional support to use in inclusive settings.

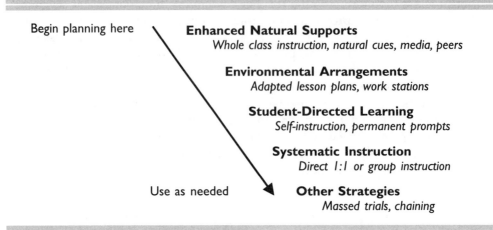

natural supports available to students in educational settings include (1) whole-class and small-group instruction, (2) individual teacher assistance, (3) natural cues and consequences, (4) media and technology, and (5) peer assistance.

Whole Class and Small Group Instruction

In the general education class or in job orientation, participants frequently receive large- and small-group instruction. This group instruction may involve lectures, media presentations, discussions, and other methods designed to present information to a number of participants at one time. The strategies that the teacher uses to help all students participate in group lessons are forms of "natural supports." Sometimes the only enhancement needed is to create the opportunity for students with moderate and severe disabilities to participate in group instruction.

Other students may be able to benefit from group instruction if they receive help in focusing their attention (Wolery, Alig-Cybriwsky, Gast, & Boyle-Gast, 1991; Wolery, Ault, & Doyle, 1992). For example, Schoen and Ogden (1995) had all students in a small group write a sight word before one student read it. Teachers may also focus students' attention by using a verbal prompt (e.g., "Everyone look") or by having students make a motor movement (e.g., "Raise your hand when you hear the word . . . "). Students may also need to be offered alternative ways to respond. For example, a nonverbal student may hold up a card or picture to answer a question. Some students may need ongoing individualized prompting to maintain attention in the group lesson. A paraprofessional, peer, or job coach may sit beside such a student, helping him or her keep pace in the book or other materials as the teacher lectures.

Individual Assistance

In many learning contexts, another of the "natural supports" available is individual assistance from the teacher or other expert. In the media center, a librarian can help with selecting books or using the computer. In a new job, the supervisor will frequently help new employees understand their job expectations. In a team sport or dance class, the coach or instructor will often give individual prompts. In the community, staff members at an information booth in the mall or a museum can offer help. When such support is provided to an individual with disabilities, it is important not to bypass or compete with these sources of support. Instead, the individual can be prompted to ask for help from the appropriate person in the setting.

Natural Cues and Consequences

The goal in most instruction is that students learn to respond to the natural cues and consequences in their environments in performing their daily routines (Ford & Mirenda, 1984). The bell is a natural cue for going to class, and a tardy slip may be the natural consequence for not making it on time. Entering the lunchroom is the natural cue to get in line to purchase lunch. Coming to the cashier is the cue to pay, and the natural consequence of paying is getting to go sit and eat lunch. When educators are providing instructional support to students with moderate and severe disabilities, it is important to focus on these natural cues and consequences. In their research demonstrating how to focus prompting on natural cues, Colyer and Collins (1996) stated the price of an item in the same way cashiers do (natural cue) before giving a prompt. They then used a prompt hierarchy to help a student respond if this natural cue was not sufficient. When using classroom or school community simulations, teachers can incorporate natural cues and consequences (Nietupski, Hamre-Nietupski, Clancy, & Veerhusen, 1986; Westling & Fox, 1995). For example, in having students practice ordering at a restaurant, the teacher can use a copy of the actual menu.

Media and Technology

The Internet, cable television, and other new types of technology are additional natural supports that are becoming increasingly important resources. Students with disabilities, who may lack the reading skills that were once needed to conduct research in the library, can now access audiovisual material through Internet sites, educational television, and videos. Teachers can also prepare materials such as videotapes or computer slides of students performing activities in their own communities. If a teacher wants to do a unit on shopping in a department store, the student can be instructed in how to access a Web site or home shopping menu for that store to plan (or even make) the purchase. If the teacher has a computer-accessible camera, the student can be photographed at the store to create a file for discussion and review. The student can also create his or her own Web page about shopping and other activities.

Peer Assistance

Another form of natural support is peer assistance. Peers can serve as tutors, buddies, or helpers, with positive benefits for both the students with disabilities and the peers who are nondisabled (Hunt, Staub, Alwell, & Goetz, 1994). In recruiting peers, Downing and Eichinger (1996) recommend that participation be voluntary. They suggest recruiting peers to assist students with disabilities by doing the following:

1. Ask students if they would like to interact with a given student and give opportunities to do so.
2. Ask the teacher who might benefit academically, socially, or emotionally from working with a student with disabilities.
3. Ask the school counselor, especially at the secondary level, for nominees.
4. Assign students to cooperative learning groups to help establish relationships.
5. Have students with disabilities join extracurricular activities and clubs.
6. Ask the school council or other school leaders if they are interested in supporting some students.

A peer assistant may need some information about the student's disability and some training in his or her own duties. If the student with the disability uses augmentative communication, the peer assistant may need an orientation to understand this system. If the peer will be offering specific prompting, some practice may be needed. In contrast, some "peer buddy" relationships will evolve naturally from interactions between students. When this occurs, professionals do not need to "formalize" the relationship with special training unless the peer assistant asks for help.

The specific duties of the peer assistant can vary. The assistant may help direct the student's attention to the teacher; help get materials ready; offer assistance for mobility (e.g., push a wheelchair); or serve as a buddy during lunch, recess, or assemblies (Downing & Eichinger, 1996). Peers may also be recruited to provide systematic instruction or work in cooperative learning groups, as described in Chapter Twelve of this book.

Environmental Arrangements

A second type of instructional support is the arrangement of the environment to encourage the student's learning and adaptive behavior. These strategies are sometimes called "classroom management" or "classroom organization"; however, they can also apply to other environments, such as community job sites. Teachers prepare the environment for learning through the physical arrangement of the classroom and learning materials and through planning the use of instructional time with well-organized schedules and lesson plans.

Weekly Lesson Plans, Schedules, and Thematic Units

A well-organized teacher will have a written schedule for each day of the week. Special education teachers must often create individual schedules for each student to incorporate participation in general education classes, therapy, community-based instruction, job training, and other opportunities. If the special education teacher is in transition from having a self-contained class to supporting inclusion in general education, developing a daily schedule that is consistent with the schedule for the rest of the school can be a step toward this transition. The students' individual schedules can then be developed from this master schedule. A well organized schedule is an important form of natural support that can help a student anticipate and prepare for each day's routine. Table 4.1 illustrates the use of a master schedule. In this example, the special education students are partially included in general education classes, as Helen Thomas's sched-

TABLE 4.1. An Example of a Master Schedule and an Individual Student's Schedule

Special education teacher's master schedule	Special education teacher's priorities for instruction	Schedule for individual student (Helen Thomas) showing general education inclusion
7:15–7:30: Buses arrive 7:30: Homeroom	Arrival routine Greetings Orientation and mobility	7:30: Begin day in Mr. Sherman's fourth grade with peer buddy who escorts from bus
7:45: Math	Students develop their daily schedule, using pictures or objects Time telling (related to schedule) Students count money for lunch or community outing Also, assistant provides personal care/restroom assistance 1:1 during this time	7:45: Math, in Mr. Sherman's room Velcro schedule with peer Individual math folder Number entry on computer with peer
8:45: Reading	Sight words and daily living application (e.g., reading and preparing snack, reading and making grocery list) Fridays: Media center	8:45: Functional reading in special education class
9:45: Physical education	9:45: Physical education with Mr. Sherman's class (coteaching)	9:45: Physical education—go with Mr. Sherman's class
10:30: Language arts Wednesdays: Third-graders go to music with Ms. Haskin's class; assistant goes with them	Language arts—small-group communication training, using a snack or craft activity to create need to communicate Tuesdays and Thursdays: Students practice communication with peer tutors from Mr. Sherman's class while using leisure materials	10:30: Leave PE with Mr. Sherman's class and go with them to Ms. Jordan's language arts. Tuesdays: Speech therapist plans activities and provides direct therapy
11:15: Lunch	Lunch in cafeteria, using peer buddy program; encourage social skills	11:15: Comes to lunch with Ms. Jordan's class, but also has peer buddy
12:00: Mondays and Wednesdays: Social studies Tuesdays and Thursdays: Science or health Fridays: Coteach health with Ms. Haskins in third grade; fourth- and fifth-graders go to music with Mr. Sherman	Use videos, books, newspaper to introduce concepts, followed by hands-on activities emphasizing fine motor skills, choice making, daily living skills (1:1 assistance in restroom by teaching assistant)	12:00: In special education class, including occupational therapy on Wednesday in context of hands-on activities Also, work on daily living Systematic Instruction Plans
1:00: Life skills	Mondays and Wednesdays: Community-based instruction Tuesdays: Purchases at school store Thursdays: Classroom chores Fridays: Seasonal/holiday/cultural activity with combined classes	1:00: Mondays: Community-based instruction with special ed. teacher Tuesdays and Thursdays: Science with Mr. Sherman's class Wednesdays: Art with Mr. Sherman's class Fridays: Special activity with combined classes
2:00: Departure routine	Departure skills (e.g., putting coat on, carrying bookbag, finding bus)	2:00: Dismissed with Mr. Sherman's class; to bus with peer escort

Note. Helen Thomas is a fictitious student.

ule reflects. The special education teacher's master schedule is developed to be consistent with the general education class activities, and thus to make it easier to foster this inclusion. This schedule is written for upper-elementary-level students (third through fifth grades) and reflects planning for one student in particular. The special education teacher will develop a similar schedule for each student.

Besides a master schedule, a second crucial form of planning teachers use is the written weekly lesson plan. This plans outlines material to be covered during each day and time of the day. The special education teacher's weekly lesson plans should incorporate both the students' IEP priorities and the broader curricular areas to be addressed. When planning for inclusion, the special education teacher should obtain a copy of the general education teacher's weekly lesson plans, in order to develop adaptations for the students with moderate and severe disabilities.

Besides having both written schedules and weekly lesson plans, teachers can encourage learning through the physical layout of their classrooms. A model program that focuses on environmental supports for students with autism is TEACCH (Schopler, Mesibov, & Hearsey, 1995) . Many of the TEACCH adaptations have applicability across a broad range of students and settings; for example, they have been used in general education classrooms and on job sites, as well as in special education classrooms. Three of the key TEACCH adaptations are the use of visual cues in a student's environment, an individualized schedule, and "work systems." First, the classroom environment is arranged so that the same activities occur in the same areas each day. Picture, word, and object cues are placed in these areas to assist the student in knowing the function of each area of the room. Picture and word cues are also used to help the student know what social behavior is expected. In teaching a small-group lesson, the teacher may have symbols for taking turns and for watching quietly. As each student is called on, the teacher shows the student's name and the symbol for taking a turn. The other students are told to watch quietly.

Second, every student has his or her own schedule. Depending on a student's current reading skills, this schedule may include objects, picture–word combinations, or just words. The schedule may be large (a wall chart) or small enough to carry in a pocket or on a clipboard. Students refer to the schedule at the beginning of each activity, remove the card or object that depicts the activity (or check the word with a pencil), and then go to the appropriate area to start the task. Examples of three types of schedules are shown in Figure 4.2.

A third principle of the TEACCH model is to encourage students to learn to do independent work through the use of "work systems." Students have their own work spaces, which may be separated by dividers to minimize distractions. In these spaces, called "work stations" students perform independent tasks that teachers assign. Teachers may sometimes assign a series of tasks as shown in Figure 4.3. In this system, Mark will have six tasks to complete before he can play. At the beginning of each task, he removes the card and starts to work. When all six tasks are complete, he can play with a leisure material of his choice. Although the work system shown in Figure 4.3 has been constructed on a piece of poster board that creates a study carrel at the student's desk, some students may use a clipboard or small flipchart instead. The challenge in using work systems is to select work that students can do independently and that is meaningful (functional). Critics of the TEACCH model question the value of work stations because they may not provide opportunities for students to learn new skills or

FIGURE 4.2. Three types of schedules used in the TEACCH model. From Lord, Bristol, and Schopler (1993). Copyright 1993 by Plenum Press. Reprinted with permission.

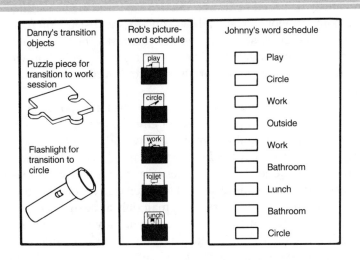

FIGURE 4.3. An individual work system that is designed for Mark to complete six tasks (see cards in slots) before he plays (see card on right). The work system is built from poster board and creates a study carrel at Mark's desk. For students who do not need a carrel, the cards can be placed on a clipboard or flipchart. From Lord, Bristol, and Schopler (1993). Copyright 1993 by Plenum Press. Reprinted with permission.

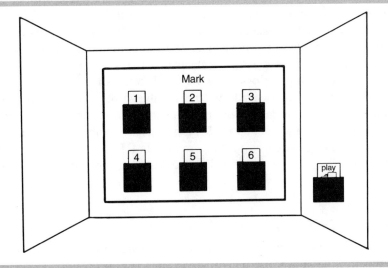

even to perform functional activities (Smith, 1996). Students need opportunities to receive direct, systematic teacher instruction to acquire new skills and should not spend
their entire day in work stations. Work stations are designed to help students practice
(maintain) previously acquired skills and participate in inclusive settings like general
education classrooms and jobs, where all-day, one-to-one instruction may not be available or desirable. To the greatest extent possible, the tasks chosen should be appropriate to the general education context (e.g., academic tasks) or should provide opportunities to practice life skills using real materials (e.g., community-validated job tasks, age-
appropriate hobby materials).

Whereas the TEACCH model relies on visual cues and on organizing students'
work into concrete units, another alternative for environmental arrangements is to simplify materials so that the student can more readily make the desired response. Elsewhere, a colleague and I (Browder & Lim, 1996) have described applications of engineering principles to make job tasks simpler. For example, by decreasing the total
movement distance in performing a task, a worker can reduce fatigue and become
more productive. This may involve arranging materials to be in closer proximity to the
student, or teaching the student to use more efficient movements when performing a
task like vacuuming. Sometimes it will involve using adaptive equipment to simplify
the movements needed, such as an adaptive switch to operate a blender, an electric stapler, or a photocopying machine that will staple and collate. In general, when planning
environmental adaptations, the teacher asks, "Is there a way that the student could perform this task better, or without assistance, if the materials or setting were designed to
encourage this?"

Student-Directed Learning

A third form of instructional support is student-directed learning. Whereas environmental arrangements are used to enable students to perform responses in their repertoire with little or no assistance, student-directed learning strategies are designed to
help students teach themselves new skills. One strategy that may be used to encourage
student-directed learning is "within-stimulus prompting" (Eckert & Browder, 1997). In
this strategy, visual (or auditory) prompts are placed within the materials themselves
rather than delivered by the teacher. One way to present these prompts is to give the
student access to computer software such as Edmark Functional Reading, which helps
students make correct responses. Another strategy is to use what are called "permanent
prompts." These may include color-coding materials or arranging materials in a certain
sequence, so that students can learn how to make the correct responses by responding
to these stimuli. Students can also be taught to instruct themselves using scripts, pictures, or audiotapes (Wehmeyer, Agran, & Hughes, 1998), and to problem-solve when
encountering a challenge such as missing materials (Hughes, Hugo, & Blatt, 1996).
These and other strategies for student-directed learning are described more fully in
Chapter Six.

Systematic Instruction

Although natural supports, environmental arrangements, and student-directed learning can all be effective and economical instructional supports, students also need the

opportunity to receive direct, systematic instruction. Systematic instruction utilizes teaching strategies derived from applied behavior analysis, such as task analysis, prompting, and feedback. One form of this instruction is called "discrete-trial instruction," because the student is given specific, defined "trials" or opportunities to respond. Lovaas (1981) developed a specific curriculum and format for discrete-trial instruction, which have been used broadly with young students with autism. Other researchers, such as Wolery et al. (1992), have developed behavioral approaches to teaching that are based on making decisions about the design of prompts and feedback. Some professionals have described how to apply systematic instruction in job-training contexts (Test & Wood, 1997). The term "systematic instruction" is used in the present book to refer to teaching focused on specific, measurable responses that may either be discrete (singular) or a response chain (e.g., task analysis), and that are established through the use of defined methods of prompting and feedback based on the principles and research of applied behavior analysis. For more information on these basic principles and research, the reader is referred to texts that describe applied behavior analysis (e.g., Alberto & Troutman, 1990) and systematic instruction (Snell & Brown, 1993; Westling & Fox, 1995; Wolery et al., 1992). Many examples of the applications of these principles and research can be found in descriptions of instruction throughout this book.

To implement systematic instruction, teachers will follow four steps:

1. Define the skills (responses) to be acquired.

   - Develop a data sheet and method to assess these skills.
   - Write an objective for mastery.

2. Define the specific methods to use in instructing the skills.

   - Determine the prompting and feedback system.
   - Write a Systematic Instruction Plan.

3. Implement the Systematic Instruction Plan frequently (e.g., daily).

   - Determine who will teach the plan, when it will be taught, and where.
   - Teach daily until mastery occurs or a change is made in the plan.

4. Review student progress regularly (e.g., biweekly) and modify instruction as needed.

   - Chart student performance.
   - Review progress, using data-based decision rules.
   - Modify the Systematic Instruction Plan as needed.

Figure 4.4 provides an example of a form that can be used in developing a Systematic Instruction Plan. Figure 4.5 shows a Data Collection Form that can be used in assessing progress. Blank versions of these two forms are provided in the Appendix to this book.

In the example shown in Figures 4.4 and 4.5, the teacher targeted teaching the student Betty Wilson[2] to purchase a soda. The soda machine was a popular place for socializing in Betty's high school; there was also a vending machine on her job site. Betty

---

[2]Betty Wilson's example is fictitious.

FIGURE 4.4. A sample Systematic Instruction Plan.

Systematic Instruction Plan

Student: _Betty Wilson_   Date plan written: _October 18_

Target skill: _Purchase a soda_   Routine for skill: _Break or lunch_

Objective: _When she indicates she wants a soda, Betty will purchase a soda by performing all steps of the task analysis correctly for 2 of 2 days._

Format

Materials: _$1 bill; access to vending machine that uses $1 bills_

Setting and teacher: _Job coach after work; peer tutor or SpEd teacher at lunch_

Number of trials: _One opportunity per day_

Instructional Procedures

Prompting:

    Specific prompt(s) to be used: _Verbal, model, physical guidance_

Fading (check one):

    _____ None (simultaneous prompting)

    _____ Time delay: ____ Progressive _or_ ____ Constant

    _X_ Least intrusive prompts

    _____ Most to least intrusive prompts

    _____ Graduated guidance

    _____ Stimulus fading or shaping

    _____ Other (describe) _____

    Fading schedule: _Give least assistance needed to perform response._

Feedback:

    Correct: _Specific praise for each step correct—e.g., "Good, you put the dollar in the slot."_

    Fading schedule for praise: _After 2 weeks, only praise independent responses._

    Error correction: _Block error and use next level of prompt._

Generalization Procedures

Train across vending machines

Other notes:

Ignore/block efforts to kiss trainer. Praise her for returning to task. After she completes the task, shake hands with Betty and talk with her as she drinks her soda.

FIGURE 4.5. An example of a standard Data Collection Form, which can also be used to summarize progress as a graph. +, independent, correct response; −, no response; V, verbal prompt required; M, model required; P, physical guidance required.

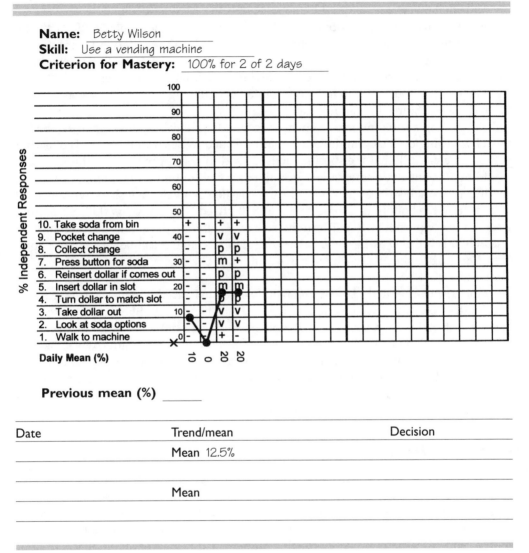

enjoyed being with people and drinking canned soda. She had already shown an interest in purchasing her own soda by approaching the machine. Based on her interest and the opportunity of her high school setting, purchasing a soda was included as one of Betty's short-term objectives on her IEP, under the annual goal for Betty to "Increase independence in daily living skills that can be used both at school and in the community."

After selecting this priority skill, the teacher identified a method for monitoring Betty's progress. She defined the target skill as "Purchase a soda" on the Systematic Instruction Plan (see Figure 4.4). To be sure the skill had a functional use in the student's daily routine, the teacher also noted the routine for the skill. In Betty's case, she could purchase a soda during lunchtime or break routines. Next, the teacher wrote down the specific objective, which was copied directly from the short-term objective on Betty's IEP. Note that this was a complete behavioral objective as described in Chapter Two, including the antecedent for responding ("When she indicates she wants a soda."), the response to be made ("Betty will purchase a soda . . . "), and the criterion for mastery (" . . . by performing all steps of the task analysis correctly for 2 of 2 days"). The condition "When she indicates she wants a soda . . . " would occur when Betty went up to a vending machine and touched it to indicate an interest in having a soda (Betty was nonverbal and used gestures to communicate).

Purchasing a soda involves a chain of responding. This response chain can be defined by writing each step in the order that is needed to perform the task. The teacher noted on Betty's IEP that the specific method used to assess progress for this objective would be "task-analytic assessment." On the data Collection Form (see Figure 4.5), the specific task analysis was written. On this particular chart, a task is written (and scored) from the bottom up. To be sure that Betty needed to learn this skill, the teacher gave her the opportunity to perform the task on 2 different days with no assistance. In research, this is called a "baseline" assessment; in teaching, it can be viewed as a "pretest." During baseline, Betty was able to do one step: She could "Take soda from bin" as shown in Figure 4.5.

Once the teacher had verified that Betty needed to learn this skill, she was ready to develop the rest of the Systematic Instruction Plan (Figure 4.4). She described the format for instruction by noting the materials needed (a $1 bill and access to a vending machine accepting such bills); the setting and teacher (job coach after work, peer or teacher at lunch); and the number of trials, which would be one opportunity a day. Next the teacher determined what specific instructional procedures would be used, including the prompting and feedback procedures. These procedures are now described in further detail.

Prompting and Feedback

In a behavioral paradigm, learning occurs when an individual consistently makes a response in the presence of a specific, discriminative stimulus. The response becomes consistent in the presence of the stimulus because of reinforcement that occurs contingent on the response. The discriminative stimulus can be thought of as the "cue to respond" and is the natural cue to which a student will respond when a teacher is not present. For example, in Betty's case (see Figure 4.4), the natural cue was the vending machine. The reinforcement for using the machine was the soda. Sometimes students cannot make the responses to gain access to the reinforcement. For example, Betty could not operate the machine, even though she indicated that she wanted a soda by touching the machine and looking at others' sodas (responses that might have worked to get a soda in her past!). To teach correct responding, "prompting" is used. Prompts are also stimuli to respond. In fact, effective prompts lead to a student's making the correct response. But prompts are not natural cues. Instead, they are stimuli that are added to a discriminative stimulus or natural cue to help the student make the target response. For example, gestures, verbal directions, a model, or physical guidance are all forms of prompting. Most of the time, a teacher or other trainer delivers these prompts. These are called "response prompts" because the teacher helps the student make the response (Wolery et al., 1992). If instead, the prompt is embedded in the materials—for example, by color-coding the materials or arranging them in an easy-to-hard sequence—these are called "stimulus prompts" (Eckert & Browder, 1997).

For Betty Wilson, the teacher chose to use a "prompt hierarchy." That is, the teacher used a series of prompts. If Betty did not perform a step of the task analysis with a verbal direction (e.g., "Put the dollar in the slot"), the teacher would use a model (e.g., showing her how to insert the dollar). If Betty still could not perform the step, the teacher would guide her to make the response. This hierarchical method of prompting has been widely validated by research with individuals with moderate and severe disabilities (Doyle, Wolery, Ault, & Gast, 1988). Although Betty could now operate the vending machine with the help of these prompts from the teacher, she would always be dependent on the teacher unless these prompts were faded. "Fading" is removing prompts so that stimulus control is transferred from the prompts (in this case, the teacher's help) to the discriminative stimulus (i.e., natural cues).

On the form for the Systematic Instruction Plan (see Figure 4.4 and the Appendix) six different prompt-fading methods are listed. These prompt-fading systems are described in Table 4.2. For more extensive information on such systems, the reader is referred to Wolery et al. (1992). Also, examples of these systems can be found in later chapters of this book.

Another part of the instructional procedures in the Systematic Instruction Plan (see Figure 4.4 and the Appendix) is "feedback." During early acquisition, the teacher will usually respond to every correct response with praise. When this praise is descriptive of the correct response, the student is more likely to make the connection between the response and teacher approval. For example, Betty's teacher would say, "Good, you put the dollar in the slot," rather than simply "Good." Sometimes a teacher may choose to use "instructive feedback," in which the teacher gives more information about the response (Werts, Wolery, Holcombe, & Gast, 1995). For example, Betty's teacher might say, "Good, you put the dollar in the slot. You could also use four quarters in this slot." These praise statements will need to be faded so that the student learns to complete the task without teacher attention. In the case of Betty (see Figure 4.4), the teacher only praised independent responses after the first 2 weeks of instruction. A student also needs feedback when an error is made. Usually, error correction instructs the student on the correct response and does not repeat, or give attention to, the error. If Betty, while learning the vending machine task, were to try to put the dollar in the coin return slot, her teacher might say, "No, put the dollar in *this* slot" and model the correct response. Betty's teacher might also block the error by holding her hand in front of the student's hand while showing the correct response.

Generalization

"Generalization" is the final component of the Systematic Instruction Plan and can be defined as responding to untrained settings, materials, or people. It is important for students to be able to use their skills across the many variations they encounter in daily life. Several effective strategies can be used to encourage generalization (Stokes & Osnes, 1988; Liberty, Haring, White, & Billingsley, 1988). One of the most effective is to

TABLE 4.2. Prompt-Fading Systems for Use in Systematic Instruction Plans

Prompt-fading system	Type of prompts used	How fading is implemented	Example
Simultaneous prompting	Usually one specific response prompt, such as a verbal model of the answer, is used.	Prompt is "dropped." Student is tested on ability to respond with no prompt.	Ms. Jefferson modeled how to count to 5 and had Jason repeat. After several repetitions, she had Jason count to 5 without a model.
Time delay	One specific response prompt is used.	At first, teacher gives prompt with the target stimulus (no delay). Over trials, the prompt is delayed by a few seconds. If these delays are incremental, it is called "progressive time delay." If one specific delay interval is used, it is called "constant time delay."	Ms. Cohen said, "Show me the word 'bread,'" as she pointed to the correct answer (gesture prompt). On the next trial she said, "Show me the word 'bread,'" but waited 2 seconds before pointing to the correct answer. If constant delay, she would also wait 2 seconds on the next trials. If progressive delay, the next trials would be at 2, 4, 6, and 8 seconds.
Least intrusive prompts	A hierarchy of response prompts is used.	On each teaching trial, the teacher waits for the student to make the response with no help, and then uses the hierarchy of prompts until the correct response is made.	Mr. Valdez waited for Tanisha to begin to zip her coat. When she did not, he said, "Zip your coat," and waited again for a response. If Tanisha still did not begin to zip, Mr. Valdez repeated the verbal direction and showed her how to pull the zipper up (model). He waited again for a response. If no response occurred, he helped Tanisha pull the zipper up (physical guidance).
Most to least intrusive prompts	Teaching begins with one response prompt that is highly effective, but may be intrusive (e.g., physical guidance). Then a less intrusive prompt is used (e.g., verbal direction).	Teacher will usually set a specific number of days or trials to use the more intrusive prompt and then switch to a less intrusive prompt.	To help Salvatore learn to cut vegetables with a sharp knife, Ms. Saunders used hand-over-hand guidance at first (physical prompt). After 10 days, she told Salvatore what to do as he used the knife (verbal prompt).
Graduated guidance	Physical prompting is always used, but only with as much guidance/physical pressure as needed.	The teacher decreases the amount of physical guidance used as the student's response improves.	To help John learn to hit a baseball off a tee, Mr. Kim used hand over hand guidance to teach him to swing. As John's swing improved, Mr. Kim used less and less physical pressure until John could swing alone.
Stimulus fading or shaping	Stimulus prompts are used—either coding the correct response with colors, pictures, or other features, or arranging the materials in an easy-to-hard sequence.	Extra cues like color or pictures can be diminished in size or brightness over time. In an easy-to-hard sequence, the distractions are made more like the target stimulus.	Ms. Rizzuto helped Carl find his locker by using a large orange sticker. Over time, the sticker was cut smaller and smaller until it was only a tiny dot, and then no mark was used at all (stimulus fading).

Note. All students mentioned in this table are fictitious.

"train sufficient exemplars." That is, the teacher introduces students to the variations that exist in their environments during instruction. For vending machine use, Betty's teacher did this by training Betty on a variety of machines.

Sometimes, in developing a Systematic Instruction Plan, the teacher will include other notes about the student's individual needs. Betty was learning social interactions appropriate for the setting and her age (16). Working with her in close physical proximity often resulted in her hugging and kissing her trainer. The teacher planned to block these attempts by holding her hand up and praising Betty for returning to task. Once the Systematic Instruction Plan was written, Betty's teacher was ready to begin teaching and monitoring progress.

Other Special Strategies

The forms of instructional support described can be used to address all or most of a student's educational needs. By beginning with natural and environmental supports and adding more direct instruction as needed, students' participation in inclusive environments can be enhanced. But for some students, even direct, systematic instruction will not be adequate for mastery of their IEP objectives. These students will need other individualized strategies that build on systematic instruction principles but alter the typical context for using the skill to enhance more rapid acquisition. These modifications may include using massed trials in which the student practices making the response repeatedly with only small intervals between repetitions, or using special materials in which students master an easy-to-hard learning sequence. For example, if a student is expected to choose a specific picture to request a break, he or she may need massed trials of instruction in a tutorial session dedicated to learning to choose between pictures. Or, if learning to put on a shirt is too difficult, the teacher may introduce an oversized shirt and then gradually offer shirts closer to the student's size. Sometimes the teacher may use chaining, in which only one step of a task analysis is taught at a time, and additional steps are added simply until the student masters the entire skill. Changing the context in which the skill is used should be introduced *after* trying systematic instruction in the student's typical routine because of the additional training that may be required for the student to generalize the skill. Other strategies focus on generalization in particular. For example, if a student does not generalize the skill, additional instruction may be provided with new materials, settings, or people. Again, by teaching skills in the context of the typical routine, the need for generalization training can be minimized.

EVALUATING ONGOING PROGRESS

The IDEA requires an IEP to state how the student's progress toward the annual goals will be measured, and how the parents will be informed of progress at least as often as parents of children without disabilities. This progress report must also include the extent to which the progress is sufficient to enable the student to achieve the goals by the end of the IEP year (Council for Exceptional Children [CEC], 1998). To be able to meet this requirement, teachers need methods to (1) measure skills, (2) summarize progress, and (3) determine whether this progress is adequate.

Methods for Measuring Skills

In developing the IEP, teachers will often rely on indirect assessments such as past records and parent interviews, because of the complexity of trying to create opportunities to observe students in a wide variety of life skills tasks. In contrast, to measure progress on the IEP, direct assessment of skills is both feasible and desirable. Direct assessment is possible if the teacher defines the exact responses the student is expected to make when performing the skill. These responses should be both *observable* and *measurable.* In the example shown in Figure 4.4, the skill was to use the vending machine. The exact responses Betty was to make are shown in Figure 4.5 and were written in the format of a task analysis. A task analysis is one of several options for designing a scale of measurement for life skills. These options are listed and illustrated in Table 4.3 and are described below.

Many high-priority skills can be measured by using one of these forms of measurement. In writing a task analysis, the teacher will usually perform the skill and then write down the responses in sequence. Each step usually begins with an action verb (e.g., "Put," "Fix," "Clean"). These statements can be used as verbal prompts when the task is being taught. Research on task-analytic assessment suggests that it may be important to break the task down into smaller, more specific responses for some students (Crist, Walls, & Haught, 1984; Thvedt, Zane, & Walls, 1984). A student who has mastered many self-care skills may be ready to learn the entire routine for getting ready for school as shown in Table 4.3; other students may need to focus on the single-skill task analysis of brushing teeth. Sometimes teachers may include steps that are nonessential to the task for teaching purposes. For example, Betty might read aloud the price when she was using the vending machine, in order to practice number reading. These nonessential steps should be excluded when task mastery is being determined (Williams & Cuvo, 1986). In the workplace and other settings where the speed with which a student performs a task is important, the teacher may choose to apply engineering principles to define the task analysis (Lin & Browder, 1990). An example of an engineering task analysis (the "therbligs" example) is shown in Table 4.3.

Some skills are not performed as a chain of responses, and task-analytic assessment is therefore not applicable. Communication and functional academics are two skill areas that often do not lend themselves to task analysis. Sometimes, even when the skill does involve a chain of responses, only one or two discrete responses may be targeted for a student with significant disabilities. For example, two discrete responses for a student with complex physical challenges during handwashing may be to choose which scented soap to use by eye gazing, and to wet her hands by moving them under the faucet. When discrete responses are the focus, a repeated-trial assessment is the best choice. Depending on the student's objective, these repeated trials may focus on a single response or a set of responses, and may be given together at one point in time or across the day. Sometimes the teacher does not initiate trials, but simply counts the number of times a student makes the target response during the day.

Most teachers may find that they can measure all, or nearly all, of their students' IEP objectives via task-analytic and repeated-trial assessments. These methods lend themselves well to daily data collection and data-based decisions, as described in the next sections. Other options for measuring IEP objectives include using permanent products and time-based assessments. These methods may be especially useful for ob-

TABLE 4.3. Options for Using Direct Assessment to Measure Progress on the IEP

Type of assessment	When to use	Variations and examples
TASK-ANALYTIC ASSESSMENT	Use for skills that involve a chain of responding (e.g., setting a table, putting on a coat, using a photocopier).	• *Single-skill task analysis:* Brushing teeth. • *Full-routine task analysis:* Getting ready for school. • *Repeated task analysis:* Setting the table. • *"Therbligs" task analysis (units of movement used in time and motion study):* Grasp towel.

Examples in detail

• *Single-skill task analysis*

1. Turn on water.
2. Wet toothbrush.
3. Open toothpaste.
4. Squeeze paste on brush.
5. Brush front teeth.
6. Brush front side teeth.
7. Brush molars.
8. Brush inside teeth.
9. Brush tongue.
10. Rinse brush.
11. Turn off water.
12. Close toothpaste.
13. Put away brush.

• *Full-routine task analysis*

1. Get up when alarm rings.
2. Take shower.
3. Put on clothes.
4. Dry hair.
5. Clean up bathroom.
6. Fix breakfast.
7. Eat breakfast.
8. Put dishes in sink.
9. Brush teeth.
10. Leave for bus.

• *Repeated task analysis*
1. Place mat on table.
2. Put plate on mat.
3. Put fork on left of plate.
4. Put knife on right.
5. Put spoon by knife.
6. Put napkin by fork.
7. Place second mat on table.
8. Put plate on mat.
9. Put fork on left of plate.
10. Put knife on right.
11. Put spoon by knife.
12. Put napkin by fork.

• *"Therbligs" task analysis*
1. BH: Grasp towel.
2. BH: Move to table.
3. BH: Release towel.
4. LH: Hold towel at center.
5. RH: Grasp left edge.
6. RH: Move left edge to right edge.
7. RH: Release towel.
8. BH: Grasp lower corners.
9. BH: Move lower to upper corners.
10. BH: Release corners.
11. RH: Hold towel at center.
12. LH: Grasp left edge.
13. LH: Move to right edge.
14. LH: Release towel. (BH, both hands; LH, left hand; RH, right hand)

Type of assessment	When to use	Variations and examples
REPEATED-TRIAL ASSESSMENT	Use when the skill involves a discrete response (e.g., reading a word, pointing to picture, stating time, nodding "yes").	• *Single response, repeated trials:* Pointing to own name—"Sally." • *Set of responses, repeated trials:* Reading sight words. • *Distributed trials:* Using schedule to find next activity. • *Frequency count:* Number of times picture wallet was used.

(cont.)

TABLE 4.3. *(cont.)*

Examples in detail

• *Single response, repeated trials*	• *Set of responses, repeated trials*	• *Distributed trials*	• *Frequency count*
1. Point to "Sally."	1. "milk"	1. 8:00: Homeroom	Monday: 3
2. Point to "Sally."	2. "eggs"	2. 8:45: Science	Tuesday: 0
3. Point to "Sally."	3. "juice"	3. 9:30: Reading	Wednesday: 4
4. Point to "Sally."	4. "cereal"	4. 10:15: Math	
5. Point to "Sally."	5. "toast"	5. 11:00: Lunch	
6. Point to "Sally."	6. "pancakes"	6. 11:45: P.E.	
7. Point to "Sally."	7. "waffles"	7. 12:30: Life skills	
8. Point to "Sally."	8. "hash browns"	8. 1:15: Community	
9. Point to "Sally."		9. 2:00: Bus	
10. Point to "Sally."			

Type of assessment	When to use	Variations and examples
PERMANENT PRODUCT SCORING	Use when the skill produces a permanent product, such as a worksheet, project, or computer printout.	• *Percent or number correct of permanent product:* Number of prices matched correctly; percent of envelopes stamped correctly. • *Scoring rubric for permanent product:* Stamped signature on a document.

Examples in detail

• *Percent or number correct of permanent product*	• *Scoring rubric for permanent product*
13 of 20 prices matched correctly. 45% of envelopes stamped correctly.	4—Name is neat, legible, and complete. 3—Name is legible but slightly smeared or faint. 2—Name is partially legible but may be smeared and faint. 1—Name is barely legible because too faint or smeared. 0—Name is not legible.

Type of assessment	When to use	Variations and examples
TIME-BASED ASSESSMENT	Use when the purpose is to get student to perform the skill within a given time frame.	• *Rate:* Number of envelopes stuffed per hour. • *Latency:* Number of seconds before pushing buzzer for help. • *Duration:* Number of minutes taken to clean motel room on job site.

Examples in detail

• *Rate*	• *Latency*	• *Duration*
Stuffed 50 envelopes per hour.	Waited 15 seconds until pushed buzzer for help.	Took 90 minutes to clean motel room on job site.

jectives in which students are gaining fluency or improving quality in already acquired skills.

To conduct the assessment of the target skills, the teacher has two options. The first is to conduct a test of how well the student performs the skill without teacher prompting or feedback. When this test is conducted prior to beginning instruction, it is called "baseline assessment." For example, before teaching Betty to use the vending machine, the teacher gave her the chance to do so without help (as noted earlier). She escorted Betty to the machine in the student commons and waited for Betty to try to purchase a soda. When Betty was not able to do a step within 5 seconds, the teacher did it for her without comment. This was what is called a "repeated-opportunity" assessment, because Betty got the opportunity to try each step. (Sometimes the teacher may simply end the test when the first error occurs or when no response occurs in a given time frame; this is called a "single-opportunity" assessment.) The teacher scored her Data Collection Form (Figure 4.5), putting a minus by each step Betty did not do and a plus by the step she completed (picking up the soda). The teacher repeated this same procedure the next day at the vending machine in front of the grocery store. At this site, Betty did not perform any responses correctly (see Figure 4.5). In a repeated-trial assessment, a teacher will usually present each trial and wait about 3–5 seconds for a student to respond (e.g., to read each site word). The teacher scores a data sheet for each response.

Besides using testing, a second option for measuring progress is to record data during instruction. Betty's teacher only used testing two times as a baseline assessment before she began teaching her to use a vending machine (see the first two columns of data in Figure 4.5). After this baseline, the rest of the data were recorded when she was teaching Betty. Because she needed to focus on prompting Betty through each step of the task analysis, she recorded data immediately after Betty got her soda. When teaching in public settings, she was careful to collect the data out of public view, so as not to stigmatize Betty. Figure 4.5 shows 2 days of data collection during instruction (see the third and fourth columns of data). Note that the teacher recorded the highest level of prompting needed for Betty to perform each step of the task analysis. On the first day of instruction, Betty walked to the machine without help, but needed verbal prompts (V) to look at the soda options and take the dollar from her pocket. She needed physical guidance to match the dollar to the slot picture (P), but was able to insert the dollar with a model (M). She then needed physical guidance (P) to insert the dollar again when it came out. With the teacher's model (M), she pressed the button for a soda, but needed physical guidance (P) to collect her change. She pocketed her change with just a verbal reminder (V) and then picked up the soda without help (+). (See the scoring in the third column of Figure 4.5.)

Figure 4.6 provides an example of a repeated-trial assessment. Jeremy Johnson[3] was learning to point to eight new pictures on his communication board. Jeremy's teacher collected all of the data shown in Figure 4.6 during instruction. She was able to record whether Jeremy pointed to each picture immediately after he responded. In general, teachers may want to consider collecting data on student performance during instruction, because of the investment of time testing involves. Testing may be most useful to evaluate the need for instruction (baseline assessment), to determine whether

---

[3]Jeremy Johnson's case is fictitious.

FIGURE 4.6. A second example of a standard Data Collection Form. Codes as in Figure 4.5.

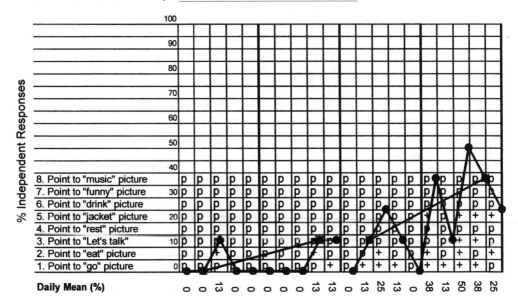

Name: Jeremy Johnson
Behavior: Use communication board
Criterion for Mastery: 100% correct for 3 of 3 days

Previous mean (%)   0.0

Date	Trend/mean	Decision
Oct. 22	Mean 3.8% Trend is accelerating	Improve antecedents
Nov. 5	Mean 21.3% Trend is accelerating	Continue with program

generalization has occurred, or to consider whether the student is overly dependent on prompting.

Some teachers may wonder whether collecting data is necessary at all. In research with teachers, many reported that they were skeptical about how representative data were (Grigg, Snell, & Loyd, 1989). However, research has also shown that teachers' evaluations of progress are more accurate when they are based on data (Holvoet, O'Neil, Chazdon, Carr, & Warner, 1983). This may be especially true when the data are variable or show a lack of progress (Munger, Snell, & Loyd, 1989). Teachers can also enhance student progress when they learn to use their data to make instructional decisions (Belfiore & Browder, 1992; Browder, Demchak, Heller, & King, 1991; Browder, Liberty, Heller, & D'Huyvetters, 1986; Farlow & Snell, 1989). To make data collection more meaningful, teachers need guidelines for summarizing progress and making instructional decisions.

Methods for Summarizing Progress

Many strategies can be found in the professional literature for summarizing data. Most rely on the use of what are called "equal-interval graphs." In an equal-interval graph, the sessions (e.g., days) on which data are collected form the horizontal axis, and the scale of measurement (e.g., percent of steps correct on a task analysis) forms the vertical axis. To save time, teachers may want to develop a standard chart that they use for graphing most skills. To minimize the amount of paper needed, the data collection sheet and graph can be combined on one page. The Data Collection Form shown in Figures 4.5 and 4.6 and found in the Appendix provides a model for how to create a combined data sheet and graph. Snell and Loyd (1991) found that teachers were more consistent in making instructional decisions when they viewed response-by-response data and level of assistance than when they reviewed graphed data alone. The Data Collection Form allows teachers to view both graphed progress and the level of assistance used for each step of the task analysis. This form was used in our research on data-based decisions (Browder et al., 1986, 1989; Belfiore & Browder, 1992), and has been widely used by teachers in the field-based programs at Lehigh University. To minimize paper management, Lehigh teachers often photocopied this form on the back of their Systematic Instruction Plan (see Figure 4.4 and the Appendix). The form has 20 columns for data, and thus can be used for 4 school weeks. When it is full, a new form is started and the old one is saved for summarizing progress across time. Another option is to use a chart that allows for longer periods of review. The chart developed by Farlow and Snell (1994) can summarize data for 3 months or more, but is not also used as a data collection sheet.

The Data Collection Form on Betty's progress in learning to use the vending machine (Figure 4.5) illustrates how the daily data are summarized. After scoring the task analysis, a teacher determines the percent of correct responses, puts a dot on the line at that percent, and also writes the percent underneath the column for that day. For example, on the first day of instruction (third column of data from the left), Betty got 2 of the 10 steps correct, which was 20%. The teacher put a dot on the line at 20%, and wrote "20" under the column for that day. The next day, Betty again got 20% correct. The teacher did the same two things; she also connected the dots across these days (not shown).

Methods for Using Data to Make Decisions

Teachers who collect ongoing data also often have rules about whether and when to change programs (Farlow & Snell, 1989). The only reasons to collect data are (1) to report student progress to parents and school administrators, and (2) to make instructional decisions. Investing the time to collect data becomes especially worthwhile when it can be used to make decisions that improve student progress. Having a set of guidelines or "rules" for making these decisions can be an important key to improving this progress (Browder et al., 1986, 1989; Farlow & Snell, 1989). The following is a description of one data-based decision system that has been extensively field-tested with students with moderate and severe disabilities, and has been evaluated through research based on real student data collected by teachers in school and adult service settings (Browder et al., 1986; Belfiore & Browder, 1992). There are three steps in using this system: (1) analyzing the data, (2) making an instructional decision based on this analysis, and (3) deciding how to implement this decision. These steps are summarized in Tables 4.4, 4.5, and 4.6.

Step 1: Analyzing the Data

In this progress-monitoring system, the teacher reviews each student's progress once every 2 weeks. Students may have several Data Collection Forms for the different skills they are learning. Once teachers have mastered this system, they can usually review these forms fairly quickly. In reviewing each Data Collection Form, the teacher makes sure that there are at least 6 data points for a review. The reason for the minimum of 6 is that this is the minimum number needed to draw a trend line using intersections. Most teachers who have used this system find that getting at least 6 days of data out of the 10 days possible in 2 school weeks is realistic. The ideal is to implement the program and take data daily. Some weeks the teacher may have all 10 data points.

Next, the teacher looks at the chart to see whether a clear-cut decision can be made. If the student has met the criteria for mastery, it is time to revise the program to focus

TABLE 4.4. Data-Based Decision System for Use in Determining Student Progress: Step 1. Analyzing the Data

1. *Have the data been recorded on a standard Data Collection Form?*
   Guideline: Collect data daily and summarize it on a standard Data Collection Form.
2. *Are the data representative of student performance?*
   Guideline: If data were collected by a substitute not trained in data collection, or if the student was ill or disruptive, the data may not be accurate. If the data are not representative, continue instruction until better data can be obtained.
3. *Are there enough data to make an instructional decision?*
   Guideline: Make decisions once every 2 weeks. At minimum, 6 days of data are needed to make an instructional decision. If fewer days of data are available, or if there has been a large break between the 2 weeks of data that might cause regression, note on the Data Collection Form that there are "insufficient data for a decision."
4. *Can a decision be made based on the daily graphed dataa for mastery during these 2 weeks, or if there have been no correct independent responses, a decision can be made. Go to the decision rules (Table 4.5).*
   Guideline: If the student met the criteria for mastery during these 2 weeks, or if there have been no correct independent responses, a decision can be made. Go to the decision rules (Table 4.5).
5. *What are the phase mean and the trend of the data?*
   Guideline: If the data are not clear-cut (i.e., clearly showing mastery or no progress), some more summarization is needed. To summarize the data further, calculate the mean of the daily performance for the 2 weeks of review. Compare this to the mean of the prior 2 weeks. Is the mean higher by at least 5% (or whatever other criterion you have set for biweekly progress)? Now summarize the trend of the data. Find the intersection of the first three points of data and mark an ×, and then find the intersection of the last three points and mark another ×. Connect the ×'s with a straight line. This line will either be going up (accelerating), going down (decelerating), or flat. When you know the mean and trend, you can go to the decision rules (Table 4.5).

TABLE 4.5. Data-Based Decision System for Determining Student Progress: Step 2. Decision Rules

Data pattern	Conclusion	Decision
1. Reached criterion during the 2 weeks.	Mastery	Develop a new plan to maintain and extend performance (e.g., fluency, generalization).
2. All data points are at 0, *or* there have been no new independent responses since instruction began.	No progress	If this is the first 2-week-period of instruction, make no changes yet. Continue instruction. After the first 2 weeks, rewrite the Systematic Instruction Plan and Data Collection Form to focus on a simpler version of the skill.
3. Trend is accelerating; mean is higher by 5% or more.	Adequate progress	Make no changes. Continue instruction.
4. Trend is accelerating or flat; mean is same as that for last decision period, or higher but by less than 5%.	Inadequate progress	Improve antecedents (e.g., prompting strategies) so that the student makes more independent, correct responses.
5. Trend is decelerating (even if mean is higher), *or* mean is lower (even if trend is accelerating).	Motivation problem	Improve motivation to perform responses correctly without assistance.

on maintenance, fluency, or generalization of the skill. If no progress has been made, the student needs the opportunity to learn a simpler response that can achieve the same outcome. Table 4.6 offers several ideas for how to simplify the response.

When the data pattern does not lead to a clear-cut decision, additional data summaries are needed. Different data-based decision systems use a variety of methods for this second level of analysis. For example, Farlow and Snell (1994) consider trends, error patterns, aim lines, and the variability of data. We (Browder et al., 1989) found that effective decisions could also be made by simply focusing on the phase mean and trend. The phase mean is easily calculated by adding the daily percentage of independent, correct responses and dividing by the total numbers of days of data. For example, in Jeremy's program during the first 10 days the daily percents were 0, 0, 13, 0, 0, 0, 0, 0, 13, and 13. The sum of these daily percents was 39; when divided by the number of days of data (10), the mean was a 3.9% increase. The mean is then compared to that of the prior phase of instruction (0% for Jeremy) or to the baseline assessment. The decision rules shown in Table 4.5 are based on a mean progress of at least 5% in 2 weeks. We (Browder et al., 1989) found that when students made progress, it was almost always by at least 5%. Also, slower progress will not result in mastery in a typical school year. For some students, this goal of a mean increase of 5% may be too low. Teachers can set a higher criterion and still follow these rules.

To determine the trend, the teacher uses a standard intersect method using the first and last three data points, as shown in Figure 4.6. In Jeremy's program, his trend was accelerating at the end of the first 2 weeks (10 days) of instruction, but his mean was not higher by 5% (it was 3.9%, compared to 0%). The teacher was then ready to consider the decision rule for this data pattern.

TABLE 4.6. Data-Based Decision System for Determining Student Progress: Step 3. Implementing the Decision to Change Instruction

To simplify the response	To improve antecedents	To improve motivation
Goal: Make it feasible for student to perform without assistance.	*Goal:* Increase the number of independent correct responses the student makes each day.	*Goal:* To help student recoup past performance after a regression, and then continue to improve.
• Use chaining: Teach only one response or one portion of the task analysis. • Use a more specific task analysis: Break it down into smaller steps. • Use a simpler motor response: Use a gross motor response or one that requires less physical control or skill. • Make the discrimination simpler: Modify the materials so that it is easier to select the correct answer. • Eliminate academic responses: Use a jig or coding to avoid the need to read or do math. • Eliminate the need for planning and positioning: Have materials preset. • Select an alternative way to achieve the same outcome: Use an entirely different response or set of materials.	• Only use the minimal prompting needed; don't overly assist. • Wait longer before giving the prompt. • Revise the prompt to focus the learner's attention more closely on the natural cues. • Make sure the learner is closer to the materials than you are. • Review the task analysis to see whether there are specific steps that are difficult for the learner. Simplify these steps or use more effective prompts for them. • Use nonspecific verbal cues like "What's next?" • Use graduated guidance; that is, fade the amount of physical assistance given. • Have a peer model the response or give the prompts. • Use self-prompting with pictures or an audiotape.	• Only praise independent correct responses. • Give less attention to errors—ignore them and prompt the next step. • Emphasize the natural consequence for performing the response. • Embed choice in instruction (e.g., when to do the task, choice of materials, choice of seating). • Involve student in self-monitoring and graphing daily performance. • Use tangible reinforcers for performance that is better than the prior day's (e.g., stickers, treats, special activity). • Vary praise statements by using different words; or make statements humorous or novel; or increase enthusiasm of praise. • Eliminate all prompting and only give feedback for correct responses. • Have a peer teach the program. • Teach the student to praise him- or herself.

Step 2: Using Decision Rules

We (Browder et al., 1986) originally derived the decision rules shown in Table 4.5 from the work of Haring, Liberty, and White (1980). Haring et al. (1980) developed their rules by studying teachers' instructional decisions to find patterns that led to student progress. These rules were further refined (Browder et al., 1989) in our research with both school-age students and adults with severe disabilities. These rules or guidelines often seem logical to teachers as they gain experience with data summaries. With this experience, they will discover that students who make no progress need simpler skills; that when progress is slow, it's because the students are relying on prompting; and that when progress regresses but a student has not been ill or absent, motivation to learn the skill may have lapsed. Until these patterns become clear to teachers, they can use Table 4.5 to find the data pattern and note the decision rule.

Step 3: Implementing the Decision to Change Instruction

Once the decision is reached, the teacher needs to know how to change instruction to improve progress. The recommendations given in Table 4.6 are based on my experience in implementing the decisions and research on teaching. A similar set of recommendations was field-tested in one of our studies (Belfiore & Browder, 1992).

In Jeremy's program, the teacher first reviewed his progress on October 22, which was the end of the first 2 weeks of instruction. Because his trend was accelerating, but the mean was not higher by 5% (it was only 3.9%, compared to 0% during the last phase), the teacher recognized that this was "inadequate progress" and that the appropriate decision was to "improve antecedents." She wrote the data pattern and decision in the space at the bottom of Figure 4.6. In reviewing the guidelines for how to improve antecedents shown in Table 4.6, the teacher decided to increase the delay between telling Jeremy to point to a picture on his communication board and prompting him with physical guidance. She also decided to fade her physical guidance by releasing his hand as he got near the picture. As the entry in Figure 4.6 for the second decision period on November 5 indicates, this decision was successful in encouraging Jeremy's progress. At the end of this second phase, his mean was 21.3%, which was higher than the previous mean of 3.9% by 17.4%. His trend was accelerating. This data pattern constituted "adequate progress" and required no change, so the decision was to "continue with program."

REPORTING PROGRESS ON THE IEP TO PARENTS

The data-based decision system that has just been described is used when the teacher has chosen to implement a Systematic Instruction Plan. As noted earlier in this chapter, these plans will be reserved for skills that are of the highest priority and that cannot be learned with less intensive forms of instruction (refer back to Figure 4.1). IEP objectives that are addressed with less intensive forms of instruction may be evaluated via permanent products (see Table 4.3), anecdotal notes on teacher observations, or direct assessment through periodic teacher tests of the student's responses. For a Systematic Instruction Plan that involves data-based decisions, a quantitative decision can be made about whether or not the student will master the objective during the current IEP year (information IDEA requires to be reported to parents). Quantitative decisions may also be possible for skills for which periodic teacher assessments will be used. In contrast, qualitative judgments can be used for evaluations completed without direct assessment data. The following illustrates how this summary was prepared for Jeremy Johnson.

Jeremy was a 7-year-old who had complex physical challenges and a severe cognitive disability. He had eight specific IEP objectives focused on several goal areas, as shown in Figure 4.7. For each IEP objective, the teacher selected the primary form of instructional support to be used and a method of assessment for each. These are also shown in Figure 4.7. For the priority objectives for which the teacher had to make data-based decisions, a summary was given for the three decisions made during the 6-week report card period. For example, in pointing to pictures on his communication board, Jeremy's initial mean was 0. His final mean was 21.3%. This reflected a

FIGURE 4.7. An example of a report to parents summarizing IEP progress.

Shadybrook Elementary School
IEP Progress Report to Parents

Student: _Jeremy Childress_   Teacher: _Ms. Samantha Jenkins_

Grade: _2_   Report Period: _1_

IEP goal/ objective/ benchmark	Primary instructional support	Method to monitor progress	Progress for past period	Expectation for mastery during current IEP year
Point to pictures on electronic board.	Systematic Instruction Plan.	Repeated-trial assessment with data-based decisions.	Made progress in last 4 weeks: Mean increase of 21.3% from 0%. Good progress.	At current rate, will master skill during this IEP year.
Make choices related to daily routine.	Systematic Instruction Plan.	Repeated trial assessment with data-based decisions.	Increase from 30% to 70%. Outstanding progress.	Mastery is anticipated in the next reporting period.
Use sight word computer software.	Systematic Instruction Plan.	Task-analytic assessment with data-based decisions.	No progress; continues to be at 0% after efforts to simplify use of software.	Mastery not anticipated—will seek advice from computer specialist for alternative software and simpler response mode.
Smile to initiate social contact with peers.	Natural supports through peer models and prompting.	Daily log from peers and general education teacher.	Smiled on four occasions during this period.	Criterion of initiating at least once daily will not be met at current rate of progress. Train peers and practice with special education teacher.
Decrease amount of time needed to be fed lunch to 20 minutes.	Self-instruction by nodding to cue assistant to give next bite of food. Environmental arrangement by using preferred foods.	Time-based assessment (number of minutes to finish lunch). Parent log.	Has decreased time to eat lunch from 55 to 40 minutes. Parent also reports Jeremy needs less time to eat at home.	Mastery anticipated by midyear.
Match numbers.	Whole-class instruction and computer practice with peer.	Permanent product: Printed computer summary of number of correct responses.	Still waiting for printer that was ordered. Peer reports that "not much" matching occurred.	Unclear. Have peer record number correct on index card until printer arrives.
Look at picture to show listening comprehension for short story.	Enhanced natural support with cues from second-grade teacher.	Anecdotal notes by second-grade teacher.	Teacher reports that Jeremy seems interested in stories. Not sure what pictures to use.	Unclear. SpEd teacher will test Jeremy with pictures once a week.
Get teacher's attention by ringing bell.	Systematic instruction plan.	Frequency count; data-based decision.	In the first 2 weeks of school, only used the bell if physically prompted. In the last month, has used the bell an average of 3 times per week.	Jeremy is making good progress toward using the bell at least once a day. Mastery projected by third quarter.

total increase of 21.3% for the 6 weeks. If Jeremy continued to make this much progress for the next 36 weeks of the school year, he could be expected to be at or near mastery. For the IEP objectives for which a qualitative assessment was used, the teacher stated what specific responses would need to be acquired for mastery by the end of the year.

SUMMARY

The two most important reasons to measure student progress are to make instructional decisions and to inform students' parents as required by the IDEA. To make instructional decisions, teachers need to begin by developing specific instructional supports for each IEP objective. Not all instructional supports will involve direct, systematic teacher instruction, especially in inclusive settings. Teachers may also augment natural supports, use environmental arrangements, and encourage student-directed learning. In contrast, all students should have opportunities to receive direct, systematic teacher instruction on IEP objectives that are of the highest priority or for which progress is not made with less intrusive forms of support. This systematic instruction will include presenting specific opportunities to perform the skills, with the teacher using preplanned, precise prompts and feedback as needed. This chapter has included information on several systems of prompting that a teacher can use.

Once IEP objectives and specific instructional supports have been developed, the teacher can select a method to measure progress. Direct assessment of IEP objectives is preferable, because it can be used to make decisions about changing instruction to increase student progress. Task-analytic and repeated-trial assessments are especially amenable to data-based decisions for IEP objectives for which systematic instruction will be used. For other IEP objectives, the teacher can use time-based assessments or reviews of permanent products.

When daily data are collected via task-analytic or repeated-trial assessment, teachers can review these data biweekly to determine whether progress has occurred. This chapter has included a data-based decision system that has been developed and refined through extensive research. Teachers are encouraged to use a standard Data Collection Form to summarize student data, and to follow guidelines for determining when and how to change instruction.

These data, and other forms of student assessment, can be summarized in an adapted report card. This report card should briefly restate each IEP objective, and should both give information on current performance and indicate whether or not mastery during the current IEP year is anticipated. Teachers may also want to include the form of instructional support being used for each objective.

Teachers are urged to remember the ultimate goal of their planning and paperwork—to improve student progress. To be efficient, teachers can often economize on this paperwork when students are making adequate progress. When such progress is not occurring, or student performance is unclear, direct daily assessment can be a worthwhile investment of teaching time if used to make instructional decisions to improve student performance.

REFERENCES

Alberto, P. A., & Troutman, A. C. (1990). *Applied behavior analysis for teachers* (3rd ed.). New York: Merrill/Macmillan.

Belfiore, P., & Browder, D. (1992). Effects of self monitoring on teaching data-based decisions and on the progress of adults with mental retardation. *Education and Training in Mental Retardation, 27,* 60–67.

Bigge, J. L., & Stump, C. S. (1999). *Curriculum, assessment, and instruction for students with disabilities.* Belmont, CA: Wadsworth.

Browder, D. M., Demchak, M. A., Heller, M., & King, D. (1991). An *in vivo* evaluation of data-based rules to guide instructional decisions. *Journal of the Association for Persons with Severe Handicaps, 14,* 234–240.

Browder, D. M., Liberty, K., Heller, M., & D'Huyvetters, K. (1986). Self-management to improve teachers' instructional decisions. *Professional School Psychology, 1*(3), 165–175.

Browder, D. M., & Lim, L. (1996). *Improving work efficiency: Job training based on engineering principles (Innovations No. 5).* Washington, DC: American Association on Mental Retardation.

Council for Exceptional Children (CEC). (1998). *Idea 1997: Let's make it work.* Reston, VA: Author.

Colyer, S. P., & Collins, B. C. (1996). Using natural cues within prompt levels to teach the next dollar strategy to students with disabilities. *Journal of Special Education, 30*(3), 305–318.

Crist, K., Walls, R. T., & Haught, P. (1984). Degree of specificity in task analysis. *American Journal of Mental Deficiency, 89,* 67–74.

Downing, J. E., & Eichinger, J. (1996). The important role of peers in the inclusion process. In J. E. Downing (Ed.), *Including students with severe and multiple disabilities in typical classrooms* (pp. 129–146). Baltimore: Paul H. Brookes.

Doyle, P. M., Wolery, M., Ault, M. J., & Gast, D. (1988). System of least prompts: A literature review of procedural parameters. *Journal of the Association for Persons with Severe Handicaps, 13,* 28–40.

Eckert, T., & Browder, D. M. (1997). Stimulus manipulations: Enhancing materials for self-directed learning. In E. M. Pinkston & D. Baer (Eds.). *Environment and behavior* (pp. 279–288). Boulder, CO: Westview Press.

Farlow, L. J., & Snell, M. E. (1989). Teacher use of student performance data to make instructional decisions: Practices in programs for students with moderate to profound handicaps. *Journal of the Association for Persons with Severe Handicaps, 14,* 13–22.

Farlow, L. J., & Snell, M. E. (1994). *Making the most of student performance data (Innovations No. 1).* Washington, DC: American Association on Mental Retardation.

Ford, A., & Mirenda, P. (1984). Community instruction: A natural cues and corrections decision model. *Journal of the Association for Persons with Severe Handicaps, 9,* 79–87.

Grigg, N. C., Snell, M. E., & Loyd, B. H. (1989). Visual analysis of student evaluation data: A qualitative analysis of teacher decision making. *Journal of the Association for Persons with Severe Handicaps, 14,* 13–22.

Haring, N., Liberty, K., & White, O. (1980). Rules for data-based strategy decisions in instructional programs: Current research and instructional implications. In W. Sailor, B. Wilcox, & L. Brown (Eds.), *Methods of instruction for severely handicapped students* (pp. 159–192). Baltimore: Paul H. Brookes.

Holvoet, J., O'Neil, G., Chazdon, L., Carr, D., & Warner, J. (1983). Hey, do we really have to take data? *Journal of the Association for the Severely Handicapped, 8,* 56–70.

Hughes, C., Hugo, K., & Blatt, J. (1996). A self-instructional intervention for teaching generalized problem solving within a functional task sequence. *American Journal of Mental Retardation, 100,* 565–579.

Hunt, P., Staub, D., Alwell, M., & Goetz, L. (1994). Achievement by students within the context of cooperative learning groups. *Journal of the Association for Persons with Severe Handicaps, 19,* 290–301.

Liberty, K. A., Haring, N. G., White, O. R., & Billingsley, F. (1988). A technology for the future: Decision rules for generalization. *Education and Training in Mental Retardation, 23,* 315–326.

Lin, C., & Browder, D. M. (1990). An application of engineering principles of motion study for the development of task analyses. *Education and Training in Mental Retardation, 25,* 367–375.

Lord, C., Bristol, M. M., & Schopler, E. (1993). Early intervention for children with autism and related developmental disabilities. In E. Schopler, M. E. Van Bourgondien, & M. M. Bristol (Eds.), *Preschool issues in autism.* New York: Plenum Press.

Lovaas, O. I. (1981). *Teaching developmentally disabled children: The ME book.* Austin, TX: Pro-Ed.

Munger, G. F., Snell, M. E., & Loyd, B. H. (1989). A study of the effects of frequency of probe data collection and graph characteristics on teachers' visual analysis. *Research in Developmental Disabilities, 10,* 109–127.

Nietupski, J., Hamre-Nietupski, S., Clancy, P., & Veerhusen, K. (1986). Guidelines for making simulation an effective adjunct to in-vivo community instruction. *Journal of the Association for Persons with Severe Handicaps, 11,* 12–18.

Nisbet, J. (1992). *Natural supports in school, at work, and in the community for people with severe disabilities* (pp. 170–256). Baltimore: Paul H. Brookes.

Schoen, S., & Ogden, S. (1995). Impact of time delay, observational learning, and attentional cueing upon word recognition during integrated small group instruction. *Journal of Autism and Developmental Disorders, 25,* 503–519.

Schopler, E., Mesibov, G. B., & Hearsey, K. (1995). Structured teaching in the TEACCH system. In E. Schopler & G. B. Mesibov (Eds.), *Learning and cognition in autism* (pp. 243–268). New York: Plenum Press.

Smith, T. (1996). Are other treatments effective? In C. Maurice, G. Green, & S. C. Luce (Eds.), *Behavioral intervention for young children with autism* (pp. 45–62). Austin, TX: Pro-Ed.

Snell, M. E., & Brown, F. (1993). Instructional planning and implementation. In M. E. Snell (Ed.), *Instruction of students with severe disabilities* (4th ed., pp. 99–151). New York: Merrill/Macmillan.

Snell, M. E., & Loyd, B. H. (1991). A study of the effects of trend, variability, frequency, and form of data on teachers' judgements about progress and their decisions about program change. *Research in Developmental Disabilities, 12,* 41–62.

Stokes, T. F., & Osnes, P. G. (1988). The developing applied technology of generalization and maintenance. In R. H. Horner, G. Dunlap, & R. L. Koegel (Eds.), *Generalization and maintenance: Life style changes in applied settings* (pp. 5–19). Baltimore: Paul H. Brookes.

Test, D. W., & Wood, W. M. (1997). Rocket science 101: What supported employment specialists need to know about systematic instruction. *Journal of Vocational Rehabilitation, 9,* 109–120.

Thvedt, J. E., Zane, T., & Walls, R. T. (1984). Stimulus functions in response chaining. *American Journal of Mental Deficiency, 88,* 661–667.

U.S. Congress, House of Representatives. (1994). *Goals 2000: Educate America Act* (H.R. 1804). (www.ed.gov/legislation/GOALS2000/TheAct)

Wehmeyer, M. L., Agran, M., & Hughes, C. (1998). *Teaching self determination to students with disabilities.* Baltimore: Paul H. Brookes.

Werts, M. G., Wolery, M., Holcombe, A., & Gast, D. L. (1995). Instructive feedback: Review of parameters and effects. *Journal of Behavioral Education, 5,* 55–75.

Westling, D. L., & Fox, L. (1995). *Teaching students with severe disabilities.* Upper Saddle River, NJ: Prentice-Hall.

Williams, G. E., & Cuvo, A. J. (1986). Training apartment upkeep skills to rehabilitation clients: A comparison of task analytic strategies. *Journal of Applied Behavior Analysis, 19,* 39–51.

Wolery, M., Alig-Cybriwsky, C., Gast, D. L., & Boyle-Gast, K. (1991). Use of constant time delay and aattentional responses with adolescents. *Exceptional Children, 57,* 462–474.

Wolery, M., Ault, M. J., & Doyle, P. M. (1992). *Teaching students with moderate to severe disabilities.* New York: Longman.

FIVE

Family-Centered Planning: A Multicultural Perspective

with Levan Lim

EMILY[1] LIVES IN SINGAPORE *and is deaf and blind. She relies on touch and smell to negotiate her surroundings. Like many unmarried young adults in her society, Emily lives with her parents. Emily tried school as a young child, but her teachers did not know how to manage her "off-task" behaviors. Her parents became her primary teachers. Although Emily's parents were never trained in special education techniques, they became highly effective in encouraging her independence. With their instruction, Emily learned to manage her personal care, to communicate discomfort, and to socialize. Emily has the skills to be home alone for short periods of time. To communicate when she is going to run an errand and leave Emily alone, her mother shows Emily her purse as a way to communicate "I'll be home soon."*

Diverse communication styles are part of Singaporean culture, and many residents are multilingual. Children with disabilities whose total vocabulary is under 50 words may have mastered these words in three languages! In Asian culture, family ties are also highly valued. In Emily's life, not only her parents but her extended family provide her with friendship and support. For example, when Emily's mother became ill, her aunt and cousins moved in with her to provide assistance as needed. Emily and her family have recently begun to learn about new options for people with disabilities to work in the community. Work is highly valued in Singaporean culture, and so the family is keenly interested in these new opportunities.

This chapter provides guidance for planning that is both family- and culture-centered. To assist someone like Emily in taking a new step like finding a community job, professionals need the knowledge and skills to know how to collaborate with families from diverse cultural backgrounds.

A family's perspective is shaped by the unique characteristics of the family and its individual members. Culture is an especially important characteristic that can shape families' perspectives (see Box 5.1). In the United States and most other countries, professionals interact with families and other professionals from diverse backgrounds in their daily work. This diversity is manifested not just in cultural differences, but also in fac-

---

[1]Emily's case is based on an actual person. The case has been disguised according to the guidelines of the American and World Psychiatric Associations for protecting confidentiality (Clifft, 1986).

Levan Lim, PhD, is a lecturer at the Schonell Special Education Research Centre, University of Queensland, Brisbane, Australia.

BOX 5.1. What is "Culture"?

The word "culture" can convey different meanings to different individuals. Simply stated, it refers to the shared norms, values, beliefs, and behaviors that are followed or expected to be followed by a particular group of people. Religion and ethnicity are two examples of differences that have created subcultures within the broader context of American (U.S.) culture. Cultural identification varies widely across cultures. For example, individuals may identify with more than one cultural group (e.g., if parents are from different cultural groups), or they may have minimal cultural identification.

---

tors such as socioeconomic status, religion, gender, generational status, and geographical location. Planning with students with moderate and severe disabilities requires particular sensitivity to these differences, because of the cultural variation in lifestyles that influence how people perform daily routines such as mealtimes and socializing (Lim & Browder, 1994). Professionals need multicultural awareness, knowledge, and skills to develop effective planning teams that include members from various cultural backgrounds. This chapter offers information to help professionals increase their multicultural competence in working with families, so that they will:

- Know the importance of having a multicultural perspective in working with families.
- Understand the influence of culture.
- Identify and use a family-centered focus in planning for students with disabilities.
- Comprehend and apply a culturally inclusive approach for this family-centered focus.

THE IMPORTANCE OF A MULTICULTURAL PERSPECTIVE IN WORKING WITH FAMILIES

One of the most important reasons to take a multicultural perspective in forming family partnerships is that individuals with disabilities and their families come from diverse backgrounds. Because educational systems have only begun to become responsive to these differences, students from backgrounds that differ from the predominant culture face a greater risk of being categorized under disability labels. For example, the overrepresentation of African Americans in special education programs has persisted, even though this reality has been recognized for over 20 years (Patton, 1998). More recently, a sharp increase in Hispanic students in the mental retardation category has been noted (Harry et al., 1995b). Besides facing a greater risk of being categorized under disability labels, students from multicultural backgrounds may also experience lower teacher expectations and poorer-quality academic programs (Misra, 1994). To enhance the educational opportunities of students with disabilities from multicultural backgrounds, it is vital for professionals to (1) learn to be culturally competent and responsive, and (2) understand systemic variables that may contribute to the dispropor-tion of certain cultural groups within special education.

Besides the overrepresentation of some cultural groups in special education, a sec-ond reason for a multicultural perspective in family–professional partnerships is the growing cultural diversity within American society. Within the United States, there are distinct cultural groups characterized primarily by ethnic differences. European Ameri-cans form the major ethnic cultural group in the United States. In addition, there are four other distinct ethnic cultural groups: Native Americans, Latino or Hispanic Amer-icans, African Americans, and Asian Americans. Moreover, each of these major groups has diverse subgroups. For example, an Asian American may be of East Indian, Chi-nese, or Japanese origin. Also, some European American groups (e.g., the Amish) have maintained strong cultural ties that are not part of the mainstream. Other individuals identify themselves more strongly with their religion (e.g., members of the Church of Jesus Christ of Latter-Day Saints, generally referred to as Mormons) or some other cul-tural variable than with their ethnic heritage. The proportions of these cultural groups are steadily changing. Demographic projections indicate that over one-third of all Americans will be from a cultural group other than the majority group of European Americans by the year 2010 (Hodgkinson, 1992). This is a considerable shift from the 1980 demographics, in which fewer than 20% of Americans belonged to a minority cul-tural group. As the demographics of the population shift toward greater heterogeneity, cultural issues and factors affect all segments of American society, including educa-tional services for children with disabilities.

A third reason for gaining a multicultural perspective in working with families of children with disabilities is that the world is quickly becoming both interdependent and multicultural. With modern technology like the World Wide Web, improved inter-national travel, and globalization trends, traditional borders are being lowered at a pace never before experienced in history as individuals, societies, and nations from cul-turally diverse backgrounds interact on a worldwide scale. Transmigration and reloca-tion of people from diverse cultures will continue into the foreseeable future. Most schools in the United States have children who have come from countries whose lan-guages and cultures differ dramatically from American culture. These children may also find that they are very different from other children whose families are from the section of the world. Many educators lack the cultural sensitivity to under-stand such differences and the challenges they create for children. For example, a Singaporean or Taiwanese individual of Chinese descent who has come to live in the United States has a very different cultural perspective from that of either a second-generation Chinese American or an individual from mainland China.

Lipsky and Gartner (1997) note that one of the most critical challenges for educa-tion is determining how to respond to this growing diversity. One important way is for professionals to be involved in international discussions about the needs of children with disabilities. In the special education literature, international, multicultural dis-course and sharing (e.g., Loxley & Thomas, 1997; Santos & Pereira, 1997), and discus-sions of social responsibility and peacemaking (e.g., Berman, 1990; Drew, 1987; Udvari-Solner & Thousand, 1996), are helping to transform perspectives and efforts. Interna-tional exchange and collaboration in special education are also on the increase (e.g., Davidson, Goode, & Kendig, 1992). In addition, descriptions of special education sys-tems and services around the world are increasingly written for an international audi-ence (e.g., Ballard, 1990; Befring, 1990; Santos & Pereira, 1997).

Besides responding to these initiatives to involve families more fully and evaluate students in the context of their culture, providing educational services in inclusive general education settings also has multicultural implications. Not only the United States, but many countries around the world, have embraced inclusion as an international educational agenda. Representatives of 92 governments and 25 international organizations have agreed upon a statement (the United Nations Educational, Scientific, and Cultural Organization [UNESCO] Salamanca statement) calling for inclusion to be the norm for the education of all children with disabilities (UNESCO, 1994). The underlying principles and goals of inclusion and multicultural education are similar and mutually compatible (Ball & Harry, 1993; Udvari-Solner & Thousand, 1996). Some of the common values in inclusion and multicultural education are (1) the creation of partnerships between school and communities (e.g., Trickett, 1997); (2) the use of natural supports (e.g., Nisbet, 1992; Storey & Certo, 1996); (3) person-centered planning and individualized supports (e.g., Bradley, Ashbaugh, & Blaney, 1994; Miner & Bates, 1997); (4) family-centered practices (e.g., Allen & Petr, 1996); (5) classrooms as learning communities (e.g., Haynes & Comer, 1996); (6) collaborative processes (e.g., Villa, Thousand, Nevin, & Malgeri, 1996); and (7) adapting curriculum to be contextually relevant and culturally responsive (e.g., Udvari-Solner & Thousand, 1996).

Understanding the Influence of Culture

As professionals try to gain a multicultural perspective, it is tempting to learn information about a cultural group and then to assume that this information creates understanding of an individual child and his or her family. The pitfall of this assumption is that it fails to recognize the heterogeneity within cultural groups, as well as the uniqueness of each child and family. Although awareness of cultural differences is beneficial and necessary for a multicultural perspective, the tendency to stereotype members of cultural groups exists. Individual diversity or variations within a cultural group (known as "idiographic" differences) are often larger than variations between cultures (the "nomothetic" differences) (Lloyd, 1987).

"Optimal theory" provides a framework for understanding the interrelationship among individual, cultural, and universal human needs. Speight, Myers, Cox, and Highlen (1991) suggest that by incorporating optimal theory into our worldview, we can appreciate a holistic view as opposed to a fragmented one of individuals. According to optimal theory, each individual can be described in terms of the following:

1. Every person is like no other person (individual values and needs).
2. Every person is like some other person in a particular cultural group (culturally specific values and needs).
3. Every person is like all other persons (common human values and needs).

Optimal theory is illustrated in Figure 5.1.

This model of viewing individuals recognizes and honors the individuality of a person, basic human needs, culturally based values, and their overlap. In a culturally pluralistic society like the United States, individuals and their families do not simply develop from a single cultural background. Instead, families are embedded within a complex, culturally diverse context where varying degrees of intergenerational differences, assimilation, and ethnic identification exist (Szapocznik & Kurtines, 1993). For

FIGURE 5.1. Optimal theory.

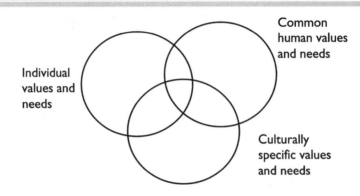

example, an individual from an Asian cultural background whose family members identify strongly with their ethnic heritage and yet have heavily assimilated into mainstream culture may have a unique fusion of cultural identities. Such a family may desire their child with disabilities to learn bicultural skills in order to function effectively in the two cultures.

Cultural Diversity and Special Education

Students with disabilities are entitled to appropriate educational services regardless of cultural differences, but the intent to deliver culturally appropriate and responsive services does not always translate into actual practice. Recent literature has critically examined the special education system and defined an implicit cultural base that affects family–professional interactions (Harry, 1992a, 1992b; Harry & Kalyanpur, 1994). This implicit cultural base, which is predominantly European American, may have a mismatch with the cultural framework of families that do not subscribe to or are unfamiliar with the cultural orientation of the professionals involved. Serious negative consequences and repercussions may be the results. For example, families may feel alienated from and disenchanted with the special education system, from which they are supposed to receive help. Also, overrepresentation of African American students and other minority groups receiving special education services may be partially due to differences in cultural assumptions (Patton, 1998). Table 5.1 provides examples of studies that have examined the responses of families from various ethnic cultural groups to special education services.

USING A FAMILY-CENTERED FOCUS IN PLANNING

A Historical Perspective on Family Involvement

The 1997 reauthorization of the Individuals with Disabilities Education Act (IDEA) enhanced the involvement of families in developing students' individualized education plans (IEPs). In contrast, professionals have not always recognized the importance of

TABLE 5.1. Research on the Responses of Various Ethnic Cultural Groups
to Special Education Services

Cultural group	Themes	Sources
African Americans	Parents became disillusioned with labeling, classroom, and curriculum issues. Absence of meaningful communication through assessment and placement processes.	Harry, Allen, & McLaughlin (1995a)
	Low-income single mothers perceived professionals as displaying disrespect, focusing on deficits, and discounting their parenting style.	Kalyanpur & Rao (1991)
	African American families listed general communication with schools as the major barrier. Families were found to offer fewer suggestions at individualized education plan (IEP) meetings and knew significantly less about what services their children were to receive than European American parents did.	Lynch & Stein (1987)
Latino Americans	Parent participation was constrained by low-context character of interactions. School district relied on formal, written communication ,which led to mistrust and withdrawal of parents.	Harry (1992a)
	Parents did not accept professional definitions of their children's disabilities. School labeling process did not recognize a child's individuality and family identity.	Harry (1992c)
	Hispanic parents were positive about children's programs, but tended not to be active participants in services provided: offered significantly fewer suggestions at IEP meetings than European American parents did.	Lynch & Stein (1987)
	Hispanic parents were not as well served by schools as were European American parents. The Hispanic parents had little understanding of education programs, did not understand materials sent home, and did not comprehend many of the technical terms used. These parents also did not generally question school decisions.	Gallegos & Gallegos (1988, cited in Westling, 1996)
	Parents felt intimidated and confused when attending IEP meetings. Majority of parents (four out of five) also expressed feelings of mistrust for teachers and other school personnel.	Zetlin, Padron, & Wilson (1996)
Native Americans	Native and Hispanic American parents reported less participation than European American parents did. European American parents were more likely to be their children's service coordinators.	Sontag & Schacht (1994)

having a family-focused approach. Simeonsson and Bailey (1990) have described four historical stages of family involvement in the education of their children with disabilities. From the beginning of the 20th century till the 1950s, parents were counseled and encouraged to relinquish their children to the care of institutions. As a result, their parenting roles were limited through sheer physical separation from their children.

In the 1950s and 1960s, amidst powerful social and political struggles on issues of equality such as the civil rights movements and the turn toward normalizing the life experiences of individuals with disabilities, parents' involvement in their children's welfare began to be deemed important. For example, the Handicapped Children's Early Education Program, established by Congress in 1968, mandated parent involvement as a requirement for receiving services. By the early 1970s, parents were actively encouraged by professionals to be involved in their children's education. Professionals identified parental needs and developed meetings and programs to meet these needs. By the mid-1970s, parents were encouraged to be teachers in carrying out interventions designed by professionals. Parent training was popular during this era of parents' becoming more formally inducted into the role of being interventionists. Once again, however, professionals were the people deciding the role of parent involvement.

The 1980s saw an increasing focus on viewing the family as a social system that included the child with disabilities. The child's outcomes were recognized as dependent on his or her interactions with other family members in this social ecology. The task of addressing the needs of the child meant also taking into account the needs and functions of the entire family as an interdependently functioning unit. Not only the parents but also the whole family, such as siblings and extended family members, became prominent in the framework for studying family involvement. Although this model was "family-focused," it still maintained professional authority in guiding families to procure and use services.

In the current era, a "family-centered" focus is defined as one in which the family's perspective is primary. The family's aspirations drive the type of support and services provided. The four models described here, and their characteristics, are shown in Table 5.2.

Understanding Family-Centered Principles

Inherent in the family-centered model is an understanding of families as individually unique and diverse in their characteristics, structures, roles, beliefs, values, coping styles, and cultural backgrounds (Darling & Baxter, 1996). Leal (1998) has noted that to be family-centered, the professional must understand the family unit in several ways. First, it is important to realize that family members influence one another. What affects one family member has the potential to affect all other members. For example, an unresolved behavior problem like a sleep disorder can have a major impact on an entire family's stress level. In contrast, a new educational opportunity for a child with a disability may help other family members feel hopeful about the future. This interdependence is influenced by the closeness of family members. In some families, all members are closely involved in each other's lives, whereas in others, family members function more autonomously.

Families also vary in their composition. A family may consist of a single parent and the child with disabilities; or may be a small nuclear family with parents and chil-

TABLE 5.2. Models of Family Involvement in the Education of Children with Disabilities

Model/paradigm	Features
Professional-centered	Professionals are the experts who decide for families. Families' perspectives are secondary. Families' involvement is minimal.
Family-allied	Professionals prescribe roles for families. Families are agents enlisted to carry out role duties. Families are "professionalized." A child-centered as opposed to a family systems approach.
Family-focused	Professionals are seen as providing a range of services that families can choose (with professional help). Families are seen as consumers with a "right to choose." Professionals guide families in procuring and using services. Families are helped to "fit" concerns with the right services.
Family-centered	Professionals are seen as instruments of families. Family needs, concerns, and aspirations drive type of support and services provided. Individualized supports and services are provided to "fit" family needs and concerns. Family perspectives are primary. Family-dominated involvement is encouraged.

Note. This table is based on the writings of Dunst, Johanson, Trivette, and Hamby (1991) and Trivette, Dunst, Boyd, and Hamby (1995).

dren; or may be a large nuclear "blended" family with parents and several children from prior marriages; or may be an extended family in which grandparents, aunts, uncles, and cousins are closely involved. A third characteristic of families is that family members are *important resources* in the life of a child with disabilities. Family members have a wealth of knowledge about the child with disabilities and often provide the ongoing stability in that child's life.

Furthermore, families change over time. During the preschool years, parents are often focused on intensive caregiving and adjusting to having a child with a disability. During the school years, school and extracurricular activities (e.g., Little League sports, Scouting) often absorb large amounts of family time. Sometimes for the family of a child with disabilities, finding inclusive opportunities requires major efforts. During the teen years, the influence of peers, emerging sexuality, and planning for the future become important themes. Parents become involved in planning for transition to adulthood. Parents of adults with disabilities adjust to changes from full-time schooling. For some parents, there will be a readjustment of expectations that they will someday be free from full-time caregiving, depending on their community's opportunities for supported living and employment for adults with disabilities. Each family is also culturally unique, as described and illustrated through optimal theory.

In being family-centered, professionals also need to recognize the methods of coping that families use. Older writings about families of children with disabilities sometimes exaggerated the stress involved, implying that such families would inevitably be dysfunctional. Or sometimes stages of adjustment were described as if families somehow graduated from one level of awareness to the next. What is now known is that all families experience stress and cope with it in a number of ways, with varying levels of success. Having a child with disabilities is one potential source of stress among the many that can affect a family. Turnbull and Turnbull (1997) have noted that some of the ways families cope with stress include positive appraisal (making the most of a situation), professional support, reframing (rethinking stressful events in terms that are more manageable), social support, and spirituality. Cultural norms concerning social support can influence how families cope with stress in rearing a child with disabilities. For example, African American mothers of children with disabilities, compared with European American mothers, have been reported to perceive less personal burden (Glidden, Kiphart, Willoughby, & Bush, 1993) and lower family stress levels (Flynt & Wood, 1989). The more positive coping outcomes may be attributed to relatively strong family networks and religious connectedness among African American families (Rogers-Dulan, 1998).

Leal (1998) recommends that professionals help families cope by doing the following:

1. *Avoiding judgment.* Coping with stress can create diverse emotional reactions, such as anger, denial, depression, guilt, and even giddiness. Professionals need to ask themselves, "Am I judging family members or trying to understand them?"

2. *Listening.* Professionals can help families cope by creating an atmosphere of trust in which families can share their feelings without fear of criticism. Also, professionals are not expected to have all the answers. Just listening is sometimes the most helpful response.

3. *Being prepared.* Professionals need to be prepared to encounter a variety of emotional reactions and not to take them personally unless they have done something to upset the parents or other family members. Anger can be a justifiable and realistic response to the treatment family members have received in the past.

4. *Refraining from saying things such as these:*

- "I know how you feel." Professionals don't know how it feels to be that family member experiencing those specific circumstances.
- "Cheer up/calm down. Things are not so bad." Such a response trivializes the person's concerns.
- "Don't worry." Parents' concern for their children should be expected and encouraged.
- "That can't be done." Problem solving involves exploring new options together as a team.
- "I'm right. You're wrong." Professionals need to be careful not to get defensive or try to argue family members out of their point of view.

Another way to work effectively with families is to share information and sources of support that may be needed. Family members may benefit from information about the child's disability, their legal rights, educational or vocational options, future services, and respite care. Professionals can also build trust with families by being flexible, accessible, and responsive to the families' needs and preferences. In research with families, Dinnebeil and Rule (1994) found that not following through with activities and scheduling meetings without consulting a family's schedule were two ways service providers detracted from a collaborative relationship. Recognizing each family's strengths not only helps the professional interact with the family with respect, but also helps to identify resources that can be beneficial in planning the student's educational program. Families may also find strength in family-to-family networking. Professionals may be able to facilitate family meetings or refer families to organizations such as the Arc.

There are some specific strategies that can be used to encourage a family to take the lead in planning (Leal, 1998; Turnbull & Turnbull, 1997). First, when a person-centered planning approach is employed, meetings can be focused on the individual with disabilities and the family. (See Box 5.2 for a discussion of the linkages among family-centered, culture-centered, and person-centered planning.) The professional can encourage the family members to tell their story in the context of these planning sessions. In shorter meetings with parents and other family members, the professional can begin with asking the members to express what they would like to discuss. Besides inviting family members to take the lead in setting the meeting agenda, professionals can also help the family clarify its priorities. Sometimes concerns that are expressed can be translated into priority statements (e.g., "I hear you saying that giving John the opportunity to continue to learn to read is important"). A professional can also learn to be a sensitive and responsive listener and respond to conflict constructively. For example, when the family appears to be resistant to a professional's recommendation, the professional can listen carefully to understand the specific objections. Family members may appear to be uncooperative for a variety of reasons. The professional's recommendations may conflict with their child-rearing or cultural values. Recommendations may be beyond their capacity to carry out, or may conflict with prior professional advice. They may not have understood the professional, or they may be basing their understanding on a previous negative experience with this or another professional. Or, as members of an empowered family, they may simply be expressing their right to make their own decision (Leal, 1998).

BOX 5.2. Family-Centered, Culture-Centered, and Person-Centered Planning

Throughout this book, the term "person-centered planning" is used to refer to putting the students' preferences and needs at the center of all planning efforts. To take this person-centered perspective, planning teams need to be "family-centered" and "culture-centered." Honoring family and cultural ties is a key component of a person-centered approach. One of the most important sources of support in the lives of many people with disabilities is the long-term commitment of their families. Many individuals with disabilities express strong preferences for maintaining family ties. Families are especially important in helping children grow into mature adults. They also teach cultural values and pride. To be person-centered requires understanding these cultural values and how they influence the individual preferences and needs of students with disabilities.

Self-Evaluation: Are My Services Family-Centered?

Allen and Petr (1996) have defined criteria for a family-centered model of service delivery. From their criteria, professionals may consider the following questions to determine whether they have a family-centered focus:

1. Do I focus on the family as the unit of attention in my interactions versus my own agenda and priorities?
2. Do I collaborate with families in making educational decisions?
3. Is the family offered choices?
4. Do I emphasize the family's strengths?
5. Have I encouraged the family members to articulate their needs and priorities?
6. Are services individualized for each student?
7. Is information sharing sensitive to this family's unique characteristics?
8. Are the special education services "user-friendly"; that is, can family members gain easy access to resources and information they need?

PROFESSIONAL PRACTICES THAT ARE BOTH FAMILY- AND CULTURE-CENTERED

To help the reader understand more about how a professional can be both family- and culturally-centered in planning with students with disabilities, several specific planning activities are described to illustrate this focus. Obviously, not every planning issue a team may encounter can be described; these examples are offered to illustrate how to think about issues that concern a student with disabilities from the perspective of the family and with sensitivity to the student's family's cultural heritage.

Encouraging Family Participation and Leadership

As summarized in Table 5.1, research on families from diverse cultural perspectives suggest that planning meetings have often not been family-centered or culturally sensitive. For example, participation by African American and Native American parents has often been less than participation by European American parents (Lynch & Stein, 1987; Sontag & Schacht, 1994). How can professionals, especially those whose cultural background differs from a particular family's, encourage family members to be leaders in planning the student's educational programs? First, professionals can be more culture-centered by communicating with or interviewing families in ways that are culturally sensitive. Dennis and Giangreco (1996) have identified the following important points in conducting culturally sensitive family interviews:

- Appreciate the uniqueness in each family.
- Be aware of the influence of your role as a professional.
- Acknowledge your own cultural biases.
- Seek new understandings and knowledge of cultures.
- Develop an awareness of cultural norms.
- Learn with families.

Second, professionals can be more family-centered by planning communication and meeting formats that offer families choices. For example, would the family prefer a home visit or a school-based meeting? Is support needed for family members to participate in the meeting, such as child care, transportation, or an interpreter? (For information on using interpreters, such as criteria for selecting interpreters, see Plata, 1993.) Does the family prefer to meet during the school day when other children are in school, or do work commitments make it essential to have the option of evening meetings? Also, are the family members more comfortable with an informal format, or would they prefer a business meeting style? Table 5.3 provides guidelines that a professional may follow when arranging planning sessions.

In the meeting itself, the professional can also strive to understand and respect the family's cultural perspective and to establish positive communication. One of the most obvious ways cultural differences manifest themselves is through communication patterns and styles. One way to understand these differences is through Hall's (1976) concept of "high-context" and "low-context" cultures. These two types of cultures have quite different communication patterns and styles. High-context cultures emphasize well-defined patterns of interaction through established hierarchies and situational cues, prefer nonconfrontational responses, and place greater value on personal styles and relations. It may seem ironic or even contradictory that though such cultures place greater emphasis on well-defined roles and formality, their members value the personal approach to communication and relations. This is because persons in high-context cultures take a longer time to "warm up" to meeting and knowing others. The well-defined patterns of interaction, depending on formalized roles and hierarchical status, provide clear boundaries and scaffolding for entering relationships where trust is gradually earned before personal sharing can occur. It is precisely because of the belief that relationships take time and demand evidence before personal disclosure can happen that personal styles and relations are highly valued. Because prime cultural values in high-context cultures are harmony and interdependence with others, well-defined patterns of interaction provide the social rules and scripts to allow people to engage ap-

TABLE 5.3. Suggested Format for Developing Planning Sessions

1. *Icebreaker.* Begin with a positive statement about the student and eagerness to meet with the family for planning the school program.
2. *Clarification.* Check with family members to determine whether they are ready to set a time for a meeting. Do other family members need to be consulted first?
3. *Purpose.* Ask what they would like to discuss at the meeting. Share your purpose (e.g., developing the IEP).
4. *Time and place.* Ask about the best time and place for the meeting. Suggest several options.
5. *Participants.* Ask which individuals the family would like to have present as members of the planning team. Be specific about anyone else you plan to invite (e.g., general education teacher). Encourage them to bring other family members or friends who are involved with the student.
6. *Support.* Discuss family needs for support to participate in a meeting (e.g., child care, transportation, interpreter). Offer supports that you have available.
7. *Format.* Describe several formats to see what they prefer. For example, would they like an informal meeting with open-ended discussion, or a business meeting format with a written agenda?
8. *Closing.* Summarize what has been planned, and check to see that this is what the family members want. End with some positive statements about the upcoming meeting with the family.

propriately in interactions, with minimal friction and conflict. Unless professionals can make sense of the meanings related to communication and interaction within high-context cultures, dissonance and conflict can occur in family–professional partnerships. Family members of high-context cultures have been labeled as evasive, passive, and "beating around the bush" in interactions with professionals belonging to low-context cultures.

Low-context cultures emphasize and encourage direct expressions of messages and feelings more than high-context cultures. European American cultures are generally considered low-context cultures. Freedom in saying what is on one's mind is seen more as an individual right and is an expected part in communicating one's needs to others. As a result, there is more reliance on what is actually said, and patterns of interaction are loosely defined. Unlike high-context cultures, where much significance is placed on the processes of interaction before trust and personal rapport can be built, low-context cultures value interactions that focus on achieving desired outcomes through expediency, direction, and "getting the job done" (Hanson, Lynch, & Wayman, 1990). Members of high-context cultures may interpret such interactions as "cold" and impersonal. On the other hand, if a member of a low-context culture initially meets a member of a high-context culture and soon after communicates personal details in an apparently personal fashion, the person from the high-context culture may interpret the other person as being superficial. Understanding cultural contexts and its implications for communication and interaction patterns can facilitate better cross-cultural communication between families and professionals. Such communication is vital to understanding and planning learning environments. It is important to note that, depending on their degree of assimilation or ethnic identification due to exposure to mainstream culture or intergenerational differences, family members may differ in communication range and style or may even have a blend of different communication patterns. The nature of acculturation within a culturally diverse society like the United States highlights the evolving and dynamic aspect of culture. For more information about specific information on communication and interaction patterns of different cultural groups within the United States, readers can refer to Lynch and Hanson's (1998) book on understanding and working with culturally diverse families.

Respecting Diverse Views of Disability

A second area where professionals can be both family- and culture-centered in planning is to respect how members of each family view the student's disability and its meaning for their family. Cultural values can influence families' views of disability (Gartner, Lipsky, & Turnbull, 1991). For example, Mary (1990) found that Hispanic American mothers reported a self-sacrificing attitude toward their children and spousal denial of disabilities more often than did African American and European American mothers. Marion (1980) noted that feelings of protection and acceptance, as opposed to shock and grief, were more typical of Mexican American and African American parents of children with disabilities. Chan (1986) noted that some Asian families viewed disability as a source of family shame.

Families can reveal much about their cultural views of disability through how they use language to construct and describe meaning out of their experiences (Lim & Tan, 1997). The Chinese word *canfei* is often used to define and describe people with disabilities. This language approximation of connoting disability is one that elicits a sense of pity and hopelessness for the person described. Similarly, European Americans have historically used terms such as "feeble-minded" and "handicapped," which have negative connotations. The term "mental retardation" is fairly well accepted among professionals in the United States, but is not an internationally accepted term or one that is acceptable to many self-advocates. Harry (1992d) and Fowler (1998) note that most Native American languages do not have words for disability, and that Native American culture has been reported as being more inclusive of individuals with disabilities.

Given these potential cultural differences, it is important to realize that an individual family's perspective on a student's disability may or may not be shared by other members of their culture. For example, although many European American professionals use the term "mental retardation," many families and individuals with disabilities from this same cultural heritage find this term stigmatizing. Or, while some Asian families may find disabilities a source of shame, others are strong advocates of school and community inclusion. Also, family members' use of language may not be indicative of their attitude toward the student, but may reflect terms professionals have used in the past. For example, a parent may use the term "trainable mentally retarded" in referring to her daughter, because this was a term she learned early in her daughter's school program. Professionals can provide parents with information on current terminology, and can advocate for the student's educational and community opportunities in ways that respect family and cultural perspectives. For example, the professional can use "I" statements and give reasons ("I like the term 'individual with disabilities' because . . . " or "I have been impressed with the progress students with disabilities have made in community jobs because . . . ") rather than criticism ("That term is no longer used" or "Sheltered workshops are segregated"). Professionals also need to remember that parents have often been the leaders in advocating for systems change to create new opportunities for individuals with disabilities. Family members are often the ones who reject stigmatizing terminology first and who help professionals know how not to underestimate their relative with a disability.

Most important, professionals can listen carefully to different families' stories of how they have come to understand their family members with disabilities. For example, Ferguson and Ferguson (1996), who are both parents and professionals, listened to and described their son's personal definition and meaning of how he saw adulthood. Family members can offer a unique understanding of an individual with disabilities. Their perspective may challenge what the mainstream culture believes about disability. Oe (1995), a Japanese father of a person with disabilities, has written:

> On a more personal level, I can imagine a very concrete example of what happens to a society that shuts out its disabled by asking myself how we ourselves—the Oes—would have turned out if we hadn't made Hikari an indispensable part of our family. I imagine a cheerless house where cold drafts blow through the gaps left by his absence; and after his exclusion, a family whose bonds grow weaker and weaker. In our case, I know it was only by virtue of having included Hikari in the family that we actually managed to weather our various crises, such as my mother-in-law's gradual mental decline. (p. 95)

Culture can influence how a family and community adapt to meet the needs of individuals with disabilities and their families. The adaptation process depends on the resilience of the family members and their community, and the degree of resilience is influenced by how the family and community are conceptualized through cultural beliefs, expectations, and practices. For example, although the incidence of schizophrenia is roughly equivalent around the world, developing countries report a much higher recovery rate than industrialized nations do (Sullivan, 1994). Social relationships and group cohesion within families and communities have been suggested as the primary factors for the higher rates of recovery in the developing countries.

On the other hand, communities can be quite harsh in their attitudes toward people with disabilities and their families. The following describes an Asian mother's perspective on how her son was treated by her neighbors:

> At one stage, K was very difficult. He would scream in public, drawing lots of attention. . . . He stripped himself. . . . He tapped/touched people whom he knew . . . probably his way of acknowledging them. He could not express himself in speech. His action was interpreted by others wrongly. He was hit at times with an umbrella and the police was called. There was a period when within a month, there would be at least be 2–3 visits by the police. I was embarrassed. People, my neighbors gathered . . . they stood and stared hoping that my son would be arrested. Everyone in the block knew him to be my child. It would not take much for someone to run up to inform me when my son stripped himself at the void deck or around the neighborhood . . . but instead, they chose the most convenient way . . . they called the police. My neighbors at one time rallied together to petition the authorities to have K placed in a HOME . . . they went round collecting signatures . . . they instigated my next door neighbor. They told my neighbor that they were unfortunate to be living next to "a family with a child like that." I was angry . . . hurt. . . . If every child like K were to be placed in a WELFARE HOME, then many such HOMES would be needed in Singapore. A welfare home is for those without a family. (Seah, 1997, p. 8)

From these two quotations, it is apparent that an important role for professionals is to advocate for and support social networks that enhance family and community resilience in coping with and dealing with disability. Extended family and community networks are influenced by culture and can be sources of both stress and support to families of children with disabilities. For instance, the degree of grandparents' involvement may be influenced by a family's culture (Turnbull & Turnbull, 1997). A challenge is for professionals to respect and negotiate with family and community members holding diverse views on disability, while mobilizing them to be sources of support rather than stress. Sandler (1998) provides suggestions for professionals to enhance the role of grandparents as a source of support rather than a source of stress, such as providing grandparents with opportunities for emotional support themselves.

Determining Educational Priorities

In addition to influencing how members of a family view their relative with disabilities, cultural and family values also influence perspectives on educational goals. Parent–professional tensions sometimes arise because of differences about what and how a student with a disability should be taught. Hamre-Nietupski, Nietupski, and Strathe (1992) investigated the educational preferences of American parents (in Iowa) of students with moderate and severe/profound disabilities in terms of the relative value they placed on functional life skills, social relationship/friendship skills, and functional academics. These authors found that the parents of students with moderate disabilities rated functional life skills most highly, followed by functional academics and social re-lationship/friendship skills, whereas parents of students with severe/profound dis-abilities rated social relationship/friendship skills most highly, followed by functional life skills and functional academics.

Lim, Tan, and Quah (2000) adapted Hamre-Nietupski et al.'s (1992) survey instru-ment to find out how parents of children with mild, moderate, and severe disabilities in Singapore valued the same set of skills. In addition, parents were asked to indicate whether they expected priority skill items within the skill areas to be performed with assistance or independently. Factor analysis of parents' ratings in Lim et al.'s (2000) study yielded four instead of three skill classifications; the category of functional life skills was separated into self-help and community-based life skills. The results showed that parents of children with moderate and severe disabilities indicated the highest pri-ority for self-help functional life skills, followed by community-based functional life skills, social relationship skills, and functional academics. Parents of children with mild disabilities also most highly valued self-help and community skills, but valued func-tional academics over social relationship skills. In another study, Lim, Tan, and Quah (1998) found that parents of young children with disabilities valued self-help functional life skills significantly more than community-based life skills, functional academics, and social relationship skills.

These studies are interesting because they suggest that some cultural differences may exist in the priorities that parents assign to educational goals. For example, the Singaporean and American parents differed in the priority given to social relationship skills compared to functional life skills. The studies also offer a model of asking parents to participate in curriculum decisions. To be both family- and culture-centered, an impor-tant part of planning an IEP is determining how much emphasis the family members want to give different curricular areas. In the Choosing Outcomes and Accommodations for Children (COACH; Giangreco, Cloninger, & Iverson, 1998) approach, family mem-bers prioritize specific curricular goals with the professional as a first step in developing the IEP. Similarly, in the assessment model described throughout this book, family and student priorities are primary tools for establishing curricular priorities.

In addition to varying in their curricular priorities, families vary in their perspec-tive on the level of independence expected at different age levels. For example, per-sonal mastery in self-help skills such as eating and toilet training may be encouraged later in some cultures than in others. In some cultures, children sleep together with adult family members in the same room, and sometimes in the same bed; in others, children sleep by themselves in separate rooms. Cultural definitions of developmental milestones can differ and affect perceptions of progress (Harry et al., 1995b). Joe and Malach (1992) noted that a Native American family remembered exactly when the child first laughed, but could not place when the child first sat or walked. By listening carefully to family members, professionals can determine what types of self-initiations will have the most meaning in the family's cultural context and which will seem less meaningful or "rushed." Sometimes a "bicultural" goal will be developed for a student. In some instances, increased independence in eating may be important at school (in or-der for the student to blend with peers from other cultures), but less important at home (where assisted eating is not stigmatizing at this age). Similarly, using a fork may be im-portant for eating the school lunch, but less relevant in a home where family members use chopsticks or bread to scoop food.

When Family and Student Priorities Seem to Conflict

A question that often arises when professionals are discussing a family-centered approach in developing educational plans is this: "What if there is a conflict between what the student wants and what the parents want? Doesn't the student's right to self-determination come first?" The potential for this conflict may seem especially strong when team members are planning for transition to adult living, as the team focuses on goals such as where the student will live and work. What if the student and family have different visions for the future?

First and foremost, professionals need to remember that in nearly every family with an adolescent (with or without disabilities) who is making the transition to adult living, there is a gradual shift of decision making from the parents to the young adult. Rarely is this process immediate or tension-free. Parents face the challenge of deciding when and how to let go, and the young adult is often ambivalent about giving up family supports, such as living at home rent-free. In some cultures, it is typical for adult children to live with their parents for long periods of time, or indefinitely. Unless professionals understand and respect these family patterns, planning meetings may lose their family focus.

The first question a professional needs to ask when a conflict seems to arise is whether the tension is between the student and the family, or between the professional's and family's values. The professional also needs to ask what "self-determination" means to the family. For families that come from a group-oriented culture, or that adhere to a religion valuing self-denial, this term may be confusing or even offensive. This does *not* necessarily mean that the family does not share the professional's conviction that the student's preferences for the future should be honored. Instead, the team needs to find more useful common language, such as "honoring student preferences." Parents and professionals can engage in a process known as "reciprocal cultural adaptation" (Correa, 1987) to learn more about and from each other's perspective to achieve important outcomes. This process involves listening carefully to find and enhance points of common understanding.

In other cases, the conflict is not a difference in communication between the family and professional, but a real difference in values. The professional may view a self-determined person as one who lives and works independent of his or her parents. To the family, this may not be a goal for any family member—with or without disabilities. Turnbull and Turnbull (1996) have critiqued the self-determination literature and made a strong case for recognizing that self-determination is itself a cultural value that needs to be carefully considered within individual family frameworks. The professional needs to listen carefully to understand what self-determination means within each family. Some people emphasize the importance of enhancing self-determination through stable and trusting relationships (e.g., Kennedy, 1996). Interdependence, which is an important strength of some cultural groups and some families, can offer a framework for self-determination. In research that illustrates this strength, Heller and Factor (1988) found that African American families were less likely than European American families to seek residential placement outside the home for their relatives with mental retardation. Instead, African American families were more likely to rely on extended familial and community supports. Such lifelong, extended family ties may also be important resources for living and employment opportunities.

Although the source of tension during planning for student self-determination may reflect conceptual misunderstanding or a professional–family difference, sometimes students and their families *do* disagree on the students' educational plan and future goals. Bambara, Cole, and Koger (1998) advise that when conflicts arise in self-determination issues with families, professionals present information so that individuals and their families can make the best-informed decisions for themselves. Sometimes the most helpful role a professional can play is to clarify that these differences exist. For example, when conducting person-centered planning meetings with a family and student, the professional may use two separate pieces of paper to record the parents' and student's preferences. Sometimes this provides important awareness for parents that their child or adolescent has distinct preferences. A second alternative to help clarify differences without being confrontational is to list all the goals suggested in the group in a brainstorming format. Then the leader can ask each planning team member to assign each goal a numerical rating of importance (e.g., 1 = not important, 5 = extremely important). This exercise can sometimes help a group see where consensus exists and where there are differences. Sometimes differences can be resolved with more discussion and careful listening; at other times, a team needs to "agree to disagree." Differences within the family are probably best resolved privately among its members, rather than in the public forum of a team meeting. Professionals with skills in family counseling may offer to facilitate these family discussions, but in the end, families have the right to decide whether such support is desirable.

Parent Training

In the 1970s, professionals sometimes held unrealistic expectations that all parents should become home teachers for children with disabilities. Much has been written about the complexities of family systems since that time. Turnbull and Turnbull (1990) describe how family systems can be conceptualized as having four main components: "family characteristics," "family interaction," "family functions," and "family life cycle."

- *Family characteristics*: Unique aspects of family relevant to characteristics of the family as a whole, members' personal characteristics, characteristics of the disability, cultural traditions and beliefs, and special challenges. Family characteristics form the input into family interaction.
- *Family interaction*: The ways family members interact with each other through roles, relationships, rules, and nature of communication on a daily and weekly basis. Family interaction processes are the means through which the family operates to meet individual and collective family needs.
- *Family functions*: The various categories of needs that family members are responsible for (e.g., what kinds of chores are performed and who performs them). They represent the output of family interaction.
- *Family life cycle*: The sequence of changes and transitions (both developmental and nondevelopmental) occurring as a result of and resulting in changing family characteristics, interactions, and functions. Families are constantly evolving and going through life changes that affect the other three components.

The extent to which parents participate in parent training programs may depend on factors such as the energy required to achieve other family functions (e.g., living in a home without modern conveniences), the family's current life cycle (e.g., needs of the parents' own aging parents), family interaction and composition (e.g., child care provided by a live-in aunt while parents work), and family characteristics (e.g., strong interdependence with relatives and the cultural belief that a child with disabilities is a blessing to be cared for by one's community). To be family-centered, professionals need to communicate with families to determine whether parent training is a priority, what factors may impede participation, and which family members assume the primary parenting role.

The success of a parent training program will also be influenced by its sensitivity to cultural perspectives on child rearing. In mainstream U.S. culture, democratic styles of parent–child interactions are highly valued. On the other hand, some cultures (e.g., some Asian cultures) have more authoritarian styles of parent–child interactions. Some Asian families practice Confucianism, which stresses harmony within the family unit, with obedience and filial piety to be shown by children to parents. Relationships between family members are hierarchical, are well defined, and follow an authoritarian model. Children are generally told what to do, and parents often consider talking or answering back by children as rude and defiant. Children who are socialized according to such parenting styles may appear quiet and passive to professionals from other cultures (Cheng, 1987).

Culture can also influence how parents inculcate discipline within their children with disabilities. Nihira, Tomiyasu, and Oshio (1987) compared the parenting strategies for regulating problem behavior in American versus Japanese families with children with mental retardation, and found culture-specific approaches to instilling discipline. Japanese mothers were found to rely more on affective ties and persuasion to gain compliance, whereas American mothers relied more on parental authority, external reward, and punishment to gain compliance. As cultures meet and interact, spillover effects from different cultures can affect parent–child interactions. For example, Laosa (1980) reported that Chicano (Mexican American) parents who possessed a higher level of formal education, and therefore were more familiar with mainstream European American cultural interactions, used more mainstream interaction patterns with their children.

Professionals can listen to and observe families interacting, to clarify what types of parent–child interactions exist for what types of occasions. There may be occasions when professionals feel that some procedures used by family members to discipline children may be aversive or unduly harsh. Laosa (1983) recommends that professionals learn what are culturally normative practices for disciplinary actions and make judgments based on the culture's standards rather than on their own professional values. Professionals can strive for a balance between respecting cultural styles for parent–child interaction and encouraging families to try to evaluate alternative interventions (Harry, 1992d). Parent training sessions can provide an effective format for teaching these alternatives if presented in such a way that parents do not feel that their culture or personal values are being criticized. Professionals can offer training in behavioral support with many examples of positive procedures, and then give families the opportunity to suggest further ideas, while not embarrassing the families by criticizing specific punishments used in the past.

Advocacy for Families and Individuals with Disabilities

Planning with individuals with disabilities often involves the need for advocacy for the person to gain access to new opportunities and services. Alper, Schloss, and Schloss (1995) encourage professionals to improve the quality of educational services through four types of advocacy: "self-advocacy," "social support advocacy," "interpersonal advocacy," and "legal advocacy." Self-advocacy consists of assisting people to speak or act on their own behalf to improve their quality of life. This form of advocacy can be led by individuals with disabilities themselves. Social support advocacy involves promoting the general interests of a particular individual or group of individuals. A common example of this type of advocacy is improving community attitudes toward a certain group of people (Alper et al., 1995). The sharing of families' stories through the print and electronic media, such as the mother's perspective on how her son was treated by her neighbors in Singapore (presented earlier in this chapter), can make professionals as well as the public more sensitive to the experiences of families of persons of disabilities. Social support advocacy can empower family members to offer their unique perspectives to enhance disability awareness. Interpersonal advocacy involves direct interactions with relevant parties centered on the needs of key participants. Some individuals with disabilities will need the support of family members who have strong negotiation skills. For example, siblings of people with disabilities can be effective advocates (McLoughlin & Senn, 1994). Finally, legal advocacy consists of formal recourse to state and federal laws in order to claim prescribed rights. Parents have the right to legally request an inclusive placement for their child.

Professionals need to respect a family's choice of advocacy roles. In some cases, the parents or the individual with disabilities may invite an extended family member (such as a grandparent or aunt) to help express priorities in an IEP meeting. Some families exercise their right to use legal advocacy when other negotiations have failed. Professionals can also encourage family members as advocates, while being sensitive to the family's culture and values. In working with families who come from countries where education is seen as more of a privilege than a right, professionals can encourage interpersonal advocacy by helping families understand their right to influence the IEP process. How such interpersonal advocacy takes form is also important. Families from high-context cultures may be more at ease with professionals who exhibit professionalism, but are also personable and flexible (e.g., in scheduling meetings). Also, professionals who are used to people stating opinions directly and frankly may need to listen carefully to the more subtle styles some families use in advocating for their relatives with disabilities. Sometimes social support advocacy, in which professionals share different cultural attitudes toward disability so that families can begin to be aware of and explore other options of perceiving and treating disability, is helpful.

MAKING ASSESSMENT AND PLANNING FAMILY- AND CULTURE-CENTERED

This chapter has provided a brief overview of cultural diversity and family-centered planning models. A person-centered planning approach requires being much more meaning- and context-based, compared to traditional decontextualized views of the learner (Perrone, 1991, 1994). Planning teams whose members take a contextual view will soon find a need to understand family systems and cultural values. Once professionals are committed to a family- and culture-centered approach, specific actions can be taken to incorporate these values into the planning process. These actions are outlined in Table 5.4.

The actions outlined in Table 5.4 include engaging in lifelong learning, gaining competence for working on multicultural teams, and staying focused on student and family priorities and strengths. As professionals grow in a family- and culture-centered focus, they will discover other actions they can take to incorporate these values in their work. Such learning is not always easy. Gallimore, Dalton, and Tharp (1986) studied the effects of culturally responsive training on teachers and found that while teachers were able to learn to adapt their teaching styles (in this instance, to Hawaiian culture), they also experienced stress, anxiety, and resentment in the early stages of training. Although gaining multicultural awareness and skills can be disconcerting for profession-

---

TABLE 5.4. Making Assessment and Planning Both Family- and Culture-Centered

Engage in lifelong learning about culture and family systems.

- Know the rationale for a family- and culture-centered approach.
- Learn more about the influence of culture.
- Learn more about family systems theory.
- Clarify personal values about family values and multiculturalism.
- Utilize books, courses, or in-service training on culture- and family-centered approaches.
- Learn about the cultures of the students to be taught.
- Get to know students and their families as individuals.

Apply family- and culture-centered values when working as part of a team.

- Follow the family's lead in all phases of planning—setting the agenda, arranging meetings, forming the team, and developing the meeting format.
- Conduct family interviews in culturally sensitive ways.
- Involve interpreters if necessary.
- Avoid making generalizations about a family based on culture; honor the students and family's lead in defining what is most important to them.
- Remember that diversity exists within cultures. Avoid having preset expectations of a family, based on an experience with a family from a similar cultural background.
- Remember that diversity exists within families. Respect the inclusion of extended family members. Honor whichever individuals families choose as their primary spokespersons.
- Learn with families.

Focus on the student's and family's strengths and priorities.

- Honor the family's and student's preferences and priorities, to incorporate their cultural and family values. (The professional does not need to ask, "What are your cultural and family values?", but simply "What are your preferences and priorities for this plan?")
- When setting goals, also turn to the student and family to validate criteria for mastery. Their perspective can ensure that criteria are sensitive to cultural standards.
- Encourage family members to focus on their strengths and those of their relative with disabilities.
- Encourage both self-advocacy and advocacy by family members on behalf of the student with disabilities.
- When reviewing differences in a student's performance between school and home, consider how these may reflect emerging biculturalism when school and home reflect different cultures.

als, it can also provide both personal and professional growth. For example, Harry, Torguson, Katkavich, and Guerrero (1993) had student teachers become involved with families from a cultural background different from their own. The student teachers were required to interview the parents, participate in community-based activities with the parents and children, and observe the parents at their annual review meetings. Some of the participants reported that the course taught them as much about themselves as about the families they interviewed.

There are many different types of planning activities in which professionals will need to use family- and culture-centered skills. Three of the most frequent types of planning meetings are planning and implementing an IEP meeting, implementing the IEP itself (i.e., planning curriculum and instruction), and planning for positive behavioral support. Each of these is now described, with examples of using a family- and culture-centered focus.

Planning and Implementing an IEP Meeting

Turnbull and Turnbull (1986) have listed step-by-step suggestions for involving parents throughout the stages of the IEP conference, which include preconference preparation, initial conference proceedings, review of evaluation and current levels of performance, development of goals and objects, and determination of placement and related services. Procuring the involvement and participation of families of culturally diverse backgrounds through these stages can be a challenge for professionals, especially if professionals' cultural backgrounds are not similar to those of the families they serve. When parents from culturally diverse backgrounds are encountering the special education system for the first time, Marion (1980) recommends that professionals do the following during the initial stages of preconference preparation and conference proceedings:

- Inform parents of relevant laws, their legal rights and responsibilities, available programs, and procedures for assessing children.
- Equip parents with this information by using forms (e.g., an IEP form) and literature that are available in the parents' own language and if necessary employing interpreters who can better explain the information to the parents in their own language.

Harry et al. (1995b) also recommends that to be culturally inclusive, a professional should try to work out convenient times for meetings with a family. In addition, the professional should allow extended time for explaining results of evaluations, and should provide information on current level of functioning through alternative assessment approaches such as authentic assessment, portfolio assessment, multiple intelligences, and person-centered planning profiles. As described throughout this book, contextually relevant assessment cannot just focus on a student's factual recall and skills; it must also focus on his or her understanding, problem solving, and relating to others (Udvari-Solner & Thousand, 1996). Portfolio assessment and person-centered planning profiles are tools for viewing students' strengths more broadly than simple skills lists (Terry-Gage & Falvey, 1995). As Harry et al. (1995b) note, such alternatives may also communicate better across cultures.

Implementing the IEP

A family- and culture-centered approach does not end with the completion of the IEP. An ongoing partnership with families is needed throughout the school year. For example, family participation can enrich planning for curriculum and instruction. Most curriculum guides for students with moderate and severe disabilities stress selecting skills that are relevant to the students' current and future environments (Ford et al., 1989; Wilcox & Bellamy, 1987). To be culturally inclusive, curriculum will also use students' cultures as a resource for their education (Kea & Utley, 1998) and will enhance lifelong cultural networks (Harry et al., 1995b). When families from diverse cultural backgrounds are included in curriculum planning, education becomes more relevant for the students' current and future environments.

Similarly, families may have invaluable ideas in planning instruction. They may make unique suggestions for job training and community-based instruction, or may think of new ways to include students in general education. Forman, Minick, and Stone (1993) stress that giving more attention to contextual factors, such as learning conditions in a classroom, interpersonal relationships, and the setting for learning, can be an important way to make education more culturally inclusive. Also, using resources from a learner's home and community environment within the school context can make instruction more culturally sensitive (Franklin, 1992).

Tharp (1989) has identified four classes of variables that can affect how culturally diverse students learn: "social organization," "sociolinguistics," "cognition," and "motivation."

Social organization is the way that teaching, learning, and performance are organized and managed in the classroom (McCormick, 1990). For example, peer tutoring in same-sex triads and dyads works well for Hawaiian American students, because such groupings reflect cultural values (Vogt, Jordan, & Tharp, 1987). Students from African American backgrounds may respond well to teaching that has high levels of verbal interaction and greater verve (Franklin, 1992). Similarly, sociolinguistics and communication styles can have an impact on the learning experience. In some cultures (e.g., Navajo), it may take longer periods of time to respond in conversation. Some cultures view overlapping speech as an interruption (rudeness), but many individuals from Hawaiian culture interpret it as a sign of interest and involvement in conversation (McCormick, 1990). Such cultural differences may also be reflected in how teachers from different cultures pose questions (White, Tharp, Jordan, & Vogt, 1989). In addition, the language of instruction may influence how well students learn. Duran and Heiry (1986) found that students with moderate and severe disabilities from Spanish-speaking homes performed best in learning vocational tasks when the language of instruction was Spanish. In contrast, Rohena-Diaz (1998) found that such students performed equally well in learning sight words with Spanish or English instruction if instruction was systematic and students had other opportunities to converse in their native language. Families can help planning teams make important decisions about the language of instruction (e.g., need for bilingual support). It would be unfair to students to disqualify them from bilingual services because of their cognitive disability. In contrast, not all students from Spanish-speaking homes need or want instruction in Spanish.

Educational programs also sometimes emphasize the cognitive styles of the predominant culture. Tharp (1989) found that schools typically use verbal analytic thinking (more typical of European Americans) rather than visual/holistic thinking (more typical of Native Americans). Similarly, teaching students to self-monitor their performance may be familiar to students from individualistic cultures, but may be unusual for students from collectivist cultures like Asian countries. Gudykunst et al. (1989) found that students from the United States and Australia were more likely to engage in self-monitoring than were students from Japan, Taiwan, and Hong Kong, who were more likely to view themselves in the context of the group.

Motivation is a fourth variable in which culture influences how children learn. For example, Vogt et al. (1987) note that praise and direct confrontation are not effective techniques to motivate students from some collectivist cultures (e.g., Navajo). Rather, a stern group lecture may be more effective.

As described earlier, professionals can make instruction more culturally sensitive by learning more about each student's cultural group and by getting to know each student and family as individuals. Sometimes it may be useful to describe instructional alternatives to family members and ask them for feedback on how well these will work with a student. Table 5.5 provides a list of questions professionals might discuss when consulting with family members about what works best for an individual student.

Planning Positive Procedures for Challenging Behavior

Sometimes a team must focus on developing positive procedures for challenging behavior. This process can also incorporate a family- and culture-centered approach. Typically, planning for challenging behavior begins with a functional assessment to identify variables that affect behaviors. Variables can consist of antecedents or discriminative stimuli that trigger behavior, consequences of behavior, and setting events belonging to the broader context that influence the likelihood of the behavior occurring (Horner & Carr, 1997). Functional assessment has been demonstrated as an effective method to analyze the relationships between variables within an environmental context and to suggest interventions or modifications for curricular activities. Research studies (e.g., Bambara, Koger, Katzer, & Davernport, 1995; Dibley & Lim, in press) have used functional assessment to demonstrate that the lack of choice over what, when, and how to perform activities can affect task initiations and problem behaviors of individuals with disabilities.

Although the literature on the use of functional assessment has increased considerably in the past decade, little has been written to address the context of culture as a potential variable to explain the motivational basis of behavior or to develop culturally appropriate intervention strategies. In a study that did address cultural influence, Richardson, Kline, and Huber (1996) applied qualitative methods to investigate the impact of family culture on the development of self-management skills in an individual with developmental disabilities, and found that culture had a large impact on the use of such skills.

A beginning point in considering the role of culture in a student's behavior is to involve the family at all stages of planning. Mullen and Frea (1995) note that parents, through greater access to opportunities for interaction and greater personal knowledge of their children, can help facilitate desired behavior and skill development through an understanding of functional assessment methods. Parents can also provide extended

TABLE 5.5. Issues to Consider When Consulting with Families to Plan Culturally Inclusive Instruction

---

Strategy: Use of materials

> *Question:*
> What materials will the student encounter when performing this skill at home or in the community?
>
> *Sample answers:*
> Rice cooker and wok for meal preparation; Spanish sight words for use at the neighborhood grocery store.
>
> *Question:*
> What materials might increase the student's interest in this activity?
>
> *Sample answers:*
> Chopsticks as a symbol for "eat" in daily schedule; music in native language played while working on task.
>
> *Question:*
> What materials might help this student perform better?
>
> *Sample answers:*
> Cultural magazine to get ideas to initiate conversation.

Strategy: Instructional format

> *Question:*
> What are some choices we might encourage at school and home?
>
> *Sample answers:*
> Which artwork to give to Grandmother; which chore to perform first.
>
> *Question:*
> How does this student learn best?
>
> *Sample answers:*
> Group instruction with group contingencies; faster or slower pace of instruction; same-sex dyads for peer instruction.
>
> *Question:*
> How do you think the student will respond when I help (prompt) the student by (1) telling what to do (verbal)? (2) physically guiding?
>
> *Sample answers:*
> Give the student more time to answer, because fast answers may be viewed as rude; we use a lot of physical contact (or we do not usually use physical contact).

---

information, due to the proximal nature of parent–child interactions (Koegel, Schreibman, Britten, Burke, & O'Neill, 1982). Parental observations of children in their natural environments can provide invaluable functional assessment information for identifying relevant variables related to behaviors and skills. Parents are usually aware of their children's idiosyncratic styles and topographies of interaction. Through their partnerships with professionals as functional assessors, parents can also learn about the functional dynamics and reciprocal nature of their own interactions with their children. Through such self-awareness, parents can become better at regulating their own parenting and communication styles in order to teach new behaviors and skills to their children.

In addition to these benefits of involving families in functional assessment, families from culturally diverse backgrounds offer perspectives on the cultural relevance of the behavior displayed. Every culture has its own definition of what constitutes good or bad manners. Gestures that are considered rude vary widely across cultures. In some Asian cultures, gesturing with the index finger is considered rude. To gesture "Come here" to someone, it may be appropriate to use a downward, repeated motion of fingers toward the palm, but not an upward curl of the index finger. Without this information, a professional could make a serious cultural blunder in teaching a student to request assistance by gesturing "Come here" with the index finger. In contrast, a team that is honoring the lead of a family will be able to identify a culturally appropriate alternative skill. Consider the case of a Native American student whose family views a certain animal (e.g., an owl) as a bad omen. The planning team may not understand the function of a nonverbal student's protesting behavior in a general education class where the teacher asks him or her to sit beside a bulletin board displaying owls. Halle and Spradlin (1993) have noted that setting events can have an important influence on behavior. Such setting events can be either *durational and concurrent* events or *prior and historical* events. For example, serving an Asian child milk (many persons of Asian descent are not used to drinking milk, or actually cannot digest lactose) may create discomfort that influences behavior for the remainder of the day (durational event). Or a boy from a Latino family who gets teased about chores considered inappropriate for his gender may react negatively when introduced to these tasks some months later by a teacher at school (prior event).

In planning interventions, cultural perspectives also need to be respected. For some individuals from Hispanic and other cultures, the spiritual realm is a part of everyday reality (Duran, 1988). The family may choose to involve priests or other members of the clergy in intervention planning, and to use religious rituals (e.g., prayer) as part of their home-based intervention. One mother known to us sprinkled holy water to remove undesirable spirits from her children's bedroom when they were agitated during sleep.

Any alternative behaviors that are chosen to teach students to perform as replacements for the problem behavior need the family's endorsement. Higginbotham and Marsella (1987) note that culturally inappropriate interventions can produce "dysfunctional cultural change," in which an individual receives reduced or harmful care. In some cultures, reinforcement procedures that draw attention to the child and his behavior may isolate him or her from a community and family that use primarily collectivist forms of reward.

SUMMARY

This chapter has described the importance of being both family- and culture-centered in planning with students with moderate and severe disabilities. Being family- and culture-centered is part of person-centered planning, because understanding students' needs and preferences requires understanding both their family system and cultural background. It is essential to get to know students and their families as individuals. According to optimal theory, families have some values in common with all people, some values in common with their cultural group, and some values that are unique to their individual family system. Because of this, it is not surprising that wide variation exists among families of students with students with special needs, even among families from the same cultural background.

A family-centered approach entails more than forming a partnership with families. Instead, it involves encouraging and empowering families to take the lead in planning with students with disabilities. The families' preferences and values play a dominant role in determining current and future priorities. Professionals can become more family-centered by involving families in all stages of the planning process. Some of the specific areas that require a family- and culture-centered focus are IEP development, IEP implementation (i.e., curriculum and instructional planning), and positive behavioral support for problem behavior. For students to gain skills that will be relevant to their current and future environments, family input is needed to understand what will be most relevant within the students' cultural and family contexts. Some of the actions professionals can take to encourage this input are to involve families in planning meetings and agendas, to honor their priorities, and to validate the skills selected and the criteria for mastery of these skills.

About Being Beth's Aunt[2]

I (Diane M. Browder) had been in the field of special education for 10 years when Marjorie Elizabeth Browder—"Beth"—was born to my older brother Mike and his wife, Susan. Several years later, we learned that her diagnosis was Angelman's syndrome. At 9 months of age, Beth went to a children's rehabilitation center for an inpatient diagnosis. By the end of the week, the labels "mental retardation" and "cerebral palsy" were assigned to Beth and pierced the hearts of our entire extended family. The diagnosis occurred in the early 1980s, when few professionals were talking about being family-centered. The diagnostic team meetings did not include any family members. My brother finally negotiated for me to be present at a team meeting because I was also a professional. Some team members objected to my presence, noting that I would not be objective because I was a family member. The team meeting itself was surreal as I watched professionals describe every one of my niece's deficits in detail. No one considered her strengths. They also analyzed the family members: Had we accepted her mental retardation? If I had not been Beth's aunt, the professionals' attitudes would not have seemed unusual to me, since I had been trained in a diagnostic model and participated in many similar meetings. But sitting there as the "patient's" aunt, I could not help realizing that we—the members of Beth's family—knew her, and that after many hours of tests and observations, the professional team still did not. That meeting was for me a turning point in my professional career. It was the day Beth and her parents became my mentors. It was the day I began learning to listen to families.

REFERENCES

Allen, R. I., & Petr, C. G. (1996). Towards developing standards and measurements for family-centered practice in family support programs. In G. Singer, L. Powers, & A. Olson (Eds.), *Redefining family support: Innovations in public–private partnerships* (pp. 57–86). Baltimore: Paul H. Brookes.

Alper, S., Schloss, P. J., & Schloss, C. N. (1995). Families of children with disabilities in elementary and middle school: Advocacy models and strategies. *Exceptional Children, 62,* 261–270.

Ball, L. M., & Harry, B. (1993). Multicultural education and special education: Parallels, divergences, and intersections. *Educational Forum, 57,* 430–437.

[2]I share this true story about Beth with the permission of her parents, Michael and Susan Browder—Diane M. Browder.

Ballard, K. D. (1990). Special education in New Zealand: Disability, politics, and empowerment. *International Journal of Disability, Development, and Education, 37,* 109–124.

Bambara, L. M., Cole, C. L., & Koger, F. (1998). Translating self-determination concepts into support for adults with severe disabilities. *Journal of the Association for Persons with Severe Handicaps, 23,* 27–37.

Bambara, L. M., Koger, F., Katzer, T., & Davenport, T. A. (1995). Embedding choice in the context of daily routines: An experimental case study. *Journal of the Association for Persons with Severe Handicaps, 20,* 185–195.

Befring, E. (1990). Special education in Norway. *International Journal of Disability, Development, and Education, 37,* 125–137.

Berman, S. (1990). Educating for social responsibility. *Educational Leadership, 48,* 75–80.

Bradley, V. J., Ashbaugh, J. W., & Blaney, B. C. (1994). *Creating individual supports for people with developmental disabilities: A mandate for change at many levels.* Baltimore: Paul H. Brookes.

Chan, S. (1986). Parents of exceptional Asian children. In M. K. Kitano & P. C. Chinn (Eds.), *Exceptional Asian children and youth* (pp. 36–53). Reston, VA: Council for Exceptional Children.

Cheng, L. L. (1987). *Assessing Asian language performance: Guidelines for evaluating limited-English-proficient students.* Rockville, MD: Aspen.

Clifft, M. A. (1986). Writing about psychiatric patients: Guidelines for disguising case material. *Bulletin of the Menninger Clinic, 50,* 511–524.

Correa, V. I. (1987). Involving culturally diverse families in the educational process. In S. H. Fradd & M. J. Weismantel (Eds.), *Meeting the needs of culturally and linguistically different students: A handbook for educators* (pp. 130–144). Boston: College-Hill Press.

Darling, R. B., & Baxter, C. (1996). *Families in focus: Sociological methods in early intervention.* Austin, TX: Pro-Ed.

Davidson, P. W., Goode, D. A., & Kendig, J. W. (1992). Developmental disabilities related education, technical assistance, and research activities in developing nations. *Mental Retardation, 30,* 269–275.

Dennis, R. E., & Giangreco, M. F. (1996). Creating conversation: Reflections on cultural sensitivity in family interviewing. *Exceptional Children, 63,* 103–116.

Dibley, S., & Lim, L. (in press). Providing choice making opportunities within and between daily school routines. *Journal of Behavioral Education.*

Dinnebeil, L.A., & Rule, S. (1994). Variables that influence collaboration between parents and service coordinators. *Journal of Early Intervention, 18,* 349–361.

Drew, N. (1987). *Learning the skills of peacemaking.* Rolling Hills Estates, CA: Jalmar.

Dunst, C. J., Johanson, C., Trivette, C. M., & Hamby, D. (1991). Family-oriented early intervention policies and practices: Family-centered or not. *Exceptional Children, 58,* 115–126.

Duran, E. (1988). *Teaching the moderately and severely handicapped student and autistic adult.* Springfield, IL: Charles C Thomas.

Duran, E., & Heiry, T. (1986). Comparison of Spanish only, Spanish and English, and English only with handicapped students. *Reading Improvement, 23,* 138–141.

Ferguson, P. M., & Ferguson, D. L. (1996). Communicating adulthood: The meanings of independent living for people with significant cognitive disabilities and their families. *Topics in Language Disorders, 16,* 52–67.

Flynt, S. W., & Wood, T. A. (1989). Stress and coping of mothers of children with moderate mental retardation. *American Journal of Mental Retardation, 94,* 278–283.

Ford, A., Schnorr, R., Meyer, L., Davern, L., Black, J., & Dempsey, P. (1989). *The Syracuse Community-Referenced Curriculum Guide for students with moderate and severe disabilities.* Baltimore: Paul H. Brookes.

Forman, E. A., Minick, N., & Stone, C. A. (1993). *Contexts for learning: Sociocultural dynamics in children's development.* New York: Oxford University Press.

Fowler, L. (1998). Native American communities: A more inclusive society? *TASH Newsletter, 24,* 21–22.

Franklin, M. E. (1992). Culturally sensitive instructional practices for African-American learners with disabilities. *Exceptional Children, 59,* 115–122.

Gallimore, R., Dalton, S., & Tharp, R. G. (1986). Self-regulation and interactive teaching: The effects of teaching conditions on teachers' cognitive activity. *Elementary School Journal, 86,* 612–631.

Gartner, A., Lipsky, D. K., & Turnbull, A. P. (1991). *Supporting families with a child with a disability: An international outlook.* Baltimore: Paul H. Brookes.

Giangreco, M.F., Cloninger, C.J., & Iverson, V.S. (1998). *Choosing Outcomes and Accommodations for Children* (2nd ed.). Baltimore: Paul H. Brookes.

Glidden, L. M., Kiphart, M. J., Willoughby, J. C., & Bush, B. A. (1993). Family functioning when rearing children with developmental disabilities. In A. P. Turnbull, J. M. Patterson, S. K. Behr., D. L., Murphy, J. G. Marquis, & M. J. Blue-Banning (Eds.), *Cognitive coping, families, and disability* (pp. 183–194). Baltimore: Paul H. Brookes.

Gudykunst, W. B., Nishida, T., Leung, K., Gao, G., Bond, M. H., Wang, G., & Barraclough, R. A. (1989). A cross-cultural comparison of self-monitoring. *Communication Research Reports, 6,* 7–12.

Hall, E. T. (1976). *Beyond culture.* Garden City, NY: Doubleday/Anchor.

Halle, J. W., & Spradlin, J. E. (1993). Identifying stimulus control of challenging behavior. In J. Reichle & D. P. Wacker (Eds.), *Communicative alternatives to challenging behavior: Integrating functional assessment with intervention strategies* (pp. 83–109). Baltimore: Paul H. Brookes.

Hamre-Nietupski, S., Nietupski, J., & Strathe, M. (1992). Functional life skills, academic skills, and friendship/social relationship development: What do parents of students with moderate/severe profound disabilities value? *Journal of the Association for Persons with Severe Handicaps, 17,* 53–58.

Hanson, M. J., Lynch, E. W., & Wayman, K. I. (1990). Honoring the cultural diversity of families when gathering data. *Topics in Early Childhood Special Education, 10,* 112–131.

Harry, B. (1992a). An ethnographic study of cross-cultural communication with Puerto Rican-American families in the special education system. *American Educational Research Journal, 29,* 471–494.

Harry, B. (1992b). Restructuring the participation of African-American parents in special education. *Exceptional Children, 59,* 123–131.

Harry, B. (1992c). Making sense of disability: Low-income Puerto Rican parents' theories on the problem. *Exceptional Children, 59,* 27–40.

Harry, B. (1992d). *Cultural diversity, families, and the special education system.* New York: Teachers College Press.

Harry, B., Allen, N., & McLaughlin, M. (1995a). Communication versus compliance: African-American parents' involvement in special education. *Exceptional Children, 61,* 364–377.

Harry, B., Grenot-Scheyer, M., Smith-Lewis, M., Park, H. S., Fu, X., & Schwartz, I. (1995b). Developing culturally inclusive services for people with severe disabilities. *Journal of the Association for Persons with Severe Handicaps, 20,* 99–109.

Harry, B., & Kalyanpur, M. (1994). Cultural underpinnings of special education: Implications for professional interactions with culturally diverse families. *Disability and Society, 9,* 145–165.

Harry, B., Torguson, C., Katkavich, J., & Guerrero, M. (1993). Crossing social class and cultural barriers in working with families. *Teaching Exceptional Children, 26,* 48–52.

Haynes, N. M., & Comer, J. P. (1996). Integrating schools, families, and communities through successful school reform: The school development program. *School Psychological Review, 25,* 501–506.

Heller, T., & Factor, A. (1988). Permanency planning among black and white family caregivers of older adults with mental retardation. *Mental Retardation, 26,* 203–208.

Higginbotham, H. N., & Marsella, A. J. (1987). International consultation and the homogenization for psychiatry in Southeast Asia. *Social Science and Medicine, 27,* 553–561.

Hodgkinson, H. L. (1992). *A demographic look at tomorrow.* Washington, DC: Institute of Educational Leadership.

Horner, R. H., & Carr, E. G. (1997). Behavioral support for students with severe disabilities: Functional assessment and comprehensive intervention. *Journal of Special Education, 31,* 84–109.

Joe, J. R., & Malach, R. S. (1992). Families with Native American roots. In E. W. Lynch & M. J. Hanson (Eds.), *Developing cross-cultural competence: A guide for working with young children and their families* (pp. 89–119). Baltimore: Paul H. Brookes.

Kalyanpur, M., & Rao, S. S. (1991). Empowering low-income, black families of handicapped children. *American Journal of Orthopsychiatry, 61*, 523–532.

Kea, C. D., & Utley, C. A. (1998). To teach me is to know me. *Journal of Special Education, 32*, 44–47.

Kennedy, M. J. (1996). Self-determination and trust: My experiences and thoughts. In D. J. Sands & M. J. Wehmeyer (Eds.). *Self-determination across the life span: Independence and choice for people with disabilities* (pp. 37–50). Baltimore: Paul H. Brookes.

Koegel, R. L., Schreibman, L., Britten, K. R., Burke, J. C., & O'Neill, R. E. (1982). A comparison of parent training to direct clinic treatment. In R. L. Koegel, A. Rincover, & A. L. Egel (Eds.), *Educating and understanding autistic children* (pp. 260–279). San Diego, CA: College-Hill Press.

Laosa, L. M. (1980). Maternal teaching strategies in Chicano and Anglo-American families: The influence of culture and education on maternal behavior. *Child Development, 51*, 759–765.

Laosa, L. M. (1983). Parent education, cultural pluralism, and public policy: The uncertain connection. In R. Haskins & D. Adams (Eds.), *Parent education and public policy* (pp. 331–345). Norwood, NJ: Ablex.

Leal, L. (1998). *A family-centered approach to people with mental retardation (Innovations No. 14)*. Washington, DC: American Association on Mental Retardation.

Lim, L., & Browder, D. M. (1994). Multicultural life skills assessment of individuals with severe disabilities. *Journal of the Association for Persons with Severe Handicaps, 19*, 130–138.

Lim, L., & Tan, A. G. (1997). *Language, identity, and culture as mediators to parental coping with disability*. Paper presented at the Second Regional Conference on English in Southeast Asia, Kuala Lumpur, Malaysia.

Lim, L., Tan, A. G., & Quah, M. L. (1998). Parental perspectives on curriculum priorities on their young children with disabilities. *Early Child Development and Care, 144*, 91–99.

Lim, L., Tan, A. G., & Quah, M. L. (2000). Singaporean parents' curriculum priorities for their children with disabilities. *International Journal of Development, Disability, and Education, 47* 77–87.

Lipsky, D. K., & Gartner, A. (1997). *Inclusion and school reform: Transforming America's classrooms*. Baltimore: Paul H. Brookes.

Lloyd, A. (1987). Multicultural counseling: Does it belong in a counselor education program? *Counselor Education and Supervision, 26*, 164–167.

Loxley, A., & Thomas, G. (1997). From inclusive policy to the exclusive real world: An international review. *Disability and Society, 12*, 273–291.

Lynch, E. W., & Hanson, M. J. (Eds.). (1998). *Developing cross-cultural competence: A guide for working with young children and their families* (2nd ed.). Baltimore: Paul H. Brookes.

Lynch, E. W., & Stein, R. C. (1987). Parent participation by ethnicity: A comparison of Hispanic, Black and Anglo families. *Exceptional Children, 54*, 105–111.

Marion, R. L. (1980). Communicating with parents of culturally diverse exceptional children. *Exceptional Children, 46*, 616–623.

Mary, N. L. (1990). Reactions of black, Hispanic, and white mothers to having a child with handicaps. *Mental Retardation, 28*, 1–5.

McCormick, L. (1990). Cultural diversity and exceptionality. In N. G. Haring & L. McCormick (Eds.), *Exceptional children and youth* (pp. 47–75). Columbus, OH: Charles E. Merrill.

McLoughlin, J. A., & Senn, C. (1994). Siblings of children with disabilities. In S. Alper, P. J. Schloss, & C. N. Schloss (Eds.), *Families of students with disabilities: Consultation and advocacy* (pp. 95–122). Boston: Allyn & Bacon.

Miner, C. A., & Bates, P. E. (1997). The effect of person centered planning activities on the IEP/transition planning process. *Education and Training in Mental Retardation and Developmental Disabilities, 32*, 105–112.

Misra, A. (1994). Partnership with multicultural families. In S. K. Alper, P. J. Schloss, & C. N. Schloss (Eds.), *Families of students with disabilities: Consultation and advocacy* (pp. 143–179). Needham Heights, MA: Allyn & Bacon.

Mullen, K. B., & Frea, W. D. (1995). A parent–professional consultation model for functional analysis.

In R. L. Koegel & L. K. Koegel (Eds.), *Teaching children with autism: Strategies for initiating positive interactions and improving learning opportunities* (pp. 175–188). Baltimore: Paul H. Brookes.

Nihira, K., Tomiyasu, Y., & Oshio, C. (1987). Homes of TMR children: Comparison between American and Japanese families. *American Journal of Mental Deficiency, 91,* 486–495.

Nisbet, J. (1992). *Natural supports in school, at work, and in the community for people with severe disabilities.* Baltimore: Paul H. Brookes.

Oe, K. (1995). *A healing family.* New York: Kodansha America.

Patton, J. M. (1998). The disproportionate representation of African Americans in special education: Looking behind the curtain for understanding the problems. *Journal of Special Education, 32,* 25–31.

Perrone, V. (1991). *Expanding student assessment.* Alexandria, VA: Association for Supervision and Curriculum Development.

Perrone, V. (1994). How to engage students in learning. *Educational Leadership, 51,* 11–13.

Plata, M. (1993). Using Spanish-speaking interpreters in special education. *Remedial and Special Education, 14,* 19–24.

Richardson, G. M., Kline, F. M., & Huber, T. (1996). Development of self-management in an individual with mental retardation: A qualitative case study. *Journal of Special Education, 30,* 278–304.

Rohena-Diaz, E. (1998). *A comparison of English and Spanish instruction in teaching sight words to students with moderate mental retardation who are linguistically diverse.* Unpublished doctoral dissertation, Lehigh University.

Rogers-Dulan, J. (1998). Religious connectedness among urban African American families who have a child with disabilities. *Mental Retardation, 36,* 91–103.

Sandler, A. G. (1998). Grandparents of children with disabilities: A closer look. *Education and Training in Mental Retardation and Developmental Disabilities, 33,* 350–356.

Santos, D., & Pereira, M. (1997). Brazilian concepts of special education. *Disability and Society, 12,* 407–425.

Seah, F. (1997). Pain: An integral part of growth. *The Pentagon, 1,* 7–8.

Simeonsson, R. J., & Bailey, J. B. (1990). Family dimensions in early intervention. In S. J. Meisels & J. P. Shonkoff (Eds.), *Handbook of early childhood intervention* (pp. 119–149). Cambridge, England: Cambridge University Press.

Sontag, J. C., & Schacht, R. (1994). An ethnic comparison of parent participation and information needs in early intervention. *Exceptional Children, 60,* 422–433.

Speight, S., Myers, L., Cox, C., & Highlen, P. (1991). A redefinition of multicultural counseling. *Journal of Counseling and Development, 70,* 29–36.

Storey, K., & Certo, N. J. (1996). Natural supports for increasing integration in the workplace for people with disabilities: A review of the literature and guidelines for implementation. *Rehabilitation Counseling Bulletin, 40,* 62–76.

Sullivan, P. (1994). Recovery from schizophrenia: What we can learn from the developing nations. *Innovation and Research, 3,* 7–16.

Szapocznik, J., & Kurtines, W. M. (1993). Family psychology and cultural diversity: Opportunities for theory, research, and application. *American Psychologist, 48,* 400–407.

Terry-Gage, S., & Falvey, M. A. (1995). Assessment strategies to develop appropriate curricula and educational programs. In M. A. Falvey (Ed.), *Inclusive and heterogeneous schooling: Assessment, curriculum, and instruction* (pp. 59–110). Baltimore: Paul H. Brookes.

Tharp, R. G. (1989). Psychocultural variables and constants: Effects on teaching and learning in schools. *American Psychologist, 44,* 349–359.

Trickett, E. J. (1997). Developing an ecological mind-set on school-community collaboration. In J. L. Swartz & W. E. Martin, Jr. (Eds.), *Applied ecological psychology for schools within communities: Assessment and intervention* (pp. 139–163). Mahwah, NJ: Erlbaum.

Trivette, C. M., Dunst, C. J., Boyd, K., & Hamby, D. W. (1995). Family-oriented program models, helpgiving practices and parental control appraisals. *Exceptional Children, 62,* 237–248.

Turnbull, A. P., & Turnbull, H. R. (1986). *Families, professionals, and exceptionality: A special partnership.* Columbus, OH: Charles E. Merrill.

Turnbull, A. P., & Turnbull, H. R. (1990). *Families, professionals, and exceptionality: A special partnership* (2nd ed.). Columbus, OH: Charles E. Merrill.

Turnbull, A. P., & Turnbull, H. R. (1996). Self-determination within a culturally responsive family systems perspective: Balancing the family mobile. In L. E. Powers, G. H. S. Powers, & J. Sowers (Eds.), *Promoting self-competence in children and youth with disabilities: On the road to autonomy* (pp. 195–220). Baltimore: Paul H. Brookes.

Turnbull, A.P., & Turnbull, H.R. (1997). *Families, professionals, and exceptionality: A special partnership* (3rd ed.). Upper Saddle River, NJ: Charles E. Merrill.

Udvari-Solner, A., & Thousand, J. S. (1996). Creating a responsive curriculum for inclusive schools. *Remedial and Special Education, 17,* 182–192.

United Nations Educational, Scientific, and Cultural Organization (UNESCO). (1994). *The Salamanca statement and framework for action on special needs education. World conference on special needs education: Access and equality.* New York: Author.

Villa, R. A., Thousand, J. S., Nevin, A, I., & Malgeri, C. (1996). Instilling collaboration for inclusive schooling as a way of doing business in public schools. *Remedial and Special Education, 17,* 169–181.

Vogt, L. A., Jordan, C., & Tharp, R. G. (1987). Explaining school failure, producing school success: Two cases. *Anthropology and Education Quarterly, 18,* 276–286.

Westling, D. L. (1996). What do parents of children with moderate and severe disabilites want? *Education and Training in Mental Retardation and Developmental Disabilites, 31,* 86–114.

White, S., Tharp, R. G., Jordan, C., & Vogt, L. (1989). Cultural patterns of cognition reflected in the questioning styles of Anglo and Navajo teachers. In D. M. Topping, D. C. Crowell, & V. N. Kobayashi (Eds.), *Thinking across cultures: The Third International Conference on Thinking* (pp. 79–91). Hillsdale, NJ: Erlbaum.

Wilcox, B., & Bellamy, G. T. (Eds.). (1987). *The Activities Catalog: An alternative curriculum for youth and adults with severe disabilities.* Baltimore: Paul H. Brookes.

Zetlin, A. G., Padron, M., & Wilson, S. (1996). The experience of five Latin American families with the special education system. *Education and Training in Mental Retardation and Developmental Disabilities, 31,* 22–28.

SIX

Promoting Self-Determination in Planning and Instruction

with Sharon Lohrmann-O'Rourke

THE FIRST TIME A TRANSITION MEETING WAS HELD *for John[1], there was one crucial omission—John. Not only was John not at the meeting physically, but his perspective was not well represented. The team members that gathered were sincerely committed to John, but they had not yet fully realized that this was John's future. When they talked about employment, they discussed options for people with intensive support needs. They discussed John's ongoing need for personal care and assistance for ambulation. But they did not consider John's interests and how they might help create a good job match. When they talked about future living arrangements, they discussed how the family felt overwhelmed in caring for John. They reviewed supported living options. But no one talked about what was important to John in his home environment. When they wrote his IEP, the team members targeted excellent skills that were functional and relevant to John's environments, but none put John in charge of his learning experience.*

This chapter describes how to promote self-determination for students with moderate and severe disabilities through both the assessment and learning processes.

"Self-determination" is a broad construct that generally describes the extent to which individuals exert control over their lives (Brown & Cohen, 1996). Self-determination is a complex multidimensional process that is difficult to define. Among the essential characteristics are internal motivation, skill abilities, and a supportive and responsive environment (Bambara, Cole, & Koger, 1998; Brown, Gothelf, Guess, & Lehr, 1998; Field & Hoffman, 1994; Wehmeyer, 1998). The interaction of these three variables is what creates conditions ripe for self-determined behavior. The concept of self-determination has emerged as a guiding principle of service provision for children and adults with disabilities. Kamii (1991) has argued that autonomy should be considered a primary outcome of education. In contrast, students like John may lack autonomy in part because of the challenges of their disabilities; but more so because of the way people in their environments respond to their disabilities.

Autonomy in the early stages of life occurs in the form of basic skill development

---

[1]Although John is not a real person, the case of the "missing student" is unfortunately based on real meetings.

Sharon Lohrmann-O'Rourke, MEd, is a doctoral student in special education at Lehigh University, Bethlehem, Pennsylvania.

(e.g., walking, toileting). These early successes produce feelings of pride and begin to develop a foundation upon which later successes are built (Brown & Cohen, 1996). For young children with disabilities, successes are often harder to come by. Physical or cognitive limitations make the acquisition of "steppingstone" tasks (e.g., walking) a more challenging, and thus slower, process. Slower acquisition, coupled with well-intentioned but overly intrusive instructional strategies (e.g., frequent verbal prompts), limits opportunities for the young child with disabilities to have autonomous experiences. As the child grows older, opportunities for critical thinking are also in jeopardy. Fearing the outcomes of bad choices or poor decision making, many caregivers guide the child's safe passage into adulthood by making all or most decisions on his or her behalf.

Unfortunately, without autonomous experiences, a pattern of dependency develops that can thwart the emergence of self-determination. Such a pattern often results in the individual's experiencing "learned helplessness" that permeates functioning in all areas of life, subsequently defeating his or her desires to act in self-directed and autonomous ways. Nirje (1972), an early writer on the concept of self-determination, warned that dependency or a perceived lack of control creates poor self-perceptions and fuels negative images of one's abilities. More recently, Field and Hoffman (1994) have proposed that internal awareness plays a key role in achieving and maintaining self-determination. As such, poor self-perceptions emerging from learned helplessness and limited autonomous experiences may diminish a person's internal motivation to act in self-determined ways. In addition, an absence of autonomous experiences may contribute to a sense of hopelessness, making it even less likely that individuals with more severe disabilities will have the internal motivation needed to act in self-determined ways (Palmer & Wehmeyer, 1998).

Planning teams may recognize the need to promote self-determination in specific, intentional ways for individuals with moderate and severe disabilities who either may have learned helplessness or may not yet know how to direct their own learning. The team may have omitted the most basic step of having the student participate in past planning endeavors or of honoring the student's preferences. This chapter has a twofold purpose. First, it describes how to make the student the center of the planning process. Second, it describes how to assess the student's skills and opportunities in self-determination, and how to develop an individualized educational plan (IEP) with this focus.

MAKING THE STUDENT THE CENTER OF THE PLANNING PROCESS

Promoting Student Participation in Planning Meetings

In Chapter Two, the steps for using ecological assessment have been described, including (1) reviewing past records, (2) conducting person-centered planning with the family and student, (3) encouraging self-determination, and (4) developing a personalized curriculum. During each of these steps, the student should be the center of the planning process. There is a popular self-advocacy poster that says, "Nothing about me without me." An important starting point for any planning team is to develop the format and environment of their meetings so that the student can be a full team member. In their qualitative research, Whitney-Thomas, Shaw, Honey, and Butterworth (1998) found that students were more likely to participate in planning meetings when the size and structure of the meetings were matched to the students' conversational style. Students were also more likely to participate when the conversation was relevant to their daily lives and experiences. In addition, the team members' behavior and response to the students affected the extent to which the students participated.

Students can learn to lead their own meetings. Leadership skills may be especially appropriate for older students (e.g., at transition meetings). To teach this leadership, teachers can use the format demonstrated by Koger and Bambara (1995). These researchers taught two adults to lead their own planning meetings by using a photo album that contained pictures to prompt them through each step of the meeting. In advance of the formal meetings, the participants practiced these steps in mock meetings with a teacher who used systematic prompting and feedback for each pictured step. They then were able to lead their own formal individualized habilitation plan meetings

---

BOX 6.1. Making Planning Meetings Student-Friendly

1. Plan the meeting with the student—the place, the time, and the agenda. For students who do not have these planning skills, consider their preferences (favorite settings, most alert times of the day).
2. If the student needs support to be present and active in the meeting, identify who will provide the necessary support (e.g., teacher, paraprofessional, family member).
3. Encourage all team members to interact with the student before the meeting begins.
4. If possible, have the student call the meeting to order (e.g., ring a bell, pound a gravel) and announce the agenda (e.g., pass out a written agenda). If this is not possible, begin the meeting by "introducing" the student and mentioning some of his or her recent achievements.
5. Encourage older students to run their own meetings (e.g., by showing pictures to initiate each new topic on the agenda). Reinforce younger students' initiations and create opportunities for them to take turns in the flow of the conversation. For students who lack conversational skills, create opportunities for the students to respond to what is being said.
6. Talk with a student, rather than about the student. When reviewing the student's achievements or other information, begin by acknowledging the student directly.
7. Try to maintain a "no negative comments" rule. When discussing problems the student is encountering, do so in a way that is gentle and respectful.
8. Decide how to respond if the student tires of the meeting and wants to leave (e.g., will the meeting end?). If the team decides to continue the meeting, make notes of any decisions that will need to be reviewed later with the student.
9. For students with limited communication skills or who are passive in meetings, invite someone (e.g., advocate, peer) whose only role in the meeting is to be sure that the student's participation is encouraged and acknowledged, and who will remind the group of the student's preferences whenever relevant.

with a team of staff, family, and friends. Box 6.1 contains suggestions for making planning meetings "student-friendly" for all participants.

The ecological assessment process will usually involve one or more informal person-centered planning meetings prior to a formal IEP meeting. As described in Chapter Two, these should be planned to encourage family involvement. Sometimes the family will include friends and extended family members who may choose not to participate in the formal IEP meeting, but who want to show their support for the student in this informal planning context. This process is called "person-centered" because it focuses on the student—his or her story, interests, goals, likes, and dislikes. At this meeting, the team will often generate a list of the student's preferences. If the student lacks sufficient symbolic communication to help make this list, the teacher and other planning team members will want to extend this list through systematic preference assessment.

Systematic Preference Assessment

Although team brainstorming is an important process to begin identifying a learner's preferences, a systematic preference assessment provides a means for a student who uses nonsymbolic communication to sample items or events (Lohrmann-O'Rourke & Browder, 1998). The student's responses to those items and events are then interpreted as relative indicators of preference. Direct observation of the student interacting with sampling options may be more accurate than soliciting information from third parties (Lohrmann-O'Rourke & Browder, 1998). Although caregivers are excellent resources for beginning to identify a student's preferences, research has shown that direct observation of individuals with severe disabilities sometimes conveys a different perspective (e.g., Green et al., 1988; Green, Reid, Canipe, & Gardner, 1991; Foxx, Faw, Taylor, Davis, & Fulia, 1993; Parsons & Reid, 1990). Furthermore, when items are not clearly disparate (e.g., most and least liked), it may be more difficult for caregivers to interpret preferences.

In contrast, a systematic preference assessment can also yield limited or skewed information if it is not well designed. Elsewhere (Lohrmann-O'Rourke, Browder, & Brown, in press), we have recommended conducting socially valid preference assessments. Assessments that are socially valid result in three positive outcomes for the learner. First, once items and events are identified as preferred, caregivers and instructors can embed opportunities for access to these preferences into the student's everyday life. Knowing a person's preferences should not preempt offering choices, but rather should enrich the options for this choice. For example, if Sam's[2] teacher knows that he likes to listen to classical music when doing independent work, she can have some tapes available. Because having these tapes on hand requires some preparation, the teacher needs to know Sam's preferences in advance. In contrast, knowing that Sam likes orange juice versus milk may be meaningless if Sam can choose either one in the school's cafeteria line each day. A second way to make the systematic preference assessment more meaningful is to use this information to promote opportunities for self-expression and self-determination. Helping a learner to understand his or her own likes and dislikes is critical for life planning and decision-making (Field & Hoffman, 1994). The student might learn to communicate likes and dislikes during conversation training, or make a scrapbook of "favorites." A third way to make the assessment more useful is to create ways for the student to sample new items and to have new experiences.

[2]Sam is a fictitious student.

Sampling a new experience is sometimes called a "situational assessment" (see Chapter Two). Through sampling new options, the student may acquire new or more informed preferences.

The components of conducting a systematic preference assessment include (1) defining the assessment purpose, (2) selecting a range of sampling options, (3) determining what form the sampling options will take, (4) developing an assessment schedule, (5) defining a response, (6) identifying presenters and activity partners, and (7) presenting sampling options (Lorhmann-O'Rourke & Browder, 1998; Lohrmann-O'Rourke et al., in press). Table 6.1 contains a summary of the preference assessment components, which are now be described in further detail.

Defining the Assessment Purpose

A preference assessment can be used for a variety of purposes. Sometimes the focus may be to determine any basic preferences (e.g., food, clothing), so that a student's likes and dislikes can be honored when the team is planning personal care. Sometimes information on preferences is needed to help create opportunities for job training or supported living. Knowing the student's leisure interests can be useful in planning extracurricular activities at school. To be sure that the time invested in creating ways for the student to sample options is meaningful, the planning team can ask, "How will this information be used to promote the student's self-determination?"

Selecting a Range of Sampling Options

Once the assessment purpose and outcomes are understood, the next step is to begin selecting options for sampling. Selecting items for assessment can be a straightforward process, or may require a bit of creativity to ensure sufficient sampling variation. It is often helpful to identify categories of sampling options first. For example, Figure 6.1 illustrates a vocational assessment for Pauola[3], a ninth-grade student just entering high school. Pauola's teacher identified three categories of sampling options (clerical, custodial, and food service). Organizing potential sampling options into categories helps an instructor ensure a sufficient range of possibilities. In another example, Frank was interested in new leisure activities. Categories for Frank, who had just turned 18, included hobbies, outdoor activities, sports, restaurants, and clubs.

Once categories are identified, the next task is to begin selecting activities that sample the range of variation. For Pauola, tasks such as photocopying, delivering messages, and organizing supply closets were all duties she might perform while working in an office. By sampling a range of possible activities, she would have sufficient information to make decisions regarding which jobs she most preferred. Frank would be sampling some new hobbies by touring an auto race track and its memorabilia shop, meeting baseball players at spring training to get their autographs, visiting a state park with wheelchair trails, meeting a radio station DJ and then going to a record store, having coffee at a nearby college campus, and trying the school chorus.

Determining What Form Sampling Options Will Take

Once a pool of sampling options is identified, the next decision point is to determine what form the options will take. Sampling options can either be presented in their actual forms or represented with symbols or objects (Lohrmann-O'Rourke & Browder, 1998). Representations may include pictures, scale replicas, videotape clips, a portion of the actual task or activity, or some other image such as a menu or flyer. To determine what form the sampling options will take, the teacher should consider several questions. First, what experience or exposure has the learner had with the sampling options? When sampling options are new and unfamiliar, it may be helpful to have students experience the actual item or event. This provides them with the opportunity to develop familiarity, interact with materials, experience atmosphere, and so forth. A second question is this: Can the learner associate a representational object or image with the actual activity? For instance, when presented with a video image of a hiking trail and an auto race, is the learner able to differentiate between the two and recall a previous experience at those establishments? If the learner has not yet developed this association, one alternative is to identify an object or picture and teach a communicative label associated with the sampling option (Browder, Cooper, & Lim, 1998). For example, Pauola's instructor took pictures of her sampling each of the job tasks that she seemed to enjoy. Once a small pool of preferred options had been identified, she then taught Pauola to associate each picture with each actual activity, thus allowing Pauola to make choices about what job tasks she wanted to work on.

Developing a Sampling Schedule

The purpose of developing a schedule is to ensure that the learner has the opportunity to experience sampling options within the typical environment in which they would occur. The schedule consists of determining where and when sampling opportunities will occur. Whenever possible, the learner should sample items and events in the locations where they typically occur. For example, a student interested in finding a job will have a more accurate experience if sampling occurs at actual employment sites as opposed to simulated settings in the high school classroom. Belfiore, Browder, and Mace (1994) compared drink preferences in community coffee shops versus a vocational center. They found that participants were more likely to make choices and demonstrate distinct preferences in the coffee shops as opposed to the vocational center. Similarly, Nozaki and Mochizuki (1995) found that one participant made different choice selections based upon the setting she was in.

In addition to selecting the setting, consideration must be given to how many choices will be offered at one time when scheduling the preference assessment. Much of the research on preference assessment has used "massed trials," in which the researcher gives the participant 10 or more consecutive trials to choose between two or more objects. The student chooses and briefly samples an option, and then immediately moves to the next set (Lohrmann-O'Rourke & Browder, 1998). In contrast, if "distributed trials" are used, the participant makes choices within his or her typical routine. Distributed trials may produce more representative information, in that the learner is experiencing the item or event under natural conditions. Sometimes, however, a teacher may use massed trials when many possible options exist and these options can easily be presented in a classroom setting (e.g., snack foods, toys). This strategy may also be efficient when the learner has had previous experience with the items or events being sampled, and trials provide a brief reminder of what is available (e.g., video clips of job sites that have been tried in the past year).

The final consideration when developing a schedule is the longevity of the assess-

TABLE 6.1. Components of Preference Assessments and Recommended Practices

Assessment component	Recommended practices	Examples
1. Defining the assessment purpose.	A. Defining the immediate context. B. Determining lifestyle enhancement. C. Selecting instructional components.	A. Food and drink choices. B. Locating a new place to live. C. Task materials, reinforcers.
2. Selecting a range of sampling options.	A. Developing categories of sampling options. B. Defining the available sampling variation within each category.	A. Foods, school materials, outerwear for cold weather, leisure materials. B. Leisure materials: Computer game, Velcro checkers, foosball, darts.
3. Determining what form sampling options will take.	A. Considering previous exposure to sampling options. B. Teaching communicative labels for objects or pictures.	A–B. Actual items; pictures (photographs or line drawings); videotape clips; computer-generated images.

4. Developing a sampling schedule.	A. Where?
	  i. Typical settings.
	  ii. New settings.
	
	B. When?
	  i. Massed in brief trials.
	
	  ii. Distributed across the day.
	  iii. Combination of massed and distributed.
	  iv. Specially scheduled events.
	
	C. Assessment longevity.
	  i. Conducting assessments over time.
		i. Within the classroom.
		ii. Attending a self-advocacy meeting for the first time.
		
		i. When the learner is familiar with the items available (e.g., toys in the classroom).
		ii. Different types of materials for instruction.
		iii. Narrowing job interests to schedule job tryouts.
		iv. Touring housing options with a realtor.
		
		i. Scheduling sampling opportunities over several weeks with different presenters and activity partners.

154

5. Defining a response.	ii. Periodically introducing new sampling options into the routine.	ii. Trying out new restaurants or nightclubs as they open in the area.
	A. Discrete responses.	A. Approaching (i.e., reaching with hand in direction of sampling option).
	B. Multicomponent responses.	B. Manipulation for at least 30 seconds plus sustained eye contact with materials for at least 15 seconds, plus positive vocalizations while manipulating item.
	C. Collateral responses.	C. Task completion or social interaction with activity partner.
	D. Refusal responses.	D. Pushing item away, expelling item from mouth.
	E. Termination response.	E. Signing "finished," walking away from activity partner.
6. Identifying presenters and activity partners.	A. Selecting presenter/activity partners familiar with the learner.	A. Teacher, family member.
	B. Selecting presenters/activity partners typical to the setting or activity.	B. Inviting friends or family to accompany the learner to a new restaurant.
7. Presenting sampling options.	A. Number of items.	
	i. Developing familiarity with materials; teaching early approach/choice responses.	i. Single-item presentation (e.g., going to the movies).
	ii. Identifying preference hierarchies; offering more complex choice options.	ii. Paired-items presentation (e.g., markers or crayons) or group presentations (e.g., magazine rack at a bookstore or toys available in a play area).
	B. Access.	
	i. Typical to the sampling option or setting.	i. Going up for seconds at a buffet line.
	ii. Age-appropriate.	ii. Unlimited time for an adult, time-limited for a child.

FIGURE 6.1. Example of a systematic preference assessment plan for Pauola.

Systematic Preference Assessment Plan

Section 1. Assessment Purpose: (*1*) *To identify job task interests, in preparation for procuring two or more sites for community-based job training next year; and (2) to begin developing a resume for Pauola that illustrates her vocational skills.*

Section 2: Sampling Options

Category	Variation 1	Variation 2	Variation 3	Variation 4	Variation 5
Clerical	Photocopying	Organizing supply closets	Delivering messages/ materials to teachers	Cutting paper into memo- size scraps	Shredding confidential documents
Custodial	Wiping tables	Loading dishes in dishwasher	Laundry	Emptying garbage and recycling	Cleaning bathrooms
Food service	Setting up trays and silverware	Loading salad bar	Putting drinks in ice bucket	Setting up prepared sandwiches on counter	Serving hot food

Section 3: Location and Schedule

Site 1 (Presbyterian Church)	Site 2 (Food Mart)	Site 3 (Eisner & Co. Accounting)	Site 4 (Califon Chiropractic)
Mon: 8:35–10:15	12:25–2:35	——	——
Tues: ——	——	8:35–10:15	12:25–2:35
Wed: 12:25–2:35	8:35–10:15	——	——
Thurs: ——	——	12:25–2:35	8:35–10:15

Section 4: Response Definitions

Primary response	Definition	Collateral response	Definition
Engagement	Duration: Remains engaged in activity for at least 5 minutes.	Smiling	Pauola will smile and laugh when enjoying an activity.
Initiation	Latency: Approaches activity/ task within 15 seconds of teacher prompt or natural cue.	Positive vocalizations	High-pitched noises that sound likes squeaks or squeals are positive vocalizations.
Choice making	Selection: Points to a picture/ actual task when provided with a two-item choice.	Grinding/ grunting	Grinding teeth or deep grunting sounds indicate nonpreference

(cont.)

FIGURE 6.1. *(cont.)*

Section 4: Response Definitions *(cont.)*

Primary response	Definition	Collateral response	Definition
——	——	Frequent stops	Frequent stops in the middle of what she is doing, and not starting again until prompted, indicate nonpreference

Section 5: Presentation Procedures

1. For first-time activities, provide Pauola with a model of what the activity looks like. Then assist Pauola to briefly try each new activity.
2. Present Pauola with a choice of two activities and provide the verbal prompt, "Pauola, what would you like to do?"
3. Provide a 15-second delay for Pauola to make a choice.
4. Observe Pauola's response, using the primary and collateral definitions.
5. Provide Pauola with the activity she selects.
6. If no response, re-present the activity pair along with a model of what is required.
7. If no response, present a different activity option.
8. After Pauola responds to the choice pair, provide access to the activity.
9. Allow Pauola to continue engaging in the activity until the activity is completed or until she indicates that she wants to stop (see collateral definitions for nonpreference).
10. If the activity has no natural end, provide Pauola with an option to terminate the activity after 15 minutes of engagement, and then in 5-minute increments after that.
11. If Pauola initiates terminating the activity or does not seem to be enjoying what she is doing, provide her with a new activity choice pair.

ment. One-time assessments may produce information about what a person likes at that point in his or her life, but as time progresses it is likely that the person's preferences may evolve or change (Mason, McGee, Farmer-Dougan, & Risley, 1989). For example, many teachers have noted that "she used to love that," or "that used to be his favorite, but now he is not interested." To be current, preference assessments must be both updated and ongoing.

Defining a Response

A key component of systematic preference assessment is observing the focus person's response to items and events being sampled. It is this response that is then interpreted as an indicator of preference or nonpreference. In some ways, defining a response is a pivotal step in the assessment process. If a response is not clearly defined or well understood, the individual's intended meaning can easily be misinterpreted. Typically, researchers have either defined discrete responses (e.g., depressing a microswitch) or multicomponent responses (i.e., combinations of several discrete behaviors) (Hughes, Pitkin, & Lorden, 1998; Lohrmann-O'Rourke & Browder, 1998). Discrete responses are commonly used when the learner is asked to make a choice between two items. For example, as Section 4 of Figure 6.1 indicates, the criteria for preference in Pauola's case were that Pauola remain engaged for at least 5 minutes, approach the task within 15 seconds, and/or point to the picture or task. The evaluator also included some "collateral responses" that could indicate Pauola's preferences. Pauola would smile and laugh when enjoying an activity, but would grind her teeth or make grunting noises when displeased. As illustrated in Pauola's example, response definition will often include several behaviors as indicators. In their review of research, Hughes et al. (1998) noted that including collateral behaviors can enhance preference definitions and make it more likely that correct interpretations will be made. These collateral behaviors may include affect (as shown in Pauola's example), or may include task completion, problem behaviors, or pointing to or naming the task. By observing multiple responses, the evaluator is also more likely to determine dislikes as well as likes.

Identifying Presenters and Activity Partners

The extent to which assessment presenters and activity partners are familiar with and have a rapport with the learner has not been fully investigated. Nozaki and Mochizuki (1995) found that their participant's choice selections varied, depending upon the activity partner present. Although not conclusive, this study does indicate that assessment presenters may influence how the focus person responds to items and events being sampled. To make assessment as natural as possible, presenters and activity partners selected should be familiar with the learner and have a basis for rapport. Rapport is important to be sure that idiosyncratic communications are not overlooked (e.g., a student's patting the table to protest) and that the student is comfortable trying new options.

Presenting Sampling Options

Another planning decision is whether to offer the student one option at a time to sample or to set the preference assessment up in a choice format. In research on preference assessment, evaluators have used three formats: Items are presented individually, in pairs, or in array of three or more (Lohrmann-O'Rourke & Browder, 1998). Foster-Johnson, Ferro, and Dunlap (1994) presented one activity related to a child's IEP at a time, and then observed the extent to which the student interacted with and manipulated the materials. In another example, Dattilo and Rusch (1985) presented pairs of leisure activities, using microswitch activities and eye gaze as indicators of preference. In a final example, Windsor, Piche, and Locke (1994) presented an array of food and drink choices, observing the participant's choices. Presenting a single item at a time is beneficial when a learner has not developed choice-making skills or does not have any previous experience with the sampling option, but overall this type of presentation may be more time-consuming than paired or group presentations may be. Paired presentations can also help to shape early choice-making behaviors by pairing highly disparate choices (e.g., most and least preferred). DeLeon and Iwata (1996) note that preference hierarchies (i.e., first, second, and third choices) can be identified by presenting a group of items at one time, and then, as the individual makes a selection, removing the item from the array on the next offering. The presentation method will also need to match the type of item or event being sampled. For example, food and drink options can easily be paired, but events (e.g., extracurricular school activities) may need to be experienced individually.

Because the idea of a preference assessment is to "sample" options, the amount of access may be small. Grocery stores often offer a small sample of a beverage or food to entice a shopper to buy it, but they do not offer an entire serving. Similarly, movie previews offer a small sample of several options. In the same way, the evaluator will usually create opportunities to try small amounts of the food, materials, or activities. For example, Frank toured the baseball diamond and auto track at no financial cost on special days that were open to the public to encourage people to attend main events. From these tours, he could decide whether to invest the time and money to pursue these leisure events. Sometimes sampling is not feasible, and instead it is more normalized or informative to try an entire routine. To try out a job, it may be important to work an entire shift or several days; to try a school club, it may be important to experience an entire meeting; to try a new restaurant, the diner will usually order an entire meal.

Summary

To summarize how to plan a systematic preference assessment, Pauola's example in Figure 6.1 is reviewed briefly. The purpose (see Section 1 of Figure 6.1) was to begin selecting sites for community-based job training during her high school years. The sampling options were three types of jobs (see Section 2). For the next 2 years, Pauola would have the opportunity to repeat this sampling to select new options for the coming year. In this way, Pauola was building a resume of brief employment experiences prior to taking a part-time job in her last years of school (ages 18–21). Sampling tryouts were scheduled at times that met these criteria: (1) They were convenient to the employer, and (2) they were times when Pauola would be able to experience the typical activities of the site. As shown in Section 4, specific responses were defined to consider in determining Pauola's preferences, since she did not currently have a symbolic system of communication. Finally, as shown in Section 5, the teacher who developed this assessment wrote some specific guidelines to use with Pauola at the sites, since a job coach would be taking Pauola for these sampling sessions.

ASSESSING SKILLS AND OPPORTUNITIES IN SELF-DETERMINATION

The ability to act in self-determined ways stems from competency in several skill areas, as well as from environments that promote the use of these skills. Because self-determination is a complex, multifaceted concept, teachers may find it difficult to know how to promote it in educational contexts (Browder, Wood, Test, Karvonen, & Algozzine, in press). Research in which teachers were surveyed about this concept revealed that even though they viewed self-determination as an important educational outcome, most did not include goals related to this priority on their students' IEPs (Agran, Snow, &

Swaner, 1999). Although promoting self-determination is more than teaching a set of specific skills, this instruction can be an important starting point if the educational environment is also designed for students to use their new skills.

Wehmeyer, Agran, and Hughes (1998) have developed a conceptual model for self determination that can be useful in defining skills for IEP objectives. They describe self-determination as having the essential characteristics of autonomous functioning, self-regulation, psychological empowerment, and self-realization. Psychological empowerment and self-realization include outcomes such as self-understanding, self-awareness, and positive self-efficacy. Autonomous functioning and self-regulation include the following "skills" components: (1) decision making; (2) independent living, risk taking, and safety; (3) problem solving; (4) choice making; (5) goal setting and attainment; (6) self-observation, evaluation, and reinforcement; and (7) self-instruction (see Figure 6.2). (Components 6 and 7 are often collectively called "self-management.") In this text, independent living, risk taking, and safety are discussed in Chapters Nine and Ten. The other skills involved in autonomous functioning and self-regulation, together with self-advocacy (an aspect of psychological empowerment), are discussed below in further detail.

FIGURE 6.2. A conceptual model of self-determination, showing its essential characteristics and component elements. Solid lines show direct relationships; dashed lines show indirect relationships. From Wehmeyer, Agran, and Hughes (1998). Copyright 1998 by Paul H. Brookes Publishing Co., Inc, Reprinted with permission.

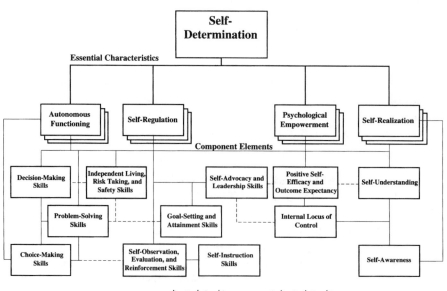

Published Curricula on Self-Determination

In recent years, numerous curricula on self-determination have been published (see Field, Martin, Miller, Ward, & Wehmeyer, 1998, or Wood, Test, Karvonen, Browder, & Algozzine, 1999, for summaries of these curricula). These curricula emphasize different perspectives on self-determination. Some focus on self-advocacy (Van Reusen & Bos, 1990), whereas others focus on skills such as planning, goal setting, and self-regulation (Martin & Huber-Marshall, 1995; Powers, 1998). A few focus on life skills such as home management, time management, budgeting, and occupational planning (Holub, 1995). Several of these curricula are shown in Table 6.2. These published curricula offer a starting point for planning self-determination instruction. In contrast, teachers will also need to personalize curricular goals, because these published guides often rely on academic and communication skills (e.g., reading a passage and discussing it) that make them too difficult for many students with moderate and severe disabilities. The following sections will help to make the skills components of self-determination achievable for students who do not have reading and conversation skills.

Self-Management

"Self-management" refers to an array of skill-based interventions used to change or maintain one's own behavior (Shapiro & Cole, 1994). Teaching a student the skills needed to change or maintain his or her own behavior is one strategy to promote self-determination. Although these strategies sometimes involve academic or symbolic communication skills, students with more severe disabilities can also acquire these skills when the specific responses to be used in self-management are properly adapted (Browder & Shapiro, 1985). Self-management interventions have been applied in a variety of situations, including employment, daily living situations, social/conversation settings, and school settings.

In using self-management, students often need to begin by learning to observe and record their own behavior, which is called "self-monitoring." For students who do not have writing skills, alternatives such as placing objects in slots or rings on a stick can be used instead of marking a tally when the behavior occurs. In their study on self-monitoring, Koegel and Koegel (1990) had children and adolescents with autism make a mark or affix a sticker following intervals where no stereotypical behavior occurred. An alarm watch signaled the end of an interval, and the students would then note whether or not they had engaged in the stereotypical behavior. At first the students needed the teacher's systematic prompting and reinforcement to perform this skill, but over time they were able to self-monitor without assistance. This self-awareness was an important step toward minimizing such behavior.

In the workplace, individuals often need to *increase* behavior—for example, to meet productivity standards. Employees may need not only to self-monitor, but also to use self-evaluation and goal setting to meet acceptable levels of productivity. "Self-evaluation" is a process of evaluating one's own performance compared to a standard or set objective. In teaching self-evaluation using a method that did not require counting skills, Grossi and Heward (1998) incorporated a shaded area on a recording form as a concrete visual representation of an established goal, against which participants

TABLE 6.2. Published Curricula on Self-Determination

Name of curriculum	Authors	Publisher and address
It's My Life: Preference-Based Planning for Self-Directed Goal Meetings	Emilee Curtis and Milly Dezelsky	New Hats, Inc. HC 64 Box 2509 Castle Valley, UT 84532 1-435-259-9400
Choicemaker Self-Determination Transition Curriculum: Take Action Choosing Employment Goals The Self-Directed IEP	Laura Huber-Marshall, James E. Martin, Laurie Lee Maxson, Patty Jerman	Sopris West, Inc. 4093 Specialty Place Longmont, CO 80504 1-800-547-6747
Self-Determination: The Road to Personal Freedom	Leslie Martin and Dale Carter	Self-Determination Team Protection and Advocacy System 1720 Louisiana N.E., Suite 204 Albuquerque, NM 87710 1-505-256-3100
Take Charge and Take Charge for the Future	Laurie Powers	Oregon Health Sciences University Child Development and Rehabilitation Center P.O. Box 574 Portland, OR 97202-0574 1-503-232-9154
The Self-Advocacy Strategy for Education and Transition Planning	Anthony Van Reusen, Candace Bos, Jean Schumaker, Donald Deschler	Edge Enterprises, Inc. P.O. Box 1304 Lawrence, KS 66044 1-785-749-1473
Steps to Self-Determination	Sharon Field and Alan Hoffman	Pro-Ed Publishing Company 8700 Shoal Creek Blvd. Austin, TX 78757-6897
Whose Future Is It Anyway?	Michael Wehmeyer and Kathy Kelchner	The Arc National Headquarters 500 East Border St., Suite 300 Arlington, TX 76010 1-888-368-8009
Next S.T.E.P.	A. S. Halpern, C. M. Herr, N. K. Wolf, J. E. Lawson, B. Doren, M. C. Johnson	Pro-Ed Publishing Company 8700 Shoal Creek Blvd. Austin, TX 78757-6897
Putting Feet on My Dreams: A Program in Self-Determination for Adolescents and Young Adults	Ann Fullerton	Dept. of Special and Counselor Education Portland State University P.O. Box 751 Portland, OR 97207-0751 1-503-725-4486
It's Your Choice: Planning for Life after High School	Gail Schwartz	Full Citizenship, Inc. 211 E. 8th St., Suite F Lawrence, KS 66044 1-785-749-0603

could compare their performance. Participants could then determine whether they had met the goal or needed to work faster. Depending on the flexibility of the workplace, workers may set their own goals for their performance during a certain time period (e.g., number of shelves to stock before break).

Another way to increase independence and productivity at the workplace is to reduce the need for trainer prompting and cueing. Grossi (1998) used a tape with music in the background to prompt participants on a variable (30- to 90-second) schedule to continue working. The auditory cue first asked whether the person was working; this was followed by a specific prompt to stay on task. The auditory prompt assisted participants to increase both the amount of time on task and the accuracy of task responses.

A third option is to use picture or sight word checklists. Traviss-Garff and Storey (1998) taught three adults in supported employment to maintain an appropriate appearance by following individualized multistep checklists illustrating how to complete their hygiene tasks. Training consisted of modeling each step on the checklist and then providing guided practice to promote independent use. The participants kept track of their performance by either checking off each step or keeping track on a calendar. When the adults met their goals, they self-selected and self-obtained a reinforcer (e.g., a crossword puzzle, a six-pack of soda). Similarly, Browder and Minarovic (2000) taught adults in supported employment to initiate jobs by following a sight word checklist. After mastering the sight words, participants used Agran and Moore's (1994) "did–next–now" strategy, in which they did a step, read the next step, and then performed the step.

Pictures can also be useful tools to help students self-initiate conversation. Hunt, Alwell, and Goetz (1988) taught three students in high school with limited verbal skills to use a communication book that included pictures and phrases of various topics to promote interaction with typical peers. A system of most to least intrusive prompts (consisting of physical, trainer proximity, and verbal prompts) was used to instruct the students to use the picture book and to take turns. In addition to successfully increasing appropriate interactions, the students also decreased inappropriate behaviors that had previously been occurring during social interactions.

Students who are verbal, or who use alternative communication systems, can be taught to use "self-instruction" or "self-talk" to keep a conversation going. Hughes, Harmer, Killian, and Niarhos (1995) taught high school students with mental retardation a self-instruction strategy to promote conversational interactions. The self-instruction strategy taught included (1) stating the problem ("I want to talk"), (2) stating the response ("I need to look and talk"), (3) evaluating the response ("I did, I talked"), and (4) self-reinforcement ("I did a good job"). These researchers found that it was important to teach self-instruction by using multiple exemplars (e.g., different settings and conversation partners) to promote generalization. In a follow-up study, Hughes, Killian, and Fischer (1996b) demonstrated that peers who were nondisabled could teach this self-instructional strategy to classmates with disabilities.

If the target skill has been mastered but is not used, the teacher may want to focus on self-reinforcement. For example, Newman, Buffington, and Hemmes (1996) used a self-reinforcement strategy to increase the appropriate conversation of adolescents with autism. In their investigation, participants initially received reinforcement (i.e., tokens that could be later exchanged for a preferred item or event) from the experimenters.

Then the participants learned to self-administer the tokens following appropriate conversation.

Another option for self-management is the use of a personalized schedule. Bambara and Ager (1992) taught three adults to self-schedule home- and community-based activities on their calendars. Using a task analysis, the instructor modeled each step of the scheduling activity and then provided each adult with corrective feedback. In addition to learning the scheduling routine, participants significantly increased the number and variety of self-directed activities selected.

Table 6.3 provides a summary of some of the self-management strategies, target skills, and common uses teachers may consider in targeting this area for the IEP.

Choice Making

Over the past decade, choice making has received increased attention among teachers and researchers. A body of research now demonstrates how individuals with moderate and severe disabilities make choices, and supports the advantages of increasing their opportunities to do so (Kern Vorndran et al., 1998). Sometimes students with severe disabilities need direct instruction to learn choice-making responses because of the lack of past opportunities to use this skill.

Brown, Belz, Corsi, and Wenig (1993) and Brown and Gothelf (1996) recommend embedding choice-making instruction in natural routines. These authors identify several types of choices available within typical routines:

- Choices within an activity (e.g., "Do you want the red or green marker?").
- Choices between two or more activities (e.g., bowling or a movies).
- Choices of when to start, terminate, or refuse to engage in an activity.
- Choices about who to do the activity with and where it will occur.

By using these guiding questions as a basis for designing choice-making instruction, teachers can expose students to a variety of different types of choices and can expand the sophistication of their choice-making skills.

To prepare for this choice-making instruction, Bambara and Koger (1996) recommend selecting options based on a learner's likes and identifying a choice-making response. The teacher can then select routines or activities to present the choice pairs, and can plan how to present the opportunities to use this response. The choice-making response may be highly individualized, depending on a student's current skills. For example, some students can point, others may reach toward an option, and still others may use eye gazing. Belfiore and Toro-Zambrana (1994) illustrate how to define this response for instruction by using a four-step task analysis:

1. Move the arm in the direction of the target object.
2. Make contact with the target stimulus.
3. Grasp the target object.
4. Manipulate the target object adaptively.

By defining choices as specific, observable behaviors, the teacher can assess the individual's level of independence and can plan systematic prompting if needed.

TABLE 6.3. Self-Management Skills

Self-management strategy	Examples of target skills for Instruction	Common applications
Self-instruction or self-prompting	• Specific verbal statements (e.g., "Stop, take a deep breath, keep looking"). • Following picture, audiotape, or sight word instructions.	• Acquisition of a new skill (e.g., to prepare a recipe, find a new classroom). • Increasing fluency of an existing skill (e.g., social interaction). • Generalizing learned skills to a new situation (e.g., checking hygiene at home and work).
Self-monitoring	• Recognizing the presence or absence of a target behavior. • Recording the behavior with a sticker on a picture chart, mark on a checklist, object in a bin, ring on a stick, etc.	• Reducing problem behaviors. • Using prior to self-evaluation (e.g., determining amount of work performed, number of times communication wallet used). • Encouraging self-awareness (may be sufficient to change behavior).
Self-evaluation	• Setting a goal (e.g., bin of towels to fold by break, folder of work to complete, number of rooms to clean in motel). • Comparing performance to goal (e.g., is bin/folder empty?). • Rating performance using a set standard (e.g., OK/not OK, thumbs up or down).	• Improving productivity at the workplace. • Completion of independent seatwork at school. • Achieving social goals like initiating conversation.
Self-reinforcement	• Recognizing reinforceable performance (e.g., OK or thumbs up). • Identifying a preferred reinforcer (e.g., pointing to object on shelf, selecting from picture, locating bag with treats, selecting sticker). • Obtaining the reinforcer.	• Acquisition of a new skill (e.g., if brushed teeth with only verbal prompts, put sticker on chart). • Maintenance of an existing skill (e.g., when completed all work in folder, find toy on shelf). • Maintenance of reductions in problem behavior (e.g., if kept hands to self during math, select fruit-scented marker or other special material to use during next lesson). • Maintenance of increases in desired behaviors (e.g., if kept pace with cashier while bagging groceries, have soda break).
Self-scheduling	• Selecting object, picture, or sight word for each activity. • Sequencing items for daily, weekly, or other schedule. • Following schedule by checking each item between activities (e.g., removing item to box after completed).	• Planning leisure activities. • Performing work tasks. • Keeping doctor appointments. • Following class schedule.

When a choice is abstract—for example, between settings or activities—the student may need to learn to associate a symbol with these options prior to being able to communicate a choice. Browder et al. (1998) demonstrated how to do this through a three-fold assessment and instructional process to teach choice making for leisure activities. The first step involved assessing each individual's activity preferences to select specific options. In this assessment, a teacher took a participant to different settings and timed the duration of his or her participation. Next, the researchers taught communicative labels for these newly identified preferences, using an object associated with each activity (e.g., a golf ball for golf, a library card for the library). Once the participants learned each object as a name for each activity, the participants were given the opportunity to use the objects to choose between two activities.

Another important dimension of choice making is the skill to request a change (in the activity, materials, etc.) when students do not like their initial selection. For example, Kennedy and Haring (1993) taught participants to make changes in leisure activities via a microswitch system. To teach this dimension of choice making, a pool of preferred activities was first identified. Using constant time delay, the participants were prompted to press a microswitch that activated a tape-recorded message requesting a change in the activity. All participants were successful in learning to use the microswitch to request activity changes. Figure 6.3 lists potential choice-making skills and serves as a planning chart for the team's use in developing the IEP.

Decision Making and Problem Solving

Although it is important for individuals with disabilities to make choices in the context of their daily routines, it is also important for them to have the skills and opportunities to make important life decisions and to solve problems when they arise. Kishi, Teelucksingh, Zollers, Park-Lee, and Meyer (1988) found that adults with disabilities were significantly less likely to have opportunities to make decisions about day-to-day events (e.g., what to wear) and life-planning events (e.g., whom to live with). Limited opportunities may stem from the perception that individuals with significant disabilities are not prepared to make decisions that affect their lives. In a study of perceptual and psychological factors that influence decision making, Wehmeyer (1993) found that students with disabilities were more likely to encounter barriers and experience anxiety during the decision-making process. Furthermore, these students relied on other people and external variables (e.g., luck and fate) to make decisions on their behalf (Wehmeyer, 1993). Consistent with Wehmeyer's findings, Hickson, Golden, Khemak, Urv, and Yamusah (1998) also found that individuals with disabilities were less prepared than their typical peers to use decision-making processes and were more likely to seek assistance from others. In addition, Wehmeyer and Kelchner (1994) found that adults with mental retardation had limited interpersonal cognitive problem-solving skills. Given these findings, decision-making and problem-solving skills may be crucial components of personalized curricula and IEPs for students with moderate and severe disabilities.

Problem solving, like choice making, can often be taught in the context of daily routines. Hughes, Hugo, and Blatt (1996a) taught problem solving to five high school students by using self-instruction and training across many examples in their daily routines. The steps the participants learned to use to solve each problem were as follows: (1) State the problem, (2) state the response, (3) self-evaluate, and (4) self-reinforce

FIGURE 6.3. Choice-making skills: Planning chart for targeting IEP goals.

Planning Chart for Choice-Making Skills

Choice-making skill	Examples	Priority for student's IEP?
1. When offered object, chooses it by looking at it, reaching for it, or asking for it.	• When shown jacket, looks at it until assisted to wear it. • When offered beverage, reaches toward glass.	
2. When offered highly preferred and strongly nonpreferred items, chooses preferred item: • Food • Clothing • School materials	• When offered juice (likes) versus water (dislikes), moves hand toward juice. • When shown poncho (likes) versus buttoned jacket (dislikes), looks at poncho.	
3. Protests if given nonpreferred item.	• Vocalizes loudly if teacher puts on wrong jacket. • Says "no" if given water.	
4. Chooses between two or more preferred items.	• Takes one cookie from assortment on tray. • Chooses one toy from closet.	
5. Chooses between activities by using sight words, pictures, or objects that represent the activities.	• Chooses whether to watch a video or take a walk, using miniature magnets (e.g., television vs. shoe). • Chooses whether to go for chicken or burger by pointing to logo of preferred restaurant.	
6. Requests a change in selection.	• Puts item down and reaches for another. • Indicates "no" after eating some of the chosen food and looks at other options on the table.	
7. Chooses when to do an activity and/or when to end it.	• Creates own object schedule for order to do chores. • Selects item from folder to do first. • Ends lesson by giving teacher "stop" card (without hitting).	
8. Chooses with whom to do an activity.	• Sits by peers of choice at lunch. • Helps select job coach.	

(Hughes et al., 1996a). Gomez and Bambara (1996) taught problem solving by having participants consider several alternatives in response to a problem situation. In this study, three adults living in group homes and supported living situations learned to use self-instruction statements (e.g., "Look in the closet," "Look under the sink," "Look next to the bed") to locate lost items during cooking, bathroom, and bedtime routines. The advantage of teaching participants to consider several options when they confront problems is that instruction can build on choice-making skills and may be more likely to achieve a solution. Agran and Wehmeyer (2000) recommend the following problem-solving training sequence that includes consideration of alternatives: (1) state the problem, (2) state one or more solutions, (3) verbally choose a solution or state the direction in which to proceed, (4) self-evaluate, and (5) self-reinforce. Box 6.2 provides two examples of how similar problem-solving strategies might be used.

Obviously, not all decision making occurs in response to problems. In a problem situation, the solution is usually not immediately obvious. Some alternatives need to be tried. In contrast, in a decision, one or more alternatives may be apparent, but the person is not sure which is best. It can be difficult to select from a wide range of appealing items on a menu, or from several different types of shoes, it can be even more difficult to make decisions such as whether or not to take an available job. Individuals with moderate and severe disabilities may lack both the information needed to make a decision and the skills to compare options and make a selection. Foxx et al. (1993) and Faw, Davis, and Peck (1996) provide two examples of how to teach individuals with disabilities to assess and evaluate residential options. To assess the availability of lifestyle preferences, Foxx et al. (1993) developed lifestyle preference photo albums for each participant. The albums contained pictures of preferences that were determined by conducting a systematic preference assessment with each participant. For instance, a

---

BOX 6.2. Learning to Solve Problems: Two Examples

Example for a Student Who Is Verbal

1. *Define the problem:* "I want to go to the homecoming game, but I don't have a ride."
2. *Consider alternatives:* "Ride with my sister Janice; ask Mom to take me; ask one of my lunch buddies if I can go with them."
3. *Select one solution:* "Ask my sister Janice. If she won't do it, ask a lunch buddy."
4. *Self-evaluate:* "Janice said no; I asked my lunch buddy Peter; he said yes."
5. *Self-reinforce:* "I did it!"

Example for a Student Who Uses Nonsymbolic Communication

1. *Identify the problem:* Pauses when discovers restroom door will not open.
2. *Try alternatives:* Try again; wait for someone to exit if restroom is in use; get key from classroom; use another restroom (but not hit or yell).
3. *Experience effect:* Walk through open door.

participant might want to live in an apartment near a bus line with a roommate. Via modeling and role playing, the participants were taught to ask questions about available residential options by using the picture album as a permanent prompt (e.g., "Is it near a bus stop?"). Individuals who do not have the skills needed to rate options can still learn decision making. Helping students select pictures to develop a holiday menu can help shape their skills in decision making. Also, helping individuals develop their own books about likes and dislikes can later be used in helping them make decisions. Figure 6.4 is an example of a discrepancy analysis chart that can be used to evaluate a student's problem-solving and decision-making skills

Leadership, Life Planning, and Goal Setting

In a follow-up study of positive adult outcomes, Wehmeyer and Schwartz (1997) found that students engaging in self-determined behaviors were more likely to experience positive postschool outcomes 1 year after graduation. Although a possible link between positive adult outcomes and self-determined behavior exists (Wehmeyer & Schwartz, 1997), Grigal, Test, Beattie, and Wood (1997) found that students with moderate and severe disabilities were less likely to be responsible for carrying out plan components, despite having advocacy and legal activities included in their transition plans. One explanation may be that some students with disabilities lack the ability to lead their teams to set goals, plan for goal achievement, and implement plan components. Even when these skills exist, barriers in the environment may prevent full participation. For example, Whitney-Thomas et al. (1998) found that students were more likely to participate in planning meetings when the size and structure of the meetings were matched to the learners' conversational style.

Despite the importance of teaching leadership and goal-setting skills, very few empirical examples exist to guide recommendations. However, several curricula are available that include strategies and lessons for teaching leadership and goal-planning skills. For example, the Self-Directed IEP (Martin, Huber-Marshall, Maxson, & Jerman, 1996) and the other components of the Choicemaker Self-Determination Curriculum (Martin & Huber-Marshall, 1995) encourage teaching a student to develop skills such as beginning the meeting by stating its purpose, asking for feedback from team members, and closing the meeting by summarizing decisions. Wehmeyer et al. (1998) also recommend using planning meetings as a forum for learning leadership skills. They stress instruction in several areas, including running a meeting (e.g., using teamwork and participation skills, staying on topic, listening without interrupting) and developing good group dynamics skills (e.g., clarifying questions and answers).

Self-Advocacy

Cunconan-Lahr and Brotherson (1996) defined "self-advocacy" as occurring when "people speak or act on their own behalf to improve their quality of life, effect personal change, or correct inequities" (p. 352). Although many service providers believe that developing self-advocacy skills are important, the perception that individuals with disabilities may not possess the ability to develop and use these skills is a barrier created by the service system (Wolfe, Ofiesh, & Boone, 1996). Despite the existence of federal mandates (e.g., the Americans with Disabilities Act), many individuals with disabilities

FIGURE 6.4. A discrepancy analysis chart to plan instruction in problem solving and decision making. (The student described here, Cathy, is not a real person).

Discrepancy Analysis Chart for Problem Solving/Decision Making

Effective problem-solving steps	Student's current response	Skills to target for instruction
1. Identify the problem.	Cathy becomes passive when she encounters a problem on her job site. She sits until told what to do next.	Teach Cathy to pause only briefly before using problem-solving steps.
2. Identify alternatives.	Cathy is nonverbal and cannot state alternatives.	Have Cathy demonstrate at least two things she could do next for several problems that she has encountered.
3. Try one alternative as a solution.	Cathy does not initiate until someone else solves the problem.	Prompt and praise Cathy for trying one or more alternatives, even if she is not successful on the first try.
4. Self-evaluate whether solution was effective.	Cathy has not experienced this because she has not initiated solutions. She will not be able to communicate her solution verbally.	Teach Cathy to use a thumbs-up sign when something she tries works.

Effective decision-making steps	Student's current response	Skills to target for instruction
1. Identify the decision to be made.	Cathy does not seem to realize that she will need to decide whether to stay in this job tryout or change to a new site next month.	Help Cathy create a decision poster showing her in this job or a new option (shown with blank space and question mark).
2. Identify the options.	Cathy has not experienced any other job tryout—this is her first site.	Take Cathy on a tour of other sites and have her take pictures of them for her decision poster. Show her how each one of these could be placed in the blank spot on her poster.
3. Review own likes and dislikes to know how to decide.	Cathy has made a scrapbook with pictures and symbols of likes and dislikes.	Help Cathy match her pictures to her "likes" in her scrapbook.
4. Make the decision.	Cathy may not fully understand the implications of this decision (i.e., that she won't go back next month if she chooses another option).	Have Cathy put one picture on the poster and arrange for her to try this site.
5. Evaluate the decision.	If Cathy is pleased, she will work. If not, she will sit and resist any prompting.	This silent protest actually works well in letting people know when she is displeased. If she is displeased, use problem solving to help her initiate what to do next.

do not feel the sense of empowerment needed to pursue their rights (Brotherson, Cook, Cunconan-Lahr, & Wehmeyer, 1995). Systemic barriers offer one explanation for why many individuals with disabilities do not act on their own behalf; personal characteristics (e.g., disability severity) of the focus individuals offer another (Wolfe et al., 1996). Although systemic barriers are often difficult to overcome, personal characteristics can be enhanced to provide the focus individuals with both the skills and motivation needed to act on their own behalf. For example, Cunconan-Lahr and Brotherson (1996) recommend training advocacy skills in three areas: (1) using effective communication; (2) locating others with similar advocacy needs; and (3) developing personal characteristics (e.g., self-confidence) that promote advocacy. In addition to these skill areas, Wehmeyer et al. (1998) recommend teaching learners about their rights. For example, high school students should understand the legal requirements for an effective transition plan, as well as their right to make their own educational decisions at the age of majority (e.g., whether to continue in school after age 18). Adults should understand about laws such as the Fair Housing Act amendments of 1988 (Brotherson et al., 1995).

PROMOTING SELF-DETERMINATION IN THE EDUCATIONAL ENVIRONMENT

Teaching skills that enable a learner to act in self-determined ways is an important component of the instructional process. A second critical feature is the extent to which the learning environment creates opportunities for the student to use those skills, and also supports and honors expressions of self-determination. The teacher who has the goal of promoting self determination can conduct an ecological inventory of the classroom and school, and can ask questions such as those shown in Table 6.4. Several of these variables are now described in more detail.

TABLE 6.4. Inventory of Educational Environments to Consider Ways to Promote Self-Determination

IEP meetings

1. Do all students attend their IEP meetings?
2. Are students being taught to participate in, and (when possible) lead, their meetings?
3. Does the meeting format encourage a student's participation?
4. Are the student's preferences incorporated throughout the planning process?
5. Does the IEP contain skills in self-determination?

Instruction

1. Does the student have ongoing opportunities to make choices in daily routines?
2. Does the student receive instruction in self-determination skills?
3. Is the student encouraged to use self-directed learning strategies?
4. Is prompting designed to encourage independence/not prompt dependency?

Classroom and school environment

1. Do students have the opportunity to make decisions about school and classroom activities?
2. Are students involved in solving problems that arise?
3. Are there opportunities for students with moderate and severe disabilities to develop leadership skills?
4. Do students have a way to protest policies and decisions they dislike?

Availability of Choice- and Decision-Making Opportunities

Everyday Choices and Decisions

Adults and children with disabilities are less likely to have frequent and diverse choice options available to them (Houghton, Bronicki, & Guess, 1987; Kishi et al., 1988; Stancliffe & Wehmeyer, 1995). In response, several researchers have begun investigating the effects of choice making on various behaviors, as well as ways to integrate choice-making opportunities within a learner's typical day (Bambara, Koger, Katzer, & Davenport, 1995; Kern et al., 1998; Lancioni, O'Reilly, & Emerson, 1996). Bambara et al. (1995) illustrated how to embed choice opportunities throughout an individual's day by identifying typical and routine activities and creating choice options in task analyses for vacuuming, dusting, and dessert preparation. For example, when washing hands before cooking, a participant was offered liquid or bar soap. During a dusting routine, the participant was offered a choice of spray polish or a pretreated dust cloth.

Moes (1998) offered numerous choices during a homework routine, such as selecting the homework assignment, choosing what problem to do first, determining what materials (e.g., markers or pencil) to use, and so forth. Higher rates of correct responding and fewer rates of problem behaviors were observed for all three children who participated. Similar positive results have been found for providing a choice of tasks (e.g., Dunlap et al., 1994; Dunlap, Kern-Dunlap, Clarke, & Robbins, 1991; Seybert, Dunlap, & Ferro, 1996), of preferred activities (e.g., Koegel, Dyer, & Bell, 1987), and of response options (e.g., Peck, 1985).

Lohrmann-O'Rourke and Yurman (in press) gave participants the opportunity to make a change in the materials selected by repeatedly (i.e., once every minute) offering choices throughout the session. These researchers offered the participants the opportunity to continue with the previously selected option or to select a new activity option. They found that the participants made diverse choices from session to session (e.g., choosing the same item repeatedly in one session vs. choosing lots of different items in another session).

Life-Planning Decisions and Choices

Offering relatively simple choices throughout the day can have a tremendous impact on the development of self-determination. But it is also important to create opportunities for choices and decisions that affect life planning. Less research has been conducted on this important topic. Winking, O'Reilly, and Moon (1993) illustrated how to consider preferences to create good job matches for individuals who were not able to communicate their employment choices directly. By creating ways for the individuals to sample a variety of jobs, the researchers were able to infer their employment preferences from their responses on the job sites. Having learners involved in developing their own IEPs or transition plans, as described earlier in this chapter, can also help promote life planning.

Prompting Strategies

Systematic instruction is an effective instructional methodology to promote acquisition of target skills (Wolery & Schuster, 1997). However, overly intrusive prompting systems may create a dependency on caregivers or instructors. When instructors introduce prompting and feedback, they run the risk of creating barriers to the development of self-determination (Brown & Gothelf, 1996; Brown et al., 1998). Prompting systems that promote self-determination contain three important characteristics. First, the prompts selected are the least intrusive possible and are carefully matched to an individual's learning style. It may be possible to provide an indirect verbal prompt (e.g., "What's next?") in place of a direct verbal prompt (e.g., "Turn on the vacuum"). Second, the instructor allows a sufficient latency period prior to providing a prompt. Some learners may need additional time to process events in their environment. Third, in using the prompt system, the instructor is careful to pace the use of multiple cues. Prompts provided in rapid succession may be difficult to process and confuse an individual, resulting in either an incorrect response or no response at all. If unaware of this, the instructor may provide a more intrusive prompt (e.g., physical assistance) to assist the person to complete the step, when in fact a more deliberately paced presentation of prompts may be preferable.

Task Analyses

As described in Chapter Four, task analyses are common instructional tools for teaching a wide range of skills. The purpose of a task analysis is to break a given activity into discrete component steps for instruction (i.e., what is done first, second, etc.). Each step is defined as an observable and measurable response. Brown and Gothelf (1996) note that a task analysis can either effectively promote self-determination (e.g., by including choice and initiation responses) or inhibit self-determination (e.g., by including only instructor-directed steps). In their research, Bambara et al. (1995) and Cooper and Browder (1998) have illustrated how to embed choice opportunities into typical task analyses. These researchers took everyday activities such as purchasing and washing hands, and created choice opportunities for each step of each task analysis. Table 6.5 compares two task analyses for toothbrushing, a common instructional activity. The first task analysis is completely instructor-driven, with little opportunity for self-initiation or choice. In contrast, the second task analysis incorporates opportunities for the

TABLE 6.5. Standard and Choice Task Analyses

Standard task analysis	Choice task analysis
1. Go to bathroom.	1. Brush teeth now or after breakfast.
2. Pick up brush.	2. Select a bathroom (upstairs or downstairs).
3. Wet brush.	3. Pick up brush.
4. Put toothpaste on brush.	4. Wet brush.
5. Brush teeth.	5. Select toothpaste flavor.
6. Spit toothpaste out.	6. Put toothpaste on brush.
7. Rinse toothbrush.	7. Brush teeth.
8. Put toothbrush in holder.	8. Spit toothpaste out.
9. Rinse mouth.	9. Rinse brush first or rinse mouth first.
10. Wipe mouth with towel.	10. Complete the second choice (mouth or brush).
	11. Put brush away.
	12. Select towel to wipe mouth.
	13. Wipe mouth.

learner to select materials, locations, and the time to begin. In addition to the construction of the task analysis, the order in which steps are followed can either promote or inhibit self-determination. Many routines include some flexibility in the sequence of responding. For example, in the choice task analysis shown in Table 6.5, the student can decide whether to rinse the brush or mouth first.

SUMMARY

Self-determination becomes an important part of the ecological assessment process in two ways. First, to be "person-centered," the team will be sure to include the student by having him or her physically present and by considering the student's preferences in all planning efforts. If feasible, an older student should lead the planning sessions. Some students may be able to share this leadership with a facilitator by calling the meeting to order and showing pictures to initiate the topics to be discussed. The meeting should also be designed to encourage the student's participation. This may be achieved by planning the meeting with the student and by focusing the group on the student's comments and preferences. Sometimes identifying the student's preferences will require systematic preference assessment. This chapter has described in detail how to design a systematic preference assessment. The evaluator needs to determine the assessment purpose, options that can be chosen, and the general format for this process. The meaningfulness of systematic preference assessment depends on whether these options and format are relevant to the student's daily life.

The second way self-determination is considered in the ecological assessment process is in identifying specific skills to target for the IEP. This chapter has provided specific examples of skills in self-management; choice making; problem solving and decision making; leadership and goal setting; and self-advocacy. Although published curricula exist that can serve as guides in planning this instruction, teachers may need to adapt these resources for students with more significant disabilities.

Teaching students self-determination skills will only produce important outcomes if students have the opportunity to use these responses daily in their educational environments. The last part of this chapter has described ways that teachers can encourage the use of self-determination in their daily classroom and school environments.

REFERENCES

Agran, M., & Moore, S. (1994). *How to teach self-instruction of job skills (Innovations No. 3).* Washington, DC: American Association on Mental Retardation.

Agran, M., Snow, K. & Swaner, J. (in press). Teacher perceptions of self-determination: Benefits, characteristics, strategies. *Education and Training in Mental Retardation and Developmental Disabilities, 34,* 293–301.

Agran, M., & Wehmeyer, M. (1999). *Teaching problem solving to students with mental retardation (Innovations No. 15).* Washington, DC: American Association on Mental Retardation.

Bambara, L. M., & Ager, C. (1992). Using self-scheduling to promote self-directed leisure activity in home and community settings. *Journal of the Association for Persons with Severe Handicaps, 17,* 67–76.

Bambara, L. M., Cole, C. L., & Koger, F. (1998). Translating self-determination concepts into support for adults with severe disabilities. *Journal of the Association for Persons with Severe Handicaps, 23*, 27–37.

Bambara, L. M., & Koger, F. (1996). *Opportunities for daily choice making (Innovations No. 8)*. Washington, DC: American Association on Mental Retardation.

Bambara, L. M., Koger, F., Katzer, T., & Davenport, T. A. (1995). Embedding choice in the context of daily routines: An experimental case study. *Journal of the Association for Persons with Severe Handicaps, 20*, 185–195.

Belfiore, P. J., Browder, D. M., & Mace, C. (1994). Assessing choice-making and preference in adults with profound mental retardation across community and center-based settings. *Journal of Behavioral Education, 4*, 217–225.

Belfiore, P. J., & Toro-Zambrana, W. (1994). *Recognizing choices in community settings by people with significant disabilities (Innovations No. 2)*. Washington, DC: American Association on Mental Retardation.

Brotherson, M. J., Cook, C. C., Cunconan-Lahr, R., & Wehmeyer, M. L. (1995). Policy supporting self-determination in the environments of children with disabilities. *Education and Training in Mental Retardation and Developmental Disabilities, 30*, 3–14.

Browder, D. M., Cooper, K., & Lim, L. (1998). Teaching adults with severe disabilities to express their choice of settings for leisure activities. *Education and Training in Mental Retardation and Developmental Disabilities, 33*, 228–238.

Browder, D. M., & Minarovic, T. (2000). Using sight words and self-management to teach supported employees to follow a schedule. *Education and Training in Mental Retardation and Developmental Disabilities, 35*, 78–89.

Browder, D. M., & Shapiro, E. (1985). Application of self-management to individuals with severe handicaps: A review. *Journal of the Association for Persons with Severe Handicaps, 10*, 200–208.

Browder, D. M., Wood, W. M., Test, D. W., Karvonen, M., & Algozzine, B. (in press). A map for teachers to follow in reviewing resources on self-determination. *Remedial and Special Education*.

Brown, F., & Cohen, S. (1996). Self-determination and young children. *Journal of the Association for Persons with Severe Handicaps, 21*, 22–30.

Brown, F., Belz, P., Crosi, L., & Wenig, B. (1993). Choice diversity for people with severe disabilities. *Education and Training in Mental Retardation, 28*, 318–326.

Brown, F., & Gothelf, C. R. (1996). Self-determination for all individuals. In D. H. Lehr & F. Brown (Eds.), *People with disabilities who challenge the system* (pp. 99–121). Baltimore: Paul H. Brookes.

Brown, F., Gothelf, C. R., Guess, D., & Lehr, D. H. (1998). Self-determination for individuals with the most severe disabilities: Moving beyond chimera. *Journal of the Association for Persons with Severe Handicaps, 23*, 17–26

Cooper, K. J., & Browder, D. M. (1998). Enhancing choice and participation for adults with severe disabilities in community-based instruction. *Journal of the Association for Persons with Severe Handicaps, 23*, 252–260.

Cunconan-Lahr, R., & Brotherson, M. J. (1996). Advocacy in disability policy: Parents and consumers as advocates. *Mental Retardation, 34*, 352–358.

Dattilo, J., & Rusch, F. R. (1985). Effects of choice on leisure participation for persons with severe handicaps. *Journal of the Association for Persons with Severe Handicaps, 4*, 194–199.

DeLeon, I. G., & Iwata, B. A. (1996). Evaluation of a multiple-stimulus presentation format for assessing reinforcer preferences. *Journal of Applied Behavior Analysis, 29*, 519–534.

Dunlap, G., dePerczel, M., Clarke, S., Wison, D., Wright, S., White, R., & Gomez, A. (1994). Choice making to promote adaptive behavior for students with emotional and behavioral challenges. *Journal of Applied Behavior Analysis, 27*, 505–518.

Dunlap, G., Kern-Dunlap, L., Clarke, S., & Robbins, F. R. (1991). Functional assessment, curricular revision, and severe behavior problems. *Journal of Applied Behavior Analysis, 24*, 387–397.

Faw, G. D., Davis, P. K., & Peck, C. (1996). Increasing self-determination: Teaching people with mental retardation to evaluate residential options. *Journal of Applied Behavior Analysis, 29*, 173–188.

Field, S., & Hoffman, A. (1994). Development of a model for self-determination. *Career Development for Exceptional Learners, 17,* 159–169.

Foster-Johnson, L., Ferro., J., & Dunlap, G. (1994). Preferred curricular activities and reduced problem behaviors in students with intellectual disabilities. *Journal of Applied Behavior Analysis, 27,* 493–504.

Foxx, R. M., Faw, G. D., Taylor, S., Davis, P. K., & Fulia, R. (1993). "Would I be able to . . . ?": Teaching clients to assess the availability of their community lifestyle preferences. *American Journal of Mental Retardation, 98,* 235–248.

Gomez, O., & Bambara, L. M. (1996). *Teaching complex problem solving using multiple exemplars.* Paper presented at the annual convention of the Association for Persons with Severe Handicaps, New Orleans, LA.

Green, C. W., Reid, D. H., Canipe, V. S., & Gardner, S. M. (1991). A comprehensive evaluation of reinforcer identification process for persons with profound multiple handicaps. *Journal of Applied Behavior Analysis, 24,* 537–552.

Green, C. W., Reid, D. H., White, L. K., Halforn, R. C., Brittain, D. P., & Gardner, S. M. (1988). Identifying reinforcers for person with profound handicaps: Staff opinion versus systematic assessment of preferences. *Journal of Applied Behavior Analysis, 2,* 31–43.

Grigal, M., Test, D. W., Beattie, J., & Wood, W. M. (1997). An evaluation of transition components of individualized education programs. *Exceptional Children, 63,* 357–372.

Grossi, T. A. (1998). Using a self-operated auditory prompting system to improve the work performance of two employees with severe disabilities. *Journal of the Association for Persons with Severe Handicaps, 23,* 149–154.

Grossi, T. A., & Heward, W. L. (1998). Using self-evaluation to improve the work productivity of trainees in a community-based restaurant training program. . *Education and Training in Mental Retardation and Developmental Disabilities, 33,* 248–263.

Hickson, L., Golden, H., Khemka, I., Urv, T., & Yamusah, S. (1998). A closer look at interpersonal decision-making in adults with and without mental retardation. *American Journal of Mental Retardation, 103,* 209–224.

Holub, T. (1995). *Becoming self-determined.* Madison, WI: Madison Metropolitan School District.

Houghton, J., Bronicki, G. J., & Guess, D. (1987). Opportunities to express preferences and make choices among students with severe disabilities in classroom settings. *Journal of the Association for Persons with Severe Handicaps, 12,* 18–27.

Hughes, C., Harmer, M. L., Killian, D. J., & Niarhos, F. (1995). The effects of multiple-exemplar self-instructional training on high school students' generalized conversational interaction. *Journal of Applied Behavior Analysis, 28,* 201–218.

Hughes, C., Hugo, K., & Blatt, J. (1996a). Self-instructional intervention for teaching generalized problem-solving within a functional task sequence. *American Journal of Mental Retardation, 100,* 565–579.

Hughes, C., Killian, D. J., & Fischer, G. M. (1996b). Validation and assessment of a conversational interaction intervention. *American Journal of Mental Retardation, 100,* 493–509.

Hughes, C., Pitkin, S. E., & Lorden, S. W. (1998). Assessing preferences and choice of persons with severe mental retardation. *Education and Training in Mental Retardation and Developmental Disabilities, 33,* 299–316.

Hunt, P., Alwell, M., & Goetz, L. (1988). Acquisition of conversation skills and the reduction of inappropriate social interaction behaviors. *Journal of the Association for Persons with Severe Handicaps, 13,* 20–27.

Kamii, C. (1991). Toward autonomy: The importance of critical thinking and choice making. *School Psychology Review, 20,* 382–388.

Kennedy, C. H., & Haring, T. G. (1993). Teaching choice making during social interactions to students with profound multiple disabilities. *Journal of Applied Behavior Analysis, 26,* 63–76.

Kern, L., Vorndran, C. M., Hilt, A., Ringdahl, J. E., Adelman, B. E., & Dunlap, G. (1998). Choice as an intervention to improve behavior: A review of the literature. *Journal of Behavioral Education, 8*, 151–169.

Kishi, G., Teelucksingh, B., Zollers, N., Park-Lee, S., & Meyer, L. (1988). Daily decision making in community residences: A social comparison of adults with and without mental retardation. *American Journal of Mental Retardation, 92*, 430–435.

Koegel, R. L., Dyer, K., & Bell, L. K. (1987). The influence of child-preferred activities on autistic children's social behavior. *Journal of Applied Behavior Analysis, 20*, 243–252.

Koegel, R. L., & Koegel, L. K. (1990). Extended reductions in stereotypic behavior of students with autism through a self-management treatment package. *Journal of Applied Behavior Analysis, 23*, 119–127.

Koger, F., & Bambara, L. M. (1995). *Teaching adults to direct their own planning meeting*. Paper presented at the 21st annual convention of the Association for Applied Behavior Analysis, Washington, DC.

Lancioni, G. E., O'Reilly, M. F., & Emerson, E. (1996). A review of choice research with people with severe and profound developmental disabilities. *Research in Developmental Disabilities, 17*, 391–411.

Lohrmann-O'Rourke, S., & Browder, D. M. (1998). Empirically based methods to assess the preferences of individuals with severe disabilities. *American Journal of Mental Retardation, 103*, 146–161.

Lohrmann-O'Rourke, S., Browder, D. M., & Brown, F. (in press). The search for meaningful outcomes: Guidelines for socially valid systematic preference assessments. *Journal of the Association for Persons with Severe Handicaps.*

Lohrmann-O'Rourke, S., & Yurman, B. (in press). Assessment and intervention of mouthing behaviors with a young boy with multiple disabilities: The influence of establishing operations. *Journal of Positive Behavioral Intervention, 3.*

Martin, J. E., & Huber-Marshall, L. (1995) Choicemaker: A comprehensive self-determination transition program. *Intervention in School and Clinic, 30*(3), 147–156.

Martin, J. E., Huber-Marshall, L., Maxson, L. L., & Jerman, P. (1996). *Self-Directed IEP.* Longmont, CO: Sopris West.

Mason, S. A., McGee, G. G., Farmer-Dougan, V., & Risely, T. R. (1989). A practical strategy for ongoing reinforcer assessment. *Journal of Applied Behavior Analysis, 22*, 171–179.

Moes, D. R. (1998). Integrating choice-making opportunities within teacher-assigned academic tasks to facilitate the performance of children with autism. *Journal of the Association for Persons with Severe Handicaps, 23*, 319–328.

Newman, B., Buffington, D. M., & Hemmes, N. S. (1996). Self-reinforcement used to increase the appropriate conversation of autistic teenagers. *Education and Training in Mental Retardation and Developmental Disabilities, 31*, 304–309.

Nirje, B. (1972). The right to self-determination. In W. Wolfensberger (Ed.), *The principle of normalization in human services* (pp. 176–193). Toronto: Leonard Crainford.

Nozaki, K., & Mochizuki, A. (1995). Assessing choice making of a person with profound disabilities: A preliminary analysis. *Journal of the Association for Persons with Severe Handicaps, 20*, 196–201.

Palmer, S. B., & Wehmeyer, M. L. (1998). Students' expectations of the future: Hopelessness as a barrier to self-determination. *Mental Retardation, 36*, 128–136.

Parsons, M. B., & Reid, D. H. (1990). Assessing food preferences among persons with profound mental retardation: Providing opportunities to make choices. *Journal of Applied Behavior Analysis, 23*, 183–195.

Peck, C. A. (1985). Increasing opportunities for social control by children with autism and severe handicaps: Effects on student behavior and perceived classroom climate. *Journal of the Association for Persons with Severe Handicaps, 10*, 183–193.

Powers, L. (1998) *Take Charge.* Portland: Oregon Health Science University.

Seybert, S., Dunlap, G., & Ferro, J. (1996). The effects of choice-making on the problem behaviors of high school students with intellectual disabilities. *Journal of Behavioral Education, 6*, 49–65.

Shapiro, E. S., & Cole, C. L. (1994). *Behavior change in the classroom: Self-management interventions.* New York: Guilford Press.

Stancliffe, R., & Wehmeyer, M. L. (1995). Variability in the availability of choice to adults with mental retardation. *Journal of Vocational Rehabilitation, 5,* 319–328.

Traviss-Garff, J., & Storey, K. (1998). The use of self-management strategies for increasing the appropriate hygiene of persons with disabilities in supported employment settings. *Education and Training in Mental Retardation and Developmental Disabilities, 33,* 179–188.

Van Reusen, A. K., & Bos, C. S. (1990). I-PLAN: Helping students communicate in planning conferences. *Teaching Exceptional Children, 23*(4), 30–32.

Wehmeyer, M. L. (1993). Perceptual and psychological factors in career decision-making of adolescents with and without cognitive disabilities. *Career Development for Exceptional Individuals, 16,* 135–146.

Wehmeyer, M. L. (1998). Self-determination and individuals with significant disabilities: Examining the meaning and misinterpretations. *Journal of the Association for Persons with Severe Handicaps, 23,* 5–16.

Wehmeyer, M. L., Agran, M., & Hughes, C. (1998). *Teaching self-determination to students with disabilities: Basic skills for successful transition.* Baltimore: Paul H. Brookes.

Wehmeyer, M. L., & Kelchner, K. (1994). Interpersonal cognitive problem-solving skills of individuals with mental retardation. *Education and Training in Mental Retardation and Developmental Disabilities, 29,* 265–279.

Wehmeyer, M. L., & Schwartz, M. (1997). Self-determination and positive adult outcomes: A follow up study of youth with mental retardation or learning disabilities. *Exceptional Children, 63,* 245–256.

Whitney-Thomas, J., Shaw, D., Honey, K., & Butterworth, J. (1998). Building a future: A study of student participation in person-centered planning. *Journal of the Association for Persons with Severe Handicaps, 23,* 119–133.

Windsor, J., Piche, L. M., & Locke, P. A. (1994). Preference testing: A comparison of two presentation methods. *Research in Developmental Disabilities, 15,* 439–455.

Winking, D. L., O'Reilly, B., & Moon, M. S. (1993). Preference: The missing link in the job match process for individuals without functional communication skills. *Journal of Vocational Rehabilitation, 3,* 27–42.

Wolery, M., & Schuster, J. W. (1997). Instructional methods with students who have significant disabilities. *Journal of Special Education, 31,* 61–79.

Wolfe, P. S., Ofiesh, N. S., & Boone, R. S. (1996). Self-advocacy preparation of consumers with disabilities: A national perspective of ADA training efforts. *Journal of the Association for Persons with Severe Handicaps, 21,* 81–87.

Wood, W., Test, D., Karvonen, M., Browder, D., & Algozzine, R. (1999). Resource list. In *Self Determination National Synthesis Project, University of North Carolina at Charlotte* [Online]. Available: http://www. uncc. edu/sdsp [July 26, 2000].

SEVEN

Functional Reading

WHEN JULIANNE[1] BEGAN SCHOOL, *it was difficult to predict what academic skills she would master. Because of her severe problem behavior, developmental delay, and unusual speech patterns, she received several diagnoses over the years. At age 7, her teachers provided Julianne with instruction from a basal reading series, but it soon became clear that this approach was ineffective for her. They then tried using a series designed for literacy that used a direct instruction approach. Julianne received daily, intensive instruction in either a small-group or 1:1 format. Although she would learn some components of the lessons, these were quickly forgotten. When Julianne was 12, she was still on the first-grade reading level. Although she enjoyed reading lessons, her lack of progress discouraged both her parents and teachers.*

Julianne's middle school teacher suggested that while they should not give up on literacy, Julianne should also have the opportunity to learn words useful in daily living. This new focus on functional words "clicked" for Julianne. She began not only to learn to read words from flash cards, but to recognize and use these words in the community. For example, at a fast-food restaurant, she read "Whopper" and began to say, "I want Whopper." She also began to read her teachers' names and other words in her school environment. Julianne's high school teacher tried linking these familiar words into simple stories (e.g., "I go to Burger King. I get a Whopper") and had some success with getting Julianne to read passages. By the time Julianne was 18, she had an excellent sight word vocabulary. She could find items on a grocery list and look up some entries in the Yellow Pages (e.g., "pizza"). Although she never learned to read books, Julianne gained important reading skills for adult living.

This chapter describes an approach for students like Julianne who may not attain literacy, but who can benefit from sight word instruction.

"Functional reading" involves being able to recognize specific sight words and use them in the performance of daily routines. Most reading instruction targets the outcome of literacy; that is, students are expected to be able to read whatever printed material they may encounter. Literacy requires that students have a large sight word vocabulary, skills to decode words, and fluency in passage reading. For a person to be

---

[1]Julianne is a real person; I had the joy of knowing her during most of her school career. Her name and specific details have been changed to protect her confidentiality, consistent with the World and American Psychiatric Association's guidelines for disguising case material (Clifft, 1986).

able to read newspapers and other materials encountered in adult life, a minimum achievement of a fifth-grade reading level is needed. The goal of literacy is the ideal outcome for all students, regardless of the type or level of disability. Many excellent texts have been written on ways to teach reading to students with special needs that target the outcome of literacy (e.g., Carnine, Filbert, & Kameenui, 1997). In addition, many published curricula are available that can help students attain this goal (e.g., Engelmann & Bruner, 1995; Engelman, Hanner, & Haddox, 1989).

By contrast, this chapter targets planning curricula for individuals with special needs who will not achieve the outcome of literacy. Some of these students may have made limited progress in a literacy program, but have progressed so slowly that achieving a literacy outcome is not tenable. For example, an adolescent may read on a primer or first-grade level after 8 years of instruction in reading. Such a student needs a new direction in reading that will encourage faster progress and teach skills that have immediate use. Other students may make no progress at all in a literacy approach. For example, a 10-year-old student may not have learned the alphabet or any phonetic analysis. Such a student may also benefit from functional reading. Sometimes functional reading can create success for students and become a foundation for again trying to attain literacy. Some adult learners have not had the opportunity to learn from the newer, powerful approaches to teaching reading. Once they have opportunities to learn sight words, they may begin to progress quickly in functional reading and move on to try an adult literacy class. From this comparison to literacy, the characteristics of functional reading can be summarized as follows:

- Functional reading focuses on learning specific sight words with immediate functional use.
- It provides an alternative way to learn reading skills beneficial to daily life when literacy is not being achieved.
- It provides quick success in reading that may encourage the future pursuit of literacy, but if not, it provides skills that have both immediate and long-term use.

In contrast to the goal of literacy, the goal of functional reading is to master words that facilitate performing activities in a person's daily routine. For example, functional reading can make it easier to prepare food according to product label directions. With some reading, it can be easier to review food options on a menu and find items in a grocery store. Getting through the day can be easier when an individual knows some key words on a personal schedule or job list, or on community or school signs. In general, the outcomes for a functional reading program are that a person will be able to (1) use printed words to make choices (e.g., music selection); (2) comprehend the words needed to manage activities at home (e.g., food preparation, medication directions), in the community (e.g., grocery words, menus), at work (e.g., job schedule), and at school (e.g., schedules, room names); (3) make safe responses when encountering warning words (e.g., "Do not enter"); and (4) through increased skills in reading, gain new opportunities (e.g., taking up hobbies that involve some reading, participating more fully in general education lessons, trying a literacy program). Being able to "read" for the first time, even if what is read is a small list of sight words, can be an important source of pride for students and their families.

A substantial body of research now exists on sight word instruction (Conners, 1992; Browder & Lalli, 1991). A recent review of this research (Browder & Xin, 1998) found that these overall procedures have been highly effective in enhancing sight word acquisition. This review also identified several options for teaching sight words. The present chapter builds on this strong research foundation on sight words to offer guidelines for assessment and curriculum planning.

CURRICULUM SELECTION

One of the most critical decisions to be made in a functional reading program is that of curriculum selection. One alternative is to use a commercial curriculum that focuses on sight words. Several of these curricula are shown in Table 7.1. For example, the Edmark Reading Program has several variations that target different types of sight words. This program was built on a strong foundation of research on stimulus shaping (Eckert & Browder, 1997). The advantage of a published curriculum is that it reduces the planning time needed to develop the sight word training program. The Edmark Reading Program also can be taught through computer-assisted instruction.

The disadvantage of a published curriculum is that it may not achieve the desired outcomes for functional reading. Since the words in the curriculum were not chosen for a specific learner and setting, they may not be the most useful. When a student will only acquire a small sight word vocabulary, it is crucial to choose these few words carefully, based on the individual's needs and preferences. Commercial curricula may provide comprehension activities (e.g., picture–word matching), but they rarely offer ways to teach and measure functional use. Without a focus on functional use, students may simply become "word callers" instead of functional readers. With young students, teachers have the possibility of introducing a larger sight word vocabulary and may want to use a combination of a commercial curriculum and some individualized sight word training. For older students, it may be better to select an individualized vocabulary.

The way to select an individualized sight word vocabulary is through the use of ecological inventories. To conduct ecological inventories for functional reading, the teacher and planning team list the student's current environments (e.g., school classes, home, favorite stores) and activities that can involve some reading. From these activities, key words can be identified for sight word instruction. This process can be described further by considering some of the specific types of sight words that might be targeted.

Sight Words for Choice and Self-Direction

When considering a student's activities that may involve reading, it is important to ask how the student's choices and self-direction within these activities may be enhanced with some sight word reading. For example, one of the most important words a student may learn is his or her name. Name recognition makes it possible for the student to know which items (e.g., desk, backpack, lunchbox, books, etc.) are his or her own belongings in a group setting (e.g., a classroom). Later in life, name recognition will be

TABLE 7.1. Published Curricula for Teaching Functional Reading

- Edmark Reading Program, Level 1, Second Edition
- Edmark Functional Word Series
  Edmark Corporation
  P.O.Box 97021
  Redmond, WA 98073-9721
  1-800-362-2890
  http://www.edmark.com

- Words That Work—A Life Skills Vocabulary Program
- Survival Vocabulary Words and Stories
- Stories About Me
  PCI Educational Publishing
  2800 NE Loop 410, Suite 105
  San Antonio, TX 78215-1525
  1-800-594-4263

- Reading Links
  Steck-Vaughn Company
  P.O.Box 690789
  Orlando, FL 32819-9998
  1-800-531-5051

- Developing Everyday Reading Skills
- Life Skills Reading
  Educational Design, Inc.
  47 W. 13th St.
  New York, NY 10011
  1-800-221-9372

- Reach for Reading
  Modern Curriculum Press
  13900 Prospect Rd.
  Cleveland, OH 44136
  1-800-321-3106

- SRA Specific Skills Series
- Reading for Understanding
  Science Research Associates (SRA), Inc.
  155 N. Wacker Dr.
  Chicago, IL 60606
  1-888-SRA-4543
  http://www.sra4kids.com

- Word Wise CD-ROM
- Looking for Words CD-ROM
  Attainment Company
  P.O. Box 930160
  Verona, WI 53593-0160
  1-800-327-4269

important in activities such as identifying personal mail and punching in at a time clock at work. Some teachers begin functional reading by teaching name recognition because of its broad and long-term applicability.

Any words related to a student's preferences can also provide motivation to learn sight words and create options for choice making. In their research, McGee, Krantz, and McClannahan (1986) taught reading to young children with autism in the context of toy play. When a student reached for a toy, the teacher showed two sight words and said, "Give me the word _____." This procedure can be taken one step further by placing the toys in storage boxes with students' name labels on the outside. Students can ask for preferred toys by pointing to their own labels. Similarly, teachers may have students indicate preferences for restaurants by pointing to one of several logos. Or students may be given menus of options for free time. Students may enjoy learning to read the names of favorite television shows and finding them in the television guide, or learning to read the names of sodas to be able to pick their favorites from a vending machine. Almost anything of high interest to a student may be a source for sight word selection.

Sight words can also be used for self-management. A colleague and I (Browder & Minarovic, 2000) encouraged independence within competitive jobs for adults with moderate mental retardation by teaching key sight words that served as directions for job tasks (e.g., "sweep," "dishwasher," "bagging"). After receiving tutoring in reading the words, the adults learned self-instruction on the job by following a checklist that contained these words. As each job was completed, a participant checked off the word for that task (e.g., "trays") and read the word for the next task (e.g., "garlic bread").

Sight Words for Daily Living

Another important way to select sight words is to choose those that can enhance performance of activities of daily living. These activities may include food preparation, housecleaning, clothing care, or home maintenance. In the research on sight words, several studies have focused on teaching recipe words (Browder, Hines, McCarthy, & Fees, 1984; Collins, Branson, & Hall, 1995; Gast, Doyle, Wolery, Ault, & Farmer, 1991b). For example, in the study by Collins et al. (1995), high school students with moderate mental retardation learned to read the directions to prepare hot chocolate, muffins, and microwave popcorn. The students learned to read the words from flash cards, but also read them from three different brands for each type of food with the help of peer tutors. After prompting a student to read each sight word, a peer tutor gave instructive feedback on what the word meant. For example, after teaching the word "stir," the tutor demonstrated stirring with a spoon. In generalization probes, the students had the opportunity to prepare the foods in a home economics room or a nearby home by following the products' directions, which included the target sight words.

Another reason to teach product labels in the home is to encourage the safe use of products. Collins and Stinson (1995) and Collins and Griffen (1996) taught students with moderate mental retardation to read product warning labels. In the study by Collins and Stinson (1995), students learned words like "precaution," "physician," "harmful," "induce vomiting," and "ingestion." After a student read each word, a teacher gave instructive feedback on the word's meaning. Although students mastered the words and learned some of their meanings, generalization to actual product labels in the store was weak. In contrast, Collins and Griffen (1996) used actual products to teach reading product labels. They rendered the products safe by closing them with duct tape. Some of the products used were liquid bleach, spray oven cleaner, and laundry detergent. Students learned to read the product warning label words from the actual products, and generalized these words to several other brands of the same products. They also learned to make a "safe response," which was either to give the product to an adult or put it in a storage area.

Teaching from actual product labels can be an important way to teach sight words for functional use. Another alternative is to create instruction booklets that a student will use for self-instruction while performing household tasks. In our research we (Browder et al., 1984) taught adults with moderate and severe mental retardation to follow one-word instructions written in teacher-made books to perform three types of household tasks: cooking, laundry, and making phone calls. The participants learned the words during the sight word drill and then learned to use the books to perform the activities. With the booklets, the participants were also able to perform a second, similar task without further instruction.

Another option for teaching sight words for the home is to teach a participant to read and use lists. These may be either "to-do" lists or shopping lists. For example we (Lalli & Browder, 1993) taught participants to read chores and grocery lists. Participants were able to use the list to self-initiate chores and to shop from the grocery list once the words were mastered.

Some students may benefit from learning to read and classify words by food groups, as illustrated by Kennedy, Itkonen, and Lindquist (1994). An alternative way to teach such words may be to teach students to read menus (e.g., school menus) and to identify the food groups represented in the day's items. Older students may also plan menus to include the four food groups. Wilson, Cuvo, and Davis (1986) taught adults to use menu planners and a menu form that helped them maintain a balanced diet and stay within their budget. This planning was taught in a "functional skills cluster" that included planning and shopping for groceries to prepare the selected menu items.

Sight Words for Community Access

Sight words can also be taught that will help an individual utilize community resources more effectively. Many adults find that shopping for groceries from a list helps to save time and money. Several researchers have illustrated how to teach grocery sight words (Gast, Ault, Wolery, Doyle, & Belanger, 1988; Lalli & Browder, 1993; Schuster, Griffen, & Wolery, 1992). For example, Gast et al. (1988) taught words like "candy," "fruit," "pasta," "tea," "spices," "meats," "rolls," "potatoes," "popcorn," "cereal," "olives," "pizza," "lettuce," "broccoli," and "grapefruit." Teachers can identify which grocery words to teach by asking students and their families what their preferences are. Also, the grocery shopping can be combined with teaching food preparation by having students learn to read and shop for the ingredients that will be needed.

Shopping can also be easier if an individual knows how to read aisle marker words. To teach grocery shopping, Schuster, Morse, Griffen, and Wolery (1996) taught words like "pasta," "fragrances," " gift wrap," "cosmetics," " stuffing," "Gatorade," and so on from words identified in an area store. Similarly, Karsh, Repp, and Lenz (1990) taught grocery aisle marker words, but focused on generalizing the word reading to several types of stimulus materials (e.g., the words written in varying typefaces or type sizes). Karsh and Repp (1992) used a similar generalization approach, but focused on department store signs such as "service," "cosmetics," "sportswear," and "jewelry."

Individuals also may gain better community mobility by learning to read key signs. Singleton, Schuster, and Ault (1995) taught participants to read signs like "KOA," "Denny's," "restroom," "Food Mart," "barber," "phone," "quiet," "thin ice," and "keep out." Through instructive feedback, they also taught a simple meaning for each word. For example, for "Denny's," the associated meaning was " 'Denny's' means pancakes." Similarly, Cuvo and Klatt (1992) and Schloss et al. (1995) taught community signs. Schloss et al. (1995) focused on teaching students with behavior disorders to read signs in leisure settings, including a swimming pool, arcade, bowling alley, and hiking trail. Students found the signs as part of a scavenger hunt. Students also may benefit from learning to read words on menus in restaurants to make selections (e.g., "hamburger," "soda," "French fries," "pizza," "soup"). Knowing words like "restroom," "men," and "women" can be useful in locating restrooms.

Community access may also be encouraged by teaching students to read words that help them plan for their next outing. Students may learn to read the calendar of events in the newspaper or a sports schedule. We (Browder & Shear, 1996) taught students to read weather words from a newspaper's weather reports. After the students practiced reading the words, the teacher discussed what type of clothing would be needed, according to the weather report.

Sight Words for Personal Safety

When the concept of teaching sight words to individuals with developmental disabilities first emerged, professionals sometimes referred to this curriculum as "survival words." Sometimes the words selected for "survival" had little relevance to the students' daily lives. For example, learning to read the word "stop" is probably not critical unless an individual is planning to drive. A more salient cue for pedestrians to pause before crossing a street is the curb. Similarly, the word "railroad" alerts drivers to stop and look for a train, but is less crucial than attending to railroad tracks when a person is walking. The community signs that are critical also vary widely from community to community. The best way to teach sight words for safety is to survey the community and the students' activities to find specific signs they will encounter (e.g., "Do not enter"), and then to teach these specific signs along with a safe response. For example, Collins and Griffen (1996) had students give hazardous household products to an adult or put them in storage as a safe response to reading the labels, as noted above. Similarly, students might show the safe response as walking away from signs that say "Danger," "Keep out," and "No trespassing."

Sight Words for General Education Access

As students gain greater access to general education, some words may be chosen for their relevance to these settings. Students may be taught to read the words on their daily schedule or key words on frequent handouts, such as "name" and "date." For example, Wolery, Werts, Snyder, and Caldwell (1994) selected peer tutors to teach students with moderate developmental disabilities to read words such as "girls," "boys," "pencil," and "notebook." If the sight word instruction will serve as a bridge to a literacy program, teachers may select high-frequency words such as those on the Dolch word list. Other words should also be included in the sight word instruction, however, since it is difficult to teach functional use of academic words such as those from the Dolch list. Sometimes specific words encountered frequently in an academic class may be chosen (e.g., science or social studies vocabulary words). When academic words are being selected, planning for comprehension is necessary. For example, a student may read each word and give a brief meaning.

Table 7.2 gives examples of sight word selection for general education inclusion and the other types of activities described above.

Special Curriculum Considerations

When teachers or teams are making curriculum decisions about the sight words to be taught and their corresponding functional activities, special considerations may be needed for students with unique needs, such as being linguistically diverse, having challenging behavior, or being unable to master words. When students are bilingual or otherwise linguistically diverse, consideration needs to be given both to the context and format of instruction and to the language of instruction (Rohena-Diaz & Browder, 1996). Duran (1985) found that students with moderate and severe disabilities who came from Spanish-speaking homes acquired sight words more easily when they were related to familiar activities. The ecological inventory approach recommended in this chapter for selecting sight words is consistent with Duran's (1985) approach, in that it focuses on students' own environments and activities in identifying target words. We (Rohena-Diaz & Browder, 1996) have recommended considering the written language

TABLE 7.2. Examples of Sight Words for a Functional Reading Program

Activity	Examples of words	Functional use
Choosing materials or activities	"music," "snack," "video game," "walk outside," "rest," "movie"	Picking material or activity from a menu and then completing it
Reading or making a menu	"pizza," "tossed salad," "hoagies," "apple pie," "sliced peaches"	Reading school lunch menu; using a menu planner
Food preparation	"stir," "bake," "microwave," "minutes," "let cool," "remove cover"	Preparing food or beverage according to product directions
Home management	"dust," "dishes," "pay bills," "sweep," "call doctor"	Using a "to-do" list
Dining out	"ice cream," "coffee," "soda," "pancakes," "hamburger"	Ordering from a menu
Shopping	"milk," "bread," "onions," "cereal," "birthday card," "deodorant"	Making purchases using a list
Planning a leisure activity	"Freedom Basketball," "Regal Cinema," "pancake breakfast," "One Day Tours," "hiking club"	Scanning calendar and leisure section of newspaper for key events and finding times
Going to work	"schedule," "Paul Davis" (student's name), "Butztown Road" (bus name), days of week for schedule	Finding correct bus; identifying name on time card; reading job schedule
Participation in general education	"math," "reading," "science," "page," "name," "Date," "Ms. Thomas," "cafeteria," "gym," "East Hills Middle School"	Finding correct text for lesson listed on board or schedule; writing name, date; identifying room by teacher's name on door; finding cafeteria

encountered in the students' home community, as well as the students' age, when the age of instruction is selected. An adolescent student from a Latino community in which most street and community signs are in Spanish may focus on learning Spanish sight words. In contrast, an elementary student who comes from a home in which Spanish is the primary language, but who lives in a community where most signs are in English, will probably benefit more from learning English sight words.

Rohena-Diaz (1998) explored the issue of whether Spanish or English was preferable as the language of instruction for students from Spanish-speaking homes who were learning English sight words. Students did well in either approach when the instructions followed an explicit script. The teacher also spoke informally with the students in Spanish between lessons. Rohena-Diaz concluded that in many cases, students from linguistically diverse homes may benefit more from learning English sight words taught with English instructions if (1) there are other opportunities to build rapport with their teacher in their native language; (2) the words on signs in their home community are in English; and (3) the sight word English instruction is explicit and consistent (e.g., "Look at the word, read the word").

A second special need that may be encountered in the selection of sight words is challenging behavior and/or low motivation to learn academic skills. Schloss et al. (1995) provided motivation to learn sight words by choosing words from recreational settings and teaching them in a scavenger hunt format. In general, motivation may be increased by teaching students words from highly preferred activities. Students may also be directly involved in choosing the words they want to learn.

Some students (e.g., some students with severe mental retardation) do not master sight words even with intensive instruction. An alternative is to teach students to "read" pictures or photographs by selecting key pictures in the same way as words would be selected, and using the same systematic instructional strategies that are described below for sight words. In their research, Wolery et al. (1991) used a progressive time delay procedure to teach students to name ("read") pictures of community workers (e.g., veterinarian, secretary, butcher, cashier). To encourage some sight word acquisition, they introduced the printed name of each worker on a flash card as instructive feedback (e.g., after a student identified the veterinarian, the teacher showed the word "vet"). Some students learned the words through this instructive feedback; for others, this sight word preview decreased the time needed to learn the words in later sessions. Wolery et al. (1991) replicated these results using restaurant signs (e.g., for Little Caesar's, Wendy's). Similarly, Singleton et al. (1995) taught community signs, as noted earlier. Some of these signs contained sight words (e.g., "phone," "quiet," "thin ice"), and others contained a company logo (e.g., "Denny's," "KOA"). Students in this study learned the meanings of the signs and could identify them. Similarly, photographs or pictures may be used to teach a student's schedule, community options, directions for preparing a favorite food, or other activities.

ECOLOGICAL ASSESSMENT IN FUNCTIONAL READING

Given the wide array of functional sight words, assessment is needed to pinpoint the words that are most appropriate for a specific student. As described in Chapter Two, the steps in developing personalized curriculum goals for individual students include

(1) reviewing prior records, (2) conducting person-centered planning with the student and his or her parents, (3) assessing the student's preferences, and (4) building curriculum by moving from general to specific assessments (curriculum checklists, ecological inventories, discrepancy analyses, situational assessments). These steps are now described for two students who needed functional reading programs.

Mr. Burke was developing a functional reading program for two elementary school students with autism, Chad and Jason.[2] Chad was 10 years old and scored on the primer level (below first grade) on a standardized test of reading ability. His prior records and his parents reported that he knew several words, including: "men," "women," "exit," "hamburger," "coke," "McDonald's," and "quiet." Chad rarely spoke (he was selectively mute), but read words by pointing to the correct choice when several flash cards were placed in front of him. He could also identify most letters of the alphabet in this way. Jason, a 9-year-old with autism, was skilled in decoding words. He could read passages from easy-reading library books aloud. In contrast, he could not answer questions about what he had read and would usually repeat the questions he was asked. When oral reading samples were used to test Jason, he seemed to have a second-grade reading level, based on his rate and error patterns. When standardized tests that included comprehension were used, he seemed to be below a first-grade level.

In conducting person-centered planning with Chad's family, Mr. Burke discovered that Chad had begun to make progress in reading when he was 7 years old, but that he seemed to need to relearn the same skills each year. They were eager for him to acquire some reading skills that would be usable in daily living. Chad himself showed moderate interest in reading. He would complete short reading lessons that had a clear beginning and end. He also liked doing matching seatwork tasks, including matching letters.

When Mr. Burke met with Jason's parents, he learned that they liked to read to him each night and encouraged him to read library books. They realized that he had outgrown young children's books (e.g., *Sesame Street* books), but were not sure what alternative to encourage.

In conducting preference assessments to begin generating vocabulary, Mr. Burke noted that Chad had a strong interest in auto racing. He considered the possibility of teaching Chad to identify the names of some drivers and cars. Jason did not have a specific outside interest like Chad's, but he did show a preference for quiet areas like the library and for illustrated books. Mr. Burke noted that these preferences could be honored in planning Jason's materials and reading activities.

To pinpoint more specific needs for Chad's reading program, Mr. Burke began by getting a better understanding of Chad's sight word vocabulary. Because Chad had been exposed to several years of reading instruction, Mr. Burke thought he might have a larger vocabulary than the list found in his prior records indicated. Using the words shown in Figure 7.1, Mr. Burke screened Chad's functional reading vocabulary. He also consulted with the school's reading specialist to get a list of high-frequency words (e.g., Dolch words). Because Chad responded best to short sessions, Mr. Burke introduced one set of words each day for several days. He also adapted the assessment to use Chad's pointing response with familiar materials (i.e., he rewrote the words on index

[2]Chad and Jason are based on my experience in designing reading programs for several students with autism and other developmental disabilities, but are not real people themselves.

FIGURE 7.1. Functional Reading Inventory

Functional Reading Inventory

Directions: Check all words the student can read on sight (you may have a nonverbal student find words in the column as you read them in random order). Note whether functional use is mastery (M), partial mastery (PM), not mastered (–), or unknown (?).

Functional vocabulary	Check words read	Functional use	Mastery, partial mastery, not mastered, or unknown
Food words Hamburger Hot dog Grilled cheese Chicken nuggets Chicken patty Sandwich Tacos Burritos Carrot Apple Grapes Salad Cheese Eggs Bacon Sausage Biscuit Bagels Cereal Toast Pancakes Waffles Ham Meatloaf Potatoes Rice Stir-fry Macaroni and cheese Spaghetti Pizza *(Adapt these words for student's food preferences.)*		1. Reads school menu and chooses to buy/not buy lunch. 2. Follows grocery list with known words. 3. Orders from menu using known words.	

(cont.)

FIGURE 7.1. *(page 2 of 4)*

Functional vocabulary	Check words read	Functional use	Mastery, partial mastery, not mastered, or unknown
Daily living words *Chores:* Vacuum Dust Laundry Sweep Dishes Feed pet Clean room *Preparing convenience foods:* Stir Heat Cover Microwave Conventional oven *Using microwave oven:* Start Stop Cooking time *Using washer/dryer:* Hot Cold Warm Normal Perm press High Low Medium *(Adapt these words to specific materials in student's home.)*		1. Follows a chores list. 2. Follows directions on label to prepare convenience foods. 3. Prepares simple recipes. 4. Sets dials on washer/dryer. 5. Separates edible and nonedible groceries.	
Community and safety words *Aisle markers:* Hardware Garden Automotive Pharmacy Women's Men's Children's Clothing		1. Finds location by using familiar street signs and landmarks. 2. Uses aisle markers in department store to find items. 3. Avoids areas with warnings. 4. Can find emergency contacts.	

(cont.)

FIGURE 7.1. *(page 3 of 4)*

Functional vocabulary	Check words read	Functional use	Mastery, partial mastery, not mastered, or unknown
Community and safety words (cont.) Safety: Exit Entrance Do not enter Police Phone Information Emergency call button Fire alarm *(Adapt these words to student's community.)*			
School words (also found in community sites) Cafeteria Auditorium Office Men Women Boys Girls Staff only Lounge Date Name Address Phone number *(Assess recognition of own name, teacher's name, name of school, and name of city.)*		1. Finds major areas of school. 2. Locates own restroom. 3. Locates own belongings and gives basic information on forms.	

Self-scheduling
DAYS
  Monday
  Saturday
  Wednesday
  Thursday
  Sunday
  Friday
  Tuesday
		1. Follows a schedule by using sight words.
		2. Uses a personal calendar.	

(cont.)

FIGURE 7.1. *(page 4 of 4)*

Functional vocabulary	Check words read	Functional use	Mastery, partial mastery, not mastered, or unknown
Self-scheduling (cont.) DATES 　22 　11 　15 　18 　6 　3 　31 　5 TIMES 　9:00 　1:30 　2:15 　5:45 MONTHS 　March 　February 　December 　September 　April *(Assess other dates, times, and months relevant to student.)*			
Other: *(Assess words related to student's interests and to environments such as job sites.)*		1. Uses a menu of words to select leisure activity. 2. Finds words related to interests in hobby book, newspaper, catalog, magazine. 3. Reads words needed to do job or other individual activity.	

cards). From this screening, Mr. Burke discovered that Chad knew 12 additional sight words. Most of these were food words. Mr. Burke decided that it would be important to keep an ongoing record of Chad's known words, to use in instruction and share with future teachers.

Mr. Burke then conducted ecological inventories of Chad's general education classes and community activities to determine additional words he might need. From these inventories, he discovered that Chad could benefit from learning to read his name, his teacher's names, school location signs ("cafeteria," "auditorium"), and additional daily living and community words.

In evaluating Jason, Mr. Burke decided to begin with a listening comprehension assessment to help determine Jason's comprehension level. He adapted the listening test from the revised Brigance Diagnostic Comprehensive Inventory of Basic Skills (Brigance, 1999). He discovered that Jason's listening level was below the lower first-grade level. Mr. Burke then decided to construct his own vocabulary test to determine how many functional words Jason understood. In collaboration with the school's speech therapist, Mr. Burke found pictures to correspond with many of the words shown in Figure 7.1. To be sure Jason understood the matching task, he first had Jason match identical pictures. Jason was able to do this independently during ongoing seatwork activities. Mr. Burke then worked with Jason in short daily sessions to have him match sight word flash cards to the photographs (e.g., "vacuum," "apple"). Mr. Burke discovered that Jason lacked comprehension of many daily living terms. He concluded that Jason's poor reading comprehension could be attributed to his limited vocabulary skills. Although Jason had mastered decoding skills that might someday lead to literacy, he would need intensive vocabulary work to comprehend what he read.

Mr. Burke decided to continue to encourage Jason's progress toward literacy by using a commercial series that emphasized comprehension. He chose the Science Research Associates (SRA) resources Reading for Understanding and the Specific Skill Series (see Table 7.1). To encourage Jason's understanding of everyday vocabulary, and to build on his interest in colorful illustrations with age-appropriate materials, Mr. Burke chose computer software from the Attainment Company called Looking for Words and Word Wise (see Table 7.1). He also used "high-interest, low-vocabulary" library books he located with the help of the school librarian. Mr. Burke tried out these materials with Jason before purchasing them. As he discovered resources that worked well with Jason, he shared them with Jason's parents as well as using them in class, so that they could help Jason develop a personal library of age-appropriate materials.

SIGHT WORD INSTRUCTION

Once the specific sight words to be taught have been chosen through the curriculum-planning process, methods are needed to develop a Systematic Instruction Plan. Because of the wealth of research literature on teaching sight words, there are many options for developing this plan. These options and guidelines for their use are now described by reviewing various components of the Systematic Instruction Plan.

Instructional and Objective Format

Instructional Objective

In defining the specific instructional objective, the teacher needs to decide how many words to present at a time and the criterion for mastery. Also, will progress monitoring be based on the teaching data, or will there be separate probes? The number of words taught at a time will depend on a student's rate of progress. In the research, students have been taught as few as 1 word at a time (Karsh et al., 1990) or 2 words at a time (Collins & Stinson, 1995), or as many words as 10 in a set (Browder & Shear, 1996). When several sets of words are taught to mastery, students may continue to expand their vocabulary. For example, the objective may be for a student to master 10 cooking sight words taught in sets of 2. The criterion for mastery should be applied to each word, so that as it is mastered, a new word can be added to the set. The learned word can be reviewed periodically. It may also be beneficial to intermix known words with the unknown words to enhance acquisition (Browder & Shear, 1996). The number of days the student needs to read a word for it to be considered mastered is also an individual decision. Often the criterion of 2 or 3 consecutive days has been used in the research literature (e.g., Wolery et al., 1991). This criterion might apply either to a sight word probe given at the beginning of the lesson or to the training data. For example, an objective might be the following: "Given cooking words presented on flash cards in a probe, Gordon[3] will master 10 cooking words in sets of 2 by reading each word independently for two consecutive probes." The student also needs to learn to apply these new reading skills. Thus a companion objective for Gordon might be as follows: "When given a sight word–picture recipe book, Gordon will complete at least five out of six recipes attempted with edible food."

In addition to these primary objectives, teachers may also want to maximize instructional time by using instructive feedback (Werts, Wolery, Holcombe, & Gast, 1995). One of the best ways to use instructive feedback is to give the meaning of the word after praising the student for saying it. For example, Singleton et al. (1995) gave the meanings for each community sign taught. After students identified the sign (e.g., "barber"), the teacher would say, "Good, this word is 'barber.' 'Barber' means a person who gives you a haircut." Collins and Stinson (1995) explained product warning words similarly: "Good, the word is 'irritant.' An eye 'irritant' means a product that can hurt your eyes." A companion objective for Gordon might be this: "When encountering the 10 target new food words on flash cards or in recipes, Gordon will state whether that food needs to be refrigerated, for 80% of the words." Gordon might learn this by feedback that tells him, "Yes, Gordon, you read 'eggs'; eggs need to go in the refrigerator." This feedback can even be from another curricular area. For example, in teaching math flash cards, Whalen, Schuster, and Hemmeter (1996) gave feedback on sight words by saying, "Good, the sum is 4. This word is 'cheese' " (showing a flash card of the word "cheese").

Instructional Format

Material Preparation. Once the objective is known, materials can be prepared. A simple procedure is to write the sight words on index cards to be used as flash cards. If

---

[3]Gordon is a fictitious student.

peer tutors will be involved in the instruction, it may be beneficial to have a sight word folder, with instructions for the tutor and the sight words enclosed (Barbetta, Miller, Peters, Heron, & Cochran, 1991; Wolery et al., 1994). For example, Wolery et al. (1994) placed the sight words in a binder with one word per page and the peer tutor instructions on the back. Computer presentation of the sight words is another alternative (Baumgart & VanWalleghem, 1987). Although an interactive computer program may be ideal, teachers can also present the sight words in any word-processing program by typing one word centered on a page in a large font to be used with teacher or peer instruction.

The limitation of using a flash card approach is that students may not generalize reading the words to real materials. Cuvo and Klatt (1992) addressed this generalization issue by using videotapes of the words versus teaching the words in the community or on flash cards. For their participants with moderate and mild mental retardation, all three methods worked well. In contrast, Collins and Stinson (1995) found that participants with moderate mental retardation did not generalize well from flash cards of product warning label words to the actual items found in a grocery store. In subsequent research by Collins and Griffen (1996), actual products were used to teach the words, and several different brands were probed. In teaching instruction booklets, we (Browder et al., 1984) taught the words from the actual booklets rather than using separate flash cards. In deciding on the materials to use, teachers may want to consider both the students and settings. Flash cards and sight word folders may blend better in general education settings. Students may then receive periodic training to generalize the words to actual products through private tutoring or community-based instruction.

Some sight words are found in the community with distinctive natural cues, such as the company or product logo or a special typeface (e.g., the soda name Sprite as it appears on a can or bottle has a special typeface and a green background). When these words are being taught in the classroom, it may be most efficient to teach them using these natural cues, so that students can benefit from the cues. Store flyer coupons provide one option for finding words printed distinctively.

If students need to be able to read a word across a variety of printed styles, a general-case approach to teaching may be needed. Karsh et al. (1990) and Karsh and Lenz (1992) developed the task demonstration model as a general-case approach. In this model, several sets of flash cards are made for each sight word. These sets vary the following features of the flash cards: (1) the typeface of the letters, (2) the color of the letters of the word, (3) the color of the flash card, (4) the size of the letters of the word, and (5) the size of the flash card. This extra preparation of materials may be warranted when a student is being taught to read words that will be encountered in many different contexts, such as his or her name and restroom signs.

Setting and Teacher. The next teaching decisions involve whether the lesson will be taught in a group or one-to-one format, what the setting for instruction will be, and who will deliver instruction. An advantage of using a group instruction format in teaching sight words is that students may learn through observing their peers (Alig-Cybriwsky, Wolery, & Gast, 1990; Farmer, Gast, Wolery, & Winterling, 1991; Gast, Wolery, Morris, Doyle, & Meyer, 1990; McCurdy, Cundari, & Lentz, 1990). To maximize this observational learning, each student is taught a different subset of the target words. For example, each student is taught 2 of 10 target grocery words. For students to learn from each other's instruction, they must attend to it. One way to encourage attention is to call on students in an unpredictable pattern (as opposed to going around the group in sequence). In the group instruction research, teachers also used either a cue such as "Everyone look" or a more specific cue, such as having everyone spell the letters of the word presented (Alig-Cybriwsky et al., 1990) or write the word (Schoen & Ogden, 1995).

A second format consideration is the setting for instruction. Most research on sight word instruction has been conducted in either a private tutorial context or a special education classroom, but recent innovations have demonstrated that words can be taught in the community (Cuvo & Klatt, 1992; Lalli & Browder, 1993; Schloss et al., 1995) or in general education classes (Schoen & Ogden, 1995; Wolery et al., 1994). For example, Schoen and Ogden (1995) taught a small, heterogeneous group in a first-grade class sight words that had been selected from the academic materials. The small group included students with moderate mental retardation and some who were "at risk" for school failure. To cue their attention, students wrote each word on their paper before one student read it. Students learned both their own and some of their peers' words.

The setting for instruction also influences who will deliver the sight word instruction. In addition to the special education teacher, sight words have been taught by the general education teacher (Schoen & Ogden, 1995), a teacher's aide (Kamps, Walker, Locke, Delquadri, & Hall, 1990), peers who are nondisabled (Collins et al., 1995; Wolery et al., 1994), and peers who are disabled (Koury & Browder, 1986). Kamps et al. (1990) examined the impact of the person teaching, as well as of the format, on sight word acquisition for students with autism. They compared a peer tutor using a one-to-one format, a teacher's aide using either a one-to-one or group format, and a special education teacher using either a one-to-one or group format. The one-to-one instruction worked well, whether the instructor was the peer, the aide, or the teacher. Group instruction was as effective as one-to-one instruction when implemented by the classroom teacher. Although students learned in the group instruction with the aide, they had poorer on-task behavior.

When peers from general education provide the teaching, it may be implemented in either the special education class (Collins et al., 1995) or the general education class (Wolery et al., 1994). Collins et al. (1995) demonstrated how to get peers involved in a way that also met their own curricular objectives. Students from an advanced English class provided the peer instruction and used this activity for reflections in their class writing assignments. Collins et al. (1995) noted that the peers' overall teaching precision was good. Although they sometimes forgot to use praise, they were highly motivational to the students with moderate mental retardation. Peer tutors sometimes missed sessions due to other school responsibilities, but students still learned the words and formed some friendships during these sessions. Wolery et al. (1994) also found a high degree of teaching accuracy, which was encouraged by training the peers to use the instructional procedures prior to beginning the peer tutoring sessions.

From the research on these various options, it is recommended that teachers maximize instructional time by using a group instruction format for sight word instruction, and that they supplement this group instruction with one-to-one instruction by peers and classroom aides. Some of this one-to-one instruction may be geared toward encouraging functional use of the words in daily activities or community settings.

Options for Prompting and Fading: Response Prompts

Several options exist for prompting sight word reading and fading the use of these prompts. Since these procedures have all been highly effective in research, teachers are encouraged to select the method that works best for an individual student and setting. Students with severe disabilities may learn more efficiently from strategies such as time delay that minimize errors (Ault, Wolery, Doyle, & Gast, 1989), but can learn from a variety of other strategies as well (Browder & Xin, 1998). The first set of options to be reviewed is that involving "response prompts." Response prompts are teacher-delivered models or guidance in making a response. In contrast, "stimulus prompts" utilize modifications in the materials to assist the learner to respond. These various prompting and fading options are shown in Table 7.3 and are now described.

Postresponse Prompting

For some students, the best way to learn sight words is to be given the opportunity to read flash cards rapidly and without interruption from the teacher unless a mistake is made. When the correct answer is prompted after a student tries to read the word, this method is called "postresponse prompting." One method of postresponse prompting that can allow the student to read sight words with minimal teacher interruption, while keeping errors low, is to use interspersal of sight words (Browder & Shear, 1996). For example, we (Browder & Shear, 1996) taught students 2 new words interspersed with 10 known words. The teacher kept replacing the new word in the set of 10 known words as follows ("fruit salad" and "sandwich" were the new word examples in these school menu word sets):

"fruit salad, milk"
"fruit salad, hamburger, hot dog"
"fruit salad, French fries, pudding, ice cream"
"fruit salad, taco, pizza, carrots, cupcake"
"fruit salad, sandwich, taco," etc. (known words were added until 10 new words and 5 known words were read; 101 trials total)

A student may opt to hold the flash cards, replacing the new words in the set while reading. The student flips and reads the words as rapidly as possible. At the end of the set, the teacher praises the student's reading. If the student misses a word, the rapid drill pauses, and the teacher gives expanded feedback. First, the teacher has the student repeat the correct word, then trace or spell it, repeat a sentence using the word, and repeat it again. We (Browder & Shear, 1996) found that this procedure worked well for students with moderate mental retardation and severe behavior disorders. The students seemed to like to control the cards and to be able to keep the teacher from interrupting by reading all words correctly.

Another alternative for postresponse prompting is to use a simple feedback procedure. The learner reads each word, and the teacher praises accurate responses and corrects errors by stating the word. We (Lalli & Browder, 1993) found that this simple feedback procedure worked well in teaching adults with moderate mental retardation to

TABLE 7.3. Methods of Prompting and Fading Used in Teaching Sight Words

Method	Reading format	Prompt used	Example	Research
RESPONSE PROMPTING				
1. Postresponse prompting: Interspersal method	Expressive reading—student reads flash cards rapidly without interruption until error.	Interspersing high ratio of known words to reduce errors; using expanded error correction.	Expanded error correction: 1. Repeat word. 2. Spell it. 3. Trace it. 4. Repeat it.	Browder & Shear (1996)
2. Postresponse prompting: Feedback only	Can be expressive (saying word) or receptive (pointing to word).	Simple correction of any word missed.	"No, the word is 'coffee.'"	Lalli & Browder (1993)
3. Simultaneous prompting	Usually expressive	Teacher models answer on every trial, probes independent reading.	"Read 'hamburger.'"	Schuster, Griffen, & Wolery (1992)
4. Time delay: Constant time delay	Usually expressive; can be receptive.	Usually teacher models correct answer. First trials at no delay; remainder trials at delay interval of 4–5 seconds.	On first day, teacher shows each word and models it. "Read 'gym.'" On rest of days, teacher waits for student to read word 4–5 seconds before prompting.	Gast, Doyle, Wolery, Ault, & Baklarz (1991a)
5. Time delay: Progressive time delay	Usually expressive; can be receptive.	Same as constant time delay, but delay intervals change across sessions.	First day, no delay; then 2 seconds, 4 seconds, 6 seconds, 8 seconds.	Browder, Hines, McCarthy, & Fees (1984); Collins & Stinson (1995)
6. Least intrusive prompts	Expressive or receptive.	Teacher gives several levels of assistance until student says word.	Teacher gestures toward word, points to correct word, guides student's hand to point to correct word.	Gast, Ault, Wolery, Doyle, & Belanger (1988); Karsh & Repp (1992)
STIMULUS PROMPTS				
1. Stimulus fading	Can be expressive or receptive.	Correct word is highlighted with color or picture cue, which is faded across trials.	Correct word is highlighted with red; over trials, red highlighting is faded until all letters are black.	Lalli & Browder (1993)
2. Stimulus shaping	Always receptive.	Uses an easy-to-hard discrimination with distractor symbols and words.	The word "exit" is presented as follows: —exit— sun exit tooth exit x-ray ten eat x-ray exit	McGee, Krantz, & McClannahan (1986)
3. Task demonstration model	Always receptive.	Same as stimulus shaping, but irrelevant stimuli also vary.	In example above, "exit" is also presented in varied typefaces, colors, sizes.	Karsh & Repp (1992); Karsh, Repp, & Lenz (1990)

read words on household chores and grocery lists and could be implemented easily in community settings.

Simultaneous Prompting

Some students need procedures that will decrease or eliminate errors. For example, a student who is likely to repeat errors or become disruptive when error correction is used may benefit from an errorless learning procedure. To achieve errorless learning, the teacher prompts before the student responds (e.g., "Read the word 'men' "). The student then repeats this answer ("men"). One alternative, called "simultaneous prompting," is to continue to use this prompt on every teaching trial so that the student never makes a mistake (Schuster et al., 1992). To encourage transfer of stimulus control to the sight word versus the teacher's model, probes are provided during each teaching session. A student's performance may be enhanced over time by using an error correction during this probe and having the student repeat the correct answer (Johnson, Schuster, & Bell, 1996).

Constant Time Delay

The problem with giving the prompt on every trial is that some students may not transfer stimulus control from the teacher to the sight word. That is, they may become prompt-dependent. To transfer stimulus control (i.e., to fade the teacher model), constant time delay can be utilized (Collins & Griffen, 1996; Cuvo & Klatt, 1992; Gast, Doyle, Wolery, Ault, & Baklarz, 1991a; Gast et al., 1990). After an initial session in which the words are presented with an immediate model, the teacher can then begin to present the model at some delay interval (e.g., 4–5 seconds). (Please refer to Chapter Four to review guidelines for using time delay.)

Constant time delay is one of the most frequently used methods to teach sight words in the research literature (Browder & Xin, 1998). This method works well in a group instruction format and has been implemented both in peer tutoring (Collins et al., 1995; Wolery et al., 1994) and in a typical classroom by a general education teacher (Schoen & Ogden, 1995). This procedure is also easy to implement in community-based instruction of sight words (Cuvo & Klatt, 1992). Constant time delay has been compared to several other prompting options and found to be both effective and efficient (Doyle, Wolery, Gast, Ault, & Wiley, 1990; Gast et al., 1988).

Progressive Time Delay

Some students may need a more gradual withdrawal of the teacher's assistance. This can be achieved with progressive time delay (Browder et al., 1984; Collins & Stinson, 1995; Farmer et al., 1991; Gast et al., 1991b; Wolery et al., 1991). In the first session (or several sessions), the sight words are presented with an immediate teacher model. Then in each subsequent session (or set of sessions), the delay interval is increased by 1–2 seconds. For example, in the first session on Monday, the teacher gives the prompt with no delay. On Tuesday, the words are presented after 2 seconds of delay, on Wednesday after 4 seconds, on Thursday after 6 seconds, and on Friday (and from then on) after 8 seconds. If mistakes are made, the teacher can return to the no-delay condition and repeat this sequence.

An alternative (Browder & Minarovic, 2000) is to use progressive time delay within a session. First, the participant reads the list of sight words on a probe with no feedback. Next, the words are taught with no delay (immediate prompting). The words are shuffled and presented again after 2 seconds of delay. Then they are reshuffled and presented after 4 seconds of delay, then after 6 seconds, and then after 8 seconds. This same sequence is presented each day until all words are read correctly for 2 consecutive days on the probe.

Two concerns with progressive time delay are that it can be difficult to implement, and that it may shape waiting for the teacher's model. Progressive time delay can be difficult to implement if errors begin to occur. Ideally, the teacher will repeat the delay schedule for any missed word, but to do so may mean keeping track of different delay schedules for each word. If the words are taught in a group format, this can become especially complex. Glat, Gould, Stoddard, and Sidman (1994) also found that a participant waited for the cue to select the correct word when progressive time delay was used in a receptive reading format (pointing to the correct word). This prompt dependence was corrected by having the learner say the word before finding it.

Least Intrusive Prompts

In the system of least intrusive prompts, the teacher gives progressively more assistance until the student reads a word correctly (see the example Table 7.3). In general, the system of least intrusive prompts has *not* been an efficient strategy to teach sight words, compared to other methods such as constant time delay (Doyle, Wolery, Gast, Ault, & Wiley, 1990), progressive time delay (Gast et al., 1991b), or the task demonstration model (Karsh & Repp, 1992). This is important comparative research, because in general, the system of least intrusive prompts is a highly effective strategy that has been applied to teaching a wide variety of other skills (Doyle, Wolery, Ault, & Gast, 1988). One reason why this strategy may not be efficient in teaching sight words is the difficulty in designing a prompt hierarchy when the most straightforward way to prompt the response is to model reading the word. To actually break this model down into increasing assistance would involve giving phonetic prompts (e.g., "mmm" for "milk"), but this type of prompting has been found to be less effective than whole-word prompting (Barbetta, Heward, & Bradley, 1993).

More Options for Prompting and Fading: Stimulus Prompts

Stimulus prompting involves making modifications in materials so that the materials themselves help the learner make the correct response. Because stimulus prompting requires these special modifications, which can be time-consuming, teachers often prefer using response prompting. In contrast, the investment of time to design special materials may be warranted when they make it possible for students to self-instruct or work independently in general education or other contexts. Some students may also respond better to cues contained within the materials than to teacher prompting. The two primary methods of stimulus prompting are "stimulus fading" and "stimulus shaping." These terms are often confused or used interchangeably in the literature, but are distinctly different procedures (Eckert & Browder, 1997). Stimulus fading involves enhancing the target stimulus in some way to make it distinct from the other sight words in an array. In stimulus shaping, the changes are made in the distractor stimuli (e.g., other sight words) to make them more similar to the target word across teaching trials. This difference is illustrated in Figure 7.2. These procedures are now described.

Stimulus Fading

Stimulus fading is one of the oldest methods for teaching individuals with developmental disabilities to read sight words (Dorry & Zeaman, 1973; 1975). In most applications of stimulus fading, a picture is paired with a word to help the student read the word. Over successive trials, the picture is faded by either removing components of it or making it less salient (e.g., by repeated photocopying or the use of tissue paper). The problem that may arise in this method is that the student may not transfer stimulus control from the picture to the word, especially if the word is more prominent than the picture (Singh & Solman, 1990). That is, the student may focus on the picture and never learn to recognize the word itself. Some research on stimulus fading suggests that stimulus control may be enhanced by using within-stimulus, distinctive-feature cues (Rincover, 1978). "Within-stimulus" means putting the cue on the target stimulus (e.g., the word). "Distinctive-feature" means highlighting the visual stimulus to which the student should attend (e.g., letter shapes). To use within-stimulus, distinctive-feature

FIGURE 7.2. Illustrations of stimulus fading and stimulus shaping. From Eckert and Browder (1997). Copyright 1996 by Westview Press, a member of Perseus Books, L.L.C. Reprinted with permission.

CAR	CAT
CAR	CAT
CAT	CAR
CAR	CAT

Stimulus fading

—	car	—
car	C	box
ca	box	car
car	box	cat

Stimulus shaping

cues, the teacher highlights the letters of the target word. For example, we (Lalli & Browder, 1993) highlighted the correct word in an array of three words on three cards. One of the cards (the one with the target word) was highlighted in red; the other two cards were in black ink. Over trials, the red highlighting was made less distinct until all words looked the same. The participants were taught 8 words. To prepare the materials for stimulus fading, the trainer made a flash card using black ink for each of the 8 words. Then four additional flash cards were made for each word. The first had the word in full red highlighting. The second used more black ink and less red, as did the third and fourth, so that the fourth-faded-level card only had slight specks of red.

One way teachers may use stimulus fading is to prepare materials for student self-instruction or seatwork. Using worksheets, workbooks, or other materials that display the target word, the teacher gives this direction: "Find the word 'hamburger' in these pages." On each page of the materials, the correct word is presented with several other words, but with highlighting. The student circles the correct word. Over successive pages of the workbook or worksheets, the highlighting becomes less distinct until there is no highlighting for the correct word. The teacher may have the student trace the letters of the target word on each page with a highlighter in another color, to encourage attending to the letter shapes.

Stimulus Shaping

Another option that involves modifying the materials is stimulus shaping. In this method, no changes are made to the target word. Instead, the distractor words or symbols are changed. In the beginning, the distractor word or symbols are made to appear highly distinct from the target word. For example, in teaching the word "women," the first trial may give the distractors of just dashes (—). Over trials, the distractors are made more similar to the target word, as shown in Table 7.3 and Figure 7.2. This is called an "easy-to-hard discrimination." Similar to stimulus fading, stimulus shaping requires making a set of flash cards for the target words and then making additional sets of cards with distractor symbols and words. Often stimulus shaping is taught using worksheets with the rows of words. The student finds the word in each row, with each array containing distractor words more similar to the target word, making it harder to distinguish the target word. McGee et al. (1986) used this procedure when teaching students with autism to read words in a play setting. When the student identified a desired play material, the teacher showed the name of the material on a flash card with two distractors. Over trials of asking for the toy, the distractor flash cards became more similar to the target words.

The Edmark Reading Program is a commercial program that uses stimulus shaping. There are several versions of the Edmark Reading Program, including both workbook and computer-assisted instruction. Activities are designed for teacher-directed instruction and for independent seatwork or computer time.

Task Demonstration Model

The "task demonstration model" is a variation of stimulus shaping (Karsh et al., 1990; Karsh & Repp, 1992). In this model, variations are also made in the materials for the target word, but these are designed to encourage stimulus generalization rather than to cue the correct response. As described earlier, several variations of flash cards are made for each sight word, to encourage the student to read the word across stimulus materials. Sets of distractor words and symbols are also developed on separate flash cards, to be used in an easy-to-hard sequence with sets that are introduced in the following order of difficulty: (1) very different, (2) moderately different, and (3) slightly different.

Karsh and Repp (1992) taught teachers to use the task demonstration model during group instruction. Each student in the group was given two flash cards for each target word—one with the target word and one with a distractor.

Each student in the group had a different example of the target word and distractor. For example, if the word was "exit," each student had a flash card with the word "exit," but each flash card differed in some way (e.g., color of card, color of letter, typeface of letters). The distractor words were all different, but were "very different" from the target word. Over trials, the teacher introduced distractors that were moderately different and slightly different. When the teacher said, "Everybody touch 'exit,' " and clapped his or her hands, the students all pointed to their target word. The teacher praised correct responding. If a student made a mistake, the teacher said, "No, this is 'exit,' " and guided the student's hand to the correct flash card. The students then passed the words to the left for the next trial. All students had to get 9 out of 10 trials correct, before the teacher moved to the next level of difficulty (e.g., from very different to moderately different).

Teaching Guidelines for Selecting Prompts

As illustrated in Table 7.3 and described above, teachers have several options in choosing prompts for sight word instruction. Guidelines are needed to help make the decision about which method of prompting to use. Teachers may use more than one method. For example, a simpler procedure may be taught to a peer tutor or paraprofessional, and the teacher may supplement this with an alternative procedure. Or the teacher may use stimulus prompting for seat work and response prompting during teacher-directed instruction. The following are some questions teachers may ask in choosing these prompts:

- Which method does the student like best?
- Would it be useful to vary the prompting method or allow the student to choose the prompting method to enhance motivation?
- Is an errorless procedure needed for this student? (If so, consider time delay or stimulus prompting.)
- Who will be teaching the sight words? Which method can this teacher or tutor use most easily?
- Are options needed for seatwork? (If so, consider stimulus prompting or computer-assisted instruction.)

Stimulus Generalization: Reading Words across Varied Materials

The task demonstration model described earlier can help students learn to read words across a variety of materials. An alternative is to have a student read the words from real materials and in real settings, to augment flash card instruction. For example, Collins et al. (1995) had students read cooking words from the actual food packages of three different brands. Schloss et al. (1995) had students find words in a leisure context. These word-finding activities can be an important way to ensure that students can read their words in context.

Planning Sight Word Instruction

With these considerations, teachers can plan sight word instruction. This planning is illustrated in Figures 7.3 and 7.4. Figure 7.3 is a plan for teaching words needed on the job to a student who works in a community setting. The teacher will use progressive time delay. The teacher will go through the flash cards several times. On the first round, the teacher will give the answer immediately (no delay). On each subsequent round, the teacher will wait before giving the answer. This delay will be slightly longer during each round. In Figure 7.4, the teacher is using constant time delay to teach menu words. After a no-delay "warm-up" round, the teacher waits 4 seconds before modeling the word.

COMPREHENSION AND FUNCTIONAL USE

For a reading program to be "functional," it needs to target not only sight word instruction, but also the use of these words in daily living. Functional use requires response generalization—that is, making a second response after reading the word. For example, after reading the activity on a daily schedule, the student gets the necessary materials. Or, after reading selections on a menu, the student places an order. Unfortunately, the research literature provides few examples of functional use of sight words (Browder & Xin, 1998). Most researchers have focused on teaching word identification, but not on using the words to perform some daily activity.

Understanding Sight Word Comprehension

To plan functional use for sight words, it is important to understand how comprehension occurs. Sight word comprehension can be explained by using the principle of "stimulus equivalence"—specifically, "transitivity" (Sidman & Tailby, 1982). "Transitivity" is a mathematical term for a special type of equivalence relationship, which can be illustrated as follows:

$$
\begin{aligned}
\text{If } 6 &= 2 + 4 \text{ (A = B)}\\
\text{and } 2 + 4 &= 3 + 3 \text{ (B = C)}\\
\text{then } 3 + 3 &= 6 \text{ (A = C)}
\end{aligned}
$$

A colleague and I (Browder & D'Huyvetters, 1988) illustrated how this principle applies to the comprehension of sight words by evaluating word and object matching (figurines). We found that if a student learned to say "woman" when shown a figurine of a woman (A = B), and to say "woman" when shown the letters "w-o-m-a-n" (B = C), then the student could match the printed "w-o-m-a-n" to the figurine without further training (A = C).

FIGURE 7.3. Systematic Instruction Plan for job sight words.*

Systematic Instruction Plan

Student: _Allison_   Date plan written: _November 1, 20—_

Target skill: _Job sight words_   Routine for skill: _Following a work schedule_

Objective: _When given sight words that designate job tasks, Allison will read all words independently for 2 of 2 days._

Format

Materials: _Job checklist with sight words_

Setting and teacher: _Job coach in library before Allison starts work_

Number of trials: _One trial—all words_

Instructional Procedures

Prompting:

   Specific prompt(s) to be used: _Model reading correct word_

   Fading (check one):

   _____ None (simultaneous prompting)

   _X_ Time delay: _X_ Progressive or _____ Constant

   _____ Least intrusive prompts

   _____ Most to least intrusive prompts

   _____ Graduated guidance

   _____ Stimulus fading or shaping

   _____ Other (describe) _____

   Fading schedule: _Each session, begin with no delay (0 sec) for two trials, then two trials at each next delay level—2 sec, 4 sec, 6 sec, 8 sec. Probe independent reading at beginning of session._

Feedback:

   Correct: _Praise correct words, prompted or unprompted._

   Fading schedule for praise: _Only praise unprompted correct words after third session._

   Error correction: _Say "No, the word is . . ." and go to next trial._

Generalization Procedures

See Systematic Instruction Plan for self-initiated job routine.

Other Notes

*Allison is a fictitious student.

FIGURE 7.4. Systematic Instruction Plan for menu sight words.*

Systematic Instruction Plan

Student: <u>Simeon, Jordan, Anna</u>   Date plan written: <u>September 8, 20—</u>

Target skill: <u>Menu sight words</u>   Routine for skill: <u>Planning day</u>

Objective: <u>When given 5 frequent words from the school lunch menu, the student will read these words independently for 2 of 2 days.</u>

Format

Materials: <u>Flash cards with menu words; different set if 10 for each student</u>

Setting and teacher: <u>SpEd teacher in general education class during reading groups</u>

Number of trials: <u>4 trials per word; 20 per student</u>

Instructional Procedures

Prompting:

    Specific prompt(s) to be used: <u>Model reading correct word aloud</u>

Fading (check one):

    _____ None (simultaneous prompting)

    __X__ Time delay: _X_ Progressive *or* _X_ Constant

    _____ Least intrusive prompts

    _____ Most to least intrusive prompts

    _____ Graduated guidance

    _____ Stimulus fading or shaping

    _____ Other (describe) _____

    Fading schedule: <u>No delay (0 seconds) for 2 days, all trials; 0-second "warm-up" trial followed by 4-second delay for next week; then 4-second delay only.</u>

Feedback:

    Correct: <u>Praise correct words, prompted or unprompted.</u>

    Fading schedule for praise: <u>Only praise unprompted correct words after third session.</u>

    Error correction: <u>Say "No, the word is . . ." and have student repeat trial.</u>

Generalization Procedures

<u>See Systematic Instruction Plan for meal planning and shopping.</u>

Other Notes

<u>Focus attention in group by saying "Everybody look" and praising attending. On Fridays, probe to see who can read someone else's words.</u>

*Students are fictitious.

Transitivity can also be understood by considering why some students are "word callers," but do not understand what they read. For example, even after students learn to read the word "men" and "women" on flash cards, they may not choose the correct restroom door. This may occur because they do not yet understand whether they fit the category of "men" or "women." Or, it may be because they do not know to choose a restroom based on the signs. Either way, teaching needs to provide students with the opportunity not only to learn to read "men" and "women," but also to understand how to choose a restroom based on their gender.

Kennedy et al. (1994) illustrated why comprehension (transitivity) may not occur when the relationships to be formed are more complex. They taught students to classify foods together that belonged to the same food groups, using sight words of the food names. Whereas students could learn that "onion" went with "potato" and "potato" went with "garlic," and then automatically pair the "onion" and "garlic," they did not realize that if "garlic" went with "squash," then "onion" and "squash" were the same type of food.

Although this research is fairly complex, it illustrates the simple principle that the associations students are to make in functional use must be taught directly. If students are to learn not only to read their schedule words, but to follow a schedule, then they need instruction in both reading words and following a schedule. If students are to learn not only to read recipe words, but to cook, then instruction is needed in both recipe reading and food preparation.

Planning Functional Use

In Table 7.2, examples have been given of sight words that can be taught and their functional use. This section describes how to plan instruction in the functional use of sight words so that comprehension will occur. Although researchers often overlook the need to demonstrate functional use, the examples that do exist illustrate the varied ways this can be achieved. McGee et al. (1986) had students point to the appropriate words to choose play materials that were shelved in boxes. Teachers may teach functional use of sight words with many types of choices. For example, students may read the next day's lunch menu and choose whether to bring lunch or buy it. Or a student may read the menu in a restaurant to choose and place an order. Teachers may incorporate many other choices in the classroom with a written list of sight words. Students may pick a free-time activity from a written list of options, or choose a peer partner from a written list of names.

Another way functional use can be taught is teaching students to use sight words for self-instruction. For example, we (Browder et al., 1984) taught adults to read sight words in instruction booklets for daily living (e.g., for cooking, " chop," "stir," "spread"). After group instruction on reading the words, the learners were taught to perform the activities following each word in their booklets. Similarly, when Collins et al. (1995) taught students food preparation words, they created opportunities in the home economics room and in a neighborhood home for them to prepare the actual recipes following package directions.

Sight words can also be useful as "to-do" or "to-buy" lists. We (Browder & Minarovic, 2000) taught employees with moderate mental retardation to read sight words that related to the key tasks of their community jobs. For example, the word "carts" was the cue to gather carts from the grocery store parking lot. After instruction in learning to read the words, instruction was provided in following a "did–next–now" self-instruction strategy (Agran & Moore, 1994). The employees learned to go back to their checklists after each completed task and check it off while saying, "I did that." They read the next word and said, "Next, 'sweep.' " They then located the materials needed and said, "Now, I 'sweep.' " Similarly, we (Lalli & Browder, 1993) taught participants to follow a household chore schedule. The participants in this study were able to follow the schedule to perform the chores once the words were learned. Participants also learned words for grocery shopping and used them as components of a "to-buy" list.

If sight words are related to safety, the functional response may need to be simulated with role play. As noted earlier, in teaching product warning labels, Collins and Griffen (1996) had students show a "safe response." This safe response could be either to store the material in a safe place or to give it to an adult. Similarly, students may need to role-play avoiding areas that say "Danger" or "Do not enter."

Figure 7.5 provides an example of a Systematic Instruction Plan to teach functional use of sight words. This plan is taught concurrently with the one shown in Figure 7.4. In this plan, students learn to generate menus and a grocery list, using the food sight words they are learning in class. The teacher chooses to use a feedback procedure, since this lesson reviews material taught in a prior lesson.

PLANNING A COMPREHENSIVE FUNCTIONAL READING PROGRAM

Recommendations

Often students will have more than one sight word instruction plan as part of a comprehensive functional reading program. Kamps, Leonard, Dugan, Boland, and Greenwood (1991) conducted ecobehavioral assessment in programs for children with autism, to determine how to design effective instructional procedures. They recommend using an abundance of varied materials (e.g., manipulatives, pictures, household objects, food, clothing, etc.) and having a variety of interactions (e.g., individualization of materials, group instruction with choral responding, group instruction with serial responding, student-to-student interactions). They also found that instructional procedures were more effective when verbal responses were intermixed with motor and written responses. Effective groups were typically fast-paced sessions, with enthusiastic participation by the students and the teacher. Similarly, a functional reading program will introduce sight words and their use in a variety of ways, as described in the illustrations that follow and in Box 7.1.

Three Examples of Comprehensive Functional Reading Programs[4]

Ms. Carson collaborates with the third- to fifth-grade teachers in an elementary school. Reading is an important part of the individualized plans for the students Ms. Carson supports in these various classes. Her comprehensive reading plan includes using the

---

[4]All three of these examples are fictitious.

FIGURE 7.5. Systematic Instruction Plan for meal planning and shopping.*

Systematic Instruction Plan

Student: _Simeon, Jordan, Anna_   Date plan written: _September 8, 20—_

Target skill: _Meal planning and shopping_   Routine for skill: _Grocery shopping_

Objective: _When given a menu-planning guide, the student will plan a menu and make a shopping list with all steps of the task analysis correct for 2 of 2 days._

Format

Materials: _Menu guide showing food ideas (sight words) from each food group; grocery list with sight words to be circled from menu selections_

Setting and teacher: _Group instruction by teacher; community-based instruction to buy selected items with paraprofessional_

Number of trials: _One trial_

Instructional Procedures

Prompting:

    Specific prompt(s) to be used: _Point to word on menu or shopping list_

Fading (check one):

    ____ None (simultaneous prompting)

    _X_ Time delay: _X_ Progressive _or_ ____ Constant

    ____ Least intrusive prompts

    ____ Most to least intrusive prompts

    ____ Graduated guidance

    ____ Stimulus fading or shaping

    _X_ Other (describe) _(Feedback only)_

    Fading schedule: _None needed—feedback-only procedure._

Feedback:

    Correct: _Praise each correct response in training._

    Fading schedule for praise: _Drop praise after 1 day at 100%._

    Error correction: _Say "No, the word is . . . " (state correct word and have student repeat)._

Generalization Procedures

Vary brands of food used in menus and shopping.

Other Notes

*Students are fictitious.

BOX 7.1. **Functional Reading and General Education Inclusion**

Functional Reading is a curricular area that overlaps with general education. In the early elementary grades, students may begin learning sight words; as late as high school, teachers introduce new words related to new concepts. The difference for students with developmental disabilities is that the target words may come from activities of daily living and community settings, rather than from textbooks. Although the words themselves may differ, students may learn these by using formats compatible with general education settings (e.g., computer-assisted instruction, peer tutoring, self-instruction with seatwork). Students will probably need some direct instruction in order to learn the functional use for these words. This additional instruction in functional use will often require going beyond the general education classroom to utilize activities in other school settings or the community.

Edmark Reading Program to introduce the students to as many functional words as possible. Peers work with the students, using the classroom computers to run the Edmark software. Since the Edmark Program provides its own structure, she is able to utilize a lot of different peers with a minimum of training. In addition, each student has a list of "favorite words" that he or she is learning. Some of these words are part of free-time menus. Students are also being taught to read their classmates' names, which they practice by handing back papers in class. Ms. Carson teaches a small group in each class daily that includes the students with special needs and some peers who need extra reading help. They are working on reading package labels that are either household products or food items. For household products, they practice a "safe response," and for food, they make a snack one day a week. Ms. Carson also uses the Edmark materials to give the students with special needs reading seatwork to do when other students are working out of their texts.

In Mr. Johnson's middle school class, he has chosen not to use a commercial series, but to focus all of his instruction on the students' school and community environments. In his class, Mr. Johnson teaches Systematic Instruction Plans for reading the school menu, making grocery lists, ordering from a menu, following a schedule, and reading words frequently seen in school. To maximize instructional time, Mr. Johnson uses group instruction and gives instructive feedback (e.g., tells the meaning of each word). Students also receive community-based instruction to purchase groceries and order food in a restaurant. The students have peer escorts for their classes who help implement the schedule reading plan. For seatwork in general education classes when students cannot do the work assigned, they practice finding their key sight words in a variety of materials (e.g., doing word search puzzles, scanning newspaper ads, scanning school notices).

Ms. Gabriel's high school class operates as a resource room for students to receive specialized instruction, which is fitted in between general education classes, their community jobs, and school activities (e.g., chorus, pep club). Ms. Gabriel plans all reading instruction from these other activities. Students' Systematic Instruction Plans include reading words used in pep rally signs, job schedules, job applications, and words frequently encountered in classrooms (e.g., dates, teachers' names). Ms. Gabriel uses mostly one-to-one instruction with additional instruction, provided in context by peers, the job coach, and a paraprofessional.

SUMMARY

Functional reading instruction focuses on teaching a limited sight vocabulary of words that have immediate functional use. To select these target sight words, teachers can use ecological inventories of the student's current and future environments. Words that enhance independence in daily living routines, community mobility, and the expression of preferences can be especially useful to the student. Consideration should also be given to words that help the student function in general education contexts.

In planning sight word instruction, the teacher will need to decide how many words to teach at one time, what type of materials to use, and the setting for instruction. Students may learn sight words well through flash card drills taught in small groups, but they will also need practice to use their words in functional contexts. In teaching the words, several options exist for systematic prompting and fading including simultaneous prompting, time delay, stimulus shaping, and stimulus fading. Teachers can choose a prompting and fading system by considering which procedure is the easiest to implement and which students respond to best.

Some students master reading sight words aloud but do not demonstrate comprehension of these words. The mathematical principle of transitivity would predict that if students understand the language concept behind the word, they will be able to comprehend it once they have mastered reading it by sight. To teach the concept of the word, students need opportunities to use the words in the context of daily routines like reading a daily schedule, menu, job card, or recipe.

REFERENCES

Agran, M., & Moore, S. C. (1994). *How to teach self-instruction of job skills (Innovations No. 3)..* Washington, DC: American Association on Mental Retardation.

Alig-Cybriwsky, C., Wolery, M., & Gast, D. (1990). Use of a constant time delay procedure in teaching preschoolers in a group format. *Journal of Early Intervention, 14*, 99–116.

Ault, M. J., Wolery, M., Doyle, P. M., & Gast, D. L. (1989). Review of comparative studies in the instruction of students with moderate and severe handicaps. *Exceptional Children, 55*, 346–356.

Barbetta, P. M., Heward, W. L., & Bradley, D. M. (1993). Relative effects of whole-word and phonetic prompt error correction on the acquisition and maintenance of sight words by students with developmental disabilities. *Journal of Applied Behavior Analysis, 26*, 99–110.

Barbetta, P. M., Miller, A. D., Peters, M. T., Heron, T. E., & Cochran, L. L. (1991). Tugmate: A cross-age tutoring program to teach sight vocabulary. *Education and Treatment of Children, 14*, 19–37.

Baumgart, D., & VanWalleghem, J. (1987). Teaching sight words: A comparison between computer-assisted and teacher-taught methods. *Education and Training in Mental Retardation, 22*, 56–65.

Brigance, A. (1999). *Brigance Diagnostic Comprehensive Inventory of Basic Skills (Revised).* North Billerica, MA: Curriculum Associates.

Browder, D. M., & D'Huyvetters, K. K. (1988). An evaluation of transfer of stimulus control and of comprehension in sight word reading for children with mental retardation and emotional disturbance. *School Psychology Review, 17*, 331–342.

Browder, D. M., Hines, C., McCarthy, L. J., & Fees, J. (1984). A treatment package for increasing sight word recognition for use in daily living skills. *Education and Training of the Mentally Retarded, 19,* 191–200.

Browder, D. M., & Lalli, J. S. (1991). Review of research on sight word instruction. *Research in Developmental Disabilities, 12,* 203–228.

Browder, D. M., & Minarovic, T. (2000). The use of sight words in self-instruction training for individuals with moderate mental retardation in competitive jobs. *Education and Training in Mental Retardation and Developmental Disabilities, 35,* 78–89.

Browder, D. M., & Shear, S. M. (1996). Interspersal of known items in a treatment package to teach sight words to students with behavior disorders. *Journal of Special Education, 29,* 400–413.

Browder, D. M., & Xin, Y. P. (1998). A meta-analysis and review of sight word instruction. *Journal of Special Education, 32,* 130–153.

Carnine, D. W., Filbert, J., & Kameenui, E. J. (1997). *Direct instruction reading* (3rd ed.). Upper Saddle River, NJ: Prentice-Hall.

Clifft, M. A. (1986). Writing about psychiatric patients: Guidelines for disguising case material. *Bulletin of the Menninger Clinic, 50,* 511–524.

Collins, B. C., Branson, T. A., & Hall, M. (1995). Teaching generalized reading of cooking product labels to adolescents with mental disabilities through the use of key words taught by peer tutors. *Education and Training in Mental Retardation and Developmental Disabilities, 30,* 65–76.

Collins, B. C., & Griffen, A. K. (1996). Teaching students with moderate disabilities to make safe responses to product warning labels. *Education and Treatment of Children, 19,* 30–45.

Collins, B. C., & Stinson, D. M. (1995). Teaching generalized reading of product warning labels to adolescents with mental disabilities through the use of key words. *Exceptionality, 5,* 163–181.

Conners, F. A. (1992). Reading instruction for students with moderate mental retardation: Review and analysis of research. *American Journal of Mental Retardation, 96,* 577–598.

Cuvo, A. J., & Klatt, K. P. (1992). Effects of community-based, videotape, and flash card instruction of community-reference sight words on students with mental retardation. *Journal of Applied Behavior Analysis, 25,* 499–512.

Dorry, G. W., & Zeaman, D. (1973). The use of a faded technique in paired associate teaching of a reading-vocabulary with retardates. *Mental Retardation, 11,* 3–6.

Dorry, G. W., & Zeaman, D. (1975). Teaching simple reading vocabulary to retarded children: Effectiveness of fading and nonfading procedures. *American Journal of Mental Deficiency, 79,* 711–716.

Doyle, P. M., Wolery, M., Gast, D. L., Ault, M. J. & Wiley, K. (1990). Comparison of constant time delay and the system of least prompts in teaching preschoolers with developmental delays. *Research in Developmental Disabilities, 11,* 1–22.

Doyle, P. M., Wolery, M., Ault, M. J., & Gast, D. (1988). System of least prompts: A literature review of procedural parameters. *Journal of the Association for Persons with Severe Handicaps, 13,* 28–40.

Duran, E. (1985). Teaching functional reading in context to severely retarded and severely retarded autistic adolescents with limited English proficiency. *Adolescence, 20,* 432–439.

Eckert, T., & Browder, D. M. (1997). Stimulus manipulations: Enhancing materials for self-directed learning. In E. M. Pinkston & D. Baer (Eds.), *Environment and behavior* (pp. 279–288). Boulder, CO: Westview Press.

Engelmann, S., & Bruner, E. C. (1995). *Reading mastery.* Chicago, IL: Science Research Associates/Macmillan/McGraw-Hill.

Engelmann, S., Hanner, S., & Haddox, P. (1989). *Corrective reading.* Chicago, IL: Science Research Associates/Macmillan/McGraw-Hill.

Farmer, J. A., Gast, D. L., Wolery, M., & Winterling, V. (1991). Small group instruction for students with severe handicaps: A study of observational learning. *Education and Training in Mental Retardation, 26,* 190–201.

Gast, D. L., Ault, M. J., Wolery, M., Doyle, P. M., & Belanger, S. (1988). Comparison of constant time delay and the system of least prompts in teaching sight words to students with moderate retardation. *Education and Training in Mental Retardation, 23,* 117–128.

Gast, D. L., Doyle, P. M., Wolery, M., Ault, M. J., & Baklarz, J. L. (1991a). Acquisition of incidental information during small group instruction. *Education and Treatment of Children, 14,* 1–18.

Gast, D. L., Doyle, P. M., Wolery, M., Ault, M. J., & Farmer, J. (1991b). Assessing the acquisition of incidental information by secondary-age students with mental retardation: Comparison of response
prompting strategies. *American Journal of Mental Retardation, 96,* 63–80.

Gast, D. L. Wolery, M., Morris, L. L., Doyle, P. M., & Meyer, S. (1990). Teaching sight word reading in a
group instructional arrangement using constant time delay. *Exceptionality, 1,* 81–96.

Glat, R., Gould, K., Stoddard, L. T., & Sidman, M. (1994). A note on transfer of stimulus control in the
delayed-cue procedure: Facilitation by an overt response. *Journal of Applied Behavior Analysis, 27,*
699–704.

Johnson, P., Schuster, J., & Bell, J. K. (1996). Comparison of simultaneous prompting with and without
error correction in teaching science vocabulary words to high school students with mild disabilities. *Journal of Behavioral Education, 6,* 437–458.

Kamps, D. M., Leonard, B. R., Dugan, E. P., Boland, B., & Greenwood, C. R. (1991). The use of
ecobehavioral assessment to identify naturally occurring effective procedures in classrooms serving students with autism and other developmental disabilities. *Journal of Behavioral Education, 4,*
367–397.

Kamps, D. M., Walker, D., Locke, P., Delquadri, J., & Hall, R. V. (1990). A comparison of instructional
arrangements for students with autism served in public school settings. *Education and Treatment of
Children, 13,* 197–215.

Karsh, K. G., & Repp, A. C. (1992). The task demonstration model: A concurrent model for teaching
groups of students with severe disabilities. *Exceptional Children, 59,* 54–67.

Karsh, K. G., Repp, A. C., & Lenz, M. W. (1990). A comparison of the task demonstration model and the
standard prompting hierarchy in teaching word identification to persons with moderate retardation. *Research in Developmental Disabilities, 11,* 395–410.

Kennedy, C. H., Itkonen, T. L., & Lindquist, K. (1994). Nodality effects during equivalence class forma-
tions: An extension of sight word reading and concept development. *Journal of Applied Behavior
Analysis, 27,* 673–684.

Koury, M., & Browder, D. M. (1986). The use of delay to teach sight words by peer tutors classified as
moderately mentally retarded. *Education and Training of the Mentally Retarded, 2,* 252–258.

Lalli, J. S., & Browder, D. M. (1993). Comparison of sight word training procedures with validation of
the most practical procedure in teaching reading for daily living. *Research in Developmental Disabilities, 14,* 107–127.

McCurdy, B. L., Cundari, L., & Lentz, E. F. (1990). Enhancing instructional efficiency: An examination
of time delay and the opportunity to observe instruction. *Education and Treatment of Children, 13,*
226–238.

McGee, G. G., Krantz, P. J., & McClannahan, L. E. (1986). An extension of incidental teaching procedures to reading instruction for autistic children. *Journal of Applied Behavior Analysis, 19,* 147–157.

Rincover, A. (1978). Variables affecting stimulus fading and discriminative responding in psychotic
children. *Journal of Abnormal Psychology, 8,* 235–246.

Rohena-Diaz, E. (1998). *A comparison of English and Spanish instruction in teaching sight words to students
with moderate mental retardation who are linguistically diverse.* Unpublished doctoral dissertation,
Lehigh University.

Rohena-Diaz, E., & Browder, D. (1996). Functional reading for students with developmental disabilities
who are linguistically diverse. *Journal of Behavioral Education, 6,* 25–33.

Schloss, P. J., Alper, S., Young, H., Arnold-Reid, G., Aylward, M., & Dudenhoeffer, S. (1995). Acquisition of functional sight words in community-based recreational settings. *Journal of Special Education, 29,* 84–96.

Schoen, S., & Ogden, S. (1995). Impact of time delay, observational learning, and attentional cueing
upon word recognition during integrated small group instruction. *Journal of Autism and Developmental Disorders, 25,* 503–519.

Schuster, J. W., Griffen, A. K., & Wolery, M. (1992). Comparisons of simultaneous prompting and constant time delay procedures in teaching sight words to elementary students with moderate mental retardation. *Journal of Behavioral Education, 2,* 305–325.

Schuster, J. W., Morse, T. E., Griffen, A. B., & Wolery, T. (1996). Teaching peer reinforcement and grocery words: An investigation of observational learning and instructive feedback. *Journal of Behavioral Education, 6,* 511–534.

Sidman, M., & Tailby, W. (1982). Conditional discrimination vs. matching to sample: An expansions of the testing paradigms. *Journal of the Experimental Analysis of Behavior, 37,* 5–22.

Singh, N. N., & Solman, R. T. (1990). A stimulus control analysis of the picture–word problem in children who are mentally retarded: The blocking effect. *Journal of Applied Behavior Analysis, 23,* 525–532.

Singleton, K. C., Schuster, J. W., & Ault, M. J. (1995). Simultaneous prompting in a small group instructional arrangement. *Education and Training in Mental Retardation and Developmental Disabilities, 30,* 218–230.

Werts, M. G., Wolery, M., Holcombe, A., & Gast, D. L. (1995). Instructive feedback: Review of parameters and effects. *Journal of Behavioral Education, 5,* 55–75.

Whalen, C., Schuster, J. W., & Hemmeter, M. L. (1996). The use of unrelated instructive feedback when teaching in a small group instructional arrangement. *Education and Training in Mental Retardation and Developmental Disabilities, 31,* 188–202.

Wilson, P. G., Cuvo, A. J., & Davis, P. K. (1986). Training a functional skill cluster: Nutritious meal planning within a budget, grocery list writing, and shopping. *Analysis and Intervention in Developmental Disabilities, 6,* 179–201.

Wolery, M., Doyle, P. M., Ault, P. M., Gast, D. L., Meyer, S. L., & Stinson, D. (1991). Effects of presenting incidental information in consequent events on future learning. *Journal of Behavioral Education, 1,* 79–104.

Wolery, M., Werts, M. G., Snyder, E. D., & Caldwell, N. K. (1994). Efficacy of constant time delay implemented by peer tutors in general education classrooms. *Journal of Behavioral Education, 4,* 415–436.

EIGHT

Functional Math

WHEN JAMES,[1] **A 9-YEAR-OLD BOY** *with severe mental retardation, received his first community-based instruction at a fast-food restaurant, he had no functional math skills. The teacher asked James's mother to send some money to school for this activity. When the money arrived, the teacher put it in an envelope in her purse. The teacher watched the clock to know when to leave for this community instruction. When they arrived at the restaurant, she prompted James to wait in line and hand the cashier a card to place his order. The teacher then handed the cashier the money and helped James take his tray to his table.*

Within a few years, this activity had a totally new format because of the functional math skills James had acquired. When the teacher prompted James to check his calendar for a special event, James opened the photo album schedule and saw a picture of the restaurant. He then took a $5 bill from the budget folder he was learning to use and placed it in his wallet, with some help from his teacher. He went to the door to indicate he was ready to go. At the restaurant, James again placed his order with a picture card, but this time he took money from his own wallet to pay. When he finished eating, he took his tray to the trash can and waited there to indicate he was ready to go.

Gaining skills in time and money management can be important ways to "take charge" of one's life. Functional math skills can also provide a link to the general education curriculum for students gaining skills in inclusive settings. This chapter describes curriculum and assessment for teaching functional math.

"Functional math" refers to the basic math skills needed to perform skills of daily living; it includes money management, time management, measurement, counting, and simple computation. In a typical general education curriculum, students learn the number and computation skills needed to perform these tasks by the end of second grade. By contrast, acquiring the functional use of these skills to manage time and money is a lifelong learning experience for most people. Individuals with developmental disabilities often have not mastered the basic math skills needed in activities of daily living and will need to learn these concurrently with their applications to time and

---

[1]The example of James is based on an actual student. His name and other details have been changed to protect his confidentiality, consistent with the guidelines of the World and American Psychiatric Associations for disguising case material (Clifft, 1986).

money management. By focusing on the match encountered in daily living, teachers can also adapt many math activities found in the general education math curriculum for students with moderate and severe disabilities. This chapter describes curriculum for teaching basic math in the context of daily living skills and recommends ways to simplify the math skills needed through the use of adaptations.

MONEY MANAGEMENT SKILLS

One of the most efficient and effective ways to teach functional math is to focus on teaching money management. Individuals with developmental disabilities often lack autonomy in their personal financial management. Sometimes they may even have few opportunities to make decisions about how to spend or save their money.

Money management has several components: (1) knowing how much money one has (computation and record keeping), (2) knowing how to gain access to one's money (banking), (3) knowing how much money one can spend (budgeting), (4) knowing how to spend it (purchasing), and (5) knowing how to use money to make money (saving and investing) (Browder & Grasso, 1999). Most of the research on teaching individuals with developmental disabilities to use money has focused on teaching them to know how to count and spend their money (Browder & Grasso, 1999). It is important in a functional math program to help individuals learn these varied aspects of money management.

Computation and Purchasing

Students with developmental disabilities may be highly motivated to learn how to use money to purchase preferred items. Computation and purchasing are excellent starting points for instruction in money management and in functional math in general. Students with a broad range of abilities can learn to use money and make purchases independently, depending on the complexity of the money skills taught. A skill sequence for teaching money computation and purchasing is shown in Table 8.1.

Preselected Money Amounts

When students have no counting or money recognition skills, purchasing can still be taught by accommodating for this skill deficit through preselecting the money amount needed. Such an accommodation may be the best approach when the learner is older (e.g., an adult) or needs to learn the concept that money is needed to gain access to goods. It is not a functional approach to postpone opportunities to make purchases until a student learns to count or name money, because the student may never learn the purpose of these skills.

A support person (e.g., a teacher or paraprofessional) can help an individual with disabilities who cannot count money prepare for purchasing by placing the exact money needed in his or her wallet. For example, in teaching adults with severe mental retardation to purchase a snack in a fast-food restaurant or grocery store, McDonnell and Laughlin (1989) gave each person two $1 bills. Similarly, Storey, Bates, and Hanson (1984) gave adults with mild to severe mental retardation a $1 bill to purchase coffee. If the person lacks the fine motor skills to use a wallet, the money may be carried in a

TABLE 8.1. An Easy-to-Hard Skill Sequence for Teaching Money Computation and Purchasing

Money skill	Example	Reference
1. Use a preselected amount of money to make purchase.	Teacher places two $1 bills in wallet.	McDonnell & Laughlin (1989)
2. Use response classes for types of purchases.	Student learns to use quarters for vending machine, $1 for convenience store, and a $5 for lunch.	Gardill & Browder (1995)
3. Use $1 bills only and compute next-dollar amount.	If purchase is $3.45, student says "Four" and counts out four $1 bills.	McDonnell & Ferguson (1988)
4. Use $1, $5, or $10 bill and compute next-dollar amount.	If purchase is $6.75, student says "Seven," selects a $5 bill and two $1 bills, and counts up to 7.	Frederick-Dugan, Test, & Varn (1991)
5. Compute coins, counting by 5's.	Student learns to count nickels, then dimes, then quarters, using counting by 5s.	Lowe & Cuvo (1976)
6. Discriminate money equivalence.	Student learns that two quarters and five dimes are the same.	Frank & Wacker (1986); Stoddard, Brown, Hurlburt, Manoli, & McIlvane (1989)
7. Read price and find exact money amount.	Given price $2.56, student selects two $1 bills, two quarters, a nickel, and a penny.	Cuvo, Veitch, Trace, & Konke (1978)

pocket or given to the person at the time of the purchase. At this first step in the money and purchasing skills sequence, the person is simply learning to exchange money for desired items.

Using Response Classes

Many people in today's fast-paced society simplify their money management by making purchases with certain types of money. For example, when a person is getting gas, a $20 bill may be used. Or, when the person is going to a fast food restaurant for lunch, a $5 bill is selected. A $1 bill may be used for coffee or a soda at convenience store. People who choose to use specific bills may save their change or convert it into bills at the bank.

Similarly, individuals with developmental disabilities can learn to associate specific denominations of money with classes of purchases. In one study (Gardill & Browder, 1995), three classes of money were taught: Students learned to discriminate among quarters, a $1 bill, and a $5 bill. Through tabletop instruction via picture examples, the students learned to select quarters for a variety of vending machine purchases, a $1 bill for going to a convenience store, and a $5 bill for buying lunch. As prices change, these skills need to be retrained. Many vending machines now take $1 bills, and some beverages in convenience stores cost more than $1. Given the limitation that retraining will be needed after prices increase, the response class method of teaching money use can enable students to make purchases independently when the students have not been able to learn strategies that require counting or other more complex math skills. An example of a Systematic Instruction Plan for teaching money response classes is shown in Figure 8.1.

Next-Dollar Strategy

The "next-dollar strategy," also called the "one-more-than technique," involves giving the cashier one more dollar than the stated price. This method has gained popularity in the research literature and has been used with individuals with autism (Haring, Kennedy, Adams, & Pitts-Conway, 1987), mild to moderate mental retardation (Colyer & Collins, 1996; Van den Pol et al., 1981), moderate mental retardation (Denny & Test, 1995; Frederick-Dugan, Test, & Varn, 1991; McDonnell & Ferguson, 1988), and moderate to severe mental retardation (Test, Howell, Burkhart, & Beroth, 1993; Westling, Floyd, & Carr, 1990).

In teaching the next-dollar strategy, the teacher often begins with flash card training in a classroom setting. In their study, Colyer and Collins (1996) used 75 flash cards with prices from $.01 to $5.00. They also used real money ($1 bills) and a variety of items that the students could buy during instruction. They surveyed the stores and found that cashiers always stated the price; only in some settings, however, was the price visible on the cash register. Based on this information, the teacher trained the students to select the next-dollar amount based on the stated price. The teacher used a hierarchy of least intrusive prompts that encouraged use of the natural cues of the stated price and printed price (if available), as shown in Box 8.1.

Sometimes the teacher used a number line to help the student find the number that was one more than the stated price.

The next-dollar strategy can be useful across a large variety of small purchases. The accommodation needed to use the next-dollar strategy is for the person to carry only $1 bills in his or her wallet. Change that accumulates each week can be converted into $1 bills at the bank.

For larger purchases, the person may learn to use a debit card. A debit card func-

---

BOX 8.1. The "One More Than" Technique for Counting Money

1. The teacher stated the price and waited for the student to count out the next-dollar amount ("Five ninety-seven").
2. If there was no response, the teacher showed a flashcard of the written price ($5.97) and restated it verbally ("Five ninety-seven").
3. If there was no response, the teacher used an expanded verbal cue sometimes used by cashiers ("Five dollars and ninety-seven cents").
4. If there was still no response, the teacher gave explicit directions on how much was needed ("Five dollars and ninety-seven cents. Give me five dollars and one more dollar for the cents").
5. If there was still no response, the teacher modeled how to count out the next-dollar amount ("One, two, three, four, five, and one more dollar for the cents").

FIGURE 8.1. Systematic Instruction Plan for selecting money amount.*

Systematic Instruction Plan

Student: _Robin, John, Sue_   Date plan written: _September 15, 20—_

Target skill: _Select money amount_   Routine for skill: _Purchasing_

Objective: _When given a choice among quarters, a $1 bill, and a $5 bill, the student will select the correct money amount for a given purchasing activity on 2 of 2 days._

Format

Materials: _Real money, pictures of items_

Setting and teacher: _Classroom teacher in class and other school settings—group instruction; weekly in community during purchasing_

Number of trials: _During classroom instruction, 10 trials on each of the three types of purchases—vending machine, convenience store, and lunch—across the three students_

Instructional Procedures

Prompting:

    Specific prompt(s) to be used: _Picture of each type of money; gesture_

Fading (check one):

    ____ None (simultaneous prompting)

    _X_ Time delay: ____ Progressive or _X_ Constant

    ____ Least intrusive prompts

    ____ Most to least intrusive prompts

    ____ Graduated guidance

    ____ Stimulus fading or shaping

    _X_ Other (describe) _Eliminate pictures of money after first week_

    Fading schedule: _4 sessions at 0-second delay; then 4-second delay until mastery._

Feedback:

    Correct: _Specific praise—"Good! That's a dollar for buying a soda at the 7–11!"_

    Fading schedule for praise: _Eliminate praise after correct response for 2 days_

    Error correction: _Say "No" and show correct response._

Generalization Procedures

Weekly use in store; also training in cafeteria, school vending machines, school store.

Other Notes

*The three students are fictitious.

tions similarly to a credit card, but the transaction is deducted from the checking account like a check. To use a debit card, the person need only be able to sign his or her name to the credit slip. If the purchase exceeds the amount in the checking account, the transaction will be denied. Individuals with developmental disabilities may benefit from learning to use debit cards to make periodic purchases for items such as clothing and food. Debit cards can also be used in many places for obtaining cash from a bank machine, paying for haircuts, buying movie tickets, and a wide variety of other uses. The drawback of debit cards is that they make it easy to drain a checking account without adhering to a budget. Teaching budgeting is discussed later in this chapter.

Next-Dollar Strategy with Mixed Currency

When students master the next-dollar strategy, they may be able to master the use of mixed currency. When this strategy is used for more than minor purchases, it is more convenient to carry a mix of bills (e.g., $1, $5, and $10 bills) than a large number of $1 bills. Denny and Test (1995) taught adults with moderate mental retardation to use the next-dollar strategy with mixed currency to make purchases up to $20. Students learned to count up from the highest bill they could use. They also learned to set aside a dollar for the next-dollar amount, rather than rounding up the price. This extra dollar was set aside as the "cents pile." The skill sequence they followed was as follows:

1. One-more-than strategy, using the "cents pile" strategy for prices up to $4.99. (If cashier said, "Three eighty-two," the learner laid aside a $1 for the cents and counted out another three $1 bills.)
2. "Counting on" from a $5 bill for purchases from $5.00 to $9.99. (If the cashier said, "Seven thirty-two," the learner laid aside a $1 bill for the cents, then selected a $5 bill, and then counted out two more $1 bills to make the $7.
3. "Counting on" from a $10 bill for prices from $10.00 to $14.99.
4. "Counting on" from a $5 bill and a $10 bill for prices from $15.00 to $20.00.
5. Mixed practice with all different combinations.

A Systematic Instruction Plan for the next-dollar strategy is shown in Figure 8.2.

Coin Computation

In general education, students often learn coin recognition and computation as their first money skills. In the current economy, few items can be purchased efficiently with coins, because most things cost more than $1. Even vending machines are converting to the use of $1 bills, as noted above. Given this economic reality, it may not be a useful investment of time to teach individuals with developmental disabilities the complex skills of coin computation. In contrast, if students have mastered the use of currency (e.g., the next-dollar strategy with mixed currency), mastery of coin computation increases their flexibility and independence in money use. For example, students may gain skills for working as cashiers.

Lowe and Cuvo (1976) developed a simplified method to teach coin computation by teaching students to count all coins by 5's, using their fingers for self-prompting. The skill sequence they used appears in Box 8.2.

FIGURE 8.2. Systematic Instruction Plan for next-dollar strategy.*

Systematic Instruction Plan

Student: Garland Jennings   **Date plan written:** January 1, 20—

Target skill: Next-dollar strategy   **Routine for skill:** Purchasing

Objective: When making a variety of purchases under $20.00, Garland will give the cashier one more dollar than the stated price for 10 of 10 trials on 2 consecutive days in training and for 2 of 2 days in the community.

Format

Materials: $1 bills

Setting and teacher: Library before work by job coach

Number of trials: 10

Instructional Procedures

Prompting:

   Specific prompt(s) to be used: System of least intrusive prompts: (1) Say price, (2) show price, (3) restate price in dollars, (4) model counting $1 more than price.

Fading (check one):

   _____ None (simultaneous prompting)

   _____ Time delay: _____ Progressive *or* _____ Constant

   __X__ Least intrusive prompts

   _____ Most to least intrusive prompts

   _____ Graduated guidance

   _____ Stimulus fading or shaping

   _____ Other (describe) _____

   Fading schedule: Use least assistance needed on each trial.

Feedback:

   Correct: Specific praise—"Perfect! That's six dollars."

   Fading schedule for praise: Intermittent after first week

   Error correction: Repeat trial with all levels of prompt

Generalization Procedures

Train in store weekly.

Other Notes

*Garland is a fictitious student..

BOX 8.2. **Lowe and Cuvo Coin Counting Technique**

1. Counting nickels to $1 by 5's, using the index finger ("pointer") to move and count each coin.
2. Counting dimes to $1 by 5's, using the index and middle fingers to count each dime (i.e., making the "victory sign" with the fingers).
3. Counting a mix of nickels and dimes by 5's, beginning with the dimes ("victory sign" fingers) and then the nickels ("pointer").
4. Counting quarters by 5's, using all fingers (the "hi" sign).
5. Counting a mix of quarters, dimes, and nickels by 5's.
6. Counting pennies with the mix by counting all silver coins first by 5's, then "counting on" pennies by 1's.

Discriminating Money Equivalence

To have the maximum flexibility with money, individuals need to be able to use money interchangeably. For example, if an item costs $12.36, a shopper can use a variety of money amounts: (1) a $20 bill, (2) two $10 bills, (3) a $10 and a $5 bill, (4) a $10 and three $1 bills, (5) three $5 bills, or (6) a $10 bill, two $1 bills, and exact change. Not all students will master this level of complexity; such students can make purchases efficiently by using the next-dollar strategy. In contrast, students who master both using currency and computing coins may benefit from moving on in their money computation and purchasing skills to learn money equivalences.

Stoddard, Brown, Hurlburt, Manoli, and McIlvane (1989) used the principle of transitivity to teach stimulus equivalence for various combinations of coins to match prices. Participants were given coins and prices on cards, and were taught to construct matches. Students first learned to make an exact match (e.g., a quarter to a quarter) and matched the coin(s) to a price (in this case, $.25). Then they learned (1) two dimes and a nickel, (2) two dimes and five pennies, and (3) five nickels. This complex research primarily focused on how levels of equivalence relationships were formed. To translate this into an instructional program, the teacher could teach the student to make pairs:

> Two $5 bills = $10.00 (A = B)
> A $10 bill = $10.00 (C = B)
> Two $5 bills = A $10 bill (A = C)

Based on the mathematical principle of transitivity that if A = B and B = C, then A = C (see Chapter Seven), students might be able to match the two $5 bills and the $10 bill after learning the first two matches. Some other matches to consider that use frequently used coins and currency are as follows:

> Five $1 bills = one $5 bill
> Two $10 bills = one $20 bill
> Four quarters = one $1 bill
> One quarter = two dimes and a nickel

Using Exact Change

If a person stands at a cash register and observes the general public making transactions, it quickly becomes apparent that most people rarely use exact change to make purchases. Students can become completely independent in making purchases and not use exact change. Two reasons some individuals *do* use exact change are to keep close track of their money and to avoid accumulating change. Individuals with developmental disabilities may have limited resources. It may not always be possible to have a $5 bill to purchase lunch every day, but it may be possible to buy lunch for $2 or $3 each day by keeping close track of change. Individuals who master the use of coins and currency, and who have some understanding of money equivalences, have the potential to learn to count exact change. Being able to compute exact change can also be a vocational skill if a person is interested in working as a cashier. Cuvo, Veitch, Trace, and Konke (1978) taught exact-change computation up to 50 cents in four response classes: (1) 1–4 cents, (2) 5–9 cents, (3) 10–45 cents, and (4) 11–49 cents. Students learned to count back change from a purchase from the lowest to highest coin combination. For example, if the correct change was 16 cents, the person would select a penny, a nickel, and a dime.

Record Keeping

Although the skills described are focused on making purchases, they can also be utilized to teach individuals to count their money so that they know how much they have prior to planning purchases or outings. These money skills should correspond with the money strategy being taught. For example, individuals learning to count the next-dollar amount will count their money in $1 bills. A support person (e.g., a teacher or parent) can facilitate this by converting the money to $1 bills. Counting the amount of money on hand is a step toward the next money management skill—budgeting. Besides counting the money one has on hand, a second step in beginning to follow a budget is to keep a spending record. After each monetary transaction, or at the end of the day, the individual can record the amount of money spent in a notebook (or can record it by using computer software such as Microsoft Excel). By recording even the smallest purchases, the person can gain awareness of where his or her money is going. Recording purchases requires gaining skill in writing or typing numbers. As skill in writing numbers increases, students can also learn to write the names of numbers to write checks ("Twenty-two dollars & 50/100—").

Budgeting, Saving, and Planned Purchases

To gain control over personal finances, individuals with developmental disabilities need not only to know how to spend money, but also how to develop a budget. A simple way to teach budgeting that requires few to no computation skills is to teach the person spending habits. For example, a young child may be given a money notebook with pockets for lunch money, school pencils, savings, and toys. In a spending-habits approach, the child learns to take out the preselected amount each day for lunch. On Monday, he or she may also take the pencil money (e.g., a quarter). Once a month, after receiving the allowance, the child can buy a small toy. Similarly, an adult with disabilities can learn to pay all bills on payday, then divide what is left into budget envelopes for a one-time purchase (e.g., clothes, pleasure item), a monthly recreational event (e.g., movies), weekly groceries, and daily cash for a soda. A budget for an individual who is paid every 2 weeks and who has $100.00 after paying the bills might look like this.

EXAMPLE OF A SIMPLE BUDGET

WEEK ONE ENVELOPES

Groceries	$25.00 (use debit card)
Special purchase	$10.00 ($10 bill)
Daily snack	$7.00 (take out $1 bill each day)
Lunch out 1 day	$8.00 ($5 bill and three $1 bills)

WEEK TWO ENVELOPES

Groceries	$25.00 (use debit card)
Recreation	$10.00 ($10 bill)
Daily snack	$7.00 (take out a $1 bill each day)
Lunch out 1 day	$8.00 ($5 bill and three $1 bills)

Another alternative in teaching budgeting is to teach planned purchases. In planning purchases, individuals use store flyers and a calculator or number line to determine whether they can buy desired items. For example, Gaule, Nietupski, and Certo (1985) taught young adults with moderate and severe mental retardation to plan their grocery purchases on a number line divided into 50-cent intervals. As each grocery item was selected from a shopping aid with pictures and prices of food, the participants colored the appropriate number of intervals on the number line. The participants could select items that did not exceed the number of intervals they had on their number line. Matson (1981) also used a shopping aid, but foods were listed in columns by price from small items (under 50 cents) to more expensive items (over $10).

Matson and Long (1986) and Nietupski, Welch, and Wacker (1983) also focused on planning grocery purchases, but taught participants with moderate and mild mental retardation to use a calculator. Selected items were added on a calculator and subtracted from the budgeted amount. Frederick-Dugan et al. (1991) used a similar procedure but focused on a broad range of purchases (food, clothing, and hygiene items). The participant learned that as long as the calculator did not register a negative value, the selected items could be bought.

A simple way to begin teaching planned purchases is to have students plan a single purchase. For example, a store flyer for a discount department store (e.g., Kmart) can be used. The student cuts out or circles possible items to buy on the next trip to that store (e.g., candy, cassette tape, shirt). The cost of each item is subtracted from the allowance for a special purchase. When the subtraction does not yield a negative number, the item can be filed as "can buy." Just prior to going to the store, the student can pick something from this file to buy.

Budgeting can also be encouraged by teaching comparison shopping. To be able to comparison shop, students need to be able to determine which of two prices is less.

Sandknop, Schuster, Wolery, and Cross (1992) taught students to select the lower-priced grocery item in a pair. Semiautomatic price tags found in the community grocery store were used for instruction. A number line was used with the numbers arranged vertically, so that the students could see which number was "lower." Students first learned to compare prices in a skill sequence of prices that required the least discrimination (first number different) to those that required the most discrimination (all numbers in price except the last one the same). Students worked through the task analysis until they were able to determine which price was lower. The teacher used constant time delay beginning with no delay, of a model and verbal description. Once students got all steps correct with the no-delay prompt, the delay level for the prompt moved to 5 seconds.

Another aspect of budgeting is paying bills. LaCampagne and Cipani (1987) taught individuals with mild mental retardation to pay bills by focusing on the three skills of (1) writing a check, (2) recording the check in a checkbook, and (3) preparing the bill to be mailed. To teach these skills, the teacher used real materials, including actual bills and checks. Each skill was task-analyzed and taught with forward chaining in a group instruction format. For example, the first step was to enter the payee's name on the check. All students were taught to perform this skill to mastery before the next step (writing the date) was introduced.

A difficult money management skill for many people (both with and without disabilities) is saving money. Sometimes savings plans are not useful because they have no specific goal or purpose. Individuals with developmental disabilities will need specific savings goals to understand the purpose of this aspect of money management. For example, for the individual using the simple budget shown above to be able to purchase a sweatshirt that costs $30.00, he or she may forgo making a special purchase or using money for recreation for the first 2-week pay period, to be able to buy the sweatshirt at the beginning of the next pay period. To help the person visualize the savings goal, a picture of a sweatshirt can be drawn on an envelope with three miniature pictures of $10 bills. The person checks off each picture of a $10 bill as it is placed in the savings envelope. When the third picture is checked off, the sweatshirt can be purchased.

Banking Skills

Most people keep their money in a bank rather than making all financial transactions with cash. Individuals with developmental disabilities can also learn banking skills, such as making deposits and withdrawals. For example, Bourbeau, Sowers, and Close (1986) taught students with mild mental retardation to make deposits and withdrawals in a classroom simulation, and then demonstrated that they could generalize these skills to a community bank. Students may benefit from self-paced instruction booklets to practice skills such as making deposits, making withdrawals, and balancing a checkbook (Cuvo, Davis, & Gluck, 1991; Zencius, Davis, & Cuvo, 1990). It can also help students to state each numeral aloud before entering it in a check register (Wacker et al., 1988).

In recent years, people have begun to use automatic teller machines (ATMs), more often than cashiers to do their banking. McDonnell and Ferguson (1989) taught both cashier and ATM skills to individuals with moderate mental retardation, implementing all instruction in the community. In contrast, Schafer, Inge, and Hill (1986) designed a simulated ATM, because teaching this skill in the community could result in the machine's taking the person's ATM card if mistakes were made. The simulation was constructed of plywood and had paper for the video screen messages and painted numerals.

A task analysis for teaching withdrawing cash from an ATM is shown in Figure 8.3. This task analysis was designed for Henrietta Johnson,[2] a middle school student with autism, whose ecological assessment for math is described at the end of this chapter. The teacher instructed Henrietta in the use of an ATM, using a classroom simulation (a box made to look like an ATM). On the first 2 days, she conducted a baseline assessment or pretest for Henrietta by observing what Henrietta could do prior to instruction. Henrietta was not able to insert her card or do any of the other steps. On the subsequent days, the teacher used the system of least intrusive prompts (see Chapter Four for a description of this procedure). She scored the highest level of prompt that Henrietta needed to perform each step. For example, on October 4 (the third column of data), Henrietta needed verbal direction (v) or a model (m) for every step. But on the next day, October 5, she waited for the cue for her password and for her request without any reminders (+). By the time the teacher made an instructional decision on October 13, Henrietta had begun to make good progress. The trend of her data (percent of independent, correct responses each day) was accelerating. That is, she was getting more steps correct without help. The last day of data shown on this graph is October 16. Henrietta continued to do well; however, the teacher noted that Henrietta consistently needed help on all the steps that required reading the machine's cues. Since Henrietta was continuing to make good progress, the teacher decided to wait until the end of the current decision period (October 27) before deciding whether Henrietta would need some additional instruction on reading the machine's cues. Also, the teacher put an asterisk by October 6 (see top of fifth column) there to remind her that this day's data were taken with a *real* ATM in the community. She was pleased that Henrietta's performance was similar in the community to what it had been in the classroom the day before. Given this generalization, the teacher decided to continue community-based training of this skill about once every 2 weeks.

Using Commercial Materials to Teach Money Management Skills

In taking a functional approach to money management skills, teachers will want to use materials that are real, or at least as realistic as possible. Many students with moderate and severe disabilities will need opportunities to use real currency to learn its value and purpose. However, keeping cash on hand in a classroom for instructional purposes may not be practical because of potential theft. Many commercial materials provide "play money" that is realistic. Also, students who are physically challenged may need other ways to learn about money besides physically manipulating it. Commercial materials that use software can provide the opportunity to learn how to count and spend money with simplified physical responding. With this experience, students can take charge of how their money is spent, even if they must rely on others to handle the money during community purchases. Table 8.2 provides a list of commercial materials for teaching money management.

---

[2]Henrietta Johnson is a fictitious student.

FIGURE 8.3. Use of a standard Data Collection Form to track Henrietta's progress in learning to use an ATM. The teacher made a decision about Henrietta's progress after two weeks. Because Henrietta's data showed a positive acceleration and a higher mean, no changes were needed; her progress was good.

Name: Henrietta Johnson
Skill: Withdraw cash from an ATM
Criterion for Mastery: All steps correct (100%) for 2 of 2 days

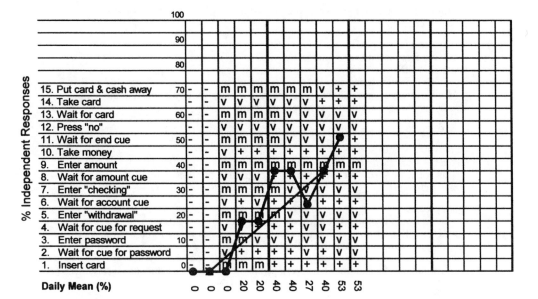

% Independent Responses

15. Put card & cash away	70
14. Take card	
13. Wait for card	60
12. Press "no"	
11. Wait for end cue	50
10. Take money	
9. Enter amount	40
8. Wait for amount cue	
7. Enter "checking"	30
6. Wait for account cue	
5. Enter "withdrawal"	20
4. Wait for cue for request	
3. Enter password	10
2. Wait for cue for password	
1. Insert card	0

Daily Mean (%) 0 0 0 20 20 40 40 27 40 53 53

Previous mean (%) 0.0

Date	Trend/mean	Decision
Oct. 13	**Mean** 24.7% Trend is accelerating	Continue with program
	Mean	

TABLE 8.2. Commercial Materials for Teaching Money Management

Materials for teaching money recognition and counting

Money Big Box
Available from Science Research Associates (SRA)
1-888-SRA-4543
www.sra4kids.com
    Coin value dominoes, coin stamps, coin puzzles, amusement park game.

Touch Money
Available from Edmark Corporations
1-800-362-2890
www.edmark.com
    Interactive computer software to count coins; terrific for students with
physical challenges.

Dollars and Cents Kit
Available from Attainment Company
1-800-327-4269
www.attainmentcompany.com
    Money recognition available with realistic money, money mats, and stickers;
also available as a computer software program.

Materials for teaching money management

Dollars and Cents Series
Available from Edmark Corporation (see above)
    This software series includes money recognition, simulated purchasing, and
making change.

Money Games
Available from Attainment Company (see above)
    Budget City and Budget Town are two board games that can be used to teach
spending, writing checks, and budgeting.

Note. For full mailing addresses for the companies listed here, see Chapter Seven, Table 7.1.

TIME MANAGEMENT

A second important area of functional math is time management. Just as money management involves much more than knowing how to make a purchase, time management involves more than being able to state the time. Time management involves being able to conduct advanced plans (calendar planning), develop and adhere to a daily schedule, and determine when to make transitions to arrive at scheduled activities on time. To master these time management skills requires knowing not only how to read a clock and calendar, but also how to plan ahead. A skill sequence for time management is shown in Table 8.3.

Using Picture and Object Schedules

Some individuals may not be able to read numbers or drawings of clocks, but may be able to learn to manage their daily schedule by using pictures or objects. For a picture schedule, the teacher may photograph the student performing each activity or use line drawings of activities. For an object schedule, the teacher should select an object associated with an activity (e.g., a swimsuit for swimming). Some individuals

TABLE 8.3. A Curriculum Sequence for Teaching Time Management

Skill	Example
1. Use pictures or objects to know what to do next.	Before each activity, the student is shown a picture of the activity or object associated with it, and is then prompted to go to that area or get needed materials.
2. Use clock hand placements to know when to make transitions.	The student is given a drawing of a clock with the hands at 3:15 (both hands on the 3). The student learns to get his or her bookbag ready for the bus when the clock hands are in this position.
3. Use clock hands or digital times to follow a full day's schedule.	An employee begins each job task by matching digital times on schedule to times on watch. He or she then performs task for that time.
4. Use a calendar to create a schedule.	A young adult looks at wall calendar in morning and enters time he or she will be meeting a friend for lunch in a daily schedule book (e.g., a Daytimer).
5. Follow exact times during day on a digital watch.	An individual can state time when asked (reads three- or four-digit time) and can initiate activity at a specific time (e.g., home economics begins at 9:23).
6. Read month, days, and year. Plan activities with a calendar.	An adolescent plans activities for March by filling in soccer practices and planning to go to movies on March 14.
7. Tell time on an analog clock or watch.	A child can read a clock or watch to determine hour and minutes (may be taught to nearest quarter hour).

may learn to use symbolic objects for activities (e.g., a refrigerator magnet depicting French fries for dining out; a magnet depicting a computer for math class). Just prior to each activity, the teacher will have the student select the object or picture for that activity. For example, my colleagues and I (Browder, Cooper, & Lim, 1998) taught adults with severe mental retardation who had no symbolic communication system to associate specific objects with activities (e.g., a golf ball for golfing, a towel for aerobics, a library card for the library, and a name tag for attending a club). Just prior to a person's going to an activity, the teacher showed the person the target object and a distractor (e.g., a paper clip, a stapler). Using constant time delay, the teacher physically guided the person to select the correct object. This was repeated 10 times before the person began the activity. After a few training days, the teacher pointed to the correct object and waited 4 seconds before using physical guidance during each of the 10 training trials. When students selected the correct object consistently, the teacher waited 4 seconds before pointing to the correct choice. Once the participants mastered associating objects with their activities, they then were able to choose activities by using the objects.

In the TEACCH program for students with autism, an "object schedule" is used. An object is chosen for each activity of the day and displayed on some type of object board (Schopler, Mesibov, & Hearsey, 1995). For example, a set of shelves, a large travel case with clear compartments, or boxes might all be used to house the objects for each activity. Just prior to each activity, a student is prompted to remove the object that symbolizes what to do and proceed to the area where the activity takes place. As students gain proficiency using life-size objects, smaller symbolic objects are introduced (e.g., a magnet with a miniature basketball for gym, or a magnet with a miniature hamburger for lunch). Later, pictures and words are introduced.

An example of a data-based assessment for teaching a student to follow an object schedule is shown in Figure 8.4. In this example, Kevin Thomas[3] was learning to follow a schedule with eight objects for eight activities. Kevin Thomas was an elementary school boy with severe mental retardation and mild cerebral palsy. He was nonverbal, but could communicate some needs (e.g., eating) by gesturing to what he wanted. He currently used no symbolic communication. He walked with a walker and was able to grasp and release objects. He currently had no academic skills. The teacher was helping Kevin learn to anticipate activities by selecting an object to be used next. At the beginning of the day, Kevin was supposed to get a poster with the name of the month and Velcro it to the top of a wall calendar. When the calendar lesson was over, he was to go back to his "schedule shelf" and take out the paper towels that he would use in the restroom. After using the restroom, he was supposed to take out a computer disk and carry it to the third-grade class where he had math (including computer work). However, Kevin had never used an object schedule before, and he did not yet comprehend what the teacher wanted him to do. To prompt him, the teacher used physical guidance to help Kevin select an object and take it to the next activity (i.e., put the object in the pouch on his walker and go to the correct area for the next lesson).

For the first 2 days, the teacher gave physical guidance for Kevin to grasp the correct object as soon as he walked to his schedule shelf. On the third day, she began to fade her assistance by waiting 4 seconds (see Chapter Four for more information on time delay). For the first 2 weeks, Kevin relied on the teacher's physical guidance for all except three responses. On the 14th and 15th, he took out the dollars for lunch independently. On the 18th, he picked up his photographs for his communication lesson. Using the decision rules described in Chapter Four, the teacher realized that this rate of progress was too slow for mastery to be achieved this school year. To encourage more independence (more +'s in Figure 8.4), the teacher decided to increase the amount of time she waited before prompting Kevin (delay interval) to 15 seconds. With this change, Kevin showed better progress in the last 2 weeks. Although he did not do well on the 31st (last column), his overall trend was accelerating, and his mean was higher. The teacher decided to wait 2 more weeks before deciding whether further changes were needed.

Using Distinctive Clock Hand Placements for Transitions

Even if individuals are unable to read numbers and tell time, they may be able to learn to recognize distinctive clock times. For example, the hands of a clock are together pointing up at 12:00 and they form a straight vertical line at 6:00. Learning to recognize these distinctive times can be easier than reading digital clock numbers for some individuals with developmental disabilities. In this approach, the teacher makes a line

[3]This is another fictitious example, Kevin Thomas is not a real person.

FIGURE 8.4. Use of a standard Data Collection Form to track Kevin's progress in learning to use an object schedule. When the teacher evaluated his progress after the first 2 weeks, his trend was level and his mean was only slightly improved (from 0 to 3.8%). After his prompting system was improved, Kevin made better progress in the next 2 weeks (from 3.8% to 13.8%). **p**, physical guidance required. Other codes as in Figure 8.3.

Name: Kevin Thomas
Skill: Follow an object schedule
Criterion for Mastery: 6 of 8 objects for 3 of 3 days

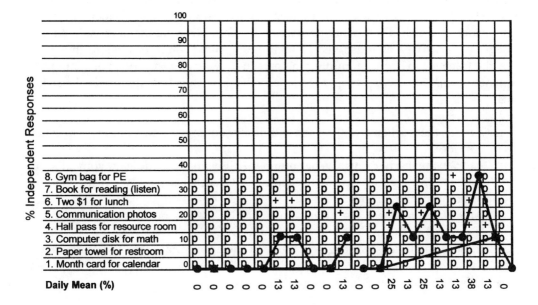

Previous mean (%) _0.0_

Date	Trend/mean		Decision
	Mean 3.8%	Trend is level	Improve antecedents
			Increase delay interval before using physical guidance
	Mean 13.8%	Trend is level	Continue with program

drawing of a clock showing the time the person needs to begin a transition. If the person needs to meet a 1:00 bus, the distinctive clock hands may be 12:30 (nearly straight vertical line) combined with a natural cue (after the noon television news ends). The teacher can teach the person to "read" these clock times, using the methods suggested for sight words in Chapter Seven. For example, the teacher may show the times on flash cards and use time delay. Additional prompting may be needed at first for the person to follow the times during the actual daily schedule.

Following a Full Day's Schedule

Once students can recognize a distinct time to begin an activity, they may move on to learn to follow a full day's schedule by using either distinctive analog clock times or a digital clock or watch. The teacher prepares a schedule showing the time for a student to begin each activity, as illustrated in Figure 8.5. About 5 minutes before the target time, the teacher can begin prompting the person to watch for the time. For example, a sequence of least intrusive prompts sequence to begin a transition at 9:30 may be as follows:

1. At 9:25, the teacher says, "It's about time for something new. Let me know when it's close."
2. At 9:29, the teacher says, "What number will be in the middle on your [digital] watch?" If there is no correct response, the teacher says, "Watch for the 3 to come up in the middle!"
3. At 9:30, the teacher says, "What time is it?" If there is no correct response, say, "See the 3 in the middle and the 0 at the end. It's 9:30."
4. If the student does not begin to move to the appropriate area or get materials, the teacher says, "What do you do at 9:30?" If there is no response, the teacher tells the student and helps to get materials.

At any point, if the student tells time and begins to make the transition, the teacher says, "Excellent time telling! Thanks for getting ready!"

FIGURE 8.5. An example of a daily schedule.

Time	Activity
8:15	Homeroom
8:47	Language Arts
9:35	Reading
10:23	Math
11:01	Science
11:49	Lunch
12:36	Metal Shop
1:34	Community
3:15	Bus or Pep Club

Using a Calendar to Create a Schedule, and Calendar Reading

Whether or not individuals have learned to follow a schedule all day, they may be able to master using a calendar to plan a special activity. Bambara and Ager (1992) taught individuals with moderate mental retardation to self-schedule a leisure activity. The participants used a calendar planner. Through role play of a task analysis to do planning and prompting, the participants learned to select a picture of a desired activity, to place it on the calendar at the time they wanted to do it, and to contact a staff member if support was needed (e.g., transportation). Each day, the participants checked their calendars for special preplanned events.

If a student is going to learn to use the calendar fully (see skill 6 in Table 8.3), some sight word instruction may be needed to teach reading the months of the year and days of the week. If students cannot read numbers, they may also practice reading the numbers of the days. Methods described in Chapter Seven, such as feedback, time delay, or simultaneous prompting, can all be used to teach number reading. Number reading can also be taught using the task demonstration model (Repp, Karsh, & Lenz, 1990), in which an easy-to-hard discrimination is used. At first, the student is shown the number with two highly different distractors:

giraffe   12   men

Over time the distractors become more similar, so that the discrimination becomes harder:

it   42   12

Following Exact Times with a Digital Watch

As students gain skills in using a calendar and specific times to follow a schedule, the next step is to learn to read a digital watch for exact times to begin activities. At this level, rather than "watching for the 3" (as in skill 3 in Table 8.3), the person receives instruction to read numbers from 0 to 59 to be able to read any digital time. As mentioned above, to teach the times, the teacher can use sight word instructional methods. For example, Karsh and Repp (1992) used the task demonstration model (discussed above) to teach students to read exact digital times. Similarly, the teacher may use flash cards with constant time delay to teach these times. It may be necessary to teach the times in small skill clusters (e.g., hours from 1 to 12; minutes from 00 to 15, 16 to 30, 31 to 45, and 46 to 59).

Telling Time on an Analog Clock or Watch

One of the most difficult time management skills is to tell time on an analog clock or watch. Although this skill is taught early in math series in elementary education, individuals with developmental disabilities who do not learn time telling in these early years may benefit from the alternatives for time management shown in Table 8.3. By wearing a digital watch, an individual can avoid the need to learn to tell time on an analog watch. In contrast, students who have mastered reading numbers to 12 and can recognize some analog clock configurations may be successful in learning to tell time on an analog clock or watch. The best approach to this time-telling instruction may be to follow a skill sequence. An early resource on time telling (Thurlow & Turnure, 1977) suggested the following sequence: (1) discriminating the minute and hour hands, (2) telling time to the hour (o'clock), (3) telling time to the half hour, (4) telling time to the quarter hour, and (5) telling time to the minute. Students are taught one skill in the sequence to mastery (e.g., hour hand vs. minute hand) before the next skill is introduced. Commercial materials may be beneficial in teaching analog time. Several resources are shown in Table 8.4.

BRIDGING TO MATH LITERACY: COMPUTATION AND PROBLEM SOLVING

Some students with moderate and severe disabilities may be able to achieve basic math literacy, in which they are able to solve math problems encountered both in daily living and within traditional academic materials (e.g., textbooks, worksheets, computer software). At this level, students will be able to perform the four basic operations of addition, subtraction, multiplication, and division, and to compute fractions and decimals. Students will understand number concepts and be able to solve basic word problems. Students who are not able to memorize math facts may benefit from learning to use a calculator in solving problems. The revised Brigance Diagnostic Comprehensive Inventory of Basic Skills (Brigance, 1999) can be useful in pinpointing specific math skills to target. Table 8.5 provides a summary of some of the skills listed in this inventory.

When a student's rate of mastery, age, and interest in math suggest the need to go beyond the basics of money and time management, it is beneficial to choose a commercial curriculum to approach math literacy systematically. This commercial curriculum may be a textbook adopted by the school district or a remedial series that streamlines instruction to focus on basic skills. Some of these basic skills math programs are shown in Table 8.6.

TABLE 8.4. Commercial Materials for Teaching Time Management

Time Big Box
Available from SRA
1-888-SRA-4543
http://www.sra4kids.com
    Clocks and calendar, clock stamp, clock puzzles, sequential picture cards.

Timescales
Available from Attainment Company
1-800-327-4269
    A Windows/Mac CD-ROM that introduces analog and digital time in three modules—Hour, Minute, and Time to Time. Can be adjusted for level of difficulty.

Time Families Game
Available from PCI Educational Publishing
1-800-594-4263
    Teaches time to nearest quarter hour, using a game board format and flash cards.

Note. Again, for full mailing addresses for the companies listed here, see Chapter Seven, Table 7.1.

TABLE 8.5. Some of the Math Skills Included in the Revised Brigance Diagnostic Comprehensive Inventory of Basic Skills

I. Numbers
   A. Recognizes numbers
   B. Arranges numbers in order
   C. Understand ordinal numbers
   D. Writes numbers as dictated
   E. Identifies odd and even numbers
II. Number facts
   A. Addition facts
   B. Subtraction facts
   C. Multiplication facts
   D. Division facts
   E. Computes with calculator (addition, subtraction, multiplication, division)
III. Computation of whole numbers
   A. Addition of whole numbers
   B. Subtraction of whole numbers
   C. Multiplication of whole numbers
   D. Division of whole numbers
IV. Percents
V. Time
VI. Money
VII. Fractions
VIII. Decimals
IX. U.S. customary measurement and geometry
X. Metrics

TABLE 8.6. Commercial Materials for Teaching Basic Math Literacy

Available from SRA (1-888-SRA-4543 or http://www.sra4kids.com):
Math Explorations and Applications
   A research-based basal math program for each grade level.
Spectrum Math
   Student workbooks and computer software for independent practice of basic skills (available in Spanish); suitable for all age levels.
Schoolhouse Math
   Drill and practice for grades 1–4.
Merrill Building Skills in Math
   Affordable basic math program.
Available from Edmark Corporation (1-800-362-2890 or http://www.edmark.com):
Show Me Math
   Software to teach basic math facts; can be used with Edmark Touch Window for students with physical challenges.
Access to Math
   Computer software that provides talking math worksheets; these can be teacher-customized.
Bake and Taste
   Software simulates preparing a recipe; students practice following directions and measuring; requires some reading skills.
Available from Attainment Company (1-800-327-4269):
Math Bundle CD-ROM
   A Windows/Mac CD-ROM for teaching basic math facts; no numbers greater than 20; illustrated with an animated movie.
Available from Steck-Vaughn Company (1-800-531-5051):
Mastering Math
   Math series with an easy-to-read presentation; workbooks for grades 1–6.
Early Math
   Colorful workbooks for K–2 math skills; appropriate for young children.

EXAMPLES OF ASSESSMENT
AND PLANNING FOR FUNCTIONAL MATH INSTRUCTION

This chapter has provided descriptions of many of the functional math skills that can be beneficial in daily living. In using the "broad-to-specific" method of ecological assessment, the teacher or other professional will begin by (1) determining the student's current level of performance in math, (2) setting priorities with the family, and (3) considering the student's preferences. These steps are usually taken as part of the overall planning process for the individualized education plan (IEP) described in Chapter Two. The case of Henrietta, introduced earlier in this chapter, is used here to illustrate how the portion of this planning related to math may evolve.

Henrietta was a middle school student with autism whose parents highly valued academic instruction. Henrietta could read about 20 sight words, count to 50, and recognize numbers to 100. She could add single-digit numbers to 10 by drawing and counting lines for each number to be added. In summarizing her current level of performance for the IEP, the special education teacher noted that Henrietta had made no progress in the prior year's instruction to increase her addition skills. Henrietta enjoyed attending general education classes. She could also complete simple worksheets, such as circling numbers on a page.

To further summarize Henrietta's skills, the teacher used the Functional Math Curriculum Checklist, shown in Table 8.6. From this checklist, the teacher realized that Henrietta needed to learn to use a personal calendar, to begin to use budget envelopes, to develop her own schedule, and to keep up with her own money in a wallet or purse. In conducting an ecological inventory of the consumer math class targeted for Henrietta's inclusion, the teacher discovered that the students in this class often copied problems from their textbook. Many of the problems required addition and subtraction of two- to four-digit numbers. Because Henrietta had some concept of addition, but had not been able to master addition facts, the teacher decided to instruct her in the use of a calculator so that she would be able to do some problems in the consumer math class. The teacher would also adapt each assignment by choosing with the general education teacher one to two problems for Henrietta to do, and then photocopying and enlarging them so Henrietta could write directly on the page. To make the IEP objectives related to time management more specific, the teacher conducted a discrepancy analysis, comparing Henrietta's skills to those of a peer who was the same age. This is what she found.

DISCREPANCY ANALYSIS RELATED TO TIME MANAGEMENT

Henrietta	Her friend Julia (nondisabled)	Ideas for instruction
Relies on others to know next activity	Goes to class when bell rings; anticipates time using watch/clock	Use of digital watch
Asks daily about special events	Keeps a personal calendar in her bedroom	Sticker calendar
Has leisure activities planned for her	Chooses leisure activities with friends and asks parents	Self-scheduling of leisure activities

FIGURE 8.6. Functional Math Curriculum Checklist

Skills	Mastery	Partial mastery	No progress
Money management			
I. PURCHASING			
1. Hands cashier money for purchase.			
2. Gets money out of wallet/purse/pocket.			
3. Spends money in preset categories (e.g., $1 for soda, $5 for lunch).			
4. Uses $1 bills and counts next-dollar amount.			
5. Uses $1, $5, $10 bills and counts next-dollar amount.			
6. Uses coins (except pennies) by counting all of them by 5s.			
7. Counts coins by 25, 10, 5.			
8. Selects equivalent money amounts (e.g., two $5 bills = a $10 bill).			
9. Reads price and takes out exact money amount (e.g., $5.79).			
II. MONEY RECORD KEEPING AND BUDGETING			
1. Puts money in a piggy bank or money box.			
2. Spends money from preset envelopes.			
3. Divides own money into envelopes as simplified budget.			
4. Records amount of money spent.			
5. Follows a preset budget for 1 month.			
6. Develops own budget and follows it for 1 month.			
III. BANKING			
1. Signs/marks/stamps name on check to be cashed.			
2. Hands deposit or check to be cashed to cashier.			
3. Puts money in purse, wallet, pocket.			
4. Uses debit card to make purchases.			
5. Uses ATM.			

(cont.)

FIGURE 8.6. *(page 2 of 3)*

Skills	Mastery	Partial mastery	No progress
Money Management (cont.)			
III. BANKING *(cont.)*			
6. Writes checks.			
7. Balances checkbook.			
IV. SAVING			
1. Puts money in savings envelope/box/piggy bank weekly for 1 month.			
2. Saves for specific item using picture of item, and savings envelope.			
3. Deposits money in a savings account with specific saving goal.			
Time Management			
I. SCHEDULING			
1. Selects correct object for an activity for at least three activities.			
2. Selects object for each activity in an object schedule.			
3. Selects miniature/symbolic objects for activity in schedule.			
4. Follows a picture schedule.			
5. Follows a picture schedule with some written times.			
6. Follows word schedule with times.			
7. Creates and follows own schedule (self-schedules).			
II. TELLING TIME			
1. Anticipates events that happen at the same time each day by moving to area or seeking out materials.			
2. Recognizes one or two clock times that are distinctive (e.g., nearly vertical hands for 12:30).			
3. Recognizes specific digital times for activities by matching numbers.			
4. Tells time on analog clock to nearest hour.			

(cont.)

FIGURE 8.6. *(page 3 of 3)*

Skills	Mastery	Partial mastery	No progress
Time Management (cont.)			
II. TELLING TIME *(cont.)*			
5. Tells time on analog clock to nearest half hour.			
6. Tells time on analog clock to nearest quarter hour.			
7. Tells time to the nearest 5 minutes on analog clock.			
8. Tells time to the minute on analog clock.			
III. USE OF A CALENDAR			
1. Finds current day on wall calendar with prior days marked out.			
2. Points to month, day, year.			
3. Identifies current month, day, year.			
4. Finds current month, day in a pocket calendar.			
5. Uses stickers or words to mark special events on calendar.			
6. Plans leisure or other activities with a personal calendar.			
Basic math skills: Bridge to general education			
1. Rote-counts to 10. (Note whether student can count higher than 10. If so, to what number can student count?)			
2. Counts objects to 5.			
3. Counts objects to 10. (Note here whether student can count higher than 10. (If so, what is largest number of objects student can count correctly?)			
4. Enters number in calculator using matching.			
5. Performs addition and subtraction with calculator.			
6. Knows addition facts.			
7. Knows subtraction facts.			
8. Writes numbers.			

The functional math needs of Kevin (also introduced earlier in this chapter) were quite different from Henrietta's. Because of Kevin's age and previously limited opportunities in general education, his parents, like Henrietta's, highly valued academic instruction for him. Kevin showed a preference for colorful software materials and other materials with bright lights or colors. In summarizing Kevin's current level of performance, the special education teacher noted that Kevin currently had no basic or functional math skills. He had learned to go with an escort to make a purchase, but did not yet handle money. In looking at the Functional Math Curriculum Checklist (Figure 8.6), Kevin's teacher decided to focus on the simplest skill in each of a few categories. For Kevin, these were as follows:

- Handing money to a cashier.
- Putting money in a money box to keep it safe.
- Using an object schedule.
- Finding the current day on a wall calendar with prior days marked off.
- Counting and recognizing numbers to 5.

In conducting an ecological inventory of the third-grade class and interviewing the general education teacher, Kevin's teacher discovered that he would have opportunities to use money not only during lunch, but also in a weekly trip to the school store. Together, the teachers decided it would be good for Kevin to practice daily for this trip to the store by making a simulated classroom purchase of supplies. The general education teacher also used computers in math. Although the third-grade software was too difficult for Kevin, she was glad to include recommended alternatives. The teacher suggested trying the Edmark software Show Me Math (see Table 8.6) because of the Edmark Touch Window to simplify responding, its colorful display, and its introduction of numbers. Kevin's teacher then used a situational assessment in which she had him try out the software. She discovered that Kevin had no skills in using a computer. He would need prompting to attend to the screen and touch the Touch Window. She decided to develop a task analysis for using the computer that she would teach Kevin daily in the resource room, and that she would train a peer to use in helping him when the class did computer work. Her task analysis was as follows:

1. Turn computer on.
2. Look at screen.
3. Press "Enter" after teacher/peer types in password.
4. Look at screen.
5. Press "Enter" after teacher/peer selects program.
6. Look at screen and listen to directions.
7. Touch number on screen.
8. Press "enter."

When the teacher shared Kevin's program with his parents, they were pleased that he would be working on a computer and learning numbers. They agreed with the importance of his learning to use money, but asked that he learn to count it. Together, they decided that the teacher would count the dollars aloud as Kevin handed the money to the cashier.

SUMMARY

Money and time management are the primary ways basic math is encountered in daily living. This chapter has described skill sequences for teaching money and time management skills. Mastery of these skills may depend on making the math responses simpler. For example, in money management the next-dollar strategy may be used, so that the person can rely on counting by $1 bills. In time management, a digital watch or clock may be selected instead of an analog timepiece. Once such adaptations are made to simplify the math responses needed, a person with developmental disabilities will often be able to master the money or time management skill through systematic instruction.

In conducting ecological assessment for curriculum planning in functional math, the teacher or other professional should begin by considering the student's current level of skill and the parents' and student's preferences. For some students, functional math instruction may form a significant portion of the IEP. For others, a few basic skills may be selected. In selecting skills, the teacher can begin with a general curriculum checklist such as the one shown in Table 8.6. A personalized curriculum can be developed for the student by using ecological inventories, discrepancy analyses, and situational assessments, as described for the cases of Henrietta and Kevin. When meaningful and functional skills are selected and taught, students can gain increased autonomy in the use of their finances and time.

REFERENCES

Bambara, L., & Ager, C. (1992). Use of self-scheduling to promote self-directed leisure activity in home and community settings. *Journal of the Association for Persons with Severe Handicaps, 17*, 67–76.

Bourbeau, P. E., Close, D. W., & Sowers, J. A. (1986). An experimental analysis of generalization of banking skills from classroom to bank settings in the community. *Education and Training in Mental Retardation, 21*, 98–107.

Brigance, A. (1999). *Brigance Diagnostic Comprehensive Inventory of Basic Skills (Revised).* North Bullerica, MA: Curriculum Associates.

Browder, D. M., Cooper, K., & Lim, L. (1998). Teaching adults with severe disabilities to express their choice of settings for leisure activities. *Education and Training in Mental Retardation and Developmental Disabilities, 33*, 226–236.

Browder, D. M., & Grasso, E. (1999). Teaching money skills to individuals with developmental disabilities: A review. *Remedial and Special Education, 20*, 297–308.

Clifft, M. A. (1986). Writing about psychiatric patients: Guidelines for disguising case material. *Bulletin of the Menninger Clinic, 50*, 511–524.

Colyer, S. P., & Collins, B. C. (1996). Using natural cues within prompt levels to teach the next dollar strategy to students with disabilities. *Journal of Special Education, 30*(3), 305–318.

Cuvo, A. J., Davis, P. K., & Gluck, M. S. (1991). Cumulative and interspersal task sequencing in self-paced training for persons with mild handicaps. *Mental Retardation, 29*(6), 335–342.

Cuvo, A. J., Veitch, V. D., Trace, M. W., & Konke, J. L. (1978). Teaching change computation to the mentally retarded. *Behavior Modification, 2*, 531–548.

Denny, P. J., & Test, D. W. (1995). Using the one-more-than technique to teach money counting to individuals with moderate mental retardation: A systematic replication. *Education and Treatment of Children, 18*(4), 422–432.

Frank, A. R., & Wacker, D. P. (1986). Analysis of a visual prompting procedure on acquisition and generalization of coin skills by mentally retarded children. *American Journal of Mental Deficiency, 90,* 468–472.

Frederick-Dugan, A., Test, D. W., & Varn, L. (1991). Acquisition and generalization of purchasing skills using a calculator by students who are mentally retarded. *Education and Training in Mental Retardation, 26*(4), 381–387.

Gardill, C. M., & Browder, D. M. (1995). Teaching stimulus classes to encourage independent purchasing by students with severe behavior disorders. *Education and Training in Mental Retardation, 30,* 254–264.

Gaule, K., Nietupski, J., & Certo, N. (1985). Teaching supermarket shopping skills using an adaptive shopping list. *Education and Training of the Mentally Retarded, 20,* 53–59.

Haring, T. G., Kennedy, C. H., Adams, M. J., & Pitts-Conway, V. (1987). Teaching generalization of purchasing skills across community settings to autistic youth using videodisc modeling. *Journal of Applied Behavior Analysis, 20,* 89–96.

Karsh, K. G., & Repp, A. C. (1992). The task demonstration model: A concurrent model for teaching groups of students with severe disabilities. *Exceptional Children, 59,* 54–67.

LaCampagne, J., & Cipani, E. (1987). Training adults with mental retardation to pay bills. *Mental Retardation, 25,* 293–303.

Lowe, M. L., & Cuvo, A. J. (1976). Teaching coin summation to the mentally retarded. *Journal of Applied Behavior Analysis, 9,* 483–489.

Matson, J. L. (1981). Use of independence training to teach shopping skills to mildly mentally retarded adults. *American Journal of Mental Deficiency, 86,* 178–183.

Matson, J. L., & Long, S. (1986). Teaching computation/shopping skills to mentally retarded adults. *American Journal of Mental Deficiency, 91*(1), 98–101.

McDonnell, J. J., & Ferguson, B. (1988). A comparison of general case in vivo and general case simulation plus in vivo training. *Journal of the Association for Persons with Severe Handicaps, 13,* 116–124.

McDonnell, J., & Ferguson, B. (1989). A comparison of time delay and decreasing prompt hierarchy strategies in teaching banking skills to students with moderate handicaps. *Journal of Applied Behavior Analysis, 22,* 85–91.

McDonnell, J., & Laughlin, B. (1989). A comparison of backward and concurrent chaining strategies in teaching community skills. *Education and Training in Mental Retardation, 24*(3), 230–238.

Nietupski, J., Welch, J., & Wacker, D. (1983). Acquisition, maintenance, and transfer of grocery item purchasing skills by moderately and severely handicapped students. *Education and Training of the Mentally Retarded, 18,* 279–286.

Repp, A. C., Karsh, K. G., & Lenz, M. W. (1990). Discrimination training for persons with developmental disabilities: A comparison of the task demonstration model and the standard prompting hierarchy. *Journal of Applied Behavior Analysis, 23,* 43–52.

Sandknop, P. A., Schuster, J. W., Wolery, M., & Cross, D. P. (1992). The use of an adaptive device to teach students with moderate mental retardation to selected lower priced grocery items. *Education and Training in Mental Retardation, 27,* 219–229.

Schafer, M. S., Inge, K. J., & Hill, J. (1986). Acquisition, generalization, and maintenance of automated banking skills. *Education and Training in Mental Retardation, 21,* 265–272.

Schopler, E., Mesibov, G. B., & Hearsey, K. (1995). Structured teaching in the TEACCH system. In E. Schopler & G. B. Mesibov (Eds.), *Learning and cognition in autism* (pp. 243–268). New York: Plenum Press.

Stoddard, L. T., Brown, J., Hulbert, B., Manoli, C., & McIlvane, W. J. (1989). Teaching money skills through stimulus class formation, exclusion, and component matching methods: Three case studies. *Research in Developmental Disabilities, 10,* 413–439.

Storey, K., Bates, P., & Hanson, H. B. (1984). Acquisition and generalization of coffee purchasing skills by adults with severe disabilities. *Journal of the Association for Persons with Severe Handicaps, 9,* 178–185.

Test. D. W., Howell, A., Burkhart, K., & Beroth, T. (1993). The one-more-than technique as a strategy for counting money for individuals with moderate mental retardation. *Education and Training in Mental Retardation, 28*, 232–241.

Thurlow, M. L., & Turnure, J. E. (1977). Children's knowledge of time and money: Effective instruction for the mentally retarded. *Education and Training of the Mentally Retarded, 12*, 203–212.

Van den Pol, R. A., Iwata, B. A., Ivanic, M. T., Page, T. J., Neef, N. A., & Whitley, F. P. (1981). Teaching the handicapped to eat in public places: Acquisition, generalization, and maintenance of restaurant skills. *Journal of Applied Behavior Analysis, 14*, 61–70.

Wacker, D. P., Berg, W. K., McMahon, C., Templeman, M., McKinney, J., Swarts, V., Visser, M., & Marquardt, P. (1988). Evaluation of labeling-then-doing with moderately handicapped persons: Acquisition and generalization with complex tasks. *Journal of Applied Behavior Analysis, 21*, 369–380.

Westling, D. L., Floyd, J., & Carr, D. (1990). Effects of single setting versus multiple setting training on learning to shop in a department store. *American Journal of Mental Retardation, 94*, 616–624.

Zencius, A. H., Davis, P. K., & Cuvo, A. J. (1990). A personalized system of instruction for teaching checking account skills to adults with mild disabilities. *Journal of Applied Behavior Analysis, 23*, 245–252.

NINE

Community and Leisure Skills

with Karena J. Cooper

RANDY[1] WAS A 16-YEAR-OLD BOY *who lived with his mother, father, brother, sister, and dog named Charlie in a small town. He enjoyed playing ball, moving to music, playing with Charlie, and eating good food. Randy had been medically diagnosed with severe mental retardation and autism. He used nonsymbolic communication skills, such as pointing toward an object he wanted. Randy was able to walk, but had a wide gait because of his difficulties with balance. After Randy turned 16, his family began to talk with his teacher about how to help Randy have a more interesting life outside of school. They were concerned that Randy spent most of his evenings and weekends playing ball on the living room floor, watching children's videos he had outgrown, or sitting on the back porch watching the dog. Sometimes in the summer, he would help his father pick vegetables in the garden. Randy's mother, Mrs. Schwit, told his teacher that summers and vacations had become a challenge because Randy was bored. She was also worried about Randy's future. She had heard that Mrs. Rollo's daughter graduated from school and was now at home all day with nothing to do.*

This chapter describes how the school and family can work together to help students gain greater access to their communities and find meaningful leisure pursuits. Some students, like Randy, may need ongoing support to pursue these options after high school. Other students may gain the skills and awareness they need to be able to travel through their communities independently. Whether teams are planning for ongoing support or independence, community-based instruction provided by the school can be an important resource in training students for adulthood.

With the appropriate support, all students, no matter what their types or levels of disability may be, can participate actively in their communities. The purpose of teaching community and leisure skills is not to get students "ready" to be part of their communities, but instead to help them benefit from these experiences more fully. An important way that schools can prepare students for both current and future community and leisure opportunities is to get them directly involved in these activities through "community-based instruction." Community-based instruction involves teaching students sys-

---

[1]The case study of Randy, described throughout this chapter, is based on our experience in designing community-based instruction with people like him, but Randy himself is not a real person.

Karena J. Cooper, PhD, is an assistant professor of special education at Western Carolina University, Cullouhee, North Carolina.

tematically and directly in community contexts, such as banks, restaurants, stores, and recreation centers. This instruction prepares students to generalize skills to environments beyond the school, to different peers, and to diverse materials. Students also learn to respond to natural cues and consequences that will enable them to participate in activities more fully and with less assistance from others. Some of these activities are essential to daily living, such as learning to use a bank or buy groceries. Others focus on enjoyment and being with friends, such as going to the movies, taking a dance class, or joining a Little League team. Opportunities for individuals with disabilities to get involved in recreational programs are increasing.

Community and leisure skills are included in nearly all life skills curricula (e.g., Ford et al., 1989; Loyd & Brolin, 1997; Giangreco, Cloninger, & Iverson, 1998; Wilcox & Bellamy, 1987). The benefits of teaching students skills directly in community contexts have also been well documented by research (Snell & Browder, 1986). Many school districts follow guidelines for offering community-based instruction that had been developed by experts like Nietupski, Hamre-Nietupski, Houselog, Donder, and Anderson (1988). Community-based instruction first became a priority in the early 1980s, when many educational programs for students with moderate to severe disabilities were segregated and used instruction that was not age-appropriate or functional. Professionals emphasized community-based instruction to focus on the importance of teaching students useful skills (Brown et al., 1983). Many teachers adopted this priority and provided both community-based instruction and classroom activities focused on these skills. For example, teachers used "simulations," in which students practiced skills like paying a cashier in their classroom contexts (Nietupski, Hamre-Nietupski, Clancy, & Veerhusen, 1986).

Although community-based instruction continues to be important for students with moderate and severe disabilities, many professionals now see the need to plan this time carefully so that it does not compete with school inclusion. Removing only children with disabilities from classrooms to learn community skills can stigmatize them and emphasize their differences from peers. Moreover, when children with disabilities are removed from the regular education class they may miss valuable instruction and socialization time. Also, it is unusual to see children in the community during typical school hours, which may work against the goal of helping students "blend" into their community contexts.

Given these issues, it may be tempting for administrators to eliminate community-based instruction, and in doing so to reduce costs and potential risks to student safety. This would be a serious loss for students with moderate and severe disabilities, who may not generalize skills from school to community contexts unless directly trained to do so (Snell & Browder, 1986). Community-based instruction may also be a highly preferred and motivational activity for many students. As schools encourage students' self-determination, it is important to listen to their choices about their school activities. Community-based instruction provides a way for schools to form partnerships with area businesses. For example, educators can work with business leaders in planning this instruction (Aveno, Renzaglia, & Lively, 1987). Rather than discontinuing this important resource, schools should update their approach to it, so as to minimize the competition between school inclusion and community-based instruction.

To update this approach, educators can use four strategies: (1) reconsidering who participates in community-based instruction, (2) focusing on generalization, (3) involving peers who are nondisabled, and (4) expanding the school day or working with after-school programs. First, school districts may want to reconsider who participates in community-based instruction by using a set of criteria, rather than a blanket policy that all students with disabilities should receive this training. For example, Rosalyn (see below) only participated in one or two community-based instruction sessions per month, because she was in elementary school and had many other priorities. In contrast, Randy, who was in high school, had an individualized education plan (IEP) that targeted daily community-based instruction. It may be appropriate for some elementary students to have *no* community-based instruction beyond the incidental learning that occurs in school field trips. Other elementary students may have behavioral challenges in community contexts or special skill needs that make this a high priority for them and their families. In updating community-based instruction policies, educators may want to use criteria such as in Box 9.1 to determine who participates in such a program.

Community-based instruction programs can also be updated by focusing on generalization. If students are instructed to generalize, they will be able to use the skills taught in untrained contexts. Horner, McDonnell, and Bellamy (1986b) demonstrated how to achieve generalization by careful planning about which settings to use in training, in an approach called "general-case instruction." Teachers train the "general case" by selecting settings that sample the range of variation found in the community. For example, training in settings that have automated, push, and pull doors may enable students to use any door encountered in the community in the future. Although general-case instruction focuses on training in multiple community settings, Westling and Floyd (1990) found that students can sometimes learn to generalize from just *one* community context if this is augmented by school-based practice. This school-based practice can be designed as a close simulation of what occurs in the community (Nietupski et al., 1986). For example, a teacher may set up a simulated grocery store in a school storage area and have students practice finding items on their lists and paying for them at a cash register. Or students may practice ordering from real menus the teacher obtains from local restaurants. Teachers may also encourage generalization by using more school settings to teach community skills. Students may go to the school store daily to practice purchasing. Teachers may urge par-

---

**BOX 9.1. Criteria to Determine Students' Need
for Community-Based Instruction**

1. How important is community-based instruction to the family?
2. To what extent is community-based instruction a preferred activity for the student?
3. How many years does the student have left in school to learn community skills?
4. Are there specific skill deficit issues that need to be addressed in community settings (e.g., problem behavior when the family tries to take the student to grocery store)?
5. Can these skills be addressed by training the student across more environments within the school?
6. Is the student beyond the typical age to be in public school (19–21)?
7. What will the student miss at school when he or she is in the community?

ents to let students purchase their lunches, rather than bringing them, so that the students can practice waiting in line and paying.

To update community-based instruction, teachers can also include children who do not have disabilities in a unique form of cooperative learning (Moon, Komissar, Friedlander, Hart, & Kiernan, 1994, Schleien, Green, & Heyne, 1993). During these small-group activities, all students work together to achieve a common goal. A science class may go to the park to take water samples. This class activity may also offer an opportunity for students with severe disabilities to practice skills like street crossing and carrying a wallet with emergency information. Leisure activities provide other opportunities to participate with children who are nondisabled (Moon et al., 1994). These may include after-school activities, in-school clubs, and community outings (e.g., taking a gym class to the YMCA for swimming).

A fourth way to update community-based instruction is to expand the school day to incorporate these after-school options. This option can be expensive and may not be feasible for some districts. In contrast, districts that have already expanded their school day for older students or have provided after-school care for younger students may be able to incorporate community-based instruction during this time.

SELECTING SKILLS FOR COMMUNITY AND LEISURE INSTRUCTION

Once the decision has been made that community-based instruction is important for an individual student, the planning team needs to prioritize specific skills for this training. An ecological assessment can be used for this prioritization, including (1) getting background information on the student; (2) conducting person-centered planning with the family and student; (3) promoting student self-determination; and (4) using ecological inventories, situational assessments, and curriculum guides, and (5) developing the student's personalized curriculum and IEP.

Summarizing Prior Records

Before any community-based instruction is implemented for a student with disabilities, it is critical for the teacher to get to know the student and plan instruction in the community. A community-based instruction plan should begin with a review of the student's prior school records (see Figure 9.1). Specifically, information from the student's records should include (1) medical information, (2) previous community-based instruction on community or leisure skills and any progress the student made, (3) problem behavior, (4) student preferences, and (5) family preferences. This information is crucial for "risk management," as well as for developing appropriate instruction. Risk management is the set of strategies used to minimize any risks to student safety and well-being, and may include school district policies that must be followed (e.g., requirement for written parental consent; well-defined procedures for medical emergencies; written procedures for behavioral support).

An example of reviewing prior records is shown in Figure 9.1. Rosalyn[2] was an 11-

---

[2]The case study of Rosalyn, used throughout the rest of this chapter, is based on our experiences in designing community-based instruction for people like her, but Rosalyn is not a real person.

FIGURE 9.1. A summary of Rosalyn's prior records, as a first step toward implementing community-based instruction.

Summary of Prior Records

Name of student: Rosalyn Brown

Date: 8/23/2—   **Age:** 11

Medical Information

1. Medical conditions: Rosalyn has asthma, which is a lung disease that creates difficulty for her in breathing after physical exertion or in the presence of irritants (specifically, cigarette smoke, and perfume) and allergens (cats and pollen).

2. Medication and possible side effects: Rosalyn takes albuterol to stop an asthma attack. The liquid albuterol may be given if she begins wheezing. This medication may cause dizziness, headache, lightheadedness, heartburn, loss of appetite, nervousness, trembling or sweating, or even heart palpitations.

3. Medically related restrictions on activities or limitations on the environments that the student may attend: Rosalyn's physician recommends that she have some modified exercise, but that her physical activities be limited to those that are not overly strenuous.

Previous Community-Based Instruction and Progress

1. Skills taught in the community: Last year Rosalyn received community-based instruction in selecting and checking out books on tape from the library, going to the grocery store, using her wheelchair to move through a checkout counter, and sampling music CDs at a music store.

2. Student progress: By the end of last year, Rosalyn had mastered with 80% accuracy selecting and checking out books and tapes from the library; she was able to partially participate in the task of buying groceries with 50% accuracy; and she was able to partially participate in music selections with peers with 50% accuracy. She did not make progress on moving her own chair through a checkout line and needed more help with nonvisual orientation to do this.

3. Student preference: Rosalyn participated most during the public library activities.

Disruptive Behavior

1. Behaviors the student demonstrates: Rosalyn will scream loudly and throw her head back against her chair, almost flipping the chair over backward.

2. Behaviors that occur most frequently: Rosalyn will scream and push her head back when she is frustrated with a task and when her initial protests of pulling away and making soft vocalizations ("nnnn") are ignored. This usually occurs when she is asked to do puzzles at school or hand out art supplies; if her music is turned off; or if she is told she has to leave her friends at lunch.

(cont.)

FIGURE 9.1. *(cont.)*

3. **Possible functions of the student's behavior, or what the student gets when he or she demonstrates the disruptive behavior:** This behavior works to enable Rosalyn to refuse undesired tasks, as the teacher will usually offer an alternative task. It is also used to protest discontinuation of highly preferred activities and occasionally results in an activity's being reintroduced (e.g., peer comes back to console her).

4. **How can this behavior be prevented in community contexts?** Use the same training Rosalyn receives at school to shake her head "no" while vocalizing "nnnn" to refuse or protest. Offer choices of activities. When a preferred activity has to be discontinued, offer her choices such as what to do next, how fast she'd like to be pushed in her chair, and what to sing during the transition. Keep her schedule consistent with her peers (e.g., she leaves the activity at the same time they do).

5. **What can be done to stop the student's challenging behavior once it is started?** Once Rosalyn has started to demonstrate her disruptive behavior in the community, the teacher will step back and wait for Rosalyn to calm herself (which is usually within a few minutes). Then the teacher should prompt Rosalyn to shake her head "no" and respond to a choice (see point 4 just above.)

6. **Additional planning to reduce risk of problem behavior in community settings:** The teacher should explain to Rosalyn where they are going and what she will be doing, both verbally and with key objects from the activities (e.g., musical instrument). This is especially important when making a transition between settings. Next, the teacher should follow the behavior plan, and be prepared for an emergency by carrying a cell phone and emergency numbers (ambulance, parents' work numbers). The teacher is trained in first aid that may be needed if Rosalyn flips back out of her chair. This written emergency and first aid plan has been approved by Rosalyn's parents.

year-old girl with multiple disabilities. Using a variety of gestures and manual signs, Rosalyn could communicate well with her sixth-grade companions at Southeast Middle School. She smiled and laughed when her friends argued over who was her best friend or complimented her on her cool shoes. Rosalyn was blind, had cerebral palsy on one side of her body (hemiplegia), and uses a wheelchair for mobility. She had also been diagnosed as severely mentally retarded. Rosalyn's planning team was considering ways to use both school and community activities to enhance her leisure interests. Since some of these activities required travel away from school, the team began by summarizing Rosalyn's support needs from her prior records as shown in Figure 9.1.

Person-Centered Planning with the Student and Family

DeLeo (1994) defines "person-centered planning" as a process that included (1) identifying the person's hopes, interests, accomplishments, and skills; (2) clarifying the future vision for the person; (3) identifying life goals; (4) identifying steps to reach the goals by including community supports; and (5) identifying the personal actions and services needed to achieve the goals. In addition to helping identify skills for instruction, this type of planning helps the team determine the importance of community-based instruction in the student's overall program. Randy's family decided that community-based instruction and leisure skills were the highest priorities for their son at this point in time. In contrast, Rosalyn's family wanted her to have community-based instruction, but they did not want this training to supplant other priorities (e.g., taking music, eating lunch with her friends, and taking more general education classes). They

TABLE 9.1. Questions to Identify Family and Student Preferences for Community and Leisure Skills Instruction

1. Community leisure

- What does your family do for fun?
- What does your child/teen like to do most for fun?
- What places does your family enjoy going to during community outings?
- What does your child/teen enjoy doing for fitness?
- Does your child/teen play or socialize with other children/teens after school and on the weekend? If so, what do they do for fun? If not, are there activities children/teens in the neighborhood do in which you would like your child/teen to participate?
- Are there any leisure activities that have not been explored, but may be of interest to your child/teen?

2. Family values and customs

- What holidays does your family celebrate?
- What does your family like to do on these holidays?
- Are there community activities related to these activities that might be appropriate for students to attend during the school day? Are there ways we can participate in celebrating a holiday while your child/teen is at school?
- Are there activities, foods, or places that are *not* appropriate for us to use in teaching community or leisure skills because of your family's values or customs?

3. Safety in the community

- Do you have any concerns about your child's/teen's participation in community-based instruction? If so, what are they?
- Does your child/teen cross the street independently?
- Does your child/teen have skills in personal safety (e.g., not talking to strangers, locating police for assistance, showing an identification card if he or she is are lost)?
- Can your child/teen use a public phone to call for assistance or get directions?
- Does your child/teen ever go into the community without an adult (e.g., with friends)?
- How does your child/teen respond if treated rudely in public (e.g., stared at)?
- How does your child/teen respond if his or her rights are violated (e.g., not served by waiter, ignored by cashier)?

4. Participation in community activities

- Does your child/teen go shopping with your family? If so, what does he or she do while you shop? What does your child/teen *like* to do most while shopping?
- Does your child/teen eat in restaurants with you? Which restaurants are family favorites? What are your child's/teen's favorite places to eat? What are his or her favorite foods and beverages to order?
- Are there other community settings where your child/teen goes that we have not discussed (e.g., bank, post office, church/temple)? What does your child/teen do there? Is this an activity your child/teen likes to do?

were also eager for her to participate in more extracurricular activities. After determining how much emphasis to give to community-based instruction in the school schedule, the teams for Randy and Rosalyn identified specific student and family preferences for each student. Table 9.1 provides some questions that might be used in learning more about these preferences.

Promoting Student Self-Determination during Community and Leisure Skills

Browder, Bambara, and Belfiore (1997) describe the importance of promoting self-determination in developing community-based instruction. Using O'Brien's (1987) five essential outcomes for lifestyle enhancement, they note that community-based instruction should be designed not only to encourage competence through skill acquisition, but also to enhance the person's community presence, respect, and choice. One of Randy's previous teachers had made the mistake of focusing only on how he learned to make purchases, without considering these other issues. She took Randy and his classmates to the store, but decided where they would shop and what they would purchase (e.g., class supplies or items for a menu the teacher had selected). At the cash register, she used loud verbal directives and excessive physical guidance to help Randy take out his money. Other customers would stare or move to another checkout counter. In contrast, his current teacher adopted a person-centered focus. Randy took turns with his classmates selecting the store by touching one of three picture logos of popular area stores from store flyers (e.g., Wal-Mart). He chose what to purchase by scanning the shelf and putting an object in the cart. The teacher minimized the prompting Randy needed at the checkout counter by teaching him to hand the cashier either a debit card or a bill large enough to cover the purchase.

Besides designing community-based instruction to enhance student competence, choices, and respect, teachers can also promote self-determination through having students participate in planning what they will do and learn. Newton, Horner, and Lund (1991) note the importance of having students present when planning future goals and activities. The following description shows how Randy's team made his preferences the center of their planning meeting.

How Randy Let His Team Know about His Leisure Preferences

Randy's IEP team included himself, his mother, his father, his sister, his special education teacher, his homeroom teacher, his physical education teacher, a transition specialist, and two 11th-grade boys who were interested in becoming Randy's friends. Randy's meetings were designed so that Randy would be comfortable. Because Randy did not like to sit in hard chairs, they held the meeting in a lounge and used a coffee table rather than a conference table. At the first meeting, Randy stood beside his mother's chair, holding her hand as she provided a lot of the information needed during the person-centered planning process (e.g., his history, his interests, their goals). As others began to talk at greater length about Randy's interests, he would sometimes walk over to their chairs. When Randy and his family got home, he began to bring his mother items from his room related to activities they had discussed. She encouraged him to keep bringing her what he liked, and then took these to his next meeting (e.g., movie ticket stubs, baseball glove, tennis balls, cassette tapes). At the next meeting, his mother prompted Randy to hold up each one of these items as the team talked more about making this activity a goal. He seemed to enjoy participating in the meeting in this way. The other 11th-grade boys in the meeting began to clap for their favorites (e.g., while making comments about their favorite sports stars or movies); Randy began to clap after he held up each item as well. As the discussion progressed, the teacher asked Randy's mother whether she had any concerns about his community-based instruction. She stated that taking Randy to activities in the community was worrisome because of occasional toileting accidents. When she began talking about his accidents, Randy stood up, let go of his mother's hand, and began to make loud noises. The team interpreted this as a request not to talk about this issue at the meeting. His teacher offered to discuss options for managing incontinence with Randy and his mother in private later, and changed the topic to reviewing some extracurricular activities Randy might enjoy.

Helping Students Who Lack Symbolic Communication Skills Express Preferences

Not all students will have Randy's unique ability to show people objects to help them understand his preferences. Randy was especially skilled in using objects to communicate, because he did not need contextual cues to know what they symbolized. For example, he could hold up a tennis ball when others talked about tennis, without needing to be at a tennis court or seeing others dressed for tennis to understand what this meant. For students who do not have this level of symbolic communication, the team can determine the students' preferences on leisure and community activities based on their ongoing participation and choices.

We (Browder, Cooper, & Lim, 1998) assessed the leisure preferences of adults with severe disabilities who had limited communication skills by first reviewing past teaching records to determine patterns of participation and refusal. We reviewed records on participation in over 30 activities that had been sampled over several years. These lists contained a wide variety of activities, such as craft classes, bingo, volunteer mailings for area politicians, volunteer work at a food bank, fitness activities at the YMCA, and fishing in local parks. As part of the program's ongoing services to identify preferences, staff members had taken notes on whether participants engaged in the activities or refused. After selecting activities that the participants rarely refused (e.g., golfing, exercise class, viewing magazines), we made arrangements for them to go to these activities on a regular basis, but in two different settings (community vs. day program). We timed the duration of their participation in the activities with a stopwatch to discern which of the two settings they preferred. The timing ended when a person said, "No," walked away, or dropped the leisure materials. After several weeks, setting preferences could be inferred from how long the participants stayed engaged in the activities.

In applying these strategies, teachers might time how long students engage in various community and leisure activities, and take notes on responses that may convey preference (e.g., smiling vs. frowning, looking at objects vs. looking away, vocalizing pleasure vs. displeasure). Keeping notes on choices students make during ongoing community and leisure activities can also be useful in determining preference patterns. Through using these strategies with Rosalyn, the teacher discovered her music preferences. Rosalyn would participate much longer in classroom chores with upbeat music like rock or oldies than she would with "easy-listening" music or no music at all. Rosalyn's teacher also kept notes on her choices and discovered that she often chose leisure materials that made sounds (e.g., musical instrument, tape player, electronic games) or ones that were squeezable (e.g., Nerf ball, stuffed animal). She rarely chose items that had bumpy or complex surfaces (e.g., textured ball, pinball maze).

In addition to these indirect methods of preference assessment, teachers can also teach choice-making skills that can later be used to assess preference. We (Browder et al., 1998) taught participants to associate an object with each setting and activity. For example, a golf ball symbolized playing golf, and a library card symbolized going to the library to view magazines. Each object chosen for as a symbol for instruction was one a student would use in the activity. After intensive instruction in picking the symbol for each activity, the participants mastered selecting the correct one. We could then create opportunities for participants to ask to go to specific settings by choosing between these objects.

Another way to promote student self-determination in leisure and community skills is to encourage choice making during these activities. Much of the research literature on choice making has focused on students' choosing between items they will use or consume (e.g., toys or food) in a school, workshop, or experimental setting (Lancioni, O'Reilly, & Emerson, 1996). In contrast, community resources and leisure activities provide a wide variety of opportunities for choice making. In another study, we (Cooper & Browder, 1998) demonstrated how these choices could be embedded in a community purchasing routine. The young adults with severe disabilities who participated were given choices before each of five different steps of the purchasing task analysis. The teacher conducted a baseline assessment to determine how many choices the participants would make. For example, before entering the restaurant, the teacher would stand back to see which door a participant chose (e.g., by touching it or trying to open it). Other choices the staff observed were (1) menu items (from pictures), (2) condiments, and (3) seating. Once the teacher determined which choices the learner could make, specific instruction was used to teach participants how to make the other choices. In this instruction, the teacher made two options clear (e.g., "Which door?" while pointing to two doors). Showing these specific options was faded using time delay (Chapter Four provides more information on time delay). If a student made a choice, the teacher commended this choice. If not, the teacher said, "I'm not sure which one. I'll help you choose," and guided the student's hand to indicate a choice. The following description indicates how the teacher used a similar strategy with Rosalyn during community-based instruction to pick out a purchase.

Assessing and Teaching Rosalyn Choices in a Community Routine

When they got out of the van on one community outing, Rosalyn's teacher asked her to pick who she would like to have help push her into the store. Rosalyn's friends stated their names, offered to push her, and held out their hands to see whether she would touch one to make a choice. She laughed, but did not choose, so the teacher helped her into the store. Her friends suggested looking at jewelry. They let Rosalyn hold two types of necklaces, but she dropped each one as if uninterested. When they tried accessories, she held on to a pair of furry earmuffs and would not release it. She continued to hold the earmuffs as they went to the music section. The music section had a listening center to enable customers to sample CDs. The teacher and peers played CDs for Rosalyn and watched her reaction. She became animated and smiled when they played a certain group. Because Rosalyn only had enough money to purchase one item, they needed to see whether she could choose between the earmuffs and the music. Using creativity, one of the friends went and got a second pair of earmuffs, and held it in one hand and the earphones for the music (still playing) in the other. After placing each one on her head and letting her touch each, they waited to see whether she would reach for one, but she did not respond. The teacher said that she would work more on choosing between objects at school. For now, it seemed that the first pair of earmuffs (which Rosalyn still held) was a strong first choice, so they assisted her to purchase it at the cash register. From this assessment, the teacher targeted teaching Rosalyn to accept or refuse help with her wheelchair and to choose between objects in making a purchase (they would work on this by going to the school store prior to their next outing).

Teaching Self-Management

Self-management is another component of self-determination. In their review of the literature, Hughes and Agran (1993) identified several strategies that have been used in community contacts. One of these is self-instruction, in which students learn to use pictures or verbal statements to perform a new skill or solve a problem. In applying this strategy, a teacher can help a student learn to cope with being lost in a store by using a series of verbal statements. The student will (1) state the problem ("I am lost in the store"), (2) state a plausible response ("I can ask the cashier to help me"), (3) enacting this response, and (4) evaluating the response and verbally reinforcing oneself ("All right, I did it! The man helped me find Dad"). Chapter Six discusses this and other components of self-management in greater detail.

Curriculum Building Blocks

By considering a student's preferences and skills needed to enhance self-determination, a teacher has an important beginning point in selecting community and leisure skills. To build the student's curriculum further in this area, the teacher can use ecological inventories, situational assessment (e.g., discrepancy analyses), curriculum lists, and other strategies. The first two of these are described here.

Ecological Inventories

As described in Chapter Two, an ecological inventory is a process of surveying the student's current and future environments to determine specific skill needs. One way to conduct such a survey for leisure skills is to use Ford et al.'s (1989) five categories: (1) school and extracurricular activities, (2) home or neighborhood activities that can be done alone, (3) home or neighborhood activities that can be done with family or friends, (4) community activities with family and friends, and (5) activities for physical fitness. When planning with Randy, his team used these five areas to generate ideas to expand his leisure skills, as shown in Figure 9.2.

Another way to conduct ecological inventories is visit sites to identify needed skills. In a book chapter entitled "Finding or Creating Fun in Your Community," Moon et al. (1994) recommend traveling around the student's neighborhood and looking for (1) places where students the same age are playing, (2) places with activities that may be of interest to the student, and (3) places that just might be fun. Browder (1991) has described an ecological inventory process that involves visiting a site to gain informa-

FIGURE 9.2. Ecological inventory of five leisure areas: Randy's example

Ecological Inventory of Leisure Areas

I. School and extracurricular activities

• *Initially*

Randy does not participate in extracurricular activities; however, he does have leisure time at school. He usually watches videos or looks out the window while passing his ball back and forth between his hands.

• *Possible future ideas from the team*

Join the band and play a percussion instrument; assist with the tennis or soccer team; play computer games with peers during breaks from lessons; learn to play the tabletop paper football game some students play in the cafeteria; go to a school dance.

II. Home or neighborhood activities that can be performed alone

• *Initially*

Randy likes to play with balls (especially baseballs and tennis balls), play a harmonica, listen to music, play with his dog, and watch videos.

• *Possible future ideas from the team*

Select from a variety of leisure activities on a shelf in the family room. These may include a collection and an album of sports cards, a radio, a toy to play with the dog, teen magazines and sports magazines (Baseball Weekly, Tennis Weekly), a hand-held electronic game, and a family photo box that has drawers of pictures. He could have a shelf in the garage for things to play with in the yard, including a tug-of-war rope for the dog, a Nerf ball that makes a sound when thrown, horseshoes, a soccer ball and net, and a water gun.

III. Home or neighborhood activities to do with family and friends

• *Initially*

Randy will sometimes help his father in the garden. He does not visit other homes or have friends who visit.

• *Possible future ideas from the team*

Play soccer with his sister and other teens in the neighborhood; hit a tennis ball with a friend or his father; visit a neighbor to play with the neighbor's dog; play a computer game with other teens (get him games that will attract other teens to his house as well); go to neighborhood teens' sports events; go with other teens to a movie.

(cont.)

FIGURE 9.2. *(cont.)*

IV. Community activities to do with family and friends

- *Initially*

Goes to grocery store with mother.

- *Possible future ideas from the team*

Parents' dream is to go to church with Randy as a family and participate in fellowship activities after the service. Team dreams for Randy also include going to the mall, shopping, eating out with friends or family, playing billiards with friends, and going to under-21 coffee house.

V. Activities for physical fitness

- *Initially*

Sometimes runs around house so family members will chase him. Otherwise, not much exercise.

- *Possible future ideas from the team*

Playing tennis, soccer, bike riding (he has a special three-wheeled bike that he has not learned to ride), dancing, talking walks around the neighborhood, and walking the mall.

tion to plan community-based instruction. This process involves both viewing the site and interviewing people who work at the setting. Figure 9.3 provides an example of this type of ecological inventory that was used in planning for Randy. Scott, one of the teens on Randy's team, suggested trying the local billiard hall because it was popular with other guys their age. Randy's mother was hesitant because she was not sure whether Randy would be safe there. Randy's teacher visited the site and talked with Randy and his mother about this option.

Situational Assessment

After sites are identified through ecological inventories, it is important to give students the opportunity to try out new leisure and community opportunities. For example, Randy needed the opportunity to see the billiard hall for himself and try this new activity. One way to summarize the information found during such tryouts is with a discrepancy analysis. In a discrepancy analysis, the evaluator compares the student's performance to that of an individual who is nondisabled, as shown in Table 9.2.

PLANNING FOR SPECIFIC LEISURE SKILLS AND ACTIVITIES

Considerations in Selecting Leisure Skills and Activities for Instruction

Moon et al. (1994) define "leisure" and "recreation" as any activities or programs that people participate in for fun, relaxation, diversion, or amusement; they note that this element of having fun is what differentiates leisure or recreation from any other type of activity. Leisure activities should also provide choices for participants and should be

FIGURE 9.3. Ecological inventory based on a site visit to assess a possible leisure activity for Randy.

Ecological Inventory: Site Visit

Site: The 8 Ball Billiard Hall   **Interviewee:** Mr. Panzo (owner of the billiard hall)

Date: September 23, 20—   **Student:** Randy Schwit

1. Describe the site.

The 8 Ball Billiard Hall is located on North Main St. This small facility is near Central Bank and Rosie's Diner. Inside the site, there are 10 pool tables and an area with vending machines and chairs. There is a small counter where Mr. Panzo sits watching television and renting pool supplies. There is one single-person restroom. No alcohol is served in this facility.

2. What leisure activities are available in this site?

Playing pool, using vending machine, socializing at the tables.

3. What is the site's schedule?

The billiard hall is open from 4:00 in the afternoon until 10:00 P.M. on Monday through Friday. On Saturdays and Sundays it is open from 9:00 A.M. until 9:00 P.M. Tables can be rented by the hour.

4. How accessible is the site? What orientation and mobility skills are required?

Because playing billiards is a turn-taking game, there are both opportunities for standing up and walking around the table and for sitting on a high bar-like stool to take a break. Some mobility is needed to get to the vending machines and the public phone or snack bar; they are located at the far end of the building. There are no stairs either in or outside the facility. The front door of the facility is wheelchair-accessible.

5. What safety considerations need to be considered for this activity or site?

Mr. Panzo says that people rarely get hurt playing billiards. He is strict about no "roughhousing" and no drugs or alcohol. The local police usually drop in once or twice each day—mostly because of their interest in the billiard games!

6. Is any special equipment or clothing required?

Equipment is provided when a table is rented. Dress is casual (teens wear jeans and T-shirts).

7. What types of communication and social skills are required?

Requesting a table, conversing with peers, joking. The patrons are often loud and boisterous in this site (jumping up and down, bumping chests, playing loud music on CD players they bring, teasing each other).

8. What natural reminders (cues) and rewards (contingencies) are available?

Mr. Panzo keeps players' deposits if they don't return the equipment to him, if they leave the area trashy, or if they are asked to leave for misconduct. He usually will give one warning. The teens often tell each other what ball to shoot and give each other lots of humorous feedback.

(cont.)

9. What is the owner's response to using the site for instruction?

Mr. Panzo said he would open one morning for teaching Randy and some classmates to play pool. Randy would be welcome to come back after school during regular hours. Mr. Panzo said, "Anybody who pays and behaves is welcome."

10. Will escorted assistance in restrooms or for eating or dressing be acceptable?

The restroom can be used privately with assistance if needed, but assistance would be stigmatizing in this small setting.

11. What is the recommendation for the student sampling this site?

This site does seem safe and accessible. The challenge is that the site operates during after-school hours. The school can help by teaching Randy and some classmates to play billiards during the morning when Mr. Panzo opens for us, but arrangements also need to be made for him to sample this site during after-school hours.

TABLE 9.2. Discrepancy Analysis Used as Part of a Situational Assessment of a Community Setting

Grocery Shopping			
Grocery-shopping routine	Randy's responses	Responses of nondisabled peer (Sara Mason, age 16)	Implications for instruction
Context	I took him to his family's favorite store.	I observed Sara and her father shopping together.	Most teens do not yet grocery-shop alone.
Communication after entering the store	Yelling and smiling due to excitement.	A little small talk and asked her father for a purchase.	Point to choices without yelling.
Staying with companions	Ran away from teacher three times.	Stayed near cart pushing it; left once to look at something.	Stay near cart or walk over to look at something briefly.
Pushing the cart	Wanted to push cart; able to negotiate aisles except when hit display; began to run with cart at end.	Pushed cart for a while, then let father do it.	Push cart around displays; walk slowly; take turns.
Matching coupons to items	Would not hold or attend to coupons.	Found coupon items.	Use coupons for special treat to find, place in cart, and then eat after leaving the store.
Putting items in the cart	Tried to eat apples and other preferred foods he could reach while walking through the store.	Put items in the cart.	Place items in cart (grocery-shop after lunch when less hungry).
Purchasing	Sat on a bench near checkout counters.	Helped bag groceries; father put items on counter and paid.	Put items on counter. OK to rest on bench if tired.

age-appropriate and community-integrated. Leisure activities help participants escape from stress, socialize with peers, and improve physical fitness. Despite these potential benefits, many students with severe disabilities may have an excess of free time with few leisure options.

The most important way to select leisure skills and activities for instruction is through preference assessment. Typically, a student is exposed to a variety of leisure materials and activities, and his or her reaction is noted. Schleien et al. (1993) note that the teacher may evaluate preference by looking at the following:

1. How the student displays affect in the presence of the leisure activity (e.g., increased smiles, change in vocalizations, increased concentration or interest, or displeasure with the leisure materials).
2. How strongly the student indicates an attraction to particular objects over others (e.g., by approaching, reaching for, discarding, or touching and manipulating the objects).
3. How long the student shows interest (e.g., the duration of eye contact or visual acuity with materials).
4. How long the student engages in the activity (e.g., duration of manipulation of the materials or of active engagement in the activity).

Besides preference, a second consideration in selecting leisure skills and activities is the extent to which they foster social interaction and inclusion. Rynders et al. (1993) synthesized the research literature on improving integration outcomes for children with severe disabilities through cooperatively structured recreation activities. They found that proximity alone does not ensure interactions. Instead, adults may need to structure activities to encourage student interaction. They also found that some activities (e.g., board games, volleyball) foster interaction more than others. Rynders et al. (1993) also note that students who participate who are nondisabled may need reassurance that their peers with disabilities can benefit from the activities. These students may need information on how to provide assistance.

Rynders, Schleien, and Mustonen (1990) applied these strategies in a study that evaluated the effectiveness of offering an integrated outdoor education camp for children with and without disabilities. The activities were traditional summer camp activities that were organized by adults to facilitate opportunities for all the children (e.g., crafts, swimming, meal preparation, fishing, boating, hiking, dancing, hay rides, etc.). The students with disabilities were taught specific skills (e.g., preparation for swimming) as well as being given numerous opportunities for socialization. The following section gives examples of specific leisure skills and activities that can be taught in typical leisure environments.

Examples of Leisure Skills and Activities

Leisure Skills and Activities for School

School itself provides not only an educational environment, but also a recreational one with offerings of extracurricular activities, such as clubs, sports, and chorus or band. Sometimes educational activities also provide a context to learn leisure skills. For example, LeGrice and Blampied (1994) taught students to operate a VCR and a computer at school; they used a self-management strategy with video prompting of taped models of each step to correct student errors. Sometimes extracurricular activities may need to be modified to include all children. Bernabe and Block (1994) conducted a study to evaluate the effects of modifying the rules of a girls' softball league to facilitate the inclusion of a child with severe disabilities. The researchers asked members of the league, the team, the parents, and coaches whether modifications were needed, and if so, which ones. As a result of this collaboration, the student with disabilities was able to participate and gain high rates of peer acceptance. In some classrooms, teachers allow students to play board games when they complete their work. Students may need systematic instruction to be able to play these games. Wall and Gast (1997) taught caregivers how to use constant time delay to teach individuals with severe disabilities to play a variety of games. These games included horseshoes, checkers, Bottle Topps, Jenga, Uno, croquet, and dominoes. Similarly, peer tutors may assist students to play board games available in a general education classroom. Figure 9.4 provides a checklist that can be used in choosing leisure skills and activities for school.

Leisure Skills and Activities for Time Alone

Most people have some leisure interests that they enjoy pursuing alone (e.g., reading, jogging, needlework). Similarly, students with disabilities also need to develop enjoyable ways to spend time alone. At school, teachers can encourage students to select and use leisure materials during their free time. For example, Rosalyn's teacher taught her to go to a set of shelves that were filled with leisure materials and that were easily accessible to her (only 1 foot high). Figure 9.5 gives examples of leisure skills and activities for times alone.

Leisure Skills and Activities with Friends and Family in the Community

Most of the leisure skills and activities described for school or for use alone can also be done with friends and family in the home, neighborhood, or community. There are also additional leisure opportunities in community settings. For example, Schleien, Mustonen, and Rynders (1995) designed and implemented a cooperatively structured art education class at the local museum. The classes included both children with and without disabilities. In the classes, the children increased their participation in the art activities, as well as their cooperative interactions. Taylor, McKelvey, and Sisson (1993) taught students to order takeout pizza and rent a video at a video store. Vandercook (1991) selected games teens enjoy, such as pinball and bowling at the local YMCA and a bowling alley. Using decreasing assistance and peer partnerships, the instructors successfully taught the students with severe disabilities to engage in these activities.

One way that schools can help students become more involved in community recreation opportunities is by implementing summer programming in recreational versus school settings. Hamre-Nietupski et al. (1992) used a variety of settings for the implementation of students' extended school year services. These included playground programs, week-long camps, and swimming. By planning jointly with the

FIGURE 9.4. A checklist for choosing leisure skills and activities for school.

Checklist of Leisure Skills and Activities for School

Skills/activities	Mastery	Partial mastery	Not tried yet
Skills			
Indicate preference while sampling new activity			
Decide which activity to join			
Go to meeting to join activity			
Request assistance if needed in participating in the activity			
Participate actively with the group			
Greet and socialize with others during the activity			
Identify when the activity is ended			
Help in cleaning up after the activity			
Examples of activities			
School newspaper			
School band or chorus			
Sporting events (football, soccer, swimming, cheerleading, etc.)			
Science or environmental clubs, 4-H clubs			
Student government bodies			
Foreign-language interests			
Art class activities (e.g., drawing, ceramics, painting)			
Gym class activities (e.g., sports, gymnastics, aerobics)			
Drama club, school plays			
Service groups			
Board games			
Others (specify)			

FIGURE 9.5. Checklist of Leisure Skills and Activities for Time Alone

Skills/activities	Mastery	Partial mastery	Not tried yet
Skills			
Select an activity			
Locate materials to begin the activity			
Determine where to engage in the activity			
Begin the activity			
Use materials appropriately			
Terminate activity			
Put materials away			
Examples of activities			
Play with a pet			
Play computer games			
Watch a video (operate VCR)			
Look at, display collections (baseball cards, stamps, football cards, dolls, etc.)			
Play tossing games (Velcro darts, jacks, horseshoes, etc.)			
View a book or magazine			
Listen to music (use a CD or cassette player or turn on radio)			
Water plants			
Do art/craft activities (painting, stenciling, latch hooking, cutting/pasting and coloring [for children under 10] etc.)			
Others (specify)			

program's staff, the special educators were able to develop creative adaptations for participation. For example, students with disabilities used a dowel stick or broom handle to roast hot dogs and large foam dice when playing a table game. Similarly, Rynders et al. (1990) found that students with severe disabilities who participated in an integrated camping experience not only learned new daily living skills (e.g., dressing for swimming), but also increased their social interactions. Some more ideas for getting students involved with friends and family in community leisure activities are shown in Figure 9.6.

Leisure Skills for Fitness

An important consideration in developing leisure skills that will improve strength, stamina, and overall cardiovascular fitness is to find activities that the student will participate in on a continuing basis. Students need to explore different options for fitness activities. Some people prefer to exercise with a group or partner. These group activities can also foster social interaction. Ellis, Wright, and Cronis (1996) observed students with moderate and severe disabilities in regular gym classes, and found that more interactions occurred in grouped activities. Initially, a participant may need direct instruction to participate in an exercise program. We (Cooper & Browder, 1997) taught adults with severe disabilities to perform a specific water exercise, and then encouraged peers who were nondisabled to help the participants maintain their skills. Other students may prefer a self-managed exercise routine. Ellis, Cress, and Spellman (1990) taught students with moderate mental retardation to walk in either the school hallways or on a treadmill, using self-monitoring. To keep track of their distance, the students put a baton in a basket after completing each lap in the hallway, or set a timer on the treadmill. These participants improved the duration of their exercise over time by setting increasingly higher goals for themselves (e.g., more batons in the basket). Whereas some individuals like to focus on one specific fitness activity such as walking or swimming, others prefer "cross-training." To encourage a diversified fitness plan, Zhang, Gast, Horvat, and Dattilo (1995) taught four students with severe disabilities bowling, throwing, and putting (all in a school gym).

Besides increased fitness, exercise can have other benefits. In training students to play basketball in the Special Olympics in Turkey, Gencoz (1997) observed concurrent reductions in their problem behavior. The Special Olympics has a long tradition of promoting fitness for athletes with disabilities, and for some students, participation in this program is highly valued. However, students also need the opportunity to be active in inclusive school and community fitness programs. Schleien, Green, and Heyne (1993) describe how inclusive opportunities can be created in three ways: (1) Students with disabilities can be integrated into generic recreation programs (e.g., Little League, dance classes, physical education at school); (2) students who are nondisabled can be recruited to participate in a special program ("reverse mainstreaming"); or (3) a new program can be developed that includes all students from the onset ("zero exclusion"). Whatever type of program is selected, students with moderate and severe disabilities will often need systematic instruction to learn how to participate in the activities. Figure 9.7 provides a checklist teachers can use in considering what skills and activities to teach.

FIGURE 9.6. A checklist for choosing community leisure skills and activities.

Checklist of Community Leisure Skills and Activities

Skills/activities	Mastery	Partial mastery	Not tried yet
Skills			
Select an activity			
Identify persons to invite to join in the activity			
Schedule the activity			
Select money that is needed			
Go to the activity			
Purchase needed items			
Participate in the activity			
Socialize during breaks			
End activity			
Return home			
Examples of activities			
Community events (fairs, carnivals)			
Getting coffee			
Eating out			
Playing pool			
Swimming			
Movies			
Girl or Boy Scouts			
Participation with local theater group			
Library			
Miniature golf			
Museum			
Nature walks			
Church activities			
Sports events			
Others (specify)			

FIGURE 9.7. Leisure Skills for Fitness

Checklist of Leisure Skills for Fitness

Skills/activities	Mastery	Partial mastery	Not tried yet
Skills			
Select an activity for exercise			
Collect materials necessary for exercise			
Set a goal for amount of exercise			
Select a location for exercise			
Select partner (optional)			
Begin exercise activity			
Maintain exercise for goal			
Gradually slow down exercising			
Complete exercise			
Replace materials			
Say goodbye to partner (if any) and leave location			
Examples of activities			
Jump rope			
Yoga or stretching			
Tennis			
Hockey			
Swimming			
Bike riding			
Walking, hiking			
Roller skating or in-line skating			
Running, jogging			
Aerobics			
Soccer			
Dancing			
Softball, baseball			
Others (specify)			

SKILLS FOR COMMUNITY ACCESS

Gaining skills for community access can enhance both the student's and family's quality of life. In a survey of parents of preschoolers, Ehrmann, Aeschleman, and Svanum (1995) found that parents of children with disabilities reported more fear and risk in taking their children to community settings, and consequently participated in fewer community activities, than a comparison group of parents of children who were non-disabled. Because students with moderate and severe disabilities may have had fewer of these family experiences, they often need community-based instruction during their school years to prepare for the transition to adult living. Students with moderate and severe disabilities may also be more receptive to instruction in community contexts. Belfiore, Browder, and Mace (1993) observed adults with profound mental retardation in community- and center-based settings, and found that participants were more alert (e.g., awake and making eye contact) when in the community. Such differences in behavior may also be interpreted as preference. Belfiore, Browder, and Mace (1994) examined setting contrast again, and found that these same participants would choose a beverage and indicate a preference (e.g., for juice vs. water) in the community context, but were inactive or had no clear preference in the center.

Assessing Generalization of Community Skills

In assessing students' skills in the community, it is important to consider generalization across settings, activities, materials, and people. In a review of the community literature, Westling and Floyd (1990) found general-case instruction to have the most impressive generalization outcomes. In this procedure, the teacher identifies the "universe" of desired generalization conditions, identifies the variations of the relevant stimuli and responses in the universe, and then teaches the student to respond appropriately under all appropriate stimulus conditions (Horner et al., 1986b). Several researchers have demonstrated the benefits of using this approach to teach various community skills: purchasing in a fast-food restaurant (McDonnell & Ferguson, 1988), operating vending machines (Sprague & Horner, 1984), purchasing groceries (Horner, Albin, & Ralph, 1986a), crossing streets (Horner, Jones, & Williams, 1985), using public phones (Horner, Williams, & Steveley, 1987), and asking for help (Chadsey-Rusch, Drasgow, Reinoehl, Halle, & Collet-Klingenberg, 1993). An example of how to evaluate a student's level of skill generalization is shown in Figure 9.8. The advantage of conducting a generalization assessment is that teachers can identify how much variety needs to be included in instruction. Some students may generalize from teaching in only *one* community setting. Westling, Floyd, and Carr (1990) found that students with severe disabilities were able to generalize their shopping skills, whether their instruction was conducted in a single department store or multiple stores. In contrast, most research on general-case instruction documented the need for training across settings. Again, each student's needs can be determined best through direct assessment.

Safety Skills

Besides generalization, consideration also needs to be given to whether or not students practice community safety. Watson, Bain, and Houghton (1992) taught seven students

FIGURE 9.8. An assessment of Randy's generalization of a particular skill (purchasing food at a concession stand).

Assessment of Student's Skill Generalization

Student: Randy Schwits   Skill: Purchase at concession stand

Generic task analysis	Settings				Implications for instruction and accommodations
	High school football stadium	Pete's Hot Dog Stand	Community fundraisers	Jackson Arena	
1. Approach stand.	Stands are on perimeter. Randy could not negotiate walking through the crowd. (−).	Stand has large hot dog on top. Randy walked to it. (+)	Volunteers knew Randy and invited him to their table. (+, with natural support).	Stands are in hallway. Randy could not negotiate crowd. (−)	Practice weaving through crowd with companion.
2. Wait in line.	Long wait; began to vocalize loudly. (−)	No waiting. (omit step)	Volunteers served him ahead of others. (omit step)	Long wait; sat on floor. (−)	Go at "off" times. Practice standing and waiting.
3. Make choice.	Bobbed head toward someone's hot dog. (−; chose, but stigmatizing)	Looked at hot dogs intently. (+)	Grabbed bag of hot dog buns. (−; chose, but inappropriate)	Did not choose (−).	Point to options or use eye gazing to choose.
4. Inform cashier.	Teacher told cashier. (−)	Pete recognized his eye gaze as an order. (+)	Volunteers recognized grabbing (−; not appropriate).	Teacher told cashier. (−)	Learn to use picture order card.
5. Take out money.	Teacher physically guided. (−)	Teacher guided (−)	Volunteers gave it to him. (omit)	Teacher guided. (−)	Learn to take dollar from pocket.
6. Give money.	Handed money to cashier. (+)	Handed money to Pete. (+)	Not applicable. (omit)	Handed money to cashier. (+)	Generalize.
7. Take food items.	Grasped hot dog on tray. (+)	Grasped hot dog on napkin. (+)	Grasped hot dog alone. (+)	Hot dog in bag; took bag. (+)	Generalize.
8. Find place to sit/ stand to eat.	Stood and ate in line—would not move. (−)	Ate while standing at Pete's counter. (−)	Stood at table and ate. (−)	Followed escort to tables. (+)	Learn to walk with food away from counter.
No. steps correct	2 of 8	5 of 7	3 of 5	3 of 8	

between the ages of 6 and 8 to respond to the inappropriate invitations of strangers. The children were taught a "no–go–tell" response: (1) to say, sign, or gesture "No" to the stranger; (2) to move away from the stranger within 15 seconds; and (3) to tell a safe adult about the invitation from the stranger. Skills such as stranger awareness are crucial if a student will be alone in public, even briefly (e.g., to look at toys while the parents are in a nearby aisle). Older students who will be traveling to work and other sites need additional skills to seek help when needed. These include skills such as showing an identification card to officials and staying in safe areas. Using progressive time delay, Collins, Stinson, and Land (1993) taught students with moderate mental retardation to use public pay phones. Students were able to generalize this skill to a public phone when taught either in a classroom simulation or the community. Figure 9.9 provides examples of safety skills.

Shopping Skills

Shopping can focus on purchasing essentials such as groceries, or on purchasing recreational items such as CDs. Researchers who have taught shopping usually focus on the entire routine, from entering the store until the purchase is complete (McDonnell & Horner, 1985); however, they may also select steps using "backward chaining," in which students learn the last steps and then add new steps until the entire routine is learned (McDonnell & Laughlin, 1989). Purchasing also provides an excellent opportunity for students to generalize sight word reading and money management skills, as described in Chapters Seven and Eight. Figure 9.10 gives examples of shopping skills.

Skills for Purchasing Meals and Snacks

Dining at a restaurant or buying a snack can be a leisure activity as well as a means to eat. Traditionally, researchers have focused on the steps needed to make and consume the food. Teachers can be creative in using school settings to help prepare students for purchasing food in public. Gardill and Browder (1995) taught middle school students to use specific money amounts for food purchases at a school vending machine, in the cafeteria, in classroom simulations, and during community trips to fast-food restaurants. School simulations can be made realistic by obtaining materials from community sites, such as menus, paper cups, place mats, trays, and other items. In school, the student can practice the communication and money skills that often take more practice than community outings allow. Sowers and Powers (1995) not only used a simulation, but also invited parents to school to learn how to implement the training in their family trips to restaurant settings. Figure 9.11 lists some of the skills for purchasing meals and snacks.

Pedestrian and Transportation Skills

Community mobility will increase opportunities for the student to gain access to community resources (some essential skills for community mobility are summarized in Figure 9.12). Nearly all students will need to know how to cross streets safely, but not all will cross independently. For some students, learning to cross safely with an escort is an important alternative. Some students will gain more sophisticated skills, such as

FIGURE 9.9. A checklist for assessing community safety skills.

Safety Skills Checklist

Skills	Mastery	Partial mastery	Not tried yet
Avoid strangers			
Avoid unsafe areas of community			
Refuse drugs, cigarettes, or alcohol			
Show identification card to officials only (police, store security)			
Carry an identification card			
State name, address, phone number for officials (police, store security)			
Locate correct restroom			
Respond to fire alarm			
Communicate need for help			
Keep money safe			
Use pay phone			
Make 911 calls			
Use a first aid kit for minor injuries			
Use seat belts			

FIGURE 9.10. A checklist for assessing shopping skills.

Shopping Skills Checklist

Skills	Mastery	Partial mastery	Not tried yet
Enter the store			
Use a cart or basket			
Locate items			
Ask for help if items not found			
Choose specific item(s)			
Take item from shelf			
Place item in the basket			
Wait in the checkout line			
Greet cashier			
Pay for the item(s)			
Carry package			
Leave the store			

FIGURE 9.11. A checklist for assessing skills for purchasing meals and snacks.

Skills Checklist for Purchasing Meals and Snacks

Skills	Mastery	Partial mastery	Not tried yet
Choose where to go			
Select money needed for outing			
Choose food items			
Express choice to waiter or cashier			
Pay for food			
Choose where to sit or express preference to restaurant host/hostess			
Interact with companions while eating or drinking			
Dispose of trash			
Choose when to leave			
Use vending machine			
Generalize across variety of restaurants			

FIGURE 9.12. A checklist for assessing community mobility skills.

Community Mobility Skills Checklist

Skills	Mastery	Partial mastery	Not tried yet
Cross street by staying with escort			
Cross street independently			
Walk familiar route in community, using landmarks			
Communicate desired destination, using speech or augmentative system (e.g., pictures)			
Request a ride			
Ride in a car or van safely			
Ride school bus safely			
Get on and off school bus safely			
Ride bus or subway with help to find destination			
Ride bus or subway without assistance			

crossing streets using walk signs and traffic lights, and judging the speed of cars (Horner et al., 1985). Other students may learn to tell their escorts how to assist them. For example, Reid and Hurlburt (1977) taught students with physical disabilities to touch a picture to show where they wanted to be wheeled. Sometimes students need to learn how to negotiate a specific route, such as getting to a bus stop or finding a job site. Learning to read community signs and other landmarks may be helpful.

In some communities like Randy's, the primary form of mobility is cars. Randy needed to acquire skills to ask for a ride and to ride safely in a variety of cars. Wearing his seat belt was an important priority. In other communities, public transportation (e.g., buses or subway trains) is frequently used. To master using public transportation, students will typically need direct training in the community. Classroom simulations may help students practice some skills (e.g., paying fare), but cannot replace *in vivo* experiences (Browder & Bambara, 2000).

SUMMARY

Increased access to community settings can enhance the quality of life for individuals with moderate and severe disabilities and their families. Providing community-based instruction will often be a priority for students whose curriculum focuses on life skills. With creative planning, this community-based instruction can be augmented by training in school simulations and activities. As in all ecological assessment, reviewing the student's records, planning with the student and family, and identifying preferences are important prerequisites to initiating community-based instruction. When the focus is on leisure skills, teachers may target not only skills for community recreation, but also activities that can be done alone at school or home. Fitness is another important area for leisure instruction. Community access skills include safety, shopping, purchasing meals and snacks, and community mobility. Many of these activities can also be used to encourage choice making.

REFERENCES

Aveno, A., Renzaglia, A., & Lively, C. (1987). Surveying community training sites to insure that instructional decisions accommodate the site as well as the trainees. *Education and Training in Mental Retardation, 22,* 167–175.

Belfiore, P. J., Browder, D. M., & Mace, F. M. (1993). Effects of community and center-based settings on the alertness of persons with profound mental retardation. *Journal of Applied Behavior Analysis, 26,* 401–402.

Belfiore, P. J., Browder, D. M., & Mace, F. M. (1994). Assessing choice-making and preference in adults with profound mental retardation. *Journal of Behavioral Education, 4,* 217–225.

Bernabe, E. A., & Block, M. E. (1994). Modifying rules of a regular girls' softball league to facilitate the inclusion of a child with severe disabilities. *Journal of the Association for Persons with Severe Handicaps, 19,* 24–31.

Browder, D. M. (1991). *Assessment of individuals with severe disabilities: An applied behavioral approach to life skills assessment* (2nd ed.). Baltimore: Paul H. Brookes.

Browder, D. M., & Bambara, L. (2000). Home and community. In M. Snell & F. Brown (Eds.), *Instruction of students with severe disabilities.* Upper Saddle River, NJ: Merrill/Prentice-Hall.

Browder, D. M., Bambara, L., & Belfiore, P. (1997). Using a person-centered approach in community based instruction for adults with developmental disabilities. *Journal of Behavioral Education, 7,* 519–528.

Browder, D. M., Cooper, K., & Lim, L. (1998). Teaching adults with severe disabilities to express their choice of settings for leisure activities. *Education and Training in Mental Retardation and Developmental Disabilities, 33,* 226–236.

Brown, L., Nisbet, J., Ford, A., Sweet, M., Shiraga, B., & York, J. (1983). The critical need for non-school instruction in programs for severely handicapped students. *Journal of the Association for the Severely Handicapped, 8,* 71–77.

Chadsey-Rusch, J., Drasgow, E., Reinoehl, B., Halle, J., & Collet-Klingenberg, L. (1993). Using general-case instruction to teach spontaneous and generalized requests for assistance to learners with severe disabilities. *Journal of the Association for Persons with Severe Handicaps, 18,* 177–187.

Collins, B. C., Stinson, D. M., & Land, L. (1993). A comparison of in vivo and simulation prior to in vivo instruction in teaching generalized safety skills. *Education and Training in Mental Retardation, 28,* 128–142.

Cooper, K. J., & Browder, D. M. (1997). The use of a personal trainer to enhance participation of older adults with severe disabilities in community water exercise class. *Journal of Behavioral Education, 7,* 421–434.

Cooper, K. J., & Browder, D. M. (1998). Enhancing participation for adults with severe disabilities in community-based instruction. *Journal of the Association for Persons with Severe Handicaps, 23,* 252–260.

DeLeo, D. (1994). *Reaching for the dream!: Developing individual service plans for persons with disabilities.* St. Augustine, FL: Training Resource Network.

Ellis, D. N., Cress, P. J., & Spellman, C. R. (1990). Using timers and lap counters to promote self-management of independent exercise in adolescents with mental retardation. *Education and Training in Mental Retardation, 27,* 51–59.

Ellis, D. N., Wright, M., & Cronis, T. G. (1996). A description of the instructional and social interactions of students with mental retardation in regular physical education settings. *Education and Training in Mental Retardation and Developmental Disabilities, 31,* 235–242.

Ehrmann, L. C., Aeschleman, S. R. & Svanum, S. (1995). Parental reports of community activity patterns: A comparison between young children with disabilities and their nondisabled peers. *Research in Developmental Disabilities, 16,* 331–343.

Ford, A., Schnorr, R., Meyer, L., Davern, L., Black, J., & Dempsey, P. (1989). *The Syracuse Community-Referenced Curriculum Guide for students with moderate and severe disabilities.* Baltimore: Paul H. Brookes.

Gardill, M. C., & Browder, D. M. (1995). Teaching stimulus classes to encourage independent purchasing by students with severe behavior disorders. *Education and Training in Mental Retardation and Developmental Disabilities, 30,* 254–264.

Gencoz, F. (1997). The effects of basketball training on the maladaptive behaviors of trainable mentally retarded children. *Research in Developmental Disabilities, 18,* 1–10.

Giangreco, M. F., Cloninger, C. J., & Iverson, V. S. (1998). *Choosing Outcomes and Accommodations for Children* (2nd ed.). Baltimore: Paul H. Brookes.

Hamre-Nietupski, S., Nietupski, J., Krajewski, L., Moravec, J., Riehle, R., McDongal, J., Sensor, K., & Cantine-Stull, P. (1992). Enhancing integration during the summer: Combined educational and community recreation options for students with severe disabilities. *Education and Training in Mental Retardation, 27,* 68–74.

Horner, R. H., Albin, R. W., & Ralph, G. (1986a). Generalization with precision: The role of negative teaching examples in the instruction of generalized grocery item selection. *Journal of the Association for Persons with Severe Handicaps, 11,* 300–308.

Horner, R. H., Jones, D. N., & Williams, J. A. (1985). A functional approach to teaching generalized street crossing. *Journal of the Association for Persons with Severe Handicaps, 10,* 71–78.

Horner, R. H., McDonnell, J. J., & Bellamy, G. T. (1986b). Teaching generalized skills: General case instruction in simulation and community settings. In R. H. Horner, L. H. Meyer, & H. D. Fredericks (Eds.), *Education of learners with severe handicaps: Exemplary service strategies* (pp. 289–314). Baltimore: Paul H. Brookes.

Horner, R. H., Williams, J. A., & Steveley, J. D. (1987). Acquisition of generalized telephone use by students with moderate and severe mental retardation. *Research in Developmental Disabilities, 8,* 229–248.

Hughes, C., & Agran, M. (1993). Teaching persons with severe disabilities to use self-instruction in community settings: An analysis of application. *Journal of the Association for Persons with Severe Handicaps, 18,* 261–274.

Lancioni, G., O'Reilly, M., & Emerson, E. (1996). A review of choice research with people with severe and profound developmental disabilities. *Research in Developmental Disabilities, 17,* 391 - 411.

LeGrice, B., & Blampied, N. M. (1994). Training pupils with intellectual disability to operate educational technology using video prompting. *Education and Training in Mental Retardation and Developmental Disabilities, 29,* 321–330.

Loyd, R. J., & Brolin, D. E. (1997). *Life Centered Career Education: Modified curriculum for individuals with moderate disabilities.* Reston, VA: Council for Exceptional Children.

McDonnell, J. J., & Ferguson, B. (1988). A comparison of general case in vivo and general case simulation plus in vivo training. *Journal of the Association for Persons with Severe Handicaps, 13,* 116–124.

McDonnell, J. J., & Horner, R. H. (1985). Effects of *in vivo* versus simulation-plus-*in vivo* training on the acquisition and generalization of grocery item selection by high school students with severe handicaps. *Analysis and Intervention in Developmental Disabilities, 5,* 85–91.

McDonnell, J. J., & Laughlin, B. (1989). A comparison of backward and concurrent chaining strategies in teaching community skills. *Education and Training in Mental Retardation, 24,* 230–238.

Moon, S., Komissar, C., Friedlander, R., Hart, D. & Kiernan, W. (1994). Finding or creating fun in your community. In S. Moon (Ed.), *Making school and community recreation fun for everyone: Places and ways to integrate* (pp. 63–84). Baltimore: Paul H. Brookes.

Newton, J. S., Horner, R. H., & Lund, L. (1991). Honoring activity preferences in individualized plan development: A descriptive analysis. *Journal of the Association for Persons with Severe Handicaps, 16,* 207–212.

Nietupski, J., Hamre-Nietupski, S., Clancy, P. L., & Veerhusen, K. (1986). Guidelines for making simulation an effective adjunct to in-vivo community instruction. *Journal of the Association for Persons with Severe Handicaps, 11,* 12–18.

Nietupski, J., Hamre-Nietupski, S., Houselog, M., Donder, D. J., & Anderson, R. J. (1988). Proactive administrative strategies for implementing community based programs for students with moderate/severe handicaps. *Education and Training in Mental Retardation, 23,* 138–146.

O'Brien, J. (1987). A guide to life-style planning. In B. Wilcox & G. T. Bellamy (Eds.), *A comprehensive guide to the Activities Catalog: An alternative curriculum for youth and adults with severe disabilities* (pp. 175–189). Baltimore: Paul H. Brookes.

Reid, D. H., & Hurlburt, B. (1977). Teaching nonvocal communication skills to multihandicapped retarded adults. *Journal of Applied Behavior Analysis, 10,* 591–603.

Rynders, J., Schleien, S., Meyer, L., Vandercook, T., Mustonen, T., Colond, J., & Olson, K. (1993). Improving integration outcomes for children with and without severe disabilities through cooperatively structured activities: A synthesis of research. *Journal of Special Education, 26,* 386–407.

Rynders, J., Schleien, S., & Mustonen, T. (1990). Integrating children with severe disabilities for intensified outdoor education: Focus in feasibility. *Mental Retardation, 28,* 7–14.

Schleien, S., Green, F., & Heyne, L. (1993). Integrated community recreation In M. E. Snell (Ed.), *Instruction of students with severe disabilities* (pp. 526–549). New York: Charles E. Merrill.

Schleien, S., Mustonen, T., & Rynders, J. (1995). Participation of children with autism and nondisabled peers in a cooperatively structured community art program. *Journal of Autism and Developmental Disorders, 25,* 397–413.

Snell, M. E., & Browder, D. M. (1986). Community-referenced instruction: Research and issues. *Journal of the Association for Persons with Severe Handicaps, 11,* 1–11.

Sowers, J., & Powers, L. (1995). Enhancing the participation and independence of students with severe physical and multiple disabilities in performing community activities. *Mental Retardation, 33,* 209–220.

Sprague, J. R., & Horner, R. H. (1984). The effects of single instance, multiple instance, and general case training on a generalized vending machine use by moderately and severely handicapped students. *Journal of Applied Behavior Analysis, 17,* 273–278.

Taylor, J., McKelvey, J., & Sisson, L. (1993). Community-referenced leisure skill clusters for adolescents with multiple disabilities. *Journal of Behavioral Education, 3,* 363–386.

Vandercook, T. (1991). Leisure instruction outcomes: Criterion performance, positive interactions, and acceptance by typical high school peers. *Journal of Special Education, 25,* 224–227.

Wall, M. E., & Gast, D. L. (1997). Caregivers' use of constant time delay to teach leisure skills to adolescents or young adults with moderate or severe intellectual disabilities. *Education and Training in Mental Retardation and Developmental Disabilities, 32,* 340–356.

Watson, M., Bain, A., & Houghton, S. (1992). A preliminary study in teaching self-protective skills to children with moderate to severe mental retardation. *Journal of Special Education, 26,* 181–194.

Westling, D. L., & Floyd, J. (1990). Generalization of community skills: How much training is necessary? *Journal of Special Education, 23,* 386–406.

Westling, D. L., Floyd, J., & Carr, D. (1990). Effect of single setting versus multiple setting training on learning to shop in a department store. *American Journal of Mental Retardation, 94,* 616–624.

Wilcox, B., & Bellamy, G. T. (1987). *The activities catalog: An alternative curriculum for youth and adults with severe disabilities.* Baltimore: Paul H. Brookes.

Zhang, J., Gast, D., Horvat, M., & Dattilo, J. (1995). The effectiveness of a constant time delay procedure on teaching lifetime sport skills to adolescents with severe to profound intellectual disabilities. *Education and Training in Mental Retardation and Developmental Disabilities, 30,* 51–64.

TEN

Home and Personal Living Skills

KELLY[1] WAS A BEAUTIFUL 16-YEAR-OLD *with golden brown eyes. Because of her large extended family and supportive friends, she had a full schedule with many community activities. Her family and friends hoped that Kelly would someday have a home of her own. Kelly had severe mental retardation and mild cerebral palsy. The greatest challenges to her family, friends, and future dreams were in the areas of home and personal living skills. After 11 years of training in using the toilet and washing her hands, she still needed help with both skills. Although her parents and friends took her to a wide variety of social settings, they didn't always know what to do about her eating problems. They also did not know how to address the more complex issues of how she would help take care of a home. As an older teen, Kelly needed the opportunity to take charge of her own personal life—to make decisions about her own likes and wants.*

This chapter provides ideas for teaching home and personal living skills not only for students who will master self-care and independent living, but also for students like Kelly who will need ongoing support.

Nearly all published curricula for students with moderate and severe disabilities include home and personal living skills. Focusing on home and personal living skills is important for several reasons. First and foremost, the acquisition of skills for caring for a home and personal needs can increase an individual's dignity and autonomy. In their meta-analysis of the research on deinstitutionalized adults with severe and profound intellectual disabilities who moved into community placements, Lynch, Kellow, Thomas, and Wilson (1997) found that the most pronounced gains occurred in self-care. In contrast, Uehara, Silverstein, Davis, and Geron (1991) found more intense medical, adaptive behavior, self-care, and self-preservation needs among individuals with developmental disabilities who had been placed in nursing home settings. Individuals with significant disabilities can improve their self-care when given the education and opportunity to do so.

A second reason to focus on skills for home and personal care is to respond to caregiver concerns. In a survey of family members of young adults with severe disabilities,

---

[1]Kelly's case study, presented throughout this chapter, is based on a real person. Her name and other details have been changed to protect her confidentiality, consistent with the guidelines of the World and American Psychiatric Associations (Clifft, 1986).

Thorin and Irvin (1992) discovered that self-care, sexuality, and getting along with others were the most frequently mentioned concerns. By teaching individuals with severe disabilities more self-care skills, educators can help lessen their dependence on caregivers and their need for more intensive forms of support. The acquisition of home and personal care skills can also make it easier to gain community opportunities. Although individuals who need ongoing support for personal care *can* live in the community and hold competitive jobs, the more personal independence such persons acquire, the easier it becomes for them to gain access to these opportunities.

Perhaps for these reasons, home and personal care skills are the most frequently found content areas in any curriculum for students with severe disabilities. A large body of research now exists on how to teach skills such as eating, dressing, using the toilet, toothbrushing, housekeeping, food preparation, and laundry skills (Konarski & Diorio, 1985; Westling & Fox, 1995). Despite the popularity of focusing on home and personal living in research and other resources, updated guidelines are needed for developing a student's personalized curriculum and individualized education plan (IEP). Much of the research in this area is 10–20 years old. Although personal and home care skills certainly do not become outmoded, some of the older research does not reflect current instructional technology. Often the research and curricula reflect an assumption that students will become fully independent in these skills; however, not all students will become independent in their daily routines, but instead will rely on lifelong caregiver support. Guidelines are needed to select skills that will encourage autonomy and personal dignity even when lifelong care may be necessary. Many older resources on self-care and home living also lack current perspectives on self-determination and cultural diversity. Home and personal care skills are indeed "personal." The way individuals perform these routines are influenced by their cultural background, family traditions, and personal preferences. New guidelines are needed that take a "person-centered" perspective on home and personal care skills.

Guidelines are also needed to consider how to address home and personal care skills in inclusive school settings. Personal care skills are typically mastered in the early preschool years, and so teaching them to school-age students can be stigmatizing. How do teachers adapt personal care instruction to school settings? Furthermore, some home and personal living skills (e.g., toileting, sex education) are among the most private issues in our society. How do teachers respect students' privacy in these matters? This chapter provides guidelines for developing a curriculum in home and personal living, and for selecting skills for individual students through ecological assessment.

ECOLOGICAL ASSESSMENT FOR HOME AND PERSONAL LIVING

Summarizing Prior Records

An excellent starting point for planning instruction in home and personal living skills is to scan a student's prior educational records, to determine what the student has previously been taught and to note any particular issues related to teaching home and personal living skills. For example, are there food or other allergies? What medications does the student take, and do any of these require food restrictions or have side effects (e.g., frequent urination) that may affect the acquisition of personal care skills? What earlier instruction did the student receive in home and personal care skills, and what progress was made? Figure 10.1 is an example of a personal care routine planning sheet for students who need intensive support. At this first step, a teacher can note any special allergies, food restrictions, or other issues. The teacher can also make notes about how the student currently performs daily routines.

Planning with the Family for Home and Personal Care Skill Instruction

After obtaining some background information on the student that is relevant to planning home and personal care instruction, the teacher should consult with the family to plan individually for the student. Sometimes the best way to discuss some of these personal issues is in a private conversation with the primary caregiver (e.g., often the mother). Table 10.1 gives a guide for some of the questions that might be explored with caregivers during this planning.

Encouraging Student Self-Determination in Daily Routines

After consulting with the family, the teacher will begin to have a clearer idea of the responses the student typically makes in daily routines and the need for caregiver support. Students need the opportunity to be active participants in their daily routines. Even if they will not become fully independent, they can achieve goals of "partial par-

FIGURE 10.1. Example of a chart for planning instruction in daily personal care routines.*

Chart for Planning Instruction in Daily Routines

Student: Wanda Burgh   **Age:** 12   **Teacher:** Ms. Hunter

Medication notes: Diamox (anticonvulsant; may cause thirst and increased urine output), Beconase (anti-inflammatory respiratory tract medication; may cause sneezing and nose irritation).

Allergy notes: Severe allergy to animal fur; peanuts can be life-threatening.

Dietary restrictions: No peanuts or recipes with peanut oil; encourage fluid intake; underweight—keep notes on food and fluid intake.

Other medical notes: Has been seizure free for almost 1 year. High risk for pressure sores and skin irritation—check skin daily; keep skin in buttocks area clean and dry.

Family preferences: Personal care for toileting by females only in private setting; make detailed notes about any seizure and call parents the day of the seizure; family does not consume alcohol or caffeine and limits sweets to special occasions, according to religious custom.

Student's preferences: Wanda does not like acidic foods and juices (e.g., tomato sauce, orange juice); she has a strong preference for dairy products (e.g., yogurt, cheese sauce).

*This example is based on my work in planning instruction in personal living skills with individuals with moderate and severe disabilities, but Wanda Burgh is not a real person.

TABLE 10.1. Questions for Caregivers about Support and Instruction in Daily Routines

1. *Tell me about your son's/daughter's mealtimes.*

- Who prepares the food? Does your son/daughter help?
- How well does your son/daughter eat?
- What assistance, if any, do you give to help him or her eat?
- What are his or her favorite foods?
- What does he or she dislike?
- Are there certain foods that are off limits because of allergies, a special diet, or religious customs?
- Are there any medical concerns related to your child's eating?

2. *Let's talk about your child's toileting needs.*

- Does your child indicate the need to use the toilet? To be changed?
- Does your child use diapers? If so, is this all the time or at certain times? How often does he or she need to be changed? Are there any special concerns?
- If not in diapers, does your child ask to use the toilet?
- Do you take your child to the toilet on a schedule? How often?
- Does your child have toileting accidents? How often?
- What does your child do for him- or herself in the restroom?
- Are there any special concerns related to toileting?

3. *Let's talk about how your child gets dressed.*

- How does your child get dressed and ready for school?
- If you dress your child, does the child do anything for him- or herself?
- Who chooses your child's outfits? Can your child choose his or her clothing?
- Are there any special concerns related to dressing?

4. *What other skills should we emphasize in your child's daily routine?*

- Chores and housekeeping? If so, what specific skills?
- Grooming skills like hair and nail care?
- Telephone use?
- Other?

5. *Are you interested in having your child receive sex education at school?*

- What topics should be addressed in this sex education?
- Are there topics that you prefer not be taught at school or at this age?

6. *Is there anything else you would like to share that will help me meet your child's unique needs and respect your family's customs?*

---

ticipation" (Ferguson & Baumgart, 1991). That is, students can learn to make independent responses within their daily living routines. It is important that teachers target specific, measurable, *independent* responses that students will eventually be able to make without teacher guidance. If IEP objectives focus on responses made with teacher guidance, students remain passive in their daily routines. A teacher may work strenuously guiding a student through a routine, while the student learns little to nothing about what to do. Although physical guidance and other forms of support may be used initially to teach correct responding, *it is essential that the target response be one that the student is physically capable of making without teacher assistance.* These observable, measurable responses that the student is physically capable of making can be called "active responses."

Although focusing on active responses is essential for students to participate more in their daily routines, being "active participants" is still not a sufficient goal for instruction. Teachers need to consider the overall goal of encouraging student self-determination (Wehmeyer, 1992). Students need to be able to "take charge" of their daily routines as they mature into adulthood. An adult can require extensive personal care, but still can be "in charge" of that care through directing the caregiver's actions. Helping students "take charge" can occur through creating opportunities to make choices in personal routines and to initiate/terminate the steps of the activity. Students' personal dignity can also be encouraged by respecting the students' privacy and using materials appropriate to the students' chronological age and setting. Figure 10.2 provides an example of a chart used by one teacher to plan a student's active participation during school arrival, lunch, and restroom use.

Defining a Personalized Curriculum

Using a chart of the type shown in Figure 10.2, the teacher can begin to define the student's personalized curriculum for home and personal living skills. This curriculum can be further developed through using general-to-specific assessment procedures, as described in Chapter Two. For a general inventory of the student's home and personal living skills, the teacher can use a published curriculum (e.g., Ford et al., 1989; Loyd & Brolin, 1997; Giangreco, Cloninger, & Iverson, 1998; Wilcox & Bellamy, 1987) or the checklists that are provided for each home and personal care area later in this chapter. This broad-based assessment may be especially important for the student who has already mastered some of these skills. This information can be used to help summarize the student's "current level of performance" on the IEP.

A teacher may also generate a curriculum by using "ecological inventories" of a student's current and future environments (Brown et al., 1979). By observing and interviewing people in these environments, the teacher can generate specific skills to teach this particular student. Using the "subenvironments" or rooms of a home is one way to organize a curriculum for home and personal care. The following shows an ecological inventory of skills needed for the home for a student named Matt[2] who was moderately disabled.

ECOLOGICAL INVENTORY

Environment: Matt's Family Home

Subenvironment: Kitchen.
   Activities: Prepare food; eat; wash dishes; store food.

Subenvironment: Bathroom.
   Activities: Use the toilet; shower; brush teeth; wash hands; groom hair; clean the bathroom.

Subenvironment: Bedroom.
   Activities: Sleep; dress; do various leisure activities; clean up.

Subenvironment: Laundry room.
   Activities: Sort, wash, dry, fold clothes.

Subenvironment: Living room.
   Activities: Watch TV; play video games; eat popcorn.

[2]Matt is a fictitious student.

FIGURE 10.2. Example of a chart for planning active participation for students who may need ongoing support in their daily routines.*

Chart for Planning Active Participation in Daily Routines

Student: Shania Johnson   **Age:** 13   **Teacher:** Mr. Rodriguez

Routine/skills	Responses to be more active	Choice making responses	Responses for student to "take charge"	Considerations for appropriateness to age and setting
Arrival				
1. Go from bus to classroom	• Help with transfer to chair		• Nod for bookbag to be put on chair • Look up to be wheeled	
2. Take off coat	• Lift right arm as coat is removed	• Choose if coat on chair or hook	• Vocalize when ready to take coat off	
3. Put belongings away	• Grasp/release refrigerator door to help put lunchbox away		• Nod to indicate taking lunch box out	
Mealtime				
1. Get lunch	• Grasp refrigerator door	• Use eye pointing to indicate choice of seat	• Indicate lunchtime by pointing to object schedule	
2. Open containers		• Use eyepointing to indicate which container to open first (order in which to eat lunch)		
3. Eat	• Scoop food after spoon placed in bowl		• Use eye contact to indicate when ready for next bite of food	• Use spare T-shirt (not a bib) for spills
4. Clean up lunch	• Release containers in lunchbox after placed in hand		• Vocalize to indicate when finished lunch	

(cont.)

*As in Figure 10.1, this example is based on my work, but Shania Johnson is not a real person.

FIGURE 10.2. *(cont.)*

Restroom				
1. Go to restroom			• Point to picture of "Women" for restroom to indicate when ready to go	• Use universal sign for "women"—not picture of a toilet
2. Use toilet	• Help lift buttocks for pants down • Help with transfer on/off toilet		• Indicate when ready to get off toilet by vocalizing	• Use single-person restroom for privacy
3. Wash hands	• Turn water on • Move hands toward water • Release paper towel in trash	• Choose wall or pump soap, paper towel or hot-air dryer		

Because a typical school day does not take place in the home environment and subenvironments, an ecological inventory is also needed of the school environment, with special consideration given to daily living and self-care skills. In using school contexts, the teacher identified the following activities for Matt.

ECOLOGICAL INVENTORY

Environment: Matt's elementary school

Subenvironment: Classroom.
  Daily living/self-care skills: Clean up room; put coat on and take it off; tie shoes if come untied; may prepare food as special activity.

Subenvironment: Boys' restroom.
  Daily living/self-care skills: Use toilet; wash hands; comb hair; zip and button pants; straighten shirt; may brush teeth.

Subenvironment: School cafeteria.
  Daily living/self-care skills: Choose food; make salad at salad bar; eat; scrape dishes.

Subenvironment: Gym and playground.
  Daily living/self-care skills: Coat off/on; tie shoes if come untied; drink water from water fountain.

A comparison of the two lists for Matt reveals that some skills had relevance for both his home and school settings. In contrast, some skills would not be used in Matt's elementary school (e.g., washing dishes, taking a shower) unless opportunities were created for their use. Teachers may want to emphasize those skills that have applicability across settings and consult with parents about how to generalize and expand on these at home (e.g., from scraping a school tray to scraping and rinsing dishes at home). In other instances, when a certain home or personal living skill is a high priority, opportunities may need to be created to address these skills at school. For example, Matt could be taught showering skills during community-based instruction in swimming at the YMCA.

Encouraging Active Participation

When students lack many of the skills represented in either a published curriculum or a teacher-generated ecological inventory, it can be difficult to know what skills to target. Parental and student preferences and self-determination considerations can help in setting priorities. Students can become active participants in any routine, depending on the specificity of the responses targeted and the amount of the routine selected. For example, Jonathan[3] had mastered most personal care skills. In his transition years, he was gaining independence for adult living. In learning the skills he would need for getting to work in the morning, Jonathan followed a picture schedule at home. His job coach, Mr. Toney, was giving him additional instruction at school on getting ready for work (e.g., shaving, combing his hair) in the locker room before he went to his job in the community. Mr. Toney prepared the following task analysis for Jonathan's prepraration-for-work routine.

ROUTINE TASK ANALYSIS

1. Get up when alarm rings.
2. Take a shower.
3. Comb hair.
4. Shave.
5. Straighten bathroom.
6. Get dressed.
7. Fix cereal and juice.
8. Finish eating by 7:15.
9. Put dishes in sink.
10. Get bookbag and wallet.
11. Leave for the bus.

In contrast, Matt, who was 10 years old, was focusing on learning to make his own breakfast. He had learned to work with his father in getting showered and dressed; he also selected his own clothes, with some help in matching. Although Matt still had a lot of skills to learn in his morning routine, preparing breakfast was selected as the teaching focus because of Matt's preference for food preparation activities. Matt would be working on this skill during the school's breakfast program. His task analysis for preparing breakfast follows. When Matt's task analysis is compared to Jonathan's, it becomes evident that Matt was focusing on just one specific activity *within* a morning routine.

[3]Jonathan is also a fictitious student.

SPECIFIC SKILL TASK ANALYSIS

1. Get a bowl and spoon.
2. Choose a cereal.
3. Pick up milk and juice.
4. Open box of cereal.
5. Pour into bowl.
6. Open milk carton.
7. Pour milk on cereal without spilling.
8. Open juice.
9. Eat breakfast.
10. Clean up by taking bowl and trash to cleanup counter.

Wanda (see Figure 10.1) was a 12-year-old girl who needed intensive assistance in her daily routines. She currently relied on her parents and teachers for all of her eating, dressing, toileting, and home management routines. To help Wanda become more active in her morning routine, the teacher targeted these responses, which she would teach upon Wanda's arrival at school. Although Wanda, like Matt, was focusing on breakfast, her responses were selected for encouraging active, partial participation when receiving assistance to eat.

TASK ANALYSIS FOR PARTIAL PARTICIPATION IN A DAILY ROUTINE

1. Press switch to ring chime to begin breakfast.
2. Point with eyes toward food held at eye level to choose between two foods (e.g., oatmeal and yogurt).
3. Lift head slightly to indicate ready for each bite of food.
4. Lower head to refuse food.
5. Move hand across tray to help clean up after breakfast.

Sometimes the teacher will want to pinpoint skill needs further by using situational assessments in which the student tries a new activity. The teacher may use a task analysis to summarize the student's performance for a skill like preparing banana pudding.

EXAMPLES OF HOME AND PERSONAL LIVING CURRICULA

Eating Skills

Considerations for Instruction in Eating Skills

Perske, Clifton, McLean, and Stein (1977) described the ideal mealtime as having the following characteristics:

- Feeling of comradeship and belonging.
- Relaxing and being less defensive.
- Communicating in many ways (with voice, eyes, body, taste, smell, and touch).

- Laughing and feeling joyful.
- Being accepted exactly as you are and being glad you are *you*.
- Making choices.
- Having all the time you need.
- Heightening all the senses.
- Feeling full, satisfied, and relaxed.
- Taking in nutrition for growth and good health.

Having an ideal mealtime can be difficult for an individual with severe disabilities, because of deficits in both eating and social skills. Learning skills in this area may make it easier for students to focus on the social context of mealtimes such as school lunch periods. In contrast, students who will need long-term assistance to eat also need the opportunity for peer socialization at lunch. Teachers should seek a balance between the goals of socialization and nutrition during school lunch periods. This can be done by reserving direct, systematic instruction only for the highest-priority skills. This direct instruction may also occur in some private tutoring sessions rather than at lunchtime. As Chapter Four has described, many other sources of instructional support can be used to help students become more self-sufficient at meals. Being with peers who model eating skills is a form of natural support during school lunches. The teacher may use environmental arrangements, such as giving a student a spoon with an enlarged grip, a plate with raised edges, and a rubber mat to make it easier to eat. Sometimes the teacher or a peer can simply prepare the food further for simplified eating (e.g., a hamburger can be cut into bite-size pieces). Students may also use self-instruction. For example, wiping the mouth after each bite is one way for a student to pace him- or herself to avoid gorging the mouth with food.

Some students (e.g., a student who is tube-fed or who gags easily when eating) may need to eat in private, to preserve lunchtime as a social context. Other students will need direct, systematic instruction to learn some basic eating skills. This direct instruction need not occupy the entire meal. The teacher and student may go to the cafeteria early to work on eating whatever menu items need a spoon (e.g., applesauce), and then the student is free to eat the remainder of lunch (finger foods like burrito and carrot sticks) with friends. A student who needs to be fed may enjoy having a peer who is nondisabled provide this assistance. This assistance may be provided just before everyone gets into the cafeteria, or during the busy activity of the regular lunchtime, depending on the student's needs and preferences. When a student needs direct instruction, the teacher will probably use a task analysis of the skill and systematic prompting, as described in Chapter Four. For example, to teach self-feeding, Collins, Gast, Wolery, Holcombe, and Leatherby (1991) used this task analysis:

1. Grasp spoon.
2. Scoop food.
3. Raise spoon to lips.
4. Open mouth.
5. Put spoon in mouth.
6. Remove spoon.
7. Lower spoon.

Collins et al. (1991) used constant time delay to teach eating with a spoon, drinking from a cup, and napkin use. Eating skills also lend themselves well to the use of graduated guidance, in which physical assistance is gradually withdrawn as the student masters each motor response. For example, in a study by Azrin and Armstrong (1973), the teacher began by molding his or her hand around the student's to help the student lift the spoon to and from the mouth. As the student began to master the movement with the spoon, the teacher faded this physical pressure to a gentle touch. The guidance was then faded to the forearm, elbow, upper arm, and finally the shoulder.

Systematic instruction can also be used to teach a mealtime routine (e.g., eating lunch in the cafeteria). Kohl and Stettner-Eaton (1985) created a task analysis with many specific steps—32 steps for going through the cafeteria line! They also task-analyzed eating and cleaning up. These researchers then demonstrated how fourth-graders who were nondisabled could serve as trainers of cafeteria skills. The peers used a "feedback-only" method of instruction, in which they praised or corrected each response as it occurred. Task analyses and systematic prompting can also be used to teach students family-style dining. Wilson, Reid, Phillips, and Burgio (1984) used a system of least intrusive prompting to teach students to set the table, pass and serve themselves food, and clear the table.

Eating Problems

Sometimes an assessment will reveal that a student has eating problems. These problems may reflect the need for specific skill instruction. A student who grabs others' food may need to learn the concept of table boundaries, as Kelly did.

How Kelly Learned to Eat Her Own Food. Having Kelly at the dinner table with the family had become extremely difficult, because she would grab food from others' plates and from the serving dishes. Her grabbing often resulted in foods' and beverages' being spilled. When her teacher assessed Kelly's eating skills, she discovered that Kelly did not seem aware of the boundaries of her own food. She also lacked the ability to ask for a food item not put on her plate by a family member, because she had few communication skills. To assist Kelly, the teacher got her a bright, distinctive placemat to use at school and home. As Kelly ate, the teacher would frequently point to Kelly's place setting and say, "Look, you have more potato salad," or "Here, you still have juice to drink." She also taught Kelly to extend her hand in the direction of the food that she wanted. For example, when she wanted margarine for her bread, she would "hover over" the margarine dish with her hand until served. The teacher also discovered that Kelly sometimes did not recognize that she still had food on her plate, because it became mixed together as she tried to eat everything with a spoon. The teacher organized Kelly's food with separate dishes for finger foods, items to be eaten with a spoon, and items to be speared with a fork. She taught Kelly to eat one food at a time, using the method that worked best. Kelly could still be in charge of her meal by selecting the order in which to eat each item. Once she had learned to ask for food by extending her hand, to eat food within the boundary of her placemat, and to keep foods separate, Kelly began to eat her meals without grabbing food.

Methods for Dealing with Eating Problems. In research conducted with a student who grabbed food, Smith, Piersel, Filbeck, and Gross (1983) found that seating the student alone and reinforcing the student with favorite foods for not stealing food were effective. Over time, the student was able to rejoin her peers. Some researchers have found that students' table manners improve when the dining environment is made more appealing. Hendrickson, Akkerman, and Speggen (1985) and VanBiervliet, Spangler, and Marshall (1981) demonstrated that skills improved in family-style dining compared to large, residential cafeterias.

Students who eat too rapidly or who gorge themselves with food risk choking. Both Luiselli (1988) and Knapczyk (1983) found that teacher-delivered pacing prompts were effective for students to slow their rate of eating. In this method, the teacher cues the student when to take the next bite, and these cues are gradually faded. Teachers can also help students use self-pacing. For example, by using a napkin between each bite, the student can slow the rate of eating. Wayne[4] learned to pace his eating by setting a 10-second timer between each bite. While waiting for the timer to ring, Wayne would chew. When the timer sounded, he swallowed and took another bite. The teacher rewarded Wayne for eating his lunch while using self-pacing by giving him a special treat at the end of the meal. After several weeks, Wayne was able to eat at a safe pace without using the timer. Eventually, the teacher was also able to fade the use of the treat. Sometimes teachers will need to use reinforcement to increase the rate of eating for students who eat extremely slowly (Luiselli, 1988).

Other students' eating problems focus on the quantity or types of food that they will eat. Kelly, the student described above, rarely indicated that she had had enough to eat. Instead, she would continue eating large quantities of food, with resultant weight gain. Her parents discovered that if they gave her a low-fat, high-fiber diet, and then dry popcorn or fresh vegetables to eat at the end of a meal until the family finished, Kelly was willing to stop eating when the family did. Some students refuse food or will only eat a limited number of foods (e.g., only cereal). Sometimes the problem of eating limited types of food can be resolved by giving the student a bite of a highly preferred food after each bite of a nonpreferred food (Riordan, Iwata, Finney, Wohl, & Stanley, 1984). Over time the student can be required to take more bites of the nonpreferred food to get the preferred food. Students who do not show any food preferences may need some other form of reinforcement, such as toy play after each bite of food (Riordan et al., 1984).

Figure 10.3 is a checklist of some eating and drinking skills that may be considered in planning instruction and dealing with problems in this area.

Food Preparation

Learning to prepare food is important not only because of the nutrition it provides, but also because of the personal enjoyment and socialization associated with food. Families and friends often celebrate important events with food. Most individuals have specific food likes and dislikes. Food preferences also may reflect individuals' cultural heritage. To consider these many functions of food in the lives of a student, a teacher should be-

---

[4]Wayne is a real person; his name has been changed and other steps have been taken to protect his confidentiality, consistent with the recommendations of the World and American Psychiatric Associations (Clifft, 1986).

FIGURE 10.3. A checklist for assessing eating skills.

Eating and Drinking Skills Checklist

Skills	Mastery	Partial mastery	Not mastered
Eating			
Take food from a spoon and swallow			
Chew food			
Choose between two food items			
Indicate when full/finished eating			
Expresse desire to eat			
Feed self finger foods			
Use a napkin			
Use a spoon			
Eat a sandwich			
Pace eating (avoid stuffing mouth)			
Spear with a fork			
Eat without spilling			
Drinking			
Swallow from cup held by someone			
Choose between two drinks			
Hold own glass to drink			
Drink from a soda can			
Drink from a mug			
Drink from water fountain			
Drink through a straw			

gin by conferring with the family about ideas for instruction. The family may identify some of the student's favorite foods and share ideas from the family's typical menus or snack items. The student's parents can also provide information on food restrictions. The teacher can then further assess the student's food preferences through systematic preference assessment (Lohrmann-O'Rourke & Browder, 1998). To conduct this assessment, the teacher can select several potential foods that the student may like. Then, by introducing two foods at a time, the teacher can record which food the student chooses. After several trials of sampling food, some specific food likes and dislikes may emerge.

To assess and teach specific food preparation skills, the teacher may want first to prepare easy-to-follow directions to encourage the student's self-direction. Researchers who have taught individuals with moderate and severe disabilities to prepare food have used sight word instruction books (Browder, Hines, McCarthy, & Fees, 1984), picture books (Griffin, Wolery, & Schuster, 1992), a cassette tape player with audiotaped directions (Trask-Tyler, Grossi, & Heward, 1994), and a communication board with picture overlays and voice output (Mechling & Gast, 1997). Commercial cookbooks, developed for individuals with limited reading skills, such as the *Home Cooking Cookbook*, can also be especially useful (see Table 10.3, below). Singh, Oswald, Ellis and Singh (1995) demonstrated how to teach individuals with profound cognitive disabilities to follow a picture cookbook. They task-analyzed each step of the recipe preparation and provided systematic prompting. Figure 10.4 is a checklist of some of the skills that may be considered in teaching students to prepare a wide variety of foods.

Food preparation can also be an excellent opportunity to teach additional skills such as the basic food groups, nutritional value of food, and safe food handling. Jones and Collins (1997) embedded extra information about safe food handling and nutrition in the instructive feedback they gave while teaching adults with moderate mental retardation to prepare food. For example, after telling the participants to fill the cup with water to make a hot chocolate mix, they said something like "Drink at least 6 glasses of water a day for your health." Later they assessed the students' mastery of this additional information by asking them questions like "How much water should you drink?" Using food preparation can be a creative way to teach these more complex concepts.

Dressing and Grooming Skills

Dressing and grooming are important ways in which individuals express their personal style. This personal style may change over time, with the middle school years being a time when students are keenly aware of their appearance. Often in teaching dressing and grooming, teachers have focused on mechanics such as how to brush teeth, comb hair, or put on a shirt. Although these mechanics are important, students also need the opportunity to make choices about their appearance. By focusing on self-determination, teachers can encourage students to take pride in their appearance. Even students who rely on caregivers to be dressed can direct that care through choosing clothes and accessories to develop and express a personal style.

To encourage the development of a personal style, the teacher can begin assessment for dressing and grooming through systematic preference assessment. For a student who can discriminate pictures and can communicate symbolically, the teacher can use clothing catalogs and magazines to explore preferences. The student may develop a

FIGURE 10.4. A checklist for assessing food preparation skills.

Food Preparation Skills Checklist

Skills	Mastery	Partial mastery	Not mastered
Choose between two foods to prepare by asking, pointing, nodding, looking, or using other means of communication			
Plan simple snack of food and beverage			
Plan meal using major food groups			
Use blender to make beverage by pressing button or using adaptive switch			
Rinse fresh fruit and vegetables			
Help prepare food by pouring contents from package and stirring (e.g., pudding, cake mix, drink mix)			
Prepare snack or sandwich that requires stacking and spreading (e.g., peanut butter crackers, chicken sandwich)			
Use microwave for food or beverage (e.g., prepare hot dog, hot chocolate, popcorn): • Read and set cooking time • Use matching to set time • Use coding to set time • Set time, but only with assistance			
Follow simple recipe, using: • Photographs • Audiotape • Sight words • Directions on package • Picture cookbook			
Pour beverages			
Set the table			
Bake frozen item in oven (e.g., frozen casserole, pie) • Read and set temperature • Use matching to set temperature • Use color coding • Set oven temperature, but only with assistance			
Prepare "heat and eat" stovetop item (e.g., soup, canned pasta)			
Chop and cut (e.g., fresh fruit or vegetables, refrigerator cookies)			
Prepare convenience food, following package or picture instructions (e.g., stir-fry meal)			
Coordinate preparing several foods at once to serve a meal			
Measure ingredients			

scrapbook of favorite styles. In collaboration with the family, the teacher can then focus community-based instruction on shopping for clothing items or accessories that create this style. For students who do not recognize pictures and use nonsymbolic communication, the teacher should create opportunities to sample different options. For example, does the student like smooth or textured fabrics? Sweatshirts or velour? Does the student visually attend longer to certain colors or accessory items?

Andrea[5] was a young adult with severe physical and cognitive disabilities, who showed a keen interest in things that sparkled. Her teacher collaborated with her mother to help Andrea purchase bracelets, hair accessories, shirts with sequins, and other items that Andrea seemed to enjoy. When the teacher styled Andrea's hair during the day, she gave her a choice of hair accessories by holding up two options; Andrea expressed her choice by reaching for one of these. In these ways, the people who provided support to Andrea helped translate her preference for objects that sparkled into a personal style of dressing.

After giving first priority to the student's style preferences, the teacher can consider what mechanics of dressing and grooming to teach. Collaborating with the family in this planning is essential. Kelly's mother was hesitant when the teacher suggested instructing Kelly in how to take off her shirt; her mother feared that she would begin doing so in public! Because Kelly was 16, and larger than her mother, dressing her was becoming increasingly difficult. Together, the teacher and Kelly's mother selected some responses Kelly could make that would make dressing her less physically demanding (e.g., raising her legs when her pants were put on). They also selected responses that helped put Kelly more in charge of dressing. (For further details, see the discussion of Kelly at the end of this chapter.)

Nearly all of the research on teaching dressing and grooming skills has focused on the mechanics of these skills, rather than on choice or style. The contribution of this research is that it provides important clues for defining the specific responses to be taught and how to teach them. Alberto, Jobes, Sizemore, and Doran (1980) taught students to put on a pullover sweater and elastic outer pants, using forward chaining. That is, they taught the students one specific response (the first response) in putting on the clothing item. When this was mastered, they then had the students do the first step and then taught the second. In contrast, Sisson, Kilwein, and Van Hasselt (1988) taught students the entire task analysis for putting on socks, elastic-waist pants, and pullover shirts, but used graduated physical guidance to help the students perform each step. These physical prompts were systematically faded. They taught these three clothing items and found that students were able to generalize to three similar items. Reese and Snell (1991) were also able to teach the entire task analysis for putting on and taking off coats and jackets, but they used oversized garments as well as graduated guidance to help students succeed. Over time, the size of the garments and physical guidance were faded until the students were independent.

Some students have physical challenges that make it impossible for them to dress and groom themselves. For such students, specific responses can be chosen to encourage their active participation in these routines. For example, Snell, Lewis, and Houghton (1989) taught students with multiple disabilities to partially participate in a tooth-

---

[5]Andrea is not a real person.

brushing routine. The skills they targeted were for each student to (1) open the mouth wide, (2) keep it open while the teacher brushed one area, and (3) close the mouth with lips touching. This was repeated four times as the teacher brushed four areas of the mouth. Then the student was to (1) drop the head toward the basin, (2) spit, and (3) lift the head. Finally, the teacher had each student help with drying the face by (1) turning the head to one side and (2) turning the head to the other side as the teacher held the towel on the mouth. This partial participation might also include responses such as looking up to ask to have the next section of the mouth brushed, and choosing the flavor of toothpaste. Figure 10.5 is a checklist that can be used for assessing specific dressing and grooming skills.

In conducting situational assessments of dressing and grooming skills, it is also important to consider how context influences responding. Students may do more when they are in the presence of peers who perform these skills for themselves. Schoen, Lentz, and Suppa (1988) demonstrated that students with Down's syndrome made some gains in using a water fountain and washing their face simply by observing their peers. Alberto et al. (1980) also found greater gains for dressing skills in a group instruction format. Some dressing skills lend themselves well to group contexts. For example, adolescent girls often enjoy grooming when they are around peers who are doing the same (e.g., trying new hairstyles and makeup). In contrast, some dressing and grooming skills are personal. Performing them in a group may inhibit responding and violate a student's privacy. Students may also demonstrate higher skill levels if assessed at the appropriate time and context for using these skills. Freagan and Rotatori (1982) found that adults with moderate to profound cognitive disabilities learned skills like deodorant use, toothbrushing, and hand washing faster when taught during the natural times and contexts, compared to artificial times. Students may be much more proficient in washing hands when they are anticipating lunch than if they are simply taken to the restroom at an artificial time for an assessment of this skill.

Using the Toilet

Societal expectations for the age at which children master bowel and bladder control vary culturally, but nearly all cultures expect complete continence by the time a child reaches school age. Although incontinence can occur at any age, due to illness or to physical or mental changes, if it is not managed well it can be both highly stigmatizing and unhealthy for the incontinent individual and others in his or her environment. The reasons why gaining bowel and bladder control is delayed or arrested for individuals with moderate and severe disabilities are varied. These can include neurological damage, slower awareness of internal cues of the need to void, less ability to learn from being asked to use the toilet, and difficulty in communicating to others the need for assistance in using the toilet (Snell & Farlow, 1993).

There are three options for bowel and bladder management: (1) learning to use the toilet based on internal cues about bladder and bowel fullness, (2) going to the toilet on a time schedule that prevents accidents, and (3) using sanitary products or other alternatives (e.g., catheterization) in lieu of using the toilet. If at all possible, teaching students to use the toilet on their own initiative is the ultimate goal, because it encourages personal dignity. Several studies have demonstrated that some students with severe

FIGURE 10.5. A checklist for assessing dressing and grooming skills.

Dressing and Grooming Skills Checklist

Skills	Mastery	Partial mastery	Not mastered
Dressing and undressing			
1. Choose between two clothing options			
2. Select outfit for the day			
3. Choose accessories for personal style			
4. Move arms and lift legs to help in dressing			
5. Communicate to caregiver when help is needed in dressing (e.g., look up to get shirt on; vocalize to get sweater off; ask for help with fastening pants)			
6. Pull down pants in restroom			
7. Take off clothing: • Shoes • Socks • Jacket or sweater • Pants • Shirt • Unfasten Velcro • Unsnap • Unbutton • Unzip			
8. Get dressed: • Put on jacket, coat • Put on elastic-waist pants, underpants • Put on large T-shirt, sweatshirt • Put on tube socks • Put on jeans (may not zip them) • Fasten Velcro fasteners • Snap • Zip • Button			
Toothbrushing			
1. Choose between two toothpastes			
2. Ask for help with toothbrushing (e.g., look at/ point to toothbrush)			
3. Participates with caregiver in toothbrushing by opening/closing mouth			

(cont.)

FIGURE 10.5. *(page 2 of 2)*

4. Spit out toothpaste			
5. Brush own teeth			
Washing hands or face			
1. Ask for help with washing hands or face (e.g., point to sink)			
2. Choose between two types of soap			
3. Determine whether water is comfortable temperature (e.g., nod, smile)			
4. Participate in washing by: • Moving hands towards water • Moving face back and forth against cloth			
5. Grasp/release paper towel in trash			
6. Wash own hands when told			
7. Initiate washing hands and face			
Other grooming			
1. Ask for help with combing/styling hair			
2. Comb/style own hair			
3. Use makeup (optional)			
4. Care for nails			
5. Leave restroom groomed for public: • Clothing straight • Zippers and fasteners closed • Hair neat • Hands washed • Face clean • Makeup on neatly (optional)			
6. Shower or bathe: • Choose bath products to use (e.g., soap, shampoo) • Wash body • Shampoo hair • Shave (if applicable) • Apply deodorant			

disabilities can master toilet training (Azrin & Foxx, 1971; Hobbs & Peck, 1985). Students can also be prompted to use the toilet on a schedule, and can be allowed to make extra trips when they initiate these (Richmond, 1983). However, not all students master using the toilet and may need the support of incontinence products (e.g., disposable underpants or diapers) to avoid the stigma of public incontinence. Whichever option for bowel and bladder management is chosen, the student may receive various levels of assistance and instruction, as illustrated in Figure 10.6. In using this form to plan for support for toileting needs, the teacher first selects the method of management. For Henry,[6] the goal is for him to learn to use the toilet on a schedule. Because he is a preteen (age 12) and has frequent accidents, he will also wear a sanitary product until he masters the toilet-training schedule (pull-up disposable underpants). The teacher then plans support needs related to the method selected. The goal is for Henry to ask for help by using a picture to go to the toilet when told it is time. In the restroom, Henry will learn to assist by pulling his pants up and down (the teacher will help with fastening and zipping for now). He will also be in charge of disposing of his disposable underpants when soiled and will learn to put on a new pair of underpants. Because Henry seems to be reinforced by the attention he receives when he voids in public, the use of disposable underpants will also resolve this problem.

If the goal of the bowel or bladder management program is using the toilet based on either internal cues or a schedule, the teacher will need to determine when to take the student to the toilet. If the goal is internal cues, it is best to prompt the student to go just before an accident would typically occur. To determine when this is, the teacher can keep daily data for a week or two by checking the student every 15 minutes to determine whether he or she is dry or has voided. An example of a data collection chart the teacher may use is shown in Figure 10.7. In contrast, when training a student to use the toilet on a schedule, the teacher may begin with a frequent schedule (e.g., every 30 minutes) and reinforce the student if he or she voids. The schedule is then increased by 15-minute increments up to about 2 hours. Some students will not achieve a 2-hour pattern and will need a more frequent voiding schedule. An alternative method to schedule training is to pick one time of day for the student to use the toilet (e.g., after lunch), and then to add additional time periods of the day (Fredericks et al., 1981). Students may also need training and support to generalize their toilet skills across community and other environments. This can be done by making sure all those who provide support to the student are following the management plan for toileting (Dunlap, Koegel, & Koegel, 1984).

Sometimes, in assessing a student's toileting needs, the teacher will identify problems related to the toileting routine. Gray and Boswell (1999) recommend solutions from their work with students with autism. A few of these are as follows:

PROBLEM	POTENTIAL SOLUTION
1. Student resists sitting on toilet.	• Have student practice sitting with clothes on; fade to underwear, then no underwear.
	• Help student understand how long to sit by playing a tape or using timer.

2. Flushing—student either fears it or is overinterested.

- Use visual or verbal signal when time to flush: "Ready, set, go."
- Flush when student is away from toilet; gradually transfer to student flushing.

3. Student plays in toilet water.

- Let student hold a toy as a distraction.
- Have student use padded lap desk while seated.

4. Student (boy) does not aim in toilet when standing.

- Use a target (e.g., a piece of cereal).

5. Student uses large quantities of toilet paper.

- Use facial tissue or put clothespin to show where to tear off.

6. Student resists being cleaned.

- Try different material (e.g., "wet wipes").

Housekeeping and Laundry

For many individuals (with and without disabilities), mastering housekeeping and laundry skills involves not only learning to perform the specific tasks required, but acquiring the habit of doing so on a regular basis. In many families, these tasks are shared by each member. In planning for a student with moderate or severe disabilities, the teacher can plan with the student and family what the student's responsibility will be in contributing to the upkeep of the home. Consideration can also be given to the skills that have potential for career development. For example, learning to fold towels may lead to a job in a commercial laundry.

Most researchers who have focused on housekeeping and laundry skills have used a task analysis of specific skills, such as bedmaking (McWilliams, Nietupski, & Hamre-Nietupski, 1990), using a key (Ivancic & Schepis, 1995), or using a washing machine (Browder et al., 1984; Miller & Test, 1989). The teacher may want to begin with a more broad-based assessment like the checklist shown in Figure 10.8. It may be helpful to share this checklist with the student and family to determine not only what the student can do, but what is most relevant for instruction at this time. Then, when specific skills have been chosen, a task analysis can be used for ongoing monitoring of the student's progress. Students who cannot master the entire task can still be active participants by learning specific responses (e.g., carrying dishes to the sink, wiping the table, or grasping soiled clothes and releasing them into the washer).

Teachers may also want to assess whether students can manage completing chores on a given schedule. Following a chore schedule can be useful not only for home living, but also as a step toward job training. Pierce and Schriebman (1994) taught children with autism to use a picture album to complete chores such as setting the table, making the bed, making a drink, getting dressed, and doing laundry. Once a student learned the meaning of each picture and how to perform the task, the therapist was able to leave the area and the child could complete each step of the task by following the pictures. Anderson, Sherman, Sheldon, and McAdam (1997) taught adults with mental retardation to self-schedule their activities for after-work hours by sequencing photos in an album after they got home.

FIGURE 10.6. Form for planning assistance for bowel and bladder management needs.

Bowel and Bladder Management Plan

Student's name: Henry Bartholomew   **Age:** 12   **Date:** November 4, 20—

Method to Be Used

_____ Student will use toilet based on internal cues.

Comments: _____

_____

  X Student will use toilet on a specific time schedule.

Comments: Goal is for Henry to learn to use toilet once every hour.

_____

_____ Student will use: X incontinence products; _____ catheterization; _____ other (specify).

Comments: Henry will stay in disposable underpants until he is accident-free.

_____

Support Needs

1. Initiation

_____ Student will take care of needs without prompting.

Comments: _____

_____

_____ Student will be prompted to take care of needs on own.

Comments: _____

_____

_____ Student will ask for help.

Comments: _____

_____

  X Student will be prompted to ask for help.

Comments: Prompt Henry to indicate picture for toilet when it is time to go.

_____

_____ Caregiver will initiate toileting.

Comments: _____

_____

(cont.)

FIGURE 10.5. *(page 2 of 2)*

2. Using the toilet or alternative methods

_____Student will perform all steps independently.

Comments: _____

_____

_____Student will be prompted to perform all steps, with goal of independence.

Comments: _____

_____

_X_ Interactive; student will perform some steps without prompts.

Comments: Henry can remove and discard disposable underpants without assistance.

_____

_X_ Interactive; student will be prompted to perform some steps.

Comments: Prompt Henry to help push pants down, to sit down on his own, and to put on disposable underpants.

_____Caregiver will do all assistance.

Comments: _____

_____

3. Accident management

_____Student will manage own cleanup.

Comments: _____

_____

_____Student will be prompted to manage own cleanup, with goal of independence.

Comments: _____

_____

_____Interactive; student will perform some steps without prompts.

Comments: _____

_____

_X_ Interactive; student will be prompted to perform some steps.

Comments: Attention for accidents seems to have increased Henry's incontinence. Using disposable underpants can limit cleanup to restroom; prompt Henry to assist with this.

_____Caregiver will provide all cleanup.

Comments: _____

_____

FIGURE 10.7. Chart for recording child's pattern of elimination to plan a toilet-training schedule. (U, urination; BM, bowel movement; D, dry.)

Elimination Pattern Chart

	Sunday	Monday	Tuesday	Wednesday	Thursday	Friday	Saturday
7:00	U—pants	U/BM—pants	U—pants	U—pants	U—pants	U—pants	U—pants
8:00	D	D	D	D	D	D	D
9:00	U—pants	U—pants	D	U—pants	U—pants	D	D
10:00	D	D	U/BM—toilet	D	D	U/BM—pants	U—pants
11:00	U—pants	U—pants	D	U/BM—pants	U—pants	D	U—pants
12:00	D	U—pants	D	D	D	U—pants	D
1:00	U—toilet	D	U—pants	U—pants	U—pants	D	U—pants
2:00	D	U—pants	U—pants	D	D	U—pants	U—pants
3:00	U—pants	D	D	U—toilet	U—pants	D	D

Sex Education

One of parents' primary concerns about their older children's transition to adulthood is the issue of sexuality (Wolfe & Blanchett, 1997). Two important reasons students with severe disabilities need sex education are to manage their own sexuality and to avoid abuse or harassment. Given the confusion and mixed messages in American society about sexuality, students with cognitive disabilities may find it especially difficult to learn what is acceptable behavior for inclusive settings. McCabe and Cummins (1996) found that adults with mild mental retardation, compared to college students who were nondisabled, were less knowledgeable and more negative about sex, but also had more experience with pregnancy and sexually transmitted disease.

The challenge of teaching sex education to individuals with cognitive disabilities is that care must be taken that educational activities do not themselves become abusive or violate students' privacy. In school settings, teachers providing sex education to students who are nondisabled use lectures and audiovisual presentations. Some students with cognitive impairments are not able to comprehend materials in these formats. However, using one-to-one instruction or more specific materials may violate a stu-

FIGURE 10.8. A checklist for assessing housekeeping and laundry skills.

Housekeeping and Laundry Skills Checklist

Skills	Mastery	Partial mastery	Not mastered
Kitchen/lunchroom			
1. Wipe table or tray after eating			
2. Carry dishes to sink (or tray to cleanup area)			
3. Wash dishes in sink			
4. Load dishwasher			
5. Clean sink			
6. Clean floor			
Living areas			
1. Dust with choice of dusters (e.g., feather, cloth)			
2. Straighten living area			
3. Vacuum: • Vacuum entire room, including under furniture • Vacuum main floor area • Help by turning vacuum on/off			
4. Strip bed: • Help by putting pillow on chair			
5. Make bed: • Help by pulling covers up • Help by putting pillow on bed			
Bathroom			
1. Clean tub			
2. Clean toilet			
3. Clean sink			
4. Clean floor			
Laundry			
1. Put clothes in hamper			
2. Sort clothes for washing			
3. Use washer and dryer: • Help by putting clothes in • Help by pulling clothes out • Do all steps except setting dial • Perform all steps without help			
5. Fold towels and washcloths			
6. Fold clothes			

dent's legal rights or offend parents. Some planning teams may decide to include more explicit sexuality training, in collaboration with parents and school authorities. In one case, Epps, Stern, and Horner (1990) used a task analysis and systematic prompting to teach young women with cognitive disabilities menstrual care. Lumley, Miltenberger, Long, Rapp, and Roberts (1998) taught avoiding abuse via a "no–go–tell" sequence. With the review and approval of a human rights committee, they also probed the participants' reactions to simulated harassment in natural settings.

Some students may need help to learn the concept of privacy. This may be addressed by teaching them to discriminate between the private and nonprivate zones of their bodies. They may also need to learn differential social responses. For example, students may learn to give a wave rather than a hug to acquaintances, and to reserve hugs for close friends and family. The Circles Program provides color cue training and videos that can be useful in teaching social/sexual boundaries (see Table 10.3, below). This program may be acceptable to parents who do not want explicit sexual content taught. In contrast, Sexuality Education for Persons with Severe Developmental Disabilities provides explicit slides to help teach students behaviors that are private versus public (see Table 10.3, below). Table 10.2 offers questions that might be considered in assessing a student's needs for a sex education program.

TABLE 10.2. Questions to Consider in Planning a Sex Education Curriculum for a Student with Moderate or Severe Disabilities

---

1. *Why is sex education being considered at this time?*
- How old is the student?
- Does the student have specific behaviors that are causing concern?
- Do community risks exist?
- Have the parents made a specific request?
- Other reasons (specify)?

2. *What is the school district's policy on sex education?*
- Have you (the teacher) talked with an administrator about this policy?
- How is sex education provided for students who are nondisabled?
- Can this student be included in this general program? If so, how? If not, why not?

3. *What are the parents' and student's preferences?*
- What are the parents' preferences regarding sex education?
- To what extent has the student shown interest in sexual issues?

4. *Which of the following should be included in the student's sex education program?*
- Names of private body parts and their function
- Social expectations for private body zones (e.g., "Don't touch others in these areas," "Keep these areas covered")
- How to avoid abuse or harassment ("No, go, tell")
- Social interactions appropriate for different relationships (e.g., "Wave, don't hug")
- Specific behaviors that are private versus public
- Intercourse and reproduction
- Birth control
- Avoiding sexually transmitted disease
- Other:

5. *How should the sex education program be designed?*
- Who, where, what materials?
- Procedural safeguards (human rights protection)?

REVIEWING QUALITY INDICATORS IN THE HOME
AND PERSONAL LIVING CURRICULUM

Several published curricula and other materials for teaching home and personal living skills to students with disabilities are available (see Table 10.3). By using those materials, ecological inventories, guidelines for active participation, and situational assessments, the teacher can select the appropriate skills to teach a particular student. Once this selection has been made, it may be helpful to review some of the quality indicators that have been mentioned at the beginning of this chapter. These can be illustrated by considering the curriculum that was developed for Kelly, the 16-year-old student with severe cognitive impairments and mild cerebral palsy. Table 10.4 summarizes the skills targeted for Kelly in the home and personal living domain.

1. *Does a curriculum contain skills that encourage active, partial participation for a student who will not attain independence in his or her daily routines?* Kelly would probably need lifelong care in her daily routines. Despite intensive instruction for most of her life, Kelly still needed assistance to dress, eat, and use the toilet. This ongoing need for support was partly due to her physical challenges, which made it difficult for her to perform some of the motor responses needed to perform these skills. Despite these lim-

TABLE 10.3. Commercial Materials for Teaching Home and Personal Living Skills

Attainment Company
P.O. Box 930160
Verona, WI 53593-0160
1-800-327-4269

    Keeping House Curriculum
    Looking Good Curriculum (e.g., dental hygiene, bathing, dressing)
    Home Cooking Curriculum and *Home Cooking Cookbook*
    Look 'n' Cook Program and *Look 'n' Cook Cookbook*
    Select-A-Meal Curriculum
    What People Wear (focuses on dressing for the weather and different occasions)
    Life Skills Games Series (Cooking Class Game, Look Good Game, Eating Skills Game)

James Stanfield Company, Inc.
PO Box 41058
Santa Barbara, CA 93140
1-800-421-6534
http://www.stanfield.com

    The following are all videotapes (often humorous) for teaching skills; each includes a teacher's guide.
Hygiene for Males and *Hygiene for Females*
Grooming for Males and *Grooming for Females*
Dress Makes a Lasting Impression (on dressing with style)
Home of Your Own (about roommates, lending and borrowing, sharing expenses)
Circles I: Intimacy and Relationships (uses color coding to teach social distance and relationship
    building)
Circles II: Stop Abuse
Sexuality Education for Persons with Severe Developmental Disabilities
The Gyn Exam
Janet's Got Her Period
No–Go–Tell (designed for young children; to prevent physical abuse)

TABLE 10.4. Curriculum Items in the Home and Personal Living Domain for Kelly, a 16-Year-Old Student with Severe Disabilities

Dressing

- Choose shirt or jacket by nodding
- Ask for help with dressing by taking clothing to assistant (e.g., coat to teacher)
- Nod to indicate when ready for help in dressing (e.g., to put coat on or tie shoes)
- Lift legs and arms to assist when being dressed
- Keep shoes on at school
- Wear glasses all day at school

Eating

- Use spoon without spilling
- Spear appropriate foods with a fork
- Put glass on table to indicate when finished (not throw it)
- Choose entrée in lunch line
- Find favorite seat
- "Dump" tray contents in garbage can while holding silverware

Using the toilet/grooming

- Use toilet every 2 hours without accidents
- Request use of toilet by patting side
- Wash hands with assistance to turn on/off water
- Choose (by reaching for) "body mist" or flavored lip gloss

Food preparation

- Microwave a hot dog (favorite food)
- Make air-blown popcorn (low-calorie snack)
- Take dishes to sink
- Rinse dishes (loves water)

Housekeeping and laundry

- Put soiled clothes in bag or hamper
- Wipe table area after eating
- Use feather duster to dust
- Put clothes in washer/pull out of dryer

Sex education

- Shake hands or give "high fives" versus giving tight body hugs
- Avoid physical contact in public settings (especially with strangers)
- Help change sanitary pad (pull adhesive strip, throw old pad in trash)
- Learn receptive language for "private zones," "period"
- Keep "private zones" of body covered when around other people
- Refrain from touching genital area except when on toilet or in own bedroom

itations, Kelly did not have to be a passive recipient of care. Some of the skills that were chosen to make her more active included lifting her arms and legs to assist with dressing, using a spoon and fork, washing her hands (performing all steps except turning the faucet off and on), and putting her soiled clothes in a bag or hamper.

2. *Does a curriculum encourage a student's self-determination?* Kelly could become not only active, but more "in charge" of her daily routines as she made the transition to adult living. Kelly could become more self-determined by making choices in her routines. For example, she would learn to choose clothing, lunch entrees, and toiletry items. Kelly would also begin the process of directing her own care. For example, she would be taught to ask for help in dressing and to nod when ready to be dressed. She

would find her own seat in the lunchroom, and would put her glass down to show when she was finished with lunch. Her preferences were also being encouraged in her curriculum. For example, because Kelly loved hot dogs, she would have the opportunity to learn how to prepare them. She also might enjoy learning to rinse the dishes, since she loved water.

3. *Does the curriculum honor parental preferences and cultural values?* Kelly's parents had three primary concerns. They wanted her to wear her glasses, because her vision was limited. They also requested that food preparation activities take into consideration Kelly's tendency to gain weight easily. If she became obese, it might become physically impossible for her parents to provide her care. Finally, her parents were concerned that Kelly become "accident-free" by using the toilet consistently. Because she had no way to indicate the need to use the toilet, her mother had her urinate on a 2-hour schedule, but had to "guess" when bowel movements would occur. The curriculum would include teaching Kelly to indicate the need to toilet. Because Kelly did not comprehend pictures and could not make manual signs, she would use the gesture of patting her waist to indicate this need.

When asked about sex education, Kelly's parents were wary about what the teacher would address. They had strong personal values in this area related to their religious heritage. Kelly's 18-year-old sister, Heather, who accepted these family values, dressed modestly and valued sexual abstinence. Heather was the one who expressed concern that Kelly might give people the wrong impression with her close-contact body hugs and indifference about whether her clothes covered her. When the teacher suggested that Kelly's sex education at this time might focus on learning to respect others and her own personal boundaries, her parents agreed that this would be important. Her curriculum focused on learning new ways to greet others (handshakes and "high fives") and social customs regarding privacy.

4. *Can the items on a curriculum be taught in an inclusive school setting without violating a student's privacy?* Kelly's dressing skills could be addressed in a typical school setting by focusing on her outerwear (coats, jackets, sweaters). Her mother would send in more than one item, and Kelly would then decide how heavy an item she wanted to wear outside when changing classes. Her eating skills could also be addressed in a school cafeteria. With some help from a peer who was nondisabled, and with discreet prompting by her teacher, Kelly could learn the additional skills targeted for this setting. Using the toilet was more challenging to plan in a high school setting. Kelly's teacher had an adapted restroom in her classroom. Since Kelly needed assistance in the restroom, she would use this private setting rather than one of the school's more public restrooms. Kelly would also learn about her "private zones" during this time. For food preparation and housekeeping, Kelly would have the opportunity to learn some of these skills by enrolling in home economics. The teacher would also be providing a tutoring session for Kelly and other classmates with disabilities during a time when the home economics room was available.

5. *Are all of the skills in a curriculum functional and age-appropriate?* All of the skills in Kelly's curriculum were *functional*. That is, these skills would be used on an ongoing basis in her daily routines. Most high school students are self-reliant when it comes to self-care, and Kelly would not be learning self-care skills the way a preschooler would. Instead, she would be "taking charge" of the assistance she needed by indicating when she was ready to dress or use the toilet and when she was finished eating. She would

also be learning food preparation and housekeeping skills that are typical activities for teens (preparing snacks, doing chores). Learning social customs about keeping private bodily areas covered and greeting others in an age-appropriate way would also encourage respect and dignity for Kelly as a young woman.

SUMMARY

Home and personal living skills are important to both individual dignity and increased opportunities for independence in community settings. Even when lifelong care may be necessary, students can learn to take charge of personal care by making choices and initiating responses in their daily routines. When support for personal living and home skills are required, it is important to honor individuals' self-determination and personal values. For example, not all people have the same tastes in food and clothing styles. Sometimes these preferences are influenced by the student's cultural background, which should be honored in planning.

When conducting ecological assessment to plan instructional support for home and personal living skills, teachers may target teaching an entire routine like getting ready for work, a specific skill like eating cereal, or partial participation like choosing a food and nodding when ready to be fed. The choice teaching target will depend on the student's current skills and the challenges of his or her disability.

Home and personal living instruction may address skills in several areas, including eating, food preparation, dressing and grooming, toileting, and sex education. A wealth of research exists on teaching self-care and daily living skills, some of which has been reviewed in this chapter to illustrate the content and method for such instruction.

REFERENCES

Alberto, P., Jobes, N., Sizemore, A., & Doran, D. (1980). A comparison of individual and group instruction across response tasks. *Journal of the Association for Persons with Severe Handicaps, 5,* 285–293.

Anderson, M. D., Sherman, J. A., Sheldon, J. V., & McAdam, D. (1997). Picture activity schedules and engagement of adults with mental retardation in a group home. *Research in Developmental Disabilities, 18,* 231–250.

Azrin, N. H., & Armstrong, P. M. (1973). The "mini-meal": A method for teaching eating skills to the profoundly retarded. *Mental Retardation, 11*(1), 9–11.

Azrin, N. H., & Foxx, R. M. (11971). A rapid method of toilet training the institutionalized retarded. *Journal of Applied Behavior Analysis, 4,* 89–99.

Browder, D. M., Hines, C., McCarthy, L. J., & Fees, J. (1984). A treatment package for increasing sight word recognition for use in daily living skills. *Education and Training of the Mentally Retarded, 19,* 191–200.

Brown, L., Branston, M. B., Hamre-Nietupski, S., Pumpian, I., Certo, N., & Gruenewald, L. (1979). A strategy for developing age appropriate and functional curricular content for severely handicapped adolescents and young adults. *Journal of Special Education, 13,* 81–90.

Clifft, M. A. (1986). Writing about psychiatric patients: Guidelines for disguising case material. *Bulletin of the Menninger Clinic, 50,* 511–524.

Collins, B. C., Gast, D. L., Wolery, M., Holcombe, A., & Leatherby, J. G. (1991). Using constant time delay to teach self-feeding to young students with severe/profound handicaps: Evidence of limited effectiveness. *Journal of Developmental and Physical Disabilities, 3,* 157–179.

Dunlap, G. Koegel, R. L., & Koegel, L. K. (1984). Continuity of treatment: Toilet training in multiple community settings. *Journal of the Association for Persons with Severe Handicaps, 9,* 134–141.

Epps, S., Stern, R. J., & Horner, R. H. (1990). Comparison of simulation training on self and using a doll for teaching generalized menstrual care to women with severe mental retardation. *Research in Developmental Disabilities, 11,* 37–66.

Ferguson, D. L., & Baumgart, D. (1991). Partial participation revisited. *Journal of the Association for Persons with Severe Handicaps, 16,* 218–227.

Ford, A., Schnorr, R., Meyer, L., Davern, L., Black, J., & Dempsey, P. (1989). *The Syracuse Community-Referenced Curriculum Guide for students with moderate and severe disabilities.* Baltimore: Paul H. Brookes.

Freagon, S., & Rotatori, A. F. (1982). Comparing natural and artificial environments in training self-care skills to group home residents. *Journal of the Association for the Severely Handicapped, 7,* 73–86.

Fredericks, H. D. B., Grover, D. N., Baldwin, V. L., Moore, W. G., Toews, J., Aschbacher, V., & Templeman, T. P. (1981). *Toilet training the handicapped child* (4th ed.). Monmouth, OR: Instructional Development.

Giangreco, M. F., Cloninger, C. J., & Iverson, V. S. (1998). *Choosing Outcomes and Accommodations for Children* (2nd ed.). Baltimore: Paul H. Brookes.

Gray, D., & Boswell, S. (1999). Applying structured teaching principles to toilet training. *The Spectrum, 15*(3), 6–9.

Griffin, A. K., Wolery, M., & Schuster, J. W. (1992). Triadic instruction of chained food preparation responses: Acquisition and observational learning. *Journal of Applied Behavior Analysis, 25,* 257–279.

Hendrickson, K. C., Akkerman, P. S., & Speggen, L. (1985). Dining arrangements and behavior of severely mentally retarded adults. *Applied Research in Mental Retardation, 6,* 379–388.

Hobbs, T., & Peck, C. A. (1985). Toilet training people with profound mental retardation: A cost effective procedure for large residential settings. *Behavioral Engineering, 9,* 50–57.

Ivancic, M. T., & Schepis, M. M. (1995). Teaching key use to persons with severe disabilities in congregate living settings. *Research in Developmental Disabilities, 16,* 415–423.

Jones, G. Y., & Collins, B. C. (1997). Teaching microwave skills to adults with disabilities: Acquisition of nutrition and safety facts presented as nontargeted information. *Journal of Developmental and Physical Disabilities, 9,* 59–78.

Knapczyk, D. R. (1983). Use of teacher-paced instruction in developing and maintaining independent self-feeding. *Journal of the Association for Persons with Severe Handicaps, 8,* 10–16.

Kohl, F. L., & Stettner-Eaton, B. A. (1985). Fourth graders as trainers of cafeteria skills to severely handicapped students. *Education and Training of the Mentally Retarded, 20,* 229–245.

Konarski, E. A., & Diorio, M. S. (1985). A quantitative review of self-help research with the severely and profoundly mentally retarded. *Applied Research in Mental Retardation, 6,* 229–245

Lohrmann-O'Rourke, S., & Browder, D. M. (1998). Empirically based methods of preference assessments for individuals with severe disabilities. *American Journal of Mental Retardation, 103,* 146–161.

Loyd, R. J., & Brolin, D. E. (1997). *Life Centered Career Education: Modified curriculum for individuals with moderate disabilities.* Reston, VA: Council for Exceptional Children.

Luiselli, J. K. (1988). Improvement of feeding skills in multihandicapped students through paced-prompting interventions. *Journal of the Multihandicapped Person, 1,* 17–30.

Lumley, V. A., Miltenberger, R. G., Long, E. S., Rapp, J. T., & Roberts, J. A. (1998). Evaluation of a sexual abuse prevention program for adults with mental retardation. *Journal of Applied Behavior Analysis, 31,* 91–101.

Lynch, P. S., Kellow, J., Thomas, J., & Willson, V. L. (1997). The impact of deinstitutionalization on the adaptive behavior of adults with mental retardation: A meta-analysis. *Education and Training in Mental Retardation and Developmental Disabilities, 32,* 255–261.

McCabe, M. P., & Cummins, R. A. (1996). The sexual knowledge, experience, feelings, and needs of people with mild intellectual disability. *Education and Training in Mental Retardation and Developmental Disabilities, 31,* 13–21.

McWilliams, R., Nietupski, J., & Hamre-Nietupski, S. (1990). Teaching complex activities to students with moderate handicaps through the forward chaining of shorter total cycle response sequences. *Education and Training in Mental Retardation, 25,* 292–298.

Mechling, L. C., & Gast, D. L. (1997). Combination audio/visual self-prompting system for teaching chained tasks to students with intellectual disabilities. *Education and Training in Mental Retardation and Developmental Disabilities, 32,* 138–153.

Miller, U. C., & Test, D. W. (1989). A comparison of constant time delay and most-to-least prompts in teaching laundry skills to students with moderate retardation. *Education and Training of the Mentally Retarded, 24,* 363–370.

Perske, R., Clifton, A., McLean, B. M., & Stein, J. I. (Eds.). (1977). *Mealtimes for severely and profoundly handicapped persons: New concepts and attitudes.* Baltimore: Paul H. Brookes.

Pierce, K. L., & Schriebman, L. (1994). Teaching daily living skills to children with autism in unsupervised settings through pictorial self-management. *Journal of Applied Behavior Analysis, 27,* 471–481.

Reese, G. M., & Snell, M. E. (1991). Putting on and removing coats and jackets: The acquisition and maintenance of skills by children with severe multiple disabilities. *Education and Training in Mental Retardation, 26,* 398–410.

Richmond, G. (1983). Shaping bladder and bowel continence in developmentally retarded preschool children. *Journal of Autism and Developmental Disorders, 13,* 197–205.

Riordan, M. M., Iwata, B. A., Finney, J. W., Wohl, M. K., & Stanley, A. E. (1984). Behavioral assessment and treatment of chronic food refusal in handicapped children. *Journal of Applied Behavior Analysis, 17,* 327–341.

Schoen, S. F., Lentz, F. E., & Suppa, R. J. (1988). An examination of two prompt fading procedures and opportunities to observe in teaching handicapped preschoolers self-help skills. *Journal of the Division for Early Childhood, 12,* 349–358.

Singh, N. N., Oswald, D. P., Ellis, C. R., & Singh, S. D. (1995). Community-based instruction for independent meal preparation by adults with profound mental retardation. *Journal of Behavioral Education, 5,* 77–92.

Sisson, L. A., Kilwein, M. L., & Van Hasselt, V. B. (1988). A graduated guidance procedure for teaching self-dressing skills to multihandicapped children. *Research in Developmental Disabilities, 9,* 419–432.

Smith, A. L., Jr., Piersel, W. C., Filbeck, R. W., & Gross, E. J. (1983). The elimination of mealtime food stealing and scavenging behavior in an institutionalized severely mentally retarded adult. *Mental Retardation, 21,* 255–259.

Snell, M. E., & Farlow, L. J. (1993). Self-care skills. In M. E. Snell (Ed.), *Instruction of individuals with severe disabilities* (pp. 380–441). New York: Macmillan.

Snell, M. E., Lewis, A. P., & Houghton, A. (1989). Acquisition and maintenance of toothbrushing skills by students with cerebral palsy and mental retardation. *Journal of the Association for Persons with Severe Handicaps, 14,* 216–226.

Thorin, E. J., & Irvin, L. K. (1992). Family stress associated with transition to adulthood of young people with severe disabilities. *Journal of the Association for Persons with Severe Handicaps, 17,* 31–39.

Trask-Tyler, S. A., Grossi, T. A., & Heward, W. L. (1994). Teaching young adults with developmental disabilities and visual impairments to use tape-recorded recipes: Acquisition, generalization, and maintenance of cooking skills. *Journal of Behavioral Education, 4,* 283–311.

Uehara, E. W., Silverstein, B. J., Davis, R., & Geron, S. (1991). Assessment of needs of adults with developmental disabilities in skills nursing and intermediate care facilities in Illinois. *Mental Retardation, 29,* 223–231.

VanBiervliet, A., Spangler, P. F., & Marshall, A. M. (1981). An ecobehavioral examination of a simple strategy for increasing mealtime language in residential facilities. *Journal of Applied Behavior Analysis, 14,* 295–305.

Wehmeyer, M. (1992). Self-determination and the education of students with mental retardation. *Education and Training in Mental Retardation, 27,* 302–314.

Westling, D. L., & Fox, L. (1995). *Teaching students with severe disabilities.* Upper Saddle River, NJ: Prentice-Hall. Pp. 384–415.

Wilcox, B., & Bellamy, G. T. (Eds.). (1987). *The activities catalog: An alternative curriculum for youth and adults with severe disabilities.* Baltimore: Paul H. Brookes.

Wilson, P. G., Reid, D. H., Phillips, J. F., & Burgio, L. D. (1984). Normalization of institutional mealtimes for profoundly retarded persons: Effects and noneffects of teaching family style dining. *Journal of Applied Behavior Analysis, 17,* 189–201.

Wolfe, P. S., & Blanchett, W. J. (1997). Infusion of sex education curricula into transition planning: Obstacles and solutions. *Journal of Vocational Rehabilitation, 8,* 143–154.

E L E V E N

Communication and Social Skills

with Kim Ware

BY THE TIME JORDAN[1] WAS 8 YEARS OLD, *he had received many diagnoses for his disability. These included severe mental retardation, autism, oppositional defiant disorder, obsessive–compulsive disorder, and attention-deficit/hyperactivity disorder. Jordan's family moved to a new, large school district that was well known for its services for children with autism. Jordan's first days at his new school were extremely difficult. He had frequent outbursts of screaming, head banging, and running from the classroom. When his teacher, Ms. Washington, talked with Jordan's mother, she learned that these behaviors had been problematic since Jordan was young. Jordan's mother, Ms. Holdren, reported that Jordan's previous school had used restrictive procedures to cope with his behavior, such as putting Jordan by himself in a "fenced-in" area of the classroom where he received minimal instruction. Ms. Washington asked about Jordan's communication skills, noting that he had not used any speech or other symbolic communication during his first days and would not use the communication board his former school had sent for him. Ms. Holdren said that Jordan had never learned to use this board. She also shared that Jordan sometimes spoke, but these vocalizations were usually exact repetitions of something he had heard (echolalia).*

This chapter provides guidelines for developing curriculum in communication and social skills by using an ecological assessment model. When students are relying on problem behavior for communication, as Jordan did, a functional assessment and positive behavioral supports also become an important part of this planning process.

Communication skills are often among the top priorities for students with disabilities. To be able to communicate with peers facilitates social interactions in inclusive settings. Many instructional interactions rely on communicative responses. Self-determination is also promoted through self-expression. Without an effective means of communication, individuals with moderate and severe disabilities can fall victim to the phenomenon of "learned helplessness" (Guess, Benson, & Siegel-Causey, 1985). If individuals are not able to influence others through their communicative efforts, they may stop trying to

---

[1]Jordan's case study, which is used throughout this chapter, is based on a real person. His name and other details have been changed to protect his confidentiality, consistent with the recommendations of the World and American Psychiatric Associations (Clifft, 1986).

Kim Ware, MEd, is a teacher of students with autism in Bethlehem, Pennsylvania.

do so and relinquish control of their daily lives to their caregivers. In contrast, some students may not become passive when their communicative efforts are unrecognized, but instead develop problem behaviors because they lack more sophisticated means of self-expression (Carr et al., 1994; Durand, 1990).

The three major components of communication are "form," "content," and "function." When the "form" of communication is speech, teachers focus on "syntax," including such skills as sentence structure, grammar, and inflection. When the form is an "augmentative" or "alternative" communication system (a nonspeech system), the teacher focuses on teaching the student to use this system effectively. The "content" of communication includes vocabulary and the topics discussed. "Function" is the purpose of the communication. In recent years, professionals have shifted the focus of communication training from a focus on the specific "forms" of expression to an emphasis on its "function" (Reichle & Sigafoos, 1994). "Functional communication skills" are also called "pragmatic" or "practical communication" skills (Dyer & Luce, 1996). In earlier training methods, an individual with moderate and severe disabilities might engage in training drills, such as identifying the names of pictures, imitating movements, following instructions, using a sentence, or speaking more clearly. Such drills focus on the "form" of communication and may not generalize to functional use of communication in daily routines. Current best practice in communication training skills is to teach the student to expand functional use by learning to make requests, initiate social routines, gain attention, and exercise other interactive skills.

Three other communication concepts that are important to curriculum planning are "intentionality," "comprehension," and "augmentation." McLean and Snyder-McLean (1988) have described the development of intentionality in communication. In their first months of life, infants will often engage in behavior that their caregivers "translate" as having meaning, even if the infants are expressing no intent. For example, if a baby fusses in a certain way that a caregiver translates as "I'm hungry," and the baby gets food, the baby will probably learn to use that style of fussing to get fed. This then becomes a "primitive" form of communication. Primitive forms of communication are actions that have occurred often enough to become conditioned. In some cases, a student may pull away from undesired items or interactions, or may close his or her eyes when overwhelmed. Some authors call this the "perlocutionary stage" of language development (Bates, 1979). Over time, a child learns to use communication with more intention. This level of communication is called "conventional" and may include such acts as extending the hand to ask for more, turning the head to end a task, or sitting forward to ask to be moved. This stage of language development typically occurs at about 9 months of age and is called the "illocutionary stage" of language development (Bates, 1979). The third level is "referential" communication. At this level, the student can use either speech or some type of symbols to communicate. For example, the student can now ask for food by showing a picture of it, by signing "eat," or by saying "eat." Referential communication is both intentional and symbolic. In typical child development, this stage occurs at about 13 months of age and is called the "locutionary stage" (Bates, 1979). Older students with moderate and severe disabilities may not use symbolic communication, but may have a rich repertoire of intentional communication that they achieve nonsymbolically. Interpretation and social responsiveness to efforts to communicative acts are essential to shape this intentionality. Because nonsymbolic communication can sometimes be difficult to interpret, caregivers may overlook students' expressions. An important part of a communication assessment is to consider all the ways a student may be using communication signals.

Communication is also "expressive" and "receptive." Expressive communication is the production of a communication act, such as showing someone a picture, moving toward a desired object, or asking about the day's schedule. Receptive communication is the comprehension of someone else's communication. Students with moderate and severe disabilities do not always have even development in their expressive and receptive communication skills. For instance, a student who uses nonsymbolic communication may be able to understand short spoken phrases, and thus to understand most of what is said to him or her. Other students may need concrete symbols (such as objects or manual signs), paired with verbalizations, to be able to understand. Some students may use speech and be able to talk in phrases or short sentences, but may still need concrete referents like picture symbols to be able to understand others' speech fully. In assessing communication skills, an evaluator needs to be careful not to make assumptions about a student's receptive communication skills based on his or her expressive skills, or vice versa.

An augmentative system of communication may be used to assist students who have either expressive or receptive communication problems. Augmentative systems can be "aided" or "unaided" (Lloyd, 1985). In an aided system, the student uses a device such as a picture wallet, communication board, or computer system. In an unaided system, the student needs no special equipment, but instead uses either hand gestures or manual signing. In assessing communication, the evaluator considers what types of augmentative communication might help the student be more effective in social contexts.

Table 11.1 provides a summary of some of the terms used in communication training.

DEVELOPING CURRICULAR PRIORITIES FOR COMMUNICATION SKILLS

In the ecological assessment model described throughout this book, the evaluator begins by getting to know the student, conducting person-centered planning with the student and family, and considering ways to promote the student's self-determination, both in the planning process and through future instruction. In developing the curricular priorities, the evaluator may use ecological inventories, curriculum charts, and situational assessments, as described in Chapter Two. In communication, the evaluation team also may need to plan for an augmentative or alternative communication system.

Augmentative and Alternative Communication Systems

Although professionals have been introducing augmentative and alternative communication systems (hereafter referred to as "AAC systems") to individuals with disabilities for many years, the result has not always been enhanced functional communication. In a survey of consumers, Wehmeyer (1998) found that over a third of AAC system users were somewhat to very dissatisfied with the evaluation and training they received in

TABLE 11.1. Terms Used in Communication Training

Term	Application in speech	Application in augmentative and alternative communication
	Intentionality	
Primitive (*illocutionary*)	Prespeech acts interpreted with intent	Actions to which others will respond to encourage intentional communication
Conventional (*perlocutionary*)	Prespeech acts that child uses to influence others (e.g., reaching)	Recognized as nonsymbolic communication; may be primary mode of communication
Referential (*locutionary*)	Intentional use of speech to communicate with others	Use of augmentative or alternative communication systems (symbols such as pictures, words, manual signs); may be aided (with materials) or unaided (e.g., gestures, signs)
	Components of communication	
Form	Syntax—sentence structure, grammar	Type of system used (e.g., nonsymbolic, manual signs, picture wallet, electronic board)
Content	Semantics—vocabulary and meaning	Vocabulary (symbols)
Function	Pragmatics—social use of language	Pragmatics—functional/social use of communication system

using their system. Goetz and Hunt (1994) note that there are three important premises in planning an AAC system:

1. All persons communicate.
2. All communication is multimodal.
3. All communication requires partners.

In planning a system, it is important to realize that the person is already using some means of communication. These means may include nonsymbolic actions and problem behaviors, as well as symbols or speech. Introducing a new system is more likely to enhance functional use of communication if it builds on, or directly replaces, these alternatives. Communication is also multimodal. To express a message, a person may use facial expression, hand gestures, body language, and proximity, as well as speech. Similarly, individuals who use AAC systems typically need more than one aid or technique to communicate (Vanderheiden & Lloyd, 1986). The fact that communication requires partners means that no matter how attractive an AAC technique may be to a planning team, if it does not affect others in the student's environment, it is not functional.

In assessing the student to select an AAC system, the team also needs to consider how easily the person will be able to master the symbol system. A picture symbol system will require the visual acuity to discriminate between pictures, as well as the comprehension skills to use the pictures symbolically. Some individuals may need to use objects instead of pictures. Others may need direct training to recognize these objects as symbols and may rely primarily on nonsymbolic communication while learning these associations. Other students may be able to use printed sight words or a combination of speech and symbols.

Besides the ability to discriminate symbols, motor skills and ambulation are considerations. Manual signs such as those used in American Sign Language can be convenient because they require no special materials; however, some students may not have the dexterity to produce signs. An electronic communication board with voice output can be highly effective in helping others understand the message, but may be most practical for a student with a wheelchair and lap tray. Some of the considerations in selecting an AAC system for a particular student are illustrated in Figure 11.1.

In planning for Jordan, the boy described at the beginning of this chapter and in Figure 11.1, the team noted that he relied primarily on nonsymbolic communication in the form of problem behavior. Although he had been trained on an electronic picture communication board, he had not mastered its use. He also showed a strong dislike for the board by resisting his teacher's prompting to use it. Ms. Washington discovered that Jordan lacked a pointing response—a lack that would make independent use of the board difficult. A good alternative for Jordan seemed to be the Picture Exchange Communication System or PECS (Bondy & Frost, 1994), because he could already grasp and release objects. In this system, Jordan would first learn to make a physically assisted exchange. For example, a highly preferred toy or edible would be placed on the table (preference assessment is described in Chapter Six). He would be assisted to exchange a picture the teacher placed in his hand for the object. In the second phase, Jordan would learn to give the picture spontaneously to obtain the object. To promote this, the teacher would lay the picture on the table. As Jordan began to give her the picture without prompting, the teacher would move away from the table and look away to require Jordan to be persistent in his response. In later phases, Jordan would learn to discriminate between more than one picture at a time, to use the pictures in a communication book, and to respond to questions like "What do you want?"

In selecting an AAC system, most planning teams will include a member who is a speech therapist and who is trained to conduct a comprehensive evaluation of these needs. Light, Roberts, Dimarco, and Greiner (1998) recommend that this evaluation include (1) a determination of any possible limitations in sensory-perceptual functioning, (2) assessment of receptive and expressive language skills, (3) consideration of the types of symbols the person understands, (4) evaluation of the person's ability to organize communicative information, (5) evaluation of the person's fine motor skills, and (6) determination of the environmental supports (e.g., people) that will encourage use of the augmentative device.

Situational Assessments and Ecological Inventories

Kaiser (1993) recommends a twofold approach to the process of selecting skills for functional communication training: (1) determining the student's current communication skills, and (2) conducting ecological inventories to identify what the student needs to learn for his or her current and future settings. Teachers may use a variety of methods to determine a student's current communication skills. Brady and Halle (1997)

FIGURE 11.1. A chart for recording considerations in selecting an AAC system.

Considerations in Selecting an Augmentative or Alternative Communication System

Student: Jordan Holdren   **Evaluator:** Ms. Karen Washington

System	Currently used by student?	If used, what symbols/ elements used?	How well does system match student's current motor, academic, and other skills?	How appropriate is system for student's social settings?
Symbols				
Nonsymbolic	Problem behaviors.	Screams, bangs head, runs.		
Gestures	Does not point or use other gestures.		Resists being prompted to point.	
Manual signs	Does not use.		Focus on gross motor signs that can be formed easily.	School peers may not understand these signs.
Objects	Does not use.		Can grasp and release objects.	Peers and teachers may understand object use; not always practical to carry objects.
Pictures	Does not use— tried with a communication board.		Because has good grasp and release, consider use of picture exchange vs. board.	Peers and teachers would probably understand pictures; more portable than objects.
Sight words	Does not read.		Difficult— introduce later with sight word training.	Understandable and may be more acceptable in academic settings.

(cont)

FIGURE 11.1. *(cont.)*

System	Currently used by student?	If used, what symbols/ elements used?	How well does system match student's current motor, academic, and other skills?	How appropriate is system for student's social settings?
Display				
One symbol at a time	Does not use symbols.		A good starting point.	Easy for others to understand, but limits "conversation."
Picture communi-cation board	Has a board—not currently used.	Current board has "eat," "toilet," "Hi," "rest."	Discontinue board for now.	Can introduce more options.
Wallet or notebook	Does not use.		A next step.	Can enhance conversation, offer more options.

identify the three primary methods teachers use. The first alternative is to interview people who are familiar with the student, such as the parents and other family members. The information to be obtained from this interview may include the forms the student currently uses to communicate, their communicative functions, and the contexts in which they are most likely to use these skills. In identifying Jordan's skills, his mother noted that most of his speech was an exact replication of something he had been told or heard on television (echolalia). His sister said that Jordan would sometimes talk when they played alone, but she had never heard him talk in public.

A second option to determine the student's current skills is to conduct direct observations. This can be achieved by keeping information on the student's responses during typical routines in the natural contexts. To organize this information, the evaluator may want to record information for each function of communication. Several experts have described the pragmatic functions of communicative utterances (Dyer & Luce, 1996; Kaiser, 1993; McLean & Snyder-McLean, 1988; Reichle & Sigafoos, 1994). Although the specific functions vary across these resources, most include behaviors that are instrumental (e.g., requesting) and social. Sometimes students will use words or symbols in noninteractive ways (e.g., to entertain themselves). The evaluator can consider which of these functions are currently in the student's repertoire by summarizing notes that are kept across several days. Figure 11.2 lists the primary functions of communication and illustrates how each was assessed for Jordan.

In addition to these pragmatic functions, Reichle and Sigafoos (1994) recommend giving consideration to how a student initiates, maintains, and terminates social interactions. For example, a child on the playground may initiate being pushed in a

FIGURE 11.2. Pragmatic functions of communication and an example of assessing these functions in the context of typical school routines.

Assessment of Pragmatic Functions of Communication in Context

Student: Jordan Holdren   **Evaluator:** Ms. Karen Washington

Pragmatic function	Context for assessment	Student's response	Possible skills for instruction
Instrumental functions			
Request help	Preferred food was in clear container that was difficult to open; toy rolled under shelf	• Handed food container to me. • Reached under shelf and screamed to try to get toy; banged head on wall when not successful.	• Teach to hand picture for food or toy. • Teach to reach toward lost toy without screaming.
Request food or object	Favorite toy was on high shelf but within eyesight; when gave out pretzels, "forgot" Jordan at first.	• Tried to jump to toy and screamed; when not successful, pinched me. • Stole peer's pretzels.	• Teach to hand picture for object. • Encourage persistence with picture if ignored at first. • Have him ask peers to share by moving hand toward their food.
Request attention	Gave student seatwork task and was "busy" at desk.	• Sat passively; did not attempt task. • After 10 minutes, ran from room.	• Teach to use buzzer or raised hand for attention, or to walk to teacher's side and tap shoulder.
Request action	Delayed lunch and appeared to get ready for an after-lunch activity.	• As soon as saw materials for after-lunch lesson, began to scream and bang head on desk.	• Teach to use a picture or object schedule (request activity with picture or object).
Protest	Began to remove highly preferred toy.	• Screamed and physically resisted.	• Teach to say "no" or shake head "no."
End activity	Worked with student on a long, tedious task.	• Shoved materials on floor and began to bang head on desk.	• Have him use color cue card for "break."
Social functions			
Get social attention ("show off")	Played musical game with lots of attention to peers.	• Passive; stood by himself and looked at hands.	• Teach game.

(cont)

FIGURE 11.2. *(cont.)*

Pragmatic function	Context for assessment	Student's response	Possible skills for instruction
Social Functions *(cont.)*			
Take turns	Gave student a preferred toy and asked to have a turn with it.	• Ignored requests; moved away when I tried to use it with him.	• Teach turn taking by passing object.
Greet	Said "Hello" to student in morning; had peers greet him.	• Ignored greetings; no eye contact.	• Teach to wave a greeting and look at person briefly.
Start conversation (e.g., by directing person's attention to object or asking a question)	Had student sit near peer with a picture or object related to an activity they did together.	• Ignored picture and peer; when peer began to converse, Jordan walked away.	• Teach to initiate conversation by sharing object of interest.
Clarify communication	When student communicated, said, "What? I don't understand."	• When Jordan moved toward his jacket at the end of the day, I said, "What?" He used echolalia: "Put your coat on! Put your coat on!"	• Jordan will try a second response, but this is sometimes problem behavior (screaming). Teach him to try a second and third form of communication (e.g., gesture, picture) if someone does not understand.
Acknowledge	Tried to get student to acknowledge communication about some highly preferred event.	• I told Jordan I would talk to "Mommy" today. I tried this several times. Each time Jordan paused from his play and looked up.	• Jordan acknowledged by pausing and looking in a new direction. Teach to look at speaker to acknowledge.
Request a social routine	Tried to get Jordan involved in a game of simple responses, and to see if he would ask to do it again.	• I made a game of trying to put Jordan's small hat on me and acting frustrated. He laughed and gave me the hat to do it again.	• Jordan will request a social routine! Expand this to other fun exchanges peers can use.

swing by taking the teacher's hand and walking to the swingset. The student may maintain the interaction by saying "more" or moving his or her body in swinging motion whenever the swing slows. When tired of swinging, the student may vocalize in protest or say "stop." In Jordan's case, he liked Ms. Washington's trying to put his hat on. He remembered this game the next day and took her the hat to initiate an interaction. After she went through her comic way of trying to put it on, she handed it to Jordan, but he gave it back (maintaining the interaction). To see whether Jordan would end this, the teacher continued to play the game for a while. Finally, Jordan became very excited. He began screaming, ran in circles, and then ran from the room. This was his way of ending one routine (the hat game) and starting a new one ("Catch me"). Because his running was potentially dangerous, Ms. Washington decided to teach Jordan to relax after several exchanges by taking deep breaths and then to decide whether to continue with the hat game or an alternative. He made this choice by picking up either the hat or a second toy, both of which were placed on a tray. Ms. Washington also taught him to accept her ending of the routine by using deep breaths and a picture for "finished."

In addition to interviewing significant others and using direct observation during a student's typical routines, the evaluator may also want to use "structured probes," in which many communication responses are sampled in a short period of time through activities that are used to prompt communication (Brady & Halle, 1997). These activities can also be used in teaching communication. Kaiser (1993) offers several recommendations for these activities, including (1) introducing interesting materials; (2) placing highly desired materials out of reach, to see whether a student will request them; (3) giving inadequate portions or "forgetting" to serve a student when giving out snacks, to see whether the student will protest or request; (4) offering choices; (5) creating situations where the student will need assistance; and (6) creating silly situations, to determine whether the student will comment or question them (e.g., wearing an inappropriate hat, as Ms. Washington did).

In addition to assessing the student's current skills in order to develop curricular ideas, the planning team may also want to use ecological inventories to determine skills the student may need in the future. The team may consider the communication needed to interact with peers on the bus, in the hall, and in the cafeteria. Specific skills may be needed during instructional interactions with general education teachers. The family may note skills that are needed at home and in community settings (e.g., a store or a recreational setting). The following is an example of an inventory that was completed for Jordan.

ECOLOGICAL INVENTORY TO IDENTIFY COMMUNICATION AND SOCIAL SKILLS

SETTING

School cafeteria.

COMMUNICATION OPPORTUNITIES

Students in line talk as they wait their turn. Cafeteria workers greet children and joke with them. Students ask for choice of entrée. Students talk with each other as they eat, and they sometimes share food. When peers are unkind, students will say "Stop it" or move to a new table (sometimes teachers intervene).

SKILLS NEEDED

Jordan cannot currently wait in line—needs waiting skills and means to communicate as he waits. He needs a greeting response. He will need a method to communicate food choice, since he may not speak or point (e.g., by nodding "yes" when shown "this one"). He needs a way to interact with peers during lunch (e.g., sharing pictures). He will need a protest for unkind peers when teacher is not nearby to intervene (e.g., moving away or walking to teacher).

Generalization

Generalization occurs when a student performs a skill in a new setting or with new people or materials. Generalization of communication skills is especially important, because of the varied contexts in which these skills are used. Two ways that this generalization can be encouraged are through the use of "general-case instruction" (Chadsey-Rusch & Halle, 1992) and "milieu teaching" (Kaiser, 1993). In general-case instruction, the teacher trains communication responses across a range of examples that are representative of what students encounter in their daily routines. For instance, to teach a student to generalize asking for help, training may be conducted with the special education teacher, the general education teacher, and a peer. The student may also be taught to generalize the help response across activities such as eating, dressing, doing seatwork, and using a locker. Sometimes the teacher will give the student novel situations to see whether the response has generalized. For example, after teaching the student to request help with the exemplars described, the teacher may then assess if the student can use the skill with the paraprofessional (new person) and while cleaning out a desk (new skill).

Milieu teaching involves prompting target communicative responses in the context of natural routines. These may include opportunities that the learner initiates, those that the teacher creates, or ones that occur naturally in the day's events. For instance, if the student is looking for a pencil, the teacher might prompt him or her to say, "I need a pencil." To assess generalization, the teacher can keep notes on the extent to which the student uses skills across people, situations, or materials, as shown here for Jordan.

ASSESSMENT OF GENERALIZATION OF COMMUNICATION SKILLS

Skill: Show green "break" card to end activity.

SETTINGS, PEOPLE, OR ACTIVITIES	*USED OR NOT USED?*
SETTINGS	
Special class	Used
Cafeteria	Not used—doesn't want to end lunch?
Gym	Not used—protested with screams

Speech	Trained and used
PEOPLE	
Mother	Used
Ms. Washington (teacher)	Trained and used
Mr. Newcomb (speech therapist)	Used
Barry Jacobs (peer)	Not used—pinched him
Kim McNealy (peer)	Not used—walked away
ACTIVITIES	
Sight word training	Not used—no protest
Picture training	Used to end lesson
Practice with money	Not used—screamed
Science class	Not used—ran out of room

ASSESSING SOCIAL SKILLS

In using a pragmatic approach to communication training, the teacher focuses on social and communicative skills concurrently. For students with moderate and severe disabilities, social skills training usually focuses on (1) enhancing communication, (2) promoting social inclusion, and/or (3) planning for problem behavior. Self-determination skills, as described in Chapter Six, are another are also a type of social skills. To encourage social inclusion, researchers have demonstrated several effective strategies. One of the most effective is to create opportunities for students to participate in general education (Kennedy, Shukla, & Fryxell, 1997). General education contexts offer numerous opportunities for students to see models of social behavior, practice new skills, and obtain feedback. (Methods to promote inclusion are described in Chapter Twelve.)

To benefit from these opportunities, some students with moderate and severe disabilities will need instructional support. Peer support strategies are especially appealing, because they facilitate social participation with students who are nondisabled as students learn new social skills. Peers may provide systematic instruction, curricular adaptations, social interaction, and support for problem behavior (Shukla, Kennedy, & Cushing, 1999).

"Social skills" can be broadly defined as any responses that are interactive with another person. Many of the personal care, home living, community, and employment skills described in other chapters of this book are interactive. Some social skills are more specifically related to influencing others and developing friendships; these skills are the focus of this section of this chapter. Haring and Ryndak (1994) recommend selecting specific social skills for instruction by assessing the student and the supports available in the environment. These authors note that four primary social interaction skills have been identified in the social skills literature: social initiation, social responsiveness to others, turn taking, and duration of social interaction.

Social Initiation

"Social initiation" is any response that begins an interaction with another person. Students who do not use speech may rely on alternatives for this initiation. Hunt, Alwell, and Goetz (1988) taught students with severe disabilities to use photo albums with pictures of activities, pets, and family members to initiate interactions with peers who were nondisabled. Similarly, Storey and Provost (1996) taught workers with severe disabilities to use communication books with pictures of hobbies, family members, sports, pets, shopping, foods, vacation, and other items to share interests with coworkers. Gaylord-Ross, Haring, Breen, and Pitts-Conway (1984) taught students with autism to share gum or a cassette tape player. Other forms of nonverbal initiation may include pointing to an object of interest, waving or stating a greeting, or sitting near a peer. To encourage verbal initiations, Krantz and McClannahan (1998) taught young boys with autism to interact by using specific scripts. The boys learned to approach a peer with a toy and say "Look" (to share an object of interest) or "Watch me" (while playing with the toy). Once these scripts were mastered and faded, the boys generalized their skills to unscripted interactions and new activities.

Social Responsiveness

A second social skill is responding to the initiations of others. If students are unresponsive, peers may lose interest in initiating contact with them. Nonverbal skills students may learn to be socially responsive include making eye contact, waving, nodding, shaking hands, and smiling. Students who are verbal may also rehearse specific scripts to use in a social context. These responses may be based on current lingo for the student's age and social setting (e.g., "What's up?")

Turn Taking

Turn taking is assessed by counting the number of turns that occur in an interaction. Turn taking is what keeps an interaction going after the initial greeting and response. Students who are nonverbal may take turns by passing objects, playing a game, or responding to a peer's remarks with a nod or shake of the head. Students who are verbal may need to practice conversational turn taking.

Duration of Social Interaction

Students can also work on increasing the amount of time they spend interacting with a peer. An evaluator may time the duration of an interaction with a stopwatch to determine whether interactions increase over time. To increase the duration of interactions, the teacher may use such strategies as interactive games, cooperative learning, or peer tutoring. Shukla et al. (1999) had peers in a middle school context adapt materials and requirements in a general education class. These strategies not only increased the engagement of the students with severe disabilities in the lesson, but also increased the duration of their social interaction with peers.

Environmental Supports

Assessment of students' social skills should also include consideration of the environmental supports for these skills. The evaluator may want to keep a record of the number of opportunities students have to be with friends. This may include recording data on the names of participants, the types of activities, the relationship of the participants to each other, and the level of support within the environment (Kennedy, Horner, & Newton, 1989). Teachers may also want to consider friendship patterns in a classroom. To identify friendships in an elementary class in which a student with moderate or severe disabilities is included, a teacher may ask peers to answer questions such as (1) "Whom do you like to play with?" (2) "Whom would you like to work with on a class project?" and (3) "Whom would you invite to a birthday party?" From these replies, the teacher can identify peer groups. Encouraging the student's interaction with one student in a large peer group may create opportunities for multiple friendships. These nominations can also help the teacher determine whether the student with severe disabilities is currently included in a peer group.

PLANNING FOR PROBLEM BEHAVIOR

Planning teams may focus on communication and social skills to encourage inclusion, to promote self-determination, or to help students overcome their "learned helplessness." In other cases, like Jordan's, the initial focus of planning is problem behavior. Considerations of communication and social skills develop from hypotheses that are formed about why the student engages in this behavior. This section briefly reviews a format teams can use for this planning, with a focus on communication training. For more information, the reader is encouraged to consult the comprehensive assessment descriptions provided by Durand (1990), Carr et al. (1994), Demchak and Bossert (1996), or O'Neill, Horner, Albin, Storey, and Sprague (1990). Most approaches to planning for problem behavior begin with a functional assessment.

Functional Assessment

A "functional assessment" is a process used to determine how problem behavior functions in the student's environment. A successful functional assessment will provide (1) an operational definition of the behavior or class of behaviors, (2) identification of variables that will predict when the behavior will occur, (3) hypotheses about the consequences that are maintaining the behavior, and (4) verification of the predictors and consequences (Horner, O'Neill, & Flannery, 1993). Similarly, Carr et al. (1994) recommend that functional assessment should be a three-step process of describing, categorizing, and verifying information.

Describing the Behavior

The first step in conducting a functional assessment is to describe the behavior in observable, measurable terms. Sometimes the problem behavior is not one response, but a set of behaviors. When this occurs, definitions are developed for each behavior in the set. In the beginning Jordan's team needed to clarify what they meant by "problem behavior." For example, one team member said that Jordan was "noncompliant." As the team defined Jordan's exact responses, they decided that "pushing" was a better term, since this described exactly what he did. Also, another team member questioned the term "tantrums," and suggested that "screaming" and "head banging" were more descriptive of what Jordan actually did. Here is how the team eventually defined Jordan's set of problem behaviors.

DEFINITIONS OF JORDAN'S PROBLEM BEHAVIORS

Head banging: Hitting the head against the table, wall, or other surface one or more times.

Running: Fast movement that results in leaving the classroom, the building, or other supervised area (e.g., the playground).

Pinching: Grasping the skin of another person.

Screaming: Vocalizing in a loud high-pitched sound; may be only a sound or may also include words; may include crying.

Pushing: Pushing materials or people away from his immediate area; may include throwing materials out of his area or giving strong shoves to people.

Sometimes professionals recommend evaluating the seriousness of the behavior at this stage (Meyer & Evans, 1989). Is the behavior dangerous, disruptive, or simply different? When behaviors are dangerous and seriously disruptive, the team members may need to develop a crisis management plan before they continue their planning efforts. Carr et al. (1994) recommend that this crisis management follow five procedures:

1. When feasible, *ignore* the behavior problem.
2. *Protect* the individual and others from any physical harm.
3. *Restrain* the individual momentarily during episodes of problem behavior.
4. *Remove* anyone who is in the vicinity who is in danger because of the behavior.
5. Use *cues* that evoke nonproblem behavior (e.g., "Show me your pictures").

Crisis management is a *temporary* strategy to prevent physical harm while a team develops a more effective strategy to prevent the behavior. In Jordan's case, the team members could not ignore his head banging, because he could hurt himself. For crisis management, they decided that his head should be momentarily restrained to get him to stop banging. His running was also dangerous, and so the team decided that the teacher or another professional would momentarily restrain him by blocking the door and holding his arm. For his pinching, professionals would move themselves or other students out of his reach when he moved toward their arms (his most likely pinching area). Although Jordan's screaming was disruptive, it was not dangerous, so the team members decided that this behavior should be ignored. They also decided that his pushing materials and people should be ignored for now, but that other students would be moved so as not to get hurt. In addition, Jordan would be told to sit in a different seat as a cue to engage in a nonproblem behavior.

Describing the Environmental Variables

Once the problem behavior is defined and plans are in place for crisis management, the team can begin to describe the environmental variables that may predict or maintain the behavior. This is often done through the use of an "ABC analysis." An ABC analysis is a description of the antecedent (A) of the behavior (B) and the consequence (C) that follows it. The teacher and other members of the team working with the student can make notes about the behavior in this format. Carr et al. (1994) recommend describing the "A" or antecedent as the "interpersonal context" in which the behavior occurs. The "C" or consequence is the "social reaction" to it. An ABC analysis using this format might look like the example given below for Jordan. Carr et al. (1994) recommend keeping each occurrence of behavior on a separate index card, so that it will be possible to categorize them later in forming hypotheses.

ABC ANALYSIS OF PROBLEM BEHAVIOR

Student: Jordan Holdren   Date: September 9, 20—

A. Antecedent: (interpersonal context)	B. Problem Behavior	C. Consequence (social reaction)
	8:45—Morning arrival	
I was helping another student put his bag away. Jordan got his sweatshirt tangled on his arms as he tried to take it off.	Jordan screamed and banged his head against the wall.	I went to Jordan, held his head for a moment, and then removed his sweatshirt. I said, "You need help."
	10:15—Reading lesson	
I was teaching Jordan and another student sight words on flash cards in a massed-trial format.	Jordan pulled his hand away when I tried to get him to point to the correct card. He then pushed the cards off the table and pinched his classmate.	The classmate began to cry. I comforted the classmate and then told Jordan to sit at his desk. He went and sat down, but began screaming. The screaming was so loud I could not continue teaching, but I continued to ignore him. It lasted for over 15 minutes.
	12:00—Lunch	
We arrived in the cafeteria. We got there a bit late and there was a line. I walked to the line with the students and stood near Jordan.	Jordan began to scream. He dropped to the floor and began to bang his head on the floor.	I held his head briefly and then told him to sit at a table for lunch. I sat with him while a cafeteria worker brought his tray.

<u>2:00—Classroom</u>

There was some classroom confusion when an observer arrived. Students began to vocalize and move around as I tried to answer the observer's questions.	Jordan began to bang his head on his desk.	I went to Jordan and held his head briefly.
The observer began to talk with Jordan after I held his head.	Jordan gave the observer a hard shove and began to bang his head again.	I asked if the observer was OK. Then I held Jordan's head again and asked the observer to move to the other side of the room.

Two alternatives to ongoing anecdotal notes are (1) to use team brainstorming about the events that surround the occurrence of the behavior, and (2) to chart the occurrence of the behavior on a scatterplot. Bambara and Knoster (1998) have illustrated how team brainstorming can lead to developing global as well as specific hypotheses about the behavior. The team brainstorming often focuses on the quality-of-life issues that may be contributing to the problem behavior.

Sometimes the team may choose to use a scatterplot analysis (Touchette, MacDonald, & Langer, 1985). In this method, a teacher or other professional records whether or not each behavior occurs during each period of the day. In the O'Neill et al. (1990) approach, this scatterplot also categorizes the behavior by the setting events (e.g., difficult task, transition, interruption). These data can help the team see patterns that may relate to environmental variables. For example, if Jordan continued to engage in problem behaviors during reading, this might indicate the need for some specific planning in this curricular area.

Forming Hypotheses about the Behavior

After notes are taken on the behavior for several days, the team is ready to categorize the behavior according to its function. Authors vary in how they classify the functions of behavior (Carr et al., 1994; Durand, 1990; O'Neill et al., 1990), but all emphasize that most problem behavior has a communicative function. Donnellan, Mirenda, Mesaros, and Fassbender (1984) identify these interactive functions of behavior as (1) requests, (2) negations, (3) declarations/comments, and (4) declarations of feelings. In contrast, some behavior may not be communicative. Donnellan et al. (1984) note four non-interactive functions of behavior: (1) self-regulation, (2) rehearsal, (3) habit, and (4) relaxation/tension release. Table 11.1 is a guide to help teachers and others consider the function of the problem behavior.

To determine the function of behavior, the members of the planning team review their ABC analyses to see how they fit the categories shown in Table 11.2. As noted above, Carr et al. (1994) recommends keeping each ABC entry on a separate index card so that they can be grouped together to find commonalties. For each ABC entry, the teacher or other evaluator may want to write a hypothesis for that occurrence. These can be written by asking the question "What did the person want to have hap-

TABLE 11.2. Functional Assessment: A Guide for Identifying the Function of Behavior

1. Is the behavior **nonsocial**?

   Example: Student engages in behavior when no one is nearby. People in the student's environment do not respond to the behavior in any way.
   Possible function: Relaxation/tension release; stimulation when bored; alleviation of medical problem/pain; involuntary (e.g., tic).
   Communication: "I'm tense," "I hurt," "I'm bored."

2. Is the behavior a form of **obtaining preferences?**

   Example: Student gets objects, activities, and food with this behavior either from people or by bypassing people (e.g., grabbing).
   Possible function: Requesting or choice making when student does not have the skills to get preferred items in other ways or when preferences are denied.
   Communication: "I want this."

3. Is the behavior a method to gain **social attention?**

   Example: Student behavior gets attention (even if scolding or reprimands), affection, playful interactions, or affirmation.
   Possible function: Greeting; humor; showing off; initiating or maintain social interaction.
   Communication: "Look at me!", "Let's have fun together!"

4. Is the behavior used to **refuse what is disliked or no longer appealing?**

   Example: Student behavior ends a lesson, avoids a task, avoids a person, or shortens time spent on task.
   Possible function: Refusal; termination of activity or of interaction; protest.
   Communication: "No!", "I need a break," "Please don't bother me," "I don't like this."

5. Is the behavior used to **express feelings?**

   Example: Behavior suggests that student is anticipating a highly preferred event, confused about what comes next, frustrated by problem or task, afraid of situation, or excited and happy.
   Possible function: Commenting or complaining.
   Communication: "I'm excited," "I'm afraid," "I'm confused," "I'm frustrated."

6. Is the behavior used to **get help?**

   Example: Student's behavior causes others to find a missing item, to get needed supplies, or to complete a task.
   Possible function: Getting help.
   Communication: "Help me."

pen by engaging in this behavior?" (Carr et al., 1994). Sometimes it helps to have two people ask this question separately and then compare notes to see whether there is consensus on the hypothesis. From these individual hypotheses, some overall hypotheses can be generated to use in developing behavioral support. Bambara and Knoster (1998) recommend writing two types of summary hypotheses—specific and global. The specific hypotheses summarize the information from the ABC analyses. These help the team understand what is happening in the immediate context when the behavior occurs. In contrast, global hypotheses guide the team to consider lifestyle issues that may be contributing further to the problem behavior. These may include such issues as an inappropriate or restrictive school placement, poorly developed curricular goals, inadequate instruction, a lack of choice-making opportunities, or few social supports.

Ms. Washington began developing hypotheses for Jordan's behavior by writing a hypothesis for each of her ABC entries. She asked the school psychologist to review these entries and to develop hypotheses as well. As she reviewed her own and the psychologist's notes, Ms. Washington began to see patterns in Jordan's behavior. From these patterns, she wrote the following specific summary hypotheses.

> ### HYPOTHESES ABOUT THE FUNCTIONS OF JORDAN'S BEHAVIOR
>
> 1. When Jordan is unable to solve a problem such as a tangled sweatshirt, he screams and bangs his head to express his frustration and to get help.
> 2. When Jordan wants an activity to end, he will push materials or people, pinch, and/or scream to escape the situation.
> 3. When Jordan wants to shorten the time he has to wait or stand, he will drop to the floor and bang his head.
> 4. When Jordan is confused about what comes next or what is expected of him, he will bang his head or push people and materials away.

In addition to these specific hypotheses, the team members reviewed two global summary hypotheses: (1) Jordan used problem behavior because he had limited alternatives to communicate; and (2) he had been in a restrictive setting during his prior school year, in which there were few social opportunities.

Verifying the Hypotheses

In a functional assessment, after describing the behavior and categorizing it to form hypotheses, the team collects information to verify these hypotheses. In research, and in some applied settings, the evaluator will collect data to test these hypotheses, either by creating simulations of the problem contexts or by using naturally occurring events. For example, if the hypothesis is that frustrating situations set the occasion for the behavior, the evaluator may test this assumption by creating minor frustrations (e.g., giving the student a difficult-to-open food container). Testing the hypothesis about problem behavior through systematic data collection is called a "functional analysis" and can either be experimental (using contrived conditions) or naturalistic (Horner et al., 1993). In many applied settings, however, the team members may not have the time or resources to conduct a functional analysis. Instead, they will verify their hypotheses by designing positive behavioral support related to their assumptions and collecting ongoing data to determine whether there is a decrease in the problem behavior and an increase in the use of alternatives.

Whether the team is using a functional analysis or verifying hypotheses through evaluation of a behavioral intervention, not all hypotheses will be verified. Sometimes the team needs to review the ABC analyses again and form new hypotheses. At other times, team members may need to go beyond the ABC analyses to consider "setting events" (Carr et al., 1994; Horner et al., 1993). Setting events are situations that occur at some time preceding the behavior and that influence how the student responds to later events. Because these events occur at some earlier point in time, they will not usually be reflected in an ABC analysis. They can, however, be identified by keeping notes and brainstorming about what else has happened during the student's day. Setting events can be physiological, physical, or social. An example of a physiological setting event is an illness like a headache. When Jordan had a headache, he might push away tasks that he would perform on other days. Physical events are things like classroom noise, temperature, and visitors. In Jordan's ABC analyses, he began to bang his head one day when students in his classroom became noisy and an observer was present (see above). On another day when the teacher was distracted, but there was no noise or observer, Jordan sat quietly. A social setting event may be an earlier interpersonal conflict. On a day when Jordan had a substitute bus driver who was loud and demanding, Jordan began screaming as soon as the teacher asked him to take off his coat. When team members cannot find consistency in their ABC entries, or when some entries are atypical, they may want to begin collecting information on the student's entire day to look for the influence of setting events.

Positive Behavioral Support

A functional assessment is key to successful behavior change. In earlier eliminative approaches to problem behavior, interventionists would focus on trying to reduce behaviors without the benefit of knowing their functions. Meyer and Evans (1989) note that such strategies are often ineffective and sometimes may result in a student's missing out on instruction and other opportunities until the problem behavior is controlled. In contrast, positive behavioral support is assessment-based and links interventions to hypotheses about the functions of behavior. It is also proactive, involving the teaching of alternative skills. Moreover, positive behavioral support honors the dignity and preferences of the individual (Bambara & Knoster, 1998).

Carr et al. (1994) recommend five strategies for positive behavioral support: (1) building rapport, (2) conducting functional communication training, (3) building tolerance for delay of reinforcement, (4) embedding demands, and (5) offering choices. Carr et al. (1999) demonstrated the effectiveness of using a combination of these five strategies in designing comprehensive support for three individuals with mental retardation and other disabilities (cerebral palsy, autism). The students' problem behaviors included tantrums, property destruction, aggression, and self-injurious behavior. After an assessment phase in which the team described, categorized, and verified the function of the participants' behavior, they developed a five-component intervention package for each person. Parents, teachers, job coaches, and group home staff found this five-component intervention to be efficient and usable in natural contexts. They also noted both socially valid and long-term changes in problem behavior (1½ to 2½ years later).

Building Rapport

Building rapport is a precursor to communication training. In this approach, the teacher becomes associated with highly preferred items and activities, and encourages simple communication. Carr et al. (1994) describe building rapport as follows:

> The idea is for you and the individual displaying behavior problems to interact with one another within a context of sharing entertaining and rewarding activities and generally enjoying each other's company. . . . Ultimately, rapport building is intended to establish a friendship between you and the person with disabilities, a friendship that can provide a basis for teaching that person that there are other ways besides problem behavior for achieving important goals. (p. 114)

To build rapport, the teacher makes a list of foods, games, topics of conversations, and activities that the person prefers. These are then offered "noncontingently"; that is, the person does not have to work for them or ask for them. Rapport has been achieved when the person initiates interactions with, and/or stays in close proximity to, the teacher. Although some of these items may later be used in communication training, the teacher (and others) will continue to offer some activities and items noncontingently to maintain rapport and enhance the student's quality of life.

Conducting Functional Communication Training

Once rapport is established, the teacher has created an environment conducive to functional communication training. Functional communication training has received broad empirical support as an effective intervention for problem behavior (e.g., Horner et al., 1993; Carr et al., 1994). In functional communication training, the student learns to use a symbolic or nonsymbolic communicative response as an alternative to the problem behavior (Carr & Durand, 1985). These alternatives are sometimes called "replacement behaviors" (Demchak & Bossert, 1996). Whenever possible, these alternatives achieve the same function as the problem behavior, but more effectively or efficiently. Belfiore, Browder, and Lin (1993) taught a man with limited speech to say "no" as an alternative to self-injurious behavior that had functioned to escape nonpreferred situations. When the man lifted his arm to bite it, the teacher would block the self-injury and prompt him, "Tell me 'no'!" When the man said "no," the teacher terminated the activity immediately. Once the man mastered saying "no," he no longer engaged in arm biting. Dunlap and Fox (1999) designed comprehensive support plans for young children with autism that included long-term supports, prevention strategies, replacement skills, and consequences. Some of the replacement skills they taught included (1) using nonverbal signals to request social interaction, as opposed to wandering or hyperventilating; (2) requesting "help," saying "want," stating "no," or making a choice instead of engaging in prolonged tantrums; (3) requesting an activity choice by using a visual schedule and stating "no" instead of head banging and screaming; and (4) asking "up" (for a hug) instead of biting, pushing, and dumping shelves.

Planning functional communication training is the same as using a pragmatic approach to communication training, as described earlier in this chapter. The only difference is that in addition to overall enhancement of communication skills, specific replacement skills are chosen based on the function of the problem behavior. Sometimes the alternative skills chosen will not be communication per se. Students may learn alternatives such as sitting quietly, waiting, or self-management of their routines. Here are the replacement skills that the team selected for Jordan.

REPLACEMENT SKILLS FOR JORDAN

FUNCTIONAL COMMUNICATION TRAINING

1. Communicate "help." Jordan will use a red 3 x 5 index card with the word "help" and a picture of a child receiving help from a teacher. When Jordan encounters a problem and begins to vocalize (a precursor to screaming and head banging), Ms. Washington will prompt him to give her the red card. She will then give him the assistance he

wants. After Jordan gives her the card as soon as she approaches him, Ms. Washington will begin to stay a small distance from him, so that he will initiate seeking help by moving to her and handing her the card.

   2. Communicate "I need a break." Jordan will use a green card with the word "break" and a picture of a child resting. When Jordan begins to resist an activity by moving to push the materials or Ms. Washington, she will prompt him to give her his green "break" card. When he does, he will be given time to himself (no demands). Once Jordan masters giving the teacher the green card without prompting, she will introduce a delay in granting the break to encourage longer participation in lessons. She will hold her hand up and say, "Wait a few minutes for break." At first, the wait will be only a few seconds. Over time, the wait signal will be increased to 5 minutes.

OTHER ALTERNATIVE SKILLS

   1. Waiting skill. When Jordan has to wait a turn in a group activity, or while getting lunch, he will hold a small beanbag. This will be his signal to stand or sit quietly until the teacher or peer removes the beanbag.

   2. Self-management. Prior to lunch, Jordan will review a picture story about what to do at lunch. Each page will show Jordan doing a step of the lunch routine successfully. Jordan and his teacher will read this story together each day before lunch.

Building Tolerance for Delay of Reinforcement and Embedding Demands

In the early stages of functional communication training, the student may not spend much time in instruction. For the use of alternatives to be effective, the reinforcement for their use must be frequent and powerful. If a student communicates "I want a break," the end to the activity should be as quick as it would be if the student threw the materials. If a student says, "I want to talk," the teacher will shift attention to the student as quickly as he or she once did for hitting a peer.

   This early stage of functional communication training is important to establish the use of these alternative responses, but students also need to be encouraged to participate in instruction. One way to achieve this is to teach students to tolerate a delay of reinforcement. In Jordan's example, after he mastered use of the "break" card, the teacher would introduce a delay in giving the break. She would then gradually increase the length of time until the break was granted. Students who seek teacher attention by raising their hand or saying, "I want to talk" can also learn to wait for this response. If a student begins to engage in the problem behavior again, the delay interval may be too long. The teacher should shorten the delay and increase it more gradually (e.g., by intervals of a few seconds). Sometimes the student may request a preferred activity or object. In the beginning, the teacher should reinforce this immediately, if possible. Over time, the activity or object may be given after a delay or after another activity takes place. For example, the teacher may say, "You can play the video game after you finish this lesson."

   Teachers can also encourage participation in learning through "embedding." Embedding is used when students refuse to participate in a task that is important to their education and overall quality of life. Embedding is also called "interspersal training" and "behavioral momentum," and has been found to be effective in reducing problem behavior (Dunlap & Koegel, 1980; Mace et al., 1988). In this procedure, stimuli that set the occasion for problem behavior (e.g., riding the bus, going into the restroom, or taking medication) are paired with stimuli that set the occasion for appropriate behavior (e.g., music, friendly conversation, or a favorite toy). If Jordan consistently refused to participate in his reading lessons, Ms. Washington might embed presentation of the reading materials with presentation of a preferred toy (e.g., a truck). She would escort Jordan to the lesson area, but begin by letting him play with the toy. Then she would ask Jordan to do a few trials of reading the words before playing with the toy again. She would continue to intersperse reading with toy play until the lesson was complete.

Carr et al. (1999) effectively used music to encourage a boy to participate in household chores. His mother offered him three choices of chores. When he refused to select one, his mother played his favorite music tape. After 2 minutes, she turned the music off. When he asked to hear it again, his mother said, "Sure, you can have more music, but let's do some work." Then she represented the three options, and the boy chose a chore to do. Sometimes teachers can encourage participation by making the materials or activities of a lesson more appealing. They may use a game format, brightly colored materials, computer software, or other options to entice students to engage in the lesson.

Providing Choices

Providing choices to a student can be another effective way to reduce problem behavior (Dyer, Dunlap, & Winterling, 1990). These choices can be embedded in the student's daily routines. Offering choices during instruction may also promote student participation. The student may choose between materials to use, places to sit, and tasks to do first. Chapter Six provides more information on how to increase choice-making opportunities.

Other Options

Many other options exist for positive behavioral support. These options can be characterized as "antecedent strategies," "consequence strategies," and "lifestyle changes." Building rapport, functional communication training, embedding, increasing tolerance for a delay in reinforcement, and offering choices are all antecedent strategies. Antecedent strategies are those that are introduced *before* the behavior occurs, with the intent of preventing the problem. In their research, Dunlap and Fox (1999) used several other antecedent strategies, which they called "prevention strategies." Some of these included increasing choices, increasing leisure and social opportunities, providing transition warnings, simplifying language when making requests, pairing verbal requests with gestures or visual aids, and using an activity schedule. Bambara and Knoster (1998) recommend teaching coping and tolerance skills, such as controlling anger, relaxation, and persisting during difficult tasks.

Consequence strategies can also be used to prevent problem behavior by reinforcing use of alternative skills or the absence of the problem behavior. In behavioral terms, these strategies are called "differential reinforcement of incompatible (or alternative) behavior" (DRI) or "differential reinforcement of other behavior" (DRO). In Jordan's case, the teacher used a token economy for participating in lessons without engaging in problem behavior. At the end of each lesson in which none of the defined problem behaviors occurred, Jordan received a ticket (like those used at carnivals for rides and prizes). At the end of each day, he had a menu of options he could purchase, depending on the number of tickets he had earned. Teachers may also use consequences in a preventive manner by responding to the earliest forms of the problem behavior and prompting the alternative response. When Jordan moved his hands toward materials to shove them, his teacher quickly guided his hands to show her the "break" card instead. Sometimes crisis management will still be needed if the problem behavior occurs. Crisis management is also a consequence strategy.

Students can also learn to self-manage these behavioral strategies, as described in Chapter Six. Jordan began using self-instruction to manage his behavior at lunch. He used a form of a "social story," in which he read what would happen when he went to lunch. Social stories have been shown through research to be an effective strategy to teach social skills (Swaggert, Gagnon, Bock, & Earles, 1996). Because Jordan's reading skills were limited, his story was a photo album showing him doing each step of the lunch routine. His teacher taught him to read the phrases that go with each picture—for example, "I wait. I hold my beanie bear" (his favorite beanbag toy). Jordan might also learn to self-manage his token reinforcement program by taking a token from a basket and placing it in a bin at his desk after each lesson that he did well.

Finally, Bambara and Knoster (1999) encourage planning teams to consider the lifestyle changes that may encourage prosocial behavior. Lifestyle enhancement will rarely be as systematic as a functional assessment. Instead, teams need to use the person-centered planning strategies described in Chapter Two. Some of the lifestyle changes Bambara and Knoster (1999) give as examples are helping a student develop friendships, incorporating choices across daily routines, developing an action plan to move a student to a more inclusive setting, sampling prospective jobs, and helping the student participate in after-school activities. For Jordan, moving to a class in a public school created new options for him. His team began to brainstorm ways to include him in general education classes as well, based on his preferences. They decided to begin with physical education, since Jordan's running was his only form of exercise. The team discovered that Jordan enjoyed any type of game or activity that involved fast movement like running or jumping. A future goal was to get Jordan involved in a community sport like soccer.

SUMMARY

Communication and social skills are top priorities for many students with moderate and severe disabilities. In recent years, professionals have recognized the importance of focusing on the "pragmatics" (also known as the "functional use") of communication. Although the form and content of communication are also important, these are typically enhanced in the context of functional use. Some students use speech to communicate; others achieve symbolic communication through the use of AAC systems. These may include pictures, manual signing, communication boards, and other options. Other students do not use symbols, but rely on gestures or other nonsymbolic communication responses. What is most important to remember is that all students do communicate!

If students' communicative attempts have not been successful, they may develop "learned helplessness." Other students may rely on problem behaviors when they lack alternative skills. Most problem behaviors have communicative intent and can be eliminated by teaching students replacement skills through functional communication training. Before these replacement skills can be selected, a planning team will need to conduct a functional assessment. This functional assessment involves describing the behavior and the events that precede and follow it in the social context. Recording the antecedent, behavior, and consequences of behavior is known as an ABC analysis. From this analysis, the team can develop hypotheses about the function of the behavior and plan positive behavioral supports. Positive behavioral support relies primarily on antecedent strategies to prevent the occurrence of the problem behavior. These antecedent strategies include building rapport, functional communication training, encouraging delay of reinforcement, embedding, offering choices, and providing other environmental supports (e.g., an activity schedule). The plan may also include consequence strategies, such as reinforcing the student for the absence of the behavior or for using alternative skills. Teams may need to create a crisis management plan as a consequence when the problem behavior cannot be prevented. Finally, positive behavioral support can also involve lifestyle planning, such as encouraging choices, new opportunities, and friendships. By using positive behavioral support, a team helps the student gain appropriate social skills that will have lifelong benefits.

REFERENCES

Bambara, L. M., & Knoster, T. (1998). *Designing positive behavior support (Innovations, No. 13).* Washington, DC: American Association on Mental Retardation.

Bates, E. (1979). *The emergence of symbols: Cognition and communication in infancy.* New York: Academic Press.

Belfiore, P. J., Browder, D. M., & Lin, C. H. (1993). Using descriptive and experimental analyses in the treatment of self-injurious behavior. *Education and Training in Mental Retardation, 28,* 57–65.

Bondy, A. S., & Frost, L. A. (1994). The Picture Exchange Communication System. *Focus on Autistic Behavior, 9,* 1–19.

Brady, N. C., & Halle, J. W. (1997). Functional analysis of communicative behaviors. *Focus on Autism and Other Developmental Disabilities, 12,* 95–104.

Carr, E. G., & Durand, V. M. (1985). Reducing problem behavior through functional communication training. *Journal of Applied Behavior Analysis, 18,* 111–126.

Carr, E. G., Levin, L., McConnachie, G., Carlson, J. E., Kemp, D. C., & Smith, C. E. (1994). *Communication-based intervention for problem behavior.* Baltimore: Paul H. Brookes.

Carr, E. G., Levin, L., McConnachie, G., Carlson, J. E., Kemp, D. C., Smith, C. E., & McLaughlin, D. M. (1999). Comprehensive multisituational intervention for problem behavior in the community: Long-term maintenance and social validation. *Journal of Positive Behavioral Intervention, 1,* 5–24.

Chadsey-Rusch, J., & Halle, J. (1992). The application of general case instruction to the requesting repertoires of learners with severe disabilities. *Journal of the Association for Persons with Severe Handicaps, 17,* 121–132.

Clifft, M. A. (1986). Writing about psychiatric patients: Guidelines for disguising case material. *Bulletin of the Menninger Clinic, 50,* 511–524.

Demchak, M., & Bossert, K. W. (1996). *Assessing problem behavior (Innovations No. 4).* Washington, DC: American Association on Mental Retardation.

Donnellan, A. M., Mirenda, P. L., Mesaros, R. A., & Fassbender, L. L. (1984). Analyzing the communicative functions of aberrant behavior. *Journal of the Association for Persons with Severe Handicaps, 9,* 201–212.

Dunlap, G., & Koegel, R. L. (1980). Motivating autistic children through stimulus variation. *Journal of Applied Behavior Analysis, 13,* 619–627.

Dunlap, G., & Fox, L. (1999). A demonstration of behavioral support for young children with autism. *Journal of Positive Behavioral Interventions, 1,* 77–87.

Durand, V. M. (1990). *Severe behavior problems: A functional communication training approach.* New York: Guilford Press.

Dyer, K., Dunlap, G., & Winterling, V. (1990). Effects of choice making on the serious problem behaviors of students with severe handicaps. *Journal of Applied Behavior Analysis, 23,* 515–524.

Dyer, K., & Luce, S. C. (1996). *Teaching practical communication skills (Innovations No. 7).* Washington, DC: American Association on Mental Retardation.

Gaylord-Ross, R. J., Haring, T. G., Breen, C., & Pitts-Conway, V. (1984). The training and generalization of social interaction skills with autistic youth. *Journal of Applied Behavior Analysis, 17,* 229–247.

Goetz, L., & Hunt, P. (1994). Augmentative and alternative communication. In E. C. Cipani & F. Spooner (Eds.), *Curricular and instructional approaches for persons with severe disabilities* (pp. 263–288). Boston: Allyn & Bacon.

Guess, D., Benson, H., & Siegel-Causey, E. (1985). Concepts and issues related to choice making and autonomy among persons with severe disabilities. *Journal of the Association for Persons with Severe Handicaps, 10,* 79–86.

Haring, T. G., & Ryndak, D. (1994). Strategies and instructional procedures to promote social interactions and relationships. In E. C. Cipani & F. Spooner (Eds.), *Curricular and instructional approaches for persons with severe disabilities* (pp. 289–321). Boston: Allyn & Bacon.

Horner, R. H., O'Neill, R. E., & Flannery, K. B. (1993). Effective behavior support plans. In M. E. Snell (Ed.), *Instruction of students with severe disabilities* (pp. 184–214).New York: Macmillan/Merrill.

Hunt, P., Alwell, M., & Goetz, L. (1988). Acquisition of conversation skills and the reduction of inappropriate social interaction behaviors. *Journal of the Association for Persons with Severe Handicaps, 12,* 20–27.

Kaiser, A. P. (1993). Functional language. In M. E. Snell (Ed.), *Instruction of students with severe disabilities* (pp. 347–379). New York: Macmillan/Merrill.

Kennedy, C. H., Horner, R. H., & newton, J. S. (1989). Social contacts of adults with severe disabilities living in the community: A descriptive analysis of relationship patterns. *Journal of the Association for Persons with Severe Handicaps, 14,* 190–196.

Kennedy, C. H., Shukla, S., & Fryxell, D. (1997). Comparing the effects of educational placement on the social relationships of intermediate school students with severe disabilities. *Exceptional Children, 64,* 31–47.

Krantz, P. J., & McClannahan, L. E. (1998). Social interaction skills for children with autism: A script-fading procedure for beginning readers. *Journal of Applied Behavior Analysis, 31,* 191–202.

Light, J., Roberts, B., Dimarco, R., & Greiner, N. (1998). Augmentative and alternative communication to support receptive and expressive communication for people with autism. *Journal of Communication Disorders, 31,* 153–180.

Lloyd, L. (1985). Comments on terminology. *Augmentative and Alternative Communication, 1,* 95–97.

Mace, F. C., Hock, M. L., Lalli, J. S., West, B. J., Belfiore, P., Pinter, E., & Brown, D. K. (1988). Behavioral momentum in the treatment of noncompliance. *Journal of Applied Behavior Analysis, 21,* 123–141.

McLean, J., & Snyder-McLean, L. (1988). Application of pragmatics to severely mentally retarded children and youth. In R. Schiefelbusch & L. Lloyd (Eds.), *Language perspectives: Acquisition retardation and intervention* (pp. 255–288). Austin, TX: Pro-Ed.

Meyer, L. H., & Evans, I. M. (1989). *Nonaversive intervention for behavior problems: A manual for home and community.* Baltimore: Paul H. Brookes.

O'Neill, R. E., Horner, R. H., Albin, R. W., Storey, K., & Sprague, J. R. (1990). *Functional analysis of problem behavior: A practical assessment guide.* Sycamore, IL: Sycamore Press.

Reichle, J., & Sigafoos, J. (1994). Communication intervention for persons with developmental disabilities. In E. C. Cipani & F. Spooner (Eds.), *Curricular and instructional approaches for persons with severe disabilities* (pp. 241–262). Boston: Allyn & Bacon.

Shukla, S., Kennedy, C. H., & Cushing, L. S. (1999). Intermediate school students with severe disabilities: Supporting their social participation in general education. *Journal of Positive Behavioral Intervention, 1,* 130–140.

Storey, K., & Provost, O. (1996). The effect of communication skills instruction on the integration of workers with severe disabilities in supported employment settings. *Education and Training in Mental Retardation and Developmental Disabilities, 31,* 123–141.

Swaggart, B., Gagnon, E., Bock, S. J., & Earles, T. L. (1995). Using social stories to teach social and behavioral skills to children with autism. *Focus on Autistic Behavior, 10,* 1–16.

Touchette, P. E., MacDonald, R. F., & Langer, S. N. (1985). A scatter plot identifying stimulus control of problem behavior. *Journal of Applied Behavior Analysis, 18,* 343–351.

Vanderheiden, G., & Lloyd, L. (1986). Communication systems and their components. In S. Blackstone (Ed.). *Augmentative communication: An introduction* (pp. 49–61). Rockville, MD: American Speech–Language–Hearing Association.

Wehmeyer, M. (1998). National survey of the use of assistive technology by adults with mental retardation. *Mental Retardation, 36,* 44–51.

TWELVE

Using Ecological Assessment in Planning for Inclusion

with Barbara Wilson

SEAN[1] WAS AN 8-YEAR-OLD STUDENT *with traumatic brain injury (the result of an acci-dent when he was 5 years old). In the upcoming academic year, he would be moving from a sepa-rate school for students with physical disabilities to his neighborhood elementary school. Both Sean and his mother were anxious and excited about his future at Northern Elementary School. To help Sean make this transition to a new, inclusive setting, his teacher used an ecological as-sessment—including planning with Sean, his mother, and a team from the elementary school— in developing the individualized education plan (IEP) that will be implemented during the up-coming school year at Northern.*

In recent years, an increasing number of students with moderate to severe disabilities are being educated either partially or fully in general education settings. The Individuals with Disabilities Education Act (IDEA) legally entitles students with disabilities to be educated in general education settings to the "maximum extent" possible, although interpretations vary regarding the extent to which students with severe disabilities can be supported in general education settings. Ethical arguments for inclusion include minimizing the stigma associated with segregated programming (Fuchs & Fuchs, 1994); creating caring, supportive school communities that benefit all students; and allowing students with disabilities to form and maintain meaningful, interactive relationships with peers (Strully & Strully, 1985). Educational arguments focus on the current dual system of education, which has long been criticized as being both an inefficient and ineffective means of educating students with unique educational needs. As noted by Lipsky and Gartner (1989), "the law itself does not require the largely separate and unequal special education service system that has developed" (p. 9). Furthermore, these authors contend that financial incentives serve to maintain restrictive placements for students with unique educational needs. In addition, the quality of the education received by the students in this expensive, segregated system has been questioned (Mills & Hull, 1992).

---

[1]Sean, whose case study is used throughout this chapter, is not a real person, but his example is based on our experiences in planning for students with moderate and severe disabilities.

Barbara Wilson, EdD, is a private consultant in Allentown, Pennsylvania.

Research on the impact of including students with moderate and severe disabilities in general education classrooms has generally been supportive of these placement decisions. Early studies revealed student gains in attaining IEP objectives (Brinker & Thorpe, 1984), increased communication and social skills (Cole & Meyer, 1991), and increased peer contact both in and outside school (McDonnell, Hardman, Hightower, & Keifer-O'Donnell, 1991). More recent studies have focused on educational strategies related to high rates of student engagement (Logan, Bakeman, & Keefe, 1997); the quality and quantity of social relations between students in inclusive versus segregated settings (Grenot-Scheyer, 1994; Fryxell & Kennedy, 1995); the concerns of teachers facing inclusion (York, Vandercook, MacDonald, Heise-Neff, & Caughey, 1992); moral outcomes for general education students (Helmstetter, Peck, & Giangreco, 1994); and the impact of inclusive programming on the academic attainment of the general education students (Hunt, Staub, Alwell, & Goetz, 1994; Sharpe, York, & Knight, 1994). In almost all reported cases, inclusive programming has been linked to positive results.

With the literature base growing, a number of experts have outlined the models they used to facilitate the inclusion of students with severe disabilities (see, e.g., Jorgensen, 1998; Lipsky & Gartner, 1997; Villa & Thousand, 1995). Although the models vary in a number of ways, several themes emerge regarding the successful implementation of inclusion. First, it is imperative for the school administration to support the movement of students with disabilities into general education, and to take steps to support the changing roles of teachers. Second, professional collaboration is a frequently noted aspect of successful inclusion (see Mostert, 1998, for a detailed text on interprofessional collaboration). Finally, inclusion needs to be viewed as a process rather than an outcome. As noted by Calculator (1994) in recounting a conversation he had with an administrator involved in inclusion, "[there was a failure] to anticipate the amount of work that would then be necessary to assure these students (and their families) that students' educational needs could be met in these . . . settings" (p. xxi).

An important part of this work is the planning needed to focus the instructional priorities for students with moderate and severe disabilities. Inclusion is more than planning for such students to be present in general educational settings (temporal inclusion). It is also more than encouraging social membership in the class and school for students with moderate and severe disabilities (social inclusion). To meet students' educational needs, they must have the opportunity to learn from the curriculum and to have their unique instructional needs addressed (instructional inclusion) (see Figure 12.1). Sometimes the functional curricular priorities of students with more severe disabilities and the academic priorities of general education can seem to create a "mismatch" for instructional inclusion. Careful planning is needed to determine how to meet the individual needs of students with more severe disabilities in general educational settings. Several planning steps are offered here for this purpose. Given these steps, the planning team can decide which are necessary to best meet the needs of the individuals involved. As noted by Wilson (1999), no professional consensus has yet emerged defining the "successful inclusive experience"; therefore, it is the responsibility—and joy—of the planning team to determine, define, and evaluate inclusion based on the individual needs of the student.

FIGURE 12.1. The building blocks of inclusion.

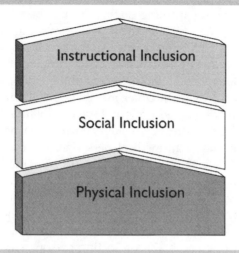

USING ECOLOGICAL ASSESSMENT TO DEVELOP THE IEP
FOR A STUDENT RECEIVING NEW OPPORTUNITIES
IN AN INCLUSIVE SETTINGS

The implementation of inclusion varies widely across the United States—from districts where all students have attended their neighborhood schools for a decade or more, to districts that continue to have separate schools for students with moderate and severe disabilities. In most localities, the goals of inclusion are still in process, and many students with moderate and severe disabilities will experience their first placements in general education classes in the years to come. Some districts that have offered inclusive services for most of their students are now implementing plans for students with more complicated needs. This section describes a team process for planning an IEP for a student who will be a full-time member of a general education class for the first time. In reviewing research on inclusion, Wilson (1999) found that the most successful inclusive efforts in the past have resulted when the following guidelines were observed:

- The planning team incorporated general and special education teachers, parents, students, and administrators.
- Administration provided support in terms of reduced caseloads, scheduling that facilitated planning, and training as needed.
- Team members maintained a flexible and creative approach to both the development of the program and ongoing problem solving needed to maintain student progress.

The first step, then, is to assemble a team that will plan for the student's IEP in the new inclusive setting. This team needs the flexibility to have one or more planning meetings prior to the formal IEP meeting, so that the members have the time to develop a foundation for success in the new placement. The team should minimally be made up of the student, the general education teacher(s), the special education teacher (whose role can be changed—as noted by Tashie et al., 1993—to that of "inclusion facilitator"), the parents of the included student, and members of the school administration (special education director, school principal). Other members include individuals who will be supporting the student in general education; these can include therapists, school psychologists or counselors, paraprofessional staffers, friends or peers of the student, and members of outside agencies (e.g., medical personnel or community service agency staff) (Snell & Brown, 1993). In the case of Sean, described at the beginning of this chapter, the special education teacher invited Sean's future general education teachers, the special education teacher, and the principal from Northern Elementary School to join Sean, his mother, his physical therapist, and her in planning the upcoming year's IEP. The team then implemented the ecological assessment model to develop the IEP, including (1) reviewing prior records, (2) conducting person-centered planning with the family and student, (3) identifying ways to enhance student self-determination, and (4) developing a personalized curriculum for Sean.

Reviewing Prior Records

In using the ecological assessment model, the first step is for the team to get to know the student, both directly through spending time with the student and in directly through reviewing prior records. At the beginning of the first team meeting, Sean's teacher used a person-centered planning strategy of telling Sean's story with the help of his mother, Ms. Walker. As his mother shared stories and photographs of Sean, his teacher summarized this story on newsprint using short phrases and illustrations. The team was deeply moved by the story of Sean's recovery from his accident. Sean had been struck by debris that flew off of delivery truck when it wrecked in front of his home while he was playing in the yard. The debris hit Sean in the head, causing traumatic brain injury. The team took time to discuss the story of Sean's remarkable recovery and to look at the newspaper story that had been written about him. His current teacher, Ms. Harper, then introduced Sean's educational program to the staff from Northern by giving them a copy of his most recent report card, which summarized his IEP objectives and current progress. Ms. Harper also used a *"profile summary"* to describe Sean's strengths and challenges in each area of the curriculum. A profile summary gives a snapshot of an individual and his or her strengths, interests, and successes (Allinder & Siegel, 1999; Downing, 1996; Ryndak & Alper, 1996). These summaries can be especially beneficial for introducing a student to a planning team in a new inclusive setting. Allinder and Siegel (1999) found that educators rated profile summaries higher than traditional assessments (i.e., technical reports) in their ability to communicate between staff and parents (although many educators still preferred traditional assessment information). The profile summary that Ms. Harper used for Sean follows.

PROFILE SUMMARY FOR SEAN WALKER

WHO IS SEAN?

Sean is an 8-year-old boy who currently attends Fields School, a specialized school for children with physical and health impairments. This has been his only school experience. Sean loves to attend Fields School. Sean likes to do academic work when he can use a computer. Sean enjoys being with people who are upbeat and positive.

SEAN'S STRENGTHS

Sean is able to use a computer and can stay focused on a software program or game that he likes for 30 minutes or more. If uncertain about what to do, Sean will wait quietly for assistance. Sean also has strong determination to master a goal once he sets it.

SEAN'S CHALLENGES

Sean has difficulty with tasks that require fine motor coordination, such as writing. He also learns sight words and math facts quickly, but has difficulty remembering them unless they are reviewed daily. Although Sean enjoys conversation, it is difficult for him to initiate it, because he has difficulty articulating what he wants to say. Sometimes his remarks seem unusual as he searches for the words he needs to express himself. Sean is still learning some daily living and personal care skills that are a challenge to him because of his physical impairments.

SEAN'S SUCCESSES

Sean's most remarkable success has been learning to walk, even though he was not expected to regain this skill. He now walks with a walker. Sean can read about a 20-word sight word vocabulary. He also knows most of his addition facts. Sean mastered writing a cursive signature last year (his own goal). Sean also recently learned to put on his jacket.

Sean's mother also wanted the team to read the neurologist's evaluation, conducted when her son was 7 years old. The neurologist described the need for Sean to have ongoing training to enhance his memory, and to be given cognitive stimulation. The principal asked several questions about the accommodations and supports used with Sean in his current school setting. Ms. Harper noted that Sean was currently in a small class with two staff members. The second staff person was a nurse, but Sean had not needed medical treatment during his last 2 years of school. His future special education teacher, Mr. Atkinson, asked Sean how he felt about going to a new school. Sean replied, "New school," which his mother interpreted as meaning he was interested.

For each planning step, the team used the form shown in Figure 12.2. This form summarizes all of the steps the team took in planning, which are described in more detail in the rest of this chapter. For the first step of reviewing Sean's prior records, the teacher recorded the team's notes under "Background on the Student" (see Figure 12.2).

FIGURE 12.2. Form to summarize steps of ecological assessment used in developing an IEP for an inclusive setting.

Summary of Ecological Assessment
for an Individualized Education Plan (IEP)

Student's Name: Sean Walker   **Date:** May 23, 20—

Planning Team: Sean, Ms. Walker (Sean's mother), Ms. Harper (current special education teacher), Mr. McBride (current physical therapist); Mr. Atkinson (special education teacher at Northern), Ms. Baker (principal of Northern), Ms. Shey (third-grade teacher at Northern), Ms. Newhart (math and computer teacher at Northern), Mr. Lopez (language arts specialist at Northern)

1. Background on Student

Sean Walker is an 8-year-old boy who has traumatic brain injury as the result of an accident at age 5. Sean made a remarkable recovery from the accident and has continued to show important progress over the last 3 years. He can now walk with a walker and speak in short phrases. Last year Sean mastered writing a cursive signature and putting on his jacket. He made good progress on learning sight words and some math facts, which he often practiced using computer software. Sean did not learn to initiate conversation. Although he talks more this year, his comments are often difficult to comprehend as he searches for the words he wants to use. He also made little progress on reading phrases. A prior evaluation by a neurologist, Dr. Jeffreys, notes that Sean needs continued training in memory strategies and cognitive stimulation.

2. Person-Centered Planning with Student and Family

Sean's mother's priorities are that he (1) be treated well by other students (social inclusion); (2) continue to learn life skills, given his excellent progress this year in learning to put on his jacket; and (3) be taught reading. Sean has expressed an interest in trying out the cafeteria. Currently he eats in his special education classroom with only five other students present.

3. Encouraging Student Self-Determination

Sean has been learning goal setting and decision making this year. He has presented the planning team with a photo album of his preferences, which he placed in rank order. His top five include food (tacos, hamburgers, French fries), working on the computer, playing computer games, swimming at the YMCA, and music. He has also presented the team with his goals, which include being able to walk without his walker and getting his own computer.

4. Development of a Personalized Curriculum

Because Sean has emerging functional academic skills, these can be used to create curricular parallels in general education. Expanding his sight word vocabulary, teaching him to read and write short phrases, and helping him build on his knowledge of math facts by learning to add are important priorities. These skills should be embedded in as many academic subjects as possible (e.g., learning sight word vocabulary in math). Sean also has priority needs related to communication, self-direction, social interaction skills, and motor development that can be taught within the typical classroom.

(cont.)

FIGURE 12.2. (cont.)

5. Recommendations for the IEP

The team has determined that the priorities for Sean's IEP include (1) functional academics (Sean wants this work to be computer-assisted), (2) continued improvement of his balance and fine motor skills (Sean's priority is to walk without his walker); (3) initiation of conversation; (4) self-direction (goal setting, self-managed seatwork); and (5) mastery of personal care skills. Sean will spend most of his day with Ms. Shey's third grade and will receive specially designed instruction from Mr. Atkinson and a teaching assistant in this context. He will also receive individual assistance for toileting and individual physical therapy sessions, based on his preference for privacy in these activities.

Person-Centered Planning with the Student and Family

Ms. Harper, Sean's current special education teacher, used a person-centered planning meeting format to help the team members get to know Sean and each other as they planned for his future IEP. She also prepared for this team meeting by talking with Sean and his mother about their hopes and fears about this major transition. Sean's mother said that she was worried about how the other students would treat Sean. It was important to her that his new plan focus on his social inclusion. She also wondered how the new setting would help Sean continue to learn some of the life skills he had been working on in his current school. She was especially pleased that he had learned to put on his jacket this year. The neurologist had told Ms. Walker that Sean might never learn to read, but Sean had surprised everyone in the past, and she wanted the school to continue to focus on this area.

In the meeting with Sean and his mother, Sean listened closely to each of her concerns. When asked about his concerns for the future, Sean asked about lunch. Ms. Harper explained how the students at Northern eat in a cafeteria (Sean currently ate in his special education room) and asked him whether he would like to try doing this when he visited his new school. Sean nodded "yes." She noted this information on her summary form. In the planning team meeting, Ms. Harper shared her notes from this meeting as a beginning point for planning Sean's curriculum (see "Person-Centered Planning with Student and Family" in Figure 12.2).

Encouraging Student Self-Determination

In the past 2 years, Ms. Harper had made it her priority to give students more choices in their daily routine and to keep notes on their preferences. She was also teaching Sean and his classmates to set and implement goals and to make decisions. She thought it would be helpful for the planning team to hear from Sean himself about his preferences and goals in their meeting. To help Sean prepare for this, they made a photo album together, showing the activities and materials he liked best. He also made the decision about the placement of the photographs to rank them in order of importance. Ms. Harper also helped Sean use the computer to type his future goals. Using clip art, Sean selected pictures to symbolize each goal, and the teacher wrote a sight word or phrase to help him remember it. At the planning meeting, after getting to know Sean, the team members watched as Sean opened his photo album to show each picture. Sometimes they asked questions. For example, when Sean showed the picture of eating a taco, Ms. Shey (the third-grade teacher at Northern) asked, "Do you like tacos, or does this mean you like to eat lunch?" When Sean said, "Tacos! Lunch!", Ms. Shey said, "Oh, both! We have tacos at Northern at least once a month." As Sean held up the pictures for his goals, Ms. Harper helped to explain these, including that Sean wanted to learn to walk without his walker and to have his own computer. She also noted that Sean preferred to do his schoolwork on the computer. Ms. Harper summarized Sean's top priorities on her planning form (see "Encouraging Student Self-Determination" in Figure 12.2).

Development of a Personalized Curriculum

In planning for inclusion, one of the most important steps is to develop the student's personalized curricular priorities so that the potential competition among academic, life skills, and socialization can be addressed on an individual level. The steps the planning team may take for this include (1) clarifying the goals for the student's inclusion, (2) conducting ecological inventories and discrepancy analyses, (3) conducting situational assessments, and (4) reviewing the age-level academic curriculum.

Clarifying Goals for Student Inclusion

One of the most basic and important steps to be undertaken by the inclusion team is to determine the goals and/or outcomes for the included student. Research has demonstrated that teachers, parents, and students involved in inclusive programming can remain unclear about the basic goals of inclusion (York & Tunidor, 1995). Given the varied potential benefits, the planning team needs to clarify what student outcomes will constitute "good inclusion" for the specific student. Although the student's IEP will specify goals and objectives for inclusion, a number of positive student outcomes may be available in an inclusive setting that are not specifically listed on an IEP. For instance, the development of a friendship network may be a very important outcome for a student with severe disabilities, but may not be specifically listed as a goal on the IEP. Similarly, the included student may be expected to learn the rudiments of the general education classroom curriculum while in the class, although that outcome is not specifically identified on the IEP. The following is the conversation the members of Sean's team had when they developed their goals for Sean's inclusion.

Ms. NEWHART (math and computer specialist at Northern): I think that addressing Sean's progress in learning basic math skills will fit in easily to the routines and activities in the math class. We also frequently use computers for individual practice. He's never been to school with students who are nondisabled, and most of his prior classmates were younger than he is. Are there skills he will need to be around other 8-year-olds?

Ms. WALKER: I'd like Sean to make some friends. He really didn't interact much with the other kids in his old class, because most of them didn't talk.

Ms. BAKER (principal at Northern): There are a lot of things we can do to encourage interactions between Sean and his classmates. We have been using a pals-for-lunch
program, peer tutoring, and some other strategies with students who are already
included at Northern. A lot of the students who are nondisabled also need these
opportunities to develop social relationships. My concern is what Sean will learn
in his general education classes. Currently, the students who are included at
Northern have mild disabilities and can do the academic work with some minor
accommodations.

Ms. SHEY (third-grade teacher at Northern): From what I've seen, Sean is used to having
a lot of individual attention. I realize that he will still need extra help with some of
his work, but I'd like to have him become more independent in the classroom. You
know—be able to find his seat, listen during group times, and use the computer independently.

Ms. HARPER (special education teacher at Northern): So in addition to making friends,
do we agree that Sean also needs to learn to be more independent in his new class
and to have curricular goals that are meaningful in his general education classes?

The team members all said, "Yes," and added a few more comments to indicate
their agreement. Ms. Harper jotted in her notes: "Friends, increased independence in
class routines, and meaningful curricular goals in general education."

Ecological Inventories

Once the student's general inclusion goals have been identified, the team can begin the
process of defining the student's personalized curriculum. As described in Chapter
Two, one step that can be used in this process is to conduct an ecological inventory of
the student's environments. In inclusion planning, conducting observations of general
education classrooms and interviews of these teachers can be especially beneficial in
planning the student's program. Because most of Sean's new teachers were present at
his planning meeting, Ms. Walker was able to have them work together to conduct an
ecological inventory of each of his classes and other school environments. Here are two
that they generated.

ECOLOGICAL INVENTORIES OF GENERAL EDUCATION SETTINGS

Environment: Language arts with Mr. Lopez.

Activities: Individual work using computer, workbooks, or handouts; cooperative learning groups; special projects using crafts or drama; teacher lecture.

Skills for Sean: Use of new software and computer; participating with group (maybe
with picture communication); composing text; sight words—"Mr. Lopez," "language
arts," dates (months), key words used to list assignments on board ("groups,"
"journal," "computer").

Environment: School cafeteria.

Activities: Purchasing lunch; making selections in lunch line or making a salad; finding a
table; conversation; cleaning up.

> <u>Skills for Sean</u>: Use of money (next-dollar strategy); communicating lunch choices to peer; motor skills to sit down at bench-style tables (use end seat); converse with props (e.g., pictures, sports trading cards).

Discrepancy Analysis

An alternative way to identify curricular needs for a student is to use a discrepancy analysis, as also described in Chapter Two. To conduct a discrepancy analysis for inclusion planning, the general education teacher or a classroom observer lists the skills and activities that the classroom students need to be independent in the classroom; these skills are then compared to the skills of the individual student being assessed. The team can then plan ways to address skill discrepancies through teaching skills or designing adaptations of these. Ryndak and Alper (1996) recommend using a decision hierarchy for developing these adaptations. This 11-step decision hierarchy is presented in Table 12.1. In using this hierarchy, the planning team begins with the first level. If that accommodation is not feasible, the team moves to the next level, and so on. The goal is to keep the student involved in the typical classroom experience as much as possible. These decisions can be used both in planning for the classroom's routine and in making ongoing decisions about the student's activities in the class.

As the team began planning Sean's curricular priorities, Mr. Atkinson first discussed this decision hierarchy with the other team members. The team then considered how Sean would respond during a typical day in the middle school. They wrote a discrepancy analysis for the day, comparing Sean's responses with the way other third-graders would cope with their day.

TABLE 12.1. Decision Hierarchy for Planning Adaptations in General Education

1. Can the student participate the same as classmates? If so, no accommodation needed. If not, go to 2.
2. Can the student participate if the environment is adapted? If so, how? If not, go to 3.
3. Can the student participate if the general education teacher's instruction is adapted? If so, how? If not, go to 4.
4. Can the student participate if the general education materials are adapted? If so, how? If not, go to 5.
5. Can the student participate if the rules/expectations for the activity are altered? If so, how? If not, go to 6.
6. Can the student participate if given personal assistance? If so, how and by whom (e.g., paraprofessional, peer)? If not, go to 7.
7. Can the student participate using the same academic content, but at an easier level? If so, what level and materials will be used? If not, go to 8.
8. Can the student participate in the general education class while learning different content? If so, what content and materials will be used? If not, go to 9.
9. Can the student participate in the general education class even if doing some activities in a different part of the room? If so, what activities will be used?

   If not, go to 10.
10. Does the student need to do a different activity in the building (not in the classroom) during this activity (e.g., quiz)? If so, what activity and where? If not, go to 11.
11. Is this general education activity irrelevant for the student (e.g., week-long statewide testing)? If so, would the time be better spent doing community-based instruction?

Note. Adapted from Ryndak and Alper (1996). Copyright 1996 by Allyn & Bacon. Adapted by permission.

DISCREPANCY ANALYSIS FOR SEAN'S PARTICIPATION
IN MS. SHEY'S CLASSROOM

Typical peer's routine in third grade	Sean's current skills	Plans to teach or adapt
1. Walks to class from bus.	Can walk with walker, but cannot find classroom.	Have Sean walk with peer guide.
2. Puts coat/book-bag in bin with name.	Will be able to do this after he is shown his bin.	Have him participate same as classmates.
3. Listens to announcements.	Does not listen unless prompted; will sit quietly.	Adapt expectations—let him sit quietly.
4. Gets out materials as directed by teacher.	Does not follow instructions given to whole class.	Adapt instructions—give a hand signal.
5. Maintains quiet as teacher talks.	Often quiet, but hums if bored, yells if angry.	Adapt environment—give him a visual cue for "quiet"; give personal assistance if angry.
6. Begins assignments written on board.	Cannot read board; usually needs verbal directions.	Adapt instruction—teach him key words as sight words; adapt materials—give him his assignments in folder.
7. Works independently for 15 minutes.	Can work for 15 minutes if able to do the task and has frequent prompts to "keep working."	Adapt instruction—teach Sean to self-monitor his on-task behavior
8. Completes assignments from book, worksheet, computer.	Writing is a challenge; can use familiar computer software; entry-level academic skills vs. third-grade.	Adapt content or level—have him work on functional reading and math; adapt materials—have him complete all assignments on computer.
9. Works cooperatively with small group.	Pleasant with other people; but quiet—does not initiate communication; may not understand curricular content.	Adapt expectations and content level—give Sean a specific contribution to make to group, related to one fact or concept.
10. Makes transition from one activity/subject to the next with teacher cue.	Will sit quietly until told what to do next; then he will follow peers.	Have him participate same as classmates.

SKILLS TO CONSIDER FOR IEP
1. To self-manage independent seatwork using a "quiet" visual cue, self-pacing with a folder of assignments, and self-monitoring of time on task.
2. To participate in a cooperative learning group.

Situational Assessment

Another way to plan for inclusion is to a give student the opportunity to try out new options, in order to gather more information about the students' needs and preferences. For example, Sean was concerned about how he would eat lunch in his new school. Because he enjoyed lunch, this also seemed a good activity to introduce him to his new placement. Ms. Harper worked with Mr. Atkinson to arrange for Sean to eat lunch at Northern Elementary School, and for her to go with him for assistance and observation. During this tryout, Sean was very quiet when confronted with the noise and activity of a typical elementary school cafeteria. He stayed close to Ms. Harper as they went through the cafeteria line. When he saw the menu options, he smiled and laughed. It was easy for Ms. Harper to determine what Sean wanted, because he reached toward each item displayed. At the end of the line, Sean did not understand that he needed to wait and pay; he became angry and began to yell. Ms. Harper let another student go through the line and pay, to show Sean what was expected. They then paid and went to the seating area. Sean wanted to sit at the first table. He needed help to sit on the bench. He began to eat his food, ignoring the other children at the table until he was finished. He liked the menu and asked for more. A girl at the table gave him her French fries. He smiled and ate them. The children at the table then got their teacher's signal to return to class. Later, when asked about the cafeteria experience, Sean nodded "yes" that he had liked it. This assessment helped to confirm what the members of the planning team had identified in their ecological assessment as Sean's skill needs (e.g., social interaction skills, communication, use of money). Ms. Harper was also surprised to discover that Sean would need some prompting to be patient with the process of paying for his lunch and to interact with peers at the table. She realized that the team had not considered the need for Sean to stand in line for as long as 10 minutes, but he did this without complaint.

Curriculum-Based Assessment

Although ecological inventories, situational assessments, and discrepancy analyses can help the team plan for how the student will participate in the general class and school routines, planning is also needed to determine ways the student can participate in the general education curriculum. Giangreco and Putnam (1991) have defined two alternatives for this curriculum planning: "multilevel curriculum selection" and "curriculum overlapping." With multilevel curriculum selection, classroom instruction is individualized within the topic area to accommodate students at varying levels. For example, in a middle school algebra class, a gifted student may be working on an enrichment activity involving advanced concepts; the majority of the students may be working on mastery of the concepts in the text; and a student with severe disabilities may be learning the numerals 1–10 and the amounts they represent. Although all students are involved in activities involving mathematics concepts, the levels of the activities they are assigned vary with their abilities and educational needs. Conversely, in curriculum overlapping, students with disabilities may be working on mastery of goals that are not part of the general education curriculum but can be adequately practiced within the overall classroom structure. An example of curriculum overlapping is to teach mobility skills by assigning a student with severe disabilities the job of passing out materials in a middle school science classroom. Hunt et al. (1994) evaluated an application of curriculum overlapping, as they developed individualized goals (motor, communication) for young elementary students with severe disabilities who were included in cooperative learning academic classes. Their research demonstrated that students could learn these curricular alternatives while their peers learned their academic content (e.g., geometry).

With some creative planning, generalization or enrichment activities that meet IEP or overall goals can be built into the classroom activities, regardless of the topic or academic demands of the general education curriculum. Planning teams rarely have the time to adapt the entire curriculum prior to a student's placement. Instead, this is usually an ongoing planning process. For IEP planning, the team may want to identify a few priorities for the student's participation in the general education curriculum. Ryndak and Weidler (1996) suggest approaching this task by considering the areas traditionally within special education curricula that have parallels in general education. Table 12.2 shows some of the parallels that an IEP planning team might consider in developing goals for specific content areas.

It is important to note at this point that some minor modifications of the general education classroom structure may be needed in order to address the needs of the included student. For example, a general education teacher may have traditionally taken morning attendance by calling out the students' names. Changing this procedure to a daily sign-in sheet, in which students sign their own names, would provide one additional opportunity for the included student to practice writing his or her name or making a distinctive mark—an opportunity that is naturally occurring and simply becomes part of the classroom routine. By creatively considering minor modifications of classroom routines, the team may manufacture additional opportunities for the student to practice individualized skills without major classroom modifications.

After considering curricular parallels (multilevel curriculum) that will enable the student to participate in the academic content of general education to the maximum extent possible, a next step is to review the student's life skills and other curricular priorities and determine how these might be addressed in the classroom context. This planning focuses on the curriculum overlapping that will be used in inclusive settings when the student with disabilities learns functional skills that do not parallel the academic content. These may include skills like personal care, communication, ambulation, and self-direction, which can be learned and practiced in a wide variety of settings. To identify these skills, the team can review a life skills curriculum or other functional skills checklists, such as the ones provided in Chapters Nine and Ten of this book. Once the skills have been identified, the team can plan how these skills can be taught in the context of the general education classroom. Many experts on inclusion have recommended using a matrix for this planning (Downing, 1996; Snell & Brown, 1993). The matrix both assists in the planning and serves as a visual planning tool. In this step, the matrix is

TABLE 12.2. Planning a Parallel (Multilevel) Curriculum for a Student with Severe Disabilities Who Is Participating in General Education

General education curricular areas	Parallel functional curriculum options
	Language arts
Reading Spelling Writing English Public speaking Journalism	• Functional reading (sight word practice; stories about functional activities; daily living reading materials) • Communication skills (picture identification and use for communication; sign language; use of electronic system) • Social interaction skills • Name writing; writing/typing lists for functional use (e.g., schedule, grocery list)
	Math and science
Elementary math Algebra Geometry Biology Chemistry Physics	• Functional math (e.g., telling time, use of calendar, use of money, measurement) • Health and safety • Number entry for job (e.g., computer, cash register) • Use of calculator
	Social studies
American history World history Government Geography	• Social interaction • Preparation for community-based instruction (banking, social services) • Leisure skills—planning travel or class field trip (maps, brochures of historic sites)
	Electives and other
Home economics Industrial arts Music Art Sports Physical education Computers	• Daily living skills (e.g., cooking and housekeeping) • Job training • Leisure skills—music, art, sports • Fitness training

filled with the included subjects or class periods (as determined from the student's schedule) across the top, and the goals and priorities along the side. With this completed, the team can then begin brainstorming activities within the classes that meet the goals.

Figure 12.3 shows the completed matrix for some of Sean's IEP priorities. Sean's first two priorities had parallels to the academic curriculum (expanding his sight word vocabulary and computing). His other goals were not academic parallels (e.g., improving balance, initiating conversation, improving finger strength), but could easily be incorporated into the activities of his third-grade classes. Not all IEP goals make sense in all contexts. For example, self-managing seatwork is not applicable in music or at lunch, when students are not doing seatwork. This matrix allowed the planning team to double-check that all stated IEP goals were addressed throughout the day.

Developing Individual Classroom Activities

Some students with severe challenges will have physical or educational needs that cannot be addressed appropriately in general education classrooms. Clearly, IEP goals such as "increased independence in the toileting routine" or "decreased resistance to oral stimulation" would be extremely stigmatizing to a student if they were practiced even in part in the general education classroom. A number of other strategies generally considered effective teaching strategies in segregated settings have been identified as not appropriate for use in inclusive programming, either because of logistical factors (they require too much assistance) or because of the stigmatizing factors that would be evident in general education (Billingsley & Kelley, 1994). In order both to meet the individual student's IEP goals and to respect the student's dignity in the classroom, it is important to identify those skills that cannot adequately or appropriately be addressed in the classroom.

For Sean, the team determined that his need to eliminate toileting accidents would need to be addressed through training him both to initiate toileting and to go on a schedule. To minimize the intrusions on his daily schedule, the teacher's assistant would take Sean to a private restroom in the school at three times during the day when the class was making transitions. If Sean asked to go at another time, the assistant would take him then as well. A second time scheduled away from the general education class was a weekly physical therapy session. Although the physical therapist consulted with the planning team about how to prompt Sean to balance and negotiate certain types of seating, Sean also needed some therapy (range-of-motion exercises) that he did not want to do in front of other children.

Sometimes IEP goals that seem to require separate or private instruction can be addressed in general education classrooms with some creativity. For example, the IEP goal "will increase independence in opening/closing clothing fasteners" appears to be a goal that would be stigmatizing when addressed in general education, as it would be inappropriate for a student with disabilities to be manipulating his or her clothing in the classroom. However, artists' smocks with a variety of fasteners (i.e., snaps, buttons, zippers) can be used by all the students when participating in art activities. Teachers can also obtain or create folders for students' seatwork that have a variety of fasteners (e.g., zipper pencil case, snap closure plastic folder).

At the end of the planning team's meetings about Sean, the members had both defined his curricular focus and identified priorities for his upcoming year's IEP (see Figure 12.2). All team members felt that they had a well-developed plan for helping Sean succeed in his new school placement. Planning for inclusion, however, does not end with the development of the IEP. Ongoing planning is needed for the continuing process of curricular integration and problem solving. This is described next.

ONGOING INCLUSION PLANNING

The ongoing phase of planning takes the process from the "generic" to the "specific." This level of planning addresses exactly how the student will be included in the classroom activities, how his or her individual goals will be addressed, and what supports will be needed. In schools and districts where inclusion has been implemented for some time, the planning challenge is often in these specifics.

FIGURE 12.3. A matrix to plan curriculum parallels and overlapping: teaching functional skills in general education contexts

Matrix for Planning Curriculum Parallels and Overlapping

IEP priorities	Classes							
	Reading	Language arts	Math	Science	Computers	Gym	Art and Music	Recess and lunch
1. Expand sight words	High-frequency words, "Ms. Shey"	Board assignmt. words, dates	"Math," "Ms. Newhart," number words	"Science"				Menu words, game words
2. Compute sums			Math facts, addition					Add costs of menu items
3. Initiate conversation	Point to story picture to start talking	Use picture to make point in small grp.	Greet students	Use pictures to share ideas with grp.			Describe day's activity	Use sports cards, pictures to start talking
4. Improve balance on uneven surfaces and when sitting	Transfer from desk to small-grp. table	Join grp. in floor activity	Steer up ramp to class			Do part of activity without walker—guide to balance		Sit on bench

5. Improve finger strength and flexibility	Hold own sight words	Pass out journals	Count objects in doing addition	Grasp and pass lab supplies	Begin learning keyboarding	Do finger flexes and games if can't do class activity	Grasp, release, paste in art	Use of spoon and fork
6. Set and implement goals	Goals for no. of words to learn	Goals for writing	Goals for using math	Goals for homework	Goals for learning new software	Fitness-level goals		
7. Self-manage seatwork	Sight word practice	Folder or computer	Folder or computer	Highlight notes with marker				
8. Put on Velcro shoes		May take off shoes when doing group work on floor				Put on shoes after stretches		

Adapting Daily and Weekly Lesson Plans

The matrix created during the development of the IEP (see Figure 12.3) provides an excellent resource for teachers to focus a student's specially designed instruction in general education contexts. However, these IEP objectives rarely provide enough focus to keep students fully involved in daily instruction. To take the next step in instructional inclusion, the special education teacher can work with the general education teacher to adapt each week's lesson plans for the student. Downing (1996) provides many examples of how classroom activities have been adapted; we mention three of Downing's examples here. For a student named Celia who had no vision and used a wheelchair, the teacher planned an alternative for her participation in a creative writing activity. Celia chose objects she liked, and then a peer incorporated these items into a story for Celia. Michael, a student who had no vision and mental retardation, was in an elementary science class that was studying insects. The teacher's daily activities for Mike were that he get the materials needed and set up the work area for the other members of his group, who would be dissecting insects. As the peers performed each step, they described them for Mike and let him tactilely explore the materials. In a high school class, Sandi, a student with mental retardation and severe quadriplegic cerebral palsy, was participating in a social studies unit on civil rights. Her peers were to read their text and watch a short video on this subject. A teaching assistant helped Sandi review the text material by referring her to the pictures and using simple phrases. Sandi then participated with the class to view the video. Sandi also used pictures to choose what rights she wanted for herself.

Developing Instructional Support

With the activities for each classroom developed, each teacher should have an idea of the type and amount of support the student will need to meet his or her goals, and can begin the process of identifying the resources available for supporting the student in general education. Supports to be considered can be personnel, such as the special education teacher, therapists, or classroom aides, or forms of natural supports, such as peers (Jorgensen, 1992).

Some classroom structures naturally facilitate student interaction and cooperation. Peer tutoring, one of the earliest forms of instruction (Osguthorpe & Scruggs, 1986), generally utilizes groupings of two students to investigate a common educational goal or to have one student instruct another. Most often, a student serving as a tutor is trained to work with a peer, which results in increased opportunities to learn in a classroom context. Both formal and informal models of peer tutoring have been reported in the literature, including "reciprocal" tutoring, in which students take turns being both tutor and tutee (Balenzano, Agte, McLaughlin, & Howard, 1993); "classwide" tutoring, in which all students participate in peer tutoring (Delquadri, Greenwood, Whorton, Carta, & Hall, 1986); and "expert" models, which utilize cross-ability or cross-age tutoring (Natasi & Clements, 1991). Utilizing peers as tutors can provide natural opportunities for reinforcing social skills, while also addressing the need for additional classroom support for students with disabilities.

Similarly, cooperative learning encourages student interaction by having small, heterogeneous groups of students work together on academic assignments (Peterson &

Miller, 1990). A large literature has demonstrated the efficacy of cooperative learning, with a number of prosocial and academic outcomes (Slavin, 1995). Although both formal (i.e., "team-assisted individualization") and informal models have been investigated, models such as the "jigsaw" approach, in which each student in a cooperative learning group is assigned a specific "role" or job, may lend themselves most easily to inclusion of a student with significant disabilities. When an individualized task that also addresses the IEP goals (e.g., counting and signing out group materials) is assigned, the peers can prompt, motivate, and reinforce skill attainment.

If peer supports are not feasible, various supports are available from school personnel. Therapists, aides, and special educators may be scheduled to assist in integrated therapy, 1:1 support, or team-teaching models. Although the use of adults as supports is often seen in schools, the results of research conducted by Giangreco, Edelman, Luiselli, and MacFarland (1997) indicate that the addition of a 1:1 aide specifically for an included student may actually function to hinder the development of social relationships between the student with disabilities and his or her peers. Consequently, adult support should be provided judiciously, with extra care taken to encourage peer interactions.

Developing Materials

Clearly, there will be times when specific, individualized materials are needed for the student with disabilities to (1) benefit from the general education lesson, (2) work on individualized goals, or (3) participate in group activities in an authentic way. Decisions about who will provide the materials and how to develop them should be made by the team.

As much as possible, additional materials should maintain the theme of the overall lesson and reflect age-appropriate norms. For example, if students in a middle school art class are working with oil-based paints—a medium that might be dangerous for a student with mouthing behaviors—safer but similar materials should be selected for the included student. In this example, a small palette of nontoxic water-based paints would be an appropriate substitution for the oil-based paints, whereas providing the student with crayons would be stigmatizing.

Developing Data Collection Systems

Data are necessary for ensuring that goals are being met, modifying instructional programs, and providing formal information for periodic progress reports. Data collection systems, however, can be labor-intensive, often requiring extensive observations and laborious graphing. Because inclusion itself requires significant planning, selecting data systems that provide critical information while remaining "user-friendly" can be a challenge to the planning team.

A number of data systems lend themselves more easily to the inclusive classroom. Portfolio assessment, a collection of a student's work across time, can provide a permanent record of progress over the course of a school year (Wesson & King, 1996). Self-monitoring, a system in which the student self-observes and records data (Shapiro & Cole, 1994), can provide another data source on the acquisition of instructional or behavioral goals. The planning team may decide to use direct, daily data as described in Chapter Four, but to limit it to the IEP objectives that are the highest priorities. These daily data may be taken by the teacher, an assistant, or a peer. Such direct, daily data can provide the information needed to determine whether the student is making gains with the supports provided for the inclusive setting.

Training Peers and Support Staff Members

Students and staff members who are unfamiliar with the supported student will need a degree of training to interact with and support a student with significant needs in general education contexts. Initially, when peers and support staffers are unfamiliar with a student's unique communication and educational needs, they may be uncomfortable interacting with the student. Giangreco, Dennis, Cloninger, Edelman, and Schattman (1993) investigated the reaction of general educators during the first year of an inclusion program, and noted that experience often served to decrease the anxiety initially reported by these educators. Other professionals suggest providing general educators with both theoretical and practical experience with individuals with disabilities before initiating inclusive education (Wisniewski & Alper, 1994). Whether training is provided prior to instituting inclusion or occurs in the general education room, it is crucial that the individuals supporting a student with disabilities be trained in strategies to maximize the inclusion experience.

Reviewing Plans to Ensure Full Classroom Membership

In planning for the specifics of inclusion, it is important to consider whether the included student is considered a classroom "member." As noted by Schnorr (1997), several guidelines help promote classroom membership of the student with disabilities, including promoting friendships, ensuring similarity between the activities done by the student with disabilities and those done by classmates, and supporting ongoing interactions among students. Two ways to encourage belonging are to reduce differences and to model interactions.

Reducing Differences

All interactions in the classroom should reflect age-appropriate, natural classroom interactions. Although this guideline is apparently simplistic, many professionals use verbal cues and reinforcement that may be stigmatizing to an included student in a general education context. For example, providing specific verbal reinforcement (i.e., "Good wiping the table, Tommy") may be appropriate in an early intervention classroom but not in a middle school class, where this type of stilted language would be apparent and stigmatizing to the student.

Similarly, the general education teacher can minimize differences by being aware of the "power structure" of the room and maintaining this structure for the student with disabilities as well. In other words, if the general education teacher assigns the work, provides feedback to individual students, and enforces classroom and school rules, he or she should fulfill these roles for the student with disabilities as well. Because an included student may be supported by an additional classroom adult (1:1 aide or special educator), there may be a tendency for the support person to implement the total program for the student. For the student to become a true member of the general education classroom, frequent and natural interactions between the general educator and the student are required.

Modeling Interactions

Just as students learn by observation, the students in the classroom will model the behavior of the adults in the room. Consequently, the behavior of the general education teacher can have a significant impact on how the student with disabilities is perceived by his or her peers. If a teacher expects, models, and reinforces respectful interactions between and among students, the students are likely to emulate these behaviors. Conversely, if a teacher is obviously uncomfortable with a student, or acts in ways that stigmatize the student, it will be those behaviors that are most prevalently exhibited by the students in the classroom.

Evaluation and Problem Solving

An important part of the ongoing process of inclusion is to evaluate both student progress and the supports the student is receiving. Sometimes the team conducts this review as a step in resolving a problem that emerges during the school year. The first step in this evaluation process is to compile whatever data are available on both the student and the strategies utilized. Sharing strategies that work and don't work will help the team avoid future failures and increase successes. Over time, the team will begin building sets of strategies that increase IEP goal acquisition and socialization for specific students.

For example, Sean's team noted that he exhibited low rates of engagement in active large-group activities, but attended when in 1:1 or small-group activities. Because many of the stated goals of the classroom required large-group activities, the teacher felt that she was unable to modify many of the activities to meet Sean's needs, although she noted that his progress on many of his stated goals, as documented in the data, was not as great as anticipated. By using a collaborative problem-solving technique similar to the one used by Salisbury, Evans, and Palombaro (1997), the team was able to identify several strategies for supporting Sean while not changing the entire structure of the classroom. Included on their list was providing Sean with a smaller "cooperative learning" group in the context of the large-group activity or teaming him with a supportive peer. With these ideas generated, the team felt comfortable with Sean's progress, and scheduled the next review for 2 weeks. To summarize this problem-solving process, a team does the following:

1. Identifies the problem.
2. Reviews any available data on the student and strategies used.
3. Brainstorms potential solutions.
4. Selects a solution for implementation.
5. Implements the solution.
6. Evaluates whether the solution was effective.

SUMMARY

Students with moderate and severe disabilities are receiving increasing opportunities for inclusion in general education settings. Many professionals no longer ask, "Does inclusion work?" Instead, they ask, "How can we make inclusion work for this student?" Making inclusion work requires the resources of a planning team. Special education teachers who try to create inclusive education alone will soon discover that they lack the resources to answer questions about curriculum and expectations for the general education setting. If they do not collaborate with general education teachers from the onset, these special educators may find themselves on the defensive when problems arise with individual students. In contrast, a team that includes the student, the parent, general educators, the special educator, therapists, and an administrator is ideal. Such a team will have the people present who are needed to make decisions.

The ecological assessment process is one alternative for planning an IEP for an inclusive setting. The advantages of this process are that it incorporates the family's and student's preferences, and that it considers the learning environment as well as the student's needs. The primary adaptation in applying this model for students who will spend most of their day in general education contexts is the need to incorporate planning for participation in the academic curriculum. This can be done by finding curriculum parallels among the student's functional skill needs (e.g., sight words), and by considering ways to teach some basic skills (e.g., motor skills, communication) at the same time other students are learning academics.

Inclusion planning is an ongoing process. Once the school year begins, continued work is needed to adapt daily lesson plans to identify activities the student can do, to develop necessary instructional supports, and to solve any problems that may arise. Ongoing planning is also needed to find ways to ensure the student's full membership in the class. Through this focused planning, a team can increase the likelihood that a student will have a successful experience in general education.

REFERENCES

Allinder, R. M., & Siegel, E. (1999). "Who is Brad?": Preservice teacher preparation of summarizing assessment information about a student with moderate disabilities. *Education and Training in Mental Retardation and Developmental Disabilities, 34,* 157–169.

Balenzano, S., Agte, L. J., McLaughlin, T. F., & Howard, V. F. (1993). Training tutoring skills with preschool children with disabilities in a classroom setting. *Child and Family Behavior Therapy, 15,* 1–35.

Billingsley, F. F., & Kelley, B. (1994). An examination of the acceptability of instructional practices for students with severe disabilities in general education settings. *Journal of the Association for Persons with Severe Handicaps, 19,* 75–83.

Brinker, R. P., & Thorpe, M. E. (1984). Integration of severely handicapped students and the proportion of IEP objectives achieved. *Exceptional Children, 51,* 168–175.

Calculator, S. N. (1994). Introduction. In N. W. Nelson (Series Ed.) & S. T. Calculator & C. M. Jorgensen (Vol. Eds.), *Including students with severe disabilities in schools: Fostering communication, interaction, and participation* (pp. xxi). San Diego, CA: Singular.

Cole, D. A., & Meyer, C. L. (1991). Social integration and severe disabilities: A longitudinal analysis of child outcomes. *Journal of Special Education, 25,* 340–351.

Delquadri, J., Greenwood, C. R., Whorton, D., Carta, J. J., & Hall, R. V. (1986). Classwide peer tutoring. *Exceptional Children, 52*, 535–542.

Downing, J. (Ed.). (1996). *Including students with severe and multiple disabilities in typical classrooms.* Baltimore: Paul H. Brookes.

Fryxell, D., & Kennedy, C. H. (1995). Placement along the continuum of services and its impact on students' social relationships. *Journal of the Association for Persons with Severe Handicaps, 20,* 259–269.

Fuchs, D., & Fuchs, L. S. (1994). Inclusive schools movement and the radicalization of special education reform. *Exceptional Children, 60,* 294–309. Giangreco, M. F., Dennis, R., Cloninger, C., Edelman, S., & Schattman, R. (1993). "I've counted Jon": Transformational experiences of teachers educating students with disabilities. *Exceptional Children, 59,* 359–372.

Giangreco, M. F., Edelman, S. W., Luiselli, T. E., & MacFarland, S. Z. (1997). Helping or hovering?: Effects of instructional assistant proximity on students with disabilities. *Exceptional Children, 64,* 7–18.

Giangreco, M. F., & Putnam, J. W. (1991). Supporting the education of students with severe disabilities in regular education environments. In L. Meyer, C. A. Peck, & L. Brown (Eds.), *Critical issues in the lives of people with severe disabilities* (pp. 379–386). Baltimore: Paul H. Brookes.

Grenot-Scheyer, M. (1994). The nature of interactions between students with severe disabilities and their friends and acquaintances without disabilities. *Journal of the Association for Persons with Severe Handicaps, 19,* 253–262.

Helmstetter, E., Peck, C. A., & Giangreco, M. F. (1994). Outcomes of interactions with peers with moderate of severe disabilities: A statewide survey of high school students. *Journal of the Association for Persons with Severe Handicaps, 19,* 263–276.

Hunt, P., Staub, D., Alwell, M., & Goetz, L. (1994). Achievement by all students within the context of cooperating groups. *Journal of the Association for Persons with Severe Handicaps, 19,* 290–301.

Jorgensen, C. M. (1992). Natural supports in inclusive schools: Curricular and teaching strategies. In J. Nisbet (Ed.) *Natural supports in school, at work, and in the community for people with severe disabilities* (pp. 179–215). Baltimore: Paul H. Brookes.

Jorgensen, C. M. (1998). *Restructuring high schools for all students: Taking inclusion to the next level.* Baltimore: Paul H. Brookes.

Lipsky, D. K., & Gartner, A. (1989). The current situation. In D. K. Lipsky & A. Gartner (Eds.), *Beyond a separate education: Quality education for all* (pp. 3–24). Baltimore: Paul H. Brookes.

Lipsky, D. K., & Gartner, A. (1997). *Inclusion and school reform: Transforming America's classrooms.* Baltimore: Paul H. Brookes.

Logan, K. R., Bakeman, R., & Keefe, E. B. (1997). Effects of instructional variables on engaged behavior of students with disabilities in general education classrooms. *Exceptional Children, 63,* 481–497.

McDonnell, J., Hardman, M., Hightower, J., & Keifer-O'Donnell, R. (1991). Variables associated with in-school and after-school integration of secondary students with severe disabilities. *Education and Training in Mental Retardation, 26,* 243–257.

Mills, R. P., & Hull, M. E. (1992). State departments of education: Instruments of policy, instruments of change. In R. A. Villa, J. S. Thousand, W. Stainback, & S. Stainback (Eds.), *Restructuring for caring and effective education: An administrative guide to creating heterogeneous schools* (pp. 245–266). Baltimore: Paul H. Brookes.

Mostert, M. P. (1998). *Interprofessional collaboration in schools.* Boston, MA: Allyn & Bacon.

Natasi, B. K., & Clements, D. H. (1991). Research on cooperative learning: Implications for practice. *School Psychology Review, 20,* 110–131.

Osguthorpe, R. T., & Scruggs, T. E. (1986). Special education students as tutors: A review and analysis. *Remedial and Special Education, 7*(4), 15–25.

Peterson, D. W., & Miller, J. A. (1990). Best practices in peer-influenced learning. In A. Thomas & J. Grimes (Eds.), *Best practices in school psychology II* (pp. 531–546). Washington, DC: National Association of School Psychologists.

Ryndak, D., & Alper, S. (1996). *Curriculum content for students with moderate and severe disabilities in inclusive settings.* Boston: Allyn & Bacon.

Ryndak, D., & Weidler, S. (1996). Application to special education curriculum areas with general education parallels. In D. Ryndak & S. Alper (Eds.), *Curriculum content for students with moderate and severe disabilities in inclusive settings* (pp. 97–121). Boston: Allyn & Bacon.

Salisbury, C. L., Evans, I. M., & Palombaro, M. M. (1997). Collaborative problem solving to promote the inclusion of young children with significant disabilities in primary grades. *Exceptional Children, 63,* 195–209.

Schnorr, R. F. (1997). From enrollment to membership: "Belonging" in middle and high school classes. *Journal of the Association for Persons with Severe Handicaps, 22,* 1–15.

Shapiro, E. S., & Cole, C. L. (1994). *Behavior change in the classroom: Self-management interventions.* New York: Guilford Press.

Sharpe, M. N., York, J. L., & Knight, J. (1994). Effects of inclusion on the academic performance of classmates without disabilities. *Remedial and Special Education, 15*(5), 281–287.

Slavin, R. E. (1995). *Cooperative learning* (2nd ed.). Needham Heights, MA: Allyn & Bacon.

Snell, M. E., & Brown, F. (1993). Instructional planning and implementation. In M. E. Snell (Ed.), *Instruction of students with severe disabilities* (4th ed., pp. 99–151). New York: Macmillan.

Strully, J., & Strully, C. (1985). Friendship and our children. *Journal of the Association for Persons with Severe Handicaps, 10,* 224–227.

Tashie, C., Shapiro-Barnard, S., Dillon, A. D., Schuh, M., Jorgensen, C., & Nisbet, J. (1993). *Changes in latitudes, changes in attitudes: The role of the inclusion facilitator.* Concord: University of New Hampshire.

Villa, R. A., & Thousand, J. S. (Eds.). (1995). *Creating an inclusive school.* Alexandria, VA: Association for Supervision and Curriculum Development.

Wesson, C. L., & King, R. P. (1996). Portfolio assessment and special education students. *Teaching Exceptional Children, 28*(2), 44–48.

Wilson, B. A. (1999). Inclusion: Empirical guidelines and unanswered questions. *Education and Training in Mental Retardation and Developmental Disabilities, 34,* 119–133.

Wisniewski, & Alper, S. (1994). Including students with severe disabilities in general education settings: Guidelines for change. *Remedial and Special Education, 15*(1), 4–13.

York, J., & Tunidor, M. (1995). Issues raised in the name of inclusion: Perspectives of educators, parents, and students. *Journal of the Association for Persons with Severe Handicaps, 20,* 31–44.

York, J., Vandercook, T., MacDonald, C., Heise-Neff, C., & Caughey, E. (1992). Feedback about integrating middle-school students with severe disabilities in general education classes. *Exceptional Children, 58,* 244–258.

T H I R T E E N

Using Ecological Assessment in Planning for Transition and Employment

with Edward Grasso

FOR DAVE STEWART,[1] *the transition from school to adult living was looming in his future, and his prospects did not look promising. Dave was an 18-year-old diagnosed with moderate mental retardation who was unhappy in his present school program. He had enjoyed his experiences of inclusion in general education, but his friends in his general education classes had graduated from high school the year before, and he was now enrolled in a segregated "life skills" training program with which both he and his mother were dissatisfied. Furthermore, Dave's frustration was manifesting itself in problem behavior, and he was beginning to acquire a reputation as a "troublemaker."*

Raetta Baker's transition to adult living seemed even more uncertain than Dave's. Raetta, a 21-year-old with severe disabilities, would graduate from high school in a year, and she had no current options for a job or leisure activities. Her parents both worked, and they worried about the impact when Raetta had neither school, work, nor other services to support her during the day. Raetta's parents also worried about where their daughter would live if they became unable to care for her. Because Raetta was much happier and more alert when school was in session, her parents worried about the negative effects of her staying home all day while waiting to find new opportunities.

This chapter focuses on the planning needed for students to transition from high school to employment and adult living. Unfortunately, the majority of individuals with moderate and severe disabilities leave high school with a cloudy future. The unemployment rate for this population continues to be extremely high. This chapter provides guidelines for developing and implementing transition plans to improve employment outcomes.

The emphasis on transition planning emerged in the 1980s, when new initiatives in supported employment demonstrated that individuals with disabilities, including those with severe disabilities, could succeed in competitive jobs (Wehman, Hill, Wood,

---

[1]The case studies of Dave Stewart and Raetta Baker are based on the employment histories of real people who were served through Lehigh University Supported Employment and Assessment Services. Their names and other facts about them have been changed to protect their confidentiality, consistent with recommendations by the World and American Psychiatric Associations (Clifft, 1986).

Edward Grasso, MEd, is director of Lehigh University Supported Employment and Assessment Services, Bethlehem, Pennsylvania.

& Parent, 1987). In contrast, the unemployment rate for this population was found to be extremely high—over 78% (Wehman, Kregel, & Seyfarth, 1985). Students and families who had reaped the benefits of a free public education found that they had no "entitlement" to adult services. For many individuals, reaching age 21 meant either finding no options or having to accept segregated day services as their only option. In response to the bleak postschool outcomes students with disabilities faced, the U.S. Congress passed PL 98-199, which put a priority on transition services by requiring an individual transition plan (ITP) to be included with older students' individualized education plans (IEPs). This encouraged school districts to conduct this planning in collaboration with other agencies (e.g., state or local division of vocational rehabilitation) so that the students would be able to receive services upon leaving school. Congress also passed the Developmental Disabilities Act of 1984, which stipulated that employment of individuals with disabilities should be a priority, and offered guidelines for providing supported employment services. "Supported employment" is paid employment in a competitive job setting with ongoing support services. In this same year (1984), the Carl D. Perkins Vocational Education Act expanded the vocational education and assessment services available to students with disabilities to include transition services. As amended in 1990, this act mandated that students be informed of their vocational opportunities at least 1 year prior to graduation, and that equal access to all vocational services be given to students with disabilities.

The focus on transition that emerged in the 1980s continued into the next decade. The reauthorization of the Individuals with Disabilities Education Act (IDEA; PL 101-476) in 1990 defined transition planning and mandated its inclusion in IEPs. "Transition" was defined as a coordinated set of services to promote movement from school to postschool activities. Transition activities must be based on a student's needs and preferences, and must include the development of employment and other adult living objectives. Since the 1997 amendments to IDEA, this transition planning must begin at age 14 with a statement of the student's transition service needs under the applicable components of the IEP, and be updated annually. By age 16, or earlier if this is deemed appropriate by the IEP team, these transition service needs are defined to include any interagency responsibilities or linkages. Although there is still much work to do before there will be adequate adult services for individuals with moderate and severe disabilities, schools can enhance these options through well-designed transition planning.

This transition planning will typically focus on a range of decisions to be made about adult life. Wehman, Moon, Everson, Wood, and Barcus (1988) recommend that transition planning focus on the following areas:

- Employment
- Postsecondary education
- Residential plans
- Financial/income needs
- Recreation/leisure needs
- Medical needs
- Counseling/case management (e.g., sex education, respite care, counseling)
- Transportation needs
- Advocacy/legal needs
- Personal/home/money management

Because earlier chapters in this text have described community and home/personal care planning, this chapter emphasizes the employment component of transition planning.

ECOLOGICALLY RELEVANT TRANSITION ASSESSMENTS

Despite the emphasis on employment in the last two decades, many individuals with moderate and severe disabilities continue to find it difficult to gain access to job opportunities. Educators can play a key role in promoting employment opportunities through planning, training, and networking. In an extensive review of the research literature and a survey of parents, advocates, and professionals, Sale, Everson, Metzler, and Moon (1991) identified four primary quality indicators for vocational transition programs: (1) community-based employment training, (2) parent and consumer involvement, (3) interagency coordination, and (4) adult service options. Adult service options include having services available in the community that students can access upon graduation, such as support for employment, transportation, self-advocacy groups, leisure options, and college programs. The school's transition coordinator can often play a key role in helping students gain access to these services upon graduation. In the past, professionals often steered students with moderate and severe disabilities toward specialized, segregated environments, such as sheltered workshops and adult day programs. More recently, new options in supported employment have created ways for adults who need long-term support to be able to obtain and maintain jobs. These services typically include a support person (e.g., an employment specialist) who may provide direct instruction in how to perform the job (job coaching), but who may also work indirectly by collaborating with the job supervisor and coworkers to encourage natural supports available in the workplace. The range of employment alternatives that may exist in the community is shown in Table 13.1.

All of the options shown in Table 13.1 are not "equal" in terms of the quality of life they create for individuals with disabilities. Griffin, Rosenberg, Cheyney, and Greenberg (1996) found that adults with mild mental retardation scored higher on measures of self-esteem and job satisfaction in supported employment versus sheltered workshops. To find a preferred, individual job in a company with good wages and benefits can have a large impact on anyone's life. Such employment can foster financial security, offer opportunities to meet new friends, and enhance self-esteem. Given these potential benefits, an individual job placement with ongoing support (e.g., funded supported employment or well-established natural supports) may be the "ideal" outcome for employment planning for most students. Opportunities for individuals with severe disabilities to obtain supported employment have been increasing, making it possible for more students to be in competitive jobs (Revell, Wehman, Kregel, & West, 1994). In contrast, some individuals may have health challenges, family considerations, or personal preferences that create the need for an adaptation of a comprehensive service (e.g., a part-time job and leisure supports). It is no longer necessary to use a segregated center (e.g., a day program) to create such adaptations. A national trend exists in which providers are exploring new, integrated options (McGaughey, Kiernan, McNally, Gilmore, & Keith, 1995; Rucker & Browder, 1997). To develop such options requires using

TABLE 13.1. Adult Service and Community Employment Alternatives That May Be Available for Students Exiting High School

Inclusive community options	Traditional segregated options
• **Regular employment:** An individual with a disability may procure and work a job with no specialized support. This category also includes individuals who are self-employed or who work in a family business, and who may receive extensive assistance from others in their environments ("natural supports"), but who do not receive funded services.	• **Sheltered workshop:** Most communities have a sheltered workshop, established as a charitable organization, to provide job training in a self-contained environment. Typically, all workers on site are disabled, and wages are substantially below minimum wage (e.g., piece rate). The work is usually subcontracted, and the workers are employed by the workshop itself. Sheltered workshops are sometimes large organizations that include work evaluations as well as training. They may also have a supported employment division. Some sheltered workshops are not accessible to individuals with more severe disabilities, who are referred instead to work activity centers or adult day programs. Sheltered workshops are often funded by the state vocational rehabilitation agency.
• **Transitional support:** Agencies such as the state vocational rehabilitation agency may offer short-term help such as an assessment, assistance for job procurement, or brief on-the-job training (a few days or weeks).	
• **Supported employment:** The community may have one or numerous companies or agencies that provide supported employment, including job placement, training, and on-the-job support for as long as the individual needs it. "Supported employment" usually refers to an individual job placement in a competitive work environment earning minimum wage or above for 20 hours per week or more. A job coach may work full-time with the individual on the job initially, and then fade this to intermittent follow-along assistance. Some agencies emphasize indirect support (e.g., collaboration with job supervisors) in a "natural supports" model. Supported employment may be funded by the state's vocational rehabilitation agency or other adult agencies (e.g., mental health/mental retardation/developmental disabilities services). In some communities, individuals can purchase these services with either private funds or "vouchers" from a funding agency.	• **Work activity center:** A work activity center has a "prevocational" focus, in that individuals are learning to do work tasks and typically are not paid. Sometimes the program may include training in motor tasks or self-care skills. These services are also often funded by the state vocational rehabilitation agency.
	• **Adult day program:** This is a center-based program that usually does *not* have a focus on employment. Sometimes training extends the school program to include life skills instruction, but not all focus on functional skills. To update their services, some adult day programs now provide community-based instruction. Some adult day programs specialize in serving individuals with significant disabilities or behavioral challenges. Day programs are typically funded by mental health/mental retardation developmental disabilities service agencies. Some may include private pay participants.
• **Adaptations of supported employment:** To create more opportunities for individuals with severe disabilities to be employed, some providers offer other forms of support. These may include placing a group of individuals with disabilities in the same job site in an "enclave" or "cluster" placement. The individuals with disabilities may also be employed by the supported employment company or agency itself, but work in integrated environments in either a "mobile work crew" or other model. Supported employment companies that employ individuals with disabilities to do work in integrated settings are sometimes called "entrepreneurial" models. Some supported employment agencies will help individuals with disabilities create their own businesses; this is called "supported self-employment." In	• **Adult day care:** Adult day care centers may be created primarily to serve older adults who are not developmentally disabled, but their clients may also include individuals with mental retardation. Some may require that these participants also be of a certain age, depending on their source of funding. Funding may either be from human service agencies (e.g., services on aging) or private pay. The focus of these services is usually caregiving. Some also provide training.

(cont.)

TABLE 13.1. *(cont.)*

Inclusive community options	Traditional segregated options
adaptations in supported employment, the participant may work less than 20 hours, earn less than minimum wage (with approval of the U.S. Department of Labor through the Handicapped Worker's Certificate), and/or work in a "carved" job created within a company to meet the needs of both the company and the individual with disabilities. Many new adaptations of supported employment are emerging as more providers seek to serve individuals with severe disabilities.	
• **Inclusive leisure support or comprehensive services:** Some companies or agencies offer either support for participation in community recreation or comprehensive services to fill the day with options beyond employment. In some communities, adult day programs have "converted" to being fully community-based by focusing on leisure and community access as well as employment options. Similarly, some supported employment agencies provide options for individuals who need full-time (e.g., all-day) support, but do not have full-time jobs.	
• **Volunteer work:** Individuals with disabilities may provide unpaid community service for organizations such as hospitals, the Society for Prevention of Cruelty to Animals, or the American Cancer Society. This volunteer work may be done on their own initiative or may be supported through an agency that offers comprehensive services as described above.	

Important Note: Individuals with moderate and severe disabilities can be found in *all* of the aforementioned types of services. Whether or not a person with significant disabilities receives a preferred job in an inclusive setting with good wages and benefits often depends on the creativity and resources of the planning team.

an individualized and creative planning process. An ecological assessment, with its person-centered planning approach, provides a format for a transition team to conduct this planning.

Rationale for Using an Ecological Approach in Transition Assessment

Special educators have often relied on standardized assessment protocols to determine students' current level of functioning on their IEPs. Not surprisingly, with the advent of transition planning, special educators searched for standardized vocational assessments to guide this planning. For students with moderate and severe disabilities, the use of standardized assessments has been widely criticized because of misapplications of tests not designed for this population (Sigafoos, Cole, & McQuarter, 1987), their insensitivity to small changes in functional behavior (Cole, Swisher, Thompson, &

Fewell, 1985), and their irrelevance to the ecologies of students' homes, communities, and work settings (Rainforth & York, 1987). In general, using standardized tests for transition planning has been criticized, because so few instruments exist that measure life skills and other adult outcomes (Clark, 1996). In contrast, ecological assessments that focus on functional skills and support needs (Spencer & Sample, 1993) and person-centered planning (Everson, 1996) can provide more useful information. As described in Chapter Two, ecological assessments have also been empirically validated as providing information that is more useful in planning (Linehan, & Brady, 1995; Linehan, Brady, & Hwang, 1991; Downing & Perino, 1992).

Conducting an Ecological Assessment for Transition Planning

Review of Prior Records

In an ecological planning process, the team begins by getting to know the student and reviewing prior records. This procedure should focus on reviewing the student's achievements, strengths, and preferences for their relevance to future employment. If the student has had prior job training, this information should be summarized. Sometimes standardized assessment information may be available in the student's file. If a formalized transition assessment is to be written, selective information from these reports may be included if they are relevant to planning or if they help the student gain access to future funding.

When Dave Stewart's transition coordinator, Mr. Lewis, reviewed his file to prepare for the first planning meeting, he found a lot of information that was not relevant to their purpose. For example, Dave had scored below the 1st percentile on the Wechsler Individual Achievement Test and in the 13th percentile on the California Verbal Learning Test. His scores on the Child Behavior Checklist were nearly all below the 60th percentile (clinically significant for problem behavior). These statistics portrayed Dave as "very deficient" and offered no concrete information on his specific academic, communication, or social skills. Mr. Lewis decided not to stigmatize Dave by repeating these scores to his new transition planning team. In contrast, information from an augmentative communication evaluation by the speech therapist and from Dave's current IEP progress report was helpful. The speech therapist noted Dave's need for skills in listening and conversational turn taking, and suggested that a visual-aid referent might help foster these skills. The most recent IEP progress reports revealed that Dave was receiving some community-based instruction in using restaurants and crossing streets, and that he had made good progress in these skills. However, these IEP progress reports also described problem behavior. After meeting Dave and talking with his mother, Mr. Lewis concluded that this behavior might be due to the mismatch between Dave's needs and his current environment. Dave was receiving all instruction in a segregated "life skills" center designed for 18- to 21-year-olds in the district. His mother reported that Dave did not like being taken out of the high school, nor did he care for the job tasks used in this setting (simulated tabletop assembly work).

In reviewing these records, Mr. Lewis was concerned about taking a positive focus in presenting Dave to the team, which included both members who were familiar with him and members who did not know him. Mr. Lewis decided that the best option was for Dave to introduce himself, followed by Mr. Lewis's reading a capacity statement about him. At their first meeting, Dave introduced himself by shaking each person's hand and smiling as the team members in turn said their names. He then showed memorabilia of his favorite college sports team and shared his dream of someday visiting that college. Next, Mr. Lewis gave this introductory statement, which he had previewed with Dave and his mother:

> "Dave, we are delighted to be gathered here as your planning team. We are first and foremost committed to helping you find *your* dream, because this is *your* future. I would like to introduce Dave to everyone. As I am sure you realize by now, Dave Stewart is a friendly and energetic young man. He has an impressive ability to start a conversation with a few words by sharing objects of interest, like his favorite basketball team. Dave is 18 years old and lives with his mother, Ms. Donna Jenkins, and his sister, Ms. Maria Stewart, who is a graduate student in psychology. Both Donna and Maria have accepted Dave's invitation to be part of this team and are here today. Dave visits his father, Bob Stewart, on alternate weekends and enjoys helping to care for his stepbrother, who is 1 year old. Dave has attended Hanover High School since he was 15. He loved being part of high school, but was confused when many of his friends in general education graduated at 18 and he didn't. Instead, he was placed in the 'life skills' training at Hanover Vocational Center. Dave's dissatisfaction with this option led to the creation of this planning team. His mother has formally requested that his IEP be reopened and that his vocational needs be reevaluated.
>
> "To offer a brief profile of Dave's skills, Dave has responded well to community-based instruction in the last year and can order food at a fast-food restaurant. He has nearly mastered crossing side streets and will soon be focusing on busier intersections. Dave also has some academic skills. He can read and write some words, and can use a calculator to add. Although Dave can often initiate a topic of conversation, he is still working on his listening skills and turn taking. Dave is currently dissatisfied with his instruction in employment and life skills at the vocational center. His mother, Dave, and the staff all agree that Dave needs new options."

In another school district, a team was planning for a student named Raetta Baker. The team's introduction to Raetta revealed a very different starting point than that for Dave. Raetta had been diagnosed with profound mental retardation and mild cerebral palsy. She was able to walk short distances, but also used a wheelchair for ambulating. She was nonverbal and did not use an augmentative system of communication. Instead, she made her desires known through vocalizations, eye gazing, and lifting her head. Raetta's team was planning for her last year of education, as she would turn 21 this year. Ms. D'Alberto, the transition coordinator, found no recent standardized assessments in Raetta's file. In contrast, Raetta's evaluations had been based on her medical and therapy reports and behavioral observations. For Raetta's meeting, Ms. D'Alberto prepared the following written profile to share with the team:

PROFILE TO INTRODUCE STUDENT TO TRANSITION PLANNING TEAM

PERSONAL INFORMATION

Raetta Baker is a young woman who will soon be 21 years old. Raetta lives with her parents, Walter and Sonia Baker. She is the youngest child and has four adult siblings who live on their own. Raetta's aunt (her mother's sister), Charlene Johnson, also lives with the family and helps care for Raetta.

SKILLS AND RECENT ACHIEVEMENTS

In the past 2 years, Raetta has improved her ability to walk short distances and get in and out of a car. She has been developing her choice-making skills and will reach toward an object to ask for it. Raetta can also feed herself and enjoys a wide variety of foods.

ONGOING SUPPORT NEEDS

Raetta relies on her caregivers for dressing and other personal care. She continues to need physical assistance when walking. Raetta wears a helmet, because her seizures are only partially controlled by medication, and the chance of a head injury during a seizure exists. Raetta sometimes becomes lethargic. She is more likely to respond well with an active schedule and frequent changes of materials or settings.

Person-Centered Planning

A key component of an ecological assessment is to conduct person-centered planning. This person-centered planning often provides an important format for family input. In their research with transition-age students, Morningstar, Turnbull, and Turnbull (1995) found that high school students *do* want their families involved in helping them plan for the future. Unfortunately, parents do not always feel welcome in school-initiated planning efforts. This may be especially true if professionals are not sensitive to cultural diversity (Sontag & Schacht, 1994). Weber and Stoneman (1986) recommend that teachers encourage family involvement by (1) letting family members know how important their input is to the planning process, (2) informing family members of specific information contained in the student's educational plans, and (3) using plain language to discuss complicated issues. When working cross-culturally, professionals can encourage input by obtaining interpreters (if needed) and being cognizant of the family's unique interaction style (Dennis & Giangreco, 1996).

Educators can also help parents prepare by sharing examples of how other students with moderate and severe disabilities have made successful outcomes. These examples may be shared through showing videotapes of individuals with severe disabilities working at integrated job sites, taking parents to job sites, inviting family members who have recently been through the transition process to describe what worked for them, and having employers who are excited about their employees with severe disabilities speak to family groups (Morton, Everson, & Moon, 1987). After this general information sharing, holding a person-centered planning meeting with the family and friends in preparation for the school's formal IEP/ITP meeting can be an important tool to make planning more family-centered. This meeting can help the family establish priorities and generate an agenda for topics to be discussed in the formal meeting.

In their research on using person-centered planning as part of the transition process, Miner and Bates (1997) held a special meeting prior to the formal IEP/ITP meeting. These researchers found that the use of person-centered planning increased the parents' participation in the subsequent school-based IEP/transition meeting. The parents who had the additional planning process also were more positive about the outcome of the IEP/ITP meeting. An important observation of the researchers was that the school-based IEP/ITP meetings were only scheduled for 30 minutes. These brief, formal meetings did not allow sufficient time for the brainstorming and team goal setting that are critical to person-centered planning. Holding a more open-ended planning meeting prior to the formal IEP/ITP meeting can be an important strategy to promote family- and student-centered planning. This work can then set the agenda for the formal process.

There are several options for person-centered planning, as described in Chapter Two. One of the most popular is "mapping," which is described in Mount and Zwernik's (1988) manual on person-centered planning. Using this format, the team creates a personal profile of the student by developing diagrams of the student's life history, current and past relationships, choice-making opportunities, community presence, and preferences. From these individual diagrams or maps, a future-vision map is developed, including desires for career, home, leisure pursuits, and socialization.

For Dave's transition assessment, Mr. Lewis conducted a person-centered planning meeting with Dave, his mother, his sister, friends, and advocates in their home prior to the formal school-based team meetings. This meeting was essential to develop trust with Dave's mother, Ms. Jenkins, who had become discouraged with the current school program. Dave and Ms. Jenkins were also more comfortable discussing their desires and concerns in their own home, with the help of some friends and professionals who had been lifelong advocates for Dave. During this meeting, this "circle of friends" helped determine that his reports of problem behavior were his way of protesting his current setting, since he had been cooperative in prior settings that he liked. They also discussed frankly the issue of Dave's "troublemaker" reputation and planned with Mr. Lewis how to help his formal, school-based transition team maintain a positive focus. They diagrammed maps for Dave and began helping him define a vision for the future. His enjoyment of community-based instruction, martial arts, sports teams, and people became important clues for helping design his future instruction.

Dave's mother also had the opportunity to articulate her preferences, which included (1) for Dave to have a "real" job someday; (2) for Dave to continue developing his academic skills in school until he was 21; (3) for Dave's prior love of being in general education classes to be considered (e.g., would college be an option after high school?); and (4) for him to pursue some of his community interests through volunteering. Dave also expressed some specific preferences, including (1) to be able to go to college like his sister (preferably the college of his favorite basketball team); (2) to work in a police department or on the radio; (3) to get paid; (4) never to be talked to like a "baby"; and (5) to be at his own meetings and sign the papers. This planning time also gave Ms. Jenkins and Dave's sister, Maria, the opportunity to articulate their priorities for what would be discussed at the IEP/ITP meeting. Mr. Lewis summarized these priorities in a "family preference profile." In addition to helping create the agenda for the transition meeting, creating a written list of family preferences, and a separate list of student preferences, can be a strategy to help parents realize that their children's priorities may differ from their own. For example, in developing the following family preference profile, the team had a frank discussion about whether or not Dave shared his family's strong preference that he stay in school until age 21. Mr. Lewis noted that as an 18-year-old, Dave had the legal status of an adult (having reached the "age of majority") and could decide his educational future. Ms. Jenkins then realized that staying in school was *her* priority for Dave, but that he might not agree unless his program was improved.

FAMILY PREFERENCE PROFILE

Student: _Dave Stewart_   Age: _18_

Participating Family Members: _Mother, Donna Jenkins; sister, Maria Stewart_

VOCATIONAL SKILL PREFERENCES
- That Dave's team determine what employment options are available.
- That Dave be given experience in real jobs.
- That Dave's interests be considered in selecting job training sites.
- That Dave obtain a community job by graduation at age 21.

EDUCATIONAL PREFERENCES
- That Dave continue receiving public school services until age 21, and that the school make every effort to encourage him to continue to pursue this education (although Dave has the right to decide to leave school now that he is 18).
- That Dave's progress be monitored, and that the family receive specific data-based reports.

At the end of the person-centered planning meeting, the family decided that Dave, his mother, his sister, and a lifelong advocate, Mr. Shelton, would attend the school-based meetings. These meetings would also be heavily attended by professionals (e.g., the principal, the supervisor of special education, the school psychologist, Dave's current teacher), because Dave's mother had made a formal request to reopen the IEP (on the advice of her personal attorney). With the understanding of Dave and his mother, and the special education supervisor, Mr. Lewis would serve as facilitator of the planning effort. The goal was to achieve an appropriate plan—one that would be acceptable to Dave, his mother, and the district. In the first school-based meeting, Mr. Lewis introduced Dave using information that had been developed in the person-centered planning meeting, as described earlier. He also shared information on Dave's preferences, interests, and goals.

Raetta's person-centered planning process followed a different format. Ms. D'Alberto conducted two school-based planning meetings for Raetta—one for transition planning, and the second to develop and formalize the IEP/ITP plan. The first, which the district called a "transition meeting," became a celebration of Raetta as she began her last year of school. Although held in a school conference room, the team of professionals, family members, and friends used the occasion to affirm Raetta by bringing refreshments and handmade cards or posters for her. This small celebration of Raetta reminded each member of the team that this was *her* meeting. This meeting also offered a time to reflect on Raetta's school history as they got ready for her exit process. From their brainstorming, the group discovered the parents' strong concern about how Raetta would spend her days after high school. Because they knew she became lethargic when not active, they worried about the potential impact of not having a job on her health and well-being. Ms. D'Alberto noted that the search for employment and other community pursuits would be a high priority for Raetta. The team would also need an action plan to help her obtain the funding needed to support these endeavors. To consider what type of employment and leisure interests to pursue, Ms. D'Alberto talked with the group about Raetta's preferences. The group noted that she liked to be clean and in quiet surroundings. She also liked to be outside, to be near plants, and to view magazines with pictures of food. From their discussions, they concluded that their primary goal was to find Raetta a job and comprehensive supports, so that her days would be both meaningful and productive after leaving high school.

Promoting Self-Determination

In their evaluation of transition programs, Grigal, Test, Beattie, and Wood (1997) found that successful transition plans included self-determination, self-evaluation, student empowerment, student-determined postschool goals, and student-selected educational experiences. In contrast, many individuals with disabilities have not been allowed to participate fully in deciding what services they are to receive, how they are to be administered, or what their outcomes should be (Brotherson, Cook, Cunconan-Lahr, & Wehmeyer, 1995). Three ways the ecological assessment process can be used to promote self-determination during transition planning are (1) to use the meetings themselves to foster leadership; (2) to encourage the student to set goals and make decisions (or, if this is not feasible, to base goal setting on the student's preferences); and (3) to assess what self-determination skills the student may need to acquire. These methods to promote self-determination are described in detail in Chapter Six. They are illustrated here for the case studies of Dave and Raetta.

In Dave's case, Mr. Lewis decided to begin teaching Dave to be an active participant in his planning meetings, with the goal that he would be able to lead the meetings in the future. Van Reusen and Bos (1994) recommend encouraging student participation in planning by giving students the skills needed to participate, providing opportunities in the meeting for them to ask and respond to questions, and helping them organize the information they will need during the meeting. Dave already had some important skills that would benefit him in planning sessions. Because he had some reading and number recognition skills, he would be able to follow written reports and charts to some extent. Mr. Lewis practiced these skills with Dave, including finding the page number of a report, and reading key words such as his name to determine whether the report was about him. Dave also prepared for his transition meeting by making a written list of questions on a handout that he would distribute. He practiced his handshake greetings and decided what to share with the team (his sports interest). He also selected materials that could help him tell the group his future interests. He and Mr. Lewis listed these as follows:

PLANNING FOR DAVE'S PARTICIPATION IN TRANSITION MEETING
WITH MATERIALS PREPARED IN ADVANCE

SYMBOL OR MATERIAL:	USED TO TALK ABOUT:
Bookmark made like a $100 bill	His desire to earn money
Picture of police station	Interest in job with police
Bumper sticker of a local radio station	Interest in job as DJ
University banner	Interest in attending college and interest in basketball
Handout of questions dictated to Mr. Lewis	His questions for the group
A special felt tip pen	Reminder that he signs everything (18 years old)

One of the IEP goals that Mr. Lewis planned to recommend for Dave was that he learn goal setting and meeting leadership. He planned to introduce Dave's planning group to the Choicemaker Self-Determination Transition Curriculum (Martin & Huber-Marshall, 1995, 1996). In one module of this curriculum, The Self-Directed IEP, participants watch a videotape of a high school student directing his own IEP meeting. The videotape helps participants learn the social skills needed for professional meetings, such as asking appropriate questions and handling disagreements. In a second videotape, students learn to break down long-term goals into short-term objectives. They then learn how to plan to attain their goals by determining performance criteria; identifying a means to obtain feedback, instruction, and other needed support; and making a schedule for action. Mr. Lewis would illustrate how this curriculum could be adapted to Dave's communication ability by having Dave set some goals in the meeting, using the materials listed above. Mr. Lewis also recommended including an IEP objective in problem-solving strategies for Dave. For example, Dave could learn to solve problems in functional activities, as described in the research of Hughes, Hugo, and Blatt (1996). (See Chapter Six, for more information on teaching problem solving.) Mr. Lewis also recommended to the team that Dave participate in a series of situational assessments to explore his job interests and skills further.

In Raetta's case, it was not feasible to have her lead her planning meeting (given her current communication and social skills), but it was important to have her present at the meeting. To promote self-determination for Raetta, Ms. D'Alberto used her preferences as the foundation for the team's goal setting. When students are not able to communicate their job interests, a systematic preference assessment can be used to help with job matching (Winking, O'Reilly, & Moon, 1993; Lohrmann-O'Rourke & Browder, 1998; Reid, Parsons, & Green, 1998). Ms. D'Alberto prepared for the transition meeting by conducting systematic preference assessments of Raetta over a 2-week period (see Chapter Six for more on preference assessment). She tried a wide range of choices in the context of Raetta's daily routines and kept notes to see whether any preferences emerged. From these notes, Ms. D'Alberto discovered that Raetta would ask for music by looking toward the tape player when it was turned off. She was most responsive with upbeat background music such as "oldies." In addition, Ms. D'Alberto discovered that Raetta would pull her hands away from any activity that soiled them (e.g., potting plants, kneading bread dough). Raetta also would lift her head and look around more when the room's lighting was bright versus dim. From these classroom activities, Ms. D'Alberto noted Raetta's preferences for upbeat music and bright lighting, and her dislike of messy work tasks. Ms. D'Alberto created a student preference profile to use in the team meeting's planning. She gave all members a copy of this profile and made a large poster to help the team remember them in creating goals for Raetta. This is what the preference profile looked like.

STUDENT PREFERENCE PROFILE

Student: _Raetta Baker_   Age: _21_

ENVIRONMENTAL PREFERENCES

- Upbeat background music
- Bright lighting
- Other people working or other activities nearby
- Being outside or near flowers

FOOD PREFERENCES

- Spaghetti
- Ice cream (not chocolate or coffee)
- Applesauce
- Dislikes hard-to-chew foods

MATERIALS PREFERENCES

- Materials with bright colors
- Pictures of flowers
- Dislikes hands becoming soiled with dirt, food, etc. (e.g., dislikes working in soil, kneading bread dough)

ACTIVITIES PREFERENCES

- Strolling at fairs or amusement parks
- Listening to siblings sing or play piano
- Family reunions
- Going to restaurants
- Sitting outside

Like Dave, Raetta could benefit from some situational assessments, so that the team would understand her preferences better. Ms. D'Alberto also would recommend an IEP objective to encourage Raetta to "take charge" of all of her personal care routines (e.g., dressing, toileting) by directing the caregiver's actions through movement and eye gazing (see Chapter Ten for specific examples). This self-determination skill would be useful with the people who would provide her support in her future job contexts.

Developing a Personalized Job Training Curriculum and Work Sites

In an ecological assessment, the priorities established through person-centered planning and self-determination strategies are used to develop a personalized curriculum for the student. It is important that any employment training be linked to real jobs that exist in a student's community. By identifying these options in collaboration with area businesses and focusing on the student's preferences, the teacher or transition coordinator can begin to determine what specific job skills the student will need to learn.

Ecological inventories. The first step in developing a student's personalized job training curriculum is to identify some specific job options in the local community that correspond to the student's preferences. This is done through an ecological inventory process. Baine (1987) notes that using ecological inventories in developing special education curricula makes it more likely that students will be taught skills that they will use in their current and future environments. In conducting an ecological inventory, the teacher or transition coordinator generates a list of options to be considered for current training and future employment. This list can be generated by (1) reading want ads in the newspaper, (2) participating in community business councils or interviewing business leaders, (3) touring major companies in the area, and (4) talking with the family about potential leads for future jobs. Throughout this process, the professional needs to keep the student's preferences in mind. Figure 13.1 illustrates the ecological inventory process used in finding sites for Dave's job training.

Situational Assessments. With the information obtained through these ecological inventories, the teacher can plan for specific job tryouts. Some job tryouts may be very brief, as part of an initial transition assessment. For example, at Lehigh University Supported Employment and Assessment Services, 40-hour assessments are conducted in which participants seeking jobs try five different job sites for 1 day each. From this brief exposure, the participants then choose the type of job to pursue for future employment. For students who still have some school years left for job exploration, this job sampling may be longer. In some cases, students may stay in each job site for one-quarter of the school year. Some students may work in more than one job site at a time (e.g., 2 days at a restaurant, 2 days in a warehouse) to be able to make a decision based on this concurrent experience. Whatever the model used, it is important for students to be able to develop a work history by trying jobs in a variety of settings.

At Dave's formal transition meeting, the team decided to create the opportunity for Dave to try a variety of jobs in the coming school year. In talking with Dave, they decided that he might benefit most from concurrent placements, to be able to make weekly comparisons of what he liked and disliked in these sites. Mr. Lewis developed a job training/tryout schedule for Dave, based both on activities he liked (police work, radio station work) and on his desire to earn money (e.g., jobs that frequently had openings and opportunities for pay increases). Using the information from his ecological inventories in further planning with Dave, his family, and the supervisor of special education, Mr. Lewis helped created the following schedule. Notice that Mr. Lewis also incorporated Dave's interest in attending college by arranging for him to try a class in public relations. Dave and Mr. Lewis chose this class because it would be helpful in his work with the drug education program hosted by the police department. Dave re-

FIGURE 13.1. Ecological Inventory of Job Skills and Training Sites

Company	Types of jobs	Sample list of job skills	Interest as host site for training?
Township Police Dept.	Law enforcement Drug education Clerical Custodial	Drug education • Showing video • Handing out materials • Interacting with children in elementary schools • Giving personal statement about refusing drugs	Yes—in drug education
Radio station	On-air DJ Programming News and weather reporting Marketing Public relations Clerical Custodial	Clerical work • Photocopying • Mailings • Filing • Making coffee • Participation in office discussions about musical selections	Yes—in assisting with clerical work; student interns are unpaid
Super Foods (grocer) (frequently has job openings)	Cashier Bagger Cart collector Custodial Produce manager	Bagger and cart collector • Greeting customer and asking, "Paper or plastic?" • Bagging groceries so items are not crushed or contaminated • Cleaning carts of trash • Stacking carts • Pushing a line of carts to cart storage area	Yes—for bagger and cart collector; will pay student intern above minimum wage
Martial arts studio (student preference)	Martial arts instructor Receptionist		No—but can take classes
Becker's Warehouse	Packaging Inventory of stock Driving fork lift Loading trucks	Loading • Finding correct inventory • Lifting and stacking boxes • Using a handtruck • Working with team in high-volume jobs	Yes—for loading; openings for full-time employment with benefits
University cafeteria	Cashier Cook Cook's assistant Dishwasher assistant	Dishwasher assistant • Clearing trays as they come down the line • Helping load dishes • Scrubbing pots and pans	Yes—for dishwasher assistant

ceived training at each job site from a job coach. When not participating in this community-based job training, Dave worked on other curricular goals at the local community college in a program newly created by the school district for 18- to 21-year-old students.

DAVE'S JOB TRAINING TRYOUT SCHEDULE

Day	Time	Site and activity
Monday	9:00–12:00	Radio station—Placed as a "student intern," along with college students (unpaid)
Tuesday	12:00–4:00	Super Foods—Work half a shift as bagger (paid)
Wednesday	11:00–1:00	University cafeteria—Clear trays on the line (school paid)
	1:00–2:30	(Audit class on public relations)
	2:30	(Training in ridings city bus home from university)
Thursday	12:00–4:00	Super Foods—Work half a shift doing carts (paid)
Friday	9:00–12:00	Police dept.—Volunteer work in drug education program
	12:30	Lunch at university
	1:00–2:30	(Audit class on public relations)

Raetta's circumstances were different from Dave's, in that as a 21-year-old student, she needed to find a job and other pursuits before the end of the 9 months she had left in school. Raetta also was not able to articulate her specific interests, as Dave was. The team needed to discover how she would respond to several job contexts to determine her preferences. To achieve this goal, the team looked at Raetta's student preference profile and brainstormed as many jobs as they could. Some of the ideas they had for job sites were these: a florist shop, the garden shop of a chain store, a music store, an office that played music in the background, a women's clothing store selling bright-colored clothes, a pizza restaurant, and an ice cream store. Ms. D'Alberto realized that Raetta would need intensive support when first placed in a job, because she had almost no employment experience. Raetta would probably also need long-term support to maintain her job. Because Raetta had few independent physical responses, it might also be necessary to "carve" a job for her—that is, to create a job that would benefit both the employer and Raetta.

Ms. D'Alberto conducted ecological inventories of a large number of sites in Raetta's community. From these, she found five sites that offered jobs related to Raetta's preferences and that were willing to cooperate for a 1-day assessment. The sites that Ms. D'Alberto found were as follows.

RAETTA'S SITUATIONAL ASSESSMENT SITES FOR JOB TRYOUTS

Site	Rationale	Carved job for Raetta
Florist	Raetta likes flowers	Discard old arrangements
Bottled-water distributor	Clean environment Friendly staff	Tear apart distribution sheets
Ice cream store	Likes ice cream Likes cleanliness	Wipe counter and seats
Dress shop	Bright colors; music	Remove old price tags
Music store	Music; lots of people	Dust shelves

For both Dave and Raetta, the person conducting the evaluation of the job tryouts used a variety of assessment tools, such as task analyses, discrepancy analyses, and repeated-trial assessments. (See Chapter Four for further information on these assessment formats.) For each job site, the evaluator wrote a one-paragraph description of how the student responded to the site. The evaluator also summarized any data collected at the site. This summary for Dave's first week on his job sites is shown in Figure 13.2.

One of the primary methods of data collection used in these job sites was task-analytic assessment. Figure 13.3 provides an example of a task-analytic assessment used with Dave when he was clearing trays in the university cafeteria. (The data chart here is similar to the Data Collection Form used in other chapters of this volume and provided in the Appendix, but some changes have been made for the job tryout situation.) For the first three trays, the job coach "probed" or tested Dave's ability to clear the trays alone. He was able to teach himself most of the task by imitating a peer. By the third tray, he could do 66% of the steps. Then, with some modeling, gesturing, and verbal prompting from the job coach, he could do each step. This last step was complicated by Dave's difficulty in keeping up with the conveyor belt. As students pushed their trays down the line, he often was not finished unloading a tray; this caused trays to collide and double up. The job coach then stopped taking data and helped Dave keep pace for the remainder of that work shift. The coach did make a mental note by looking at a wall clock with a secondhand of the number of seconds it took Dave to clear a tray versus a peer's time, in order to be able to set a goal for increasing Dave's productivity. After comparing about 10 trays each, she discovered that Dave would need to clear a tray in 10 seconds to keep up with the demands of the job during busy times, but that he was currently taking about 43 seconds.

Many of Raetta's jobs required two to three specific, motoric responses that she repeated in performing her job. For example, at the bottled-water distributing company, she tore apart order forms. At the florist, she pulled old arrangements apart, tossing the dead flowers in the garbage. Removing dress tags at the dress shop was also a grasp-and-release movement as she pulled each tag off and dropped it into a basket. For these jobs, Ms. D'Alberto used a repeated-trial assessment. Her data sheet was similar to the one shown in Figure 13.3, but instead of a task analysis, she simply wrote down the re-

FIGURE 13.2. Summary of the first week of job tryouts for Dave.

Summary of Job Tryouts

Student: Dave Stewart

Evaluators: Mr. Lewis, Transition Coordinator, and Ms. Moyer, job coach

Job site	Date	Data-based assessment	Description
Radio station	10/3	Filing: 20% of steps of task analysis correct. Social Interactions: 13 initiations; only responded to others' initiations or response on 3 of 24 (8%). On Dave's self-rating, he circled a 10 ("Terrific") for liking the job and 5 ("OK") for the work he did.	Dave was excited to be in this environment and made frequent comments to others in the environment. He smiled and said, "I like this!" several times. He will need systematic instruction to learn the filing and other tasks. The other student interns (college students) will need some training to know how to encourage Dave to take turns in conversation. They were joking about his lack of listening skills. We talked about the fact that this is an unpaid site with the other student interns. Dave said, "I don't care. It's cool!"
Super Foods	10/4	No steps correct on task analysis for bagging. Used customer greeting with 75% of the customers. On Dave's self-rating, he circled 1 ("Hate it!") for his preference for the job, and would not rate himself on how he did the job.	Dave needed continuous prompting to bag the groceries. We worked in the express lane after finding that the other aisles were too demanding for now. Dave did not like the high level of prompting needed—especially in a public setting. He sometimes stopped working and walked away. Consider self-instructional strategies and having cashier give more of the cues. Dave did enjoy the customers and greeted most of them.
University cafeteria	10/5	88% on tray clearing task analysis; unable to keep up with speed of conveyor belt. Dave circled 8 ("Good job") for his preference, and rated himself a 10 ("Perfect") for how he did the job.	Dave smiled and shook hands with the other college student workers he met. He was eager to imitate them on the assembly line. He taught himself a large part of the task by watching them! He will need practice to work at the pace needed to keep up with the conveyor belt. Consider using peer prompting for speed.

(cont.)

FIGURE 13.2. *(cont.)*

Super Foods	10/6	45% on cart collecting task analysis. After getting his paycheck, Dave now rated this job site a 10 ("Terrific"). He gave himself a 10 on performance and said, "I'm strong."	At first Dave was unhappy to be back at Super Foods. He began swearing loudly. A coworker came over and distracted him with comments about the upcoming football game. Dave was then willing to try the carts. He needed mostly verbal prompts to do the carts. He liked using his strength to push long lines of carts, and got compliments from customers about his hard work. He also got paid at the end of the shift.
Police Department	10/7	Social interactions: 12 initiations; 4 of 16 (25%) responses to others. Dave rated this job a 10 ("Terrific") on preference and an 8 ("Good") on his job performance.	Dave declared this to be his favorite job. He was exuberant about being at the police station. He asked for a uniform. The police officer with whom he was working gave him a police T-shirt to wear on the job. We rode in a police car to the elementary school. Dave loved this and made siren sounds as we drove. At the school, he was so excited it was difficult for him to become quiet to enter the school. The police officer was very firm with him about "getting serious," and he became immediately quiet. He was able to hand out the flyers to the students in the class and was quiet during the lecture. This site will be an excellent opportunity for Dave to develop his social skills.

peated responses. For example, for removing the dress tags, her data sheet included the following:

1. Grasp tag
2. Pull to remove tag
3. Drop in basket
4. Grasp tag
5. Pull to remove tag
6. Drop in basket
7. Grasp tag
8. Pull to remove tag
9. Drop in basket

FIGURE 13.3. Data Collection Form used for Dave's task-analytic assessment in the university cafeteria. +, independent, correct response; −, no response; g, gesture prompt required; m, model required; v, verbal prompt required; latency of 3–5 seconds between prompts.

Name: Dave Stewart   **Date:** 10/5
Assessment Site: University Cafeteria
Assessment Task: Clearing Trays (Competitive Rate: 10 sec/tay)

% Independent Responses							
9. Send tray down line	40	−	−	−	m	v	v
8. Discard paper goods		−	+	+	+	+	+
7. Remove paper goods	30	−	−	+	+	+	+
6. Place utensils in bin		−	+	+	+	+	+
5. Remove utensils	20	−	+	+	+	+	+
4. Place glasses in rack		−	−	−	m	v	+
3. Empty glasses	10	−	−	−	v	m	m
2. Remove glasses		−	−	+	+	+	+
1. Receive tray	0	−	−	+	g	g	g

Daily Mean (%)   0   33   66   55   55   66

Seconds to Complete One Tray: 35   45   39   45   50   42

Previous mean (%) _____

Date	Trend/mean	Decision
5-Oct-00	Mean 45.8%	for completing steps of task analysis
	43 seconds average for completing one tray	
	Competitive rate is 10 seconds per tray	

Comments: These data were taken on one day at the job site. Dave improved on this task quickly by imitating his coworkers and with some prompting from the job coach.

Ms. D'Alberto also used a form to summarize Raetta's job tryout performance (see Figure 13.4). As the form shows, Raetta's experiences were mixed. She showed a preference for the bottled-water distributor site and the dress shop. She did not get to try the music store on her first trip there because of health problems. (On a later trip to the music store, Raetta was surprisingly unresponsive again, so the team members dropped this site from their consideration. Her mother's theory was that the flashing lights and loud music might have been overwhelming.) Ms. D'Alberto then negotiated getting

FIGURE 13.4. Summary of job tryouts for Raetta.

Summary of Job Tryouts

Job site	Date	Data-based assessment	Description
Florist	10/5	No independent responses; needed full physical guidance to grasp and pull flowers; dropped flowers in trash with partial guidance. Preference: Moderate	Raetta was alert and observant when entering the florist shop. The shop had a strong smell of flowers and was brightly lit. Raetta cooperated with removing the dead flowers, but her hands became soiled. She gazed at her hands after each flower. I put disposable gloves on her hands, but this made it harder for her to grasp the flowers. She did not respond to others' social initiations because she was distracted by her hands.
Bottled-water distributor	10/12	Needed full physical guidance to separate sheets without tearing them. Preference: High for site.	The friendly staff members in this site all joked with Raetta the entire time. She was animated, smiling, and vocalizing. She cooperated with the task of tearing apart the sheets, but will need more instruction to learn this task. The staff ordered pizza for lunch, which also delighted her. She ate well and looked at the staffers as they talked. The site was also very clean.
Ice cream store	10/14	Resisted wiping counter. Preference: Strong dislike for wiping counters and for being around ice cream when can't eat it.	Raetta looked at each customer's ice cream with obvious interest. She would not wipe the counter and resisted guidance to hold the sponge. I tried having her use a paper towel and dishcloth, and having her wear a disposable glove. She resisted each and began to vocalize in protest. When she did not get ice cream to eat, she became very loud.
Dress shop	10/18	One response was independent out of 20—5%. Preference: High	Although Raetta worked in the stock room, she was focused on the brightly colored clothes. She cooperated well with the tag removal task and even did one of the last tags without assistance!
Music shop	10/25	Incomplete.	Raetta seemed lethargic before we got to the job site. On the site she was not responsive. Concerned for her health, I was taking her back to the car when she had a seizure. Because she fell against the sidewalk curb, I called for an ambulance and contacted her mother. In a follow-up call to her mother, I learned she was not hurt (she was wearing her helmet). I recommend trying this site again when Raetta feels better. We also need to consider a written emergency first aid plan to share with her future job supervisor and coworkers.

Raetta a paid job. The dress shop owner hired Raetta for two mornings per week to re-move tags. Ms. D'Alberto arranged for a job coach to provide support to Raetta on these mornings. She also began to build Raetta's week around this job. For example, she found that Raetta enjoyed delivering flowers as a volunteer in the hospital on two other days. Raetta was able to deliver the flowers while riding in an electric cart driven by another volunteer.

The eventual outcomes for both Dave and Raetta gave their transition teams much hope for their futures. Until Dave turned 21, his team continued to work in the manner described above to establish Dave's job preferences and to assess and develop his specific skills. Dave eventually found that he preferred working at Super Foods; with the help of his school's job coach, he mastered his duties as a bagger and cart collector, and took a full-time job with Super Foods after his graduation. Dave obtained services from an adult agency for long-term support in this job, with Mr. Lewis's assistance. He rode to work with Martha, a neighbor who had worked as a cashier in this store for 10 years. Dave also created a daily routine based on his needs and preferences. Because he enjoyed martial arts, he enrolled in a class in an academy that was a short bus ride from his work. During community-based instruction, he learned to ride the bus. The driver, who came to know Dave well, was a source of natural support if Dave got confused about which stop to take. A friend named Ethan in Dave's martial arts class gave him rides home from the class. They sometimes stopped to eat or play video games at an arcade. Although Dave liked the apartments he toured with his high school class, he enjoyed living at home with his mother and sister, and so he decided to continue living at home for the present. Overall, Dave was making a successful transition from school to adult living.

Likewise, Raetta's team continued to work toward building a meaningful week for Raetta and obtaining the support she would need. By the end of the school year, Raetta had a 40-hour week planned. For example, on Mondays and Wednesdays, she rode to the hospital with another volunteer (natural support). At the hospital, a community in-structor (hired with voucher from mental retardation services) helped her deliver flow-ers and eat with other volunteers in the cafeteria. Raetta went swimming at the YMCA in the afternoons and walked across the street for ice cream before returning to the YMCA, where her mother picked her up on her way home from work. On Tuesdays and Thursdays, Raetta took a cab to the dress shop (provided by vocational rehabilita-tion services), where a job coach provided the support she needed to perform this paid job. She ate lunch with her coworkers (natural supports) after the job coach left. In the afternoon, Raetta joined two other adults with disabilities for a variety of leisure activi-ties (e.g., shopping, bowling, and visiting parks) in a cooperative program that her fam-ily developed with some other families from the Arc (an advocacy organization for in-dividuals with developmental disabilities and their families). Each family paid a set amount for the services of this cooperative program each month. The Arc provided the staff person who also drove Raetta and the other participants to these leisure activities. By relying on family funds for these two afternoons, Raetta had enough voucher money for some additional 1:1 support on Fridays. On Fridays, Raetta continued to ex-pand her job experiences by sampling other jobs arranged by an employment specialist that Raetta and her parents hired with her voucher money (from the same supported employment agency that provided Raetta with a job coach in her paid job). Sometimes she took Fridays off and did special things with her family members. For example, one of her adult sisters liked to take her to the movies. When she took Fridays off, she then could use her voucher money to try some job options that were only available on the weekends or in the evenings.[2]

Skill Selection. Once specific job sites are targeted, skills for a student's transition curriculum can more easily be determined. These skills may be job-specific (e.g., removing price tags, clearing lunch trays, dusting shelves) or more generally job-related. Many of the other chapters in this text have given examples of job-related skills. For example, learning to purchase lunch, cross the street, put on a jacket, and sign one's name are all potentially job-related skills. A commercial curriculum may lack the relevance needed to prepare students to work in their own communities. Often, for example, teaching students to sort screws and bolts may be nonfunctional if there is no job like this in the community. However, teachers sometimes find these curricula to be useful in teaching students some general employment skills, such as working on a task without teacher prompting and getting read for work. Some curricula that may be used for this purpose are shown in Table 13.2.

SPECIAL CONSIDERATIONS IN TRANSITION PLANNING

Meeting Labor Law Requirements

In using community-based work placements, schools need to adhere to the Fair Labor Standards Act and should contact their local office of the U.S. Department of Labor to determine whether a student should be paid in a work placement (Moon, Kiernan, & Halloran, 1990). In general, vocational exploration should be limited to 5 hours per job, vocational assessments to 90 hours per job, and vocational training to 120 hours per job in a single school year. For a student not to be paid as a worker, the following criteria must be met (Moon & Inge, 1993):

1. Participants must be students with disabilities for whom competitive employment is not immediately available, and who will need intensive ongoing support to perform in a work setting.
2. Participation is for vocational exploration, assessment, or training and is under the general supervision of public school personnel.
3. The community-based job placement is a clearly defined part of the student's IEP/ITP and is designed for the benefit of the student.
4. The family and student must be fully informed of the job placement and must have indicated voluntary participation, with the understanding that the student is not entitled to wages.
5. The participation of the student cannot result in an immediate advantage to the business. Students must not displace regular employees or relieve them of their duties. Their work must be related to their IEPs and they must receive direct supervision of either the school staff or employees of the business.
6. Students are not necessarily entitled to employment at the end of their IEPs.

[2] The person who served as the model for Raetta's story had full funding for 40 hours per week from one source. Participants who receive services from Lehigh University Supported Employment and Assessment Services rarely need to utilize more than two sources of funding to create comprehensive supports in real-life cases. The combination of four funding sources given here is used to illustrate the various options available.

TABLE 13.2. Commercial Materials for Teaching Employment Skills

Attainment Company
P.O. Box 930160
Verona, WI 53593-0160
1-800-327-4269

- *Everyone Can Work* (for students)
  A video presenting biographies about individuals with disabilities who gained employment, developed to use as a discussion starter. There are companion *Everyone Can Work* videos to be used with employers and professionals.

- A Way to Work
  A curriculum that provides guidance to set up a vocational training program, including functional assessments, job development and matching, transition planning, and supported employment.

- *Individual Transition Plans*
  A teacher's handbook on how to design ITPs, authored by Dr. Paul Wehman, a leading expert in supported employment.

- *It's All Part of the Job*
  A video focusing on the social skills needed on the job, featuring real-life individuals with disabilities and their employers.

James Stanfield Company, Inc.
P.O. Box 41058
Santa Barbara, CA 93140
1-800-421-6534
http://www.stanfield.com

- The Transitions Curriculum
  A three-volume curriculum on personal, career, and life management. Includes objectives and teacher-developed lesson plans.

- *Job Smart*
  Training video on how to succeed on the job, use humor to illustrate how to avoid irritating the boss or coworkers, also cover getting a promotion and avoiding getting hurt.

- *Working*
  Training video to help students get and keep a job, dealing with such issues as finding the right job, being on time, understanding directions, interactions with coworkers, and being a high-quality worker.

Steck-Vaughn Company
P.O. Box 690789
Orlando, FL 32819-9998
1-800-531-5015

- The Integrator Series and Career Interests
  Two CD-ROM programs that help students explore job interests and identify skills they will need. Includes photographs of adults performing these various jobs.

- *Necessary Skills for the Workforce*
  Workbooks for students with some entry-level reading skills, to help them students learn skills like choosing a job, completing an application, and renting a home.

These regulations should not be misinterpreted as implying that students *cannot* be paid by employers during their school training placements. In Dave's case, he received above-minimum-wage pay at the grocery store site and ongoing supervision from school staff.

School-Based Vocational Training

Most transition experts recommend training high school students with moderate and severe disabilities in community jobs (Moon & Inge, 1993). In contrast, school-based programs may be used for younger students (e.g., middle school age) when community-based placements are not available. These school-based programs may utilize inclusion in vocational training classes (e.g., industrial arts), assisting school employees (e.g., in the office or cafeteria), and simulating work experiences (e.g., assembling gift baskets to sell during a holiday season). Elementary students can begin to learn work skills by taking responsibility for classroom chores. Educators should avoid the pitfall of having students do repetitive assembly work that is unrelated to options in the local community (e.g., sorting screws, assembling pens). To teach seatwork-type tasks, the teacher can survey the school and community to find real tasks (e.g., stamping mailings for a nonprofit organization or bagging materials for a school fundraiser).

Longitudinal Skill Sequences

Teachers may seek resources that define specific transition skills students can acquire across their school years. Most published transition curricula include lists of functional life skills for home, community access, or leisure. For example, Wehman et al. (1988) recommend that elementary children learn such skills as making their beds, dressing, eating meals in a restaurant, picking up their dishes after a meal, and cleaning their rooms at the end of the day to begin to prepare for the world of work. Skills checklists for community access and for personal care and home living can be found in Chapters Nine and Ten of this book, respectively. Many of these skills do "double duty" in preparing students for both work and home or work and community mobility. Some professionals have identified generic work skills, including developing strength, endurance, orienting, physical mobility, working independently, interacting with supervisors, and adapting to change (Westling & Fox, 1995). These skills are usually evaluated best in the context of a specific activity. For example, a student may have excellent endurance in a highly preferred leisure activity, but may tire easily during cleaning. Instead of using checklists to evaluate the development of longitudinal vocational skills that may not be relevant to actual jobs students pursue in the future, educators may instead use a portfolio assessment model (described in greater detail in Chapters One and Three). In this model, a student creates a portfolio of job experiences; this may include pictures of the student on the job site, performance ratings, letters of recommendation, and other information. The portfolio may contain specific skills checklists (e.g., for social skills) and data from task-analytic and other assessments (e.g., for job tasks like stocking a vending machine). The student also self-evaluates each job experience. As this portfolio is shared at each year's transition planning meeting, the team can learn about the student's achievements and continuing needs for support and training.

As the student approaches adulthood, the teacher can help the student translate this portfolio into a typed resume to use in the job search process.

THE INDIVIDUALIZED TRANSITION PLAN

The outcome of the ecological assessment process is the development of a written ITP, which is then implemented in the coming year. Students also continue to have an IEP. Whereas the IEP specifies target skills for the student to acquire, the ITP delineates action goals that the transition planning team will take. Often these action goals and student objectives can be linked. Raetta's highest priority was to develop a meaningful week of activities, including a part-time paid job and leisure activities with the ongoing support she needs. The way the team translated this priority into both action goals and specific skills is shown in Figure 13.5 for two domains—employment and leisure. Raetta also had transition goals in community and home living. Raetta's transition planning team included representatives from the outside agencies that would fund services for her, and these representatives agreed to be responsible for helping Raetta and her family apply for these resources.

SUMMARY

This chapter has used the cases of Dave Stewart and Raetta Baker to describe the process of planning the transition from school to adult living. The planning for Dave began with several difficult obstacles. His school had decided to use a segregated school site for job training for students with moderate and severe disabilities. When Dave protested, he began to receive negative progress reports about his behavior. Knowing his rights as an 18-year-old, Dave was uncertain about continuing in school. In contrast, Dave's family was eager for him to continue to receive the benefits of a public education, but their dissatisfaction with his program led them to consider legal action. To overcome these obstacles, the district made the decision to invest in a comprehensive transition assessment for Dave from an area-supported employment provider. This assessment included a review of Dave's records, person-centered planning with the family, working with Dave to promote his self-determination in both this process and his future education, and situational assessments of Dave in community job options. These situational assessments were extended into ongoing job tryouts for Dave. Mr. Lewis also helped the district in its decision to relocate Dave's educational services to the community college and to begin inclusive educational programs at this level. Because Dave's transition planning team had 3 years to work together, Dave made an easy transition at graduation when his employer at the grocery store asked him to work full-time. Because the area adult agency representatives had been involved with Dave's case for 3 years, the procurement of ongoing support for this context could also be made without starting over. An ecological assessment approach was equally applicable for Raetta, who would need ongoing, intensive support. Her team used a review of Raetta's prior records, person-centered planning, promotion of Raetta's self-determination, and situational assessments in which she tried new jobs.

In general, employment training will be much more relevant when it is conducted

FIGURE 13.5. An excerpt from the ITP for Raetta.

Individualized Transition Plan

Date: September 30, 20—
Student's Name: Raetta Baker   **Date of Birth:** 8/29/19—

Parents' Names: Walter and Sonia Baker   **Home Phone:** 899-9888
Work Phone: 787-6754
Date for Initiation of Services: September 30, 20—
Annual Review Date: September 30, 20—

Domain: Employment

Current level	Support needs	Transition action goals	Related skills for IEP implementation
Raetta has no experience in a community job. She has received training in classroom chores and community training to use restaurants and stores. She currently needs a high level of physical prompting in these activities.	• Community-based job training • 1:1 job coach	1. Provide Raetta with the opportunity to sample at least five jobs. *Person responsible:* Ms. D'Alberto. *Time frame:* In first 90 days of school. 2. Help Raetta procure a paid, part-time job that she can keep after graduation. *Person responsible:* Ms. D'Alberto, working with business council and family contacts. *Time frame:* By May. 3. Procure ongoing training and support for the job after graduation. *Person responsible:* Office of Vocational Rehabilitation case manager and mother. *Time frame:* By May.	• Participating in interview by playing video from job tryouts and handing resume folder to potential employer • Increasing job endurance to 4 hours per day. • Performance of specific job tasks (e.g., pulling price tags). • Generalization of social greeting and choice-making skills to work setting and new people.

(cont.)

FIGURE 13.5. *(cont.)*

Domain: Leisure

Current level	Support needs	Transition action goals	Related skills for IEP implementation
Raetta likes to swim and has learned to walk in shallow water. She enjoys settings with bright lights, people, and music.	• Community-based job training • Leisure coach	1. Expand Raetta's community leisure options by exploring her preferences across a wide range of activities. Person responsible: Ms. D'Alberto Time frame: Throughout the school year. 2. Get Raetta a membership at the YMCA. Person responsible: Raetta and her father. Time frame: By October 15. 3. Procure adult service that includes comprehensive support for leisure activities. Person responsible: Office of Mental Retardation case manager and mother. Time frame: By May.	• Indicating preference through participation and affect. • Choosing activities by using objects that represent them. • Self-direction of caregiving needed during leisure activities by eye gazing and movement. • Expanding responses to be used for social interaction with others in community leisure settings.

in real community jobs, and this should be a priority for high school students. Younger students can learn job skills through classroom chores or through performing other real tasks in school settings (e.g., photocopying, mailings). Transition planning and the opportunity to sample a variety of job experiences are crucial sources of support that schools can provide students with moderate and severe disabilities to help them make the transition to adult living.

REFERENCES

Baine, D. (1987). Ecological inventories and curriculum development for special education in developing countries. *Indian Psychologist*, 4(2), 1–8.

Brotherson, M. J., Cook, C. C., Cunconan-Lahr, R., & Wehmeyer, M. (1995). Policy supporting self-determination in the environments of children with disabilities. *Education and Training in Mental Retardation and Developmental Disabilities*, 30, 3–14.

Clark, G. M. (1996). Transition planning assessment for secondary-level students with learning disabilities. *Journal of Learning Disabilities*, 29(1), 79–92.

Clifft, M. A. (1986). Writing about psychiatric patients: Guidelines for disguising case material. *Bulletin of the Menninger Clinic*, 50, 511–524.

Cole, K. N., Swisher, V., Thompson, M. D., & Fewell, R. R. (1985). Enhancing sensitivity of assessment instruments for children: Graded multi-dimensional scoring. *The Journal of the Association for Persons with Severe Handicaps*, 10, 209–213.

Dennis, R. E., & Giangreco, M. F. (1996). Creating conversation: Reflections on cultural sensitivity in family interviewing. *Exceptional Children*, 63, 103–116.

Downing, J. E., & Perino, D. (1992). Functional versus standardized assessment procedures: Implications for educational programming. *Mental Retardation*, 30, 289–295,

Everson, J. M. (1996). Using person-centered planning concepts to enhance school to adult life transition planning. *Journal of Vocational Rehabilitation*, 6, 7–13.

Griffin, D. K., Rosenberg, H., Cheyney, W., & Greenberg, B. (1996). A comparison of self esteem and job satisfaction of adults with mild mental retardation in sheltered workshops and supported employment. *Education and Training in Mental Retardation and Developmental Disabilities*, 31, 142–150.

Grigal, M., Test, D. W., Beattie, J., & Wood, W. M. (1997). An evaluation of transition components of individualized education programs. *Exceptional Children*, 63, 357–372.

Hughes, C., Hugo, K., & Blatt, J. (1996). Self-instructional intervention for teaching generalized problem solving within a functional task sequence. *American Journal of Mental Retardation*, 100, 565–579.

Linehan, S. H., & Brady, M. P. (1995). Functional versus developmental assessments: Influences on instructional planning decisions. *Journal of Special Education*, 29, 295–309.

Linehan, S. H., Brady, M. P., & Hwang, C. (1991). Ecological versus developmental assessment: Influences on instructional expectations. *Journal of the Association for Persons with Severe Handicaps, 16*, 146–153.

Lohrmann-O'Rourke, S., & Browder, D. M. (1998). Empirically based methods of preference assessments for individuals with severe disabilities. *American Journal on Mental Retardation 103*, 146–161.

Martin, J. E., & Huber-Marshall, L. H. (1995). Choicemaker: A comprehensive self-determination transition program. *Intervention in School and Clinic*, 30, 147–156.

Martin, J. E., & Huber-Marshall, L. H. (1996). *Choicemaker Self-Determination Transition Assessment*. Longmont, CO: Sopris West.

McGaughey, M. J., Kiernan, W. E., McNally, L. C., Gilmore, D., & Keith, G. R. (1995). Beyond the workshop: National trends in integrated and segregated day and employment services. *Journal of the Association for Persons with Severe Handicaps*, 20, 270–285.

Miner, C. A., & Bates, P. E. (1997). The effect of person centered planning activities on the IEP/transition process. *Education and Training in Mental Retardation and Developmental Disabilities*, 32, 105–112.

Moon, M. S., & Inge, K. (1993). Vocational preparation and transition. In M. E. Snell (Ed.), *Instruction of students with severe disabilities* (pp. 556–587). New York: Macmillan/Merrill.

Moon, M. S., Kiernan, W., & Halloran, W. (1990). School-based vocational programs and labor laws: A 1990 update. *Journal of the Association for Persons with Severe Handicaps*, 15, 177–185.

Morningstar, M. E., Turnbull, A. P., & Turnbull, H. R. (1995). What do students with disabilities tell us about the importance of family involvement in the transition from school to adult life? *Exceptional Children, 62,* 249–260.

Morton, M. V., Everson, J. M., & Moon, S. (1987). Guidelines for training parents as part of interagency transition planning teams. In J. M. Everson, M. Barcus, M. S. Moon, & M. V. Morton (Eds.), *Achieving outcomes: A guide to interagency training in transition and supported employment.* Richmond: Virginia Commonwealth University.

Mount, B., & Zwernik, K. (1988). *It's never too early, it's never too late: A booklet about personal-futures planning for persons with developmental disabilities, their families, and friends, case managers, service, providers, and advocates.* St. Paul, MN: St. Paul Metropolitan Council.Governor's Planning Council on Developmental Disabilities.

Rainforth, B., & York, J. (1987). Integrating related services in community instruction. *Journal of the Association for Persons with Severe Handicaps, 12,* 190–198.

Reid, D. H., Parsons, M. B., & Green, C. W. (1998). Identifying work preferences among individuals with severe disabilities prior to beginning supported work. *Journal of Applied Behavior Analysis, 31,* 281–286.

Revell, W. G., Wehman, P., Kregel, J., & West, M. (1994). Supported employment for persons with severe disabilities: Current practice and future directions, *Education and Training in Mental Retardation and Developmental Disabilities, 29,* 256–264.

Rucker, R. E., & Browder, D. M. (1994). Conversion from sheltered to integrated employment: Current practice and future directions. *Journal of Vocational Rehabilitation, 4,* 255–264.

Sale, P., Everson, J., Metzler, H., & Moon, S. (1991). Quality indicators of successful vocational transition programs. *Journal of Vocational Rehabilitation, 1,* 47–64.

Sigafoos, J., Cole, D., & McQuarter, R. J. (1987). Current practices in the assessment of students with severe disabilities. *Journal of the Association for Persons with Severe Handicaps, 12,* 264–273.

Sontag, J. C., and Schactt, R. (1994). An ethnic comparison of parent participation and information needs in early intervention. *Exceptional Children, 60,* 422–433.

Spencer, K., & Sample, P. (1993). Transition planning and services. In C. Royeen (Ed.), *Classroom applications for school based practice* (pp. 6–48). Rockville, MD: American Occupational Therapy Association.

Van Reusen, A. K., & Bos, C. S. (1994). Facilitating student participation in individualized education programs through motivation strategy instruction. *Exceptional Children, 60,* 466–475.

Weber, J. L., & Stoneman, Z. (1986). Parental non-participation in program planning for mentally retarded children. *Applied Research in Mental Retardation, 7,* 359–369.

Wehman, P., Hill, J. W., Wood, W., & Parent, W. (1987). A report on competitive employment histories of persons labeled severely retarded. *Journal of the Association for Persons with Severe Handicaps, 12,* 11–17.

Wehman, P., Kregel, J., & Seyfarth, J. (1985). Outlook for young adults with mental retardation. *Rehabilitation Counseling Bulletin, 25,* 90–99.

Wehman, P., Moon, M. S., Everson, J. M., Wood, M., & Barcus, M. (1988). *Transition from school to work: New challenges for youth with severe disabilities.* Baltimore: Paul H. Brookes.

Westling, D. L., & Fox, L. (1995). *Teaching students with severe disabilities.* Upper Saddle River, NJ: Prentice-Hall.

Winking, D. L., O'Reilly, B., & Moon, M. S. (1993). Preference: The missing link in the job match process for individuals without functional communication skills. *Journal of Vocational Rehabilitation, 3,* 27–42.

APPENDIX
Blank Versions of Two Forms

Systematic Instruction Plan

Student: _____   Date plan written: _____

Target skill: _____   Routine for skill: _____

Objective: _____

Format

Materials: _____

Setting and teacher: _____

Number of trials: _____

Instructional Procedures

Prompting:

    Specific prompt(s) to be used: _____

Fading (check one):

    _____ None (simultaneous prompting)

    _____ Time delay: _____ Progressive or _____ Constant

    _____ Least intrusive prompts

    _____ Most to least intrusive prompts

    _____ Graduated guidance

    _____ Stimulus fading or shaping

    _____ Other (describe) _____

    Fading schedule: _____

Feedback:

    Correct: _____

    Fading schedule for praise: _____

    Error correction: _____

Generalization Procedures

Other notes

FIGURE A.2. Blank version of the standard Data Collection Form.

Name: _____

Skill: _____

Criterion for Mastery: _____

% Independent Responses

100
90
80
70
60
50
40
30
20
10
0

Daily Mean (%)

Previous mean (%) _____

Date	Trend/mean	Decision
	Mean	
	Mean	

Index

Note: Letters in italics refer to figures and tables.